Supervis

IN CANADA TODAY

SECOND EDITION

Stephen P. **ROBBINS**
San Diego State University

David A. **DE CENZO**
Towson State University

Joan **CONDIE**
Sheridan College

Laurie **KONDO**
Sheridan College

Prentice Hall Canada Career & Technology
Scarborough, Ontario

Canadian Cataloguing in Publication Data

Main entry under title:

Supervision in Canada today

2nd ed.
Previous ed. by Stephen P. Robbins, Joan L. Condie, Laurie C. Kondo
ISBN 0-13-675026-5

1. Supervision of employees. I. Robbins, Stephen P., 1943 -   .

HF5549.12.R62 1999   658.3'02   C97-932685-0

© 1998, 1995 Prentice-Hall Canada Inc., Scarborough, Ontario
A Division of Simon & Schuster/A Viacom Company

Prentice-Hall, Inc., Upper Saddle River, New Jersey
Prentice-Hall International (UK) Limited, London
Prentice-Hall of Australia, Pty. Limited, Sydney
Prentice-Hall Hispanoamericana, S.A., Mexico City
Prentice-Hall of India Private Limited, New Delhi
Prentice-Hall of Japan, Inc., Tokyo
Simon & Schuster Asia Private Limited, Singapore
Editora Prentice-Hall do Brasil, Ltda., Rio de Janeiro

ISBN 0-13-675026-5

Vice-President, Editorial Director: Laura Pearson
Marketing Manager: Sophia Fortier
Executive Developmental Editor: Marta Tomins
Production Editor: Susan James
Copy Editor: Nick Gamble
Production Coordinator: Wendy Moran
Permissions/Photo Research: Susan Wallace-Cox
Cover Design: Sarah Battersby
Cover Image: Joe Biafore
Page Layout: Arlene Edgar

Original English Language edition
published by Prentice-Hall, Inc.,
Upper Saddle River, New Jersey
Copyright © 1998, 1995

Visit the Prentice Hall Canada Web site! Send us your comments,
browse our catalogues, and more. **www.phcanada.com** Or reach
us through e-mail at **phabinfo_pubcanada@prenhall.com**

1 2 3 4 5   02 01 00 99 98

Printed and bound in the United States of America.

Photo Credits

No.	Source
Ch 1 Opener	Charles Gupton/ Charles Gupton Photography
1-7	Courtesy of Joan Condie
1-8	Courtesy of Joan Condie
1-15	John Abbott/ John Abbott Photography
1-17	Mason Morfit/ FPG International
2-1	Greg Girard/ Contact Press Images
2-7	Teri Stratford
2-11	Munro Sharp
Ch 3 Opener	Michael Barley/ Michael Barley Photography
3-1	Steve Rubin/ The Image Works
3-4	IBM
3-18	Bob Daemmrich/ Uniphoto Picture Agency
Ch 4 Opener	Bob Daemmrich / Stock Boston Inc.
4-1	Charles Gupton/ Tony Stone Images
4-3	Harris Corporation
4-8	IBM
4-11	Bettye Lanza/ Photo Researchers Inc.
4-13	John Feingersh/ Uniphoto Picture Agency
4-14	Phil Schofield
5-2	Xerox
5-4	Gabe Palmer/ The Stock Market
5-6	Gerry Gropp/ Sipa
Ch 6 Opener	Bob Daemmrich/ Stock Boston Inc.
6-1	Ralph Mercer/ Tony Stone Images
6-2	Bob Daemmrich/ Stock Boston Inc.
6-6	Robert Scott
6-7	Manpower Inc.
6-11	Mary Gascoigne
Ch 7 Opener	Terry Parke/ Terry Parke Photography
7-1	Munro Sharp
7-3	Jim Brown/ The Stock Market
7-5	James Schnepf
7-10	John Coletti/ Stock Boston Inc.
7-11	Tim Defrisco/ Allsport
7-13	Ray Fisher
Ch 8 Opener	Sikorsky Aircraft
8-1	Jay Dickman
8-4	Sikorsky Aircraft
8-5	Mike Greenlar
8-7	Jon Riley/ Tony Stone Images
Ch 9 Opener	Gary Laufman Photography
9-2	Lawrence Migdale/ Stock Boston Inc.
9-10	Walt Ennis/ W.L. Gore & Associates
9-11	Courtesy of Joan Condie
9-12	Courtesy of Joan Condie
Ch 10 Opener	Ralph Stayer/ Steve Woit
10-3	Andy Sacks/ Tony Stone Images
10-6	Pat McDonogh
10-8	UPI/ Bettmann
10-12	Terry Parke/ Terry Parke Photography
11-2	Mary Jean Giroux
11-3	Rhoda Sidney/ Stock Boston Inc.
11-5	Bruce Ayres/ Tony Stone Images
11-8	AP/ Wide World Photos
Ch 12 Opener	Kevin Horan
12-3	Kevin Horan
Ch 13 Opener	Mark Wagner/ Tony Stone Images
13-1	Will van Overbeek
13-5	Honda of American Mfg.
13-9	Steven Rubin/ JB Pictures
Ch 14 Opener	Joe Sohm/ UNICEF Photo
14-2	Kim Blake/ London Life Insurance Company
Ch 15 Opener	Marrin Rogers/ Uniphoto Picture Agency
15-3	Brad Markel/ Gamma-Liason Inc.
Ch 16 Opener	Tom Reese/ Seattle Times
16-2	Prof. E. Manjares/ Nassau Community College
16-9	Janet Gill/ Tony Stone Images
16-12	Ron Sherman/ Stock Boston Inc.

BRIEF CONTENTS

CONTENTS

BOXED FEATURES

HOW TO USE THIS BOOK

The supervisor's job has changed dramatically in recent years. Supervisors now work with a more diverse workforce in terms of race, gender, and ethnic background. Supervisors' jobs are also being affected by technological changes, a more competitive marketplace, and corporate restructuring and workflow redesign. Despite all of these changes, supervisors still need to understand the traditional elements of directing the work of others and the specific skills they need: goal-setting, budgeting, scheduling, delegating, interviewing, negotiating, handling grievances, employee counselling, and evaluating employee's performance.

The ideal way to learn a task is to find out how it is done, watch it being done, and then complete the task yourself. *Supervision in Canada Today* takes you "on the job," presenting examples of how supervisors operate in real situations, and then placing you in the first-line position where you are *making the decisions* yourself.

Chapter Outline and Objectives Each chapter begins with an outline and a list of learning objectives. This provides you a structure by which you can test whether you've learned the chapter's key concepts.

Performing Effectively These chapter introductions demonstrate each new topic's relevance to your effective performance as a supervisor. You learn to *think critically* in typical work situations.

From Concepts to Skills This section allows you to learn and practise relevant supervisory skills by combining your new knowledge and your natural talents. You assess your own progress.

Understanding the Basics Closing each chapter is a summary of the important points and terms in the chapter, and review topics for discussion.

Performing Your Job Each chapter concludes with two cases that allow you to apply your knowledge to solve real problems faced by real supervisors.

Building Your Portfolio Each part concludes with an integrative case that is based on video interviews. You have the opportunity to make critical decisions alongside real-world managers.

Margin Definitions and a Glossary provide a quick reference to new terms.

SUPPLEMENTS TO LEARNING

Instructor's Manual with a lecture guide, transparency masters, video guides, and guidelines for evaluating case responses. This manual provides the latest guidance for teaching supervision in a dynamic way.

Test Item File with 950 multiple choice, true/false, short answer, and short essay test questions. These questions are available to the instructor free with every adoption of the textbook.

Computerized Test Item File is an easy-to-access computer file. Generate your own tests or have the program select and print test questions at random. The software is free with every adoption of the textbook.

Stop-Action Video with six video cases that were chosen to accompany every major section of the textbook: Introduction; Planning and Control; Organizing, Staffing, and Employee Development; Stimulating Individual and Group Performance; Coping with Workplace Dynamics; Employee Relations; and Career Planning.

ABC News Video Library with clips from actual news stories that pertain to supervisors as they were reported by ABC News.

New in the Second edition

There are several new features and content topics that are included in this revision.

Building A Supervisory Skill We've included skill boxes throughout the text, which provide step-by-step guidelines for handling specific elements of a supervisor's job. These skills can make you a more effective supervisor once you have practiced and mastered them. They include skills such as developing budgets, conducting a performance evaluation, and managing your time.

Assessing Yourself Individuals like to get feedback about themselves that they then can use in their development. So we've included a self-assessment in most chapters. Some examples include: Are you willing to delegate? (Chapter 5). Are you effective at disciplining? (Chapter 14).

Something to Think About (and to promote class discussion) Each of these vignettes is designed to get readers thinking about an issue that affects supervisors on the job. For example, in Chapter 1, we look at the off-site employee. The boxes are designed to make readers think about all sides of an issue, and build a case (verbally in class or in a written assignment) to support a position.

Supervision in Action In several places in the text, we've presented an issue that highlights a distinction between traditional and contemporary supervisors. For example, in Chapter 9, we address motivating a diverse workforce.

Dealing with a Difficult Issue No matter where supervisors work, at some time in their careers they will be faced with a difficult issue—one that goes beyond simply following the law. These sections are designed to make learners think about situations they may face, and begin to develop a plan of action for handling ethical and moral dilemmas. For example, in Chapter 9, the issue is rewarding appropriate behaviour.

Pop Quiz Each chapter also includes at least two pop quizzes. Our experience indicates that students need more practice for tests they will take on these subjects. These questions are actual test questions that we've used before, and can serve as reinforcement for the learner. In each set, there are four questions: two multiple choice, one true/false, and one open-ended question. We also provide the answer to each question at the end of the chapter, and explain the correct response.

Supervisory jobs are similar around the world. Accountable for the work of their subordinates, all supervisors must assign, monitor, and evaluate performance, and provide feedback, training, and support. However, supervisory jobs also differ among various countries because the legal, political, and cultural context of a firm has an impact on the supervisor's job. That's why we have adapted Stephen Robbins' excellent supervisory text for the Canadian market, adding Canadian cases and quotes, and incorporating relevant Canadian legislation.

Our text offers many opportunities for students to learn from the real-life experiences of Canadian supervisors. We interviewed supervisors across our country, from Charlottetown to Nanaimo, with many stops along the way. From small communities to urban centres, these supervisors have shared their ideas and approaches to help students appreciate the challenges of being a supervisor.

For us, the reward in writing this book was the enthusiastic participation of the supervisors. When asked to tell us their stories, they were delighted with the opportunity to describe their efforts in a job that is often not fully appreciated. They, too, believe that students need to learn from the source, examining real-life applications to understand theoretical concepts. Through their eyes, students using this text will be able to glimpse the realities facing supervisors in Canada today.

In this second edition we have revised the leadership chapter and the placement of material on teams, total quality management and counselling employees. Pop quizzes have been added, and the theoretical base has been enriched by some new cases, more self-assessments, and more real-life supervisor examples.

The results of our research for this new edition reflected the emphasis on change that you'll find in this text. More than half the supervisors cited in the first edition have changed their positions since then. And their organizations continue to change: teams are increasingly mentioned, restructuring continues, the volume of demands on supervisors has remained high or has grown, and the expanding use of e-mail emphasizes the importance of communication and networking skills.

We'd love to get your feedback on the text, so feel free to contact us by e-mail:

joan.condie@sheridanc.on.ca
laurie.kondo@sheridanc.on.ca

Joan Condie
Laurie Kondo

ACKNOWLEDGEMENTS

We would like to thank the following people for their generous help in the creation of this book, contributing toward making it a truly Canadian version. It was a privilege and a pleasure to speak with so many people who clearly care about their jobs and the people with whom they work.

Terry Allan, *Holland College*
Denise Baynton, *Mary Kay*
Anne Bermingham, *2WA Consulting Inc.*
Ray Berta, *Applied Consumer and Clinical Evaluation*
Sabby Bhagrath, *Air Canada*
Don Bray, *S.C.I.L. Construction*
Tony Brown, *Sun Life Assurance Company of Canada*
Nathalie Brunet, *Kodak Canada*
Scott Burton, *Carlton Cards*
Ian Carmicheal, *Tees and Persse Brokerage*
Fred Cassidy, *Larry's Sports*
Michelle Chung
Betti Clipsham, *Motorola*
Bruce Condie, *Toronto Board of Education*
Heather Cook, *CATC, Halton Region*
David Curtis, *Green Line Investor Services Inc.*
Gerald Dandy, *Elsay Bailey Canada Inc.*
Dan Doherty, *CIBC*
John Dunn, *Harmac Pacific Inc.*
Leigh Enlund, *Bank of Nova Scotia*
Rick Finlay, *MacMillan Bathurst Inc.*
Allan Forbes, *Holland College*
Stephen Fraser
Jackie Gordon, *Halton Police Services*
Ingrid Hann, *Spar Aviation*
Joanne Hawrylyshyn, *Regional Municipality of Hamilton-Wentworth*
Peggy Hebden, *The New VR*
Paul Hickey, *Island Telephone*
Brian Jamieson, *Jannock*
Paul Jay, *Workplace News*
Adrian Jordan, *CMP Ltd.*
Colin Kirby

Jeffrey Kondo, *Toronto Dominion Bank*
Brian Lemay
David LeRoy, *Paramount Canada's Wonderland*
Elizabeth Loweth, *Canadian Centre for Ethics and Corporate Policy*
John Marshall, *Dofasco*
Pat McCallum, *Air Canada*
Brian Morrison
Wendy Nihill, *London Life Insurance Company*
Sheila Otter, *Village Wedding Belles*
Ken Pierce, *Holland College*
Kerrie Preete, *Schneider National Carrier*
Len Rak
Herman Rosenfeld, *Canadian Auto Workers Union*
Cindy Savory, *Air B.C.*
Lynn Rutherford
Kathleen Savory, *Malaspina College*
Rundell Seaman, *Seaman's Beverages*
Joe Sferrazza
Greg Sheehan, *Sheridan College*
Neil Skelding
Heather Stewart, *Diagnostic Chemicals*
Larry Sylvester, *Canada Brick*
Della Tardif
Pat Tretjack
Judy VanDuzer, *Royal York Hotel*
Mark Ward
Allan Watts, *Seaman's Beverages*
Eric White, *Appletree Wholesale Decorating*
John Williams, *Burlington Community Development Corporation*
Elizabeth Wright, *Wentworth Library Services*
Dave Zaporzon, *Dofasco*

On a personal note, we'd like to offer the following thanks:
From Joan to Len, Jenna, and Nicola: You're the best.
From Laurie to Jeff, Peter, and Dana: You teach me the important things.

PART ONE

INTRODUCTION

1. THE SUPERVISOR'S JOB AND CHALLENGES FOR THE 21ST CENTURY

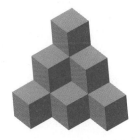

1

THE SUPERVISOR'S JOB AND CHALLENGES FOR THE 21ST CENTURY

LEARNING OBJECTIVES

After reading this chapter, you should be able to:

1. Define *supervisor*.
2. Explain the difference between supervisors, middle managers, and top management.
3. Identify the four functions in the management process.
4. Describe the four essential management competencies.
5. Explain why the supervisor's job will be increasingly important and complex in the future.
6. Describe how global competition affects the supervisor's job.
7. Explain the important role supervisors play in conveying an organization's ethical standards.
8. Define what is meant by *workforce diversity*.
9. Explain why many employees are not as loyal to their employers as they were in the past.
10. Describe the impact of constant and chaotic change on the supervisor's job.

CHAPTER OUTLINE

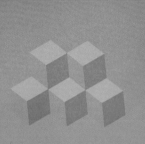

Meet two managers, Judy VanDuzer and Sabby Bhagrath. Judy has a degree in hospitality and tourism. Sabby acquired his skills in the British air force, at college in England and then, in Canada, through further coursework and exams. Judy works in the world of a busy hotel. Sabby, like the technicians he oversees, braves all manner of Canadian weather to do his job at a major international airport. Judy's staff organizes rooms, food, beverages, and other requirements for groups holding conferences or meetings at the hotel. Sabby's technicians are highly skilled individuals who have the power to ground a plane they feel is unsafe.

In spite of the differences in their jobs, Judy and Sabby have one thing in common—they're both supervisors. And, maybe somewhat surprisingly, their jobs have a very large common component. *Like what?*, you might ask. The following are just a few of the things common to the two jobs.

Judy and Sabby are both responsible for assigning work. Each must ensure that performance meets high quality standards. There are strong time demands and constant change to keep up with. They both have to handle interpersonal conflicts, and need to motivate people and evaluate performance. And they each have to advise, coach, and provide feedback to help their employees improve performance.

FIGURE 1-1

Judy VanDuzer manages catering and conference services at the Royal York Hotel in Toronto.

FIGURE 1-2

Sabby Bhagrath is an aircraft maintenance foreman for Air Canada at Pearson Airport in Toronto. He oversees the work of sixteen technicians who handle thirty to forty aircraft per shift.

This book is about the millions of Judys and Sabbys out there in organizations, and the job they do. This book will introduce you to the challenging and rapidly changing world of *Supervision in Canada Today*.

SUPERVISORS AND THE MANAGEMENT PROCESS

Supervisors work in places called organizations. Before we identify who supervisors are and what they do, it's important to clarify what we mean by the term *organization*.

An organization is a systematic grouping of people brought together to accomplish some specific purpose. Your college or university is an organization. So are sororities, charitable agencies, churches, your neighborhood convenience store, the Edmonton Oilers hockey team, the Home Depot Corporation, the Canadian Dental Association, and Mount Sinai Hospital. They are all organizations because each is comprised of three common characteristics.

Edmonton Oilers NHL Site
http://www.nhl.com/teams/edm/

First, every organization has a purpose. The distinct purpose of an organization is typically expressed in terms of a goal or set of goals. For example, the Rubbermaid Corporation set a goal of achieving 15 per cent annual growth in revenues.[1]

Second, no purpose or goal can achieve itself. It takes people to establish the purpose, as well as to perform a variety of activities to make the goal a reality.

Third, all organizations develop a systematic structure that defines the various roles of members, and that often sets limits on their work behaviours. This may include creating rules and regulations, giving some members supervisory control over other members, forming work teams, or writing job descriptions so that organizational members know what their responsibilities are.

In most traditional organizations, we can depict this structure as a pyramid containing four general categories (see Figure 1-3).

The bottom level in the pyramid is occupied by **operative employees**. These are the rank-and-file workers who physically produce an organization's goods and services. The counter clerk at McDonald's, the claims adjuster at London Life, the assembly-line worker at the Honda auto plant, and the postal carrier who delivers your mail are examples of operative employees. This category also includes many professional

Operative employees
Rank-and-file workers who physically produce an organization's goods and services

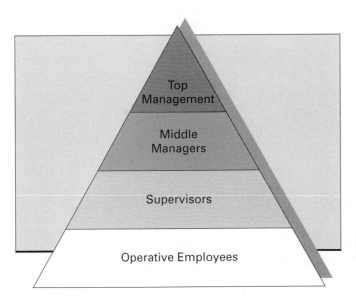

FIGURE 1-3

Levels in the organizational pyramid

people: doctors, lawyers, accountants, engineers, and computer specialists. The common characteristic these operative workers share is that they don't manage or oversee any other employees.

Now turn your attention to the top two levels in Figure 1-3. These are management positions. **Top management** is the people responsible for establishing the organization's overall objectives and developing the policies to achieve those objectives. Titles of typical top management positions in business firms include chairman of the board, chief executive officer, president, and senior vice president. Among nonprofit organizations, top management has titles such as museum director, superintendent of schools, and provincial premier. **Middle managers** include all employees below the top-management level who manage other managers. Examples of job titles held by middle managers include vice president for finance, director of sales, division manager, group manager, district manager, unit manager, and high school principal.

WHO ARE SUPERVISORS?

Returning to Figure 1-3, the only category left that we haven't described is **supervisors**. Like top managers and middle managers, supervisors are also part of management. But what makes them unique is that they oversee the work of operative employees. Supervisors, then, are the only managers who don't manage other managers. Or another way to think of supervisors is as **first-level managers**. That is, counting from the bottom of the traditional pyramid-shaped organization, supervisors represent the first level in the management hierarchy.

What kind of titles are likely to tell you that someone is a supervisor? Though names are sometimes deceptive, people with job titles like assistant manager, department head, department chair, head coach, foreman, or team leader are typically in supervisory positions.

An interesting aspect of supervisory positions is that many supervisors engage in operative tasks with their employees. For instance, the counter clerk at McDonald's may also be the shift foreman. Or the claims supervisor at London Life may also process claim forms. But even though they perform operative tasks, supervisors are still part of management. They have the authority to influence many aspects of employees' working lives. This authority may be applied to hiring, firing, promotion, transfer, layoffs, recall, assignments, scheduling, reward, discipline, and promotion.

WHAT IS MANAGEMENT?

The term **management** refers to the process of getting things done, effectively and efficiently, through and with other people. There are several components in this definition that warrant some discussion. These are the terms *process, effectively,* and *efficiently.*

Top management
The highest level of management. Those people responsible for establishing the organization's overall objectives and developing the policies to achieve those objectives.

Middle managers
All employees below the top-management level who manage other managers

Supervisors
First-level managers who oversee the work of operatives or nonmanagement employees

First-level managers
Supervisors

Management
The process of getting things done, effectively and efficiently, through and with other people. *See also* Process; Efficiency; Effectiveness.

The term **process** in the definition of management represents the primary activities supervisors perform. In management terms, we call these the *functions of management*. The next section will describe these functions.

Efficiency means doing the task right and refers to the relationship between inputs and outputs. If you get more output for a given input, you have increased efficiency. You also increase efficiency when you get the same output with fewer resources. Since supervisors deal with input resources that are scarce—money, people, equipment—they are concerned with the efficient use of these resources. Consequently, supervisors must be concerned with minimizing resource costs.

While minimizing resource costs is important, it isn't enough simply to be efficient. A supervisor must also be concerned with completing activities. We call this **effectiveness**. Effectiveness means doing the right task. In an organization, we call this *goal attainment*.

The need for efficiency has a profound impact on the level of effectiveness. It's easier to be effective if you ignore efficiency. For instance, you could produce more sophisticated and higher-quality products if you disregarded labour and material input costs—yet that would almost certainly create problems. Consequently, being a good supervisor means being concerned with both attaining goals (effectiveness) and doing so as efficiently as possible.

What Do Managers Do?

All managers engage in the **management functions**. By that we mean that they plan, organize, lead, and control. Since supervisors are part of management, we need to briefly review these four generic functions.

If you don't know where you want to go, any road will take you there. Because managers have objectives they want to achieve, they need to define those objectives and the means of attaining them. That's what **planning** is about. The planning function involves defining objectives and developing a comprehensive set of plans to integrate and coordinate the activities necessary to achieve those objectives.

Managers also have to divide work into manageable components and coordinate results to achieve objectives. We call this function **organizing**. It includes determining what tasks are to be done, who is to do them, how the tasks are to be grouped, who reports to whom, and where decisions are to be made.

Every organization contains people, and it is management's job to direct, coordinate, and motivate these people. This is the **leading** function. When managers motivate employees, direct the activities of others, select the most effective communication channel, or resolve conflicts among team members, they are leading.

The final function all managers perform is **controlling**. To ensure that things are going as they should, management must monitor activities and measure performance. Actual performance must be compared

Process
The primary activities supervisors perform

Efficiency
Doing a task right; also refers to the relationship between inputs and outputs.

Effectiveness
Doing a task right; goal attainment.

Management functions
The four managerial functions of planning, organizing, leading, and controlling

Planning
Defining objectives and the means of attaining them

Organizing
Dividing work into manageable components and coordinating results to achieve objectives

Leading
Directing and coordinating people

Controlling
Monitoring activities to ensure that objectives are being met as planned, and correcting any significant deviations

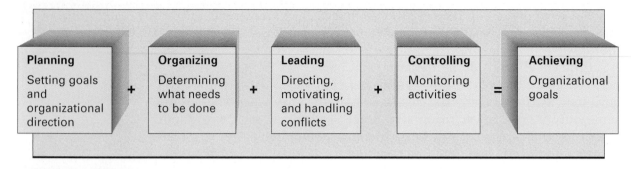

FIGURE 1-4

Management functions

with the previously set objectives. If there are any significant deviations, it is management's job to get things back on track. This process of measuring, comparing, and correcting is what we mean when we refer to the controlling function.

Does a manager's level in an organization affect how these functions are performed? For instance, does a supervisor in the accounting department at Molson Breweries do the same kind of planning as the president of Molson Breweries does? What we find is that all managers perform these four functions, but that there are important differences among the management levels. For example, top management focuses on long-term, strategic planning such as determining what overall business a company should be in, while supervisors emphasize short-term, tactical planning such as scheduling departmental work loads for the next month. Similarly, top management is concerned with designing the overall organization, while supervisors focus on designing the jobs of individuals and work groups.

A manager's level in the organization affects not only the type of planning, organizing, leading, and controlling he or she does, but also the emphasis that he or she gives to the various functions. As Figure 1-5 illustrates, supervisors spend the majority of time on leading-related activities. More specifically, in a recent study more than 650 first-level managers were asked to identify the specific tasks they felt were very important to perform their jobs successfully.[2] Figure 1-6 lists tasks that at least 50 per cent of these supervisors considered very important.

THE TRANSITION FROM EMPLOYEE TO SUPERVISOR

"It wasn't easy making the move from being one of the accountants in the department to being the supervisor. On Friday, I had been one of them. The next Monday, I became their boss. Suddenly, people that I had joked around and socialized with for years were distancing themselves from me. I could see that they were apprehensive. They weren't sure, now, if I could be trusted. I didn't think our relationship was going to be much different.

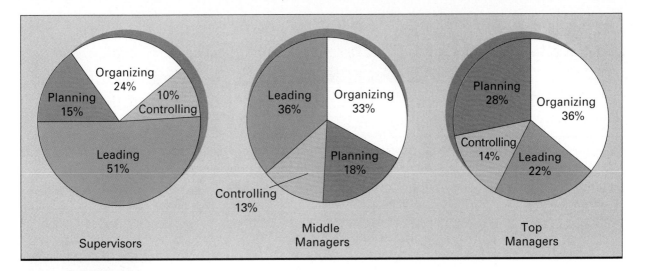

FIGURE 1-5

Distribution of time per function by organizational level. (*Source:* Adapted from T. A. Mahoney, T. H. Jerdee, and S. J. Carroll, "The Job(s) of Management," *Industrial Relations*, vol. 4, no. 2 (1965), p. 103.

- Motivate employees to change or improve their performance.

- Provide ongoing performance feedback to employees.

- Take action to resolve performance problems in your work group.

- Blend employees' goals with organization's work requirements.

- Identify ways of improving communications among employees.

- Inform employees about procedures and work assignments.

- Keep track of employees' training and special skills as they relate to job assignments to aid their growth and development.

FIGURE 1-6

Key supervisory tasks (based on a survey of more than 650 supervisors). (Based on Allen I. Kraut and others, "The Role of the Manager: What's Really Important in Different Management Jobs," *Academy of Management Executive*, November 1989, p. 287.)

Hey, we were friends. We went out for beers every Friday after work. But I'm management now. I still think I'm like them, part of the group. But they don't see me that way. Even when I join them for beers, it's not like it used to be. They have their guards up now. It's been a hard adjustment for me."

The above comments from a recently promoted accounting supervisor at Reynolds Metals Co. captures the dilemma many new supervisors face when they're promoted from the ranks. In this section, we'll look at the primary routes people take to becoming supervisors and the challenges they face in mastering a new identity.

WHERE DO SUPERVISORS COME FROM?

The majority of new supervisors are promoted from within the ranks of their own organization. The second major source of supervisory personnel is new college or university graduates. Occasionally employees of other organizations are hired to become first-line supervisors; however, this is increasingly rare. The reason is that if employers have an open supervisory position, they prefer to fill it with someone they know fairly well and who knows the organization. That favours promoting from within.

Employers tend to promote operative employees to first-line management jobs for several reasons. Operative employees tend to know the job. They understand how things are done in the organization. They typically know the people they'll be supervising. And the organization knows a lot about the candidate. When management promotes "one of its own" into a supervisory position, it minimizes risk. When it hires from outside, it has to rely on limited information provided by previous employers. By promoting from within, management can draw on its full history with a candidate. Finally, and very importantly, promoting from within acts as an employee motivator: it provides an incentive for employees to work hard and excel.

What criteria does management tend to use in deciding whom to promote into first-line managerial positions? Employees with good work records and an interest in management tend to be favoured. Ironically, good operative employees don't necessarily make good supervisors. The reason is that people with strong technical skills don't necessarily have the skills needed to manage others. We find that those organizations that successfully promote from the ranks select employees with adequate technical skills and provide them with supervisory training early in their new assignments.

Recent graduates provide the other primary source of candidates for supervisory positions. University and college programs in business provide a basic foundation for preparing for the supervisor's job. When coupled with some additional organizational training, many new university and college graduates are equipped to step into first-line management.

FIGURE 1-7

David LeRoy of Paramount Canada's Wonderland in Maple, Ontario, shows a typical internal promotion pattern: line to lead to supervisor to area manager and now senior area rides manager. His expertise will soon see a new application: on completing his college diploma, he will join the human resource department.

MASTERING A NEW IDENTITY

Moving from one middle-management job to another, or from a middle-management position to one in top management, rarely creates the anxiety that comes when one moves from being an employee to a supervisor. It's a lot like being a parent. If you already have three kids, the addition of one more isn't too big a deal. Why? Because you already know quite a bit about parenting. The trauma lies in the transition from being childless to being a parent for the first time. The same applies in management. The trauma experienced when an employee moves into first-line management is unique, and unlike anything he or she will encounter later in climbing up the organizational ladder.

A study of what nineteen new supervisors experienced in their first year on the job helps us to better understand what it's like to become a first-line manager.[3] The people in this study were fourteen men and five

FIGURE 1-8

Elizabeth Wright is a library Branch Head in Ontario's Wentworth Region. She thought she would have a lot of autonomy to make decisions, but found she "couldn't change the world after all."

women. All worked in sales or marketing. However, what they experienced would seem relevant to anyone making the employee-supervisor transition.

Even though these new supervisors had worked in their respective organizations as salespeople for an average of six years, their expectations of a manager's job were incomplete and simplistic. They didn't appreciate the full range of demands that would be made on them. Each had previously been a star salesperson. They were promoted, in large part, as a reward for their good performance. But "good performance" for a salesperson and "good performance" for a manager are very different—and few of these new supervisors understood that. Ironically, their previous successes in sales may actually have made their transition to management harder. Because of their strong technical expertise and high motivation, they had needed less support than the average salesperson. So when they became supervisors and suddenly had to deal with low-performing and unmotivated employees, they weren't prepared for it.

The nineteen new supervisors actually encountered a number of surprises. We'll briefly summarize the major ones because they capture the essence of what many supervisors encounter as they attempt to master their new identity.

Their initial view of the manager as "boss" was incorrect. Before taking their supervisory jobs, these managers-to-be talked about the power they would have and about being in control. As one put it, "Now, I'll be the one calling the shots." After a month, they spoke of being a "trouble-shooter," "a juggler," and a "quick-change artist." All emphasized solving problems, making decisions, helping others, and providing resources as their primary responsibilities. They no longer conceived of the manager's job as being "the boss."

They were unprepared for the demands and ambiguities they would face. In their first week, these supervisors were surprised by the unrelenting workload and pace of being a manager. On a typical day, they had to work on many problems simultaneously and were met with constant interruptions.

Technical expertise was no longer the primary determinant of success or failure. They were used to excelling by performing specific technical tasks and being individual contributors, not by acquiring managerial competence and getting things done through others. It took four to six months on the job for most to come to grips with the fact they now would be judged by their ability to motivate others to high performance.

A supervisor's job comes with administrative duties. These supervisors found that routine communication activities such as paperwork and exchange of information were time-consuming and interfered with their autonomy.

They weren't prepared for the "people challenges" of their new job. The managers unanimously asserted that the most demanding skills they had to learn in their first year dealt with managing people. They said they were particularly uncomfortable in counselling employees and providing leadership. As one stated, "I hadn't realized...how hard it is to motivate people or develop them or deal with their personal problems."

SOMETHING TO THINK ABOUT
•AND TO PROMOTE CLASS DISCUSSION•

Becoming a supervisor is a challenging opportunity. Some individuals look forward to "taking the helm" of a crew of workers, while others are put into this situation with little advance notice—or training. As you consider going into a supervisory position—or making yourself a more effective supervisor than you are today—think about the following two areas.

1. List five reasons why you want to be a supervisor.

   _____

   _____

   _____

   _____

   _____

2. Identify five potential problems or difficulties that you may encounter when you become a supervisor.

   _____

   _____

   _____

   _____

   _____

Do You Really Want to Be a Supervisor?

The fact that you're learning about supervision indicates that you're interested in understanding how to supervise people. What is it about supervising people that excites you? Is it the fact that you can help an organization achieve its goals? Is it the challenge of supervising others—directing their work—that interests you? Is it the fact that supervision may lead to a management position and the chance to climb the career ladder? Whatever your reasons, you need a clear picture of what lies ahead.

Supervisory positions are not easy. Even if you've been a superstar as an employee, this is no guarantee that you'll succeed as a supervisor. The fact that you are capable of doing excellent work is a big plus, but there are many other factors to consider. You need to recognize that supervising others may mean longer work hours. You're often on the job before your employees and leave after they do. Supervising can literally

FIGURE 1-9

Brian Morrison chose to leave his supervisory position and return to production. Ironically, he ended up leading his group into becoming a self-managed team, which prompted changes across the company. See Case 1.B.

be a 24-hour, seven-day-a-week job. Now, that's not to be interpreted as being on the job every hour of every day. But when you accept the responsibility of supervising others, you really never can "get away" from the job. Things happen, and you'll be expected to deal with them—no matter when they happen, or where you are. It's not unheard of to get a call while you're on vacation, if problems arise. How did someone in the organization get your vacation phone number? You probably gave it to that individual—either as required by an organizational policy, or when you "called in" to see how things were going.

You also need to recognize that, as a supervisor, you may have a seemingly endless pile of paperwork to complete. Although organizations are continually working to eliminate paperwork, a lot still remains. This may include employee work schedules, production cost estimates, inventory documentation, or budget and payroll matters.

Another matter of importance that you should consider is the effect the supervisor's job may have on your pay! In many organizations, a raise in your base pay when you become a supervisor does not translate into higher annual earnings. How so? Consider that, as a supervisor, you are no longer eligible for overtime pay. Instead, in most companies, you get compensatory time (time off). As an operative employee, however, your organization is legally required to pay you a premium rate (typically time and one-half) for overtime work. That may not be true when you become a supervisor. So if you get a $3000 raise when you become a supervisor, but earned $3500 last year in overtime, you're actually earning less as a supervisor. This is something that you'll need to discuss with your organization before making your decision to become a supervisor.

What are the paragraphs above really saying? They're telling you to think about why you want to supervise. Managing others can be rewarding. The excitement is real—and so are the headaches. You need to understand exactly what your motives are for becoming a supervisor—and what tradeoffs you're willing to make to become the best supervisor you can be.

COMPETENCIES OF SUPERVISORS

What does it take to be an effective manager? What competencies or general categories of skills does a manager need? Are these the same, regardless of the manager's level in the organization? We'll answer those questions in this section.

Management competencies General categories of skills necessary to successfully perform a managerial job

Thirty years ago, Robert Katz identified three essential **management competencies**: technical, interpersonal, and conceptual.[4] They are as relevant today as when Katz originally described them.

TECHNICAL COMPETENCE

Top management is composed of generalists. Louis Gerstner, Jr. was able to successfully move from CEO of RJR Nabisco to CEO of IBM because it wasn't necessary for him to know a great deal about the manufacturing of cookies, cigarettes or computers in order to do these jobs. The activities that consume top managers—strategic planning; developing the organization's overall structure and culture; maintaining relations with major customers, bankers, and the like—are essentially generic in nature. The technical demands of top management jobs tend to be related to knowledge of the industry and a general understanding of the organization's processes and products. But this isn't true for managers at other levels.

Most managers manage within areas of specialized knowledge: the vice-president for *finance*; the director of *computer systems*; the regional *sales* manager; the supervisor of *health claims*. These managers require **technical competence**—the ability to apply specialized knowledge or expertise. It's difficult, if not impossible, to effectively manage people with specialized skills if you don't have an adequate understanding of the technical aspects of their jobs. Of course, there are certain technical skills that are part of every manager's job and which he or she needs to be able to apply. For example, developing a budget is a technical skill in which all managers need to be competent.

Technical competence
The ability to apply specialized knowledge or expertise

INTERPERSONAL COMPETENCE

The ability to work with, understand, communicate with, and motivate other people, both individually and in groups, describes **interpersonal competence**. Many people are technically proficient but interpersonally incompetent. They might, for example, be poor listeners, unable to understand the needs of others, or have difficulty in dealing with conflicts. Since managers get things done through other people, they must have good interpersonal skills to communicate, motivate, and delegate.

Interpersonal competence
The ability to work with, understand, and motivate other people, both individually and in groups

CONCEPTUAL COMPETENCE

Managers must have the mental ability to analyze and diagnose complex situations. This ability is called **conceptual competence**. From a more theoretical viewpoint, strong conceptual abilities allow a manager to see that the organization is a complex system of many interrelated parts; and that the organization itself is part of a larger system that includes the organization's industry, the community, and the nation's economy. On a more practical level, strong conceptual abilities help managers make good decisions.

Conceptual competence
The mental ability to analyze and diagnose complex situations

POLITICAL COMPETENCE

Political competence
A supervisor's ability to enhance his or her power, build a power base, and establish the "right" connections in the organization

Supervisors need to possess **political competence**. This refers to the supervisor's ability to enhance his or her power, build a power base, and establish the "right" connections in the organization. Politics is something supervisors engage in when they attempt to influence the advantages and disadvantages of a situation.[5] It goes beyond normal work activities. Whenever two or more people come together for some purpose, each has some idea of what should occur. If one person tries to influence the situation such that it benefits him or her more than the others, or keeps others from gaining some advantage, then politics is being "played."

But not all political behaviour is negative. It doesn't have to involve manipulating a series of events, complaining about fellow supervisors, or sabotaging the work or reputation of another to further one's career. There's a fine line between appropriate political behaviour and negative politics. We'll come back to organizational politics in Chapter 12.

FIGURE 1-10

"It's important for me to know my registered representatives' job," says Mark Ward, a former branch manager for Green Line Investor Services Inc. "They use me as a point of reference and ask me questions. Being in management, I'm not doing their job on a daily basis, therefore I have to make an effort to keep up with all the changes."

COMPETENCIES AND MANAGERIAL LEVEL

While managers need to possess all three competencies, the importance each competency plays in the manager's job varies with the manager's level in the organization. Here are some general rules:

1. Technical competence declines in importance as managers rise in the organization.
2. Conceptual competencies increase in importance as managerial responsibility rises.
3. Interpersonal competencies are a constant to success, regardless of level in the organization.
4. Political competence grows in importance as managers rise in the organization.

Technical abilities have the greatest relevance for first-level managers. This is true for two reasons. First, many perform technical work as well as managerial work. In contrast to other levels of management, the distinction between individual contributor and first-line manager is often blurred. Second, supervisors spend more time on training and developing their employees than do other managers. This requires them to have a greater technical knowledge of their employees' jobs than that needed by middle- and top-level managers.

The importance of conceptual competence increases as managers move up in the organization because of the type of problems and decisions that managers make at different levels. Generally speaking, the higher a manager rises in an organization, the more the problems he or she faces tend to be complex, ambiguous, and ill-defined. This requires custom-made solutions. In contrast, first-level managers generally have more straightforward, familiar, and easily defined problems which lend themselves to more routine decision making. Ill-structured problems and custom-made solutions make greater conceptual demands on managers than do structured problems and routine decision making.

There is overwhelming evidence that interpersonal abilities are critical at all levels of management. This shouldn't come as a shock, because we know that managers get things done through other people. But supervisors are particularly in need of interpersonal competencies because they spend so much of their time in leading-function activities. Larry Sylvester, a plant manager with Canada Brick, made this point when discussing his managerial positions in the plywood, concrete precast, and brick industries. "Whatever the company produces, it's people you work with as a manager. So the skills you need are the same anywhere." In talking with dozens of practising supervisors, the one common viewpoint we have heard is the importance of "people skills" to the successful achievement of their unit's objectives.

Finally, the higher one climbs in the organization's hierarchy, the more critical political competence becomes. Because resource allocation decisions are made at higher levels in an organization, middle and top managers are "fighting" for their piece of the organizational pie. Their need to develop alliances, support one project over another, or influence certain situations, involves higher-level political skills. But don't interpret this as implying that politics is less important for supervisors. Because so much of the supervisor's job is well-defined, he or she needs strong political skills to get the unit's work completed, and to survive (see Assessing Yourself)!

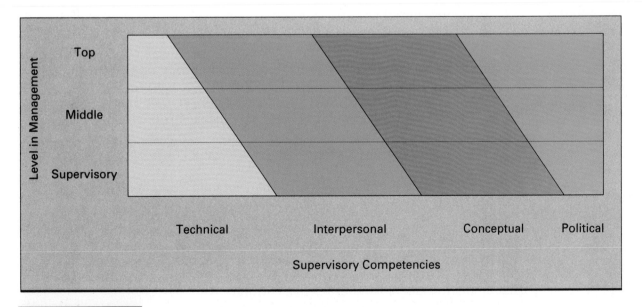

FIGURE 1-11

How competency demands vary at different levels of management

Assessing Yourself

DO YOU HAVE WHAT IT TAKES TO BE POLITICAL?

Are you an individual who likes to play politics? Is it something that you have the ability to do? Even if you prefer not to, can you "play" to protect yourself?

Undoubtedly, politics exists in every organization. Therefore, one of the first steps is understanding your political temperament. Listed below are several statements. Check True or False based on how you feel about the statement most of the time.

	True	False
1. I stay late just to impress my boss.	☒	☐
2. I do not tell others how I do things, so they don't know what I do.	☐	☒
3. I do not use gossip to my advantage.	☐	☒
4. I rarely express my opinion about my organization if my opinions are negative.	☐	☒
5. I go out of my way to make friends with powerful people.	☐	☒
6. I would not raise concerns about someone's ability to do a job, even if we were competing for a promotion.	☐	☒
7. I won't take credit for the work of someone else.	☒	☐
8. I'd tell my boss if a coworker was actively looking for a new job.	☐	☒
9. I would want my name on a group project, even though my effort was minimal.	☒	☐
10. I see nothing wrong in tooting my own horn.	☒	☐
11. I like having decorations all around my work area.	☐	☒
12. I take action only after I am sure it's ethical to do so.	☒	☐
13. I'd be foolish to publicly correct a mistake my boss made.	☐	☒
14. I'd purchase stock in my company even if it was a financial risk.	☐	☒
15. I would not play the role of "hatchet man," even if it meant a promotion for me.	☐	☒
16. I want others to fear me more than like me.	☐	☒
17. I would not join in with coworkers making fun of the boss.	☒	☐
18. Getting ahead means promoting my self-interest.	☐	☒
19. I would not want to help a coworker who makes my performance look bad.	☒	☐
20. I think it's important to be friendly with everyone at work—especially those I don't like.	☒	☐

SCORING

Give yourself one point for each response that matches those given below.

1. True	6. False	11. False	16. True
2. True	7. False	12. False	17. True
3. False	8. True	13. True	18. True
4. True	9. True	14. True	19. True
5. True	10. True	15. False	20. True

MAKING SENSE OF THE ASSESSMENT

Your political score on this assessment indicates how likely you are to use politics to gain an advantage in a situation. Scores greater than 14 indicate you have an above-average willingness to use politics to get what you want. Scores from 10 to 13 indicate you use politics mainly to protect yourself—especially from your boss and those you perceive as having power. Scores from 6 to 9 indicate you have a true belief in others—that they are fair, honest, and not likely to mistreat you. Although noteworthy, this score may indicate you don't understand organizational politics, and you may be somewhat naive in assessing the effect politics may have on you. Finally, scores less than 5 indicate an absence of ability to play politics in an organization. Remember, politics isn't always destructive—there's a constructive component that you must use to your advantage.

Source: *Winning Office Politics* by Andrew Dubrin. Copyright © 1990. Reprinted with permission of Prentice Hall.

FROM CONCEPTS TO SKILLS

It's true that supervision comes easier to some people than to others. Individuals who were fortunate enough to grow up with parents, relatives, or friends who were managers may have insights into what the job entails and role models to emulate. Similarly, those individuals whose parents helped them set realistic goals, provided positive feedback, encouraged autonomy, practiced open communication, and fostered the development of a strong self-concept have learned behaviours that will help them as managers. Also, those who have had the fortune to work for a good manager have a role model to imitate. But anyone can improve his or her supervisory abilities.

This book will help you to be an effective supervisor by focusing on both conceptual knowledge and practical skills. In the next chapter, for example, we'll discuss the importance of planning to a supervisor's success and show how setting goals is a key part of planning. Then we'll present specific techniques for helping employees set goals and provide you with an opportunity to practice and develop your goal-setting skills.

Skill
The ability to demonstrate a system and sequence of behaviour that is functionally related to attainment of a performance goal

What exactly is a skill? A **skill** is the ability to demonstrate a system and sequence of behaviour that is functionally related to attaining a performance goal.[6] No single action constitutes a skill. For example, the ability to write clear communications is a skill. People who have this skill know the particular sequence of actions to be taken to propose a project or summarize a report. They can separate primary from secondary ideas. They can organize their thoughts in a logical manner. They can simplify convoluted ideas. But none of these actions is by itself a skill. A skill is a system of behaviour that can be applied in a wide range of situations.

What are the key skills related to supervisory effectiveness? While there is no unanimous agreement among teachers and trainers of supervision, certain skills have surfaced as being more important than others. Figure 1-13 lists those key supervisory skills organized as they'll be presented in this text. In aggregate, they form the competency base for effective supervision.

Related to Planning and Control
• Goal setting
• Budgeting
• Creative problem solving
• Developing control charts

Related to Organizing, Staffing, and Employee Development
• Empowering others
• Interviewing
• Providing feedback
• Coaching

Related to Stimulating Individual and Group Performance
• Designing motivating jobs
• Projecting charisma
• Listening
• Conducting a group meeting

Related to Coping with Workplace Dynamics
• Negotiation
• Stress reduction
• Counselling
• Disciplining
• Handling grievances

FIGURE 1-13
Key supervisory skills

What Else Do I Need to Know about Supervising?

If by now you're somewhat amazed at what a supervisor has to do and the skills he or she must have to succeed in an organization, there are nonetheless several other elements that you should consider. Specifically, what are the personal issues that you should address?

One of the first things you'll need to do is to recognize that as a supervisor, you are part of management. This means that you support the organization and the wishes of management above you. Although you might disagree with those wishes, you must, as a supervisor, be *loyal* to the organization. You must also develop a means of *gaining respect* from your employees, as well as from your peers and boss. If you're going to be effective as a supervisor, you'll need to develop their trust and build credibility with them. One means of doing this is to continually keep your *skills and competencies* up to date. You must continue your "education," not only because it helps you, but also because it sets an example for your employees. It communicates that learning matters.

You'll also have to understand what legitimate power you have been given by the organization because you direct the activities of others. This legitimate power is your *authority* to act and to expect others to follow your directions. Yet, be aware that ruling with an iron fist may not work. You'll need to know when to assert your authority and how to get things done without resorting to "because I told you so." To get things done in the organization, you need to develop interpersonal skills that help you *influence* others. This is particularly true when dealing with organizational members that you don't supervise.

Finally, you'll need to recognize that organizational members differ from one another—not only in their talents, but as individuals. You'll need to be *sensitive to their needs, tolerate and even celebrate their differences,* and *be empathetic* to them as individuals. Success, in part, will begin with understanding the meaning of flexibility.

Throughout this text we'll be addressing each of these areas.

SUPERVISORY CHALLENGES FOR THE 21ST CENTURY

The world of management has changed dramatically in the last fifteen years. A few examples illustrate this point.

- Traditional national boundaries have become far less important as business firms have gone international.
- The workforce has become more diverse as new entrants are increasingly women and members of minority groups.

- Many thousands of white-collar workers have been laid off as organizations have sought to cut bureaucratic "fat."
- Jobs and decision making are increasingly done by teams rather than by individuals.
- Computers are increasingly used to process information and aid decision making.

The effects of these changes have not been limited to middle-level and upper-level managers. In many ways, these and other changes have reshaped the supervisor's job. In the remainder of this chapter, we will review some of the more significant forces that affect supervisors at the dawn of the twenty-first century.

CHANGING EXPECTATIONS OF SUPERVISORS

Forty years ago, if you asked a group of top executives what they thought a supervisor's or foreman's job was, you'd get a fairly standard answer. They'd describe a man (which it was likely to be back then) who made and enforced decisions, told employees what to do, closely watched over those employees to make sure they did as they were told, disciplined them when they broke the rules, and fired those that didn't "shape up." Supervisors were the bosses on the "operating floor" and their job was to keep the employees in line and get the work done.

If you asked top executives that same question today, you'd find a few who still hold to the supervisor-as-boss perspective. But you'd be far more likely to hear executives describe today's supervisor with terms like "trainer," "adviser," "mentor," "facilitator," or "coach." In this section, we will look at how top management, the public, and even operative employees have developed changing expectations of supervisory managers.

ROLE AMBIGUITY

The supervisor's job—unique in that it bridges both the management and operative ranks—has long had an ambiguous role. For example, each of the following offers a different viewpoint of the supervisor's role:[7]

Key person.   Supervisors serve as the critical communication link in the organization's chain of authority. They are like the hub of a wheel around which all operating activities revolve.

Person in the middle.   Because they are "neither fish nor fowl," supervisors must interact and reconcile the opposing forces and competing expectations from higher management and workers. If unresolved, this ambiguous status can create frustration and stress for supervisors.

Just another worker. To some, particularly among upper-level managers, supervisors are often seen as "just another worker" rather than as management. This is reinforced when their decision-making authority is limited, when they're excluded from participating in upper-level decisions, and when they perform operating tasks alongside the people they supervise.

Behavioural specialist. Consistent with the belief that one of the most important abilities needed by supervisors is strong interpersonal skills, we can view them as behavioural specialists. To succeed in their jobs, supervisors must be able to understand the varied needs of their staff; and be able to listen, motivate, and lead.

While each of these four role descriptions has some truth to it, each also offers a slanted view of the supervisor's job. Our point is that different people hold different perceptions of this job, which can create ambiguity and conflicts for today's supervisor.

INCREASED IMPORTANCE

Despite the differing perceptions individuals may hold about the supervisor's role, the fact is that the supervisor's job has always been important and complex, and will become increasingly so in the future.[8] Why? There are at least three reasons.

First, organizations are universally implementing significant change programs to cut costs and increase productivity. Examples of these programs include quality improvement, introduction of work teams, group bonus plans, flexible work hours, accident prevention, and stress-reduction programs. These programs tend to focus on the work activities of operative employees. As a result, supervisors have become increasingly important because they typically assume responsibility for introducing and implementing these change efforts on the operating floor.

Second, organizations are imposing extensive cutbacks in their number of employees. Stelco, Bell Canada, General Motors, IBM, CN, Woodward's, and Air Canada are just a few of the major companies that have cut thousands of jobs. Organizations have been thinning the ranks particularly of middle managers and staff-support personnel. "Lean and mean" is likely to be a major theme well into the first decade of the 2000s.

Air Canada
http://www.aircanada.ca/

The implications of these cutbacks for supervisors are clear. Fewer middle managers means that supervisors will have more people reporting directly to them. Moreover, many of the tasks previously performed by people in support units—such as work design, process flow, scheduling, and quality control—will be reassigned to supervisors and their employees. The net effect will be significantly expanded responsibilities for supervisors.

Finally, employee training is becoming more important than ever as organizations seek to improve productivity. New employees—many of them poorly schooled or immigrants with limited skill in the English language—require basic training in reading and writing. Changes in jobs brought about by computers, automation, and other technological advances require additional training among current employees in order to keep their skills up to date. Supervisors will carry the primary burden for identifying these skill deficiencies, for designing appropriate training programs, and in some cases even for providing the training itself.

FROM BOSS TO COACH

Rick Carpenter has been a supervisor at the Hershey Pasta Group for more than twenty years. When asked how his leadership style has changed over this period, he says, "I've become a facilitator rather than a direction giver." This transition is not unique to Rick Carpenter. One of the most common observations of new supervisors is that they act less as authoritative bosses and more as facilitating coaches.

The supervisor-as-boss model dominated organizations for the first eighty-five years of this century. In this model, supervisors were expected to know everything about the jobs their employees did. The boss, in fact, was assumed to be able to do every worker's job as well or better than the worker could. And because the supervisor was more knowledgeable and skilled, employees looked to him or her for direction. Supervisors responded by giving orders. Employees expected to be told what to do and supervisors did just that.

Today's supervisors are far less likely to be able to do their employees' jobs. Employees don't need or want an authority figure to tell them what to do or to "keep them in line." What they need is a coach who can listen, guide, train, assist, and empower. In their coaching role, supervisors are expected to ensure that employees have the resources they need to do a first-class job. They must also develop employees, clarify responsibilities and goals, motivate people to higher levels of performance, and represent the work group's interests within the organization.

GLOBAL COMPETITIVENESS

Many North American companies grew large and powerful following World War II because they faced modest competition. For instance, in the 1950s and 1960s, General Motors became the world's largest and most profitable corporation. Was it because GM efficiently produced first-rate

FIGURE 1-14

From boss to coach

THE BOSS	THE COACH
Decides	Guides
Directs	Develops
Orders	Shares
Controls	Empowers

Are You Comprehending
What You're Reading?

5. Supervisors in contemporary organizations are less likely than in earlier decades to be able to do their employees' jobs. True or False?

6. Interpersonal competence involves:
   a. the ability to enhance one's power base.
   b. the ability to analyze and diagnose complex situations.
   c. the ability to motivate, negotiate with, and delegate to others.
   d. the ability to apply specialized knowledge.

7. Why do technical abilities frequently have greater relevance for supervisors than for middle or top managers?

8. The ability to demonstrate a system and sequence of behaviour related to achieving a goal is:
   a. a conceptual competence.
   b. a political competence.
   c. a technical competence.
   d. none of the above.

products that were carefully matched to the needs of auto consumers? Not really. GM's success was more due to the fact that its only major competition came from two other relatively inefficient American producers—Ford and Chrysler. Now look at General Motors at the turn of the twenty-first century. It has drastically reduced costs, improved quality, and cut the time between designing a car and placing it in dealer showrooms. Did GM make these changes voluntarily? Absolutely not! It was forced to do this to meet changing global competition. Ford and Chrysler significantly improved their quality, developed innovative products like the minivan, and began selling imported cars under their names. Meanwhile, aggressive competition from companies like Honda, Toyota, Nissan, BMW, and Volvo increased pressure on GM to change in order to survive.

The GM example illustrates the fact that global competition and increased demands for quality are changing the way companies are organized and managed. Firms are taking dramatic steps to improve efficiency by cutting out layers of middle management and redesigning work around teams. They're also reorganizing departments and empowering employees to facilitate innovation, flexibility, and rapid response to changing markets.

Global competition and total quality management have been driving forces for change in the 1990s, and will continue to be such in the twenty-first century. Importantly, many of the changes they have imposed and will continue to impose on organizations will be strongly felt at the supervisory level. First-level managers will be responsible for implementing many of the changes that will be necessary to achieve global competitiveness and world-class products. Creating effective work teams, introducing pay-for-performance compensation systems, and implementing sophisticated work methods and technologies are some obvious examples of new responsibilities that are being placed on the shoulders of supervisors.

A boundaryless world introduces new challenges for supervisors. These challenges range from the way supervisors view people from foreign countries to the way they develop an understanding of minority employees' cultures. A specific challenge for supervisors is to recognize the differences that might exist and find ways to make their interactions with all employees more effective. See Supervision in Action, page 27.

DOWNSIZING, QUALITY MANAGEMENT AND REENGINEERING

DOWNSIZING

Canadian companies have been working to become "lean and mean" organizations. Organizations have cut employees from their payrolls as a result of foreign competition, mergers and takeovers, and deregulation in certain industries (like the airlines). In fact, by the mid-1990s, almost all Fortune 500 companies—like Sears, Kodak, IBM, and Toyota—had cut staff and reshaped their operations. In business terms, this action is called **downsizing**.

Organizations downsized to accomplish two primary goals: to create greater efficiency and to reduce costs. In many cases this meant that they reduced the number of workers employed by the organization. This included employees at all levels, including supervisors. Many activities were outsourced because workers outside the company with up-to-date skills could provide the services with more flexibility and lower costs.

TOTAL QUALITY MANAGEMENT

There is a quality revolution taking place in both business and the public sector.[9] The generic term that has evolved to describe this revolution is **total quality management**, or **TQM** for short. It was inspired by a small group of quality experts, the most prominent of them being the late W. Edwards Deming.

An American, Deming found few managers in the United States interested in his ideas in the 1950s. Consequently, he went to Japan and began advising many top Japanese managers on how to improve their production effectiveness. Central to his management methods was the use of statistics to analyze variability in production processes. A well-managed

Downsizing
A reduction in the workforce and reshaping of operations to create "lean and mean" organizations. The goals of organizational downsizing are greater efficiency and reduced costs.

Total quality management (TQM)
A philosophy of management that is driven by customer needs and expectations. Statistical control is used to reduce variability and result in uniform quality and predictable quantity of output.

The Cultural Variables

To date, the framework most valuable in helping managers better understand differences between national cultures is one developed by Geert Hofstede.[10] He surveyed over 116 000 IBM employees in forty countries, and found that supervisors and employees vary in four dimensions of national culture:

1. individualism versus collectivism
2. power distance
3. uncertainty avoidance
4. quantity versus quality of life[11]

Individualism refers to a loosely knit social framework in which people are expected to look after their own interests and those of their immediate family. This is made possible because of the large amount of freedom that such a society allows individuals. Its opposite is *collectivism*, which is characterized by a tight social framework. People expect others in groups to which they belong (such as a family or an organization) to look after them and protect them when they are in trouble. In exchange for this, they feel they owe absolute allegiance to the group.

Power distance is a measure of the extent to which a society accepts the fact that power in institutions and organizations is distributed unequally. A high power-distance society accepts wide differences in power within organizations. Employees show a great deal of respect for those in authority. Titles, rank, and status carry a lot of weight. In contrast, a low power-distance society plays down inequalities as much as possible. Supervisors still have authority, but employees are not fearful or in awe of the boss.

A society that is high in *uncertainty avoidance* is characterized by an increased level of anxiety among its people, which manifests itself in greater nervousness, stress, and aggressiveness. Because people feel threatened by uncertainty and ambiguity in these societies, mechanisms are created to provide security and reduce risk. Their organizations are likely to have more formal rules, there will be less tolerance for deviant ideas and behaviours, and members will strive to believe in absolute truths. Not surprisingly, in organizations in countries with high uncertainty avoidance, employees demonstrate relatively low job mobility, and lifetime employment is widely practised.

Quantity versus quality of life, like individualism and collectivism, represents a dichotomy. Some cultures emphasize the quantity of life, and value things like assertiveness and the acquisition of money and material goods. Other cultures emphasize the quality of life, placing importance on relationships and showing sensitivity and concern for the welfare of others.

Where do Canadian supervisors fit within this framework? Which cultures would be likely to involve the biggest adjustment problems for Canadian supervisors? To answer these questions, we have to identify those countries that are most and least like the Canada on the four dimensions. Canada is strongly individualistic, but low on power distance. This same pattern is exhibited by Great Britain, Australia, the United States, the Netherlands, and New Zealand. Those least similar to Canada on these dimensions are Venezuela, Columbia, Pakistan, Singapore, and the Philippines.

Canada scored low on uncertainty avoidance and high on quantity of life. This same pattern was shown by Ireland, Great Britain, the U.S., New Zealand, Australia, India, and South Africa. Those least similar to Canada on these dimensions are Chile and Portugal.

The study supports what many suspected—that the Canadian supervisor who transfers to London, New York, Melbourne, or a similar "Anglo" city has the fewest adjustments to make. The study further identifies the countries in which "culture shock" is likely to be the greatest, suggesting a need to radically modify the Canadian supervisory style.

The W. Edwards Deming Institute Web Site
http://www.deming.org/

organization, according to Deming, was one in which statistical control reduced variability and resulted in uniform quality and predictable quantity of output. That meant, from Deming's perspective, that the 64 233rd light bulb produced should have the same quality properties that the first one had. Deming developed a fourteen-point program for transforming organizations. Today, Deming's original program has been expanded into TQM—a philosophy of management that is driven by customer needs and expectations (see Figure 1-16). Importantly, the term *customer* in TQM is expanded beyond the traditional definition to include everyone who interacts with the organization's product or service, either internally or externally. TQM encompasses employees and suppliers, as well as the people who buy the organization's products or services. The objective is to create an organization committed to continuous improvement.

FIGURE 1-15

Downsizing efforts at IBM have resulted in supervisors having to become more responsive to employee needs. These IBM employees know they have more work in store for them, but their supervisor, Ted Childs (top centre) recognizes he has to let each of his employees have some control over their daily work activities. He continually encourages them to do the best they can.

1. **Focus on the customer.** The customer includes not only outsiders who buy the organization's products or services, but also internal customers (such as shipping or accounts payable personnel) who interact with and serve others in the organization.

2. **Continuous improvement.** TQM is a commitment to never being satisfied. "Very good" is not enough. Quality can always be improved.

3. **Improvement of the quality of everything the organization does.** TQM uses a very broad definition of quality. It relates not only to the final product, but also to the way the organization handles deliveries, how rapidly it responds to complaints, how politely the phones are answered, and the like.

4. **Accurate measurement.** TQM uses statistical techniques to measure every critical variable in the organization's operations. These are compared against standards or benchmarks to identify problems, trace them to their roots, and eliminate their causes.

5. **Involvement of employees.** TQM involves the people on the line in the improvement process. Teams are widely used in TQM programs for finding and solving problems.

FIGURE 1-16

The foundations of TQM

Macmillan Bathurst (MBI) has seen strong results, both within the firm and in the positive reactions of its customers, from its own continuous improvement efforts. In 1989, senior management initiated a Total Improvement Program, with each plant setting up its own projects focusing on quality issues. Changes ranged from redesigning forms and cleaning up work procedures to altering the way functions were carried out. Then the marketing department set up a program of Service, Quality, and Creativity which initiated new partnerships with customers in order to meet their needs. For example, MBI people went out to customers such as Maple Leaf Foods and found that in some cases the customer's receivers could not efficiently unload the MBI truck. So they altered the pallets used or the loading pattern of the MBI truck so that the customer's forklift could now drive onto the truck and lift off the shipping containers in minutes, instead of having to do the job by hand, taking hours. Similar communication with customers led to the reengineering of some products and the alteration of a number of processes, such as billing.

Despite both the recession and a declining market, MBI picked up market share. But they weren't content to rest on their laurels. Since 1992 they've been involved in an extensive TQM program that focuses on providing training in supervisory skills and Statistical Process Control (SPC) to staff across Canada. MBI also became the the first corrugated container manufacturer in Canada to be certified to ISO9002, an international quality standard. MBI had to meet stringent requirements to earn this certification, but in fact, the climate for change had been created and most of the necessary work had been accomplished by earlier quality projects. The main additional thrust for ISO9002 was the documentation of all activities.

The continuous improvement process at MBI has also changed the dynamics within the company. The focus on quality and objective data has led to improved problem solving within a flat and decentralized management structure, because people at all levels are now sitting down together and talking. In its training, which has been expensive and time-consuming, MBI has deliberately mixed people across functions and locations so they get to meet others in the company and better understand each other's roles. Powerful informal networks have developed. For example, the production people in New Westminster now talk with their counterparts in Winnipeg and Calgary, realizing the power of sharing information and ideas, rather than maintaining a regional posture. It has also become clear that the management philosophy has moved much closer to the "leader as facilitator and coach" than the "leader as boss" view.

REENGINEERING

Although TQM is a positive start in many organizations, it focuses on continuous improvement, or ongoing incremental change. Such action is intuitively appealing—the constant and permanent search to make things better. Today, however, companies live in a time of rapid and dynamic change. As the elements around them change ever more quickly, even a continuous improvement process may leave them behind the times.

The problem with continuous improvement is that it provides a false sense of security. It makes supervisors and managers feel like they're actively doing something positive, which is true. However, this may be today's version of rearranging the deck chairs on the *Titanic*. Why? Unfortunately, ongoing incremental change puts off facing up to the possibility that what the organization may really need is radical or quantum change. This concept is now commonly referred to as **reengineering.**[12] Reengineering occurs when most of the work being done in an organization is evaluated and altered. It requires organizational members to rethink what work should be done, how it is to be done, and how to best implement these decisions.

If you read the preceding section closely, you may be asking yourself: *Aren't these authors contradicting what they said a few paragraphs ago about TQM?* On the surface, it may appear so, but consider this: while TQM is important for organizations, and can lead to improvements for most, TQM may not always be the right thing initially. If what an organization is producing is outdated, a new improved version of the product may not help the company. Rather, major change is required. After that change has occurred, then continually improving it (TQM) can have its rightful place. Let's see how this may be so.

Assume you are the supervisor responsible for implementing some type of change in your company's roller skate manufacturing process. If you take the continuous improvement approach, your frame of reference will be a high-toe leather shoe on top of a steel carriage, with four wooden wheels. Your continuous improvement program may lead you to focus on using a different grade of cowhide for the shoe, adding speed laces to the uppers, or using a different type of ball-bearing in the wheels. Of course, your new skate may be better than the one you previously made, but is that enough? Compare your action to that of a competitor who reengineers the process.

To begin, your competitor poses the following question: How does she design a skate that is safe and fun, that provides greater mobility, and that is fast? Starting from scratch, and not being constrained by her current manufacturing process, she completes her redesign with something that looks like today's popular inline skates. Instead of your new improved leather and metal skates, you are now competing against a molded boot, similar to that used in skiing. Your competitor's skate is better than one made from leather, and has no laces to tie. Additionally, it uses four to six high-durability plastic wheels, which are placed inline for greater speed and mobility.

In this contrived example, both companies made progress. Which do you believe made the *most* progress given the dynamic environment they face? This hypothetical situation clearly reinforces why companies like Union Carbide, GTE, or Mutual Benefit Life opted for reengineering as opposed to incremental change.[13] It is imperative in today's business

Reengineering Radical or quantum change that occurs when most of the work being done in an organization is evaluated, and then altered. Reengineering requires organizational members to rethink what work should be done, how it is to be done, and how to best implement these decisions.

environment for all managers to consider the challenge of reengineering their organizational processes. Why? Because reengineering can lead to "major gains in cost, service, or time."[14] It is these kinds of gains that will take companies well into the twenty-first century.

WHAT ARE THE SUPERVISORY IMPLICATIONS OF DOWNSIZING, TQM, AND REENGINEERING?

Although downsizing, total quality management, and reengineering are activities that are initiated at the top-management levels of an organization, they do have an effect on supervisors. Supervisors may be heavily involved in implementing the changes. They must be prepared to deal with the organizational issues these changes bring about. Let's look at some of the implications.

Downsizing and Supervisors. When an organization downsizes, the most obvious effect is that people lose their jobs. Therefore, a supervisor can expect certain things to occur. Employees—both those let go and the ones that remain—may get angry. Both sets of employees may perceive that the organization no longer cares about them. Even though the downsizing decision is made at higher levels of management, the supervisor may receive the brunt of this resentment. In some cases, the supervisor may have participated in deciding which individuals to let go and which ones to keep, based on the organization's goals. After downsizing, employees who remain may be less loyal to the company.

An important challenge for supervisors will be motivating a workforce that feels less secure in their jobs and less committed to their employers. Corporate employees used to believe that their employers would reward their loyalty and good work with job security, generous benefits, and pay increases. By downsizing, companies have begun to discard traditional policies on job security, seniority, and compensation. These changes have resulted in a sharp decline in employee loyalty. As corporations have shown less commitment to employees, employees have shown less commitment to them. This impacts the supervisor's ability to motivate employees and maintain high productivity.

Downsizing may also cause increased competition among a supervisor's employees. If decisions are made to eliminate jobs based on a performance criterion, employees may be less likely to help one another. It may become every employee for him- or herself. That behaviour can defeat the team that a supervisor has built.

Finally, downsizing may foster issues for its survivors. Unless the work processes have been revamped, major tasks of jobs that were cut may still be required. Usually that means increased workloads for the remaining employees. This can lead to longer work days, creating conflicts for employees between their work and personal lives. For the supervisor, this, too, can dramatically affect work unit productivity.

TQM and Supervisors. Each supervisor must clearly define what quality means to the jobs in his or her unit. This needs to be communicated to every staff member. Each individual must then exert the necessary effort to move toward "perfection." Supervisors and their employees must recognize that failing to do so could lead to unsatisfied customers taking their purchasing power to competitors. Should that happen, jobs in the unit might be in jeopardy.

The premise of TQM, or continuous improvement, can generate a positive outcome for supervisors and employees. Everyone involved may now have input into how work is best done. The foundation of TQM is the participation of the people closest to the work. As such, TQM can eliminate many of the bottlenecks that have hampered work efforts in the past. TQM can help create more satisfying jobs—for both the supervisor and his or her employees.

Reengineering and Supervisors. If you accept the premise that reengineering will change how businesses operate, it stands to reason that supervisors will be directly affected. First of all, reengineering may leave some supervisors and employees confused and angry. When processes are restructured, some long-time work relationships may be severed.

Although reengineering has its skeptics, it can generate some benefits for supervisors. It may mean that they have an opportunity to learn new skills. They may now be working with the latest technology, supervising work teams, or having more decision-making authority. These are the same skills that may keep them marketable and help them move to another organization, should that time ever come.

Finally, as the changes we have discussed sweep across the corporate world, supervisors may see changes in how they are paid. Under a reengineered work arrangement, supervisors and their employees may be in a better position to be compensated for the work they do and to receive bonuses and incentives when they excel.

MANAGING TECHNOLOGY

Few jobs today are unaffected by advances in technology. Whether it is introducing automated robotics on the production floor, the use of computer-aided design by the engineering staff, or improving computer skills in the accounting department, these new technologies are changing the supervisor's job. Mary Jean Giroux, who oversees a retirement planning department at London Life Insurance Co., finds that advances in computer technology make her job considerably more complex. "We're being expected to find ways that our people can be more productive. The added complexity comes with learning all of the software programs and technical capabilities of the computers."

Undoubtedly, technology has had a positive effect on internal operations within organizations. How, specifically, has it changed the supervisor's job? To answer that question we need only to look at the way the typical office is set up. Organizations today have become integrated communications centres. By linking computers, telephones, fax machines, copiers, printers, and the like, supervisors can get more complete information more quickly than ever before. With that information, they can better formulate plans, make faster decisions, more clearly define the jobs that workers need to perform, and monitor work activities on an "as-they-happen" basis. In essence, technology today has enhanced supervisors' ability to more effectively and efficiently perform their jobs!

Technology is also changing where a supervisor's work is performed. Historically in organizations, the supervisor's work site was located close to the operations site. As a result, employees were in close proximity to their bosses. A supervisor could observe how the work was being done, as well as easily communicate with employees face-to-face. Through technological advancements, supervisors are now able to supervise employees in remote locations (see Something to Think About, below). Face-to-face interaction has decreased dramatically. Work, for many, occurs where their computers are. Telecommuting capabilities—linkage of a remote worker's computer and modem with coworkers and management at an office—have made it possible for employees to be located anywhere in the global village. Communicating effectively with individuals in remote locations, and ensuring that their performance objectives are being met, are some of the supervisor's new challenges.[15]

The primary implications for supervisors of advances in computer technology relate to training and overcoming resistance to change.

THE OFF-SITE EMPLOYEE

If you were to go back some 150 years in Canadian history, you'd find that it was not uncommon for most workers to be performing their jobs at home. Most goods were not mass-produced. Individuals produced a finished product and took it to a market to sell. Then along came the Industrial Revolution, which changed how work was done. Now we may be coming full circle—once again working at home. It is estimated that off-site employees comprise about one-quarter of the Canadian workforce today, and that number is expected to rise. The majority of these workers are in such professions as sales, medicine, law, accounting, and a wide range of service occupations.[16]

What benefits do you see for organizations that have work done off site? What benefits do you believe exist for employees who work at home? What are the potential problems a supervisor may face in supervising off-site workers?

Supervisors must keep up to date on the latest technologies so that they can effectively train people. Given the fact that, in the 21st century, these technological advances are likely to continue at a rapid pace, supervisors can be expected to spend an increasing amount of time training employees in their usage. And of course, rapid change is a threat to many workers. Just as they get comfortable with a specific technology, they have to adjust to a new and improved version. Change substitutes uncertainty for the known, and most people resist uncertainty. As a result, overcoming this resistance becomes an increasingly important task for supervisors.

CREATING THE PROPER ETHICAL CLIMATE

Here are a few general questions related to ethics in business: Should you tell the truth all the time? Is it right to bend the rules to your company's advantage whenever you can? Does anything go as long as you don't get caught? Now consider a couple of specific cases: Is it ethical for one of your salespeople to offer a bribe to a purchasing agent as an inducement to buy? Is it wrong to use the company telephone for personal long distance calls? Is it ethical to ask your company secretary to type personal letters?

Supervisors face **ethical dilemmas**. These are situations that require right and wrong conduct to be distinguished.

Through their comments and behaviour, supervisors are an important gauge of an organization's ethical climate. For most employees, their

Ethical dilemmas
Situations requiring one to define right and wrong conduct

FIGURE 1-18

The Canadian Centre for Ethics and Corporate Policy, located in Toronto, is a not-for-profit organization whose focus is educational. It was started in 1988 by business people concerned that profit was becoming a priority over people.

EthicScan Canada
http://www.ethicscan.on.ca/

UBC Centre for Applied Ethics Home Page
http://www.ethics.ubc.ca/

supervisor is the only contact they have with management. As such, management's ethical standards are interpreted by employees through the actions of their supervisor. If supervisors take company supplies home, cheat on their expense accounts, or engage in similar practices, they set a tone in their work groups that is likely to undermine all the efforts by top management to create a corporate climate of high ethical standards.

In some organizations, such as the Metropolitan Toronto Zoo, Scott's Hospitality Inc., and Sun Life, employees have a code of conduct to guide them in the performance of their duties. For example, Sun Life's code of business conduct includes guidelines on privacy and confidentiality, conflict of interest, environmental responsibility, fairness in employment, company records, compliance with laws and regulations, company funds and property, political support, and dealing with outside persons and organizations. They have even developed a video to help train staff in the application of these guidelines. The *Globe and Mail*'s code of conduct outlines many guidelines for editorial writers, one of which is:

> Beware any conflicts of interest. Working on stories that may involve family or friends, investments or other personal interests is prohibited. *Report on Business* staff members must regularly file investment holdings to an independent monitor and observe specific investment rules. (*Globe and Mail*, June 18, 1994)

As organizations put increased pressure on supervisors and employees to cut costs and increase productivity, ethical dilemmas are almost certain to increase.

By what they say and do, supervisors contribute toward setting their organization's ethical standards. This is illustrated in comments from Jackie Gordon, a staff sergeant with the Halton Regional Police Service:

> I tell my platoon that we can't accept gratuities in any form. It is very difficult to remain unbiased if you feel indebted to someone. It's only human nature to want to reciprocate kindness. There are several places that will offer free coffee or discounted meals to uniformed police officers, especially at night. Encouraging the police to frequent the establishment enhances security and is a deterrent for criminal activity and public nuisance complaints such as loitering. The difficulty that arises from accepting any type of gratuity is that the proprietor or the staff will have greater expectations of the police. For example, an officer stops in at a local pizza place for lunch and is given a free slice of pizza. Later that evening the officer is operating radar and stops the pizza delivery car for speeding. It would be unlikely that the officer would issue the driver a ticket.

> I suggest that officers avoid places known to offer gratuities to police, or use a drive-through where you can refuse politely without an audience. If you are in a restaurant or coffee shop and there are too many people around to discuss it, leave the full amount on the table. I emphasize it's important to refuse without offending and provide some suggestions such as "You're not very busy tonight, you could use the money" or "Look, your coffee is great, it's worth every penny" or "I get paid a lot, you'd make me feel better if...." Most importantly, I think the best way I can teach my platoon how to deal with the ethical issue is to lead by example—you won't find me drinking a coffee in a donut shop.

In situations involving ethics, it's impossible to predict what you'll face. It helps if you prepare ahead of time and anticipate how you will handle ethical dilemmas (see Building a Supervisory Skill, below).

MANAGING WORKFORCE DIVERSITY

The single most important human resource issue in the immediate future may be adapting organizational policies and practices for increasing **workforce diversity**. Only a few years ago, organizations were staffed with a predominantly white male workforce. Today, we're in the midst of a dramatic shift toward diversification.

Workforce diversity
The increasing heterogeneity of organizations with the inclusion of different groups

Figure 1-19 briefly summarizes what is going on in the Canadian labour force. In essence, along almost any dimension you choose, the workforce is becoming more diverse. Unfortunately, many company policies and practices were designed to deal with a relatively standardized employee: a white male with a wife and several children at home.

Characteristic	1950s	Today
Gender	Predominantly male	Male and Female
Race	Caucasian	Caucasian, Asian-Canadian, African-Canadian
Ethnic Origin	European descent	European descent, Asian, Middle Eastern, African
Age	20 to 65	16 to 80+ (with a higher average age)
Family Status	Single or married with children	Single, married with children, married with no children, cohabitating, dependent elders, dual-career couple, commuter relationship
Sexual Orientation	Heterosexual	Heterosexual, gay, lesbian, bisexual
Physical Abilities	Physically able	Physically able and physically challenged
Education Level	High school	About half with post-secondary education.

FIGURE 1-19

The diversification of the Canadian workforce

This may have been true in the 1950s, but it isn't anymore. The only generalization that you can legitimately make about today's workforce is that you can't generalize!

The implications of workforce diversity for management are widespread. Employees don't set aside their cultural values and lifestyle preferences when they come to work. So management must remake organizations to accommodate these different lifestyles, family needs, and work styles. Managers must be flexible enough in their practices to be accepting of others—others who are unlike them in terms of their expectation and needs at work. This will require a broad range of new policies and practices. A few examples will make this point.

- Work schedules will need to be more flexible to accommodate working parents and couples maintaining commuter relationships.
- Companies may choose to provide child care and elder care so employees will be able to give full attention to their work.
- Benefit programs will need to be redesigned and individualized to reflect more varied needs.
- Career-planning programs will need to be reassessed to deal with employees who are less willing to physically relocate for broadened job experience or promotions.

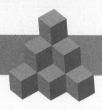

GUIDELINES FOR ACTING ETHICALLY

About the Skill

Making ethical choices can often be difficult for supervisors. Obeying the law is mandatory, but acting ethically goes beyond mere compliance with the law. It means acting responsibly in those "grey" areas, where rules of right or wrong are ambiguous. What can you do to enhance your supervisory abilities in acting ethically? We offer some guidelines.

Steps in Practising the Skill

1. **Know your organization's policy on ethics.** Company policies on ethics, if they exist, describe what the organization perceives as ethical behaviour and what it expects you to do. This policy will help you clarify what is permissible for you to do—the managerial discretion you have. It will become your code of ethics to follow.

2. **Understand the ethics policy.** Just having the policy in your hand does not guarantee that it will achieve what it is intended to do. You need to fully understand it. Ethical behaviour is rarely a "cut and dried" process. With the help of the policy as a guiding light, you will have a basis from which to resolve ethical questions in the organization. Even if a policy doesn't exist, there are several steps you can take when confronted with a difficult situation.

3. **Think before you act.** Ask yourself, why are you doing what you're about to do? What led up to the problem? What is your true intention in taking some action? Is it for a valid reason, or are there ulterior motives behind it—like demonstrating organizational loyalty? Will your action injure someone? Can you disclose to your manager or your family what you're going to do? Remember, it's your behaviour that will be seen in your actions. You need to make sure that you are not doing something that will jeopardize your role as a manager, your organization, or your reputation.

4. **Ask yourself "what if" questions.** When you think ahead about why you're doing something, you should also be asking yourself "what if" questions. For example, the following questions may help you shape your actions: What if you make the wrong decision—what will happen to you? To your job? What if your actions were described, in detail, on

your local TV news or in the newspaper? Would it bother or embarrass you or those around you? What if you get caught doing something unethical? Are you prepared to deal with the consequences?

5. **Seek opinions from others.** If it is something major that you must do, and you're uncertain about it, ask for advice from other managers. Maybe they've been in a similar situation and can give you the benefit of their experiences. If not, maybe they can just listen and act as a sounding board for you.

6. **Do what you truly believe is right.** You have a conscience and you are responsible for your behaviour. Whatever you do, if you truly believe it is the right action to take, then what others say (or what the proverbial "Monday morning quarterbacks" say) is immaterial. You need to be true to your own internal ethical standards. Ask yourself: Can you live with what you've done?

Mature workers
A group of workers born prior to 1946 who are security oriented and have a committed work ethic

Baby-boomers
The largest group in the workforce; they are regarded as the career climbers—born in the right place at the right time. Mature workers view them as unrealistic in their views and workaholics.

Baby-busters
A group of workers seen as being less committed, less rule-bound, and more into self-gratification, with an intolerance of baby-boomers and their attitudes. They are considered selfish and not willing to play by the rules.

- All employees will need training so they can learn to understand and appreciate people who are different from themselves.
- Managers will need to rethink their motivation techniques to respond to a widening range of employee needs.

Of all the levels in management, it is first-level supervisors who will be most affected by these diversifying changes in the makeup of the workforce.

In addition to the diversity brought about by such factors as lifestyle, gender, nationality, and race, supervisors must be aware of the age differences they'll encounter. Today, there are three distinct age groupings.[17] Studies have shown that their views of each other vary widely and are often negative. First, there is the mature worker, those born prior to 1946. This group of workers, born shortly after the Great Depression, is security-oriented and has a committed work ethic. While **mature workers** have until recently been viewed as the foundation of the workforce, they may be regarded by the other generational groups as having obsolete skills and being inflexible in their ways. The **baby-boomers**, born in the late 1940s to early 1960s, are the largest group in the workforce. They are regarded as the career climbers—at the right place at the right time. Their careers advanced rapidly during their initial years of employment, because organizational growth at that time was unsurpassed. Yet, the view of them by mature workers is that they are unrealistic in their views and tend to be workaholics. Finally, there are the Generation Xers, those born between 1964 and 1975. These "twentysomething **baby-busters**" are bringing a new perspective to the workforce—less committed, less rule-bound, more concerned with their own gratification, and intolerant of the baby-boomers and their attitudes.[18] As a result, they are viewed by the other two groups as being selfish and unwilling to play by the rules.

Supervisors will need to learn how to blend these three age groups in order to be effective. That is, supervisors will need to be trained to effectively deal with each group, and to respect the diversity of views that each offers.[19] Companies like the Travelers and the Hartford Insurance companies go to great lengths to train younger supervisors in how to deal with older employees. Likewise, more mature supervisors are made aware of the different work attitudes younger workers may bring to the job. Inasmuch as work attitude conflict is natural between these groups, these companies have been successful in keeping problems to a minimum by helping the various groups learn about one another.[20]

As a student, which one of the following scenarios do you find most appealing?

Scenario 1: Semesters are fifteen weeks long. Faculty members are required to provide, on the first day of each class, a course syllabus that specifies daily assignments, exact dates of examinations, and the precise percentage weights that various class activities count toward the final grade. College rules require instructors to hold classes only at the time specified in the class schedule. These rules also require instructors to grade assignments and return the results within one week from the time they're turned in.

Scenario 2: Courses vary in length. When you sign up for a course, however, you don't know how long it will last. It might go for two weeks or thirty weeks. Furthermore, the instructor can end a course any time he or she wants, with no prior warning. The length of a class also changes each time it meets; sometimes it lasts twenty minutes, while other times it runs for three hours. Scheduling of the next class meeting is done by the instructor at the end of each class. Oh yes, and the exams are all unannounced, so you have to be ready for a test at any time; and instructors rarely provide you with any significant feedback on the results of those exams.

If you're like most people, you chose Scenario 1. Why? Because it provides security through predictability. You know what to expect and you can plan for it. It may, therefore, be disheartening for you to learn that the manager's world—including the supervisor's job—is increasingly looking a lot more like Scenario 2 than Scenario 1.

We propose that tomorrow's successful supervisors will be those who have learned to thrive on chaos. They will have become adept at managing under conditions of constant and chaotic change. They'll be able to respond quickly to new laws and regulations, new competitive threats, new technological breakthroughs, and the changing demands of customers. In the coming years, victory will go to those organizations and managers who are flexible, adaptive, and able to adjust rapidly to change.

Successful supervisors must change too. They must be able to make sense out of a situation when everything appears futile. Supervisors must be able to turn disasters into opportunities. To do so, they must be more flexible in their styles, smarter in how they work, quicker in making decisions, more efficient in managing scarce resources, better at satisfying the customer, and more confident in enacting massive and revolutionary changes. Management writer Tom Peters encapsulated this scenario in one of his bestselling books: "Today's supervisors must be able to thrive on change and uncertainty."[21]

SUMMARY

This summary is organized by the Learning Objectives.

1. A supervisor is a first-level manager who oversees the work of operative or nonmanagement employees.
2. While supervisors, middle managers, and top management are all part of the managerial ranks, they differ by their level in the organization. Supervisors are first-level managers—they manage operative employees. Middle management includes all managers from those who manage supervisors up to those in the vice presidential ranks. Top management is composed of the highest level managers—responsible for establishing the organization's overall objectives and developing the policies to achieve those objectives.
3. The four functions of planning, organizing, leading, and controlling comprise the management process.
4. The four essential management competencies are technical, interpersonal, conceptual, and political competencies.
5. The supervisor's job will be increasingly important and complex in the future because of programs that focus on the work activities of operating employees, middle-management cutbacks (which have increased supervisory responsibilities), and the increased focus on training employees, which will be substantially implemented at the supervisory level.
6. Global competition requires supervisors to increase the productivity of employees and the quality of their work effort. This includes new responsibilities such as creating effective work teams, introducing pay-for-performance compensation systems, and implementing sophisticated work methods and technologies.
7. Supervisors play an important role in conveying an organization's ethical standards by what they say and do. For most employees, the supervisor is their sole contact with management, and the primary channel for conveying the ethical climate as envisioned by management.
8. Workforce diversity seeks to increase the heterogeneity of organizations with the inclusion of different groups. This includes, but is not limited to, women, members of racial minority groups, immigrants, and the disabled.
9. Many employees are less loyal to their employers because employers in recent years have become less loyal to their employees. Traditional policies on job security, seniority, and compensation have been discarded as organizations have cut costs.

10. Constant and chaotic change forces supervisors to respond quickly to new laws and regulations, new competitive threats, new technological breakthroughs, and the changing demands of customers.

KEY TERMS AND CONCEPTS

Conceptual competence
Controlling
Ethical dilemmas
First-line managers
Interpersonal competence
Leading
Management competencies
Management functions
Management process
Middle managers

Operative employees
Organizing
Planning
Political competence
Skill
Supervisors
Technical competence
Top management
Workforce diversity

REVIEWING YOUR KNOWLEDGE

1. What differentiates supervisory positions from all other levels of management?
2. Is the owner-manager of a small store, with three employees, an operative, supervisor, or top manager? Explain.
3. What specific tasks are common to all managers?
4. Contrast time spent on management functions by supervisors versus time spent by top management.
5. "The best rank-and-file employees should be promoted to supervisors." Do you agree or disagree with this statement? Explain.
6. Why is conceptual competence more important for top managers than for first-level supervisors?
7. How can a supervisor be a "key person" and "just another worker"?
8. Based on your past work experience, describe two ethical dilemmas you faced on your job. How did you handle them?
9. What challenges does workforce diversity create for first-level managers?
10. What, if anything, can organizations do to help managers and employees alike learn to thrive on constant change?

ANSWERS TO THE POP QUIZZES

1. **d. All organizations make a profit.** While almost all organizations need to make money to survive, making a profit is not a characteristic of an organization.

2. **False.** Organizational members who are responsible for establishing and meeting specific goals in a department are called middle-level managers.

3. Efficiency involves a relationship between inputs and outputs. It focuses on doing things right. Effectiveness implies goal attainment. It focuses on doing the right things. If all things are equal, effectiveness is more important because it supports reaching the goals of the organization. [Note: Don't interpret this to mean that efficiency doesn't matter. It does!]

4. **b. organizing.** The question addresses part of the definition of the organizing function.

5. **True.** Today's employees have less need for an authority figure to tell them what to do. Instead, employees need a supervisor who can listen, guide, train, and assist them.

6. **c. the ability to motivate, negotiate with, and delegate to others.** The question addresses the definition of interpersonal competence.

7. Technical abilities frequently have greater relevance for supervisors because, unlike higher-level managers, many supervisors perform technical work as well as managerial work. Also, supervisors spend more time training and developing their employees, work that requires greater technical knowledge of their employees' jobs.

8. **d. none of the above.** The ability to demonstrate a system and sequence of behaviour related to achieving a goal is a **skill**.

CASE 1.A

Judy and Sabby Revisited

Judy VanDuzer and Sabby Bhagrath (refer to Figures 1-1 and 1-2) share many similar responsibilities in their supervisory roles. They need to assign work and make sure that performance meets high quality standards. They must cope with intense time demands and a somewhat unpredictable workload. They have to handle interpersonal conflicts. They need to motivate people and evaluate their performance. They have to advise, coach, and provide feedback to help their employees improve their performance.

Judy supervises six people, all of them older than she is, who organize room, food, and beverage needs for meetings and conferences held at Toronto's Royal York Hotel. These events are an important source of revenue to the hotel and it has been host to extremely large groups and to very prestigious groups.

Sabby supervises sixteen aircraft maintenance technicians, all with college diplomas and licensed by the Ministry of Transport. They handle thirty to forty aircraft per shift and are responsible for all aspects of maintenance from engines, tires, and air conditioning to kitchen and audiovisual equipment. Their signatures are legal commitments that they have done their job thoroughly and they guarantee acceptable performance.

Both Judy and Sabby know that management knowledge and experience can be obtained in a variety of ways. They also know they must have the right knowledge and tools to be able to solve a variety of problems every single day.

RESPONDING TO THIS CASE

1. Based on the tasks and responsibilities required by a supervisor:
    a. Make a list of the similarities Judy and Sabby face in supervising their employees. Label this list "Similarities."
    b. What are the differences in Judy's and Sabby's jobs that may affect the way they supervise their employees? Make a list of these items. Label this list "Differences."
    c. Compare and discuss your two lists with those of your classmates. From the discussion, were there items you crossed off or added to your lists? Were there items that you switched from one of your lists to the other? Explain.
2. The role of a supervisor sometimes changes. When and why? Specifically, when and why would this happen for Judy? For Sabby?
3. Discuss why supervisors may need different types of training and experience. Could Judy and Sabby change places? Why or why not?
4. Explain why a) Judy, b) her employees, and c) her administrators need to understand what is expected of her in her supervisory position. Do the same for Sabby. What generalizations can you make from these expectations?

CASE 1.B

Success in the Lost Kingdom

Channel-hopping at 2 a.m. when he couldn't sleep, Brian Morrison was introduced to Deming and his TQM ideas. Despite the hour, he got excited. The words hit a nerve: "Look at everything from the point of view of quality." "The guys on the floor want to do a good job. It's management that's the problem." Brian listened and learned. But, ironically, it wasn't until he stepped down as a supervisor and returned to working as an operator that he finally had the opportunity to try out the ideas. At the end of his first month back on the shop floor, the diamond division turned a profit for the first time in three years. And it hasn't looked back since.

Back in the less productive days, Brian had reluctantly taken on the supervision of the diamond and carbide divisions (of a company that recuts dies used by clients to draw wire) when they were moved to a location across the road from the main building. Despite the physically small separation, they soon nicknamed themselves "The Lost Kingdom" because they saw so little of management. They felt very much "out of sight, out of mind" until, of course, something went wrong.

Brian was expected to set schedules and supervise productivity, but also to do the quality control job, which required hours spent over a microscope inspecting dies. With long hours, stress, and an overloaded job, Brian started showing physical problems as well as constant worry. So he asked to be relieved of the supervisory position. No one was willing to replace him.

But Brian stepped down anyway. The group was forced to handle itself as a self-directed team because there was no official leader. Brian came back to his old operative position in the team with a fresh perspective and lots of ideas. He started tackling the quality problems in the department, quietly taking advantage of the division's isolation—which had previously frustrated him.

First, he looked for bottlenecks in the line. Brian found that the rougher was spending two to three hours sorting dies before he could actually start the roughing. So Brian, with time available since he was the last on the line, started doing the sorting himself. Then he brought the crew together to examine the physical layout of equipment. This led to a redesign that successfully streamlined the layout, removing dead-ends. The crew also started cross-training so they would each have a backup. What was management's response? "Whatever you're doing, it's working so it's okay. Just let us know ahead of time in the future."

Further changes followed. The diamond division has become a completely self-directed work group, ordering its own materials and doing its own maintenance on equipment. The most recent request they've made is to be the ones who talk with customers about problems, because going through sales reps sometimes brings delays and communication problems. Brian has also asked management how it plans to deal with the aging of its staff—because the jobs involve a lot of lifting.

The company is so impressed by the changes wrought in the "Lost Kingdom" that they're asking Brian to consider introducing the new approach elsewhere in the firm. At this point Brian is reluctant.

RESPONDING TO THIS CASE

1. Although no longer a supervisor, Brian is now the informal leader of a self-managed team.
   a. What managerial functions does he seem to be carrying out?
   b. What managerial competencies does he appear to have?
2. a. What do you think Brian found difficult in his role as a supervisor? Refer to the major "surprises" supervisors typically encounter.
   b. Why would he feel more comfortable as an informal leader than as an official supervisor?
3. Explain why Deming's quality improvement ideas would appeal to Brian and to his coworkers in this manufacturing facility.
4. Imagine you are the manager/supervisor that this self-managed team now reports to. What would be your role? What would that team expect of you? What would be the challenges?

Part I: Introduction

John Erickson
Manager of A/V Services, Alliant Techsystems

John supervises a department of film/video producers, artists, photographers, and some support staff for Alliant. When John first assumed his position, he inherited a staff governed by preconceived notions. The former supervisor was controlling and judgmental. He had very traditional views of what makes an employee valuable. Women and people with technical school backgrounds were viewed as less valuable than male college graduates. John realized he had to assess the skills of his department without depending on past judgments.

During this period, Alliant was reorganizing and downsizing, and John was expected to reduce the size of his department. At the same time, demands for service were increasing, so John needed to get the most from the people in his department and acquire new staff who could adapt to the changing conditions.

1. What was probably the most important challenge that faced John Erickson when he became a supervisor? Do you think this challenge is "typical" for most supervisors (or organizations)? Why or why not?

2. How does a supervisor find the right talent for his/her department?

3. What are the elements that ensure that the "right" people are hired for, or are assigned to, the "right" jobs.

4. How can the "right" talent be developed with existing employees and new hires?

5. What did John, as a supervisor, do to assure his department would be productive? How could this example be used by any supervisor?

PART TWO

PLANNING AND CONTROL

2

SUPERVISORY PLANNING AND TIME MANAGEMENT

LEARNING OBJECTIVES

After reading this chapter, you should be able to:

1. Contrast formal and informal planning.
2. Describe how plans should link from the top to the bottom of an organization.
3. Contrast policies and rules.
4. Explain why managers create single-use plans.
5. Describe the Gantt chart.
6. Explain the information needed to create a PERT chart.
7. Describe the four ingredients common to MBO programs.
8. Contrast response time and discretionary time.
9. List the five steps to better time management.

CHAPTER OUTLINE

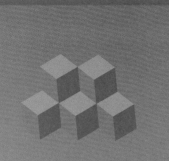

FIGURE 2-1

Jimmy Lai built a
chain of 600 stores
on the foundation of
good planning.

Jimmy Lai is a modern day rags-to-riches story.[1] Born in 1948, his early life was filled with poverty and despair. At age 12, he had to leave his family and flee to Hong Kong. Because Jimmy had little formal education, the only work he could find was labouring in sweatshops, making such garments as sweaters and gloves.

While Jimmy was unknowingly learning the clothing business, his low-paying job didn't provide him with enough money to pay for the basic necessities of life. He was often caught sleeping on work premises, for he couldn't afford a place to live. Jimmy didn't let such difficulties get the best of him. After all, he had only one way to go, and to him, that was up! He looked at this as an opportunity to better himself. He spent many of those long, cold, lonesome nights teaching himself English. Years later, his fluency with the language opened the doors for Lai to move up to supervisor of the garment factory. As a supervisor, Jimmy was able to travel abroad, gaining more insight about the knitwear business.

In 1981, Jimmy Lai started his own business—Giordano Holdings Ltd. Since then, his business has grown to over 600 shops (about 150 that he still personally supervises), selling a variety of expensive tee-shirts, polo shirts, sweaters, and jeans in Hong Kong, Japan, Southwest Asia, and China. Company sales net Jimmy about $20 million a year in profit.

How did Jimmy succeed in all these retail shops spread out over many miles? Lai has a system. In other words, he plans! He knows when inventories need to be replaced. He understands how many employees are needed to staff each store, with extra personnel on hand for peak sales periods. Jimmy also recognizes that each outlet store must maintain its profitability. He assists each store in this area by developing budgets and implementing procedures to ensure that budgets are controlled.

FIGURE 2-2

(*Source:* Creators Syndicate, Inc.; November 16, 1992. Reprinted with permission.)

WHAT IS PLANNING?

As mentioned in Chapter 1, planning encompasses defining an organization's objectives or goals, establishing the overall strategy for achieving those goals, and developing a comprehensive hierarchy of plans to integrate and coordinate activities. And for our purposes, we'll treat the terms *objectives* and *goals* as interchangeable. Each is meant to convey some desired outcome that an organization, department, work group, or individual seeks to achieve.

Does planning require that goals, strategies, and plans be written down? Ideally they should be, but they often aren't. In formal planning, specific goals are formulated, committed to writing, and made available to other organization members. Additionally, specific action programs will exist in formal planning to define the path for achieving these goals.

But many managers engage in informal planning. They have plans in their heads, but nothing is written down and there is little or no sharing of these plans with others. This probably most often occurs in small businesses where the owner-manager has a vision of where he or she wants to go and how to get there. In this chapter, when we use the term *planning* we'll be implying the formal variety. It is this formal planning that is most often required for an organization to be productive (see Something to Think About, overleaf).

PLANNING AND MANAGERIAL LEVEL

All managers should plan, but the type of planning they do tends to vary with their level in the organization.

PLANNING BREADTH

A common means for describing planning is to differentiate strategic from tactical planning. **Strategic planning** covers the entire organization, includes the establishment of overall goals, and positions the organization's products or services against the competition (see Dealing with A Difficult Issue, overleaf). Wal-Mart's strategy, for instance, is to build large stores in rural areas, offer an extensive selection of merchandise, provide the lowest prices, and then draw consumers from the many surrounding small towns. This strategy led to their recent expansion into Canada in which they bought 122 Woolco stores. Tactical planning, on the other hand, provides specific details on how overall goals are to be achieved. For example the Wal-Mart store manager in North Battleford, Saskatchewan, is engaged in **tactical planning** when developing a quarterly expense budget or making out weekly employee work schedules.

Strategic planning
Covering the entire organization, it establishes overall goals and positions the organization's products or services against the competition.

Tactical planning
Specific plans on how overall goals are to be achieved

Formalized planning became very popular in the 1960s, and, for the most part, it's still popular today. It makes sense to establish some direction. But recently, critics have begun to challenge some of the basic assumptions underlying planning.

Canadian management expert Henry Mintzberg believes that plans may create rigidity.[2] Formal planning efforts can lock organizational members into specific goals to be achieved within specific timetables. When these objectives are set, assumptions may be made that the "outside world" won't change during the time period the objectives cover. That may be a faulty assumption. Nevertheless, rather than remaining flexible—and possibly scrapping the plan—some supervisors may continue to fulfill the actions required to achieve the originally set objectives.

Other experts feel that formal plans can't replace intuition and creativity.[3] Formal planning efforts typically follow a specific methodology—making it a routine event. That can spell disaster for an organization. For instance, the rapid rise of Apple Computer Inc. between the late 1970s and the late 1980s was attributed, in part, to the creativity and anticorporate attitudes of its cofounder, Steve Jobs. However, as the company grew, Jobs felt a need for more formalized management—a style he was personally uncomfortable with. He hired a CEO (Chief Executive Officer), who ultimately ousted Jobs from his own company. With Jobs' departure came increased organizational formality—the very thing Jobs despised so much because it hampered creativity. By 1996, this one-time industry leader had lost much of its creativity, and was struggling for survival. (Eventually, Jobs was brought back on board to try to revive Apple's fortunes.)[4]

Finally, there's a perception that while formal planning may reinforce success, it may also lead to failure.[5] We have been taught that success breeds success. That's been a North American "tradition." After all, if it's not broken, don't fix it—right? Well, maybe not! Success may, in fact, breed failure in the changing world of work. It's tough to change or discard successful plans—leaving the comfort of what works for the anxiety of the unknown. Formal plans may provide a false sense of security, generating more confidence than is warranted. Consequently, supervisors often won't deliberately face that unknown until forced to do so by changes in the environment. Unfortunately, by then it may be too late!

So, given these facts, should we still plan formally? Is it worth it? What do you think?

Apple Canada
http://www.
apple.ca/

GATHERING COMPETITIVE INFORMATION

All businesses need to gather information about their competitors in an effort to plan effectively. For many, it's a game—but one that must be taken seriously. This might involve "surfing the Net" to see what new products are being released, or checking court record databases to determine what, if any, lawsuits or civil cases have been brought against a competitor. These are legitimate methods for obtaining "public information."

Some organizations pride themselves on being able to obtain competitive data in more unusual and somewhat questionable ways. They may call a competitor's office and ask questions about what the company is planning to do. Answers may not be forthcoming, but there's a chance the person on the other end of the line will be quite talkative. Other tactics may include buying some stock shares in a competitor's organization—thus getting annual reports and other information about the company that normally don't go to everyone. A company may even encourage one of its employees to take a job with a competitor—then quit and return to his or her old job after getting some "Company Private" data. Another method is to interview or hire individuals from a competing firm—who hopefully can bring with them a wealth of "inside" information.[6]

1. From your point of view, when does getting information about your competitor become corporate espionage?

2. If you were a supervisor in a Hershey's Chocolate plant, and were asked to get some information about Nestlé, how would you go about it? What kinds of tactics would you use and how far would you go to get the data? Would your position change if you knew that getting some critical data could result in your receiving a $25 000 bonus?

3. Do you believe ethical guidelines should be established to deal with the process of obtaining valuable competitive data? Explain.

For the most part, strategic planning tends to be done by top-level managers; a supervisor's time tends to be devoted to tactical planning. Both are important for an organization's success, but they are different in that one focuses on the big picture, while the other emphasizes the specifics within that big picture.

PLANNING TIME FRAME

Planning often occurs in three time frames—short-term, intermediate-term and long-term.

Short-term plans are less than one year in length. **Long-term plans** cover a period in excess of five years. Plans that cover from one to five years are called **intermediate-term plans**. A supervisor's planning horizon tends to emphasize the short-term: preparing plans for the next month, week, or day. People in middle-level managerial jobs, like regional sales directors, typically focus on one-to-three-year plans. Long-term planning tends to be done by the top executives such as vice-presidents and above.

LINKING MANAGERIAL LEVELS

It's important to keep in mind that effective planning is integrated and coordinated throughout the organization. Long-term strategic planning sets the direction for all other planning. That is, once top management has defined the organization's overall strategy and goals and the general plan for getting there, then, in descending order, the other levels of the organization develop plans.

Figure 2-3 illustrates this linking of plans from the top to the bottom of an organization. The president, vice president, and other senior executives define the organization's overall strategy. Then upper-middle managers, such as regional sales directors, formulate their plans. And so on down to first-level managers. Ideally, these plans will be coordinated through joint participation. In the case of Figure 2-3, for instance, the Vancouver territory manager would participate with other territory managers by providing information and ideas to the B.C. District Manager as she formulates plans for her entire district. If planning is properly linked, then the successful achievement of all the territory managers' goals should result in the B.C. District Manager achieving her goals. If all the district managers meet their goals, this should lead to the successful attainment of the regional sales manager's goals, and so on up each level in the organization.

KEY PLANNING GUIDES

Once an organization's strategy and overall goals are in place, management will design additional plans to help guide decision makers. Some of these will be **standing plans**. Once designed, they can be used over

Short-term plans
Plans that are less than one year in length

Long-term plans
Plans covering more than five years

Intermediate-term plans
Plans that cover from one to five years

Standing plans
Plans used over and over again for recurring activities

Single-use plans
Detailed courses of action used once or only occasionally

Policies
Broad guidelines for managerial action

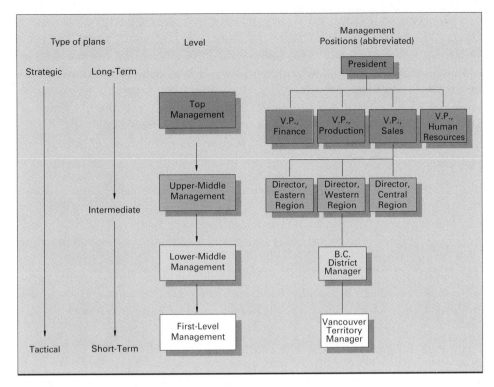

FIGURE 2-3

Planning and
managerial levels

and over again by managers faced with recurring activities. Others will
be **single-use plans**. These are detailed courses of action used once or
only occasionally to deal with problems that don't occur repeatedly.
In this section we'll review the popular types of each.

STANDING PLANS

Standing plans allow managers to save time by handling similar situations in a predetermined and consistent manner. For example, when a
supervisor has an employee who increasingly fails to show up for
work, it can be handled more efficiently and consistently if a discipline
procedure has been established in advance. In this section, we'll
review the three major types of standing plans: policies, procedures,
and rules.

POLICIES

"We promote from within wherever possible." "Do whatever it takes to
satisfy the customer." "Our employees should be paid competitive
wages." These three statements are examples of **policies**. That is, they're
broad guidelines for managerial action. Typically established by top management, they define the limits within which managers must stay as they
make decisions.

FIGURE 2-4

David Curtis of Green
Line Investor Services
says, "Part of my job
as Electronic Delivery
Systems manager was
to use the interaction
with customers to
determine the future
enhancements of our
product that cus-
tomers will want,
then sell those ideas
to senior manage-
ment and describe
them to the systems
people so they could
implement them."

Supervisors rarely make policies. Rather, they interpret and apply them. Within the parameters that policies set, supervisors must use their judgment. For instance, the company policy that "our employees should be paid competitive wages" doesn't tell a supervisor what to pay a new employee. However, if the going rate in the community for this specific job is in the range of $8.20 to $9.50 an hour, the company policy would clarify that neither a starting hourly rate of $7.75 or one of $10.00 is acceptable.

PROCEDURES

The purchasing manager receives a request from the engineering department for five computer workstations. The purchasing manager checks to see if the requisition has been properly filled out and approved. If not, he sends the requisition back with a note explaining what is deficient. If the request is complete, the approximate costs are estimated. If the total exceeds $5000, which it does in this case, three bids must be obtained. If the total had been $5000 or less, the department would have needed only to identify a single vendor and the order could have been placed.

Procedure
A series of steps for responding to a recurring problem

The previous series of steps for responding to a recurring problem is an example of a **procedure**. Where procedures exist, managers only have to identify the problem. Once the problem is clear, so is the procedure to handle it.

Procedures are more specific than policies. But, as with policies, they provide consistency. By defining the steps that are to be taken and the order they are to be done in, procedures provide a standardized way of responding to repetitive problems.

Supervisors follow procedures set by higher levels of management and also create their own procedures for their staff to follow. As conditions change and new problems surface that tend to be recurring, supervisors will develop standardized procedures for handling them. For example, when the service department of a local Ford dealership began accepting credit cards for payment, the department's supervisor had to create a procedure for processing such transactions and then carefully teach each step of the new procedure to all the service agents and cashier personnel.

RULES

Rule
An explicit statement that tells a manager what he or she ought or ought not to do

A **rule** is an explicit statement that tells a manager what he or she ought or ought not to do. Rules are frequently used by managers when they confront a recurring problem because they are simple to follow and ensure consistency. In the illustration described in the previous section, the $5000 cutoff rule simplifies the purchasing manager's decision about when to use multiple bids. Similarly, rules about lateness and absenteeism permit supervisors to make discipline decisions rapidly and with a high degree of fairness.

SINGLE-USE PLANS

In contrast to the previous discussions of standing plans, single-use plans are designed for a specific activity or time period. The most popular types of these plans are programs, budgets, and schedules.

PROGRAMS

In January 1998, an ice storm hit parts of Quebec and Ontario, causing terrible damage and knocking out power to large regions for several weeks. Businesses were especially badly affected. At a major Canadian financial institution, Lynn Rutherford, a specialist in Employment Standards, was part of the Business Recovery Planning Team at head office whose role was to advise the regions on how to handle the crisis. The team met daily to see how the situation was unfolding and what needed to be done. Among the issues they looked at were how to get information to management groups in the different areas (with no phones, faxes or e-mail); what to do about employees working in potentially dangerous conditions; whether transportation and food needed to be provided to employees; which of the many branches should be opened first; how to help employees get loans for home repairs and temporary accommodation; whether trauma teams were needed to help employees cope; and how to ensure no computers were restarted until conditions were appropriate. Lynn was on the team on behalf of HR at the bank to represent the staff and ensure their safety. What she developed with the team was a **program**—a single-use set of plans for a specific major undertaking within the organization's overall goals.

Program
A single-use set of plans for a specific major undertaking

All managers develop programs. A major program—such as building a new manufacturing plant or merging two companies and consolidating their headquarters' staff—will tend to be designed and overseen by top management, can extend over several years, and may even require its own set of policies and procedures. But supervisors frequently have to create programs for their departments. Examples include the creation of a comprehensive ad campaign for a new client by an account manager of an advertising firm, and the development of a unique training program by the regional sales supervisor for Hallmark to help her people learn the intricacies of the company's new phone-activated, computerized inventory system. Note the common thread through all these examples: These are nonrecurring undertakings that require a set of integrated plans to accomplish their objectives.

BUDGETS

Budgets are numerical plans. They typically express anticipated results in dollar terms for a specific time period. For example, a department may budget $8000 this year for travel. But budgets can also be calculated in nondollar terms, for example, employee hours, capacity utilization, or units of production. And budgets can cover daily, weekly, monthly, quarterly, semi-annual, or annual periods.

Budgets
Numerical plans

We present budgets here as planning guides. However, be aware that they are also control devices. The preparation of a budget involves planning because it gives direction. The creation of a budget tells what activities are important and how resources should be allocated to each activity. A budget becomes a control mechanism when it provides standards against which resource consumption can be measured and compared.

If there is one type of plan in which almost every manager gets involved, it's the budget. Supervisors, for instance, typically prepare their department's expense budget and submit it to the manager at the next higher level for review and approval (see Figure 2-5). Supervisors may also—depending on their needs—create budgets for employee work hours, revenue forecasts, or for capital expenditures like machinery and equipment. Once approved by higher management, these budgets set specific standards for supervisors and their departmental personnel to achieve.

SCHEDULES

If you were to observe a group of supervisors or department managers for a few days, you'd see them regularly detailing what activities have to be done, the order they are to be done in, who is to do each, and when they are to be completed. These managers are **scheduling**.

Two popular scheduling techniques that can help you prioritize activities and complete work on time are the Gantt chart and the PERT chart. In the rest of this section, we'll describe each.

The **Gantt chart** was developed early in this century by an industrial engineer named Henry Gantt. The idea was inherently simple but has

Scheduling
Determining what activities have to be done, the order they are to be done in, who is to do each, and when they are to be completed

Gantt chart
A bar graph, with time on the horizontal axis and activities to be scheduled on the vertical axis, that shows planned and actual activities

Department Expense Budget
Calender Year 1998

ITEM	QUARTER			
	1ST	2ND	3RD	4TH
Salaries/Fixed	$23 600	$23 600	$23 600	$23 600
Salaries/Variable	3 000	5 000	3 000	10 000
Performance Bonuses				12 000
Office Supplies	800	800	800	800
Photocopying	1 000	1 000	1 000	1 000
Telephone	2 500	2 500	2 500	2 500
Mail	800	800	800	800
Travel	2 500	1 000	1 000	1 000
Employee Development	600	600	600	600
Total Quarterly Expenses	$34 800	$35 300	$33 300	$52 300

FIGURE 2-5

An example of a budget that could be used as a planning guide proved extremely helpful in scheduling work activities. The Gantt chart is essentially a bar graph with time on the horizontal axis and activities to be scheduled on the vertical axis. The bars show output, both planned and actual, over a period of time. The Gantt chart visually shows when tasks are supposed to be done and compares that to the actual progress on each. As we stated, it is a simple but important device that allows managers to detail easily what has yet to be done to complete a job or project and to assess whether it is ahead, behind, or on schedule.

Figure 2-6 depicts a simplified Gantt chart that was developed for producing a book by a manager in a publishing firm. Time is expressed in months across the top of the chart. The major activities are listed down the left side. The planning comes in deciding what activities need to be done to get the book finished, the order in which they need to be done, and the time that should be allocated to each activity. Where a box sits within a time frame reflects its planned sequence. The shading represents actual progress. The chart becomes a control device when the manager looks for deviations from the plan.

Gantt charts are helpful as long as the activities being scheduled are few in number and independent of each other. But what if a supervisor has to plan a large project such as a departmental reorganization, the launching of a cost-reduction campaign, or the installation of a major piece of new equipment that requires the coordination of inputs from a

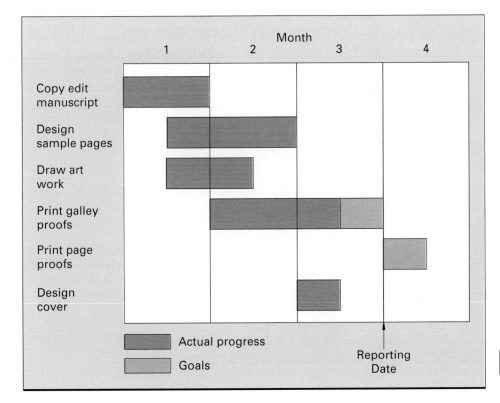

FIGURE 2-6

A Gantt chart

number of different sources? Such projects often require the coordination of hundreds of activities, some of which must be done simultaneously and some of which cannot begin until earlier activities have been completed. If you're constructing a building, for example, you obviously can't start erecting walls until the foundation is laid. How, then, can you schedule such a complex project? You could use a Program Evaluation and Review Technique (PERT) chart.

PERT chart
A technique for scheduling complex projects.

The **PERT chart** was originally developed in the late 1950s for coordinating the more than 3000 contractors and agencies working on the Polaris submarine weapon system.[7] This project was incredibly complicated, with hundreds of thousands of activities that had to be coordinated. PERT is reported to have cut two years off the completion date for the Polaris project. A PERT chart can be a valuable tool in the hands of a supervisor.

A PERT chart is a diagram that depicts the sequence of activities needed to complete a project and the time or costs associated with each activity. With a PERT chart, a supervisor must think through what has to be done, determine which events depend on one another, and identify potential trouble spots. A PERT chart makes it easy to compare what effect alternative actions will have on scheduling and costs. Thus PERT allows supervisors to monitor a project's progress, identify possible bottlenecks, and shift resources as necessary to keep the project on schedule.

To understand how to construct a PERT chart, you need to know three terms: *events, activities,* and *critical path.* Let's define these terms, outline the steps in the PERT process, and then work through an example.

Events
End points on a PERT chart that represent the completion of major activities

Activities
Time or resources required to progress from one event to another on a PERT chart

Critical path
The longest sequence of events and activities in a PERT chart

Events are end points that represent the completion of major activities. **Activities** represent the time or resources required to progress from one event to another. The **critical path** is the longest or most time-consuming sequence of events and activities in a PERT chart.

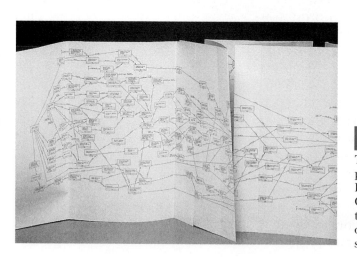

FIGURE 2-7

This photo illustrates part of a complex PERT chart used by Grumman Corp. in the design and development of a missile system.

Developing a PERT chart requires the supervisor to identify all key activities needed to complete a project, rank them in order of dependence, and estimate each activity's completion time. This can be translated into five specific steps:

1. Identify every significant activity that must be achieved for a project to be completed. The accomplishment of each activity results in a set of events or outcomes.

2. Ascertain the order in which these events must be completed.

3. Diagram the flow of activities from start to finish, identifying each activity and its relationship to all other activities. Use circles to indicate events and arrows to represent activities. This results in the diagram that we call the PERT chart.

4. Compute a time estimate for completing each activity.

5. Finally, using a PERT chart that contains time estimates for each activity, the supervisor can determine a schedule for the start and finish dates of each activity and for the entire project. Any delays that occur along the critical path require the most attention because they delay the entire project. That is, the critical path has no slack in it; therefore any delay along that path immediately translates into a delay in the final deadline for the completed project.

Now let's work through a simplified example. You're the production supervisor in the casting department at an aluminum mill. You have proposed and received approval from corporate management to replace one of the three massive furnaces that are part of your responsibilities with a new, state-of-the-art, electronic furnace. This project will seriously disrupt operations in your department, so you want to complete it as quickly and as smoothly as possible. You have carefully dissected the entire project into activities and event. Figure 2-8 outlines the major events in the furnace modernization project and your estimate of the expected time required to complete each activity. Figure 2-9 depicts the PERT chart based on the data in Figure 2-8.

Your PERT chart tells you that if everything goes as planned, it will take 21 weeks to complete the modernization program. This is calculated by tracing the chart's critical path: A–C–D–G–H–J–K. Any delay in completing the events along this path will delay the completion of the entire project. However, if it took six weeks instead of four to get construction permits (event B), this would have no effect on the final completion date. Why? Because Start–B + B–E + E–F + F–G equals only eleven weeks, while Start–A + A–C + C–D + D–G equals seventeen weeks. If you wanted to cut the 21-week time frame, you would give attention to those activities along the critical path that could be speeded up.

FIGURE 2-8

Event	Description	Expected Time (in weeks)	Preceding Event
A	Approve design	8	None
B	Get construction permits	4	None
C	Take bids on new furnace and its installation	6	A
D	Order new furnace and equipment	1	C
E	Remove old furnace	2	B
F	Prepare site	3	E
G	Install new furnace	2	D,F
H	Test new furnace	1	G
I	Train workers to handle new furnace	2	G
J	Final inspection by company and city officials	2	H
K	Bring furnace on-line into production flow	1	I,J

FIGURE 2-8

PERT data for the furnace modernization project

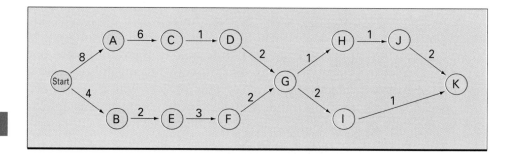

FIGURE 2-9

PERT chart

SETTING OBJECTIVES

TRADITIONAL OBJECTIVE SETTING

The traditional role of objectives in organizations was one of control imposed by top management. The president of a manufacturing firm would *tell* the production vice president what she expected manufacturing costs to be for the coming year. The president would *tell* the marketing vice president what level she expected sales to reach for the coming year. The plant manager would *tell* his maintenance supervisor how much her departmental budget would be. Then, at some later point, performance was evaluated to determine whether the assigned objectives had been achieved.

Are You Comprehending
What You're Reading?

1. Explain both the pros and cons of formal planning.
2. A supervisor develops plans to establish specific details about departmental objectives, which must be fulfilled to achieve overall organizational goals. Such plans are called:
   a. strategic plans
   b. tactical plans
   c. long-term plans
   d. detailed plans
3. Describe policies, procedures, and rules. Give an example of each.
4. A bar graph showing time on the horizontal axis and activities to be completed on the vertical axis is a Gantt chart. True or False?

The central theme in **traditional objective setting** was that objectives were set at the top and then broken down into subgoals for each level in the organization. It was a one-way process: The top imposed its standards on everyone below. This traditional perspective assumed that top management knew what was best because only it could see the "big picture."

In addition to being imposed from above, traditional objective setting was often largely nonoperational. If top management defined the organization's objectives in broad terms such as achieving "sufficient profits" or "market leadership," these ambiguities had to be turned into specifics as the objectives filtered down through the organization. At each level, managers would supply their own meaning to the goals. Specificity was achieved by each manager applying his or her own set of interpretations and biases. As shown in Figure 2-10, the result was that objectives lost clarity and unity as they made their way down from the top.

Traditional objective setting
Objectives are set at the top and then broken down into subgoals for each level in the organization.

MANAGEMENT BY OBJECTIVES

Well-managed organizations have largely discarded this traditional approach and replaced it with **management by objectives (MBO)**. This is a system in which subordinates jointly determine specific performance objectives with their superiors, progress toward objectives is periodically

Management by objectives (MBO)
A system in which subordinates jointly determine specific performance objectives with their superiors, progress toward objectives is periodically reviewed, and rewards are allocated on the basis of this progress.

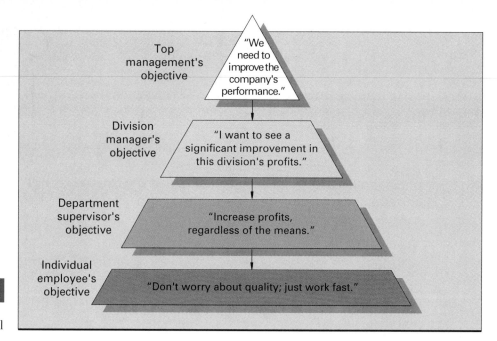

FIGURE 2-10

Traditional objective-
setting—less than ideal

Management by objectives

Digital Drucker: Peter Drucker Online
http://www.dgsys.com/~tristan/technodrucker.html

reviewed, and rewards are allocated on the basis of this progress. Rather than using goals to control, MBO uses goals to motivate people.

MBO makes objectives operational by devising a process by which they cascade down through the organization. The organization's overall objectives are translated into specific objectives for each succeeding level (for example, divisional, departmental, individual) in the organization. Because lower-unit managers jointly participate in setting their own goals, MBO works from the "bottom up" as well as the "top down." The result is a hierarchy that links objectives at one level to those at the next level.

MBO's Four Key Components

There are four ingredients common to MBO programs. These are goal specificity, participative decision making, an explicit time period, and performance feedback.

GOAL SPECIFICITY

The objectives in MBO should be specific statements of expected accomplishments. It's not adequate, for example, merely to state a desire to cut costs, improve service, or increase quality. Such desires have to be converted into tangible objectives that can be measured and evaluated. To cut departmental costs *by 7 per cent*, to improve service by ensuring that all telephone orders are processed *within twenty-four hours of receipt*, or to increase quality by keeping returns to *less than 1 per cent of sales* are examples of specific objectives.

PARTICIPATION

In **MBO** the objectives are not unilaterally set by the boss and assigned to subordinates, as is characteristic of traditional objective setting. **MBO** replaces these imposed goals with jointly determined goals. Together, the manager and the subordinate choose the goals and agree on how they will be achieved and evaluated.

TIME LIMITS

Each objective has a concise time period in which it is to be completed. Typically, the time period is three months, six months, or a year. So not only does everyone have specific objectives but also a specific time period in which to accomplish them.

PERFORMANCE FEEDBACK

The final ingredient in an **MBO** program is feedback on performance. **MBO** seeks to give continuous feedback on progress toward goals. Ideally, this is accomplished by ongoing feedback to individuals so they can monitor and correct their own actions. This is supplemented by periodic formal appraisal meetings in which superiors and subordinates can review progress toward goals and further feedback can be provided.

WHY MBO WORKS

There are several reasons why **MBO** works.

1. It gives both managers and employees clarity and direction in their jobs. Employees know what's important and the specific outcomes by which their performance will be judged.
2. **MBO** increases employee involvement, commitment, and motivation. Employees feel more empowered because they typically are given the freedom to choose the means for achieving their objectives. Additionally, the regular feedback on performance and tying of rewards to the achievement of objectives acts to stimulate employee motivation.
3. **MBO** tends to minimize the politics in performance appraisals and reward allocations. Subjective factors like an employee's effort and attitude or a boss's prejudices are replaced by objective measures of performance and rewards based on that performance.

TIME MANAGEMENT

"Our accounts have doubled in the last year with no increase in staff to handle them," says Della Tardif, Corporate Credit Manager with **IPSCO** in Regina. "I could work twenty-four hours a day for six months straight and not be finished. So every day I write down the six things I want to

FIGURE 2-11

Cheryl Munro Sharp, of London Life, participates with her boss in setting her department's goals. They are basically done on a yearly basis, but she says, "We assess the major projects pretty much once a month just to make sure that we still agree that this project takes priority over others."

London Life Insurance Company
http://www.londonlife.com

IPSCO
http://www.ipsco.com

accomplish. And I do them." Ian Carmichael, B.C. sales manager for Tees and Persse, a large food brokerage company, expresses a similar concern: "The most difficult part of my job is making time for everything, keeping everything in perspective, and making sure the right things happen in a timely fashion."

The most effective supervisors have learned how to manage their time. In this section, we'll show you that **time management** is actually a personal form of scheduling. Supervisors who use their time effectively know what activities they want to accomplish, the best order in which to take the activities, and when they want to complete those activities.

Time management
A personal form of scheduling; maximizing the allocation of the use of time

TIME AS A SCARCE RESOURCE

Time is a unique resource in that, if it's wasted, it can never be replaced. While people talk about saving time, the fact is that time can never actually be saved. It can't be stockpiled for use in some future period. If wasted, it can't be retrieved. When a minute is gone, it's gone forever.

The positive side of this resource is that all supervisors have it in equal abundance. While money, personnel, and other resources are distributed unequally in organizations, thus putting some supervisors at a disadvantage, every supervisor is allotted twenty-four hours every day and seven days every week. Some just use their allotments better than others.

FOCUSING ON DISCRETIONARY TIME

Supervisors can't control all their time. They are routinely interrupted and have to respond to unexpected crises. It's necessary, therefore, to differentiate between response time and discretionary time.

Response time
Responding to requests, demands, and problems initiated by others

The majority of a supervisor's time is spent responding to requests, demands, and problems initiated by others. We call this **response time** and treat it as uncontrollable. The portion that is under a supervisor's control is called **discretionary time**. Most of the suggestions offered to improve time management apply to its discretionary component. Why? Because only this part is manageable!

Discretionary time
The portion of a supervisor's time that is under his or her control

Unfortunately for supervisors, discretionary time makes up only about 25 per cent of their work hours.[8] Moreover, discretionary time tends to become available in small pieces—five minutes here, five minutes there. Thus it is very difficult to use effectively. The challenge, then, is to know what time is discretionary and then to organize activities so as to accumulate discretionary time in blocks large enough to be useful. Supervisors who are good at identifying and organizing their discretionary time accomplish significantly more, and the things they accomplish are more likely to be high-priority activities.

How Do You Use Your Time?

How can supervisors, or anyone for that matter, determine how well they use their time? The answer is to keep a log or diary of daily activities for a short period of time, then evaluate the data you record.

The best log is a daily diary or calendar broken down into fifteen-minute intervals. To get enough information from which to generalize, you need about two weeks of entries.

When your diary is complete, you will have a detailed time and activity log. Then you can analyze how effectively you use your time. Rate each activity in terms of its importance and urgency (see Figure 2-12). If you find that many activities received Cs or Ds, you'll find the next sections valuable. They provide detailed guidelines for better time management.

Five Steps to Better Time Management

The essence of time management is to use your time effectively. This requires that you know the objectives you want to accomplish, the activities that will lead to the accomplishment of those objectives, and the importance and urgency of each activity. We've translated this into a five-step process.

1. **Make a list of your objectives.** What specific objectives have you set for yourself and the unit you manage? If you're using MBO, these objectives are already in place.

Rate Each Activity for:

Importance

    A. Very important: must be done

    B. Important: should be done

    C. Not so important: may be useful, but is
        not necessary

    D. Unimportant: doesn't accomplish anything

Urgency

    A. Very urgent: must be done now

    B. Urgent: should be done now

    C. Not urgent: can be done some time later

    D. Time not a factor

FIGURE 2-12

Analyzing activities for importance and urgency

2. **Rank the objectives according to their importance.** Not all objectives are of equal importance. Given the limitations on your time, you want to make sure you give highest priority to the most important objectives.
3. **List the activities necessary to achieve your objectives.** What specific actions do you need to take to achieve your objectives? Again, if you're using MBO, these action plans are already laid out.
4. **Assign priorities to the various activities required to reach each objective.** This step imposes a second set of priorities. Here, you need to emphasize both importance and urgency. For example, what activities should you delegate, and which aren't urgent and can wait? This step will identify activities that you *must* do, those you *should* do, those you'll get to *when you can*, and those that can be *delegated to others*.
5. **Schedule your activities according to the priorities you've set.** The final step is to prepare a daily plan. Every morning, or at the end of the previous work day, make a list of the five or so most important things you want to do for the day (if the list grows to ten or more activities, it becomes cumbersome and ineffective). Then set priorities for the activities listed on the basis of importance and urgency.

SOME ADDITIONAL POINTS TO PONDER

FOLLOW THE 10-90 PRINCIPLE

Ten per cent of most supervisors' time produces 90 per cent of their results. It's easy for supervisors to get caught up in the activity trap and confuse actions with accomplishments. Those who use their time well make sure that the critical 10 per cent gets highest priority.

KNOW YOUR PRODUCTIVITY CYCLE

Each of us has a daily cycle. Some of us are morning people, while others are late-afternoon or evening people. Supervisors who know their cycle and schedule their work accordingly can significantly increase their effectiveness. They handle their most demanding problems during the high part of their cycle, when they are most alert and productive. They relegate their routine and undemanding tasks to their low periods.

REMEMBER PARKINSON'S LAW

Parkinson's Law says that work expands to fill the time available. The implication for time management is that you can schedule *too* much time for a task. If you give yourself an excess amount of time to perform an activity, you're likely to pace yourself so that you use up the entire time allotted.

Below are listed many of the typical factors that supervisors cite as time wasters. Check all those that apply to you in both Column A and Column B.

Column A

____ Interruptions

____ Attending meetings

____ Drop-in visitors

____ Telephone calls

____ Red tape

____ Unclear expectations

____ Lack of clear goals

____ Lack of help

____ Unrealistic time estimates

____ Too many bosses

____ Lack of motivation

Column B

____ Procrastinations

____ Too much work to do

____ Complete easy tasks first

____ Messy desk

____ Unnecessary mail

____ Can't say no

____ Failure to listen

____ Waiting for others

____ Lack of self-discipline

____ Visual distractions

____ Misplaced items

After you've checked those that apply, study your time wasters. Do they have anything in common?

Irrespective of what you checked, did you see any relationship between the items in the two columns? If you observed closely, you probably found that Column A are those things that waste your time but are not in your direct control. In Column B are time wasters we bring on ourselves. However, time management isn't that simple. Contrary to what most of us want to believe, every item in *each* columns is within our control. Many of those things in Column A that we shrug off as impossible to deal with can in fact be addressed. That's the purpose of good time management.

How will you address your time wasters? How will you face these issues? What will you do to correct your time management "problems"?

GROUP LESS IMPORTANT ACTIVITIES TOGETHER

Set aside a regular time period each day to make phone calls, do follow-ups, and perform other kinds of busywork. Ideally, this should be during your low cycle. This avoids duplication, waste, and redundancy; it also prevents trivia from intruding on high-priority tasks.

MINIMIZE DISRUPTIONS

When possible, try to minimize disruptions by setting aside a part of the day when you are most productive as a block of discretionary time. Then, try to insulate yourself. During this time—which may only be twenty or thirty minutes—limit access to your work area and avoid interruptions. Refuse phone calls or visits during this period. You can set aside other blocks of time each day to be accessible, and to initiate or return all your calls.

KNOW YOUR POLYCHRONICITY

Polychronicity
The degree to which a person prefers doing two or more things simultaneously

People differ in terms of their preference for doing one thing at a time rather than doing two or more things simultaneously. People range from being highly monochronic (focusing entirely on doing one thing at a time) to highly **polychronic** (having no difficulty writing a report, talking on the phone, eating a snack, and watching a television program simultaneously). In terms of time management, highly polychronic types are more flexible in their schedules. They're less likely to be precise in scheduling completion times for tasks; have little trouble in grouping certain tasks together to be performed during the same time period; and are more likely to add, delete, and alter their priorities as the day proceeds. Maybe most interestingly, the highly polychronic person is much better at responding to unscheduled events. An unplanned phone call, for instance, typically has little effect on the highly polychronic type's work schedule, while it is a distinct distraction and likely to interrupt the monochronic's scheduled activities.

GOAL SETTING

Now we turn to skill development and application. In this section, we introduce a skill in three parts.

1. You complete a self-assessment "Check Yourself" exercise relating to a specific supervisory skill.

2. We present some basic skill information.

3. We present a skill application on which you can practise.

For this chapter, the skill is goal setting. Each of the remaining chapters of this book will conclude with a section entitled From Concepts to Skills, which will introduce a supervisory skill using the same three-part approach.

ASSESSING YOURSELF: ARE YOU A GOOD GOAL SETTER?

For each of the following questions, check the answer that best describes your relationship with subordinates. Remember to respond as you have behaved or would behave, not as you think you should behave. If you have no supervisory experience, answer the questions assuming you are a supervisor.

THE PEOPLE WHO WORK FOR ME HAVE:

		Usually	Sometimes	Seldom
1.	Specific and clear goals.	❏	❏	❏
2.	Goals for all key areas relating to their job performance.	❏	❏	❏
3.	Challenging but reasonable goals (neither too hard nor too easy).	❏	❏	❏
4.	The opportunity to participate in setting their goals.	❏	❏	❏
5.	A say in deciding how to implement their goals	❏	❏	❏
6.	Deadlines for accomplishing their goals.	❏	❏	❏
7.	Sufficient skills and training to achieve their goals.	❏	❏	❏
8.	Sufficient resources (i.e., time, money, equipment) to achieve their goals.	❏	❏	❏

9. Feedback on how well they are
    progressing toward their goals.   ❏   ❏   ❏

10. Rewards (i.e., pay, promotions) allocated to them
    according to how well they reach their goals.   ❏   ❏   ❏

SCORING KEY AND INTERPRETATION

For all questions, give yourself 3 points for "Usually," 2 points for "Sometimes," and 1 point for "Seldom."

Total up your points. Scores of 26 or higher demonstrate a strong understanding of goal-setting techniques. A score of 21 to 25 indicates you can improve your goal-setting skills. Scores of 20 or less suggest that you have significant room for improvement.

SKILL BASICS

We presented management by objectives earlier in this chapter. Now we will take the basic concepts of MBO and turn them into specific goal-setting skills that you can apply on the job.

Let's begin by summarizing the five basic rules that should guide you in defining and setting goals.

1. **Make your goals specific.** Goals are only meaningful when they're specific enough to be verified and measured.

2. **Make your goals challenging.** Goals should be set so as to require employees to stretch in order to reach them. If they're too easy, they offer no challenge. If set unrealistically high, they create frustration and are likely to be abandoned.

3. **Impose specific time limits for accomplishment of the goals.** Open-ended goals are likely to be neglected because there is no sense of urgency associated with them.

4. **Goals should be jointly determined by the supervisor and the employee.** Participation increases an employee's goal-aspiration level. Additionally, jointly set goals are often more readily accepted, and accepted goals are more likely to be achieved.

5. **Provide feedback on performance.** Feedback lets people know if their level of effort is sufficient or needs to be increased. It can also induce them to raise their goal level after attaining a previous goal and can inform them of ways in which they can improve their performance.

Effective goal-setting skills can be condensed to eight specific behaviours. When you follow all eight you will have mastered the skill of goal setting.

1. **Identify an employee's key job tasks.** Goal setting begins by defining what it is that you want your employees to accomplish. The best source for this information is each employee's job description, if one is available. It details what task an employee is expected to perform, how these tasks are to be done, what outcomes the employee is responsible for achieving, and the like.

2. **Establish specific and challenging goals for each task.** This is self-explanatory. We should add that, if possible, these goals should be made public. When a person's goals are made public—announced in a group or posted for others to see—the individual seems to be more highly committed to them.

3. **Specify deadlines for each goal.** Again, as previously discussed, goals should include a specific time limit for accomplishment.

4. **Allow the subordinate to actively participate.** Employees are less likely to question or resist a process in which they actively participate than one that is imposed upon them from above.

5. **Prioritize goals**. When someone is given more than one goal, it is important to rank the goals in order of importance. The purpose of this step is to encourage the employee to take action and expend effort on each goal in proportion to its importance.

6. **Rate goals for difficulty and importance.** Goal setting should not encourage people to choose easy goals in order to ensure success. So goal setting needs to take into account the difficulty of the goals selected and whether individuals are emphasizing the right goals. When these ratings are combined with the actual level of goal achievement, you will have a more comprehensive assessment of overall goal performance. This procedure gives credit to individuals for attempting difficult goals even if they don't fully achieve them.

7. **Build in feedback mechanisms to assess goal progress.** Ideally, feedback on goal progress should be self-generated rather than provided externally. When an employee is able to monitor his or her own progress, the feedback is less threatening and less likely to be perceived as part of a management control system.

8. **Make rewards contingent on goal attainment.** Offering money, promotions, recognition, time off, or similar rewards to employees

contingent on goal achievement is a powerful means to increase goal commitment. When the going gets tough on the road toward meeting a goal, people are prone to ask themselves, "What's in it for me?" Linking rewards to the achievement of goals helps employees to answer this question.

APPLYING YOUR SKILLS

This is a role play exercise. Break into groups of three or four students. One student in each group will assume the role of Kelly and one will assume the role of Brad. The other students will serve as observers and evaluators.

Kelly has finally hired someone to take on part of her workload. The 80-hour weeks she was putting in running her new specialty bookstore were beginning to take the thrill out of entrepreneurship. She will continue to do all the buying but will spend less time on the shop floor. Brad, her new employee, will work full-time selling the computer books and magazines. Kelly wants to reduce her hours overall and to have more time to spend on keeping up with the new publications, especially since she is now writing a regular book review for a computer magazine.

Kelly wants to start off well with Brad. She knows he is experienced in sales and something of a computer hacker on the side. But since much of her business's future will depend on how well Brad handles himself, she has decided that they should work together to create a set of goals for him. Kelly has set up a meeting to begin this goal-setting process.

The object of this exercise is to end up with a set of goals for Brad. They might address issues such as prompt and polite attention to customer needs, handling sales appropriately (e.g., credit), maintaining store appearance, preventing shoplifting and dealing with it when it occurs, dealing with telephone inquiries, and keeping up to date with new publications.

This exercise should take no more than fifteen minutes. When completed, the observers from each group should discuss with the role players how their goal-setting session went. Focus specifically on the skill behaviours presented in this section and any problems that surfaced.

Are You Comprehending
What You're Reading?

5. When would a **PERT** chart *not* provide much help?
   a. when sequencing is important
   b. for complicated jobs
   c. for unconnected projects
   d. for jobs with many steps involved
6. How does **MBO** assist in answering the question "What's in it for me?"
7. According to the philosophy of **MBO**:
   a. Feedback occurs at the annual performance review.
   b. Goals follow a "top-down" approach.
   c. Goals typically are broad, general statements of intent.
   d. Constant feedback is provided.
8. Goal setting should encourage employees to set easy goals so that their success can be assured. True or False?

SUMMARY

This summary is organized by the Learning Objectives.

1. In formal planning, specific goals are formulated, committed to writing, and made available to other organization members. Specific-action programs will define the path for the achievement of these goals. In informal planning, plans are kept in the manager's head. Nothing is written down and there is little or no sharing of these plans with others.

2. Plans link the organization from top to bottom. Long-term strategic plans are set by top management. Then each succeeding level down the organization develops its plans. Plans at each level should help to accomplish plans for the level above and give direction for the level below.

3. Policies and rules are both standing plans. Policies are broad and leave room for managerial discretion, while rules are explicit statements that allow no discretion.

4. Managers create single-use plans to cover specific activities or time periods. They provide detailed courses of action to handle unique or nonrecurring activities.

5. The Gantt chart is a simple scheduling device. It is a bar graph with time on the horizontal axis and activities on the vertical axis. It shows planned and actual activities, and allows managers to easily identify the status of a job or project.

6. To compute a PERT chart, you need to identify all key activities needed to complete a project, their order of dependence, and an estimate of each activity's completion time.

7. Four ingredients common to MBO programs are goal specificity, participative decision making, an explicit time period, and performance feedback.

8. Response time is uncontrollable and encompasses the time one spends responding to actions initiated by others. Discretionary time is controllable and within the discretion of the individual.

9. A five-step process to better time management includes making a list of your objectives, ranking the objectives according to their importance, listing the activities necessary to achieve the objectives, assigning priorities to the various activities required to reach each objective, and scheduling your activities according to their importance and urgency.

KEY TERMS AND CONCEPTS

Activities
Budgets
Critical path
Discretionary time
Events
Gantt chart
Intermediate plans
Long-term plans
Management by objectives
PERT chart
Policies
Polychronicity

Procedures
Program
Response time
Rules
Scheduling
Short-term plans
Single-use plans
Standing plans
Strategic planning
Tactical planning
Time management
Traditional objective setting

REVIEWING YOUR KNOWLEDGE

1. Contrast the planning top managers do with that done by first-level managers.
2. Explain how budgets are both a planning and a control device.
3. How might you use a Gantt chart to schedule a group term paper for a college class?
4. What are the implications of the critical path for **PERT** analysis?
5. Contrast **MBO** with traditional objective setting.
6. Why has **MBO** proved so popular in organizations?
7. What specific things can you do, that you're not currently doing, to make you better at managing your time?
8. Why are highly polychronic people likely to be more flexible in their schedules?

ANSWERS TO THE POP QUIZ

1. Pros: **common focus, integration of efforts, preparation**
   Cons: **rigidity, dampens use of creativity**
2. **b. tactical plans.** This is the definition of tactical plans and the distinction between strategic and tactical plans.
3. Policies are broad guidelines for managerial action. Typically established by top management, they define the limits within which managers must stay as they make decisions. For example, a policy might state that a supervisor can "sign off" on purchases under $6500. A procedure defines the steps that are to be taken and the order in which they are to be done. They provide a standardized way of responding to repetitive problems. An example of a procedure would be the steps that supervisors are expected to follow when establishing, completing, and submitting their unit's budget for the coming year. A rule is an explicit statement that tells a supervisor what he or she ought or ought not to do. An example of a rule would be an organization's statements about not permitting scrap materials to be taken home by employees.
4. **True.** This is the definition of a Gantt chart.
5. **c. for unconnected projects.** For a PERT chart to be effective, there must be interdependency, or relatedness of activities. If the activities are independent of each other, no relationship exists among them. Accordingly, a PERT chart would not help in this situation.
6. MBO assists in answering the question "What's in it for me?" by showing the linkage of goal achievement and rewards. That is, money, promotions, recognition, time off, or similar rewards an employee receives are dependent on his or her meeting established work expectations.
7. **d. constant feedback is provided.** For MBO to function effectively, feedback must be continuous.
8. **False.** Setting easy goals defeats the purpose of goal setting. Instead, challenging goals should be set. The level of difficulty needs to be taken into account when reviewing/evaluating an employee's performance.

CASE 2.A

Planning at Quik Copy

Jenny Santana has worked for Quik Copy for five years. She now supervises five full-time employees and as many as twenty part-time employees who work between two and fifteen hours a week. Quik Copy is planning a promotion to bring more customers into the store during July, their slowest month of the year. The store will offer copying at half price, 20 per cent off all colour copying and business card printing, and 10 per cent off custom printing on specialty paper or card stock. To promote the use of several of their computer graphics and desktop applications, the store will give thirty minutes free time to customers who purchase thirty minutes of desktop computer time.

The July promotion will also focus on creative ways to use colour copiers and customized computer desktop applications. Jenny plans to have her employees give short creative demonstrations of colour applications and software use. She decides that seven-minute demonstrations repeated every fifteen minutes will be the best way to interest customers entering the store.

With this schedule, Jenny can run three different colour applications each hour during her four-day promotion. She will also have eight different software application demonstrations during a two-hour period. In addition, there are two touch-screen computers with five-minute general products videos from Quik Copy that she can set up in strategic locations for customers to access at any time.

Seven of her part-time employees have been trained on the various applications; however, their schedules vary. Five of these part-time employees work fifteen hours a week and the other two work ten hours a week. The store's busiest hours are 11 a.m. to 1 p.m., 4 to 6 p.m. and 7:30 to 8:30 p.m. Jenny thinks she will need at least three people to give demonstrations during these peak times.

Scheduling her employees to cover the demonstrations is a challenge. She knows she will need some flexibility because of their limited availability, but she also knows that it would not be good to have the same person give more than three or four of the eight different software demonstrations. Also, she will need employees for store coverage.

RESPONDING TO THIS CASE

1. List and briefly describe several planning elements that Jenny needs to consider in setting up her promotion.
2. In planning Jenny's promotion,
   a. identify the number of workers she will need during peak periods to cover the demonstrations.
   b. determine the schedules each worker will have and what demonstrations each will be giving.
   c. modify your list in question 1 as you find other areas that are important to the success of the promotion.
3. What alterations to Jenny's original plan should be considered now that you have looked at available workers and schedules?
4. What other elements are important to Jenny in planning her promotion? Are there factors that have not been considered in her plan? If so, what are they?

CASE 2.B

MBO at A.C. & C.E.

Shama has just been hired as the new office manager for Applied Consumer and Clinical Evaluation of Mississauga, a company mainly involved in consumer testing for packaged goods manufacturers. The woman Shama is replacing had been with the firm since its inception as a three-person enterprise, was seen as highly competent, and only left because of family demands. This is rather intimidating to Shama, despite the fact that she herself has experience as office manager at two other companies and was recognized as highly capable in those positions.

Another factor intimidating Shama about this position is that Ray Berta, the owner of the firm, uses MBO throughout the operation. Shama has never worked in an MBO environment and she knows that not only will she have to set objectives for herself, but she will also have to work with the people she supervises on their goal setting. Shama's impression is that Ray is a caring individual as well as a clever businessman, and that he wants a harmonious and happy staff as well as a profitable company. That's why she was willing to take the job.

But knowing this still doesn't ease her qualms about MBO. Ray has set up a meeting for next week when he and Shama can discuss the MBO process and begin work on her own plan for the upcoming six months.

RESPONDING TO THIS CASE

1. Discuss what it is about MBO that intimidates some people.
2. Outline the specific steps Ray should follow with Shama to ensure the MBO process works well.
3. Should he share with Shama the goals and plans of the prior office manager to help her get a feel for the job?
4. What can Shama expect to happen during the meeting and afterwards?

3

DESIGNING AND IMPLEMENTING CONTROLS

LEARNING OBJECTIVES

After reading this chapter, you should be able to:

1. Describe the control process.
2. Contrast two types of corrective action.
3. Compare preventive, concurrent, and corrective control.
4. Explain how a supervisor can reduce costs.
5. Describe what a supervisor can do to control employee behaviour.
6. List the characteristics of an effective control system.
7. Explain potential negative outcomes that controls can create.

CHAPTER OUTLINE

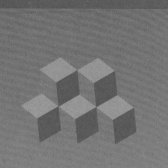

FIGURE 3-1

Well designed controls helped Harley-Davidson's revival.

Harley-Davidson
http://www.
harley-davidson.com/

In the mid-1970s, North America was going wild over motorcycles. Harley-Davidson, then owned by AMF Corp., responded by nearly tripling production to 75 000 units annually over a four-year period.[1] Along with this growth, however, came problems. Engineering and design of Harleys became dated. Quality deteriorated so much that more than half the cycles coming off the assembly line had missing parts, and dealers had to fix them before they could be sold. Harleys leaked oil, vibrated badly, and couldn't match the performance of the flawlessly built Japanese bikes. Hardcore Harley enthusiasts were willing to tolerate these inconveniences, but newcomers had no such devotion and bought Japanese bikes.

In 1973 Harley had 75 per cent of the super-heavyweight market. By 1980 its market share had plummeted to less than 25 per cent. AMF was fast losing confidence in Harley and sold the company in 1981.

Harley's new owner and supervisors worked together to introduce a number of new products, redesign and update the basic product line, and greatly improve the company's marketing programs. These actions would not have meant much if Harley hadn't also dramatically revised its production and operations practices. The new supervisors visited Honda's assembly plant in Marysville, Ohio and realized what they were up against. In response, they initiated a number of changes on Harley's production floor. A new inventory system was introduced that eliminated mountains of costly inventory parts. They redesigned the entire production system, closely involving employees in planning and working out the details. Workers were taught statistical techniques for monitoring and controlling the quality of their own work. Supervisors even worked with the company's suppliers—as has long been done by Japanese manufacturers—to help them adopt the same efficiency and quality-improvement techniques that Harley had instituted in its plants.

Harley succeeded in pulling off one of North America's most celebrated turnarounds. From the verge of bankruptcy in the early 1980s, ten years later Harley's share of the U.S. super-heavyweight market was almost 65 per cent. The company was losing money in 1982, but now is highly profitable, thanks, in part, to well-designed controls!

You've completed your planning. You know your own department's objectives and you've jointly set specific job objectives with all the people who report to you. Standing plans are in place. So, too, are your department's budgets and important schedules. Your next concern should be: How do I know if all my plans are being achieved? The answer: You don't, unless you've also developed controls!

As described in Chapter 1, controlling is the management function concerned with monitoring activities to ensure that they are being accomplished as planned and correcting any significant deviations. In this chapter, we will show you how effective supervisors perform the controlling function. Specifically, we'll detail the control process, discuss the timing of controls, identify the major areas where supervisors concentrate their control activity, describe the characteristics of effective controls, and discuss some of the potentially undesirable side effects of controls that supervisors need to be on guard against.

THE CONTROL PROCESS

The **control process**, which is derived directly from our definition, consists of three separate and distinct steps:

1. Measure actual performance;
2. Compare results with standards; and
3. Take corrective action (see Figure 3-2).

Control process
Measuring actual performance, comparing results with standards, and taking corrective action

Before we discuss each of these steps, you should be aware that the control process assumes that standards of performance already exist. These standards are actually the detailed and specific goals that we created in planning. So planning must precede application of the control process.

If management by objectives is used, the MBO-derived objectives become the standards against which actual performance is compared. This is because MBO integrates planning and control by providing

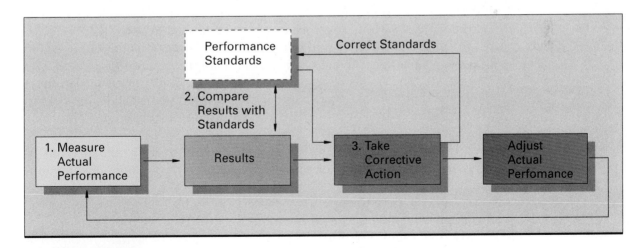

FIGURE 3-2
The control process

managers with a set of objectives or standards to be attained. If MBO is not practised, then standards are the specific performance indicators that management uses for equipment utilization, resource usage, quality, employee productivity, and the like. And these standards can be applied to individuals, teams, departments, or the entire organization. Some examples of popular performance standards include percentage of plant capacity, number of units produced per work hour, average amount of scrap per unit produced, lost work days due to injuries, absence rates, return on investment, cost per unit sold, returns as a percentage of sales, and total dollar sales per sales territory.

MEASURE ACTUAL PERFORMANCE

To determine what actual performance is, it is necessary to acquire information about it. The first step in control, then, is measuring. Let's consider both *how* we measure and *what* we measure.

HOW WE MEASURE

Four common sources of information used by supervisors to measure actual performance are personal observation, statistical reports, oral reports, and written reports.

Personal observation provides firsthand, intimate knowledge of the actual activity. As such, it is probably the most widely used means by which supervisors assess actual performance. In fact, it has even acquired its own label—MBWA or Management by Walking Around. It permits intensive coverage, since minor as well as major performance activities can be observed, as well as opportunities for the supervisor to "read between the lines." Personal observation can pick up omissions, facial expressions, and tones of voice that may be missed by other sources.

The current wide use of computers in organizations has led to supervisors increasingly relying on *statistical reports* for measuring actual performance. This measuring device, however, is not limited to computer outputs. It also includes graphs, bar charts, and numerical displays of any form that supervisors may use for assessing performance. These are described in detail later in the chapter.

Information can also be acquired through *oral reports*, that is, through conferences, meetings, one-to-one conversations, or telephone calls. The advantages of oral reports are that they are fast, allow for feedback, and permit the speaker's expression and tone of voice, as well as words themselves, to convey meaning.

Finally, actual performance can be measured by *written reports*. The strength of written reports is that they offer greater comprehensiveness and conciseness than is typically found in oral reports. They are also easier to catalogue and reference.

FIGURE 3-3

How supervisors can measure performance

FIGURE 3-4

An increasing number of supervisors are using computers to facilitate control.

WHAT WE MEASURE

What we measure is probably more critical to the control process than *how* we measure it. The selection of the wrong criteria can result in serious dysfunctional consequences (which we'll discuss later in this chapter). More importantly, what we measure determines, to a great extent, what employees will attempt to emphasize.

For instance, the office staff in the accounting department of a large health-maintenance organization is expected to be at work at 8:00 a.m. Every morning, at precisely eight o'clock, the department's supervisor walks around the office to make sure everyone is in. What he typically finds is purses and lunch bags on desks, open briefcases, coats over backs of chairs, and other physical evidence that employees have arrived. But most are down in the cafeteria having coffee. The fact is that these employees know that their supervisor checks to make sure they're in, but he isn't necessarily concerned that they're actually working. So these employees make sure that they are at the office by 8:00 a.m., because that's a control criterion their supervisor has decided is important.

Keep in mind that some control criteria are applicable to most supervisory situations while others are job-specific. For instance, since all supervisors direct the activities of others, criteria such as employee satisfaction or absenteeism rates have universal application. Almost all managers also have budgets for their area of responsibility set in dollar amounts. Keeping costs within budget is therefore a fairly common control measure.

However, in setting control criteria, you need to recognize the diversity of activities among supervisors. A production supervisor in a manufacturing plant might use measures of the quantity of units produced per day, units produced per labour hour, scrap per unit of output, or percentage of rejects returned by customers. The supervisor of an administrative unit in a government agency might use number of document pages typed per day, number of orders processed per hour, or average time required to process service calls. Sales supervisors often use measures such as percentage of market captured in a given territory, average dollar value per sale, or number of customer visits per salesperson. The key is that what you measure must be adjusted to fit the goals of the department.

Compare Results with Standards

The comparing step determines the difference between actual performance and the standard. Some variation in performance can be expected in all activities; it is therefore critical to determine the acceptable **range of variation**. Deviations in excess of this range become significant and receive the supervisor's attention. In this comparison stage, supervisors are particularly concerned with the size and direction of the variation. An example should make this clearer.

Jim Tanner is the sales supervisor at Mueller Mercedes-Porsche. Jim prepares a report during the first week of each month that describes sales for the previous month, classified by model. Figure 3-5 displays both the standard (goal) and actual sales figures for the month in review.

Should Jim be concerned about the July performance? If he focused only on Mercedes' unit sales and Porsche's average dollar sale, the answer would be "No." But there appear to be some significant deviations. The average sales price on Mercedes is far below projection. A closer look at Figure 3-5 offers an explanation. The higher-priced "S" series cars weren't moving, while the lower-priced "C" and "E" series did better than expected. On the Porsche side, almost every model had disappointing sales.

Which performance deviations deserve Jim's attention depends on what Jim and his superiors have agreed or believe to be *significant*. How much tolerance should be allowed before corrective action is taken?

The deviation on several models is very small and undoubtedly not worthy of special attention. This probably includes models where actual and standard were off by only one car. But are the shortages for the Mercedes S420, S500 and Porsche Carrera 2, 928, and 968 Coupes or the 968 Cabriolet significant? That's a judgment Jim must make.

By the way, an error in understating sales can be as troublesome as an overstatement. For instance, are the strong sales for the Mercedes C and E models a one-month abnormality, or are these models increasing in

Range of variation
The degree of acceptable variation between actual performance and the standard

Model	Goal	Actual	Over (under)
Mercedes			
C220	2	3	1
C280	4	7	3
E320	6	11	5
E320C	1	0	(1)
E420	3	5	(2)
S320	2	3	(1)
S420	5	3	(2)
S500	2	0	(2)
S600	1	0	(1)
SL320	2	1	(1)
SL500	2	1	(1)
Total units	30	34	
Total sales $	1 962 000	1 686 000	
Average sales $	65 400	49 586	
Porsche			
Carrera 2 Coupe	4	2	(2)
Carrera 2 Targa	1	1	-
Carrera 2 Cabriolet	3	2	(1)
Carrera 4 Coupe	1	0	(1)
928 Coupe	2	0	(2)
968 Coupe	4	1	(3)
968 Cabriolet	3	1	(2)
Total units	18	7	
Total sales $	1 055 000	515 000	
Average sales $	58 611	59 286	

FIGURE 3-5

Mueller Mercedes-Porsche
sales performance for July

popularity? Jim has concluded that the economy is the culprit. With the economy slow, people seem to be moving to less expensive models. Additionally, reflecting national trends, Jim's sales of Porsche cars is down across the board. But our example illustrates that both overvariance and undervariance may require corrective action.

Take Corrective Action

The third and final step in the control process is the action that will correct the deviation. It will be an attempt either to adjust actual performance or to correct the standard, or both (refer back to Figure 3-2).

There are two distinct types of corrective action. One is immediate and deals predominantly with symptoms. The other is basic and delves into the causes. Immediate corrective action is often described as "putting out fires," whereas basic corrective action gets to the source of the deviation and seeks to adjust the differences permanently. Immediate action corrects something right now and gets things back on track. Basic action asks how and why performance deviated.

Unfortunately, many supervisors rationalize that they don't have the time to take basic corrective action and therefore must be content to perpetually "put out fires." Effective supervisors recognize that they must find the time to analyze deviations and, in situations where the benefits justify such action, permanently correct significant differences between standard and actual performance.

Referring back to our Jim Tanner example, he might take basic corrective action on the positive deviation for the Mercedes C and E models. If sales have been greater than expected for the past several months, he might upgrade the standard for future months' sales of these models and increase his orders from the factory. The poor showing on all the Porsches and the upper-range Mercedes models might justify a number of actions, for instance, cutting back on orders of these cars, running a sales promotion to move the increased inventory, reworking the sales-commission plan to reward salespeople for selling Porsches and higher-priced Mercedes, and/or recommending an increase in his dealership's advertising budget.

SOME SPECIAL MEASUREMENT TOOLS

Cause-effect diagrams Diagrams used to depict the causes of a problem and to group them according to common categories such as machinery, methods, personnel, finances, or management

Flow charts Visual representations of the sequence of events for a particular process that clarify how things are being done, so that efficiencies can be identified and the process improved

Scatter diagrams Diagrams that illustrate the relationship between two variables by visually depicting correlations and possible cause-and-effect

Any discussion of how you measure would be incomplete without a discussion of the basic statistical techniques used to control variability. In this section, we'll describe the more popular statistical process control techniques.

Cause and Effect Diagrams. **Cause-effect diagrams** (also sometimes called fish-bone diagrams) are used to depict the causes of a certain problem and to group the causes according to common categories such as machinery, materials, methods, personnel, finances, or management.

As shown in Figure 3-6, these diagrams look somewhat like a fish skeleton, with the problem—the effect—as the "head." On the "bones," growing out of the "spine," are the possible causes of production problems. They're listed in order of possible occurrence. Cause-effect diagrams provide guidance for analyzing the influence that alternative courses of action will have on a given problem.

Flow Charts. **Flow charts** are visual representations of the sequence of events for a particular process. They clarify exactly how things are being done so that inefficiencies can be identified and the process improved. Figure 3-7 provides an illustration.

Scatter Diagrams. **Scatter diagrams** illustrate the relationship between two variables such as height and weight, or the hardness of a ball bearing and its diameter (see Figure 3-8). These diagrams visually

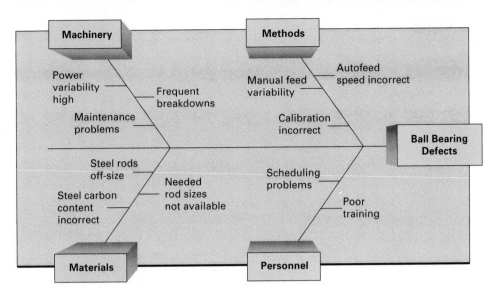

FIGURE 3-6

Example of a fish-bone diagram.

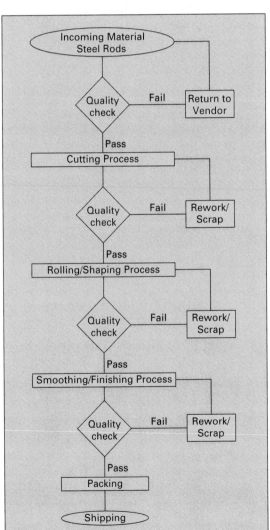

FIGURE 3-7

Example of a flow chart. (Reprinted with permission of the publisher. From *Putting Total Quality Management to Work*, p. 177, copyright © 1993 by Marshall Sashkin and Kenneth J. Kiser, Berrett-Koehler Publishers, Inc., San Francisco, CA. All rights reserved.)

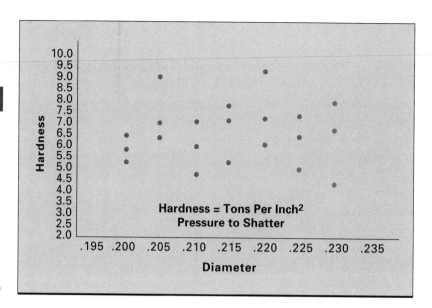
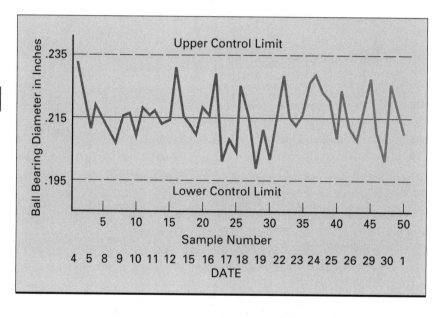
depict correlations and possible cause-and-effect. So, for instance, a scatter diagram could reveal that the percentage of rejects increases as the size of production runs increase. This, in turn, might suggest the need to reduce production runs or reevaluate the process in order to improve quality.

Control Charts. **Control charts** are the most sophisticated of the statistical techniques we'll describe. They are used to reflect variation in a system. Control charts reflect measurements of sample products averaged

Control charts
Run charts of sample averages with statistically determined upper and lower limits

1. The ultimate aim of any control system is:
   a. cost savings
   b. greater productivity
   c. higher profits
   d. achieving goals
2. Explain why planning must come before the control process.
3. Personal observation as a method for measuring performance is one of the most widely used means by which supervisors assess actual performance. True or False?
4. If a supervisor performs the job of an employee who has called in sick that day, the supervisor is:
   a. performing immediate corrective action
   b. illustrating the role of an effective supervisor
   c. performing basic corrective action
   d. none of the above

with statistically determined upper and lower limits. For instance, Coca Cola samples its one-litre bottles after they're filled to determine their exact quantity. This data is plotted on a control chart. It tells management when the filling equipment needs adjustment. As long as the process variables fall within the acceptable range, the system is said to be "in control" (see Figure 3-9). When a point falls outside the limits set, then the variation is unacceptable. Improvements in quality should, over time, result in a narrowing of the range between the upper and lower limits through elimination of common causes.

TYPES OF CONTROL

Where in the process should controls be applied? Supervisors can implement controls before an activity commences, while the activity is going on, or after the fact. The first type is called *preventive control*, the second is *concurrent control*, and the last is *corrective control* (see Figure 3-10).

PREVENTIVE CONTROL

Preventive control
Controls that anticipate and prevent undesirable outcomes

There's an old saying: An ounce of prevention is worth a pound of cure. Its message is that the best way to handle a deviation from standard is to see that it doesn't occur. Managers understand that the most desirable type of control is **preventive control** because it anticipates and prevents undesirable outcomes.

What are some examples of preventive controls? Companies such as Spar Aerospace, McDonald's, General Motors, and Air Canada spend millions of dollars each year on preventive maintenance programs for their equipment with the sole purpose of avoiding breakdowns during operations. Sport Canada requires that all federally funded coaches be certified to at least Level 4 of the National Coaching Certification Program's five levels, which requires successful completion of a long applied training program and approval from the relevant National Sport Organization. Other examples of preventive controls include hiring and training people in anticipation of new business, inspection of raw materials, practising fire drills, and providing employees with company "code of ethics" cards to carry in their wallets.

CONCURRENT CONTROL

Concurrent controls
Controls that are enacted while an activity is in progress

As the name implies, **concurrent control** takes place while an activity is in progress. When control is enacted while the work is being done, management can correct problems before they get out of hand or become too costly. This reminds us of the old saying, "A stitch in time saves nine."

Much of a supervisor's day-to-day activities involve concurrent control. When he or she directly oversees the actions of an employee, monitoring the employee's work and correcting problems as they occur, concurrent control is taking place. While there is obviously some delay between the action and the supervisor's corrective response, the delay is essentially minimal. You'll find other examples of concurrent control on factory machinery and computers. Temperature, pressure, and similar

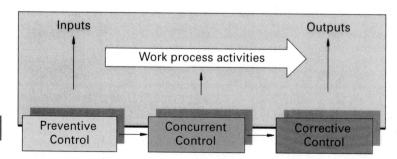

FIGURE 3-10
Three types of controls

gauges that are checked regularly during a production process, and which automatically send a signal to an operator if there is a problem, are examples of concurrent controls. So, too, are programs on computers that provide operators with an immediate response when an error is made. If the operator inputs the wrong command, the program will reject it and may even provide the correct command.

CORRECTIVE CONTROL

Corrective control provides feedback after an activity is finished, in order to prevent any future deviations.

Examples of corrective control include final inspection of finished goods, annual employee performance appraisals, financial audits, quarterly budget reports, and the like. The sales report that Jim Tanner at Mueller Mercedes-Porsche reviews each month, which we described earlier in this chapter, is an example of a corrective control.

The obvious shortcoming of corrective control is that, by the time a supervisor has the information, it's too late to do anything about what has already happened. The damage or mistakes have already occurred. For instance, where information controls are weak, a department head may only learn for the first time in August that her employees have already spent 110 per cent of the department's annual photocopying budget. Nothing she can do in August can correct the overexpenditure. What corrective control does do is alert her that there is a problem. Then she can determine what went wrong and initiate basic corrective action.

> **Corrective control**
> Provides feedback after an activity is finished, to prevent any future deviations

FIGURE 3-11

Even a bridal shop needs extensive controls to keep on top (see Case 3.B).

FOCUS OF CONTROL

What do supervisors control? Most of their control efforts are directed at one of five areas (see Figure 3-12):

- costs
- inventories
- quality
- safety
- employee performance

COSTS

Supervisors are regularly under pressure to keep their costs in line. Let's look at those cost categories and present a general program for cost reduction.

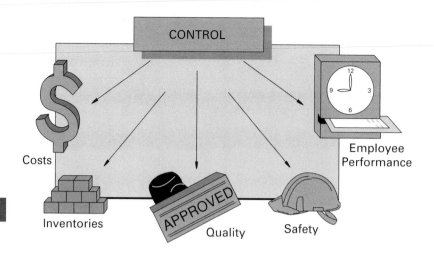

FIGURE 3-12

Focus of control

MAJOR COST CATEGORIES

The following list presents the major cost categories that a supervisor will come in contact with and which need to be monitored.

- **Direct labour costs**. Expenditures for labour that are directly applied in the creation or delivery of the product or service. Examples: Machine operators in a factory or teachers in a school.
- **Indirect labour costs**. Expenditures for labour that are not directly applied in the creation or delivery of the product or service. Examples: Cost accountants, human resource recruiters, public relations specialists.
- **Raw material costs**. Expenditures for materials that go directly into the creation of a product or service. Examples: Sheet steel at a Mazda plant or hamburger buns at a McDonalds.
- **Supportive supplies costs**. Expenditures for necessary items that do not become part of the finished product or service. Examples: Cleaning compounds at the Mazda plant or photocopying costs at Sun Life.
- **Utility costs**. Expenditures for electricity, gas, water, and similar utilities. Example: Monthly electric bill for a regional office.
- **Maintenance costs**. Material and labour expenditures incurred to repair and maintain equipment and facilities. Examples: Repair parts for equipment or jet-engine maintenance technicians at Canadian Airlines.
- **Waste costs**. Expenditures for products, parts, or services that cannot be reused. Examples: Unsold french fries at McDonalds or scrap metal at a Camco plant.

Typically, supervisors will have a budget for each major cost category. Then, by monitoring expenditures, costs can be kept within their budget plans. (See the skill module on budgeting at the end of this chapter.)

COST-REDUCTION PROGRAMS

When costs are too high, managers will implement a cost reduction program. Beginning in the late 1980s, Canadian corporations began a massive effort to reduce costs and improve their competitive position in relation to their global competitors. Much of this had a direct effect on supervisors. For instance, direct labour costs have been cut by automating jobs and redesigning work around teams that are more productive than individuals; and indirect labour costs have been slashed by laying off tens of thousands of support personnel in research, finance, human resources, and clerical functions. Budgets for training, travel, telephone calls, photocopying, computer software, office supplies, and similar expenditures have undergone significant cuts.

The following outlines a six-step program that can guide you in reducing costs in your department.[2]

1. **Improve methods**. Eliminate any unnecessary activities and introduce new work methods that can increase efficiency.
2. **Level the work flow**. Peaks and valleys in a work flow imply inefficiencies. By levelling the work flow, you can make do with fewer employees and cut down on overtime.
3. **Minimize waste**. Burning lights in unused areas, misuse of office supplies, underemployed workers, underutilization of equipment, and wasteful use of raw materials add considerably to a supervisor's departmental costs.
4. **Install modern equipment**. Budget for new equipment to replace obsolete and worn-out machinery, computers, and the like.
5. **Invest in employee training**. People, like machines, can become obsolete in that their skills become dated.
6. **Make cuts selectively**. Avoid across-the-board cuts. Some people and groups contribute significantly more than others. Make cuts where they will generate the greatest efficiencies.

INVENTORIES

Supervisors are routinely responsible for ensuring that adequate inventories of materials and supplies are available for activities under their jurisdiction. For a shift supervisor at Burger King, that would include paper products, buns, burger patties, french fries, condiments, cooking utensils, cleaning supplies, and even proper change for the cash register. For a nursing supervisor at a hospital, it might mean things like pharmaceuticals, gloves, hypodermic needles, and bed linen.

The challenge in monitoring inventory costs is balancing the costs of maintaining inventories against the cost of running out of inventory. If excessive inventory is carried, money is needlessly tied up and unnecessary storage costs are incurred. Excessive inventory also adds to insurance premiums and taxes. And, of course, there are potential obsolescence costs—if Jim Tanner gets overstocked on Porsches and the new-year models begin to arrive, he might have to sell last year's models at below cost to get rid of them. If inventories drop too low, operations can be disrupted and sales lost. A stock-out of paper can bring a publisher's printing presses to a halt. If the Burger King supervisor fails to monitor his inventory of frozen french fries, he might find himself with some very disgruntled customers. And many Mercedes and Porsche customers will expect Jim Tanner's dealership to have the model and colour they want available immediately or they'll take their business to another dealer.

A popular inventory technique that is sweeping through contemporary organizations is the **just-in-time (JIT) inventory system**. Under JIT, inventory items arrive when they are needed in the production process instead of being stored in stock. In Japan, JIT systems are called *kanban*. The derivation of the word gets to the essence of the just-in-time concept. **Kanban** is Japanese for "card" or "sign." Japanese suppliers ship parts to manufacturers in containers. Each container has a card, or kanban, slipped into a side pocket. When a production worker opens a container, he or she takes out the card and sends it back to the supplier. That initiates the shipping of a second container of parts that, ideally, reaches the production worker just as the last part in the first container is being used up. The ultimate goal of a JIT inventory system is to eliminate raw material inventories by precisely coordinating production and supply deliveries. When the system works as designed, it results in a number of positive benefits for a manufacturer: reduced inventories, reduced setup time, better work flow, shorter manufacturing time, less space consumption, and even higher quality. Of course, suppliers who can be depended on to deliver quality materials on time must be found. Because there are no inventories, there is no slack in the system to absorb defective materials or delays in shipments.

Just-in-time (JIT) inventory system
A system in which inventory items arrive when they are needed in the production process instead of being stored in stock. See also Kanban.

Kanban
In Japanese, a "card" or "sign." Shipped in a container, a kanban is returned to the supplier when the container is opened, initiating the shipment of a second container that arrives just as the first container is emptied.

Synchronizing operations: Scheduling smarter to reduce inventories
http://www.newsteel.com/features/NS9703F7.HTM

Just-in-time warehouses
http://www.newsteel.com/features/NS9707SF.HTM

Bombardier
http://www.bombardier.com/

QUALITY

With the possible exception of controlling costs, achieving high quality has become a primary focus of today's organizations. Many North American products were criticized as being shoddy in quality compared to their Japanese and German counterparts. On the other hand, companies such as Bombardier, General Electric, and Northern Telecom have thrived in the past decade by focusing on quality products or services. With this new emphasis has come increased demand on supervisors to engage in quality control.

Historically, *quality* referred to achieving some preestablished standard for an organization's product or service. Today, quality has taken on a larger meaning. We discussed this expanded perspective—called Total Quality Management—earlier in the book. Quality control, however, continues to address monitoring quality—weight, strength, consistency, colour, taste, reliability, finish, or any one of a myriad quality characteristics—to ensure that it meets our preestablished standard.

Quality control is needed at multiple points in a process. It begins with the receipt of inputs. Are the raw materials satisfactory? Do new employees have the proper skills and abilities? It continues with work in process and in all steps up to the completion of the final product or service. Assessments at intermediate stages of the transformation process are typically part of quality control. Early detection of a defective part or process can save the cost of further work on the item.

A comprehensive quality control program would encompass preventive, concurrent, and corrective controls. For example, controls would inspect incoming raw materials, monitor operations while they are in progress, and include final inspection and rejection of unsatisfactory outputs. Of course, this same comprehensive program could be applied to services. For instance, a claims supervisor for Dominion Insurance could hire and train her people to make sure they fully understand their jobs, monitor their daily work flow to ensure it is done properly and on time, review completed claims for accuracy and thoroughness, and follow up with customers to determine their degree of satisfaction with the way their claims were handled.

FIGURE 3-13

As manager of occupational health and safety at an Ontario community college, Lynn Schaule organized a training program for all the college's administrators. According to Ontario legislation, administrators are all personally liable for providing a safe and healthy workplace for their workers.

SAFETY

Fred Stillman considers safety a vital part of his job. Every morning, before his work crew arrives, he takes a tour of the warehouse. As a warehouse supervisor at Office Depot, he's looking for potential sources of accidents. He inspects the hand trucks, the forklifts, the ladders, and scaffolds. He checks the floor for loose tiles and grease. He looks over the merchandise to make sure it's been stacked properly. He makes notes about any merchandise that might be clogging aisles or walkways. And during the day, when employees are working, he's always on the lookout for "accidents in the making"—for example, employees who handle equipment improperly or fail to follow company safety procedures.

Accidents cost Canadian companies millions of dollars each year. This includes costs associated with increased absences, medical and disability claims, medical insurance, and damaged equipment. As a supervisor, you're on the front line to prevent accidents from occurring. So another area where supervisors need to focus their efforts is both preventive and corrective safety controls.

OCCUPATIONAL HEALTH AND SAFETY LEGISLATION

Canadian legislation in occupational health and safety is based on an "internal responsibility" system. This system recognizes that workers, supervisors, and employers share a common goal of preventing work-related injury or illness, and that they are all in a position to identify and prevent circumstances leading to injury or illness in the workplace. The legislation lays down rules for this joint accountability in the form of legally enacted duties, rights, and responsibilities.

For organizations under federal jurisdiction (for example, banks, airlines, post offices), the regulations governing health and safety fall under the Canada Labour Code. Health and safety matters for organizations not under federal jurisdiction are regulated by the province or territory in which the organization is located (see Figure 3-14).

The supervisor's role is an important one with respect to ensuring that health and safety regulations are followed. In fact, in Ontario, the Occupational Health and Safety Act specifies that an employer is required to appoint "competent persons" as supervisors. A "competent person" under the Act is one who

(a) is qualified because of knowledge, training, and experience to organize the work and its performance

(b) is familiar with this Act and the regulations that apply to the work

(c) has knowledge of any potential or actual danger to health or safety in the workplace

(Occupational Health and Safety Act, sections 1 and 25)

The supervisor is also expected to apply this knowledge by advising workers of hazards, giving specific instructions, procedures, and equipment to provide appropriate protection; and taking "every precaution reasonable in the circumstances for the protection of a worker."

A supervisor who fails to comply may be liable for a fine or imprisonment. Let's look at an example: On February 28, 1994, Raglan Industries Inc. of Oshawa, a company director, and a supervisor were all convicted under the Ontario Occupational Health and Safety Act. They had failed to ensure suitable lighting in a confined space during a paint spraying application despite a concern being raised by a worker. In a subsequent explosion, the worker received burns to almost 90 per cent of his body, head wounds, a fractured back, and a partially amputated hand. The supervisor's part of the conviction involved a $5000 fine.

CAUSES OF ACCIDENTS

What causes accidents? Human error and unsafe working environments.

The primary cause of workplace accidents is employees who engage in unsafe personal acts. They fail to wear safety glasses, use unsafe shortcuts to increase their output, take improper care of hazardous chemicals, or engage in horseplay around dangerous machinery. There are also some employees who are accident-prone—they are more likely than others to have accidents. These people tend to be forgetful, bored, stressed-out, or overly impulsive. This makes them more susceptible to accidents.

Jurisdiction	Main body of health & safety law	Department
Canada	Canada Labour Code	Labour
Alberta	Occupational Health and Safety Act	Environment
British Columbia	Workers' Compensation Act Workplace Act	WCB* Labour
Manitoba	Workplace Safety and Health Act	Labour - Workplace Safety and Support Services
New Brunswick	Occupational Health and Safety Commission Act Occupational Health and Safety Act	New Brunswick Occupational Health & Safety Commission
Newfoundland	Occupational Health and Safety Act	Labour
Nova Scotia	Occupational Health and Safety Act Workers' Compensation Act	Health WCB
Ontario	Occupational Health and Safety Act Workplace Safety and Insurance Act	Labour Workplace Safety and Insurance Board
Prince Edward Is.	Occupational Health & Safety Act Workers' Compensation Act	Fisheries and Labour WCB
Quebec	An Act respecting occupational health and safety An Act respecting industrial accidents and occupational disease	Occupational Health and Safety Commission
Saskatchewan	Occupational Health and Safety Act	Human Resources, Labour & Employment

* Workers' Compensation Board

FIGURE 3-14

Federal and Provincial health and safety Acts

Fred Stillman's preventive safety controls at Office Depot focused on unsafe working conditions. No department is completely immune to the possibility of being the scene of an accident. However, certain environments increase the likelihood. Noise, poor lighting, and excessive heat or cold create distracting work environments. Disorganized and messy workstations can cause accidents. Lifting heavy materials is a frequent cause of back injuries. Power equipment creates high accident potential, as does improperly-maintained equipment of any kind. Stairs, ladders, and scaffolds increase opportunities for people to fall. People who work for long periods of time on a computer are increasingly suffering from carpal-tunnel syndrome, which creates chronic pain in the wrist and fingers.

ACCIDENT PREVENTION

What can you do to prevent accidents? A number of things. Here are some actions you might consider.

1. **Match people and jobs.** Factors such as visual skills and experience have been found to be related to increased accident rates on certain types of jobs. Moreover, when employees are undergoing personal problems or other sources of stress, their potential for accidents increases on some jobs. Rotating a person temporarily to a lower-risk job, for instance, should be considered if you think their personal problems might increase accident-proneness. Or restrict the activities of an employee who is temporarily accident-prone.

2. **Engineer the job and equipment.** The proper design of job activities, work devices, protective gear, and equipment can cut down on accidents and injuries. Office workers, for instance, are less likely to suffer back problems if their desk and chair arrangement is designed to their specific work activities and body movements.

3. **Educate and train employees.** Make sure your employees know the safety rules and incorporate accident prevention into training programs. Create safety awareness by posting highly visible signs that proclaim the importance of safety, use safety committees to identify and correct potential problems, and publicize safety statistics.

4. **Enforce safety standards.** The best rules and regulations will be ineffective in reducing accidents if they are not enforced. Make regular visits to the work floor and visually check to make sure safety standards are being maintained.

5. **Reward employees for safe performance.** Make sure employee safety is viewed as important and worthwhile. Provide incentives and awards for safe performance.

EMPLOYEE PERFORMANCE

Supervisors accomplish things through other people. They need and depend on subordinates to achieve their unit goals. It is, therefore, important for them to get their employees to perform in ways they consider desirable. But how do supervisors ensure that employees are performing as they are supposed to? How do you, for example, minimize employee lateness, absenteeism, and accidents? How do you control the quantity and quality of employee effort? Obvious means include direct supervision and performance appraisals.

On a day-to-day basis, supervisors oversee employees' work and correct problems as they occur. The supervisor who spots an employee taking an unnecessary risk when operating his or her machine can point out the correct way to perform the task and tell the employee to do it the correct way in the future.

Supervisors assess the work of their employees in a more formal way by means of systematic performance appraisals. An employee's recent performance is evaluated. If performance is positive, the employee's behaviour can be reinforced with a reward such as a pay increase. If performance is below standard, the supervisor will seek to correct it or, depending on the nature of the deviation, discipline the employee.

As Figure 3-16 demonstrates, supervisors have at their disposal a considerably larger menu of behavioural control devices. In actual practice, supervisors use almost all of the options described in the figure to increase the likelihood that employees will perform as desired.

FIGURE 3-16

Behavioural control
devices

- **Selection.** Identify and hire people whose values, attitudes, and personality fit with what the supervisor desires.
- **Goals.** When employees accept specific goals, the goals then direct and limit behaviour.
- **Job design.** The way jobs are designed determines, to a large degree, the tasks that a person does, the work pace, the people he or she interacts with, and similar behaviours.
- **Orientation.** New-employee orientation defines what behaviours are acceptable and what aren't.
- **Direct supervision.** The physical presence of supervisors acts to shape employee behaviour and allows for rapid detection of undersirable behaviour.
- **Training.** Formal training programs teach employees desired work practices.
- **Regulations.** Formal rules, policies, job descriptions, and other regulations define acceptable practices and constrain undesirable behaviour.
- **Performance appraisals.** Employees will behave so as to look good on the criteria by which they will be appraised.
- **Rewards.** Pay raises, recognition, desired job assignments, and similar rewards act as reinforcers to encourage desired behaviours and to extinguish undesirable ones.

CHARACTERISTICS OF EFFECTIVE CONTROLS

Effective control systems tend to have certain qualities in common (these qualities are summarized in Figure 3-17). The importance of these characteristics varies with the situation, but the following can provide guidance to supervisors in designing their unit's control system.

TIMELINESS

Controls should alert the supervisor to a problem as soon as possible. The best information has little value if it is dated. Therefore, an effective control system must provide timely information.

ECONOMY

A control system must be economically reasonable to operate. Any system of control has to justify the benefits that it gives in relation to the costs it incurs. To minimize costs, supervisors should try to impose the least amount of control that is necessary to produce the desired results. The widespread use of computers is due to a large extent to their ability to provide timely and accurate information in a highly efficient manner.

FIGURE 3-17

Characteristics of effective controls

FLEXIBILITY

Effective controls must be flexible enough to adjust to adverse change or to take advantage of new opportunities. In today's dynamic and rapidly changing world, supervisors should design control systems that can adjust to the changing nature of departmental objectives, work assignments, and job tasks.

UNDERSTANDABILITY

Controls that cannot be understood by those who have to use them are of little value. It is sometimes necessary, therefore, to substitute less complex controls for sophisticated devices. A control system that is difficult to understand can cause unnecessary mistakes, frustrates employees, and is eventually ignored.

REASONABLE CRITERIA

Consistent with our discussion of goals in the previous chapter, control standards must be reasonable and attainable. If they are too high or unreasonable, they no longer motivate. Since most employees don't want to risk being labelled as incompetent for telling their bosses that they ask too much, employees may resort to unethical or illegal shortcuts. Controls should, therefore, enforce standards that are reasonable; they should challenge and stretch people to reach higher performance levels without being demotivating or encouraging deception.

CRITICAL PLACEMENT

Supervisors can't control everything that goes on in their department. Even if they could, the benefits couldn't justify the costs. As a result, they should place controls on those factors that are critical to their unit's performance goals. Controls should cover the critical activities, operations, and events within their unit. That is, they should focus on where variations from standard are most likely to occur or where a variation would do the greatest harm. In a department where labour costs are $20 000 a month and postage costs are $50 a month, a 5 per cent overrun in the former is more critical than a 20 per cent overrun in the latter. Hence, we should establish controls for labour and a critical dollar allocation, whereas postage expenses would not appear to be critical.

EMPHASIS ON THE EXCEPTION

Since supervisors can't control all activities, they should place their strategic control devices where they can call attention only to the exceptions. A **control by exception** system ensures that a manager is not overwhelmed by information on variations from standard. For instance, the accounts receivable supervisor at a Sears store instructs his people to only inform him when an account is fifteen days past due. The fact that 90 per cent of the store's customers pay their bills on time or no more than two weeks late means she can devote her attention to the 10 per cent exceptions.

Control by exception
Strategic control devices should call attention only to exceptions from standard

POTENTIAL NEGATIVE OUTCOMES OF CONTROLS

Controls can create their own problems. The introduction of controls comes with potential negatives that you will need to guard against. These include employee resistance, misdirection of employee effort, and ethical dilemmas for supervisors concerning control devices. Let's take a brief look at each.

EMPLOYEE RESISTANCE

Many people don't like to be told what to do or to know that they're being "checked up on." When work performance is deficient, few people enjoy being criticized or corrected. The result is that employees often resist controls. They see their supervisor, daily production reports, performance appraisals, and similar control devices as evidence that their employer doesn't trust them.

Reality tells us that controls are a way of organizational life because management has a responsibility to ensure that activities are going as planned. So what can you, as a supervisor, do to lessen this resistance?

First, wherever possible, encourage employee self-control (see Assessing Yourself). Once employees know their goals, give them the benefit of the doubt and leave them alone. Let them monitor and correct their own performance. Supplement this with regular communication so they can let you know what problems they've encountered and how they've solved them. The assumption with self-control is that employees are responsible, trustworthy, and capable of personally correcting any significant deviation from their goals. Only if this assumption proves incorrect do you need to introduce more formalized external control mechanisms.

When external controls are needed, here are a few suggestions to minimize employee resistance.

- Have employees participate in setting the standards. This lessens the likelihood that they'll view them as unrealistic or too demanding.
- Explain to employees how they will be evaluated. Surprisingly, the problem is often not the controls themselves creating resistance but the lack of understanding of how information will be gathered and how it will be used.
- Provide employees with regular feedback. Ambiguity causes stress and resistance, so it makes sense to let people know how they're doing.
- Finally, treat controls as a device for helping employees improve rather than for punishing them. Most people want the satisfaction that comes from doing their work better and want to avoid the pain and embarrassment that comes with discipline.

Assessing Yourself

HOW WILLING ARE YOU TO ENCOURAGE SELF-CONTROL?

For each of the following eighteen statements, rate each on a scale of 1 to 5, where 5 = strongly agree, 4 = agree somewhat, 3 = neither agree nor disagree, 2 = disagree somewhat, and 1 = strongly disagree.

	Strongly Agree			Strongly Disagree	
1. I'd let others do more, but it appears the jobs never seem to get done the way I want them to be done.	5	4	3	2	1
2. I don't feel I have the time to explain to others what to do.	5	4	3	2	1

3. I carefully check on others' work without letting them know I'm doing it, so I can correct their mistakes if necessary, before they cause too many problems.　　　5　4　3　2　1

4. I let others control the whole job—giving them the opportunity to complete it without any of my involvement. Then I review the result.　　　5　4　3　2　1

5. When I have given clear instructions and the task isn't done right, I get upset.　　　5　4　3　2　1

6. I feel that others may lack the commitment I have. Any task I ask them to do won't get done as well as I'd do it.　　　5　4　3　2　1

7. I'd let others control things more, but I feel I can do the job better than the person I might have given the job to.　　　5　4　3　2　1

8. I'd let others control more, but if the individual I give this responsibility to does an incompetent job, I'll be severely criticized.　　　5　4　3　2　1

9. If I were to give up control, my job wouldn't be nearly as much fun.　　　5　4　3　2　1

10. When I give up control, I often find that the outcome is such that I end up doing the task over again myself.　　　5　4　3　2　1

11. I have not really found that giving up control saves any time.　　　5　4　3　2　1

12. I tell others exactly how something should be accomplished.　　　5　4　3　2　1

13. I can't give up control as much as I'd like to because others lack the necessary experience.　　　5　4　3　2　1

14. I feel that when I give up control, I lose control.　　　5　4　3　2　1

15. I would give up control more, but I'm pretty much a perfectionist.　　　5　4　3　2　1

16. I work longer hours than I should.　　　5　4　3　2　1

17. I can give others the routine tasks, but I feel I must do nonroutine tasks myself.　　　5　4　3　2　1

18. My own boss expects me to keep very close to all details of my job.　　　5　4　3　2　1

SCORING

Total your score by adding the circled numbers for the eighteen statements.

WHAT THE INSTRUMENT MEANS

How much control you're willing to give up or share is directly related to how willing you are to assign this "authority" to others. Depending on your total score, the following interpretations can be made:

72–90 points = ineffective assignment of self-control
54–71 points = assigning self-control habits needs substantial
        improvement
36–53 points = assigning self-control habits are positive,
        but some improvement needed
18–35 points = superior assignment of self-control

Source: Reprinted by permission of the publisher from *Management Review*, May 1982 ©1982, American Management Association, New York. All rights reserved.

Misdirection of Effort

Three managers at a General Motors plant installed a secret control box in a supervisor's office to override the control panel that governed the speed of the assembly line.[3] The device allowed the managers to speed up the assembly line—a serious violation of GM's contract with the United Auto Workers. When caught, the managers explained that, while they knew what they had done was wrong, the pressure from higher-ups to meet unrealistic production goals was so great that they felt the secret control panel was the only way they could meet their targets. As described by one manager, senior GM executives would say (regarding the high production goals), "I don't care *how* you do it—just *do* it."

Have you ever been frustrated by the "service" you receive when trying to get some information, fill out a form or solve a problem? Some employees can be so fixated on ensuring that every rule is followed that they lose sight of the fact that their job is to serve the public, not hassle them! This tendency illustrates another potential problem with controls: People may misdirect their efforts in order to look good on the control criteria.

FIGURE 3-18

Employees in government offices often become so fixated on following every rule that they lose sight of what is really important.

Because any control system has imperfections, problems occur when individuals or organizational units attempt to look good exclusively in terms of the control devices while in actuality, the result is dysfunctional in terms of the organization's goals. More often than not, this situation is caused by incomplete measures of performance. If the control system evaluates only the *quantity* of output, people will ignore quality. Similarly, if the system measures activities rather than results, people will spend their time attempting to look good on the activity measures.

What can you, as a supervisor, do to minimize this problem? Two things. First, make sure that control standards are reasonable. Very importantly, this should not merely be your perception. The *employees* must believe the standards are fair and within their capability. Second, you should select and evaluate criteria that are directly related to achievement of employee job goals. If the licensing supervisor in the motor vehicle office evaluates her people on how well they follow rules rather than on how effectively they serve the needs of clients, then her employees are not going to give much attention to satisfying clients. Finding the right criteria will often mean using a multiple set of standards. For instance, the goal of "serving clients" might require the licensing supervisor to evaluate her clerks on criteria such as "greets all clients with a smile and friendly greeting," "answers all client questions without seeking outside assistance," and "solves the client's problems in one visit." In addition, the supervisor might set up a client comment box in her licensing department where individual employees could be praised or criticized on their service, and then use this feedback as one measure of how well employees were doing their jobs.

Are You Comprehending What You're Reading?

5. Because a supervisor cannot control all activities, controls should be placed on _____ activities.
   - a. risky
   - c. critical
   - b. risk-free
   - d. complex

6. Explain what is meant by just-in-time inventory systems.

7. In some jurisdictions a supervisor can be held personally liable when health and safety regulations are not followed in the workplace. True or False?

8. An annual employee performance appraisal is an example of a _____ control.
   - a. preventive
   - b. concurrent
   - c. corrective

ETHICS AND CONTROL DEVICES

Just because a supervisor *can* monitor the most minute details of an employee's work day doesn't mean he or she *should*. This has become a particularly sensitive issue in recent years as sophisticated communication systems and computer software make it possible for a supervisor's control capability to potentially interfere with an employee's right to privacy.

Supervisors at General Electric's Answering Centre record and review employees' handling of customer telephone inquiries. At Vantreight's huge flower farm in Saanichton, B.C., supervisors use handheld computers to track each picker's output. The technology now exists for "big brother" to directly and indirectly monitor employees. But is it ethical?

We have no absolute answer. It can be argued that this type of computer performance monitoring helps people do their jobs better. It enables supervisors to review employee performance and provide feedback that can improve the quality of the employees' work. But employees certainly should be aware that this monitoring is going on. Even then, studies have shown that stress-related complaints go up when employees know that somebody may be listening in on their phone calls.[4] This suggests that great care needs to be taken by supervisors as advanced technology expands their control capability.

GE Home Page
http://www.ge.com/

BUDGETING

Budgeting is an important supervisory control skill. What do you know about budgeting? The following brief self-assessment exercise can help you answer that question.

ASSESSING YOURSELF: WHAT DO YOU KNOW ABOUT BUDGETING?

For each of the following statements, record your response by circling the corresponding number.

WHEN DESIGNING AND CONTROLLING A BUDGET, I WOULD:

		Strongly Agree	Agree	Neutral	Disagree	Strongly Disagree
1.	Begin the budget process by focusing on my department's goals.	1	2	3	4	5
2.	Delegate responsibility for developing my budget to a team of employees.	1	2	3	4	5
3.	Use last period's budget as a guide for developing this period's budget, especially in times of significant departmental change.	1	2	3	4	5
4.	Use the budget process as a way to convey to upper management new programs and responsibilities that my department might pursue.	5	4	3	2	1
5.	Focus on controlling costs because expense budgets are the most frequently used supervisory budgets.	5	4	3	2	1
6.	Try to underspend my current budget because that typically results in a larger budget in the next budget period.	1	2	3	4	5

SCORING KEY AND INTERPRETATION

Add up your score. The higher your total, the better your understanding of budgeting. Individuals with scores below 20, in particular, should find the following coverage of budgeting valuable.

Skill Basics

This skill-building module deals with creating and using a budget—the planning and control tool most used by supervisors. As we noted in Chapter 2, there are many kinds of budgets—revenue (or sales), expense, profit, capital, production, cash, and advertising are popular examples. The one type of budget that almost every supervisor is involved with is the expense budget. Why? Because the supervisor is closest to where the work is actually accomplished. He or she is thus best qualified to make the most accurate judgments of what future expenses will be incurred in accomplishing unit goals. Given the universality of the expense budget, we'll use it as the focal point of our discussion.

INCREMENTAL vs. ZERO-BASE BUDGETS

The traditional budget is incremental in nature. It develops out of the previous budget. In the **incremental budget**, each period's budget begins by using the last period as a reference point. Then adjustments are made to individual items within the budget. The major problems with the incremental approach are that it tends to hide inefficiencies and waste, encourages continual increases, and hinders change. Inefficiencies tend to grow because, in the typical incremental budget, nothing ever gets cut. Each budget begins with the funds allocated for the last period—to which are added a percentage for inflation and requests for new or expanded activities. So, unfortunately, this approach to budgeting often provides money for activities long after the need is gone. And because incrementalism builds on the past, this type of budget also tends to constrain bold or radical changes.

> **Incremental budget**
> A budget that develops out of the previous budget

An option that deals directly with the incremental budget's limitations is the **zero-base budget (ZBB)**. With the ZBB, the entire budget begins from scratch and each budget item must be justified. No reference is made to previous appropriations. The major advantage to the ZBB is that all programs, projects, and activities taking place within every department in the organization are reassessed in terms of benefits and costs. The primary drawbacks of ZBB include increased paperwork and preparation time, the tendency for managers to exaggerate the benefits of activities they want funded, and the negative effect on intermediate and long-term planning. On this last point, when departmental budgets have to be completely justified every year, the potential for dramatic ups and downs in funding can create chaos for managers and make intermediate and long-term planning almost impossible.

> **Zero-base budget**
> A budget that makes no reference to previous appropriations; all items must be justified

While most organizations rely on incremental budgeting, the zero-base approach continues to have its advocates. We suggest that when organizations are developing new strategies, making major shifts in the products and services they offer, undertaking a significant reorganization, or introducing similar organization-wide change programs, managers should at least temporarily utilize zero-base budgeting. This approach will lessen the likelihood that outdated or less important activities will continue to receive their prior level of funding.

TOP-DOWN vs. BOTTOM-UP BUDGETING

Top-down budgeting
Budgets that are initiated, controlled, and directed by top management

Another decision that has to be made about budgeting is where the budget will initially be prepared. **Top-down budgeting** originates at the upper levels of the organization. Budgets are initiated, controlled, and directed by top management. This approach assumes top management is best able to allocate resources among alternative uses within the organization. These budgets are then given to middle-level and lower-level managers, whose responsibility it is to carry them out. This method has the advantage of simplifying the budgeting process and focusing attention on the organization's overall strategy and goals. However, the top-down approach has some huge disadvantages. It assumes that top management has comprehensive data on all activities within the organization. This assumption is rarely valid, especially in relatively large organizations. Since operating personnel and lower-level managers have no input, the top-down approach also does nothing to build support for and commitment to budgets.

Bottom-up budgeting
Budget requests are prepared by those who implement them and then sent to higher levels of management for approval.

Most organizations today have moved to **bottom-up budgeting**, where the initial budget requests are prepared by those who must implement them. They are then sent up for approval to higher levels of management where modifications may be suggested. When differences occur, they're negotiated. The process is followed upward until an organization-wide budget is developed. The bottom-up approach to budgeting essentially has the opposite advantages and disadvantages to those of budgets initiated from the top. Because supervisors and other lower-level managers are more knowledgeable about their needs than are managers at the top, they are less likely to overlook important funding requirements. And very importantly, lower-level managers are also much more likely to enthusiastically accept and try to meet budgets they had a hand in shaping.

THE BUDGETING PROCESS

You're a new supervisor who has been asked to submit your first budget. What do you do? The following steps will provide you with some guidance:

1. **Review the organization's overall strategy and goals.** Understanding your organization's strategy and goals will help you focus on where the overall organization is going and your department's role in that plan.

2. **Determine your department's goals and the means to attain them.** What activities will allow you to reach your departmental goals and help the organization achieve its overall goals? What resources will you require to achieve these goals? Think in terms of factors like staffing requirements, workloads, and the materials and equipment you'll need. This is also your opportunity to formulate new programs and propose new responsibilities for your department.

3. **Gather cost information.** You'll need accurate cost estimates of those resources you identified in step 2. Old budgets may be of some help. But you'll also want to talk with your immediate manager, other superiors, colleagues in similar positions, key subordinates, and use other contacts you have developed both inside and outside your organization.

4. **Share your goals and cost estimates with superiors.** Your immediate manager will need to approve your budget, so his or her support is necessary. Discuss your goals, cost estimates, and other ideas with your immediate manager and key superiors *before* you include them in your budget. This will ensure that they align with upper management's vision of your department's role and will build consensus for your proposed submission.

5. **Draw up your proposed budget.** Once your goals and costs are in place, constructing the actual budget is fairly simple. But be sure to show the linkage between your budget items and your departmental goals. You need to justify your requests. And be prepared to have to explain and sell your budget to your immediate manager and upper management. Remember that there will almost certainly be other managers competing for some of the same resources that you want.

6. **Be prepared to negotiate.** It's unlikely that your budget will be approved exactly as you submitted it. Be prepared to negotiate changes that upper management suggests and to revise your original budget. Recognize the politics in the budget process and negotiate from the perspective of building credits for future budgets. If certain projects aren't approved this time, use this point in the budget process to get some assurance that they will be reconsidered next time.

7. **Monitor your budget.** Once approved and implemented, you'll be judged on how well you carry out your budget. Manage by exception. Set variance targets that include both percentages and dollars. For instance, you could set a decision rule that says you'll investigate all monthly variances of 15 per cent or larger where the actual dollar variance is $200 or more.

8. **Keep superiors informed of your progress.** Keep your immediate manager and other relevant parties advised on how you're doing in terms of meeting your budget. This is likely to help protect you if you exceed your budget for reasons beyond your control. Also, don't expect to be rewarded for underspending your budget. In incremental budgets, underspending will only mean you'll be allocated fewer funds in the next budget period!

Applying Your Skills

You wish to attend a three-day training course in Halifax. To get approval, you need to submit a cost estimate to your supervisor. This estimate will also serve as your budget for the trip.

1. Describe how you would approach this cost estimate. For example, what information will you need and where will you get it? Remember to apply the appropriate steps of the budgeting process.

2. Create a proposed budget using cost estimates for all items. Then look at your completed budget and decide which items are negotiable and why.

3. Now take the role of the manager who will be receiving the above request.

   a) Assuming you approve the trip, would you prefer to cover the costs of the trip in advance or reimburse afterwards?

Explain why. What are the implications for control?

b) You want to encourage employee development, yet at the same time keep costs down. What kinds of expenses on the submitted budget might you decide to declare as personal expenses which the company will not cover? Which expenses should the company accept and why?

c) What "controls" might your company apply to ensure that all such travel and training expenses are both legitimate and within reason?

SUMMARY

This summary is organized by the Learning Objectives.

1. The control process consists of three separate and distinct steps: 1. measure actual performance; 2. compare results with standards; and 3. take corrective action.
2. There are two types of corrective action: immediate and basic. Immediate deals predominantly with symptoms. Basic corrective action looks for the cause of the deviation and seeks to permanently adjust the differences.
3. Preventive control is implemented before an activity begins. It anticipates and prevents undesirable outcomes. Concurrent control takes place while an activity is in progress. Corrective control is implemented after an activity is finished, and facilitates prevention of future deviations.
4. Supervisors can reduce costs in their departments by improving work methods, levelling the work flow, reducing waste, installing more modern equipment, investing in employee training, and making selective cuts that will generate the greatest efficiencies.
5. To control employee behaviour, supervisors can select employees who will fit well in the department, provide specific goals, control the design of jobs, use new-employee orientation to convey acceptable behaviour, engage in direct supervision, provide formal training, impose formal regulations, use performance appraisals, and reward desirable behaviour.
6. An effective control system should be timely, economical, flexible, and understandable; have reasonable standards and strategically placed controls; and emphasize the exception.
7. Some potential negative outcomes from controls include employee resistance, employees directing their efforts to the wrong activities, and ethical dilemmas created by advances in control technology.

KEY TERMS AND CONCEPTS

Bottom-up budgeting
Concurrent control
Control by exception
Control process
Corrective control

Incremental budget
Preventive control
Range of variation
Top-down budgeting
Zero-base budget

REVIEWING YOUR KNOWLEDGE

1. Why is it that *what* we measure may be more critical to the control process than *how* we measure it?
2. What constitutes an acceptable range of variation?
3. Which type of control is preferable—preventive, concurrent, or corrective? Why? What type do you think is most widely used in practice?
4. What is the challenge of monitoring inventory costs?
5. In terms of characteristics of an effective control system, where do you think most control systems fail? Why?
6. Why should a supervisor control "by exception"?
7. How can a supervisor lessen employee resistance to controls?
8. What can a supervisor do to minimize the problem of people trying to look good on control criteria?
9. Contrast incremental and zero-base budgets. Which is best for facilitating change? Why?
10. Why do most organizations use bottom-up budgeting?

ANSWERS TO THE POP QUIZZES

1. **d. achieving goals.** This is a basic premise of control systems. They should be designed to ensure that goals are achieved.
2. Control means examining activities to determine whether performance is acceptable. You must first have established standards of what is to be considered acceptable. Therefore you must figure out what it is you want before determining whether you have got it or not.
3. **True.** Personal observation is one of the most widely used means by which supervisors assess actual performance. It enables a supervisor to pick up verbal omissions, facial expressions, and tones of voice that may be missed by other methods.
4. **a. performing immediate corrective action.** This is the definition of immediate corrective action.
5. **c. critical.** Placing controls on critical activities is one of the elements of effective controls. It also enables a supervisor to focus on the variations from standards that are most likely to occur or where a variation would do the greatest harm.
6. Just-in-time inventory systems involve having inventory items arrive when they are needed in the production process instead of being kept in stock.
7. **True.** The text cites a specific incident at Raglan Industries in Ontario, where a supervisor was fined $5000 after a worker was badly injured.
8. **c. Corrective.** The employee appraisal provides feedback on past performance, with the intention of thereby improving future performance.

CASE 3.A

The Buck Stops Where?

Jan Roades is the Manager of the Southeastern Sales Division for a large oil company. Under her command are twenty sales reps who are responsible for the product marketing within a specific area of southern Ontario, supporting the gas stations in servicing and marketing company products. With two years on the job, Jan has earned the respect of her sales reps, who feel that she is fair in the freedom she allows while maintaining control over major policy decisions. Although Jan sees herself in a "coordinator" role, she is also actively involved in each sales area to ensure that the service is consistent throughout her division.

On reviewing the first quarter results, Jan was perturbed by the rising expense claims turned in by her reps. Thinking it was perhaps typical for the first quarter (when reps tend to think they should spend while the purse is full), Jan chose not to take any action. Now, three months later, Jan is dismayed to find that expense reports are 15% over budget. Not only that, but yesterday she received a memo from her boss pointing out the excessive expenses. Although it was an informal memo, Jan knew it was more than a subtle hint to get things back in line.

All the reps are going to be in town for a convention next week. Jan figures it will give her an opportunity to talk with them and discuss how to cut expenses. In any event, it will give her a chance to make sure they all know about the expense problem.

The convention begins and Jan tackles the expense problem in her first meeting with the reps. During a coffee break, Jan hears two of her reps discussing the expense overruns:

"Well, I guess Charlie is going to miss his Friday morning golf games. With these cuts in our expense plans, he's going to have to pay his own green fees," says Bob, the rep from Brantford.

"What do you mean?" asks Gord from London.

"Oh, every Friday Charlie takes one of his service managers to the golf course for lunch. But, before that, they play nine holes of golf. Charlie just adds it to the lunch bill so no one ever knows that the company is paying for his games."

"But wait a minute," says Gord. "Doesn't Charlie have to submit his bills with the expense report?"

"Sure, but he just hides the green fees in the total tab. Besides, he keeps the total under $100 so no one in head office ever bothers to look at the expenses."

Upset, Jan returns to the lecture room, convinced that she has been too easy on her reps and determined to clamp down on the expense process. If they're not going to play fair with her, she'll pull out every rule in the book and make sure that all procedures are followed to the letter.

Back at head office next week, Jan asks her secretary to pull all the expense forms submitted by Charlie. Sure enough, every Friday shows a submission for lunch at the golf course. The gossip was true. A quick calculation indicates that Charlie has chalked up about $300 in disguised green fees. And that's just in the first two quarters of the year.

Jan then goes through the manual on expense submissions. Although it states that all expenses over $50 are to be explained in detail, the Accounting Officer tells Jan that her department just doesn't have the time to check any expense under $100.

Jan now faces a number of options. Should she start to enforce the proper procedure for expense submissions when she knows it won't be monitored? Should she implement additional controls, given that expenses are already over budget? And what about Charlie? Most important, was there something that Jan has missed all these months, and what could she have done to have prevented the whole mess?

RESPONDING TO THIS CASE

1. Discuss how each of the three steps in the control process was applied in Jan's department. Where did the process break down?
2. Specify corrective action that Jan could implement (step 3). Explain the probable consequences.
3. Suggest three specific improvements in the control process. Identify each as a preventive, concurrent, or corrective control.

CASE 3.B

The Business of Romance

"Brides come in all shapes, sizes and personalities. But they all come in here insecure about their bodies and anxious about what they see as the most important dress purchase in their life." Sheila Otter is the owner/manager of Village Wedding Belles in Waterdown, Ontario.

Why is my shop so successful? I've got an extensive selection of dresses, I'm up on the trends—what brides are looking for—I market well, and my dresses are affordably priced. Location is not so important because brides will drive a long way for the right dress. But warm, nonthreatening, attentive and honest service is critical.

We understand our clients' needs, know what's important to them on a personal level, validate their feelings that this is an important decision for them, validate their need for detail, and then deliver what they want in exactly the way they want.

A bride will typically make three visits before purchasing a gown: first just scouting, then returning for a closer look, and finally to get approval from mother or a friend. Each visit can last a couple of hours. And the work is not over after the purchase—Sheila's staff must order the dress and accessories, tailor it to an exact fit, and have everything ready and in perfect condition for the big day.

Within Sheila's small shop are hundreds of dresses and extensive paperwork on the order for each client, so no detail is missed. It could easily fall into chaos. This would mean the end of the business. So Sheila has designed extensive controls to ensure everything is done correctly.

Sheila has special procedures and checking systems for unpacking and for ordering, and clearly outlines to staff the problems that are created when procedures aren't followed. She hires very carefully; trains new staff for months by having them work with her or with other experienced staff; gives constant feedback; and clearly outlines her expectations and standards. Both praise and suggestions for improvement are given in private, to avoid humiliation or envy on the part of others. All staff are on straight salary because commission would create competition, destroying the team effort required when a customer makes several visits and is helped by different staff members before she actually makes a decision to purchase.

Sheila herself phones in all the orders to suppliers so she can check over everything, because once a dress is ordered, it cannot be returned. She keeps an eye on seamstresses when they do customer fittings to ensure both quality work and good customer relations. She also monitors all selling activities, giving suggestions, reminders, feedback, and praise on the service provided to a customer.

Retail does not pay well, so staff turnover can be high. But it takes about eight months for Sheila's staff to come up to speed on all aspects of the store, and excellent customer service is essential to her business. So Sheila needs a strongly motivated staff that's going to stay. Besides the daily feedback, Sheila has performance reviews every four months during which staff are encouraged to express their concerns. There are regular staff meetings to share information. Sheila says it's important for her to share the "fun" part of her job, too, so whenever she's visiting a Toronto supplier she takes one of her staff (on a rotating basis) to see the new stock, express opinions, and have a paid day out with dinner included. If suppliers are visiting the shop to show Sheila their new designs, Sheila invites all the staff to see the designs and express their preferences for the shop's new line. She also gives occasional prizes to staff who most accurately predict what will be the hot-selling items.

Sheila also makes sure staff are aware of the "big picture"—how the store is doing, and what kind of money is needed for advertising, expanding inventory and making renovations on the shop. The staff understand the reality of the business, so there's no resentment that Sheila doesn't pay higher wages. And Sheila balances this with flexibility the staff would not find in many other places. She schedules around their preferred work times and accommodates their need for time off for children's sickness or activities or days off school.

And there's a family atmosphere in the shop, all staff being treated with kindness and respect. Because customers must be treated with kindness, warmth and honesty, it's important that staff feel comfortable in their work environment and support each other. Tensions can run high as the bride's wedding day approaches and staff must remain patient and courteous.

Sheila says a bridal shop would be a great setting for a sitcom, with all the mini-dramas that occur. Her job is to ensure that it's not only an interesting place to work but a profitable one as well.

RESPONDING TO THIS CASE

1. a. List the controls Sheila has in place.
   b. Which type of control is most prevalent? Why?
   c. Which of the characteristics of effective controls (Figure 3-17) apply to Sheila's controls?
2. Explain the control issues Sheila likely faces regarding:
   a. Cost categories
   b. Inventory
   c. Quality control
3. Look at the list of behavioural control devices (Figure 3-16) and select those that Sheila appears to use.
4. Explain how Sheila has avoided the problems that are sometimes created by controls.
5. If Sheila decided to open up a second shop in another location, what effect would this have on her controls?

4

PROBLEM SOLVING AND DECISION MAKING

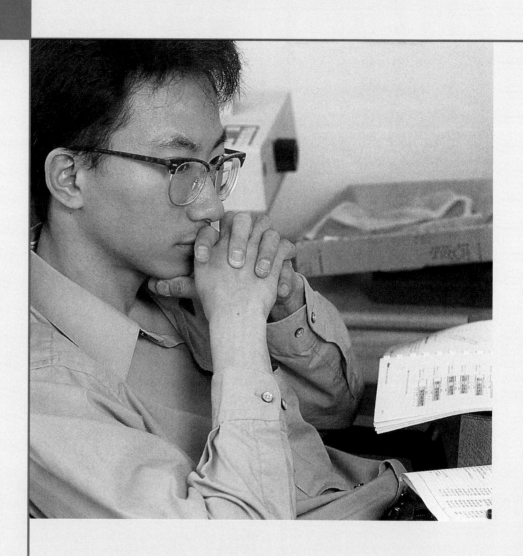

LEARNING OBJECTIVES

After reading this chapter, you should be able to:

1. List the seven steps in the decision-making process.
2. Describe expected value analysis.
3. Explain the value of decision trees.
4. Contrast data with information.
5. Describe the four types of decision styles.
6. Explain three different ethical viewpoints.
7. Compare and contrast group and individual decision making.
8. List four techniques for improving group decision making.

CHAPTER OUTLINE

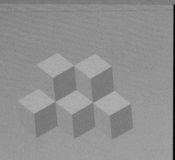

FIGURE 4-1

Cathy Hughes built her business on solid decision making.

Cathy Hughes is an individual on a mission.[1] Having spent several years studying broadcasting and working as a radio broadcaster, she dreamed of one day overseeing her own station. Cathy knew that to do this would be no easy task. A lot of information must be gathered and understood. For example, how does one go about getting licensed? How does one obtain the necessary advertising to ensure an influx of revenues to operate the station? How does one select a program format so a large listening audience can be generated—in turn bringing in more advertising dollars? Answers to such questions for Hughes meant dedicating herself to researching the facts, generating a database, and making appropriate decisions. Once prepared, and building on her knowledge and experience, Cathy launched Radio One, Inc., competing for the ever-challenging weekday morning audience in her city.

To Cathy, building and supervising a successful company requires intuition, concrete plans, business savvy, and the ability to make timely and accurate decisions. And successful she has been. What helped her along the way? One of Cathy's most important decisions was to work in almost every job in the radio business that's required to bring a radio program to life. Doing so gave her complete information to work from, and gave her greater confidence when the time came to oversee such a risky venture.

For Cathy Hughes, supervisory ability is paying off. Given the success she is having, as measured by the large "tuned-in" audience each morning, Cathy is now making decisions to expand by adding more stations and reaching into new cities.

ACOA Website:
Seamans Beverages
http://www.acoa.ca/
english/news/
atlanticprofiles/pei/info_
frame_pei_aapei07.htm

Decisions, decisions, decisions! Making decisions is what you're expected to do as a supervisor and is the reason you are paid more. Making decisions may be the toughest part of the job, but it is also very challenging and enjoyable. According to Allan Watts, the sales supervisor at Seaman's Beverages in Charlottetown, "You have to be able to think on your feet. And make a decision as soon as you can—there's nothing worse than making things drag on for weeks. Ask others for help if you need it, but make the decision soon."

What kinds of decisions will you have to make? The range is wide. For instance, suppose one of your employees has been coming to work late recently and the quality of his work has fallen off—what do you do? Or you've got a vacancy in your department and your company's human resource manager has sent you six candidates to select from—which one do you choose? Or several of your salespeople have told you that they're losing business to an innovative new product line introduced by one of your competitors—how do you respond?

Supervisors are regularly confronted with problems that require decisions. But how do supervisors learn to make good decisions? Are they born with some intuitive talent? No! There are some who because of their intelligence, knowledge, and experience are able unconsciously to analyze problems; and that can result, over time, in an impressive trail of decisions. But there are decision-making techniques that anyone can learn to help make him or her a more effective decision maker. We'll review a number of these techniques in this chapter.

THE DECISION-MAKING PROCESS

Let's begin by describing a rational and analytical way of looking at decisions. We call this approach the **decision-making process**. It's composed of seven steps (see Figure 4-2).

1. Identify the problem.
2. Collect relevant information.
3. Develop alternatives.
4. Evaluate each alternative.
5. Select the best alternative.
6. Implement the decision.
7. Follow up and evaluate.

To help illustrate this process, we'll work through a problem faced by Peggy Hebden, program director for The New VR television station in Barrie, Ontario.

IDENTIFY THE PROBLEM

The decision-making process begins with the existence of a **problem**, or an opportunity, as Peggy prefers to see it. For Peggy, it's having two half-hour program availabilities for Canadian programming in the next six months. She's looking for creative programming suggestions.

In the real world, problems don't come with neon signs identifying them as such. Many of the problems supervisors will confront aren't as obvious as Peggy's programming need. One of the most difficult tasks at this stage, then, is separating symptoms from problems. Is a 5 per cent decline in sales a problem? Or are declining sales merely a symptom of another problem, such as product obsolescence or an inadequate advertising budget? To use a medical analogy, aspirin doesn't deal with the problem of stress on the job—it merely relieves the headache symptom.

Decision-making process
The seven steps to making rational decisions

The NewVR
http://www.citytv.com/ newvr/

Problem
A discrepancy between an existing and a desired state of affairs

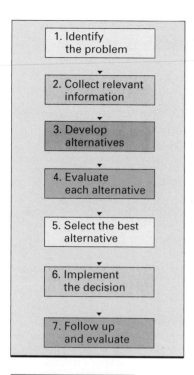

1. Identify
   the problem

   ↓

2. Collect relevant
   information

   ↓

3. Develop
   alternatives

   ↓

4. Evaluate
   each alternative

   ↓

5. Select the best
   alternative

   ↓

6. Implement
   the decision

   ↓

7. Follow up
   and evaluate

FIGURE 4-2

The decision-making process

FIGURE 4-3

Peggy Hebden of the New VR is faced with many
tough programming decisions.

COLLECT RELEVANT INFORMATION

Once you have identified the problem, you need to gather the relevant
facts and information. Why has the problem occurred now? How is it
affecting productivity in my department? What organizational policies, if
any, are relevant for dealing with this problem? What time limitations
exist for solving it? What costs are involved?

Peggy Hebden received a number of program pitches. She must consider which of these would not only serve her programming mandate
(sports and recreation) but also fulfill the sales department's needs. Some
programs are pitched as coproduction opportunities, some as straight
cash sales, and others as barter (airtime in exchange for some commercial time in the program).

DEVELOP ALTERNATIVES

Now all possible alternatives need to be identified. It is at this step in the
decision process that you demonstrate your creativity. What alternatives
exist beyond the obvious or those that may have been used previously?

Keep in mind that this step requires only that you *identify* alternatives. So no alternative—no matter how unusual—should be discarded at this stage. If an alternative isn't viable, you'll find out at the next stage. Also avoid the tendency to stop searching for alternatives after only a couple have been identified. If you see only two or three choices, you probably haven't thought hard enough. Remember that, generally speaking, the more alternatives you can generate, the better your final solution will be. Why? Because your final choice can only be as good as the best alternative you've generated.

In our example, several independent producers have been anxiously pitching their program concepts and want to have their programs broadcast on The New VR. Peggy contacts the producers and asks them to send her as much information as possible on their concepts. A full presentation and business plan are acceptable. However, a "pilot" or sample of the video is preferred.

EVALUATE EACH ALTERNATIVE

Now all the strengths and weaknesses of each alternative need to be evaluated. For example, what will each cost? How long will each take to implement? What's the most favourable outcome I could expect from each? Most unfavourable outcome?

In this step in particular, it's important to guard against biases. Undoubtedly some alternatives will look more attractive when initially identified. Others, at first glance, may seem unrealistic or exceedingly risky. As a result, you may have a tendency to prematurely favour some outcomes over others and then bias your analysis accordingly. Try to put your initial prejudices on hold and evaluate each alternative as objectively as you can. Of course, no one is perfectly rational. But you can improve the final outcome if you acknowledge your biases and overtly attempt to control them.

Figure 4-4 summarizes the highlights from Peggy's evaluations of her five alternatives. By formally writing down key considerations, it is often easier for decision makers to compare alternatives.

SELECT THE BEST ALTERNATIVE

After analysing the pros and cons for each alternative, it is time to select the best alternative. Of course, what's "best" will reflect any limitations or biases that you bring to the decision process. It depends on things such as the comprehensiveness and accuracy of the information gathered in step 2, your ingenuity in developing alternatives in step 3, the degree of risk that you're willing to take, and the quality of your analysis in step 4.

Peggy's main objectives are to attract an audience, attract advertisers, and meet her sports and recreation mandate. After analyzing her needs, and much discussion internally on which alternatives best fit current needs, Peggy chooses the Video Road Show and the Personal Watercraft Show.

Alternative	Strengths	Weaknesses
1. *Gardening Show*	Growing interest in gardening; this is a barter pitch, so would save money; currently have gardening shows on our station that could be of better quality; know and trust producers; unique approach to the subject; works well with our recreational mandate.	Risk to attract ad dollars to support genre; doesn't fit sports mandate.
2. *Video Road Show*	Very good presentation tape; targets young, 18–34 audience; great guests; barter.	Inexperienced producer; cannot do as a local production due to budget constraints; risk.
3. *Cooking Show*	Interesting concept (three young guys cooking).	Doesn't fit sports and rec theme
4. *Martial Arts Show*	Good genre; not a lot of martial arts shows available.	Risk to attract advertising
5. *Personal Watercraft Show*	Great pilot; perfect fit for sports and rec; professional pitch	None

FIGURE 4-4

Evaluating alternatives

IMPLEMENT THE DECISION

Even if you've made the proper choice, the decision may still fail if it is not implemented properly. This means you need to convey the decision to those affected and get their commitment to it. You'll specifically want to assign responsibilities, allocate necessary resources, and clarify any deadlines.

Peggy's main challenge is to ensure the Video Road Show's success despite the producer's inexperience. Peggy feels that he has a good deal of talent and the show will attract the desired 18–34 year-old audience, so it's well worth taking the risk. To reduce this risk, the New VR station agrees to provide a mentoring role for the producer to help him learn in some of the areas where he is weak.

FOLLOW UP AND EVALUATE

The last phase in the decision process is to follow up and evaluate the outcomes of the decision. Did the choice accomplish the desired result? Did it correct the problem that was originally identified in step 1?

Peggy can fairly easily evaluate the working relationship and mentoring roles by the way the finished program fits the program flow and by how it looks. However, it will take at least one month to see whether the show will gain an audience. If the audience watches, the sales department will be able to sell the program to advertisers and The New VR will be in a solid position to decide whether to extend the relationship or to go back to the drawing board.

If the follow-up and evaluation indicate that the sought-after results weren't achieved, you'll want to review the decision process to see where you went wrong. In that case, you essentially have a brand new problem and you should go through the decision process again with a new perspective.

DECISION TOOLS

A number of tools and techniques have been developed over the years to help supervisors improve their decision-making capabilities. In this section, we'll present several of them.

EXPECTED VALUE ANALYSIS

Fred Cassidy, the co-owner and manager of Larry's Sports in Hamilton, Ontario, is looking at several brands of hockey skates. Given his space and budget limitations, he can only purchase one of these brands to add to his department. Which one should he choose?

Expected value analysis could help with this decision. It permits decision makers to place a monetary value on the various consequences likely to result from the selection of a particular course of action. The procedure is simple. You calculate the expected value of a particular alternative by weighting its possible outcomes by the probability (0 to 1.0, with 1.0 representing absolute certainty) of achieving the alternative, then summing up the totals derived from the weighting process.

Expected value analysis
Calculating the expected value of a particular alternative. This is achieved by weighting its possible outcomes according to the probability of achieving the alternative, then summing up the totals derived from the weighting process.

Graves, Inc. By Pat Brady

DO YOU WANT TO ENROLL IN THE SEMINAR ON **DECISION-MAKING**?

LET ME SLEEP ON IT.

FIGURE 4-5

(©1983 by Pat Brady. Reprinted with permission.)

Alternative	Possible Outcome	Probability	Expected Value
Bauer	$ 12 000	0.2	$ 2 400
	10 000	0.6	6 000
	6 000	0.2	1 200
			$ 9 600
CCM	$ 10 000	0.4	$ 4 000
	6 000	0.5	3 000
	2 000	0.1	200
			$ 7 200
Graf	$ 9 000	0.2	$ 1 800
	6 000	0.6	3 600
	4 000	0.2	800
			$ 6 200

FIGURE 4-6

Payoff table for hockey skate decision

Let's say Fred is looking at three lines of skates: Bauer, CCM, and Graf. He's constructed the payoff table in Figure 4-6 to summarize his analysis. Based on his past experience and personal judgment, he's calculated the potential yearly profit from each alternative and the probability of achieving that profit. The expected value of each alternative ranged from $6200 to $9600. Based on this analysis, the supervisor could anticipate the highest expected value that could be reached by purchasing the Bauer line of skates.

DECISION TREES

Decision trees
A diagrammatic technique for analyzing decisions by assigning probabilities to various outcomes and calculating payoffs for each

Decision trees are a useful way to analyze hiring, marketing, investment, equipment purchases, pricing, and similar decisions that involve a progression of decisions. They're called decision trees because, when diagrammed, they resemble a tree and its branches. Typical decision trees encompass expected value analysis by assigning probabilities to each possible outcome and calculating payoffs for each decision path.

Figure 4-7 illustrates a decision facing Mike Rosen, the eastern region site-selection manager for a large bookstore chain. Mike supervises a small group of specialists who analyze potential locations and make store site recommendations to the eastern region's manager. The lease on the company's store in Moncton, New Brunswick, is expiring and the landlord has decided not to renew it. So Mike and his group have to make a relocation recommendation to the regional manager.

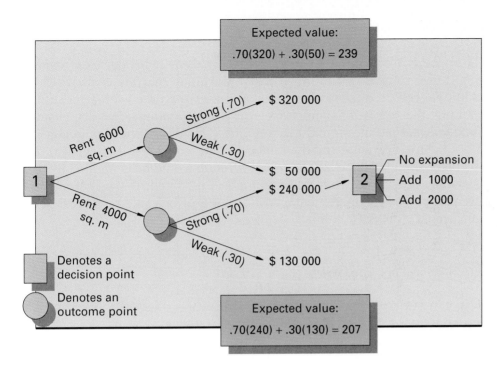

Expected value:

.70(320) + .30(50) = 239

Strong (.70) — $ 320 000

Rent 6000 sq. m

Weak (.30) — $ 50 000

1

Rent 4000 sq. m

$ 240 000 → 2

No expansion

Add 1000

Add 2000

Strong (.70)

Weak (.30) — $ 130 000

Denotes a decision point

Denotes an outcome point

Expected value:

.70(240) + .30(130) = 207

FIGURE 4-7

Decision tree and expected values for renting a large or small retail space

Mike's group has identified an excellent site in a nearby shopping mall. The mall owner has offered him two comparable locations: one with 4000 square metres (the same as he has now) and the other a larger 6000 square-metre space. Mike has an initial decision to make about whether to recommend renting the larger or smaller location. If he chooses the larger space and the economy is strong, he estimates the store will make $320 000 profit. However, if the economy is poor, the high operating costs of the larger store will mean only $50 000 in profit will be made. With the smaller store, he estimates the profit at $240 000 with a good economy and $130 000 with a poor one.

As you can see from Figure 4-7, the expected value for the larger store is $239 000 [(.70 × 320 000) + (.30 × 50 000)]. The expected value for the smaller store is $207 000 [(.70 × 240 000) + (.30 × 130 000)]. Given these results, Mike is planning to recommend the rental of the larger store space.

But what if Mike wants to consider the implications of initially renting the smaller space and then possibly expanding if the economy picks up? He can extend the decision tree to include this second decision point. He has calculated three options: no expansion, adding 1000 square meters, and adding 2000 square meters. Following the approach used for Decision Point 1, he could calculate the profit potential by extending the branches on the tree and calculating expected values for the various options.

MARGINAL ANALYSIS

Marginal analysis
Analyzing decisions in terms of their incremental costs

The concept of marginal, or incremental, analysis helps decision makers to optimize returns or minimize costs. **Marginal analysis** deals with the additional cost in a particular decision, rather than the average cost. For example, the operations supervisor for a large commercial dry cleaner wonders whether she should take on a new customer. She should consider not the total revenue and the total cost that would result after the order was taken, but rather what additional revenue would be generated by this particular order and what additional costs incurred. If the incremental revenues exceed the incremental costs, total profits would be increased by accepting the order.

MANAGEMENT INFORMATION SYSTEMS

How can supervisors improve their ability to collect the information needed for assessing problems and for accurately evaluating alternatives? The answer is to learn how to effectively use their organization's management information system.

Management information system (MIS)
A mechanism to provide managers with needed and accurate information on a regular and timely basis

A **management information system (MIS)** is a mechanism to provide managers with needed and accurate information on a regular and timely basis. It can be manual or computer-based, although recently almost all discussion of MIS focuses on computer-supported applications.

The term *system* in MIS implies order, arrangement, and purpose. Further, an MIS focuses specifically on providing management with information, not merely data. These two points are important and require elaboration.

A library provides a good analogy. Although it can contain millions of volumes, a library doesn't do users much good if they can't quickly find what they want. That's why libraries spend a lot of time cataloguing their collections and ensuring that volumes are returned to their proper locations. Organizations today are like well-stocked libraries. There is no scarcity of data. The limitation is in the ability to process it so that the right information is available to the right person when he or she needs it. An MIS has data organized in some meaningful way so you can access the information in a reasonable amount of time. **Data** are raw, unanalyzed facts such as names, numbers, or quantities. As data, these facts are relatively useless to managers. When data are analyzed and processed, they become **information**. An MIS collects data and turns them into relevant information for managers to use.

Data
Raw, unanalyzed facts

Information
Analyzed and processed data

Ten or fifteen years ago, supervisors essentially had two choices for getting the information they needed to make decisions. They could get it themselves through crude methods such as looking in files, making telephone calls, asking questions in meetings. Or, if they worked anywhere but the smallest organization, they could rely on reports generated by the

FIGURE 4-8

Ten or fifteen years ago, large mainframe computers drove an organization's MIS. Today, supervisors are end-users.

organization's data processing specialist or centralized data processing department. Today, management information systems have become decentralized; that is, decisions and control of the systems have been pushed down to the users. With decentralization has come a major change—supervisors can now take responsibility for information control. They have become **end-users**. They can access the data they need and analyze that data on their personal computers. As a result, today's supervisors need to be knowledgeable about their information needs and accept responsibility for their systems' operations.

End-users
Individuals who take responsibility for accessing and analyzing information they need on their personal computers

The good news is that sophisticated management information systems dramatically improve the quantity and quality of information available to supervisors, as well as the speed with which it can be obtained. Gone are the long delays between the appearance of a serious discrepancy and a supervisor's ability to find out about it. On-line, real-time systems allow supervisors to identify problems almost as they occur. Database management programs allow supervisors to look things up or get to the facts without either going to other people or digging through piles of paper. This reduces a supervisor's dependence on others for data and makes fact gathering far more efficient. Today's supervisor can identify alternatives quickly, evaluate those alternatives by using a spreadsheet program, pose a series of what-if questions, and finally select the best alternative on the basis of answers to those questions.

DECISION-MAKING STYLES

Each of you brings your own unique personality and experiences to the decisions you make. For instance, if you're someone who is basically conservative and uncomfortable with uncertainty, you're likely to value decision alternatives differently from someone else who enjoys uncertainty and risk taking. These facts have led to research that has sought to identify individual

1. When a Canadian Airlines ticketing supervisor observed that business was declining because more passengers were travelling with Air Canada on the Toronto to Vancouver route, she was:
   a. recognizing a problem by comparison with another unit in the organization
   b. analyzing alternatives
   c. recognizing a problem by comparison with past performance
   d. identifying relevant information
2. Explain how decision making is related to the planning process.
3. Solving the wrong problem perfectly is better than coming up with a wrong solution to a problem. True or False?
4. After implementation has been accomplished
   a. the decision-making process is complete
   b. the control function of management becomes important
   c. the alternatives are ranked
   d. the supervisor must complete written evaluation forms

decision styles.[2] To make the following discussion more personal, take ten minutes to complete the Assessing Yourself questionnaire on page 140.

The basic foundation for a decision-style model is the recognition that people differ along two dimensions. The first is their way of *thinking*. Some people are logical and rational, and process information serially. In contrast, some people are intuitive and creative, and perceive things as a whole. The other dimension addresses a person's *tolerance for ambiguity*. Some people have a high need to structure information in ways that minimize ambiguity, while others are able to process many thoughts at the same time. When these two dimensions are diagrammed, they form four styles of decision making (see Figure 4-9). These are: Directive, Analytic, Conceptual, and Behavioural.

DIRECTIVE STYLE

People using the directive style have low tolerance for ambiguity and seek rationality. They are efficient and logical. But their efficiency concerns result in their making decisions with minimal information and after assessing few alternatives. Directive-types make decisions fast and they focus on the short run.

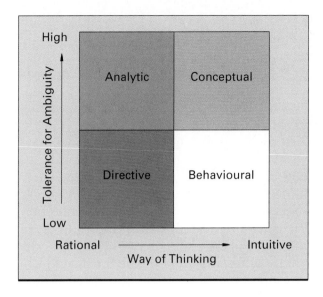

FIGURE 4-9

Decision-style model

ANALYTIC STYLE

The analytic type has a much greater tolerance for ambiguity than does a directive manager. This leads to the desire for more information and consideration of more alternatives than is true for directives. Analytic managers would be best characterized as careful decision makers with the ability to adapt or cope with new situations.

CONCEPTUAL STYLE

Individuals with a conceptual style tend to be very broad in their outlook and consider many alternatives. Their focus is long range and they are very good at finding creative solutions to problems.

BEHAVIOURAL STYLE

The final category—the behavioural style—characterizes decision makers who work well with others. They're concerned with the achievement of subordinates. They're receptive to suggestions from others and rely heavily on meetings for communicating. This type of supervisor tries to avoid conflict and seeks acceptance.

SUMMARY

Although these four categories are distinct, most supervisors have characteristics that fall into more than one. So it's probably best to think in terms of a manager's dominant style and his or her backup styles. While some supervisors rely almost exclusively on their dominant style, more flexible supervisors can make shifts depending on the situation. Referring to the Assessing Yourself results, the box with the highest score reflects your dominant style. The closer a person is to a score of 75 in each category, the greater flexibility he or she shows.

Business students, supervisors, and top executives tend to score highest in the analytic style. That's not surprising, given the emphasis that formal education, particularly business education, gives to developing rational decision-making skills. For instance, courses in accounting, statistics, and finance all stress analytical thinking.

Focusing on decision styles can be useful in helping you understand how two intelligent people, with access to the same information, can differ in the ways they approach decisions and in the final choices they make. It can also explain conflicts between supervisors and their subordinates. For example, the directive supervisor expects work to be performed rapidly and gets frustrated by the slowness and deliberate actions of a conceptual or analytic subordinate. At the same time, the analytic supervisor might criticize a decisive subordinate for incomplete work or acting too hastily. And the analytic supervisor will have great difficulty with his or her behavioural counterpart because of lack of understanding of why feelings rather than logic have been used as the basis for a decision.

Assessing Yourself

WHAT'S YOUR DECISION-MAKING STYLE?

INSTRUCTIONS

1. Use the following numbers to answer each question:
   8: when the question is *most* like you.
   4: when the question is *moderately* like you.
   2: when the question is *slightly* like you.
   1: when the question is *least* like you.

2. Each of the numbers must be inserted in the box following the answers to each question.

3. *Do not* repeat any number on a given line.

4. For example, the numbers you might use to answer a given question could look as follows: 8 2 1 4

5. Notice that each number has been used only once in the answers for a given question.

6. In answering the questions, think of how you *normally* act in your work situation.

7. Use the first thing that comes to your mind when answering the question.

8. There is no time limit in answering the questions and there are no right or wrong answers.

9. Your responses reflect how you feel about the questions and what you prefer to do, not what you think might be the *right* thing to do.

Score the following questions based on the instructions given. Your score reflects how you see yourself, not what you believe is correct or desirable, as related to your work situation. It covers typical decisions that you make in your work environment.

		I		II		III		IV	
1.	My prime objective is to:	Have a position with status	1	Be the best in my field	8	Achieve recognition for my work	4	Feel secure in my job	2
2.	I enjoy jobs that:	Are technical & well defined	2	Have a considerable variety	8	Allow independent action	1	Involve people	4
3.	I expect people working for me to be:	Productive and fast	1	Highly capable	4	Committed and responsive	2	Receptive to suggestions	8
4.	In my job, I look for:	Practical results	2	The best solutions	8	New approaches or ideas	4	Good working environment	1
5.	I communicate best with others:	In a direct one-to-one basis	8	In writing	1	By having a group discussion	4	In a formal meeting	2
6.	In my planning I emphasize:	Current problems	4	Meeting objectives	8	Future goals	2	Developing people's careers	1
7.	When faced with solving a problem, I:	Rely on proven approaches	4	Apply careful analysis	1	Look for creative approaches	2	Rely on my feelings	8
8.	When using information I prefer	Specific facts	2	Accurate and complete data	4	Broad coverage of many options	1	Limited data which is easily understood	8
9.	When I am not sure about what to do, I:	Rely on intuition	2	Search for facts	4	Look for a possible compromise	8	Wait before making a decision	1
10.	Whenever possible I avoid:	Long debates	2	Incomplete work	4	Using numbers or formulas	8	Conflict with others	1

	I		II		III		IV	
11. I am especially good at:	Remembering dates & facts	2	Solving difficult problems	1	Seeing many possibilities	4	Interacting with others	8
12. When time is important, I:	Decide and act quickly	2	Follow plans and priorities	4	Refuse to be pressured	8	Seek guidance or support	1
13. In social settings I generally:	Speak with others	8	Think about what is being said	4	Observe what is going on	1	Listen to the conversation	2
14. I am good at remembering:	People's names	2	Places we met	1	People's faces	8	People's personalities	4
15. The work I do provides me:	The power to influence others	1	Challenging assignments	4	Achieving my personal goals	8	Acceptance by the group	2
16. I work well with those who are:	Energetic and ambitious	8	Self-confident	1	Open-minded	2	Polite and trusting	4
17. When under stress, I:	Become anxious	2	Concentrate on the problem	1	Become frustrated	8	Am forgetful	4
18. Others consider me:	Aggressive	2	Disciplined	1	Imaginative	4	Supportive	8
19. My decisions typically are:	Realistic and direct	2	Systematic or abstract	1	Broad & flexible	4	Sensitive to the needs of others	8
20. I dislike:	Losing control	2	Boring work	8	Following rules	1	Being rejected	4

SCORING THE DECISION-STYLE INVENTORY

1. Add the points in each of the four columns—I, II, III, IV.
2. The sum of the four columns should be 300 points. If your sum does not equal 300 points, check your addition and your answers.
3. Place your scores in the appropriate box—I, II, III, IV.

Analytic II	Conceptual III
76	102
Directive I	Behavioural IV
59	84

Source: A. J. Rowe, R. Mason, and K. Dickel, *Strategic Management and Business Policy*. Reading, MA: Addison-Wesley, 1982, p. 217. Reproduced by permission of Alan J. Rowe.

ETHICS IN DECISION MAKING

Decision making is a prime instance of an occasion when supervisors have to confront ethical concerns (see Dealing with a Difficult Issue, page 145). For instance, one alternative may generate a considerably higher financial return than the others but might be ethically questionable because it compromises employee safety.

COMMON RATIONALIZATIONS

Through the ages, people have developed some common rationalizations to justify questionable conduct.[3] These rationalizations provide some insights into why supervisors might make poor ethical choices.

"It's not 'really' illegal or immoral." Where is the line between being smart and being shady? Between an ingenious decision and an immoral one? Because this line is often ambiguous, people can rationalize that what they've done is not really wrong. If you put enough people in an ill-defined situation, some will conclude that whatever hasn't specifically been labelled as wrong must be OK, especially if there are rich rewards for attaining certain goals and the organization's appraisal system doesn't look too carefully at how those goals are achieved. The practice of profiting on a stock tip through insider information seems often to fall in this category.

"It's in my (or the organization's) best interest." The belief that unethical conduct is in a person's or an organization's best interests nearly always results from a narrow view of what those interests are. For instance, supervisors can come to believe that it's acceptable to bribe officials if the bribe results in the organization's getting a contract, or to falsify financial records if this improves their unit's performance record.

"No one will find out." This rationalization accepts the wrongdoing but assumes that it will never be uncovered. It is often stimulated by inadequate controls, strong pressures to perform, the appraisal of performance results while ignoring the means by which they're achieved, the allocation of big salary increases and promotions to those who achieve these results, and the absence of punishment for those who get caught.

"Since it helps the organization, the organization will condone it and protect me." This response represents loyalty gone berserk. Managers come to believe that not only do the organization's interests override the laws and values of society, but also that the organization expects its employees to exhibit unqualified loyalty. Such managers believe that, even if he or she is caught, the organization will support and reward him or her for showing loyalty. Managers who use this rationalization to justify unethical practices place the organization's good name in jeopardy. This rationalization has motivated some supervisors for defence contractors to justify labour mischarges, cost duplications, product substitutions, and

Organizational ethics: Navran Associates
http://www.navran.com/Articles/articles.html#ethics

Why Ethics?
http://www.asaenet.org/Publications/AMsept97/9ethics.html

other contract abuses. While managers should be expected to be loyal to the organization against competitors and detractors, that loyalty should not put the organization above the law, common morality, or society itself.

THREE DIFFERENT VIEWS ON ETHICS

In this section we will present three different ethical positions. They can help us to see how individuals can make different decisions by using different ethical criteria.

THE UTILITARIAN VIEW

Utilitarian view of ethics
Decisions are based solely on the basis of their outcomes; the goal is to provide the greatest good for the greatest number

The first position is the **utilitarian view of ethics,** in which decisions are made solely on the basis of their outcomes or consequences. The goal of utilitarianism is to provide the greatest good for the greatest number. This view tends to dominate business decision making. Why? Because it's consistent with the goals of efficiency, productivity, and high profits. By maximizing profits, for instance, a manager can argue that he or she is securing the greatest good for the greatest number.

THE RIGHTS VIEW

Rights view of ethics
Decisions emphasize respecting and protecting the basic rights of individuals

Another ethical perspective is the **rights view of ethics.** This calls upon individuals to make decisions consistent with fundamental liberties and privileges as set forth in documents such as the Charter of Rights and Freedoms. The rights view of ethics is concerned with respecting and protecting the basic rights of individuals; for example, the right to privacy, free speech, and due process. This position would protect employees who report unethical or illegal practices by their organization to the press or government agencies on the grounds of their right to free speech.

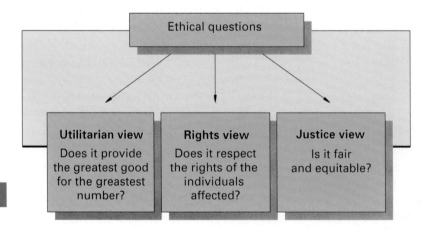

FIGURE 4-10
Three views on ethics

Dealing with a Difficult Issue

HIRING A FRIEND

In making hiring decisions, supervisors often face difficult issues. Take the following situation:

Your company is advertising for a new employee to work in your department. The person in this position will be important because the work directly affects the quality and quantity of your performance. One of your friends needs a job and you think he is qualified for the position. But you feel you *could* find better qualified and more experienced candidates if you keep looking.

What would you do? What might influence your decision? Would you tell your friend? How do you handle this sensitive situation?

THE JUSTICE VIEW

The final perspective is the **justice view of ethics**. This requires individuals to impose and enforce rules fairly and impartially so there is an equitable distribution of benefits and costs. Union members typically favour this view. It justifies paying people the same wage for a given job, regardless of performance differences, and it uses seniority as the criterion in making layoff decisions.

Justice view of ethics
Decisions seek fair and impartial distribution of benefits and costs

DISCUSSION OF THE THREE VIEWS

Each of these three perspectives has advantages and liabilities. The utilitarian view promotes efficiency and productivity, but it can result in the rights of some individuals—particularly those with minority representation in the organization—being ignored. The rights perspective protects individuals from injury and is consistent with freedom and privacy, but it can create an overly legalistic work environment that hinders productivity and efficiency. The justice perspective protects the interests of the underrepresented and less powerful, but it can encourage a sense of entitlement that reduces risk taking, innovation, and productivity.

Even though each of these perspectives has its individual strengths and weaknesses, as we noted, managers in business tend to focus on utilitarianism. But times are changing and so too must supervisors and other managers. New trends toward individual rights and social justice mean that supervisors need ethical standards based on nonutilitarian criteria.

FIGURE 4-11

Affirmative efforts to hire and promote women and minorities represent an application of the justice view of ethics.

This is a solid challenge to today's supervisor because making decisions using criteria such as individual rights and social justice involves far more ambiguities than using utilitarian criteria such as effects on efficiency and profits.

SOME ETHICAL DECISION GUIDES

There is no simple credo that we can provide to ensure that you won't err in your ethical judgments. What we can offer are some questions that you can—and should—ask yourself when making important decisions, or decisions with obvious ethical implications.[4]

1. How did this problem occur in the first place?
2. Would you define the problem differently if you stood on the other side of the fence?
3. To whom and to what do you give your loyalty as a person and as a member of your organization?
4. What is your intention in making this decision?
5. What is the potential for your intentions to be misunderstood by others in the organization?
6. How does your intention compare with the probable result?
7. Whom could your decision injure?

8. Can you discuss the problem with the affected parties before you make the decision?
9. Are you confident that your position will be as valid over a long period of time as it seems now?
10. Could you disclose your decision to your boss or your immediate family?
11. How would you feel if your decision was described, in detail, on the front page of your local newspaper?

GROUP DECISION MAKING

Decisions in organizations are increasingly being made by groups rather than by individuals. There seem to be at least two primary reasons for this. First is the desire to develop more and better alternatives. The adage "two heads are better than one" translates into groups being able to generate a greater number, and potentially a more creative set, of decision alternatives. Second, organizations are relying less on the historical idea that departments and other organizational units should be separate and independent decision units. To get the best ideas and to improve their implementation, organizations are increasingly turning over their decision making to teams that cut across traditional departmental lines. This choice requires group decision-making techniques.

InterNeg: Group Decision and Negotiation
http://interneg.carleton.ca/

ADVANTAGES AND DISADVANTAGES

Individual and group decisions each have their own set of strengths. Neither is ideal for all situations. Let's begin by reviewing the advantages that group decisions have over an individual decision maker.

1. **Provides more complete information.** A group will bring a diversity of experience and perspective to the decision process that an individual, acting alone, cannot.
2. **Generates more alternatives.** Because groups have a greater quantity and diversity of information, they can identify more alternatives than can an individual.
3. **Increases acceptance of a solution.** Many decisions fail after the final choice has been made because people do not accept the solution. If the people who will be affected by a certain solution and who will help implement it get to participate in the decision making itself, they will be more likely to accept the decision and to encourage others to accept it.
4. **Increases legitimacy.** The group decision-making process is consistent with democratic ideals and therefore may be perceived as more legitimate than decisions made by a single person.

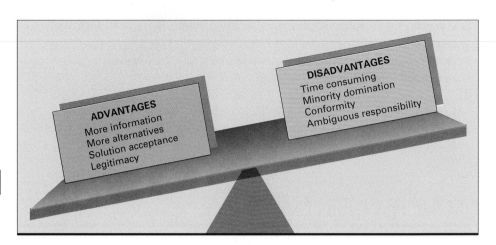

FIGURE 4-12

The advantages and disadvantages of group decision-making

If groups are so good, how did the phrase "A camel is a racehorse put together by a committee" become so popular? The answer, of course, is that group decisions are not without their drawbacks. The major disadvantages of group decision making are as follows.

1. **Time consuming.** It takes time to assemble a group. Additionally, the interaction that takes place once the group is in place is frequently inefficient. The result is that groups almost always take more time to reach a solution than an individual making the decision alone.

2. **Minority domination.** Members of a group are never perfectly equal. They may differ in terms of rank in the organization, experience, knowledge about the problem, influence with other members, verbal skills, assertiveness, and the like. This creates the opportunity for one or more members to use their advantages to dominate others in the group and impose undue influence on the final decision.

3. **Pressures to conform.** There are social pressures in groups. The desire of group members to be accepted and considered assets to the group can quash any overt disagreement and encourage conformity among viewpoints. The withholding by group members of different views in order to appear in agreement is called **groupthink**.

Groupthink
Group members withhold different views in order to appear to be in agreement.

4. **Ambiguous responsibility.** Group members share responsibility, but who is actually responsible for the final outcome? In an individual decision, it is clear who is responsible, but in a group decision the responsibility of any single member is watered down. Conscious of this, group members may not give their full effort or think through the issue as thoroughly as they would on their own.

A Guide to When to Use Group Decision Making

When are groups better than individuals and vice versa? That depends on what you mean by better. Let's look at four criteria frequently associated with "better" decisions: accuracy, speed, creativity, and acceptance.

Group decisions tend to be more accurate. The evidence indicates that, on the average, groups make more accurate decisions than individuals. This doesn't mean, of course, that all groups outperform every individual. Rather, group decisions have been found to be more effective than those that would have been reached by the average individual in the group. However, groups are seldom as good as the best individual.

If *better* is defined in terms of decision speed, individuals are superior. Group decision processes are characterized by give and take, a process that is often time-consuming.

Decision quality can also be assessed in terms of the degree to which a solution demonstrates creativity. If creativity is important, groups tend to do better than individuals. This requires, however, minimizing the forces that foster groupthink—pressure to repress doubts about the group's shared views or the validity of favoured arguments, excessive desire by the group to give an appearance of consensus, and the assumption that silence or abstention by members is a "yes" vote.

As noted previously, because group decisions have input from more people, they are likely to result in solutions that will have a higher degree of acceptance.

TYPES OF GROUP DECISION MAKING

The process used by a group to make a decision will influence the effectiveness of the decision. There is no single best process, though. The way the group should make its decision depends on the needs of the group as well as on the situation and on how much time is available.

The most commonly used method is **majority vote**. It offers the appeal of a democratic process and is as quick as it takes to get 51 per cent of the members to agree. It can leave a powerful minority very dissatisfied, however. This can harm the implementation of the decision.

Deciding by **consensus** is highly desirable. If there is sufficient time, it provides the best decisions and the most commitment to the decision. And, in practice, reaching a consensus does not mean everyone agrees absolutely but that all members are willing to support the decision, knowing that everyone has been heard and the issues have been thoroughly addressed. This decision-making method is not often used, however. Not only does it take time but it takes effort and skill, particularly on the part of the chair, to keep the discussion progressing in a constructive way.

Sometimes a group uses its power to turn the decision-making authority over to someone else. The group may choose someone deemed an **expert** to make the decision. That choice itself could be made via consensus or majority vote. A second form of decision referral is the use of **minority vote**. In its legitimate form, this involves assigning a decision to a committee made up of a few members of the larger

Majority vote
Agreement to a decision by at least 51 percent of a group's members

Consensus
Agreement to support a decision by all members of a group

Decision by expert
Decision delegated to a person with special skill or knowledge in a particular field

Decision by minority vote
Decision-making power held by a subgroup of a larger group

group. Its illegitimate form occurs when a subgroup railroads a decision through, quickly forcing a decision before real debate can occur. In either expert decision or minority vote, the advantages include putting the decision in the hands of potentially more qualified people and at the same time freeing up time for the remainder of the group.

Decision by authority after discussion Decision-making by a group leader after weighing group members' opinions

A final method of group decision making is **authority after discussion**. In this, the supervisor holds a full discussion with the whole group to hear their ideas and issues. Then the supervisor makes the final decision, which may or may not reflect the wishes of the group. In practice, this method is often similar to consensus because a group trend becomes apparent and the supervisor simply applies official approval. However, the supervisor may choose not to follow the group if the group's goals are not in the best interests of the organization.

Basically, it is a good idea to involve people in group decision making whenever there is time and the decision is pertinent to them. Group decision making can make the group more cohesive, can be an important forum for learning and sharing, and can improve motivation.

Whichever decision technique is used, it is likely that the context will often be a meeting conducted by you. And running a good meeting is a challenge, as you've probably discovered by attending meetings that were a waste of time. See "Building a Supervisory Skill: Conducting a Group Meeting" for guidance running meetings.

FIGURE 4-13

Meetings are a widely used, excellent vehicle for implementing decisions.

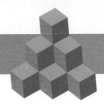

CONDUCTING A GROUP MEETING

ABOUT THE SKILL

Many supervisors report that they spend ten hours or more a week in meetings. Many of these are called and run by others. Some, however, will be conducted by supervisors. Cheryl Munro Sharp of London Life estimates that she calls 25 per cent of the meetings she's involved in, while in the other 75 per cent she is just a participant.

When it's your responsibility to conduct a meeting, do you know what to do? Experts say one-third of the time spent in meetings is a waste. What can you do to cut out that waste and make your meetings both efficient and effective? We'll provide you with the answers in this section.

STEPS IN PRACTISING THE SKILL

The following summarizes the key actions you should take as a leader to increase the likelihood that the meetings you conduct are run efficiently and effectively.

1. **Prepare a meeting agenda.** An agenda defines what you hope to accomplish at the meeting. It should state the meeting's purpose. Is the purpose only to exchange information or is it to make decisions? Will all relevant parties in the organization be included or merely their representatives? And if decisions are to be made, how are they to be arrived at? Will consensus be sought? If decisions are to be made by voting, what constitutes approval: a simple majority, a two-thirds majority? These issues should be clarified ahead of time in the agenda. The agenda should also identify who will be in attendance; what, if any, preparation is required of each participant; a detailed list of items to be covered; the specific time and location of the meeting; and a specific finishing time.

2. **Distribute the agenda in advance.** If you want specific people to attend your meeting, and particularly if participants need to do some homework beforehand, get your agenda out well in advance of the meeting. What's an adequate lead time? That depends on such factors as the amount of preparation necessary, the importance of the meeting, and whether the meeting will be recurring or is being called once to deal with an issue that has arisen and will be repeated only under similar circumstances.

3. **Consult with participants before the meeting.** An unprepared participant can't contribute to his or her full potential. It is your responsibility to ensure that members are prepared. What data will they need ahead of time? Do they have that data? If not, what can you do to help them get it?

4. **Get participants to go over the agenda.** The first thing you should do at the meeting is to get participants to review the agenda. Do modifications need to be made? If so, make them. Clarify the issues that you plan to discuss. After this review, get participants to approve the final agenda.

5. **Establish specific time parameters.** Meetings should begin on time and have a specific time for completion. It is your responsibility to specify these time parameters and to hold to them.

6. **Maintain focused discussion.** As chairperson, it is your responsibility to give direction to the discussion; to keep it focused on the issues; and to minimize interruptions, disruptions, and irrelevant comments. If participants begin to stray from the issue under consideration, intercede quickly to redirect the discussion. Similarly, one or a few members cannot be allowed to monopolize the discussion or to dominate others. Appropriate preventive action can range from a subtle stare, a raised eyebrow, or other nonverbal communication, on up to an authoritative command such as ruling someone "out of order" or withdrawing someone's right to continue speaking.

7. **Encourage and support participation by all members.** Participants were not selected randomly. Each is there for a purpose. To maximize the effectiveness of problem-oriented meetings, each participant must be encouraged to contribute. Quiet or reserved personalities must be drawn out so their ideas can be heard.

8. **Maintain a balanced style.** You need to exert the appropriate level of control. The style of leadership can range from authoritative domination to laissez-faire. The effective group leader pushes when necessary and is passive when need be.

9. **Encourage the clash of ideas.** You need to encourage different points of view, critical thinking, and constructive disagreement. Your goals should be to stimulate participants' creativity and to counter the group members' desire to reach an early consensus.

10. **Discourage the clash of personalities.** An effective meeting is characterized by the critical assessment of ideas, not attacks on people. When running a meeting, you must quickly intercede to stop personal attacks or other forms of verbal insult.

11. **Exhibit effective listening skills.** If your group meeting is to achieve its objectives, you need to listen actively rather than passively. Do whatever is necessary to get the full intended meaning from a speaker's comments. Effective listening reduces misunderstandings, improves the focus of discussion, and encourages the critical assessment of ideas. Even if other group members don't exhibit good listening skills, you can keep the discussion focused on the issues and facilitate critical thinking if *you* listen well.

12. **Bring proper closure.** Close a meeting by summarizing the group's accomplishments; clarifying what actions, if any, need to follow the meeting; and allocating follow-up assignments. If any decisions have been made, you also need to determine who will be responsible for communicating and implementing them.

TECHNIQUES FOR IMPROVING GROUP DECISION MAKING

When members of a group physically confront and interact with one another, they create the potential for groupthink. They can censor themselves and pressure other group members into agreement. There are four techniques that you might want to consider as ways to stimulate creativity in group decision making.

BRAINSTORMING

Brainstorming is a relatively simple technique for overcoming pressures for conformity that can retard the development of creative alternatives. It achieves this by using an idea-generating process that actively encourages any and all alternatives while withholding any criticism of those alternatives.

In a typical brainstorming session, the group members sit around a table. The group leader states the problem in a clear manner so it is understood by all participants. Members then "freewheel" as many alternatives as they can in a given time. No criticism is allowed, and all the alternatives are recorded for later discussion and analysis.

Brainstorming, however, is merely a process for generating ideas, not for choosing among them. The next three techniques go further by offering ways to arrive at a preferred solution.

Brainstorming
An idea-generation process that specifically encourages any and all alternatives while withholding any criticism of those alternatives

NOMINAL GROUP TECHNIQUE

Nominal group technique
A group decision technique where all members are present but operate independently

The nominal group restricts discussion during the decision-making process, hence the term **nominal group technique**. Group members are all physically present, as in a traditional committee meeting, but the members are required to operate independently. Specifically, the following steps take place:

1. Members meet as a group; however, before any discussion takes place, each member independently writes down his or her ideas on the problem.
2. This silent period is followed by each member presenting one idea to the group. Each member takes his or her turn, going around the table, presenting one idea at a time until all ideas have been presented and recorded (typically on a flip chart or chalkboard). No discussion takes place until all ideas have been recorded.
3. The group now discusses the ideas for clarity and evaluates them.
4. Each group member silently and independently assigns a rank to the ideas. The final decision is determined by choosing the idea with the highest aggregate ranking.

DELPHI TECHNIQUE

Delphi technique
A group decision technique where members act independently but need not be physically present for discussion

A more complex and time-consuming alternative is the **Delphi technique**, which is similar to the nominal group technique except that it doesn't require the physical presence of group members. This is because the Delphi technique never allows the group members to meet face to face. The following steps characterize the Delphi technique:

1. The problem is identified, and members are asked to provide potential solutions through a series of carefully designed questionnaires.
2. Each member anonymously and independently completes the first questionnaire.
3. Results of the first questionnaire are compiled at a central location, transcribed, and reproduced.
4. Each member receives a copy of the results.
5. After reviewing the results, members are again asked for their solutions. The results typically trigger new solutions or cause changes in the original position.
6. Steps 4 and 5 are repeated as often as necessary until consensus is reached.

ELECTRONIC MEETINGS

Electronic meeting
A group of individuals make decisions by communicating anonymously on computer terminals.

The most recent approach to group decision making blends the nominal group technique with sophisticated computer technology. It's called the **electronic meeting**. It has been used with great success by Royal Trust, Sears Canada, Ontario Hydro, and Met Life.

Once the technology is in place, the concept is simple. Up to fifty people sit around a horseshoe-shaped table, empty except for a series of computer terminals. Issues are presented to participants and they type their responses onto their computer screens. Individual comments, as well as aggregate votes, are displayed on a projection screen in the room.

The major advantages to electronic meetings are anonymity, honesty, and speed. Participants can anonymously type any message they want and it flashes on the screen for all to see at the push of a key. It also allows people to be brutally honest with no penalty. And it's fast because chit-chat is eliminated, discussions don't digress, and many participants can "talk" at once without stepping on others' toes. Electronic meetings offer an excellent means for supervisors and members of their department to efficiently exchange information and make decisions that affect their work group.

Experts claim that electronic meetings are as much as 55 per cent faster than traditional face-to-face meetings.[5] Supervisors at Phelps Dodge Mining, for instance, used the approach to cut the firm's annual planning meeting from several days down to twelve hours. However, there are drawbacks. Those who can type quickly can outshine those who may be verbally eloquent but are lousy typists; those with the best ideas don't get credit for them; and the process lacks the informational richness of face-to-face oral communication. This technology is currently only in its infancy. The future of group decision making is very likely to include extensive usage of electronic meetings.

FIGURE 4-14

IBM uses electronic meetings to bring together people in the company from diverse backgrounds. Many IBMers have taken part in these meetings.

5. A conceptual style of decision making reflects an individual who:
   a. thinks intuitively and has a low tolerance for ambiguity
   b. thinks rationally and has a high tolerance for ambiguity
   c. thinks intuitively and has a high tolerance for ambiguity
   d. thinks rationally and has a low tolerance for ambiguity
6. What is groupthink? What are its implications for decision making?
7. The justice view of ethics is concerned with respecting and protecting the basic freedoms of individuals, such as free speech and due process. True or False?
8. Group decisions will usually be superior to individual decisions except when:
   a. speed is a concern
   b. accuracy is critical
   c. widespread acceptance of the solution is essential
   d. flexibility is needed

CREATIVE PROBLEM SOLVING

ASSESSING YOURSELF: HOW CREATIVE ARE YOU?

How creative are you? The following test helps determine if you have the personality traits, attitudes, values, motivations, and interests that comprise creativity. It is based on several years' study of attributes possessed by men and women in a variety of fields and occupations who think and act creatively.

INSTRUCTIONS

For each statement, write in the appropriate letter:

      A = Agree
      B = Undecided or Don't Know
      C = Disagree

Be as frank as possible. Try not to second-guess how a creative person might respond.

____ 1. I always work with a great deal of certainty that I am following the correct procedure for solving a particular problem.

____ 2. It would be a waste of time for me to ask questions if I had no hope of obtaining answers.

____ 3. I concentrate harder on whatever interests me than do most people.

____ 4. I feel that a logical step-by-step method is best for solving problems.

____ 5. In groups I occasionally voice opinions that seem to turn some people off.

____ 6. I spend a great deal of time thinking about what others think of me.

____ 7. It is more important for me to do what I believe to be right than to try to win the approval of others.

____ 8. People who seem uncertain about things lose my respect.

___ 9. More than other people, I need to have things interesting and exciting.

___ 10. I know how to keep my inner impulses in check.

___ 11. I am able to stick with difficult problems over extended periods of time.

___ 12. On occasion I get overly enthusiastic.

___ 13. I often get my best ideas when doing nothing in particular.

___ 14. I rely on intuitive hunches and the feeling of "rightness" or "wrongness" when moving toward the solution of a problem.

___ 15. When problem solving, I work faster when analyzing the problem and slower when synthesizing the information I have gathered.

___ 16. I sometimes get a kick out of breaking the rules and doing things I am not supposed to do.

___ 17. I like hobbies that involve collecting things.

___ 18. Daydreaming has provided the impetus for many of my more important projects.

___ 19. I like people who are objective and rational.

___ 20. If I had to choose from two occupations other than the one I now have, I would rather be a physician than an explorer.

___ 21. I can get along more easily with people if they belong to about the same social and business class as myself.

___ 22. I have a high degree of aesthetic sensitivity.

___ 23. I am driven to achieve high status and power in life.

___ 24. I like people who are most sure of their conclusions.

___ 25. Inspiration has nothing to do with the successful solution of problems.

___ 26. When I am in an argument, my greatest pleasure would be for the person who disagrees with me to become a friend, even at the price of sacrificing my point of view.

___ 27. I am much more interested in coming up with new ideas than in trying to sell them to others.

___ 28. I would enjoy spending an entire day alone, just "chewing the mental cud."

___ 29. I tend to avoid situations in which I might feel inferior.

___ 30. In evaluating information, the source is more important to me than the content.

___ 31. I resent things being uncertain and unpredictable.

___ 32. I like people who follow the rule, "business before pleasure."

___ 33. Self-respect is much more important than the respect of others.

___ 34. I feel that people who strive for perfection are unwise.

___ 35. I prefer to work with others in a team effort rather than solo.

___ 36. I like work in which I must influence others.

___ 37. Many problems that I encounter in life cannot be resolved in terms of right or wrong solutions.

___ 38. It is important for me to have a place for everything and everything in its place.

___ 39. Writers who use strange and unusual words merely want to show off.

40. Below is a list of terms that describe people. Choose ten words that best characterize you.

❏ energetic	❏ alert
❏ persuasive	❏ curious
❏ observant	❏ organized
❏ fashionable	❏ unemotional
❏ self-confident	❏ clear-thinking
❏ persevering	❏ understanding
❏ original	❏ dynamic
❏ cautious	❏ self-demanding
❏ habit-bound	❏ polished
❏ resourceful	❏ courageous
❏ egotistical	❏ efficient
❏ independent	❏ helpful
❏ stern	❏ perceptive
❏ predictable	❏ quick
❏ formal	❏ good-natured
❏ informal	❏ thorough

	dedicated		impulsive
	forward-looking		determined
	factual		realistic
	open-minded		modest
	tactful		involved
	inhibited		absent-minded
	enthusiastic		flexible
	innovative		sociable
	poised		well-liked
	acquisitive		restless
	practical		retiring

Source: Eugene Raudsepp, President, Princeton Creative Research, Inc.

SCORING DIRECTIONS

To compute your score, circle and add up the values assigned to each item. The values are as follows:

	A Agree	B Undecided or Don't Know	C Disagree		A Agree	B Undecided or Don't Know	C Disagree
1.	0	1	2	21.	0	1	2
2.	0	1	2	22.	3	0	-1
3.	4	1	0	23.	0	1	2
4.	-2	0	3	24.	-1	0	2
5.	2	1	0	25.	0	1	3
6.	-1	0	3	26.	-1	0	2
7.	3	0	-1	27.	2	1	0
8.	0	1	2	28.	2	0	-1
9.	3	0	-1	29.	0	1	2
10.	1	0	3	30.	-2	0	3
11.	4	1	0	31.	0	1	2
12.	3	0	-1	32.	0	1	2
13.	2	1	0	33.	3	0	-1
14.	4	0	-2	34.	-1	0	2
15.	-1	0	2	35.	0	1	2
16.	2	1	0	36.	1	2	3
17.	0	1	2	37.	2	1	0
18.	3	0	-1	38.	0	1	2
19.	0	1	2	39.	-1	0	2
20.	0	1	2				

40. The following have values of 2:

energetic	dynamic	perceptive	dedicated
resourceful	flexible	innovative	courageous
original	observant	self-demanding	curious
enthusiastic	independent	persevering	involved

The following have values of 1:

self-confident	determined	informal	forward-looking
thorough	restless	alert	open-minded

The rest have values of 0.

TOTAL SCORE

95–116	Exceptionally creative		20–39	Average
65–94	Very creative		10–19	Below average
40–64	Above average		Below 10	Noncreative

SKILL BASICS

There's good news on the creativity front! Most of us have unleashed creative potential, but we get into psychological ruts. In this skill module, we want to show you how you can unleash your creative problem-solving talent.

CHARACTERISTICS OF THE EXCEPTIONALLY CREATIVE PERSON

Let's begin with the obvious. People differ in their inherent creativity. Einstein, Picasso, and Mozart were individuals of exceptional creativity. What personality characteristics do the exceptionally creative share? Generally they are independent, risk-taking, persistent, and highly motivated. They're also nonconformists who can be hard to get along with. Additionally, highly creative individuals prefer complex and unstructured tasks. Disorder doesn't make them anxious.

How widespread is exceptional creativity? Not very! A study of lifetime creativity of 461 men and women found that fewer than 1 per cent were exceptionally creative.[6] But 10 per cent were highly creative and about 60 per cent were somewhat creative. As you'll see, even if you didn't score in the exceptionally creative category on the self-assessment exercise, there are ways to improve your potential.

THE ORGANIZATION MATTERS

Your creative potential is also influenced by characteristics of the organization in which you work. For instance, rigidly structured organizations that inhibit communication between departments tend to limit creativity.

Organizational culture
A shared perception of the organization's values

Every organization has a culture. This **organizational culture** represents a shared perception of the organization's values. It's sort of an organizational equivalent of an individual's personality. That is, just as some people are open, or aggressive, or controlling, so too are organizations. The difference is that in organizational culture, all members of the organization tend to share a common understanding about the organization, how things are done in it, and the way members are supposed to behave. Certain organizational cultures can restrict creativity. Specifically, these are cultures that punish risk-taking and failure, and reward excessive loyalty and conformity.

STIMULATING YOUR CREATIVITY

Creativity is the ability to combine ideas in a unique way to make unusual associations between them. Each of us has the ability to be creative, yet some use their creativity more than others. Although creative people are sometimes referred to as "artsy," and their precise characteristics are difficult to describe, there are certain steps you can take in becoming more creative.[7]

1. **Think of yourself as creative.** Although it's a simple suggestion, research shows that if you think you can't be creative, you won't be. Just as the little train in the children's fable says, "I think I can," if we believe in ourselves, we can become more creative.

2. **Pay attention to your intuition.** Everyone has a subconscious mind that works well. Sometimes answers come when we least expect them. For example, when you are about to go to sleep, your relaxed mind sometimes comes up with solutions to problems you face. You need to listen to this intuition. In fact, many creative people keep a note pad near their bed and write down those "great" ideas when they come to them. That way, they are not forgotten.

3. **Move away from your comfort zone.** Every individual has a comfort zone in which certainty exists. But creativity and the known often don't mix. To be creative, we need to move away from the status quo, and focus on something new.

4. **Engage in activities that put you outside your comfort zone.** Not only must we think differently, we need to do things differently. By engaging in activities that are different to us, we challenge ourselves. For example, learning to play a musical instrument or learning a foreign language opens the mind up and allows it to be challenged.

5. **Seek a change of scenery.** As humans, we are creatures of habit. Creative people force themselves out of their habits by changing their scenery. Going into a quiet and serene area where you can be alone with your thoughts is a good way to enhance creativity.

6. **Find several right answers.** Just as we set boundaries in rationality, we often seek solutions that are only good enough. Being creative means continuing to look for other solutions, even when you think you have solved the problem. A better, more creative solution just might be found.

7. **Play your own devil's advocate.** Challenging yourself to defend your solutions helps you develop confidence in your creative efforts. Second guessing may also help you find more correct answers.

8. **Believe in finding a workable solution.** Like believing in yourself, you also need to believe in your ideas. If you don't think you can find a solution, one won't be found. Having a positive mental attitude, however, may become a self-fulfilling prophecy.

9. **Brainstorm with others.** Creativity is not an isolated activity. By bouncing ideas off of others, a synergistic effect occurs.

10. **Turn creative ideas into action.** Coming up with ideas is only half of the process. Once the ideas are generated, they must be implemented. Great ideas that remain in someone's mind, or on papers that no one reads, do little to expand one's creative abilities.

APPLYING YOUR SKILLS

Form groups of four or five. You are a committee of employees at Cineplex Odeon head office. The company is doing well but analysis of the statistics reveals that much of that is due to strong confectionary sales. In fact the actual box office revenues are declining. There is tremendous competition for the entertainment dollar and many people are "cocooning," choosing to stay home and watch pay-TV or a rented video. And soon, due to new technology, people may be able to pick up their phone and order a movie on demand for viewing on their TV.

You have thirty minutes for your committee to develop a list of options for Cineplex Odeon. Be prepared to discuss a) your top three recommendations, and b) what your committee believes to be its most creative option.

Yahoo / Market Guide - Cineplex Odeon Corp.
http://biz.yahoo.com/p/c/cpx.html

Cineplex Odeon
http://www.cineplexodeon.com/

SUMMARY

This summary is organized by the Learning Objectives.

1. The seven steps in the decision-making process are: 1. identify the problem; 2. collect relevant information; 3. develop alternatives; 4. evaluate each alternative; 5. select the best alternative; 6. implement the decision; 7. follow up and evaluate.

2. Expected value analysis calculates the expected value of a particular alternative by weighting its possible outcomes by the probability of achieving the alternative, then summing up the totals derived from the weighting process.

3. Decision trees are a device for analyzing decisions that involve a progression of decisions. They help decision makers visualize key decision points and outcomes.

4. Data are raw, unanalyzed facts. Data become information when they are analyzed and processed. It is information that is most relevant for making informed decisions.

5. There are four types of decision styles. The directive type is efficient and logical. The analytic type is careful, with the ability to adapt or cope with new situations. The conceptual type considers many alternatives and is good at coming up with creative solutions. The behavioural type emphasizes suggestions from others and conflict avoidance.

6. The utilitarian view of ethics makes decisions based on the greatest good for the greatest number. The rights view of ethics makes decisions consistent with fundamental liberties and privileges. The justice view of ethics seeks fairness and impartiality.

7. Group decisions are based on more complete information, more alternatives, increased acceptance of a solution, and increased legitimacy. Individual decisions take less time, have clear accountability and are not subject to pressures to conform.

8. Techniques for improving group decision making include brainstorming, nominal group technique, Delphi technique, and electronic meetings.

KEY TERMS AND CONCEPTS

Authority after discussion
Brainstorming
Consensus
Data
Decision-making process
Decision trees
Delphi technique
Electronic meeting
End-user
Expected value analysis
Expert
Groupthink

Information
Justice view of ethics
Majority vote
Management information system
Marginal analysis
Minority vote
Nominal group technique
Organizational culture
Problem
Rights view of ethics
Utilitarian view of ethics

REVIEWING YOUR KNOWLEDGE

1. Contrast symptoms with problems. Give three examples.
2. In which step of the decision-making process do you think creativity would be most helpful? In which step would quantitative analysis tools be most helpful?
3. Calculate your estimated grade average this term using expected value analysis.
4. What is meant by the expression "supervisors are increasingly becoming end-users in MIS"?
5. How might certain decision styles fit better with specific jobs? Give examples.
6. What rationalizations do people use to justify questionable conduct?
7. Which view of ethics dominates in business firms? Why?
8. When should managers use groups for decision making? When should they use individuals?
9. Contrast the nominal group technique, Delphi technique, and electronic meeting.

ANSWERS TO THE POP QUIZZES

1. **c. recognizing a problem by comparison with past performance.**
   This question reinforces the importance of properly defining a problem. That is, a problem is a discrepancy between an existing and a desired state of affairs. Past performance sets standards against which current performance is compared.

2. Planning sets the standards against which a supervisor can compare actual performance. A significant variation from the plan represents a problem—which then requires a decision about how to correct it.

3. **False.** Solving the wrong problem is a waste of time. The first step in problem solving is to identify what the problem is. Solving the wrong problem can actually make the situation worse by creating new problems.

4. **b. the control function of management becomes important.**
   Follow-up and evaluation involves determining whether the problem has been corrected. This means that actual progress is again compared to the "standard." This is the fundamental activity of control.

5. **c. thinks intuitively and has a high tolerance for ambiguity.** This is the definition of conceptual decision-making style.

6. Groupthink is a term used to reflect the withholding by group members of different views in order to appear in agreement. It affects decision making by manifesting as pressure on group members to keep doubts about the group's shared views to themselves; this silence is taken to mean a "yes" vote. Because of this pressure, poorer decisions may result.

7. **False.** This is the definition of the rights view of ethics. The justice view of ethics seeks fairness and impartiality.

8. **a. speed is a concern.** Responses *b*, *c*, and *d* are advantages of group decision making. Where speed is concerned, individuals perform better. Therefore, response *a* is the exception to the advantages of group decision making.

CASE 4.A

Norma Turok's Dilemma

When Norma Turok was promoted to assistant director of training at Brookfield General Hospital, she had mixed feelings about the job. She knew she had the background to do the work. She had developed good interpersonal skills and was frequently called on to work on special assignments that required problem solving. She also had high grades in all her community college coursework and especially liked her human resource classes, where she frequently found herself in leadership roles. Most people would describe Norma as intelligent, resourceful, motivated, and hard working.

Norma was selected for the position by the training director's manager. The manager knew Norma was energetic and creative—the two elements the training unit badly needed. Norma and the manager had had numerous conversations about personnel training and they had similar ideas about what would stimulate and motivate workers. Why, then, did Norma have reservations about the training position? Norma would have to work with two other assistant directors who had been in their positions for four and nine years respectively. Her training director also had been at the hospital for nine years, all but two of those years in her present position.

From the very beginning, Norma felt torn between wanting to forge ahead with new ideas that might ruffle some of the veterans' feathers, and trying to "fit in" by being more conservative in helping to implement the training model that had been in place for several years.

RESPONDING TO THIS CASE

1. In her new job, how can Norma make good use of the knowledge she has about decision-making styles?

2. What can Norma do to learn more about the training director and her co-assistant directors to get them to consider some of her ideas for making decisions about the direction training should take?

CASE 4.B

EDX Space Exploration, Inc.

Bradley Thornton is a technical supervisor at EDX Space Exploration, Inc. EDX is a scientific research and development company that manufacturers specialized parts and equipment used in space projects. EDX has been in business since 1969 and has grown to become a very reputable company within the space exploration and scientific community. Much of the work it does is highly technical and specialized.

Many of EDX's contracts have been awarded to them because they are willing to purchase and maintain expensive specialized equipment they need to complete a job. Many of the subcontracts they get are from large corporations and government agencies. Over the past several years, they have been very successful at winning NASA contracts.

Cuts in the military and space programs (including NASA's budget) have taken their toll on EDX. It used to be that technicians were needed on projects to keep several pieces of expensive equipment running constantly. With fewer contracts, EDX has made fewer equipment purchases. Technician expertise is not being utilized to its fullest in that there is not enough technical equipment to keep productivity at an optimum.

Brad has an important decision to make about the business. He thinks there is potential for expanding their business by seeking out contracts with smaller companies. But he also knows that EDX employees are technical people, not salespeople. He also knows that when the company tried shift work several years ago, it was not very successful. Brad has made a decision to try to solve the problem, but decides it would be better to involve his employees in the decision-making process. After all, most of the employees have been with the company for at least fifteen years.

Responding to This Case

1. If Brad already has a solution, why would he want to involve the employees in finding a solution? Is this unethical manipulation?

2. From Brad's perspective, contrast the advantages of individual versus team decision making.

3. What could result if the EDX employees do not reach the same decision that Brad has? What could result if Brad makes a decision that is not supported by the employees?

4. In groups of four to six, brainstorm alternative solutions to Brad's problem. As a group, select one solution from the alternatives. Support your decision with rationale for the solution. Would this have been the solution you would have selected without the group input? Why or why not?

Bonnie Patznick
Satellite Lab Supervisor,
Abbott-Northwestern Hospital

Bonnie had many years of experience as a lab technician, but no experience in supervision when she assumed this position. She had always worked in a hospital laborarory. Now she is responsible for six offsite laboratories, several of them inside clinics. In the hospital laboratory, quality controls were absolutely mandatory, but to her surprise, Bonnie discovered that the satellite laboratories had very few quality controls. In fact, when she insisted that quality controls be run, her staff was amazed. Bonnie was a skilled lab technician, but she had always *followed* procedures. Now she had to set up her own.

Bonnie set up an internal control system. On a weekly or monthly basis, specimens were split and sent to the hospital laboratory for testing. She introduced external controls such as outside proficiency testing. Manuals were created for each procedure. Bonnie's approach was proven successful during inspections. The staff accepted the new standards well. When they had a problem with a new freezer, it was the staff that first noted the discrepancies in their tests and reported them to Bonnie.

However, there were still problems. When one staff person went on vacation and left a trainee in charge of some expensive equipment, the equipment malfunctioned. The trainee turned the equipment off on Friday afternoon, and on Monday morning it was no longer working. When Bonnie arrived at the satellite laboratory, she spoke with the trainee and determined that the trainee had not followed the procedure. Although a procedure manual existed, the trainee had never seen it. The experienced lab technician had left notes for the trainee to follow, but unfortunately the notes were incorrect.

1. Why is it important to have quality controls?
2. If an organization has policies, procedures and controls in place, why is it possible that a supervisor may view them differently than they are viewed by an employee? How were controls viewed by Bonnie?
3. Discuss the implications of the proper amount of supervision and the benefit of controls for all employees and an organization.
4. How can a system be developed for determining, implementing, and evaluating the controls within an organization? What place does planning have in developing such a system?

PART THREE

ORGANIZING, STAFFING, AND EMPLOYEE DEVELOPMENT

5. ORGANIZING AN EFFECTIVE DEPARTMENT

6. ACQUIRING THE RIGHT PEOPLE

7. APPRAISING EMPLOYEE PERFORMANCE

8. DEVELOPING YOUR EMPLOYEES

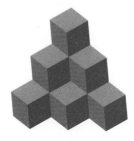

5

ORGANIZING AN EFFECTIVE DEPARTMENT

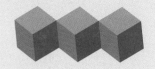

LEARNING OBJECTIVES

After reading this chapter, you should be able to:

1. Define *organizing*.
2. Describe why division of labour should increase economic efficiency.
3. Explain how the span of control affects an organization's structure.
4. Contrast line and staff authority.
5. Explain why organizations are increasingly becoming decentralized.
6. Describe functional depart-mentalization.
7. Identify the strengths and weaknesses of the matrix.
8. Explain the value of job descriptions.
9. Identify the four-step process of delegation.

CHAPTER OUTLINE

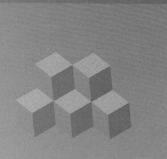

Anne Bermingham has helped numerous companies reorganize their structures.

Anne Bermingham's business is helping companies change. Consequently, she is a busy person these days. Anne is a partner in 2WA Consulting of Ancaster, Ontario, and has worked with numerous organizations (such as Hamilton Health Sciences Corporation, Northern Telecom and SAP Canada) that have reorganized themselves, creating new structures. In these cases the old structures no longer suited the organizations' environments, and were replaced by new structures that tended to emphasize downsizing, teams, and new leadership skills.

Anne facilitates the decision on what structural changes are needed and then the rolling out of the change itself, so that employees understand why the change is happening and what it will involve, and will have the skills and commitment to carry out the change effectively. Anne's role doesn't stop when the new structure is in place. New structures trigger unanticipated events that must be dealt with in order to keep the strategic focus of the change intact. So Anne continues her work with an organization well into the implementation of the new structure.

As you can see, the way in which employees are grouped together is an important consideration for an organization. And the structure within which a supervisor operates will have a large impact on that supervisor's activity and effectiveness. How many people can one person effectively supervise? When does a supervisor have the authority to make a decision and when is the supervisor limited to giving advice? What tasks can a supervisor delegate?

This chapter examines the basics of organization within a company structure and within a department, and looks at the ways in which organizational structures are changing.

In the 1920s and 1930s, as organizations got bigger and more formal, supervisors felt a need to provide more coordination of activities and tighter control over operations. Early business researchers argued that formal bureaucracies would best serve the company—and that was true sixty or more years ago. These bureaucratic structures flourished. By the 1980s, the world began to change drastically. The global marketplace, rapid technological advancements, diversity in the workforce, and socioeconomic conditions made these formal bureaucracies inefficient for many businesses. As a result, since the late 1980s many organizations have restructured to be more customer- and market-oriented, and to increase productivity.

FIGURE 5-2

This department at Xerox is organized with procedures, rules, and policies that guide employee activities.

It is critical today for an organization to have the right structure. Although setting up the organization's structure is typically done by top management in an organization (or the owner in a small business), it is important for all organizational members to understand how these structures work. Why? Because you'll understand your job better if you know why you're "arranged" as you are. For example, how many people can you effectively supervise? When do you have authority to make a decision and when is it merely advice that you're providing? What tasks can you delegate to others? Will you supervise employees who produce a specific product? Will your department exist to serve a particular customer, a geographic region, or some combination of these? You'll see how to find the answers to questions like these in this chapter. We'll look at the traditional components that go into developing an organization's structure, discuss the various ways that employees may be grouped, and look at how organizational structures change over time.

Xerox Canada
http://www.xerox.ca/

WHAT IS ORGANIZING?

Organizing is arranging and grouping jobs, allocating resources, and assigning work in a department so that activities can be accomplished as planned. The top management team in an organization typically establishes the overall organization structure. They'll determine, for instance, how many vertical levels there will be from the top of the organization to the bottom, and the extent to which lower-level managers

Organizing
Arranging and grouping jobs, allocating resources, and assigning work in a department so that activities can be accomplished as planned

FIGURE 5-3

(©1987 FatWorks Inc.
By permission of
Universal Press
Syndicate.)

"And so you just threw everything together? ...
Mathews, a posse is something you have to *organize*."

will have to follow formal rules and procedures in carrying out their jobs. In large corporations, it's not unusual for there to be five to eight levels from top to bottom; hundreds of departments; and dozens of manuals (for example, purchasing, human resources, accounting, engineering, maintenance, sales) that define procedures, rules, and policies within departments. Once the overall structure is in place, individual supervisors will need to organize their departments. In this chapter, we'll show you how to do that.

Keep in mind that our discussion here is with the *formal* arrangement of jobs and groups of jobs. These are defined by management. In addition, individuals and groups will develop *informal* alliances that are neither formally structured nor organizationally determined. Almost all employees in all organizations develop these informal arrangements to meet their needs for social contact. We'll discuss informal groups later in the book.

BASIC ORGANIZING CONCEPTS

The early writers on management developed a number of basic organizing principles that today's supervisors often use as they organize their departments.

DIVISION OF LABOUR

Division of labour (also known as work specialization) means that an entire job is broken down into a number of steps, each step being completed by a different individual. In essence, individuals specialize in doing part of an activity rather than the entire activity. Assembly-line production, in which each worker does the same standardized task over and over again, is an example of division of labour.

> **Division of labour**
> The breakdown of jobs into narrow, repetitive tasks

Until very recently, designers of organizations have felt that greater economic gains are achieved by breaking jobs down into smaller steps. In most organizations, some tasks require highly developed skills; others can be performed by the untrained. If all workers were engaged in each step of, say, an organization's manufacturing process, all would have to have the skills necessary to perform the most demanding and the least demanding jobs. The result would be that, except when performing the most highly skilled or highly sophisticated tasks, employees would be working below their skill level. Since skilled workers are paid more than unskilled workers and their wages tend to reflect their highest level of skill, it is not economical to pay highly skilled workers to do easy tasks.

Today, supervisors understand that while division of labour provides economic efficiencies, it is not an unending source of increased productivity. There is a point at which the human costs of division of labour—boredom, fatigue, stress, low productivity, poor quality, increased absenteeism, and high turnover—exceed the economic advantages. Contemporary supervisors utilize the division-of-labour concept in designing jobs but also recognize that, in an expanding number of situations, productivity, quality, and employee motivation can be increased by giving employees a variety of activities to perform, allowing employees to do a whole and complete piece of work, and joining employees together in teams.

FIGURE 5-4

The advantages of division of labour are explicitly evident on an assembly line, such as this frozen food plant. Each worker performs a narrow and standardized operation. This requires a limited range of skills and allows for increased efficiency.

SPAN OF CONTROL

Span of control
The number of subordinates a supervisor can direct efficiently and effectively

It's not very efficient for a supervisor to direct only one or two subordinates. Conversely, it's pretty obvious that the best of supervisors would be overwhelmed if he or she had to directly oversee several hundred people. This, then, begs the **span of control** question: How many subordinates can a supervisor effectively direct?

There is, unfortunately, no universal answer. For most supervisors, the optimum number is probably somewhere between five and thirty. Where, within that range, the exact span should be depends on a number of factors.

- How experienced and competent is the supervisor? The greater his or her abilities, the larger the number of subordinates that can be handled.
- What level of training and experience do subordinates have? The higher their abilities, the fewer demands they'll make on their supervisor and the more subordinates that supervisor can directly oversee.
- How complex are the subordinates' activities? The more difficult the employees' jobs, the narrower the span of control.
- How many different types of jobs are under the supervisor's direction? The more varied the jobs, the narrower the span.
- How extensive are the department's formal rules and regulations? Supervisors can direct more people when employees can find solutions to their problems in organizational manuals rather than having to go to their immediate manager.

An important trend currently taking place in organizations is for spans of control to be almost universally expanded (see Figure 5-5). It is a way for management to reduce costs. By doubling the span size, the number of supervisors you need is cut in half. Of course, this move to wider spans couldn't be effectively carried out without modifications in work assignments and improvements in skill levels. So, in order to make wider spans work, organizations are spending more on supervisory and employee training, as well as redesigning jobs around teams so individuals can help each other solve problems without needing to go to their manager. For instance, Saturn organizes work around teams, and Saturn employees spend at least five per cent of their time annually in training to facilitate team problem solving.

Something else important is taking place in organizations that involves a supervisor's span of control. This is the increased use of telecommuting. **Telecommuting** allows employees to do their work at home on a computer that is linked to their office. The big plus in telecommuting is that it gives employees more flexibility. It frees them from the constraints of commuting and fixed hours, and increases opportunities for meeting family responsibilities. For supervisors, telecommuting means managing people they rarely see. Where it is used, supervisors usually

Telecommuting
The linking by computer and modem of workers at home with coworkers and management at an office

have a fairly wide span of control. This is because telecommuters tend to be skilled professionals and clerical employees—computer programmers, marketing specialists, financial analysts, and administrative support personnel—who make minimal demands on their supervisors. Additionally, because the supervisor's computer and the employee's computer are typically networked so they can interact with each other, supervisors often are able to communicate as well or better with telecommuters than with employees who are physically in their office.

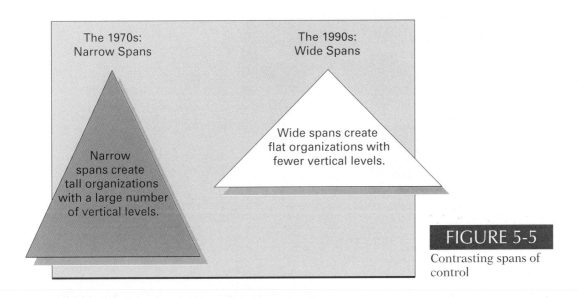

FIGURE 5-5

Contrasting spans of control

FIGURE 5-6

Pacific Bell's Steve Caulter supervises about twenty employees, most of them telecommuters. Steve himself does much of his work from home.

FIGURE 5-7

Managers at this Pitney Bowes postage-meter manufacturing plant have decentralized authority by designing work around self-directed teams.

UNITY OF COMMAND

Unity of command
The principle that a subordinate should have one and only one superior to whom he or she is directly responsible

The **unity of command** principle states that a subordinate should have one and only one superior to whom he or she is directly responsible. No person should report to two or more managers. Otherwise, a subordinate might have to cope with conflicting demands or priorities from several people at once. If this happens, employees are placed in a no-win situation. Whatever they do, they're going to upset someone.

There are occasional times when management will specifically break the unity of command. This might be necessary, for instance, when a project team is created to work on a specific problem or when a sales representative has to report to both her immediate district supervisor and a marketing specialist at head office who is coordinating the introduction of a new product. Nevertheless, these are exceptions to the rule. For the most part, when allocating tasks to individuals or grouping assignments in your department, you should ensure that each employee has one manager, and only one manager, to whom he or she directly reports.

LINE, STAFF AND FUNCTIONAL AUTHORITY

Authority
The managerial right to give orders and expect the orders to be obeyed

Authority refers to the managerial right to give orders and expect the orders to be obeyed. Each supervisory position has specific rights that are acquired from the position's rank or title. Authority, therefore, relates to one's position within an organization and ignores the personal characteristics of the individual supervisor. Employees obey individuals in authority not because they like or respect them but because of the rights inherent in their position.

There are three different types of authority relations: line, staff, and functional (see Figure 5-8, overleaf). The most straightforward and easiest to understand is **line authority**. This is the authority that gives the supervisor the right to direct the work of his or her employees and make certain decisions without consulting others.

Staff authority supports line authority by advising, servicing, and assisting, but it is typically limited. For instance, the assistant to the department head has staff authority. She acts as an extension of the department head and can give advice and suggestions, but they needn't be obeyed. However, the assistant may be given the authority to act for the department head. In such cases, she gives directives under the line authority of her boss. For instance, she might issue a memo and sign it "Joan Wilson for R. L. Dalton." In this instance, Wilson is only acting as an extension of Dalton. Staff authority allows Dalton to get more things done by having an assistant who can act on his behalf.

A third type of authority, **functional authority**, represents rights over individuals outside one's own direct areas of responsibility. For example, it is not unusual for a supervisor in a manufacturing plant to find that his immediate boss has line authority over him but that someone in corporate headquarters has functional authority over some of his activities and decisions. The supervisor in charge of a plant purchasing department is responsible to that plant's manager and the corporate director of purchasing at the company's head office.

Why, you might wonder, would the organization create positions of functional authority? After all, it breaks the unity of command principle by having people report to two bosses. The answer is that it can create efficiencies by permitting specialization of skills and improved coordination. Its major problem is overlapping relationships. This is typically resolved by clearly designating to an individual the activities over which his or her line boss has authority and those that fall under the direction of someone else with functional authority. To follow up our purchasing example, the director might have functional authority to specify corporation-wide purchasing policies on forms to be used and common procedures to be followed. All other aspects of the purchasing supervisor's job would fall under the authority of the plant manager.

Line authority
The authority that entitles a supervisor to direct the work of his or her employees, and to make certain decisions without consulting others

Staff authority
A limited authority that supports line authority by advising, servicing, and assisting

Functional authority
Rights over individuals outside one's own direct areas of responsibility

EQUATING AUTHORITY AND RESPONSIBILITY

Supervisory jobs come with authority. They also come with obligations. Supervisors are obliged to achieve their unit's goals, keep costs within budget, follow organizational policies, and motivate their subordinates. We call these obligations **responsibility**.

Responsibility
An obligation to perform assigned activities

FIGURE 5-8

Organization chart depicting line, staff, and functional authority relationships

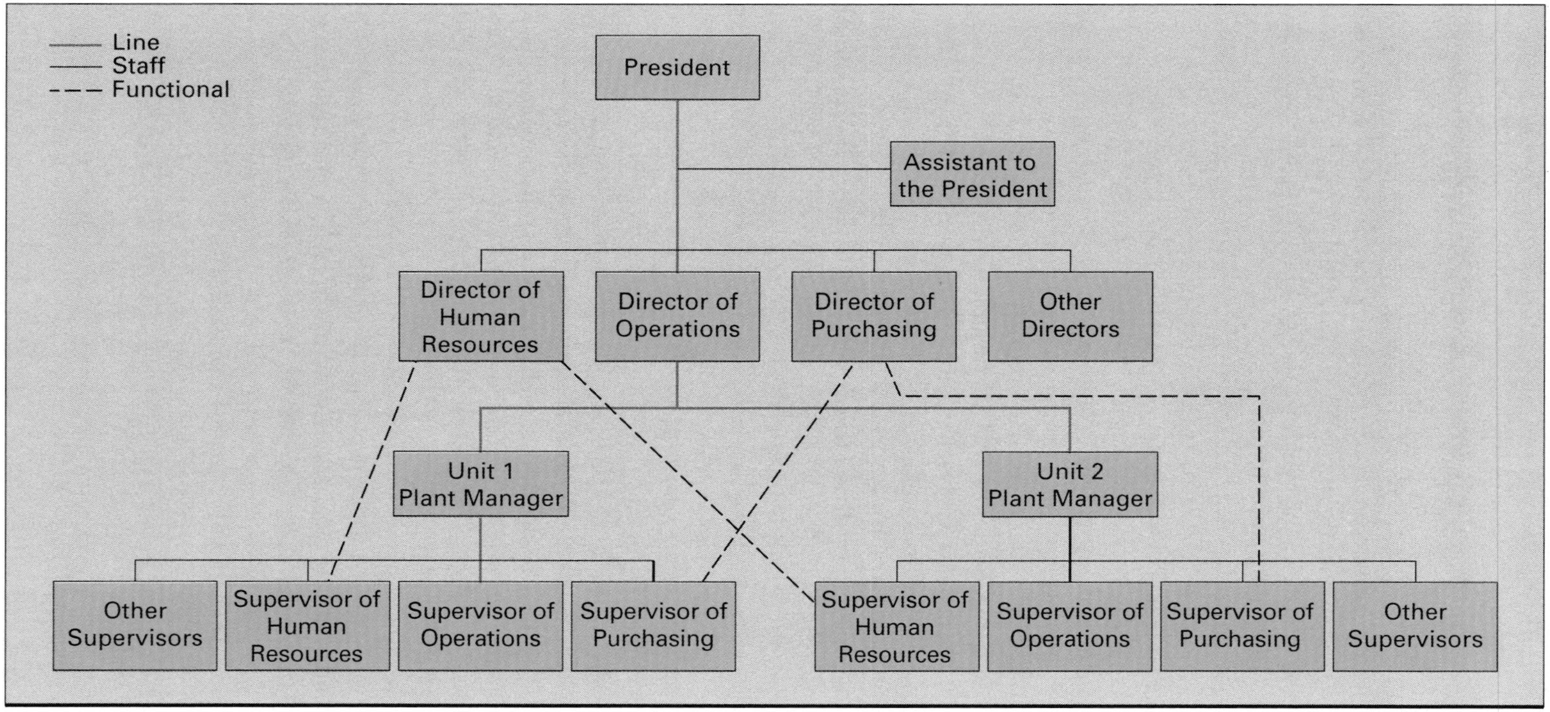

Line
Staff
Functional

President

Assistant to the President

Director of Human Resources

Director of Operations

Director of Purchasing

Other Directors

Unit 1 Plant Manager

Unit 2 Plant Manager

Other Supervisors

Supervisor of Human Resources

Supervisor of Operations

Supervisor of Purchasing

Supervisor of Human Resources

Supervisor of Operations

Supervisor of Purchasing

Other Supervisors

Authority without responsibility creates opportunities for abuse. For instance, a supervisor who isn't held responsible for his or her actions may become inclined to make excessive demands on an employee, resulting in that employee being injured on the job. Conversely, responsibility without authority creates frustration and the feeling of powerlessness. If you're held responsible for your territory's sales performance, you should have the authority to hire, reward, discipline, and fire the salespeople who work for you.

When top management creates organizational units like divisions, regions, territories, and departments—and allocates managers with specific goals to achieve and other responsibilities to fulfill—it must also give the managers enough authority to successfully carry out those responsibilities. The more ambitious and far-reaching the goals that a supervisor undertakes, the more authority he or she needs to be given.

CENTRALIZED VS. DECENTRALIZED AUTHORITY

Where does decision making lie? The design of any organization requires top management to answer this question. If the answer is "with top management," you have *centralized authority*. With centralization, problems "flow up" to senior executives, who then choose the appropriate solution. Where top management pushes decision making down to lower levels, you have *decentralized authority*.

Twenty-five years ago, centralization ruled in most organizations. Why? Top management typically had the necessary critical information and the expertise to make most key decisions. Additionally, time was not a problem. If it took a couple of months for top management to get around to making a decision, there were minimal negative consequences. That's no longer true. As jobs have become more complex, it's become nearly impossible for top managers to keep current and knowledgeable on everything going on in their organization. Moreover, the dynamics of competition make it increasingly necessary for organizations to make decisions fast. Because speedy decision making and centralization don't usually go together, top management has in recent years been forced to decentralize decision making.

Today, more than any time in recent years, supervisors and employees are being actively included in the decision-making process. As organizations have cut costs and streamlined their organizational design to respond better to customer needs, they have pushed decision-making authority down to the lowest levels in the organization and empowered employees. In this way, those people most familiar with a problem are able to quickly size it up and solve it. We'll present specific delegation skills later in this chapter, which will show you how to effectively push decision-making authority downward.

1. The principle that jobs should be broken down into the simplest of steps, with one step generally assigned to each individual, is known as:
   a. span of control
   b. line authority
   c. chain of command
   d. none of the above
2. Describe the advantages and disadvantages of the division of labour.
3. Early business experts believed top managers should have a larger span of control. True or False?
4. The main problem to be expected when the unity of command principle is ignored is that:
   a. Employees potentially have trouble coping with conflicting priorities and demands.
   b. Supervisors cannot keep abreast of what all their employees are doing.
   c. Decision making is slow.
   d. There is not enough flexibility.

GROUPING EMPLOYEES

Departmentalization Grouping departments according to work functions, product or service, target customer or client, geographic territory, or the process used to turn inputs into outputs

Early business experts argued that activities in the organization should be specialized and grouped into departments. Work specialization creates specialists who need coordination. This coordination is facilitated by putting specialists together in departments under the direction of a supervisor. Creation of these departments is typically based on the work functions being performed, the product or service being offered, the target customer or client, the geographic territory being covered, or the process being used to turn inputs into outputs. This process of grouping departments is called **departmentalization**. No single method of departmentalization was advocated by the early experts. The method or methods used should reflect the grouping that would best contribute to the attainment of the organization's objectives and the goals of individual units.

Specialization is found throughout organizations. For instance, when a company appoints vice presidents for marketing, finance, production, and research, it is dividing up organizational activities by specialization. While major decisions—such as what departments an organization will have and how they will interrelate—are typically made by top management, supervisors still make organizing decisions. These decisions are confined to activities within their own areas of responsibility. As a result, supervisors need to understand various options for organizing their departments and for grouping activities. These are, incidentally, the same options available to top managers when they make decisions about the organization's overall structure. Thus, as a supervisor, you can departmentalize on the basis of work function, product or service, geographic territory, target customer or client, or the process being used to turn inputs into outputs.

FUNCTION

One of the most popular ways to group activities is by functions performed—**functional departmentalization**. When you see a company that separates engineering, accounting, manufacturing, human resources, and purchasing specialists into common departments, you have an example of departmentalizing by function (see Figure 5-9). Similarly, hospitals use this approach when they create departments devoted to research, patient care, accounting, and so forth.

> **Functional departmentalization** Grouping activities by functions performed

Why is the functional department so popular? Because it most directly takes advantage of occupational specialization. By placing together jobs that are performed by people with the same kinds of training and experience, it is easier for people within the department to communicate with each other. It also makes it easier for the supervisor to coordinate activities, because he or she will be overseeing activities that have a somewhat common component.

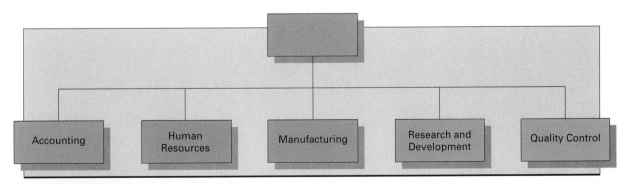

FIGURE 5-9

Functional departmentalization

PRODUCT

Another way to departmentalize is by product. This means that each major product area in the organization is under the authority of a manager who is a specialist in, and responsible for, everything to do with his or her product line.

In contrast to functional departments, **product departmentalization** creates relatively independent units. Any problem or issue that surfaces related to a product will fall under the responsibilities of that product's manager. Thus a major advantage of organizing around products is that it places ultimate responsibility for everything concerning a specific product with one manager, thus eliminating the potential for "passing the buck."

Assume Procter & Gamble used a functional organization (see Figure 5-10). If sales of its Ultra Tide laundry detergent dropped suddenly, who would be responsible? If P&G were organized along functional lines, the Sales department might blame the Advertising department. The Advertising department could say the problem was due to the way the product's container was designed and blame the Packaging Design department. The Packaging Design department could say the problem was that the detergent's strength wasn't adequate and blame the Research and Development department. This buck-passing doesn't happen with product departmentalization. Any problems or decisions relating to Ultra Tide woud lie with its product manager. It would be his or her responsibility to find the cause of the sales decline and to correct it.

GEOGRAPHY

Another way to departmentalize is on the basis of geography or territory—**geographic departmentalization**. This is particularly popular for sales and marketing units. For instance, BCE splits up its telecommunications divisions across Canada and around the world (see Figure 5-12). You also see

Product departmentalization
Grouping activities by product line

**Procter & Gamble
Global Community**
http://www.pg.com/

BCE
http://www.bce.ca/

**Geographic
departmentalization**
Grouping activities on
the basis of territory

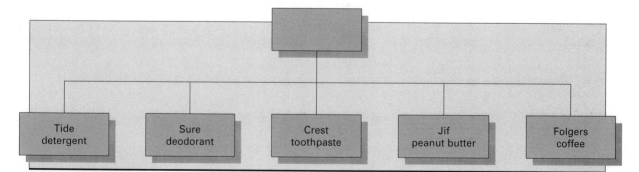

FIGURE 5-10
Product departmentalization

FIGURE 5-11

(*Source: The New Yorker*, 1975–1985.)

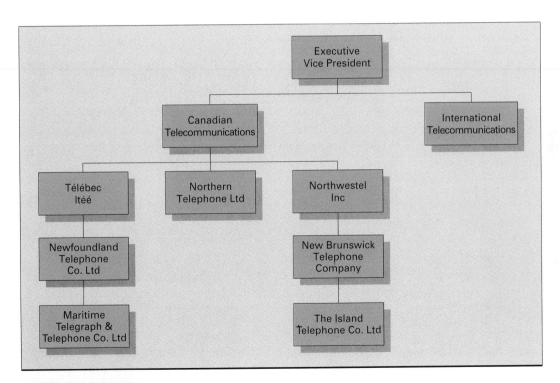

FIGURE 5-12

Geographic departmentalization

geographic departmentalization in large school districts when, for example, twelve high schools are organized so that each major territory within the district is covered. Additionally, when organizations set up international departments or divisions, they are organizing around geography.

What's the advantage to this form of departmentalization? It puts decision-making authority close to where the work is being done. If activities are physically dispersed and different locations face different types of problems, management will want to ensure that the people who make the decisions understand those differences. Paramount Publishing, for example, has marketing units in Toronto, New Jersey, London, New Delhi, Singapore, and Rio de Janeiro to reflect the unique publishing needs of the Canadian, American, European, Indian, Asian, and South American markets, respectively.

CUSTOMER

The fastest growing form of departmentalizing is by customer. Why? Because companies at the dawn of the twenty-first century are learning that success requires staying close to the customer. Organizations that lose touch with the changing needs of their diverse customer base aren't likely to be around for too long. The primary force that has driven the growth of companies such as MCI and Dell Computers has been careful listening to and response to the needs of their customers.

Where an organization has a diverse set of customers that can be grouped around common interests, concerns, or needs, then a customer form of departmentalization makes sense. For instance, most provincial governments organize departments to service different customers. The Attorney General's office is divided into criminal court, family court, and small claims court. Provincial tax offices are organized according to customer needs into commercial taxes, employer health taxes, tax grants for

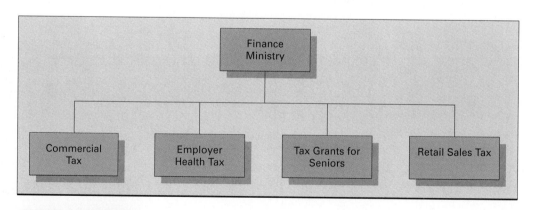

FIGURE 5-13

Customer departmentalization

seniors, and retail sales tax (see Figure 5-13). Other examples of **customer departmentalization** are universities that set up departments of evening studies or continuing education to cater to working and part-time students; and banks that separate commercial clients from individual customers.

Customer departmentalization Grouping activities on the basis of common customers

PROCESS

The final pure form of departmentalization is by process. Figure 5-14 depicts the various production departments in a Reynolds Metals plant that manufactures aluminum tubing. The metal is cast in huge furnaces; sent to the press department, where it is extruded into aluminum pipe; transferred to the tube mill, where it is stretched into various sizes and shapes of tubing; moved to finishing, where it is cut and cleaned; and finally arrives in the inspect, pack, and ship department. Since each process requires different skills and specialized equipment, this method offers a basis for the homogeneous categorizing of activities.

Reynolds Metals Company
http://www.rmc.com/

  Process departmentalization can be used for processing customers as well as products. If you have ever arrived at a major airport after an international flight, you probably went through several departments between leaving the plane and heading for home. Immigration verifies your eligibility to enter Canada, you pick up your luggage at the arrivals carousel, and the customs department verifies your purchases for import.

Process departmentalization Grouping activities on the basis of product or customer flow

BLENDING FUNCTION AND PRODUCT: THE MATRIX

The functional department offers the advantages of specialization. The product department has a greater focus on results but suffers from duplication of activities and resources. If the organization were completely organized around products—that is, if each product the company

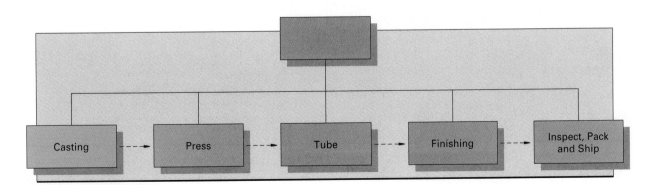

FIGURE 5-14

Process departmentalization

produced had its own supporting functional structure—the focus on results would again be high. Each product could have a product manager responsible for all activities related to that product. This, too, would result in redundancy, however, because each product would require its own set of functional specialists. Does any form combine the advantages of functional specialization with the focus and accountability that product departmentalization provides? The answer is yes, and it's called the **matrix**.

The matrix structure creates a dual chain of command. It explicitly breaks the principle of unity of command. Functional departmentalization is used to gain the economies of specialization. But overlaying the functional departments is a set of supervisors who are responsible for specific products, projects, or programs within the organization. (We'll use the terms *products*, *projects*, and *programs* interchangeably, since matrix structures can use any of the three).

Figure 5-15 illustrates the matrix structure of an aerospace firm. Notice that along the top of the figure are the familiar functions of engineering, accounting, human resources, and so forth. Along the vertical

Matrix
A structural design that assigns specialists from functional departments to work on one or more projects that are led by a project manager

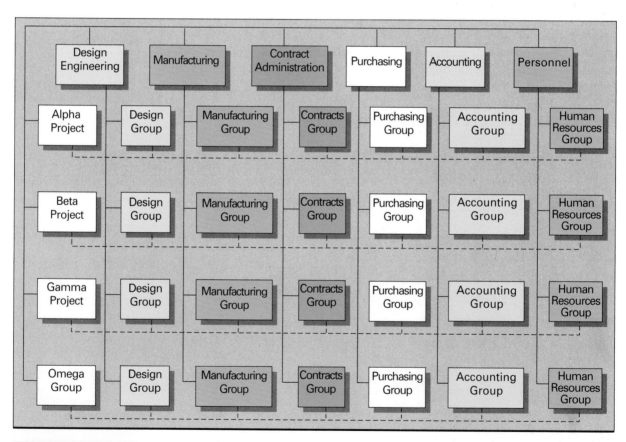

FIGURE 5-15

A matrix structure in an aerospace firm

dimension, however, have been added the various projects that the aerospace firm is currently working on. Each project is directed by a supervisor who staffs his or her project with people from the functional departments. The addition of the vertical dimension to the traditional functional departments in effect weaves together elements of functional and product departmentalization—hence the term *matrix*.

How does the matrix work? Employees in the matrix report to two managers—their functional departmental supervisor and their product or project supervisor (see Dealing with a Difficult Issue, overleaf). The project supervisors have authority over the functional members who are part of that supervisor's project team. For instance, the purchasing specialists who work on the Gamma project are responsible to both the supervisor of Purchasing and the Gamma project supervisor. Authority is shared between the two supervisors. Typically, this is done by giving the project supervisor authority over project employees relative to the project's goals, while decisions such as promotions, salary recommendations, and annual reviews remain the functional supervisor's responsibility. To work effectively, project and functional supervisors must communicate regularly and coordinate the demands upon their common employees.

The matrix creates a structure that possesses the strengths of both functional and product departmentalization, while avoiding the weaknesses of both. That is, the strength of the functional form lies in putting like specialists together, minimizing the numbers, and it allows for the pooling and sharing of specialized resources across products. Its primary drawback is the difficulty in coordinating the tasks of the specialists so that their activities are completed on time and within the budget. The product form, on the other hand, has exactly the opposite benefits and disadvantages. It facilitates the coordination among specialists to achieve on-time completion and meet budget targets, and furthermore provides clear responsibility for all activities related to a product or project. But no one is responsible for the long-run technical development of the specialists, and this results in duplication of costs.

Why Is There Movement to Simpler Employee Groupings?

Recall our discussion in Chapter 1 regarding the challenges businesses face. Two of these—downsizing and reengineering—are particularly relevant to today's changes in organizational form.[1] How? To answer this question, let's briefly review some facts regarding common structures. Many of the departmentalizations mentioned above were highly complex and formalized, and decisions were made in a centralized fashion—resulting in rigid, often massive, multilevelled structures. Although they

DO MATRIX STRUCTURES CREATE CONFUSED EMPLOYEES?

Workers in matrix structures face a difficult issue that never arose in traditional organizational structures. That is, they have at least two bosses. They are responsible to their functional supervisor, who has the responsibility to evaluate their performance and make salary increase determinations. Concurrently, these employees are responsible to their project leader for specific project tasks.

In this situation, whose authority takes precedence? Do employees give their functional supervisor's requests priority because, after all, it is this individual who handles the administrative and personnel-related paperwork? Or is it the project leader—who is more involved with the employees on a day-to-day basis—who gets the "top-billing"? Failure to complete the required tasks on the project could result in being removed from the project team—a decision that may place an employee's job in jeopardy. Are both supervisors given equal priority? Should employees simply accept that they have to serve "two masters"? What do you think?

were designed to promote efficiency, they did not easily adjust to the dynamic world around them. As a result, more emphasis today has been given to organizations that focus on simplicity. Let's look at what we mean by a simple structure.

If "bureaucracy" is the term that best describes most large organizations, "simple structure" is the one that best characterizes most small ones. A **simple structure** is defined more by what it is not than by what it is. It is not an elaborate structure.[2] If you see an organization that appears to have almost no structure, it is probably of the simple variety. By that we mean that it is low in complexity, has little formalization, and has its authority centralized in a single person. The simple structure is a "flat" organization; it usually has only two or three levels, employees who perform a variety of tasks, and one individual who makes most of the decisions.

The simple structure is most widely practised in small businesses in which the manager and the owner are one and the same. This is illustrated in Figure 5-16—an organization chart for a men's clothing retail store. Jack Singleton owns and manages this store. Although Jack employs five full-time salespeople, a cashier, and part-time weekend help, he "runs the show."

Simple structure
A non-elaborate structure low in complexity, with little formalization, and with authority centralized in a single person; a "flat" organization with only two or three levels.

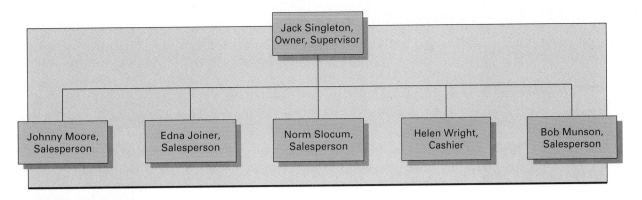

FIGURE 5-16

Jack Singleton's structure

The strengths of the simple structure should be obvious. Communications are efficient, accountability is clear, and it has flexibility to respond to the changing environment. One major weakness is that, in the past, it was viewed as effective only in small organizations. It became increasingly inadequate as an organization grew, because the low degree of formalization and high degree of centralization resulted in information overloads at the top. As size increased, decision making became slower and eventually came to a standstill as the single person in charge tried to continue making all the decisions. This often proved to be the undoing of many small businesses. The simple structure's other weakness is that it is risky: everything depends on one person. One heart attack, or a fatal auto accident on the way to work, can literally destroy the organization—for the only one who held the critical information is now gone. However, these weaknesses were not necessarily the fault of the simple structure. Rather, those in charge just couldn't give up the control that they had so enjoyed.

ARE THERE SIMPLE STRUCTURES FOR LARGER ORGANIZATIONS?

If yesterday's organizations had one feature in common, it was the rigid boundaries that separated employees from other members of the organization. Employees were often segregated by the jobs they did and rarely interacted with others in different parts of the business. A select few "ran the show." That setup may no longer provide the best advantage in organizations. Some of those boundaries are being broken down, giving employees more interaction with others whom they count on for getting jobs done. In business today, we call this arrangement the horizontal structure.

THE HORIZONTAL STRUCTURE

Horizontal structures
Very flat structures used in small businesses as well in as giant companies in which job-related activities cut across all parts of the organization

Before we begin this discussion, let's set the record straight. A horizontal structure is really nothing new. **Horizontal structures** are simply very flat structures—basically the same as what we called simple structures. What's new about them, however, is that they are being used not only in small businesses, but in giant companies like AT&T, du Pont, General Electric, and Motorola.[3] Horizontal organizations, as the term implies, means job-related activities cut across all parts of the organization. Rather than having employees perform specialized jobs and work in departments with people who do similar tasks, they are grouped with other employees who have different skills—forming a work team. These individuals come together to work toward a common objective. They are given the authority to make the necessary decisions to do the work, and are held accountable for measurable outcomes.[4] Their jobs encompass the entire work to be completed, from beginning to end—rather than focusing on individualized job tasks.[5] In a horizontal structure, control shifts from those in management to supervisors and workers.

Working in a horizontal organization brings about other changes for supervisors. For instance, supervisors reward employees for mastering multiple skills, rather than just a few specialized skills. The more jobs employees can do, the more valuable they are. Additionally, rather than being evaluated on the work one individual does, the rewards are based on how the team performs. In a horizontal organization, the supervisor's evaluations are no longer the only ones. Instead, employees are likely to be evaluated by anyone who has knowledge of their work. At General Electric, CEO Jack Welch has implemented what he calls a 360-degree appraisal process.[6] At GE, team members are evaluated by team leaders, peer members, other employees with whom they work—even customers. This evaluation system is a model coming into use in many large organizations.

FITTING EMPLOYEE GROUPING TO THE SITUATION

Although the movement toward simple structures brings with it many strengths and may provide an exciting work atmosphere, keep one thing in mind. Simple structures must be used only where appropriate. The question then arises: When does each of the different groupings work best? For example, in industries where efficiency of mass production is warranted, grouping employees by the jobs they perform may better serve the organization. The answer will depend on the environment in which you work.

Organizations group employees in a given way for a particular reason. They don't implement structures haphazardly for the fun of it. It's too expensive, and very difficult, to make these changes. When an organization does make such a change, you should learn from it. Recognize what the structure is telling you as a supervisor. If grouping employees by the job performed appears to be the norm, then your organization has made the decision that efficiency matters most. Therefore, to be successful in this element of your supervisory job, you need to focus on being efficient and continue refining your current skills. That may mean emphasizing work specialization for your employees—and yourself, too. In such an arrangement, you'll also be given clues on how best to make some of your decisions. You'll want to give greater weight to the alternatives that are most cost effective or provide greater output for a given input. Play to the strength of the employee grouping—that's usually what you'll be rewarded for.

Similar guidelines can be found in other employee groupings. For example, grouping by the product produced means that the "bigger" picture is most important. That is, achieving organizational goals is a "must," and the company is willing to use resources to do it.

ORGANIZING YOUR EMPLOYEES' JOBS

Once your departmental structure is in place, you need to organize the specific jobs of each of your employees. How do you do that? By identifying the tasks to be done, combining them into jobs, and then formalizing the process by creating job descriptions.

IDENTIFYING THE TASKS TO BE DONE

Begin by making a list of all the specific tasks with which your department has been charged. These are the tasks that, when effectively accomplished, result in your department successfully achieving its goals. Figure 5-17 illustrates a partial list drawn up by a production supervisor in a large book publishing company.

COMBINING TASKS INTO JOBS

It is unlikely that one person can do all the tasks that need to be accomplished. So the tasks need to be combined into individual jobs.

The supervisor will create jobs by separating specialized tasks, allowing each employee to become more proficient at his or her special job. So the book production supervisor will create specific jobs such as copy editor, proofreader, photo editor, production coordinator, and designer.

In addition to grouping similar tasks together, supervisors need to be sure that workloads within the department are balanced. Employee morale and productivity will suffer if some employees' jobs are significantly more difficult or time-consuming than others. The supervisor should

- Attend initial planning meeting with acquisition editor to launch a new book

- Contact with acquisition editors

- Contact with authors

- Contact with marketing personnel

- Contact with advertising group

- Contact with manufacturing buyers

- Develop production schedules for each book

- Design the internal layout of books and develop sample pages

- Draw up detailed design specifications for the computer, to be used for creating pages

- Have figures and tables drawn

- Design book covers

- Organize and direct weekly coordination meetings for each book

- Proof galleys and pages

Partial list of tasks in a book production department

take into consideration the physical, mental, and time demands that the various tasks require, and use this information to help balance the workloads among department employees.

CREATING JOB DESCRIPTIONS

Job description
A written statement of what a jobholder does, how the job is done, and why it is done

A **job description** is a written statement of what a jobholder does, how the job is done, and why it is done. It typically portrays job duties, working conditions, and operating responsibilities. Figure 5-18 illustrates a job description for a production editor in a publishing company.

Why do supervisors need to write job descriptions for each job in their department? For two reasons. First, the job description provides the supervisor with a formal document describing what the employee is supposed to be doing. It acts as a standard against which the supervisor can determine how well the employee is performing. This, in turn, can be used to make performance appraisal, feedback, wage adjustment, and training decisions. Second, the job description helps employees learn their job duties and clarifies the results that management expects them to achieve.

Job Title: Project Production Editor

Department: College Book Editorial Production

Wage Category: Exempt

Reports to: Business Team Production Supervisor

Job Class: 7-12B

Job Statement:
     Performs and oversees editing work in the areas of book specifications, design, composition, printing, and binding. May carry a number of books at the same time. Works under general supervision. Incumbent exercises initiative and independent judgment in the performance of assigned tasks.

Job Duties:

1. Identifies activities to be completed, determines sequencing, and prepares a schedule for the ten-month process.

2. Performs or contracts out copy editing of book manuscript.

3. Coordinates specifcation (size, colour, paper, covers) and design (typefaces, art) with assigned designer. Coordinates preparation of galleys and pages with manufacturing buyers and compositor.

4. Distributes scheduling-status reports to acquisition editors and others as needed.

5. Acts as liaison with authors on all production issues.

6. Checks all permissions for completeness and accuracy.

7. Responsible for maintaining in-stock date set at initial launch meeting.

8. Performs related duties as assigned by team supervisor.

FIGURE 5-18

A job description for a production editor in a publishing company

THE INCREASING USE OF TEAMS

Teams are increasingly becoming the prime vehicle around which work is being designed. Why? Because teams typically outperform individuals when the tasks being done require multiple skills, judgment, and experience. As organizations restructure themselves to compete more effectively and efficiently, they are turning to teams as a way to better utilize employees' talents. Organizations are finding that teams are more flexible and responsive to changing events than are departments or other forms of permanent groupings. They can be quickly assembled, deployed, refocused, and disbanded.

5. When an insurance claims department groups all automobile collision claims employees under one supervisor, _____ is being demonstrated.

   a. functional departmentalization
   b. geographic departmentalization
   c. process departmentalization
   d. product departmentalization

6. Identify the five different ways in which you can departmentalize, or group, your employees.

7. A strength of the matrix structure is that it capitalizes on the accountability of product departmentalization and the efficiency of work specialization. True or False?

8. Which one of the following is not reflective of the term *job description?*

   a. A job description is a written statement of what a jobholder does.
   b. A job description involves allocation of duties, assignment of authority, responsibility, and accountability.
   c. A job description defines how and why a job is done.
   d. A job description typically portrays job duties and working conditions.

Teams fall into one of three categories, depending on their objectives. Some organizations use teams to *provide advice*. For instance, they create temporary task forces to recommend ways to cut costs, improve quality, or select a site for a new plant. Some organizations use teams to *manage*. They introduce management teams at various levels in the organization to run things. However, supervisors are most likely to be involved with teams that are created to *make or do things*. They include production teams, design teams, and office teams that handle administrative work.

Companies such as Pratt and Whitney Canada, Honeywell, Motorola, Dofasco and Imperial Oil are making work teams the centrepiece in creating new work units. For instance, the Imperial Oil refinery in Dartmouth, Nova Scotia, threatened with closure just a few years ago, is now an industry leader thanks to its organizational redesign based on teams. In 1993, a cross-functional team at Pratt and Whitney Canada, of Longueuil, Quebec, produced a design for a jet engine in less than twelve months, a process that would normally take eighteen to twenty-four months.

Pratt & Whitney Canada
http://www.pwc.ca/

In organizations reorganizing work around teams, supervisors are having to learn how to effectively coordinate team activity. In many cases, management's emphasis has been on creating self-managed teams. As we'll see, this is redefining the supervisor's managerial role.

TURNING GROUPS INTO TEAMS

Groups and **teams** are not necessarily the same thing. Many formal work groups are merely individuals who sporadically interact, but who have no collective commitment that requires joint effort. That is, the group's total performance is merely the sum of the individual group members' performance.

What differentiates a team is that members are committed to a common purpose, have a set of specific performance goals, and hold themselves mutually accountable for the team's results. Teams, in other words, are something greater than the sum of their parts. Figure 5-19 illustrates how a work group evolves into a real team. The primary force that moves a work group toward a real high-performing team is its emphasis on performance.

A *working group* is a group of individuals who interact primarily to share information and to make decisions, in order to help each other perform within a given area of responsibility. Members of such a group have no need or opportunity to engage in collective work that requires joint effort, so their performance is merely the sum of each group member's individual contribution. There is no positive synergy to create an overall level of performance that is greater than the sum of the inputs.

Team
Members are committed to a common purpose, have a set of specific performance goals, and hold themselves mutually accountable for the team's results.

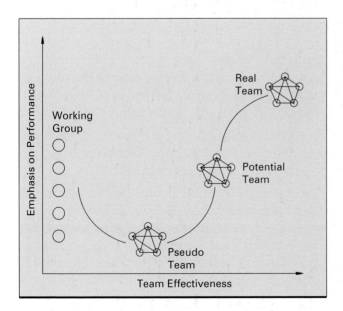

FIGURE 5-19

Comparing groups and teams

A *pseudoteam* is the product of negative synergy. The performance or output of the whole is less than the potential of the individual parts, because of factors such as poor communication, antagonistic conflicts, and avoidance of responsibilities. Even though members may call themselves a team, they're not. Because it doesn't focus on collective performance and because members have no interest in shaping a common purpose, a pseudoteam actually underperforms a working group.

"Going in the right direction but not there yet" is the best way to describe a *potential team*. It recognizes the need for, and is really trying hard to achieve, higher performance, but some roadblocks are in the way. Its purpose and goals may need greater clarity or the team may need better coordination. The result is that it has not yet established a sense of collective accountability.

The ultimate goal is to become a real team. This is a unit with a set of common characteristics that lead to consistently high performance.

BUILDING REAL TEAMS

Studies of effective teams have found that they contain a small number of people with complementary skills who are equally committed to a common purpose, goals, and working approach for which they hold themselves mutually accountable.[7] This section describes the six characteristics of real teams.

SMALL SIZE

The best teams tend to be small. When they have more than about ten members, it becomes difficult for them to get much done. They have trouble interacting constructively and reaching agreement. Large numbers of people usually cannot develop the common purpose, goals, approach, and mutual accountability of a real team. They tend merely to go through the motions. So in designing effective teams, keep them to ten people or fewer. If the natural working unit is larger, and you want a team effort, break the group into subteams. Federal Express, for instance, has divided the one thousand clerical workers at its headquarters into teams of five to ten members each.

COMPLEMENTARY SKILLS

To perform effectively, a team requires three types of skills. First, it needs people with *technical expertise*. Second, it needs people with the *problem-solving and decision-making skills* to identify problems, generate alternatives, evaluate those alternatives, and make competent choices. Finally, teams need people with good *interpersonal skills* (listening, feedback, conflict resolution).

No team can achieve its performance potential without developing all three types of skills. The right mix is crucial. Too much of one at the expense of others will result in lower team performance.

Teams don't need to have all the complementary skills at the beginning. Where team members value personal growth and development, one or more members often take responsibility to learn the skills in which the group is deficient, as long as the skill potential exists. Additionally, personal compatibility among members is not critical to the team's success if the technical, decision-making, and interpersonal skills are in place.

COMMON PURPOSE

Does the team have a meaningful purpose that all members aspire to? This purpose is a vision. It's broader than any specific goals. High-performing teams have a common and meaningful purpose that provides direction, momentum, and commitment for members.

For example, the development team at Apple Computer that designed the Macintosh was almost religiously committed to creating a user-friendly machine that would revolutionize the way people used computers. Production teams at Saturn are united by the common purpose of building a North American automobile that can successfully compete in terms of quality and price with the best of Japanese cars.

Members of successful teams put a tremendous amount of time and effort into discussing, shaping, and agreeing upon a purpose that belongs to them collectively and individually. This common purpose, when accepted by the team, becomes the equivalent of what celestial navigation is to a ship captain—it provides direction and guidance under any and all conditions.

SPECIFIC GOALS

Successful teams translate their common purpose into specific, measurable, and realistic performance goals. Just as goals lead individuals to higher performance (see Chapter 2), they also energize teams. Specific goals facilitate clear communication and help teams maintain their focus on getting results. Examples of specific team goals might be responding to all customers within twenty-four hours, cutting production-cycle time by 30 per cent over the next six months, or maintaining equipment at a level of zero downtime every month.

COMMON APPROACH

Goals are the ends a team strives to attain. Defining and agreeing upon a common approach assures that the team is unified on the *means* for achieving those ends.

Team members must contribute equally in sharing the workload and agree on who is to do what. Additionally, the team needs to determine how schedules will be set, what skills need to be developed, how conflicts will be resolved and how decisions will be made and modified. When Dofasco management gave Dave Zaporzon permission to reorganize the No. 4 pickle line on the basis of teams and empowerment, he sat down with his people, laid out the complaints, and asked them "How can we design a system to meet these concerns?" After they had created a design, it was implemented as a one-year trial with the clear understanding that the design was flexible and would be changed as needed.

MUTUAL ACCOUNTABILITY

The final characteristic of high-performing teams is accountability at both the individual and group level.

Successful teams make members individually and jointly accountable for the team's purpose, goals, and approach. Members understand what they are individually responsible for and what they are jointly responsible for.

Social loafing
The tendency of group members to do less than they are capable of individually when their individual contribution is not measured

Studies have shown that when teams focus only on group-level performance targets, and ignore individual contributions and responsibilities, team members often engage in **social loafing**.[8] They reduce their efforts because their individual contributions can't be identified. In effect, they become "free riders" and coast on the group's effort. The result is that the team's overall performance suffers. This reaffirms the importance of measuring both individual contributions to the team as well as the team's overall performance. And successful teams have members who collectively feel responsible for their team's performance.

OVERCOMING THE OBSTACLES

Critical obstacles that can prevent a team from becoming high performers include a weak sense of direction, infighting, shirking of responsibilities, lack of trust, critical skill gaps and lack of external support.

There are a number of things supervisors can do to overcome the obstacles mentioned and help teams to reach their full potential.

CREATE A CLEAR PURPOSE AND GOALS

High-performance teams have both a clear understanding of their goals and a belief that the goals embody a worthwhile or important result. Moreover, the importance of these goals encourages individuals to sublimate personal concerns to the team goals. In effective teams, members are committed to the team's goals, know what they are expected to accomplish, and understand how they will work together to achieve these goals.

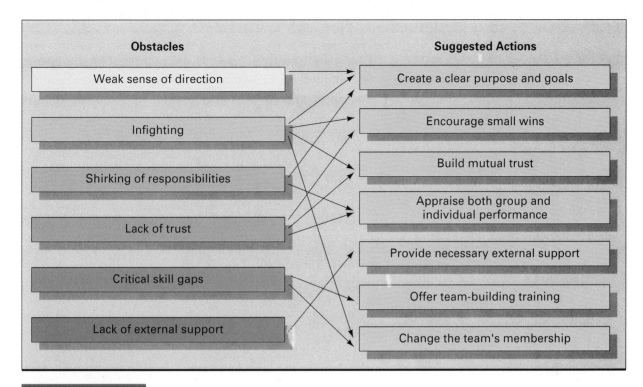

Obstacles

- Weak sense of direction
- Infighting
- Shirking of responsibilities
- Lack of trust
- Critical skill gaps
- Lack of external support

Suggested Actions

- Create a clear purpose and goals
- Encourage small wins
- Build mutual trust
- Appraise both group and individual performance
- Provide necessary external support
- Offer team-building training
- Change the team's membership

FIGURE 5-20

Creating effective teams

As a supervisor, your job is to ensure that teams under your leadership have a clear purpose and goals. Whether you participate in setting them or delegate this task to the team itself, it's your responsibility to make sure that it is accomplished.

ENCOURAGE TEAMS TO GO FOR SMALL WINS

The building of real teams takes time. Team members have to learn to think and work as a team. New teams can't be expected to hit home runs, right at the beginning, every time they come to bat. So encourage the team to begin by trying to hit singles.

Help the team identify and set attainable goals. The eventual goal of cutting overall costs by 30 per cent, for instance, can be dissected into five or ten smaller and more easily attainable goals. As the smaller goals are attained, the team's success is reinforced. Cohesiveness is increased and morale improves. Confidence builds. Success breeds success, but it's a lot easier for young teams to reach their goals if they start with small wins.

BUILD MUTUAL TRUST

Trust is fragile. It takes a long time to build and can be easily destroyed. However, there are things a supervisor can do to create a climate of mutual trust.[9]

Keep team members informed by explaining upper-management decisions and policies and by providing accurate feedback. Create a climate of openness where employees are free to discuss problems without fear of retaliation. Be candid about your own problems and limitations. Make sure you're available and approachable when employees need support. Be respectful and listen to team members' ideas. Develop a reputation for being fair, objective, and impartial in your treatment of team members. Show consistency in your actions, and avoid erratic and unpredictable behaviour. Finally, be dependable and honest. Make sure you follow through on all explicit and implied promises.

APPRAISE BOTH GROUP AND INDIVIDUAL PERFORMANCE

Team members should all share in the glory when their team succeeds, and they should share in the blame when it fails. So a large measure of each member's performance appraisal should be based on the overall team's performance. But members need to know that they can't ride on the backs of others. Therefore, each member's individual contribution should also be identified and made a part of his or her overall performance appraisal.

PROVIDE THE NECESSARY EXTERNAL SUPPORT

You're the link between the teams and upper management. As such, it's your responsibility to make sure that teams have the necessary organizational resources to accomplish their goals. That means you should be prepared to make the case to your boss and other key decision makers in the organization for tools, equipment, training, personnel, physical space, or other resources the teams may require.

OFFER TEAM-BUILDING TRAINING

Teams, especially in their early stages of formation, will need training to build their skills. Typically, these skills include problem solving, communication, negotiation, conflict resolution, and group process. If you can't personally provide this kind of skill training for your team members, look to specialists in your organization who can, or secure the funds to bring in outside facilitators who specialize in this kind of training.

CHANGE THE TEAM'S MEMBERSHIP

When teams get bogged down in their own inertia or internal fighting, allow them to rotate members. You might want to manage this change by considering how certain personalities will mesh, and reforming teams in ways that will better combine skills. If lack of leadership is the problem, use your knowledge of the people involved to create teams in which there will be a high probability that a leader will emerge.

9. Describe the six characteristics of teams.
10. Personal compatibility among members is not critical to the team's success if the complementary skills are in place. True or False?
11. Which of the following is an obstacle to creating an effective team?
    a. a weak sense of direction
    b. lack of external support
    c. shirking of responsibilities
    d. all of the above
12. "Encourage teams to go for small wins" means:
    a. Help the team identify and set major goals so they will work together towards significant accomplishments.
    b. Allow them to rotate and replace members until they achieve an effective meshing of individuals.
    c. Involve them in team-building activities aimed at creating a lot of fun and a supportive atmosphere.
    d. Break down overall goals into smaller ones which are easier to achieve.

EMPOWERING OTHERS
THROUGH DELEGATION

Empowerment
Increasing an employee's involvement in making decisions and taking responsibility for work outcomes

Contemporary supervisors need to learn to empower others. **Empowerment** means increasing your employees' involvement in their work—particularly in making decisions and taking responsibility for work outcomes. Two ways to empower people are to delegate authority to them and to redesign their jobs. In this section, we'll address delegation. In Chapter 9, we'll show you how to empower people through job design.

ASSESSING YOURSELF: ARE YOU WILLING TO DELEGATE?

Think of times when you have been in charge of a group—this could be a full-time or part-time work situation, a student work group, or similar experience. Complete the following questionnaire by recording how you feel about each statement according to this scale. Remember to be honest in your answers.[10]

5 = Strongly disagree

4 = Disagree

3 = Neutral

2 = Agree

1 = Strongly agree

When in charge of a group I find:

___ 1. Most of the time other people are too inexperienced to do things, so I prefer to do them myself.

___ 2. It often takes more time to explain things to others than to just do them myself.

___ 3. Mistakes made by others are costly, so I don't assign much work to them.

___ 4. Some things simply should not be delegated to others.

___ 5. I often get quicker action by doing a job myself.

___ 6. Many people are good only at very specific tasks, and thus can't be assigned additional responsibilities.

___ 7. Many people are too busy to take on additional work.

___ 8. Most people just aren't ready to handle additional responsibility.

___ 9. In my position, I should be entitled to make my own decisions.

SCORING KEY AND INTERPRETATION

This questionnaire gives you an idea of your willingness to empower others through delegation. Add up your score on the nine items. Possible total scores range from 9 to 45. The higher your score, the more willing you appear to be to delegate to others. A score of 36 or higher indicates a strong willingness to allow others to assume workplace responsibilities and exercise self-control in their work. Scores in the 25–35 range imply serious reluctance to give up authority and control. Scores below 25 suggest considerable room for improvement in this area.

SKILL BASICS

There is no question that effective supervisors need to be able to delegate. But supervisors tell us that it's hard for them. Why? They're typically afraid to give up control. "I like to do things myself," says Cheryl Munro Sharp of London Life, "because then I know it's done and I know it's done right." Lisa Flaherty of the Della Femina McNama advertising agency voiced a similar comment: "I have to learn to trust others. Sometimes I'm afraid to delegate the more important projects because I like to stay hands-on." In this section, we will show that delegation increases a supervisor's effectiveness and that, when done properly, still provides supervisory control.

WHAT IS DELEGATION?

Delegation is frequently depicted as a four-step process: 1. allocation of duties; 2. delegation of authority; 3. assignment of responsibility; and 4. creation of accountability.

> 1. **Allocation of duties.** Duties are the tasks and activities that a manager desires to have someone else do. Before you can delegate authority, you must allocate to a subordinate the duties over which the authority extends.

Delegation
A four-step process of allocating duties, delegating authority, assigning responsibility, and creating accountability

2. **Delegation of authority.** The essence of the delegation process is empowering the subordinate to act for you. It is passing to the subordinate the formal rights to act on your behalf. Ask yourself: Did I give my subordinate enough authority to get the materials, the equipment, and the support from others necessary to get the job done?

3. **Assignment of responsibility.** When authority is delegated, you must assign responsibility. That is, when you give someone "rights," you must also assign to that person a corresponding "obligation" to perform.

4. **Creation of accountability.** To complete the delegation process, you must create **accountability**; that is, you must hold your subordinate answerable for properly carrying out his or her duties. So while responsibility means a subordinate is obliged to carry out assigned duties, accountability means the subordinate has to perform the assignment in a satisfactory manner. Subordinates are responsible for the completion of tasks assigned to them, and are accountable to you for the satisfactory performance of that work.

Accountability
Holding a person to performing an assignment in a satisfactory manner

DELEGATION IS NOT ABDICATION

If you dump tasks on a subordinate without clarifying exactly what is to be done, the range of the subordinate's freedom, the expected level of performance, when the tasks are to be completed, and similar concerns, you are abdicating responsibility and inviting trouble. But don't fall into the trap of assuming that, in order to avoid the appearance of abdicating, you should minimize delegation. Unfortunately, this is the approach taken by many new and inexperienced supervisors. Lacking confidence in their subordinates, or fearful that they will be criticized for their subordinates' mistakes, they try to do everything themselves.

It may very well be true that you're capable of doing the tasks you delegate to your subordinates better, faster, or with fewer mistakes. The catch is that your time and energy are scarce resources. It's not possible for you to do everything yourself. So you need to learn to delegate if you're going to be effective in your job. This suggests two important points. First, you should expect and accept some mistakes by your subordinates. It's part of delegation. Mistakes are often good learning experiences for your subordinates, as long as their costs are not excessive. Second, to ensure that the costs of mistakes don't exceed the value of the learning, you need to put adequate controls in place. As we'll show, delegation without proper feedback controls that let you know when there are serious problems is abdication.

DELEGATION SKILLS

A number of actions differentiate the effective from the ineffective delega-tor. The following summarizes those actions.

1. **Clarify the assignment.** Begin by determining what is to be dele-gated and to whom. You need to identify the person best capable of doing the task, then determine if he or she has the time and motiva-tion to do the job.

    Assuming you have a willing and able subordinate, it is your responsibility to provide clear information on what is being dele-gated, the results you expect, and any time or performance expecta-tions you hold.

    Unless there is an overriding need to adhere to specific methods, you should delegate only the end results. That is, get agreement on what is to be done and the end results expected, but let the subordi-nate decide on the means. By focusing on goals and allowing the employee the freedom to use his or her own judgment as to how those goals are to be achieved, you increase trust between you and the employee, improve the employee's motivation, and enhance accountability for the results.

2. **Specify the subordinate's range of discretion.** Every act of dele-gation comes with constraints. You're delegating authority to act, but not unlimited authority. What you're delegating is authority to act on certain issues and, on those issues, within certain guidelines. You need to specify all guidelines so subordinates know, in no uncertain terms, the range of their discretion. When this has been successfully communicated, both you and the subordinate will have the same idea of the limits to the latter's authority and how far he or she can go without checking further with you.

    How much authority do you give a subordinate? In other words, how tightly do you draw the guidelines? The best answer is that you should allocate enough authority to allow the subordinate to successfully complete the task. Your level of confidence in the employee's ability should help establish appropriate guidelines.

3. **Allow the subordinate to participate.** If you allow employees to participate in determining what is delegated, how much authority is needed to get the job done, and the standards by which they'll be judged, you increase employee motivation, satisfaction, and accountability for performance.

    Be aware, however, that participation can present its own set of potential problems. For example, some subordinates are personally motivated to expand their authority beyond what they need and beyond what they are capable of handling. Allowing such people too much participation in deciding the tasks they should take on and the level of authority they must have can undermine the effectiveness of the delegation process.

4. **Inform others that delegation has occurred.** Delegation should not take place in a vacuum. The supervisor, the employee and anyone else who may be affected by the delegation act all need to be informed. This includes people outside the organization as well as inside. If you fail to follow through on this step, your subordinate's authority will probably be called into question. Failure to inform others makes conflicts likely and decreases the chances that your subordinate will be able to accomplish the delegated task efficiently.

5. **Establish feedback controls.** There is always the possibility that a subordinate will misuse the discretion that he or she has been delegated. The establishment of controls to monitor the subordinate's progress increases the likelihood that important problems will be identified early and that the task will be completed on time and to the desired specifications.

    Ideally, controls should be determined at the time of the initial assignment. Agree on a specific time for completion of the task, and then set progress dates when the subordinate will report back on how well he or she is doing and any major problems that have surfaced. This can be supplemented with periodic spot checks to ensure that authority guidelines are not being abused, organization policies are being followed, and proper procedures are being met. But too much of a good thing can be harmful. If the controls are too constraining, the subordinate will be deprived of the opportunity to build self-confidence. A well-designed control system permits your subordinate to make small mistakes, but quickly alerts you when big mistakes are imminent.

6. **When problems surface, insist on recommendations from the subordinate.** Many supervisors fall into the trap of letting subordinates reverse the delegation process: the subordinate runs into a problem and then comes back to the supervisor for advice or a solution. Avoid being sucked into reverse delegation by insisting from the beginning that when subordinates want to discuss a problem with you, they come prepared with a recommendation. When you delegate downward, the subordinate's job includes making necessary decisions. Don't allow the subordinate to push decisions back upward to you.

APPLYING YOUR SKILLS

This is a role-playing exercise. Break into groups of four to six students. One student in each group will assume the role of Chris Hall and one the role of Dale Morgan. The other students will serve as observers and evaluators.

Students playing the roles of Chris and Dale should read the Situation and his or her respective role *only*. Observers should read the Situation and *both* roles, and record observations on their Observer's Sheet.

SITUATION

CHRIS HALL is Director of Research and Development for a small pharmaceutical manufacturer. Chris has six direct subordinates: Sue Traynor (Chris's secretary), DALE MORGAN (the laboratory supervisor), Todd Connor (quality standards supervisor), Linda Peters (patent coordination supervisor), Ruben Gomez (market coordination supervisor), and Marjorie England (senior project supervisor). Dale is the most senior of the five supervisors, and is generally acknowledged as the chief candidate to replace Chris when Chris is promoted.

CHRIS HALL'S ROLE

You have received your annual instructions from the CEO to develop next year's budget for your area. The task is relatively routine but takes quite a bit of time. In the past, you've always done the annual budget yourself. But this year, because your workload is exceptionally heavy, you've decided to try something different. You're going to assign budget preparation to one of your supervisors. The obvious choice is Dale Morgan. Dale has been with the company longest, is highly dependable, and, as your probable successor, is most likely to gain from the experience. The budget is due on your boss's desk in eight weeks. Last year it took you about thirty to thirty-five hours to complete. However, you had done a budget many times before. For a novice, it might take double that amount of time.

The budget process is generally straightforward. You start with last year's budget and modify it to reflect inflation and changes in departmental objectives. All the data that Dale will need are in your files or can be obtained from your other supervisors.

You have decided to walk over to Dale's office and inform him/her of your decision.

DALE MORGAN'S ROLE

You like Chris Hall. You think Chris is a first-rate manager and you've learned a lot from him/her. You also consider yourself Chris's heir apparent. To better prepare yourself to take Chris's job, you'd like to take on more of Chris's responsibilities.

Running the lab is a demanding job. You regularly come in around 7:00 a.m. and it's unusual for you to leave before 7:00 p.m. Four of the last five weekends, you've even come in on Saturday mornings to get your work done. But, within reasonable limits, you'd try to find the time to take on some of Chris's responsibilities.

As you sit behind your desk reviewing a lab report, Chris walks into your office.

SKILL APPLICATION—OBSERVER'S SHEET

INSTRUCTIONS

This exercise should take no more than 10 to 15 minutes. When completed, representatives from each group should discuss with the entire class how their delegation exercise went. Focus specifically on the skill behaviours presented in the previous section and any problems that surfaced.

	1 Poor	2	3 Good	4	5 Excellent
1. Chris was clear in defining the assignment—expected results, deadlines	☐	☐	☐	☐	☐
2. Chris specified the range of discretion—guidelines and authority	☐	☐	☐	☐	☐
3. Chris allowed Dale to participate in the delegation process	☐	☐	☐	☐	☐
4. Chris discussed informing others of Dale's involvement	☐	☐	☐	☐	☐
5. Chris established feedback controls—times, sessions	☐	☐	☐	☐	☐

SUMMARY

This summary is organized by the Learning Objectives.

1. Organizing is arranging jobs and groups of jobs in a department so that activities can be accomplished as planned.
2. Division of labour increases economic efficiency by allocating the most difficult and complex tasks to those employees with the highest skill level and paying people less to do the less difficult and less skilled tasks.
3. The narrower the span of control, the more management levels are necessary to directly oversee activities. Wider spans create fewer managerial levels and flatter organization structures.
4. Line authority refers to the right to direct the work of subordinates. Supervisors with staff authority, on the other hand, advise, service, and assist line supervisors in accomplishing their job. So only line authority allows individuals to make decisions independently and without consulting others.
5. Organizations are becoming increasingly decentralized in order to meet competitive challenges through knowledgeable and rapid decision making.
6. Functional departmentalization means that group activities are organized around functions performed—for example, accounting, engineering, manufacturing, personnel, and purchasing.
7. The strength of the matrix is that it provides the economies of functional specialization with the accountability of product departmentalization. Its major weakness is that, because the principle of unity of command is broken, it is difficult to coordinate tasks of people who have more than one manager.
8. Job descriptions 1. provide supervisors with a formal document describing what the employee is supposed to be doing, 2. help employees learn their job duties, and 3. clarify the results that management expects.
9. Delegation consists of 1. allocation of duties, 2. delegation of authority, 3. assignment, and 4. creation of accountability.

KEY TERMS AND CONCEPTS

Accountability	Matrix
Authority	Organizing
Customer departmentalization	Process departmentalization
Delegation	Product departmentalization
Division of labour	Responsibility
Empowerment	Social Loafing
Functional authority	Span of control
Functional departmentalization	Staff authority
Geographic departmentalization	Team
Horizontal structures	Telecommuting
Job description	Unity of command
Line authority	

REVIEWING YOUR KNOWLEDGE

1. What are the limitations, if any, to division of labour?
2. How might wider spans of control lead to cost reductions for an organization?
3. What is functional authority? When is it useful to an organization?
4. What happens when authority and responsibility are out of balance?
5. What are the advantages of a) product, b) geographic, c) customer, and d) process departmentalization?
6. Why would an organization use a matrix structure?
7. Describe the four-step delegation process.
8. Is delegation synonymous with abdication? Discuss.

ANSWERS TO THE POP QUIZZES

1. **d. none of the above.** The idea that jobs should be broken down into the simplest of steps with one step generally assigned to each individual is known as **work specialization** or **division of labour**.

2. The advantages of division of labour relate to economic efficiencies. Skills are developed through repetition, less time is wasted, and training is easier and less costly. The disadvantages of division of labour are potential boredom, fatigue, stress, low productivity, poor quality, increased absenteeism and high turnover.

3. **False.** Early business experts believed top managers should have a smaller span of control.

4. **a. employees potentially have trouble coping with conflicting priorities and demands.** This is one element that early experts wanted to avoid when they identified chain of command. Conflicting priorities and demands create potential problems that can easily be avoided by having unity of command.

5. **a. functional departmentalization.** This question focuses on grouping employees by work specialization.

6. You can group your employees on the basis of function (work being done), product (product or service being generated) customer (group served), geography (location of operations), or process (work flow).

7. **True.** This statement identifies the strengths of the matrix structure, which includes combining the strengths of functional departmentalization (work specialization) and product departmentalization (accountability).

8. **b. A job description involves allocation of duties, assignment of authority, responsibility, and accountability.** Response b) actually describes the process of delegation, and has little to do with defining the term job description.

9. Teams tend to be small; require complementary skills (within the team are needed technical expertise, interpersonal skills, and problem-solving and decision-making skills); must have a common purpose and translate this into specific, measurable and realistic performance goals; agree upon a common approach; and hold members individually and jointly responsible for performance.

10. **True.** People do not need to be friends to work effectively together. Good interpersonal skills will ensure that indifference or dislike towards each other doesn't get in the way of successfully using their technical and problem-solving skills.

11. **d. all of the above**

12. **d. break down overall goals into smaller ones that are easier to achieve.**

PERFORMING YOUR JOB

CASE 5.A

Assessing Needs, Providing Feedback, and Delegating

You are the manager of a produce department in a major grocery store. On a regular basis, you review the performance of your staff with the aim of providing effective feedback to improve their behaviour. This month, you will be reviewing Chris's performance.

Chris is a new employee who has been working in your department for six months. Because Chris worked at another grocery store prior to this one, you felt that the adjustment to your department should have been made quickly. You are now reviewing the notes you have made over the past few months.

October: Chris's knowledge of the various produce items seemed very good. It appeared that on hiring, very little time would be required on product knowledge. Your store does have some specialty items, but Chris should be able to learn the required storage of these items.

December: You asked Chris to set up the display of Asian produce that was in for Christmas. Unfortunately, Chris set the fruits and "veggies" up on an unrefrigerated stand—the majority of the produce was spoiled. You guessed that Chris really didn't know as much about the produce as you assumed.

January: When the produce truck arrived for unloading, you had trouble finding Chris to help. Finally, you found Chris at the other loading dock, moving crates for the deli department. It's hard to criticize such a helpful person, but it seems that Chris is always eager to help anyone outside of your produce department.

January: You overheard a customer ask Chris for star fruit. Chris indicated that the store didn't carry it, even though it was an advertised special this week.

February: Chris seems to be having no problem relating to the other staff! You've heard that half of the female cashiers have dated Chris. Not only that, but girls are forever hanging around the produce area and you just don't believe they are all paying customers.

March: Chris volunteered to work stock one week this month to cover an ill employee. The same week, you had asked Chris to set up the audio-visual display for the advertised special in produce. The a/v was running, but Chris put the wrong product tape in the machine. You appreciate that Chris wants to help out other areas, but what about your department?

March: You're starting to wonder whether Chris can hear at all! It seems that in talking to young people, Chris is able to understand what is being said. But for some reason, he just can't understand your instructions.

RESPONDING TO THIS CASE

Discuss this manager's success in using the six delegation behaviour skills introduced in this chapter. Specifically, consider whether the manager:

1. clarified the assignments;
2. specified the range of discretion;
3. allowed the subordinate to participate;
4. informed others of the delegation;
5. established feedback controls;
6. insisted on recommendations from the subordinate.

Your answer should include:

a) an assessment of the manager's use of the above six skills;

b) your suggestions for better use of the six skills to resolve problems evident in the case.

CASE 5.B

Joan McGinty's New Job

When Joan McGinty went to work at Pampered Pets two years ago, she knew there would be plenty of interesting challenges and opportunities for her. Pampered Pets offered many services and products for their customers. The store had a wide array of pet products, diets, supplies, and equipment—and they were open seven days a week. They had a first-class grooming service and their veterinary services were popular. Their kennels were particularly noted for their personalized pet boarding. They even built specialized dog houses and shipping crates.

During the past year, the company started a pet pick up and delivery service for the convenience of pet owners who wanted to board their pets. The service had become so popular that they recently added a chauffeured "petmobile" limousine as an upscale, luxury service for pet owners who wanted special attention for their pets. When the news media did a special interest story on this new service, it gave the franchise a wonderful opportunity to show off its business and highlight its newest service—in-home pet care.

It was at this time that Joan McGinty was promoted to her new position: supervisor of in-home pet care services. Her job would need to be based on what customers wanted: all-day and all-night pet sitting or intermittent daily pet checking; personalized attention, including walking and playing with the pets; collecting newspapers and mail; watering plants and turning lights on and off; and similar services. Pet owners who would use this service would want to take the worry and stress out of their lives when they were away—and they would not have to infringe on their neighbours' goodwill to be assured that their pets were being well taken care of in their absence.

Joan's first responsibility was to make up a flyer advertising this service. She also knew it was going to be important to identify her own job responsibilities as well as those of the people she would hire, schedule, and supervise. No doubt she would need good organizational skills to provide coordinated services to customers.

RESPONDING TO THIS CASE

1. Draw the organizational chart, reflecting the addition of in-home pet care. Recommend the best reporting relationship for Joan as she heads up this new service.
2. Why is it necessary for Joan to identify her new job tasks and responsibilities? To write up a job description?
3. What tasks do you think Joan will need to do in her new job? How can she best identify these tasks?
4. Using Figures 5-16 and 5-17 as a guide, make a list of tasks that Joan will need to do on her new job. Using this list, make up a job description for Joan. Then, make up a general job description for Joan's potential house-sitters and pet care employees.
5. In groups of five or six, discuss the line and staff authority of this business. What conclusions did your group arrive at? After groups have shared their results with the class, regroup to discuss your original conclusions. On the basis of the class discussion, what conclusions would you draw now?

6

ACQUIRING THE RIGHT PEOPLE

LEARNING OBJECTIVES

After reading this chapter, you should be able to:

1. Identify key laws and regulations affecting human resource practices.
2. Define the three steps in human resource planning.
3. Explain the purpose of the job specification.
4. List the primary sources for job candidates.
5. Discuss the different problems created by accept errors and reject errors.
6. Identify the strengths and weaknesses of the best-known selection devices.

CHAPTER OUTLINE

PERFORMING EFFECTIVELY

SUPERVISORS AND THE HUMAN RESOURCES DEPARTMENT

UNDERSTANDING EQUAL EMPLOYMENT OPPORTUNITY
  Laws and Regulations
  Human Rights Legislation
  Your Role in Employment
    Equity
  EEO Goes Beyond Hiring

DETERMINING STAFFING NEEDS
  Current Assessment
  Pop Quiz
  Future Assessment
  Developing a Future Program

FROM JOB DESCRIPTIONS TO JOB SPECIFICATIONS

RECRUITING CANDIDATES
  Internal Search
  Advertisements
  Employee Referrals
  Employment Agencies
  Schools, Colleges, and
    Universities
  Professional Organizations
  Casual or Unsolicited Applicants
  Unemployment Agencies and
    Centres
  Other Sources

EMPLOYEE SELECTION
  Foundations of Selection
  Selection Devices

NEW-EMPLOYEE ORIENTATION
  *Supervision in Action: The
    Realistic Job Preview*
  Pop Quiz

FROM CONCEPTS TO SKILLS: INTERVIEWING
  Assessing Yourself: Do You
    Have Good Interviewing
    Skills?

Skill Basics
Applying Your Skills

UNDERSTANDING THE BASICS
  Summary
  Key Terms and Concepts
  Reviewing Your Knowledge
  Answers to the Pop Quizzes

PERFORMING YOUR JOB
  Case 6.A: Vance Cupples'
    Job Search
  Case 6.B: London Life

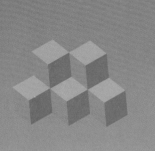

Becky Hannon dreamed of being successful.[1] As a risk taker, she wanted to pursue her individual interests. She ventured into her own business—TechSmart Inc., a software development company.

In the early days of her business, Becky made it a practice to hire family and friends. It wasn't that these individuals were the best qualified to do the jobs. Rather, many just wanted to help her—and Becky needed some workers. Before very long, a number of problems erupted. When certain tasks were needed—sometimes in a rush— some of her employees couldn't get the work done. Often, many weren't at work—they had either left work early, or simply decided to take the day off without notifying anyone. Compounding the problem was the fact that Becky didn't feel comfortable talking to these individuals about her dissatisfaction with their work behaviour. She couldn't bring herself to "play" boss with people with whom she had a personal relationship. She didn't want to hurt anyone's feelings. As a result, the problems continued and were now threatening her company's survival. Becky felt she had no choice but to crack down on her haphazardly selected workforce. Of course, the employees reacted poorly. Several friends and family members quit. She regrets that her personal relationship with most of the people she hired is, at best, strained.

Supervisors, by definition, oversee the work of other people. If supervisors have employees who lack the necesary skills, experience, or motivation, their unit is sure to be underperforming. So supervisors want qualified, high-performing people working for them. But how do they find such people? When they have a vacancy to fill, what can they do to increase the probability that they'll hire a high-performing candidate from among the applicant pool?

In this chapter, we'll address a number of key human resources issues including employee recruitment and selection. Let's start, however, by considering the role of the human resources department in staffing decisions.

SUPERVISORS AND THE HUMAN RESOURCES DEPARTMENT

Some readers may be thinking, "Sure, human resources decisions like recruitment and selection are important, but aren't they made by specialists in the human resources department? These aren't decisions that supervisors get involved in!"

It's true that large organizations have human resources departments. But the people in these departments rarely make specific staffing decisions. Rather, as staff specialists, they help supervisors by writing and placing employment ads, screening applicants, and providing legal advice on various issues. The final decision, typically, is the supervisor's. Moreover, many small organizations don't have human resources departments. In such cases, supervisors typically have sole responsibility for hiring.

Every supervisor will be involved in staffing decisions. So, regardless of the size of your organization or the presence of a human resources department staffed with specialists, there will be certain activities you need to understand. These include, at a minimum, human resources planning, how to conduct employment interviews, and techniques for new-employee orientation. Also, very importantly, every supervisor must have a fundamental understanding of the current laws and regulations governing equal employment opportunity.

UNDERSTANDING EQUAL EMPLOYMENT OPPORTUNITY

Ron Gelber had worked in the lumber business for more than twenty years, but he'd never held a management position before. About five months ago he was hired as a supervisor in the finishing department at a small lumber mill. When he recently had an opening in his department, he interviewed four candidates sent to him by the firm's human resources department. During an interview with one of the applicants, a woman who was not made a job offer, he asked her a number of questions. Two of them were "Are you married?" and "Do you have any children at home?" He didn't, however, ask those questions of the male candidates he interviewed. Ron learned today, from his boss, that this applicant has filed a discrimination suit against him and the company. When Ron's boss asked if it was true that he had asked the woman about her marital status and whether she had children, Ron responded, "Sure. I was concerned she might miss work because of family responsibilities." Ron's boss was shocked. "Let me tell you something, Ron. Regardless of your intentions, you've just gotten yourself and this company into a heck of a mess!"

Ron Gelber broke the law by asking questions of women job candidates that he didn't ask of men, questions that in fact may not even have been job-relevant. In so doing, he made himself and his employer potentially liable for damages.

This example illustrates the importance of every supervisor understanding the law and its effect on human resource practices. For supervisors in large organizations, your organization will undoubtedly provide you with specific guidelines to help ensure that you don't discriminate. You'll also probably have someone in the human resources department to turn to for advice when you face an uncertain situation. For supervisors in small organizations, where there are no formal guidelines or specialists to turn to, you must keep abreast of current laws and make sure your hiring practices are in compliance. When in doubt, you should use outside lawyers or human resource consultants for advice. As we briefly review equal employment opportunity, remember that engaging in discrimination not only exposes you and your organization to potential liability, but also deprives you of hiring the applicant who is most qualified.

LAWS AND REGULATIONS

In Canada, human rights legislation guarantees each person's right to equal opportunity for employment. Depending on your place of employment, your rights to equal treatment at work are protected by either the Federal Human Rights Act or one of the provincial acts. Although the acts vary in the categories they specify for protection, their basic intent is to prevent discrimination on the basis of race, colour, gender, religion, marital status, age or handicap. Additionally, each jurisdiction can specify additional "protected groups." The fundamental intent of all the acts is to protect equal opportunity.

HUMAN RIGHTS LEGISLATION

Human rights legislation protects job applicants from possible discriminating practices by prohibiting various questions. The following guidelines indicate which questions are not allowed on application forms.

Names
• Don't ask for maiden name, Christian name, or name changes.

Addresses
• Don't ask for addresses outside of Canada.

Age
• Don't ask about age or birth date.

FIGURE 6-2

The Nova Scotia Human Rights Act prohibits employers from discriminating against persons 40–65 years of age in any area of employment.

Sex

- Don't ask the applicant to indicate Mr., Mrs., Miss, or Ms.
- Don't ask whether the applicant is male or female.
- Don't ask about pregnancy, children, or family plans.
- Don't ask men and women to fill in different application forms.

Marital Status

- Don't ask if the applicant is married, single, divorced, engaged, separated, widowed, or common-law.
- Don't ask about a spouse.

Family Status

- Don't ask about the number of children or dependents.

National/Ethnic Origin

- Don't ask about birthplace.
- Don't ask about national origin.
- Don't ask if applicant was born in Canada.
- Don't ask if naturalized/landed immigrant.
- Don't ask for proof of citizenship.

Language

- Don't ask about mother tongue.

Race or Colour

- Don't ask any question related to race or colour, including colour of eyes, hair or skin.

Photographs

- Don't ask for photos to be attached or sent before an interview.

Religion

- Don't ask about religious affiliation, membership, or frequency of attendance at religious services.

Height and Weight
- Don't ask!

Disability
- Don't ask about disabilities or health problems.
- Don't ask about substance abuse (alcohol or drugs).
- Don't ask about psychiatric care or problems.

YOUR ROLE IN EMPLOYMENT EQUITY

Many employers will institute employment equity programs, with specific goals, to increase the number of women and minorities in their organization. As a supervisor, you will be asked to actively pursue female and minority candidates and make a good faith effort to get them into the applicant pool.

Does this mean you have to hire an unqualified applicant in order to meet employment equity goals? No! As we'll discuss shortly, before you begin looking to fill a position in your department, you need to know the skills, knowledge, and ability requirements of the job. If candidates meet these criteria, they are qualified. But the law doesn't require you to hire unqualified employees. So you should extend your search for female and minority applicants far and wide—for example, possibly placing ads in papers that are specifically targetted at multicultural groups or sending a notice of your job opening to the local disabled training centre—but you are not forced to hire any individual under this process. The objective of employment equity is to eliminate discrimination, not ensure the hiring of individuals from certain groups.

Employment Equity: A Guide for Employers
http://info.load-otea.
hrdc-drhc.gc.ca/~
weeweb/equity.htm

EEO GOES BEYOND HIRING

Equal employment opportunity goes beyond recruitment and selection of employees. It also addresses issues such as training, promotion, and eliminating discriminatorily abusive work environments.

TRAINING OPPORTUNITIES

Are you making sure *all* of your employees have equal access to training?

Do your employees need special training to learn to understand and work more effectively with individuals who are different from them? As the workforce becomes more culturally diverse, you will want to ensure that women, racial and ethnic minorities, gay employees, and members of any other group who may be perceived as "different" are not treated prejudicially by others. This may require your employees to participate in awareness and sensitivity workshops to help them better understand and work with people who are unlike themselves.

ELIMINATING SEXUAL HARASSMENT

Few workplace topics have received more attention in recent years than that of sexual harassment.

Sexual harassment generally encompasses sexually suggestive remarks, unwanted touching and sexual advances, requests for sexual favours, and other verbal and physical conduct of a sexual nature. It is considered illegal; it is a violation of the human rights legislation.

Courts have widened the test for sexual harassment to whether a comment or behaviour in a work environment "would reasonably be perceived, and is perceived, as hostile or abusive." In so doing, employees need not show they have been psychologically damaged to prove sexual harassment in the workplace, merely that they are working in a hostile or abusive environment.

From a supervisor's standpoint, sexual harassment is a growing concern because it intimidates employees, interferes with job performance, and exposes the organization to liability. To ensure that you do not have a hostile or abusive environment, you must establish a clear and strong position against sexual harassment. If higher management doesn't have a sexual harassment policy, then you need to establish one for your department. The policy should be reinforced by regular discussion sessions in which employees are reminded of the rule and carefully instructed that even the slightest sexual overture to another employee will not be tolerated. In some companies, employees have been specifically advised that they can be fired for making repeated unwelcome sexual advances, using sexually degrading words to describe someone, or displaying sexually offensive pictures or objects at work.

Sexual harassment
Sexually suggestive remarks, unwanted touching and sexual advances, requests for sexual favours, and other verbal and physical conduct of a sexual nature

DETERMINING STAFFING NEEDS

You've organized your department. You've identified the tasks that need to be done and grouped them into jobs. Now you've got to ensure that you'll have the right number and kinds of people to achieve your department's goals. We call this **human resource planning** and it can be condensed into three steps:

1. assessing current human resources
2. assessing future human resource needs
3. developing a program to meet future human resource needs

Human resource planning
Ensuring that a department has the right personnel, who are capable of completing those tasks that help the department reach its objectives

CURRENT ASSESSMENT

Begin your assessment by reviewing your current human resource status. Your goal is to create a departmental human resource inventory.

1. Sexual harassment:
   a. involves only physical conduct between male and female organizational members
   b. does not interfere with job performance
   c. holds the organization liable for the conduct of the supervisor
   d. is relevant only in large organizations
2. The objective of employment equity is to ensure the hiring of individuals from certain groups. True or False?
3. Specific staffing decions:
   a. are typically made by the human resources department
   b. are usually made by the supervisor
   c. are made as a result of multiple employee input
   d. do not have to be concerned about compliance with laws and regulations concerning hiring
4. List some questions that are prohibited in the hiring process because of their potential use for discrimination.

To build this inventory, your employees will complete forms for the human resources department. Increasingly, these files can be accessed by computer. This departmental inventory will typically include a list of your employees' names, education, training, prior employment, languages spoken, capabilities, and specialized skills. When completed, this inventory allows you to assess what talents and skills are available within your department. It lets you know what your individual employees can do.

FIGURE 6-3

"The ability to recognize and foster talent is a critical managerial skill—you're only as good as your people," says John Williams, head of the Burlington Community Development Corporation in Ontario.

FUTURE ASSESSMENT

Future human resource needs are determined by the organization's overall objectives and your departmental goals.

The organization's demand for human resources is directly related to the demand for the organization's products or services. From its estimate of total revenue, top management can attempt to establish the number and mix of human resources needed to reach these revenues. In some cases, the situation may be reversed. Revenues may be determined by human resources if the particular skills are in scarce supply, and are not available in the labour market. In recent years, this has been the case for Microsoft. This designer of computer software has more business opportunities than it can handle. Its primary limiting factor in building revenues has been its ability to locate and hire designers and programmers with the qualifications to write new software. In most cases, however, the overall organizational goals and the revenue forecast provide the major input determining the organization's human resource demand requirements.

Based on forecasts provided by upper management, you can calculate their implications for your department's operations. What will be the increase or decrease in workload? What new or changing skills will be called for?

In searching for new employees, the human resources department at Island Tel, on Prince Edward Island, uses a variety of assessment tools to attract candidates with the following qualities: self-leadership, team playing, ability and willingness to learn, an attitude of self-care and enthusiasm for life and work. These are qualities that Island Tel consider to be essential to their future success.

Island Tel Home Page
http://www.islandtel.
pe.ca/

DEVELOPING A FUTURE PROGRAM

After you've assessed both current capabilities and future needs, you'll be able to estimate shortages—both in number and kind—and to highlight areas in which your department will be overstaffed. Additionally, of course, your departmental projections will need to be combined with forecasts made by other supervisors in your organization and coordinated with the human resources department. This is important because it ensures that you can identify individuals with skills and capabilities that cut across departmental lines.

In addition, as we move to a global economy, supervisors need to consider the possibility of contracting out work to foreign countries. Assigning programming jobs to "software parks" in developing countries is a growing practice in Canada, especially when foreign export laws can result in significant savings.

FROM JOB DESCRIPTIONS TO JOB SPECIFICATIONS

You'll remember from the previous chapter that once your departmental structure is in place, you then create job descriptions. These job descriptions tell employees what they're supposed to do. Another document, closely tied to the job description, is needed before you're ready to begin efforts at recruitment and selection. This document is the job specification.

Job Title: Project Production Editor

Department: College Book Editorial Production

Job Class: 7-12B

Education:
Graduation from an accredited college or university with a specialization in creative writing, English, journalism, or equal.

Knowledge:
No prior knowledge of book production necessary.

Abilities and skills:
Ability to copy edit manuscripts; ability to organize and coordinate multiple projects simultaneously; ability to secure good working relationships with outside vendors; ability to meet deadlines; ability to express ideas clearly and concisely, orally and in writing; strong interpersonal skills; and skill in the use of Macintosh computers.

FIGURE 6-4

Job specification

Job specification
The minimum acceptable qualifications an employee must possess to perform a given job successfully

The **job specification** states the minimum acceptable qualifications an employee must possess to perform a given job successfully. It identifies the knowledge, skills, and abilities needed to do the job effectively. In large organizations, job specifications are written by specialists in the human resources department. In smaller organizations, you may develop these yourself. An example of a job specification for a book production editor is shown in Figure 6-4.

Why is the job specification important? It's the standard against which job applicants will be compared. It keeps your attention focused on the specific necessary and preferred qualifications for an individual to do a job effectively, and it assists you in determining whether candidates are qualified.

Once you've identified a vacancy in your department and have a job specification for that position, you can begin the search for the right candidate to fill that vacancy.

RECRUITING CANDIDATES

If you have a departmental vacancy, where do you look to find potential candidates to fill it? In this section, we'll review the primary sources for job candidates.

INTERNAL SEARCH

Most organizations give preference to current employees for new openings. Employees like this practice because it gives them an advantage over outsiders in applying for lateral transfers and promotions. Managers prefer internal candidates because they are more likely to be able to get detailed and accurate information on how the candidate did on prior jobs within the organization. While outside references are often vague and noncommittal, other managers within your organization can typically provide you with the full history of an internal employee's performance record. In addition, internal candidates are already familiar with the organization. They should therefore take less time to adjust to a new job.

There are several drawbacks to relying on an internal search. First, it provides a limited set of candidates. You wouldn't want to hire a second-rate employee merely because he or she was there, when excellent candidates are available outside the organization. Second, excessive reliance on internal search tends to perpetuate "inbreeding." Internal candidates are less likely to bring new ideas and fresh perspectives to the job. Third, if past hiring decisions were discriminatory, internal hiring will continue to fail the "equal opportunity" test.

ADVERTISEMENTS

The sign outside the plant reads: "Now Hiring—Experienced Machinists." The newspaper advertisement reads: "*Speech Pathologist*. Large urban hospital is looking for a speech pathologist to join our rehabilitation group. Accredited licence required. Minimum of four years experience necessary. Salary to $40 000. Call Ms. Resnick at 579-5060."

Most of us have seen both types of advertisements. When an organization seeks to communicate to the public that it has a vacancy, advertisements are one of the most popular methods.

The higher the position in the organization, or the more specialized the skills sought, the more widely dispersed the advertisement is likely to be. While advertisements for blue-collar jobs are usually confined to the local daily newspaper or regional trade journals, the search for individuals with highly specialized technical skills might include advertisements in a national periodical.

Advertisements are an excellent means of informing a wide audience of a vacancy. Also, by careful selection of the medium for the ad, you can target specific minority groups or individuals with similar interests. The major drawback of advertisements is that, unless ads are very carefully worded, they tend to attract many unqualified candidates. Cost must also be considered.

FIGURE 6-5

(©1990 FatWorks Inc. By permission of Universal Press Syndicate.)

Hopeful parents

EMPLOYEE REFERRALS

One of the best sources of individuals who will perform effectively on the job is a recommendation from a current employee.[2] The reasons are fairly obvious. Employees will rarely recommend someone unless they believe that the referral will perform adequately. Such a recommendation reflects on the recommender and, when someone's reputation is at stake, we can expect the recommendation to be based on relatively strong beliefs. Employee referrals may also have acquired more accurate information about their potential jobs. The recommender often gives the applicant more realistic information about the job than could be conveyed through employment agencies or newspaper advertisements. This information reduces unrealistic expectations. As a result of these preselection factors, employee referrals tend to be more acceptable applicants, to have a greater probability of accepting an offer if one is made, and, once employed, to have a higher job-survival rate.

There are, of course, some potentially negative features of employee referrals. For one thing, recommenders may confuse friendship with job-performance competence. Individuals often like to have their friends join them at their place of employment for social and even economic reasons. For example, they may be able to share rides to and from work. As a

FIGURE 6-6

"I don't run ads for vacancies," says Robert Scott of Southwest Doors. "When I have an opening, one or more of our people will have connections around town. They'll find good people and bring them in."

result, a current employee may recommend a friend for a position without giving unbiased consideration to the friend's job-related competence.

Employee referrals may also lead to nepotism; that is, hiring individuals who are related to persons already employed by the organization. The hiring of relatives is particularly widespread in family-owned organizations. While such actions do not necessarily meet the objective of hiring the most qualified applicant, interest in the organization and loyalty to it may be long-term advantages.

Finally, employee referrals may not help the organization in actively seeking minority and women candidates. Employees often refer someone who shares something with them—religion, demographics, race, etc. Accordingly, an organization that wants to increase the presence of protected groups must guard against over-reliance on employee referrals from members of nonprotected groups.

EMPLOYMENT AGENCIES

Employment agencies can be divided into three categories: full-service agencies, temporary help services, and executive search firms. Since the last type has little relevance to supervisors—they specialize in placing middle-level and top-level executives—we'll focus on the other two.

The typical full-service agency charges for its services. Their fees can be paid by the employer, the applicant, or on a shared basis. These agencies provide a complete line of services. They advertise the position, screen applicants against the criteria specified by the employer, and usually provide a guarantee covering six months or a year as protection to the employer, in case the applicant does not perform satisfactorily.

An increasingly popular type of employment agency is the one that specializes in temporary employees. Organizations such as Kelly and Manpower can be excellent sources of employees to fill part-time or short-term staffing needs. At the dawn of the twenty-first century, as employers look for ways to increase their staffing flexibility and at the same time keep benefit costs down, the use of contingent workers hired through temporary help services is seen as a highly attractive alternative.

Manpower Global
Home Page
http://www.manpower.com/

SCHOOLS, COLLEGES, AND UNIVERSITIES

Educational institutions at all levels offer opportunities for recruiting recent graduates. Most educational institutions operate placement services where prospective employers can review credentials and interview graduates; and many offer internship programs where you can find students who are looking for opportunities to practice on the job what they're learning. Whether the educational qualification required for the job is a high school diploma, specific vocational training, or a university background with a bachelor's, master's, or doctoral degree, educational institutions are an excellent source of potential employees for entry-level positions in organizations.

High schools or vocational-technical schools can provide blue-collar applicants; business or secretarial schools can provide white-collar staff; and colleges and universities can provide technical and professional personnel.

While educational institutions are usually viewed as sources of young, inexperienced entrants to the workforce, it is not uncommon to find individuals with considerable work experience using an educational institution's placement service. They may be workers who have recently returned to school to upgrade their skills, or alumni using their former school's placement centre.

PROFESSIONAL ORGANIZATIONS

Many professional organizations, including labour unions, operate placement services for the benefit of their members and employers. The professional organizations include such varied occupations as accountants, industrial engineers, training specialists, and seafarers.

These organizations publish rosters of job vacancies and distribute these lists to members. It is also common practice to provide placement facilities at regional and national meetings where those looking for employment and companies looking for employees can find each other.

CASUAL OR UNSOLICITED APPLICANTS

"Walk-ins," whether they reach an employer by letter, telephone, or in person, can be a major source of applicants. Although the qualification level of unsolicited applicants can depend on economic conditions, the organization's image, and the job seeker's perception of the types of jobs that might be available, this source does provide an excellent supply of stockpiled applicants. Even if there are no particular openings when the applicant makes contact with the organization, the application can be kept on file for later needs.

Applications from individuals who are already employed can be referred to many months later and can provide applicants who 1. are interested in considering other employment opportunities and 2. regard the organization as a possible employer.

Unsolicited applications made by unemployed individuals, however, generally have a short life. Those individuals who have adequate skills will usually find employment with some other organization that does have an opening. But in tough economic times, excellent prospects are often unable to locate the type of job they desire and may stay actively looking in the job market for some time.

UNEMPLOYMENT AGENCIES AND CENTRES

Provincial unemployment agencies are another source of available workers. These agencies will provide the service of posting vacancies, matching applicants, and prescreening for job openings. Increasingly, computerized files are simplifying the process of matching available workers to the skills required in available jobs.

OTHER SOURCES

In the search for particular types of applicants, nontraditional sources should be considered. For example, Employ the Disabled associations (such as Work Able in Hamilton, Ontario) can be a source of highly motivated workers; a Forty-Plus Club can be an excellent source of mature and experienced workers.

When you want to reach out and expand the diversity among applicants, sources might include urban league offices, local religious organizations, minority-oriented media, schools in low-income neighborhoods, multicultural organizations, and agencies dealing with ex-prisoners.

EMPLOYEE SELECTION

You've developed a pool of applicants. Now you need some method for screening the applicants and for identifying the most appropriate candidate. That screening method is the selection process.

FOUNDATIONS OF SELECTION

Selection is a prediction exercise. It seeks to predict which applicants will be successful if hired. "Successful" in this case means performing well on the criteria the organization uses to evaluate employees. In filling a sales position, for example, the selection process should be able to predict which applicants will generate a high volume of sales for the company.

PREDICTION

Consider, for a moment, that any selection decision can result in four possible outcomes. As shown in Figure 6-8, two of these outcomes would indicate correct decisions, but two would indicate errors.

A decision is correct when the applicant was predicted to be successful and later proved to be successful on the job, or when the applicant was predicted to be unsuccessful and would perform accordingly if hired. In the first case, we have successfully accepted; in the second case, we have successfully rejected. Thus the purpose of selection activities is to develop the outcomes shown as "correct decision" in Figure 6-8.

In selection, a supervisor is open to two different mistakes: reject errors and accept errors.

Reject errors occur when a supervisor eliminates a candidate who would have performed well on the job. The cost of reject errors might be additional recruitment and selection expenses. More significant, and potentially harmful, are the possible claims of discrimination.

Reject errors
Rejecting candidates who would later perform successfully on the job

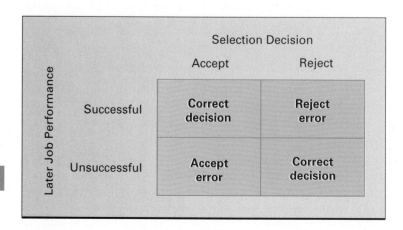

		Selection Decision	
		Accept	**Reject**
Later Job Performance	**Successful**	Correct decision	Reject error
	Unsuccessful	Accept error	Correct decision

FIGURE 6-8

Selection decision outcomes

Accept errors occur when a supervisor selects a candidate who is not able to perform the job successfully. Here, the costs of a poor decision include extra training, productivity losses, possible severance costs, and ultimately additional recruitment and selection costs. The major thrust of any selection activity is therefore to reduce the probability of making reject errors or accept errors, while increasing the probability of making correct decisions.

VALIDITY

Any selection device that a supervisor uses—such as application forms, tests, and interviews—must demonstrate **validity**. That is, there must be a proven relationship between the selection device and some relevant criterion. For example, the law prohibits management from using a test score as a selection device unless there is clear evidence that individuals with high scores on this test outperform, on the job, individuals with low test scores.

The burden is on management to show that any selection device it uses to differentiate applicants is related to job performance. For instance, while management can give applicants an intelligence test and use the results to help make selection decisions, it must be prepared to demon-strate, if challenged, that this intelligence test is a valid measure; that is, that scores on the test are positively related to later job performance.

RELIABILITY

In addition to being valid, a selection device must also demonstrate relia-bility. **Reliability** indicates whether the device measures the same thing consistently. For example, if a test is reliable, any single individual's score should remain fairly stable over time, assuming that the characteristics it is measuring are also stable.

The importance of reliability should be evident. No selection device can be effective if it is low in reliability. That is equivalent to weighing yourself everyday on an erratic scale. If the scale is unreliable—randomly fluctuating, say, ten to fifteen pounds every time you step on it—the results will not mean much. The same applies to selection devices. To be effective predictors, they must possess an acceptable level of consistency.

SELECTION DEVICES

Supervisors can use a number of selection devices to reduce accept and reject errors. The best-known devices include an analysis of the prospect's completed application form, written and performance-simulation tests, interviews, background investigations, and in some cases a physical examination. Let's take a look at each of these devices, noting their respective strengths and weaknesses.

FIGURE 6-9

Dilbert's unique selection technique. (DILBERT® reprinted by permission of United Feature Syndicate Inc.)

THE APPLICATION FORM

Almost all organizations require candidates to fill out an application (see Figure 6-10). The form might ask a prospect to give his or her name, address, and telephone number. At the other extreme, it might be a comprehensive personal history profile, detailing the applicant's activities, skills, and accomplishments. Are these forms valid?

Hard and relevant biographical data that can be verified—for example, rank in graduating class—have been shown to be valid measures of performance for some jobs.[3] Additionally, when application-form items have been appropriately weighted to reflect job relatedness—that is, points are allocated to variables such as education and experience—the device has proven a valid predictor for such varied groups as sales clerks, engineers, factory workers, clerical employees, and technicians. But typically, only a couple of items on the application prove to be valid predictors, and then only for a specific job. Supervisors are encouraged to use weighted applications for selection purposes, but it is critical that application items be validated for each job and that the items be continually reviewed and updated to reflect changes in weights over time.

WRITTEN TESTS

Typical written tests include tests of intelligence, aptitude, ability, and interest. Historically, these written tests were popular selection devices, but there has been a marked decline in their use over the past quarter-century. Why? The reason is that these tests have frequently been characterized as discriminatory, and many organizations have been unable to demonstrate that they're job related. In other words, their validity is low.

Tests in intellectual ability, spatial and mechanical ability, perceptual accuracy, and motor ability have shown to be moderately valid predictors for many semiskilled and unskilled operative jobs in industrial organizations.[4] However, remember the burden is on management to demonstrate that any test used is job-related. Since many of these tests examine characteristics that are considerably removed from the actual performance of the job itself, getting high validity scores has often been difficult across a wide spectrum of jobs. The result has been a decreased use of traditional written tests and increased interest in performance simulation tests.

Job Application

Date: _____

Name: _____
   Last   First   Middle Init.

Address: _____
   Street   City/Town   Prov.   Postal Code

Phone: (____) _____

Employment History: Last 3 Jobs

1. Employer: _____
   Address: _____
   Phone: (____) _____
   Position: _____ Salary/Rate _____

2. Employer: _____
   Address: _____
   Phone: (____) _____
   Position: _____ Salary/Rate _____

3. Employer: _____
   Address: _____
   Phone: (____) _____
   Position: _____ Salary/Rate _____

Education: Post-Secondary

1. School: _____ Degree earned _____
   Address: _____

2. School: _____ Degree earned _____
   Address: _____

Education: Secondary   Degree earned _____

Additional information: _____
_____
_____
_____

FIGURE 6-10

Application form

FIGURE 6-11

PERFORMANCE SIMULATION TESTS

What better way to find out whether an applicant can do a job successfully than by having him or her do it? The logic of this question has resulted in increased usage of performance simulation tests. Undoubtedly, the enthusiasm for these tests lies in the fact that they are based on actual job behaviours rather than on surrogates. The best-known performance simulation test is called **work sampling** and is designed for routine jobs.

Work sampling
A selection device in which job applicants are presented with a miniature replica of a job and are asked to perform tasks central to that job

Work sampling involves presenting applicants with a miniature replica of a job and letting them perform a task or set of tasks that are central to the job. Applicants demonstrate that they possess the necessary talents by actually doing the tasks. By carefully devising work samples, supervisors can determine the knowledge, skills, and abilities needed for each job. Each work-sample element is then matched with a corresponding job-performance element. For instance, for a job that involves computations on a calculator, a work sample would require applicants to make similar computations.

The results from work-sample experiments have generally been impressive.[5] They have almost always yielded validity scores that are superior to those of written aptitude, personality, or intelligence tests.

INTERVIEWS

The interview, along with the application form, is an almost universal selection device. Not many of us have ever gotten a job without one or more interviews. Unfortunately, interviews are typically poorly conducted and result in distorted findings.[6] This doesn't mean that interviews can't provide valid and reliable selection information, but rather that untrained interviewers tend to make common mistakes. For example, interviewers often hold a stereotype of what represents a "good" applicant; they often tend to favour applicants who share the interviewer's own attitudes; the order in which applicants are interviewed often influences evaluations, as does the order in which information is elicited; negative information is given unduly high weight; and interviewers forget much of the interview's content within minutes of its conclusion.

Interviews are widely used and, additionally, tend to be given considerable weight in the final selection decision. As a result, supervisors need to perfect their interviewing skills. In From Concepts to Skills at the end of this chapter, we'll present some specific guidelines to help you conduct effective employment interviews.

BACKGROUND INVESTIGATIONS

Background investigations are of two types: verification of application data and reference checks. The first type has proven to be a valuable source of selection information, whereas the latter is essentially worthless. Let's briefly review each.

Verifying the "facts" given on an application form pays dividends. The reason is that a significant percentage of job applicants—studies indicate upwards of 15 per cent—exaggerate or misrepresent dates of employment, job titles, past salaries, or reasons for leaving a prior position.[7] Confirmation of hard data on the application with prior employers is therefore a worthwhile endeavour.

The reference check is used by many organizations but is extremely difficult to justify. Whether they are work-related or personal, references provide little valid information for the selection decision. Employers are frequently reluctant to give candid evaluations of a former employee's job performance for fear of legal repercussions. In fact, one survey found that only 55 per cent of human resource executives would "always" provide accurate references to a prospective employer. Seven per cent said they would never give an accurate reference![8] Personal references should also be given little weight. Who among us doesn't have three or four friends who will speak in glowing terms about our integrity, work habits, positive attitudes, knowledge, and skills? There just isn't enough variation among personal references for them to provide supervisors with any meaningful selection information.

PHYSICAL EXAMINATIONS

For jobs that require certain physical requirements—for example, police officers, airline pilots, train engineers—the physical examination has some validity. In most cases, nowadays, the physical examination is done for insurance purposes only. Management wants to eliminate insurance claims for injuries or illnesses contracted prior to being hired.

Great care must be taken to ensure that physical requirements are job-related and do not discriminate. Some physical requirements may exclude persons with disabilities, when, in fact, such requirements do not affect job performance. Similarly, the use of height and weight requirements may discriminate against female and some ethnic minority applicants.

NEW-EMPLOYEE ORIENTATION

Orientation
The introduction of a new employee into his or her job and the organization

Once a job candidate has been selected, he or she needs to be introduced to the job and the organization. This introduction is called **orientation**.

The major objectives of orientation are to reduce the initial anxiety all new employees feel as they begin a new job; to familiarize new employees with the job, the work unit, and the organization as a whole; and to facilitate the outsider–insider transition. Job orientation expands on the information the employee received during the recruitment and selection stages. The new employee's specific duties and responsibilities are clarified, as is the way his or her performance will be evaluated. This is also the time to rectify any unrealistic expectations new employees might hold about the job (see Supervision in Action). Work-unit orientation familiarizes the employee with the goals of the work unit, makes clear how his or her job contributes to the unit's goals, and includes introduction to coworkers. Organization orientation informs the new employee about the organization's objectives, history, philosophy, procedures, and rules. This should include relevant human resource policies and benefits such as work hours, pay procedures, overtime requirements, and fringe benefits. A tour of the organization's physical facilities is often part of the organization orientation. Figure 6-12 illustrates an orientation program in one company.

Many organizations, particularly large ones, have formal orientation programs. Such a program might include a tour of the offices or plant, a video describing the history of the organization, and a short discussion with a representative from the human resources department, who describes the organization's benefit programs. Other organizations utilize an informal orientation program in which, for instance, the supervisor assigns the new employee to a senior member of the work unit, who introduces the new employee to immediate coworkers and shows him or her the locations of the rest rooms, cafeteria, coffee machine, and the like.

Supervisors will want to make the integration of the new employee into the organization and department as smooth and as free of anxiety as possible. Successful orientation results in an outsider-insider transition that makes the new member feel comfortable and fairly well adjusted, lowers the likelihood of poor work performance, and reduces the probability of a surprise resignation by the new employee only a week or two into the job.

NEW EMPLOYEE: Kim Hammond, B.Commerce in Marketing, University of Regina, 1994.

JOB TITLE: Assistant Product Planner

DEPARTMENT: Product Planning

8:00 A.M.	Report to Ms. Dennis in Human Resources Department.
8:00 – 9:00 A.M.	Ms. Dennis will: Distribute brochures describing the organization's history, products, and philosophy. Review the organization's overall structure, and the authority structure within the Product Planning department. Review HRM policies and practices.
9:30 – 10:30 A.M.	Mr. Phillips will discuss company benefits. New employee is to fill out health, tax, and other relevant forms.
10:30 – 11:30 A.M.	Tour of main building and auxiliary facilities with Ms. Dennis.
11.30 A.M. – 12:30 P.M.	Lunch with Ms. Dennis and Ms. Cosby (new employee's supervisor).
12:30 P.M. – 3:00 P.M.	Ms. Cosby will: Provide a detailed tour of the Product Planning department. Discuss daily job routine and department policies and rules. Explain job expectations. Introduce new employee to her coworkers.
3:00 P.M. – 5:00 P.M.	New employee is on her own to familiarize herself with her job.

FIGURE 6-12

A new employee orientation schedule

Supervision in *Action*

The Realistic Job Preview

Supervisors who treat the recruiting and hiring of employees as if the applicants must be sold on the job and exposed only to an organization's positive characteristics set themselves up to have a dissatisfied workforce that is prone to high turnover.[9]

Every job applicant acquires, during the hiring process, a set of expectations about the company and about the job for which he or she is being interviewed. When the information an applicant receives is inflated, a number of things happen that have potentially negative effects on the company. First, mismatched applicants who would probably become dissatisfied with the job and quit soon would be less likely to withdraw from the search process. Second, the absence of accurate information builds unrealistic expectations. Consequently the new employees are likely to become quickly dissatisfied—again leading to premature resignations. Third, new hires are prone to become disillusioned and less committed to the organization when they face the "harsh" realities of the job. In many cases, these individuals feel that they were duped or misled during the hiring process and, therefore, may become problem employees.

To increase job satisfaction among employees and reduce turnover, supervisors should provide a **realistic job preview (RJP)**. An RJP includes both positive and negative information about the job and the company. For example, in addition to the positive comments typically expressed in the interview, the candidate would be told of the downside of joining the company. He or she might be told that there are limited opportunities to talk to coworkers during work hours, that promotional advancement is slim, or that work hours fluctuate so erratically that employees may be required to work during typically off hours (nights and weekends). Applicants who have been given a more realistic job preview hold lower and more realistic job expectations for the jobs they'll be performing and are better able to cope with the job and its frustrating elements. The result is fewer unexpected resignations by new employees.

For supervisors, realistic job previews offer a major insight into the selection process. That is, retaining good people is as important as hiring them in the first place. Presenting only the positive aspects of a job to an applicant may initially entice him or her to join the organization, but it may be an affiliation that both parties quickly regret.

5. A human resource inventory is:
   a. a statement of what a current jobholder does, how it is to be done, and the accountabilities of the job
   b. a statement indicating employees' education, capabilities, and specialized skills
   c. a statement of the minimum qualifications required for job candidates to be successful on the job
   d. none of the above
6. What is the difference between reliability and validity? Is reliability alone sufficient for the selection process?
7. Negative information is frequently given more weight in an interview. True or false?
8. Name five of the primary sources for recruiting job candidates.

INTERVIEWING

ASSESSING YOURSELF: DO YOU HAVE GOOD INTERVIEWING SKILLS?

Are the following questions true (T) or false (F)? Circle what you believe is the right answer.

1. On an application form, it's illegal to ask an applicant what foreign languages he or she can read, write, or speak fluently. T F
2. It's illegal to ask an applicant about his or her past work experience. T F
3. It's illegal to ask the full names of an applicant's dependents. T F
4. It's illegal to ask an applicant's height and weight. T F
5. It's a good idea to tape record or takes notes during an interview. T F
6. A good interviewer takes control of an interview and does most of the talking. T F
7. An interviewer should avoid asking questions that can be answered with a simple yes or no. T F
8. Early in the interview, you should provide the applicant with as much detail about the job being interviewed for as possible. T F

SCORING INSTRUCTIONS

Questions 3, 4, 5, and 7 are true. Questions 1, 2, 6, and 8 are false. If you got seven or eight correct, you already have some understanding of how to conduct an effective selection interview.

SKILL BASICS

In conducting an employment interview, you're trying to get answers to three questions:

1. Can the applicant do the job?

2. Is the applicant motivated to do the job?

3. Will the applicant fit into your work group and organization? Everything you do regarding the interview—from preparation to closure—should help you to answer these three questions.

Interviewing is difficult because it is, in effect, an art. Developing the art of the interview is learning what to do and how to do it. Then it's a matter of practice to ensure your interviewing skills don't become stale from lack of use.

STEPS IN PRACTICING THE SKILL

This list summarizes the key actions in preparing for and conducting an interview.

1. **Review job description and job specification.** Reviewing pertinent information about the job provides valuable information about what you'll assess the candidate on. Furthermore, relevant job requirements help to eliminate interview bias.

2. **Prepare a structured set of questions to ask all applicants for the job.** By having a set of prepared questions, you ensure that the information you wish to elicit is attainable. Furthermore, by asking similar questions, you are able to better compare all candidates' answers to a common base.

3. **Prior to meeting a candidate, review his or her application form and résumé.** This helps you create a complete picture of the candidate in terms of what is represented on the résumé/application and what the job requires. You will also begin to identify areas to explore in the interview. Areas not clearly defined on the résumé/application that are essential for your job should become a focal point in your discussion with the candidate.

4. **Open the interview by putting the applicant at ease and providing a brief preview of the topics to be discussed.** Interviews are stressful for job candidates. By opening with small talk (e.g., the weather or the traffic) you give the candidate time to adjust to the interview setting. By providing a preview of topics to come, you are giving the candidate an "agenda." This helps the candidate to begin framing what he or she will say in response to your questions.

5. **Ask your questions and listen carefully to the applicant's answers.** Select follow-up questions that naturally flow from the answers given. Focus on the responses as they relate to information

you need to ensure that the candidate meets your job requirements. Any uncertainty you may have requires a follow-up question to further probe for the information.

6. **Close the interview by telling the applicant what's going to happen next.** Applicants are anxious about the status of your hiring decision. Be upfront with the candidate regarding others who will be interviewed and the remaining steps in the hiring process. If you plan to make a decision in two weeks or so, let the candidate know. Additionally, tell the applicant how you will respond to him or her about your decision.

7. **Write your evaluation of the applicant while the interview is still fresh in your mind.** Don't wait until the end of your day, after interviewing several candidates, to write your analysis of a candidate. Memory can fail you! The sooner after an interview you complete your write-up, the better chance you have of accurately recording what occurred in the interview.

APPLYING YOUR SKILLS

1. Break into groups of three.

2. Spend up to ten minutes writing up to five challenging job-interview questions that you think would be relevant in the hiring of new college graduates for a sales-management training program at Procter & Gamble. Each hiree will spend eighteen to twenty-four months as a sales representative calling on retail grocers. After this training period, successful candidates can be expected to be promoted to the position of district sales supervisor.

3. Exchange your five questions with another group.

4. Each group should allocate one of the following roles to their three members: interviewer, applicant, and observer. The person playing the applicant should rough out a brief résumé of his or her background and experience, then give it to the interviewer.

5. Role-play a job interview. The interviewer should include, but not be limited to, the questions provided by the other group.

6. When completed, the observer should evaluate the interviewer's behaviours in terms of the skills presented in this section.

SUMMARY

This summary is organized by the Learning Objectives.

1. All employees in Canada are protected by either federal or provincial human rights legislation. Depending on the jurisdiction, different acts specify "protected groups" with the intention of guaranteeing equal employment opportunity.

2. The three steps in human resource planning are assessing current human resources, assessing future human-resource needs, and developing a program to meet future human-resource needs.

3. The job specification, which states the minimum acceptable qualifications that an applicant needs for a job, guides supervisors in recruitment and selection by establishing the standard against which job applicants can be compared.

4. The primary sources for job candidates are an internal search; advertisements; employee referrals; employment agencies; schools, colleges, and universities; professional organizations; casual or unsolicited applicants; and nontraditional sources such as disabled and women's organizations.

5. Accept errors increase the costs to employers in the following areas: training, lost productivity, possible severance, and the recruiting and selection costs to find a replacement. Reject errors increase the number of candidates that must be screened. Additionally, they can subject the organization to charges of discrimination if members from protected groups are systematically rejected from jobs for which they are actually qualified.

6. Hard and relevant data on an application form have been shown to provide valid information, but care must be taken not to ask for information that isn't job-relevant. Some written tests demonstrate moderate validity, but they place a burden on management to support job-relatedness. Work samplings are expensive but tend to yield high validity scores. Interviews are widely used and people have confidence in them, but they are typically poorly conducted and result in distorted findings. Verification of facts on an application form is a worthwhile endeavour but reference checks provide little valid information. Physical exams as selection tools are relevant for only a small portion of jobs and care must be taken not to discriminate on the basis of physical requirements.

KEY TERMS AND CONCEPTS

Accept errors   Reliability
Human resource planning   Sexual harassment
Job specification   Validity
Orientation   Work sampling
Reject errors

REVIEWING YOUR KNOWLEDGE

1. Why do supervisors need to know the basics of employee recruitment and selection?
2. Contrast job specifications with job descriptions.
3. Why might advertisements be effective as a recruitment source?
4. Why are employee referrals called "one of the best sources" for job applicants?
5. Explain the importance of validity in a selection device.
6. Explain the importance of reliability in a selection device.
7. Why are work samples more likely to be valid than written tests as selection devices?
8. Why should a supervisor spend time orienting a new employee?

ANSWERS TO THE POP QUIZZES

1. **c. holds the organization liable for the conduct of the supervisor.** Anything of a sexual nature, where it is a condition of employment, has an employment consequence, or creates an offensive or hostile environment, is sexual harassment. Sexual harassment conduct by supervisors toward their employees can make the organization liable for their actions.

2. **False.** The objective of employment equity is to eliminate discrimination. It wishes to ensure fair treatment of all individuals.

3. **b. are usually made by the supervisor.** Although the human resources department may help by writing and placing ads and screening applicants, the final decision, typically, is the supervisor's.

4. How old are you? Are you married. Do you have children? How old are they? Your religion? Any health problems?

5. **b. a statement indicating employees' education, capabilities, and specialized skills.** This response reflects the definition of a human resource inventory.

6. Reliability reflects consistency. Validity reflects job relatedness. While a selection device can be consistently applied, it is risky if it doesn't measure something that is directly related to successful job performance.

7. **True.** Giving negative information undue weight in an interview is one of the problems that can lead to a distortion of interview findings.

8. Primary sources for recruiting job candidates include current employees, advertisements, employee referrals, employment agencies, colleges and universities, professional organizations, and employment centres.

CASE 6.A

Vance Cupples' Job Search

At the end of next semester, Vance Cupples will be graduating from Concordia College in Alberta. While attending school he has worked part-time at The Bay. He is glad he took the part-time job because not only has he learned new skills on the job, but it is likely he will be offered a full-time position there. Because Vance wants to continue learning, he feels he should also check out other career and extended learning options.

Vance's management teacher suggested he start his job search about a year before he intends to graduate. Indeed, he has found this to be very sound advice and has completed a placement file at the College. Vance has prepared several résumés outlining his background and skills. He quickly realized that just one résumé did not "do him justice" for all job vacancies. For example, in one position he highlighted the computer skills he has acquired because the job announcement stressed computer competence. For another opening, he outlined his active involvement and leadership abilities in campus student organizations. He also listed the supervisory experience he gained in his current job and two previous jobs—even though these jobs were part-time.

Vance has found there are many different ways to pursue a job search. He has found, too, that businesses use several methods for seeking qualified employees. He has responded to newspaper advertisements in the *Edmonton Examiner* and has signed up at employment agencies. He has contacted a management referral agency and has joined a regional professional organization and a community civic group. He has made a lot of friends through these contacts and is surprised at the network that has already developed for job leads. He has attended several initial interviews and has had a couple of second interviews. The job offers he has already received make him glad he started his job search early. He has found job hunting a challenge, and it is now decision time.

RESPONDING TO THIS CASE

1. In planning and implementing a systematic job search, what are the advantages for Vance as well as for the supervisors and human resources managers who have interviewed him?
2. Contrast the pros and cons of Vance staying at The Bay versus seeking a position elsewhere. Why might The Bay want to hire Vance over an outside candidate?
3. Why is the recruitment process difficult for a supervisor?
4. Research each of the recruiting mechanisms (newspaper and magazine advertisements, employment agencies, etc.) that are available to Vance and write a paper on the positive and negative aspects of each. Add your opinions and your recommendations to your paper. Be prepared to share the results with your class.

CASE 6.B

London Life

When Wendy Nihill applied to work at London Life, she knew their recruitment process was recognized internationally for its integrity and success in identifying good candidates. After being through the "process," she now feels that her impatience with what appeared to be a prolonged process was well worth the reward of working with top professionals who are proud to be working at London Life.

Initially approached by a London Life employee who recognized Wendy's professional manner in dealing with customers, she was referred to the recruiting manager of a Burlington, Ontario, office. Wendy then began a five-step process towards the offer to hire from London Life.

Step 1 Wendy was interviewed by the Burlington Staff Manager, who focused on general career interests, personal talents, aptitude, and sales knowledge. In addition, all candidates were given a career profile test to determine their perception of the industry.

Step 2 The regional Sales Manager and the Burlington Staff Manager conducted a more in-depth interview to determine her motivation to be a London Life representative, her communication skills, and her ability to "think on her feet."

Step 3 Career Presentation 1: Wendy met again with the Branch Staff Manager to discuss her career with London Life, the building steps, and greater disclosure on job expectations, career growth, and company operating practices.

Step 4 Career Presentation 2: A meeting with the two managers (Branch and Staff). This interview provided full disclosure of compensation, benefits, and taxation, and reviewed Wendy's personal budget to determine if the fixed earning of her first position was suitable. At this stage, the licensing program was discussed, with information for Wendy to review at home to determine if she wanted to pursue the licensing requirements. Wendy also spent a day in an unassigned territory with the manager as he demonstrated a rep's daily activities.

Step 5 This interview would be scheduled only after successful performance on the licensing exam. During the time that Wendy was preparing for the licensing exam, London Life provided tests every two weeks, as well as two mock exam exercises to help her prepare. (London Life does not offer employment until successful licensing by the Insurance Commission of Ontario.) At that point, Wendy's start date was confirmed, her compensation package was documented, and discussion began on available territories that might ultimately be assigned to her.

This professional, extended recruiting process fits in with the mission of London Life:

> Our business is personalized financial security. By meeting customer needs better than our competitors, we will lead our industry in Canada. We recognize that corporate integrity and superior service are essential in serving our individual and business customers. Everything we do supports our mission.

RESPONDING TO THIS CASE

1. List the advantages for London Life and the candidate that would support the length, and therefore cost, of this company's recruitment process.
2. Discuss how London Life's recruitment process enhanced the reliability and validity of their choices in hiring new employees.
3. Why would London Life be willing to spend time and money to help with the licensing exam, when at that point, the candidates are not their employees?
4. Does London Life's process adhere to legislation affecting recruitment? Why?

7

APPRAISING EMPLOYEE PERFORMANCE

LEARNING OBJECTIVES

After reading this chapter, you should be able to:

1. Contrast the three purposes of the performance appraisal.
2. Differentiate formal and informal performance appraisals.
3. Describe key legal concerns in performance appraisals.
4. Identify the three most popular sets of criteria that supervisors appraise.
5. Contrast absolute and relative standards.
6. Describe the graphic rating scale.
7. Explain the recent interest in behaviourally anchored rating scales.
8. List human errors that can distort performance appraisal ratings.
9. Identify the three variables that most often result in employee performance deficiencies.

CHAPTER OUTLINE

PERFORMING EFFECTIVELY

THE PURPOSE OF THE EMPLOYEE PERFORMANCE APPRAISAL

WHEN SHOULD APPRAISALS BE MADE?

THE SUPERVISOR'S ROLE IN PERFORMANCE APPRAISAL
  Will You Be the Sole Appraiser?
  What Forms or Documentation Does the Organization Provide?
  Setting Performance Expectations
  Providing Performance Feedback

LEGAL ISSUES IN PERFORMANCE APPRAISALS

WHAT DO WE APPRAISE?
  Pop Quiz
  Individual Task Outcomes
  Behaviours
  Traits

GATHERING PERFORMANCE DATA

PERFORMANCE APPRAISAL METHODS
  Absolute Standards
  Relative Standards
  Objectives

HURDLES IN THE WAY OF EFFECTIVE APPRAISALS
  Leniency Error
  Halo Error
  Something to Think About
  Similarity Error
  Recency Error
  Central Tendency Error
  Inflationary Pressures

OVERCOMING THE HURDLES
  Continually Document
    Employee Performance

Use Behaviourally Based Measures
Combine Absolute and Relative Standards
Use Multiple Raters
Rate Selectively
Participate in Appraisal Training

WHAT ABOUT TEAM PERFORMANCE APPRAISALS?

NOW WHAT? RESPONDING TO PERFORMANCE PROBLEMS
  What Do You Need to Know about Counselling Employees?
  Supervision in Action: Performance Appraisals in Contemporary Organizations
  Is Your Action Ethical?
  Pop Quiz

FROM CONCEPTS TO SKILLS: CONDUCTING THE APPRAISAL REVIEW INTERVIEW
  Assessing Yourself: Conducting the Appraisal Interview
  Skill Basics
  Applying Your Skills

UNDERSTANDING THE BASICS
  Summary
  Key Terms and Concepts
  Reviewing Your Knowledge
  Answers to the Pop Quizzes

PERFORMING YOUR JOB
  Case 7.A: Operating from Home Base
  Case 7.B: Cutting Costs at Great Western

"I know it's wrong," remarked Gunther Brink. "I know I should conduct performance appraisals of my people at least once a year, probably more often. But I don't. As long as my boss doesn't get on my case, I sort of ignore them. The reason is that when I do appraisals and give people feedback, we almost never agree. Everybody thinks they're doing an above average job. How can *everybody* be above average? If I believed their self-appraisals, I'd have only three kinds of people working for me—stars, all-stars, and superstars!"

Gunther Brink's comments capture the reason why a lot of supervisors find appraising employee performance to be one of their most difficult tasks. In this chapter, we'll review the performance appraisal and provide you and the Gunther Brinks of this world with some techniques that can make the appraisal and performance review a less traumatic experience.

THE PURPOSE OF THE EMPLOYEE PERFORMANCE APPRAISAL

Twenty-five years ago, the typical supervisor would sit down annually with his or her employees, individually, and critique their job performance. The purpose was to review how well they did toward achieving their work goals. Those employees who failed to achieve their goals found the performance appraisal to result in little more than their supervisor documenting a list of their shortcomings. And, of course, since the performance appraisal is a key determinant in pay adjustments and promotion decisions, anything to do with appraising job performance struck fear into the hearts of employees. Not surprisingly, in such a climate supervisors often wanted to avoid the whole appraisal process.

Performance appraisal
An evaluation and development tool. Reviewing past performance to identify accomplishments and deficiencies; and creating detailed plans to improve future performance.

Today, effective supervisors treat the **performance appraisal** as both an evaluation tool and a development tool. It reviews *past* performance—emphasizing positive accomplishments as well as deficiencies. In addition, supervisors use the performance appraisal as a means of helping employees improve *future* performance. If deficiencies are found, the supervisor can help employees draft a detailed plan to correct the situation. With emphasis on the future as well as the past, employees are less likely to respond defensively to performance feedback, and the appraisal process is more likely to motivate employees to correct their performance deficiencies. Finally, the performance appraisal functions as an important legal document. Taking action against an employee for poor performance can create a problem if the problem is not well documented, and the performance evaluation serves a vital purpose in providing the documentation necessary for any personnel action that is taken.

**Ethics Connection –
The Case of the
Performance Appraisal**
http://www.scu.edu/
Ethics/dialogue/candc/
cases/performance.shtml

WHEN SHOULD APPRAISALS BE MADE?

The performance appraisal is both a formal and an informal activity. *Formal performance reviews* should be conducted once a year at a minimum. Twice a year is better. Just as students don't like to have their entire course grade hanging on the results of one final exam, neither do employees appreciate having their careers depend on an annual review. Two formal reviews a year means less "performance" will be appraised at each review, and lessens the tension employees often associate with the formal review.

The *informal performance appraisal* refers to the day-to-day assessment a supervisor makes of an employee's performance, and the ongoing feedback the supervisor gives to the employee. The effective supervisor continually provides informal information to employees—commenting on the positive aspects of their work and pointing out any problems that surface. So while formal reviews may occur only one or twice a year, informal reviews should be taking place all the time. Moreover, when the informal feedback has been open and honest, the formal reviews will probably be less threatening to the employee and won't present any great surprises.

FIGURE 7-1

"At London Life, we do an annual performance appraisal every October," says Cheryl Munro Sharp. "But new employees get appraised after six months; that gives me a chance to talk to them about how they're doing on the job and identify any problems before they become real problems."

THE SUPERVISOR'S ROLE IN PERFORMANCE APPRAISAL

How much latitude do supervisors have in the appraisal process? The larger the organization, the more likely there will be standardized forms and procedures to follow. But, as you'll see in the next section, even small companies will tend to standardize some appraisal procedures in order to ensure that equal employment opportunity requirements are met.

WILL YOU BE THE SOLE APPRAISER?

Historically, the supervisor was the only performance evaluator of his or her employees. In fact, about ninety-five percent of all employee performance appraisals are conducted by supervisors.[1] But supervisors aren't always the sole source of pertinent performance information about employees. Employees themselves often have valuable insights to provide. So, too, do their peers. Hence, in recent years, some organizations have added self-evaluations and peer evaluations to those made by the supervisor.

Self-evaluations get high marks from employees themselves, tend to lessen employees' defensiveness about the appraisal process, and make excellent vehicles for stimulating job performance discussions between employees and their supervisors. Self-assessment should be treated as enhancing the supervisor's evaluation rather than replacing it. The use of self-evaluations, however, is fully consistent with the view of performance appraisal as a developmental rather than a purely evaluative tool.

For some elements of an employee's job, peers are better at judging performance than is the employee's supervisor. In some jobs, for instance, supervisors don't regularly observe their employee's work because their span of control is quite large or because of physical separation. If work is done in teams, the team members are often better at evaluating each other than any supervisor because they have a more comprehensive view of each member's job performance. In such instances, supplementing supervisory appraisals with peer evaluations can increase the accuracy of the appraisal process.

WHAT FORMS OR DOCUMENTATION DOES THE ORGANIZATION PROVIDE?

Most organizations require supervisors to use a standardized form to guide them in doing their performance appraisals. In some cases, top management or the human resources department will provide an abbreviated form and allow you considerable freedom in identifying and assessing job performance factors. At the other extreme, some organizations provide detailed forms and instructions that all supervisors and managers must follow (see, for example, Figure 7-2).

Our point is that supervisors rarely have complete discretion in evaluating the people who report to them. So begin by reviewing any standard forms that your organization uses for appraisals. Familiarize yourself with the information you'll be expected to provide and make sure all the people reporting to you—especially new employees—understand how and on what criteria they will be evaluated.

SETTING PERFORMANCE EXPECTATIONS

Every supervisor should be involved in determining performance standards for their employees. This principle ties back to our discussion of MBO and goal setting in Chapter 2.

Ideally, a supervisor and subordinate should jointly review the subordinate's job, identify the processes and results needed, and then determine performance standards that will define how well the results are being accomplished. Remember, before an employee's performance can be appraised, there must exist some standard against which the appraisals can be made. Supervisors must ensure that performance expectations have been defined for every employee and that employees fully understand these expectations.

PROVIDING PERFORMANCE FEEDBACK

Employees can receive performance feedback in one of two forms: it can be provided intrinsically by the work itself, or given extrinsically by a supervisor or some other external source.

In some jobs, employees regularly get feedback on how well they're doing, because the feedback is built into the job. For example, a factory worker who assembles a CD player and tests it to determine if it operates properly gets self-generated feedback on her work. Similarly, a freight clerk in a shipping department at a trucking company keeps an ongoing tally of the number of boxes he packs and the weight of each. At the end of the day, he totals the numbers and compares them to his daily goals. These calculations provide him with self-generated or **intrinsic feedback** on how he did that day.

Extrinsic feedback is provided to an employee by an outside source. If the previously mentioned factory worker routes the completed CD player on to a quality control inspector, who tests it for proper operation and makes needed adjustments, her performance feedback is extrinsic. If the freight clerk's shipping totals are calculated each day by his supervisor and posted on the department's bulletin board, his performance feedback is also extrinsic.

Center for Employee Development Home Page
http://www.
centerpointsystems.com/

Intrinsic feedback
Self-generated feedback on performance provided by the work itself

Extrinsic feedback
Performance feedback provided by an outside source

REGENTS/PRENTICE HALL
NON-EXEMPT PERFORMANCE
APPRAISAL

EMPLOYEE NAME: _____ TITLE: _____

REVIEW PERIOD: _____ — _____
Month/Year   Month/Year

SUPERVISOR'S NAME: _____ TITLE: _____

SIMON & SCHUSTER
A PARAMOUNT COMMUNICATIONS COMPANY

Writing the Appraisal
Performance Ratings

E Exceptional — Consistently exceeds expectations in major areas of responsibility.

C Commendable — Performs the job as it is defined and exceeds expectations in some of the major areas of responsibility.

I Improvement Recommended — Meets minimum requirements in most areas, but needs improvement in select areas of responsibility.

U Unsatisfactory — Does not meet minimum performance requirements. Must improve if present position is to be maintained.

PERFORMANCE FACTORS

Rate employee in each performance category. Include supporting examples for each performance factor.

E = EXCEPTIONAL
C = COMMENDABLE
I = IMPROVEMENT RECOMMENDED
U = UNSATISFACTORY

Performance Factors	E	C	I	U	Comments and Supporting Examples
Quality Consider accuracy, comprehensiveness and orderliness of work					
Quantity Consider speed and volume of work produced					
Initiative Consider the ability to think independently with minimal direction and apply new concepts and techniques					
Job Knowledge Consider the understanding of the job and the ability to apply knowledge and skills effectively					
Problem Solving/ Decision Making Consider the ability to identify, analyze and solve problems, suggest viable alternatives and analyze impact of decisions before executing them					
Judgment Consider the ability to make logical and sound decisions and to know when to act independently or to seek assistance					

Performance Factors	E	C	I	U	Comments and Supporting Examples
Punctuality Consider adherence to the work schedule and promptness in notifying supervisor of absence					
Planning and Organizational Skills Consider the ability to establish priorities, maintain schedules and manage time effectively					
Communication Consider the ability to express oneself clearly, both verbally and in writing, and to listen well					
Interpersonal Skills Consider the ability to interact diplomatically and tactfully with internal and external contacts					
Dependability Consider adherence to the work schedule, the ability to maintain confidentiality, complete work under deadlines, follow through on assignments, and be reliable and flexible					
Job Skills Consider skills in areas such as typing/word processing, computer, telephone, etc.					

OVERALL PERFORMANCE RATING

___ Exceptional   ___ Commendable   ___ Improvement Recommended   ___ Unsatisfactory

FIGURE 7-2

Employee appraisal form

PERFORMANCE SUMMARY

I. Performance vs. Goals for Past Year:

    Describe how the employee met stated goals for past year and met additional goals if applicable.

II. Goals for Upcoming Year:

    List quantifiable goals with timetables for completion.

PERFORMANCE SUMMARY

III. Strengths

    Identify employee unique strengths in relation to performance factors previously listed.

IV. Areas for Improvement

    Identify areas in which employee can focus to achieve improved performance.

PERFORMANCE SUMMARY

V. Personal Growth and Development

    Describe activities to be undertaken that will maximize the employee's career development. These may include educational programs, counseling, on-the-job training, etc.

_____   _____
Supervisor's Signature   Date

EMPLOYEE'S COMMENTS
Your comments are beneficial to the performance appraisal process. Additional comments may be attached on a separate page if desired.

THE EVALUATION AND COMMENTS WERE DISCUSSED WITH THE EMPLOYEE

Employee's Signature and date	
Supervisor's Signature and date	Title

FIGURE 7-2

continued

FIGURE 7-3

These shipping employees at a chemical plant record their data, which will be tallied by their supervisor and posted the next day for extrinsic feedback.

FIGURE 7-4

As supervisor of an Oakville, Ontario, child care centre which is also a training centre for Early Childhood Education students, Pat Tretjack must give effective feedback to students as well as staff.

Every supervisor should provide his or her employees with ongoing extrinsic feedback, even if their jobs are rich in the intrinsic variety. This aim can be accomplished through informal performance reviews—ongoing comments that let an employee know how he or she is doing—and through formal performance reviews on a semiannual or annual basis.

LEGAL ISSUES IN PERFORMANCE APPRAISALS

A great many lawsuits have arisen because supervisors said or did something that their employees believed adversely affected them. For instance, a supervisor told an employee that he had downgraded the employee's evaluation because he had taken off work for religious holidays; another employee argued that her supervisor's appraisals were arbitrary and based on subjective judgments; and a third employee was awarded damages because his supervisor failed to follow the company's performance appraisal policies and procedures.

Maybe the two most important legal facts you need to keep in mind concerning performance appraisals are:

1. Performance appraisal policies and procedures, as set forth in organizational handbooks, are being increasingly construed by the courts as binding unilateral contracts; and
2. You must do everything possible to avoid prejudice and discrimination.

Does your company have a published handbook that describes its performance appraisal procedures? If so, the courts in most provinces consider it a binding contract. The organization can be held accountable if those procedures are not followed or are followed improperly. If the handbook states, for instance, that appraisals must be performed annually or that supervisors will counsel employees to correct deficiencies, then you are obliged to fulfill these commitments. On the other hand, the courts have generally supported giving supervisors a wide range of discretion when their organizations have no published performance appraisal policies, so long as fairness and equity are not compromised. So, if your organization has a published handbook that covers its policies on performance appraisal, make sure you fully understand its contents.

The second point above reminds us that human rights laws require that all human resource practices be bias-free—including employee performance appraisals. The appraisal criteria, methods, and documentation must be designed to ensure that they are job-related. They must not create an unfair impact on any protected group. For instance, appraisal judgments must be neutral regarding an employee's race, colour, religion, age, sex, or national origin. An increasing number of organizations are providing supervisory training in the mechanics of performance appraisal specifically to minimize the likelihood that discrimination might occur in the appraisal process.

Another issue that supervisors need to be aware of is the potential charge of defamation of character. Under the law, "qualified privilege" allows you as a supervisor to point out performance problems. In law, it is your duty to honestly, without malicious intent, inform employees of unsatisfactory performance. Your duty may also be extended to other company supervisors who are considering promotions or transfers of employees who are not fulfilling their job requirements.

WHAT DO WE APPRAISE?

The criteria that supervisors choose to appraise when evaluating employee performance will have a major influence on what employees do. For instance, in an employment agency that served workers seeking employment and employers seeking workers, employment interviewers were appraised by the number of interviews they conducted. Consistent with the thesis that the evaluation criteria influence behaviour, the interviewers tended to focus on the number of interviews they conducted rather than the placement of clients in jobs.[2]

The preceding example demonstrates the importance of criteria in performance appraisal. This, of course, begs the question: What should supervisors appraise? The three most popular sets of criteria are individual task outcomes, behaviours, and traits.

1. A performance appraisal can be used:
   a. as a criterion against which the effectiveness of a selection device can be evaluated
   b. to determine if employees are in need of training
   c. to demonstrate compliance with equal employment opportunity regulations
   d. all of the above
2. What is the difference between intrinsic and extrinsic feedback?
3. You and each employee should jointly review the employee's job, identify what needs to be done, and establish performance standards that will define how well the results are accomplished. True or False?
4. Which one of the following statements is correct regarding the legal implications of performance evaluations?
   a. Supervisors are concerned with documenting performance appraisals because the courts are more closely examining policies and procedures.
   b. Supervisors are concerned with documenting performance appraisals because documentation can demonstrate that the process was proper and bias-free.
   c. Supervisors are concerned with documenting performance appraisals because they want to ensure that performance is evaluated on job-related criteria.
   d. All of the above

INDIVIDUAL TASK OUTCOMES

If the ends count, rather than the means, then supervisors should evaluate an employee's task outcomes. If task outcomes were used, a carpet cleaner might be judged on the number of square yards he was able to clean per day. A salesperson could be assessed on overall sales volume in her territory, dollar increase in sales, and number of new accounts established.

Behaviours

Evaluating employees on behaviour requires the opportunity to observe employees or devise a system for reporting to you on specific behaviour criteria. Using the previous examples, behaviours of a carpet cleaner that could be used for performance appraisal purposes might include promptness in reporting to work sites or thoroughness in cleaning equipment at the end of the work day. Pertinent behaviours for the salesperson could be average number of contact calls made per day or sick days used per year.

In many cases, it is difficult to identify specific outcomes that can be directly attributable to an employee's actions. This is particularly true of personnel in staff positions and individuals whose work assignments are intrinsically part of a group effort. In the latter case, the group's performance may be readily evaluated, but the contribution of each group member may be difficult or impossible to identify clearly. In such instances, it is not unusual to appraise the employee's behaviour.

Traits

When you rate people on the degree to which they are dependable, confident, aggressive, loyal, cooperative, and the like, you are judging traits. Experts seem to agree that traits are inferior to both task outcomes and behaviours as appraisal criteria.[3] The reason is that traits refer to potential *predictors* of performance, not performance itself. So the link between traits and job performance is often weak. Additionally, traits typically have a strong subjective component. What, for instance, does *aggressive* mean? Is the meaning "pushy," "dominating," or "assertive?" Your evaluation of someone on this trait is largely determined by what the term means to you. Despite the drawbacks of traits, they are still widely used in organizations for appraising employee performance.

GATHERING PERFORMANCE DATA

Once performance standards have been set, expectations communicated, and appraisal criteria defined, you need to gather performance data. This is an activity every supervisor can and should do.

The best approach is to gather performance data on a continuous basis. Don't wait until a week or so before the appraisal interview. You should keep an ongoing journal for each of your employees, in which you record actual incidents (behaviours and/or outcomes) that affect his or her job success or failure. Such documentation reduces the potential for errors caused by relying on your memory of recent events, and provides

FIGURE 7-5

Many organizations still place a high importance on traits such as effort and dependability in their appraisal system.

supportive evidence to back up your eventual ratings. Remember that the more opportunities you have to observe your employee's behaviour at first hand, the more accurate your performance appraisals are likely to be.

PERFORMANCE APPRAISAL METHODS

Once you have your data, you can begin your actual performance appraisals, using either the forms provided by the organization or your own rating forms. The object is to replace the "global impression" each of us creates about someone else's overall performance with a systematic procedure for assessing performance. This systematic procedure increases the accuracy and consistency of results.

There are three different approaches for performing appraisals. Employees can be appraised against 1. absolute standards, 2. relative standards, or 3. objectives. No single approach is always best; each has its strengths and weaknesses. However, keep in mind that your choice may be affected by the human resource policies and procedures in your organization.

ABSOLUTE STANDARDS

The use of absolute standards means that employees are not compared against any other person. Included in this approach are the following methods: the written essay, critical incidents, the checklist, graphic rating scales, and behaviourally anchored rating scales.

WRITTEN ESSAYS

Probably the simplest method of appraisal is to write a narrative describing an employee's strengths, weaknesses, past performance, potential, and suggestions for improvement. The **written essay** requires no complex forms or extensive training to complete. But the results often reflect the ability of the writer. A good or bad appraisal may be determined as much by the supervisor's writing style as by the employee's actual level of performance.

CRITICAL INCIDENTS

Critical incidents focus attention on those employee behaviours that are crucial in ensuring that a job is executed effectively. The supervisor writes down examples that describe what the employee did that was especially effective or ineffective. The key here is that only specific behaviours, not vaguely defined personality traits, are cited. A list of critical incidents provides a rich set of examples from which the employee can be shown those behaviours that are desirable and those that call for improvement.

CHECKLISTS

With a **checklist**, a supervisor uses a list of behavioural descriptions and checks off those behaviours that apply to the employee. As Figure 7-6 illustrates, you merely go down the list and check off yes or no to each question.

A major drawback to checklists is the cost. Where an organization has a number of job categories, checklist items must be developed for each category.

Written essay
A performance appraisal technique in which an evaluator writes out a description of an employee's strengths, weaknesses, past performance, and potential, and then makes suggestions for improvement

Critical incidents
A performance appraisal technique in which an evaluator lists key behaviours that separate effective from ineffective job performance

Checklist
A performance appraisal technique in which an evaluator uses a list of behavioural descriptions and checks off those behaviours that apply to the employee

	Yes	No
1. Are supervisor's orders usually followed?	____	____
2. Does the individual approach customers promptly?	____	____
3. Does the individual suggest additional merchandise to customers?	____	____
4. Does the individual keep busy when not servicing a customer?	____	____
5. Does the individual lose his or her temper in public?	____	____
6. Does the individual volunteer to help other employees?	____	____

FIGURE 7-6
Sample of items from a checklist

Graphic rating scale
A performance appraisal technique in which an evaluator rates a set of performance factors on an incremental scale

One of the oldest and most popular methods of appraisal is the **graphic rating scale**. An example of some graphic rating scale items is shown in Figure 7-7.

Graphic rating scales can be used to assess factors such as quantity and quality of work, job knowledge, cooperation, loyalty, dependability, attendance, honesty, integrity, attitudes, and initiative. However, this method is most valid when subjective traits such as loyalty or integrity are avoided, unless they can be defined in specific behavioural terms.

With the graphic rating scale, you go down the list of factors and note that point along the scale or continuum that best describes the employee. There are typically 5 to 10 points on the continuum. In the design of the graphic scales, the challenge is to ensure that both the factors evaluated and the scale points are clearly understood by the supervisor doing the rating.

Why are graphic rating scales so popular? Though they don't provide the depth of information that essays or critical incidents do, they are less time-consuming to develop and administer; they allow for easy numerical tallying and comparison; and, in contrast to the checklist, there is greater standardization of items, so that comparison with other employees in diverse job categories is possible.

Performance Factor	Performance Rating				
Quality of work is the accuracy, skill, and completeness of work.	**1** Consistently unsatisfactory	**2** Occasionally unsatisfactory	**3** Consistently satisfactory	**4** Sometimes superior	**5** Consistently superior
Quantity of work is the volume of work done in a normal workday.	**1** Consistently unsatisfactory	**2** Occasionally unsatisfactory	**3** Consistently satisfactory	**4** Sometimes superior	**5** Consistently superior
Job knowledge is information pertinent to the job that an individual should have for satisfactory job performance.	**1** Poorly informed about work duties	**2** Occasionally unsatisfactory	**3** Can answer most questions about the job	**4** Understands all phases of the job	**5** Has complete mastery of all phases of the job
Dependability is following directions and company policies without supervision.	**1** Requires constant supervision	**2** Requires occasional follow-up	**3** Usually can be counted on	**4** Requires very little supervision	**5** Requires absolute minimum of supervision

FIGURE 7-7

Example of graphic rating scale items

BEHAVIOURALLY ANCHORED RATING SCALES

Behaviourally anchored rating scales (BARS) have received a great deal of attention in recent years. These scales combine major elements from the critical incident and graphic rating scale approaches: Supervisors rate their employees based on items along a continuum, but the points are examples of actual behaviour on the given job rather than general descriptions or traits.

Behaviourally anchored rating scales specify definite, observable, and measurable job behaviours. Examples of job-related behaviours and performance dimensions are found by obtaining specific illustrations of effective and ineffective behaviour for each performance dimension. These behavioural examples are then translated into a set of performance dimensions, each dimension having varying levels of performance. The results of this process are behavioural descriptions, such as *anticipates, plans, executes, solves immediate problems, carries out orders*, and *handles emergency situations*. Figure 7-8 provides an example of a BARS.

Studies conducted on the use of BARS indicate that this method of appraisal tends to reduce rating errors. But its biggest plus may stem from the dimensions BARS generates rather than from any particular superiority of behaviour anchors over trait anchors. The process of developing the behavioural scales is valuable in and of itself for clarifying to both the employee and supervisor which behaviours reflect good performance and which bad.

However, BARS is not without its drawbacks. It, too, suffers from the distortions inherent in most rating methods. BARS is also costly to develop and to maintain.[4]

Behaviourally anchored rating scales (BARS) A performance appraisal technique in which an evaluator rates employees on specific job behaviours derived from performance dimensions

Relative Standards

In the second category of performance appraisals—relative standards—employees' performance is evaluated by comparing it against other employees' performance. We'll discuss two relative methods: group order ranking and individual ranking.

GROUP ORDER RANKING

Group order ranking requires supervisors to place their employees into particular classifications, such as "top one-fifth" or "second one-fifth." So if you have twenty employees and you're using the group-order ranking method, only four of your people can be in the top fifth, and, of course, four also must be relegated to the bottom fifth (see Figure 7-9).

The advantage of this group ordering method is that it prevents supervisors from inflating their evaluations so everyone looks good, or homogenizing the evaluations so everyone is rated near the average—outcomes that are not unusual with the graphic rating scale. The predominant

Group order ranking A performance appraisal approach that groups employees into ordered classifications

Performance dimension scale development under BARS for the dimension "Ability to Absorb and Interpret Policies for an Employee Relations Specialist."

This employee relations specialist

	9	could be expected to serve as an information source concerning new and changed policies for others in the organization
could be expected to be aware quickly of program changes and explain these to employees	8	
	7	could be expected to reconcile conflicting policies and procedures correctly to meet HRM goals
could be expected to recognize the need for additional information to gain a better understanding of policy changes	6	
	5	could be expected to complete various HRM forms correctly after receiving instruction on them
could be expected to require some help and practice in mastering new policies and procedures	4	
	3	could be expected to know that there is always a problem, but go down many blind alleys before realizing they are wrong
could be expected to incorrectly interpret guidelines, creating problems for line managers	2	
	1	could be expected to be unable to learn new procedures even after repeated explanations

FIGURE 7-8

Sample BARS for an employee relations specialist (*Source:* Reprinted from *Business Horizons*, August 1976. Copyright 1976 by the Foundation for the School of Business at Indiana University.)

disadvantages surface when the number of employees being compared is small. At the extreme, if you are assessing only four employees, all of whom may actually be excellent, you are forced to rank them into top quarter, second quarter, third quarter, and bottom quarter! Of course, as the sample size increases, the validity of relative scores as an accurate measure also increases.

Another disadvantage, which plagues all relative measures, is the zero-sum consideration. This means that any change must add up to zero. For example, if there are twelve employees in your department performing at different levels of effectiveness, then by definition three are in the top quarter (sometimes called *quartile*), three in the second quarter,

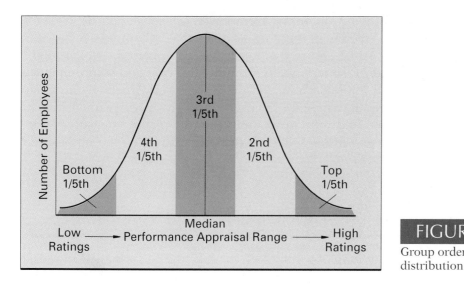

FIGURE 7-9

Group order ranking
distribution

and so forth. The sixth-best employee, for instance, would be in the second quarter. But if two of the workers in the third or fourth quarters were to leave the department and not be replaced, then the sixth-best employee would drop into the third quarter. Because comparisons are relative, an employee who is mediocre may score high only because he or she is the "best of the worst"; in contrast, an excellent performer who is matched against tough competition may be evaluated poorly, when in absolute terms his or her performance is outstanding.

INDIVIDUAL RANKING

The **individual ranking** method requires supervisors to list all their employees in order from the highest to lowest performer. In this method, only one can be "best." This method also assumes that differences between people are uniform. That is, in appraising thirty employees, it is assumed that the difference between the first and second employee is the same as that between the twenty-first and twenty-second. This method allows for no ties—this can be an advantage because it forces supervisors to confront differences in performance levels. But its major drawback is that, in those situations where differences are small or nonexistent, this method magnifies and overemphasizes differences.

Individual ranking
A performance appraisal approach that ranks employees in order from highest to lowest

OBJECTIVES

The final method for appraising performance is the use of objectives. This is essentially an application of management by objectives (MBO), which we introduced in Chapter 2.

With this method, you and your employee will set standards to assess performance by agreeing on measurable goals that encompass key results for achievement. At the end of the objective-setting period—which might be monthly, quarterly, semiannually, or annually—you and your employee can sit down and appraise how well he or she performed. If the goals were carefully chosen to capture the essential performance dimensions in the employee's job, and written so they could be readily measured, they should provide you with a fairly accurate appraisal of the employee's overall job performance.

HURDLES IN THE WAY OF EFFECTIVE APPRAISALS

Expert Marketplace: Sample Performance Appraisal
http://www. expert-market.com/ client/find/demo.html

While you and your employer may seek to make the performance appraisal process free from personal biases, prejudices, and idiosyncrasies, a number of potential problems can creep into the process. As a supervisor, you can try to avoid distorted performance appraisals by recognizing the following errors.

LENIENCY ERROR

Leniency error
The tendency to appraise a set of employees too high (positive) or too low (negative)

Every appraiser has his or her own value system that acts as a standard against which appraisals are made. Relative to the true or actual performance an individual exhibits, some appraisers mark high and others low. The former is referred to as positive **leniency error**, and the latter as negative leniency error. When appraisers are positively lenient in their evaluations, an employee's performance is rated higher than it actually should be. Conversely, a negative leniency error underrates performance, giving the individual a lower appraisal than deserved.

If all employees in an organization were appraised by the same person, there would be no problem. Although there would be an error factor, it would be applied equally to everyone. The difficulty arises when we have different raters with different leniency errors. For example, assume that Jones and Smith are performing the same job for different supervisors, but they have absolutely identical job performance. If Jones's supervisor tends to err toward positive leniency, while Smith's supervisor errs toward negative leniency, we might be confronted with two dramatically different performance appraisals.

HALO ERROR

Halo error
A tendency to rate an individual high or low on all factors due to the impression of a high or low rating on some specific factor

The **halo error** is a tendency to rate an individual high or low on all factors as a result of the impression of a high or low rating on some specific factor. For example, if an employee tends to be dependable, you might become biased toward that individual and rate him or her high on many desirable traits.

Nearly everything you've been reading so far in this chapter can be directly applied to your classroom. Every day you come to class, every quiz or test you take, and any assignments you turn in are evaluated in some form. You're being appraised—even if you hadn't thought about it that way.

Let's look at how you are evaluated. More than likely, your instructor has laid out his or her grading policy in the course outline. Is it based on absolute standards, relative standards, objectives—or a combination of all of these? For example, on an exam based on a hundred points, your grade on that exam is being rated against an absolute standard. If your instructor curves the exam, some relative standards are appearing. Maybe the final grade in the course is determined by how well you met certain goals (objectives). Of course, the list could go on.

Consider how you are evaluated. Do you believe it meets the three purposes of evaluations—feedback, development, and documentation? If you had the opportunity to redesign the evaluation component of your class, what would you recommend? (Of course, you realize that "no evaluation" is not acceptable!)

The halo effect confronts the people who design teaching appraisal forms for college students to fill out in order to evaluate the effectiveness of their instructors. Students tend to rate a faculty member as outstanding on all criteria when they are particularly appreciative of a few things he or she does in the classroom. Similarly, a few bad habits—showing up late for lectures, being slow in returning papers, or assigning an extremely demanding reading assignment—might result in students evaluating the instructor as "lousy" across the board.

SIMILARITY ERROR

When appraisers rate other people giving special consideration to those qualities they perceive in themselves, they are making a **similarity error**. For example, the supervisor who perceives himself as aggressive may evaluate others by looking for aggressiveness. Those who demonstrate this characteristic tend to benefit, while others are penalized.

Similarity errors hurt an organization if the rated quality does not further the organization's success.

Similarity error
Giving special consideration when rating others to those qualities that the evaluator perceives in himself or herself

Recency error
The tendency for evaluators to recall and give greater importance to employee job behaviours that have occurred near the end of the performance-measuring period

Most of us can remember more vividly what happened yesterday than what happened six months ago. This creates the potential for the **recency error** to surface in performance appraisals.

The recency error results in evaluators recalling, and then giving greater importance to, employee job behaviours that have occurred near the end of the performance-measuring period. So if supervisors have to complete an appraisal form on each of their employees every June 1, those accomplishments and mistakes that took place in May tend to be remembered while those behaviours exhibited the previous November tend to be forgotten. Given the reality that we all have good days and bad days—even good and bad months—and that they don't occur at the same time for all employees, a semiannual or annual review may be significantly biased by employee behaviours just prior to their supervisor's review.

CENTRAL TENDENCY ERROR

It's possible that, regardless of who the appraiser evaluates and what characteristics are used, the pattern of evaluation will remain the same. It is also possible that a supervisor's ability to appraise objectively and accurately will be impeded by a failure to use the extremes of the appraising scale. This reluctance to assign extreme ratings, in either direction, is the **central tendency error.**

Central tendency error
A reluctance by an evaluator to use the extremes of the appraising scale

Raters who are prone to the central tendency error avoid the "excellent" category as well as the "unacceptable" category, and assign all ratings around the "average" or midpoint range. By failing to use the extreme ratings, the pattern of evaluation becomes the same for all employees. For example, if a supervisor rates all subordinates as 3, on a 1 to 5 scale, then no differentiation among the subordinates exists. And by suppressing differences, employees' work performances appear considerably more homogeneous than they really are.

INFLATIONARY PRESSURES

A clerical employee at a large insurance company was disappointed by the small salary increase she received following her recent performance review. After all, her supervisor had given her an 86 overall rating. And she knew that the company's appraisal system defined "outstanding performance" as 90 and above, "good" as 80 to 89, "average" as 70 to 79, and "inadequate performance" as anything below 70. This employee was really bewildered when she heard from some friends at work that her pay increase was below the company average. You can imagine her surprise when, after meeting with the assistant director for human resources, she learned that the "average" rating of clerical personnel in the company was 92!

FIGURE 7-10

The effective supervisor regularly documents information on her employees' performance.

This example illustrates a potential problem in appraisals—inflationary pressures. This problem arises when supervisors both minimize differences among their subordinates *and* push all evaluations into the upper range of the rating scale.

Inflationary pressures have always existed, but they have become more of a problem over the past three decades. As equality has grown in importance, and fear of retribution from disgruntled employees who fail to achieve excellent appraisals has increased, there has been a tendency for evaluators to be less rigorous and to reduce the negative repercussions from the appraisal process by generally inflating or upgrading evaluations.

OVERCOMING THE HURDLES

Just because there are potential hurdles to effective appraisals, supervisors shouldn't give up on the process. There are several things you can do to help overcome these hurdles.

CONTINUALLY DOCUMENT EMPLOYEE PERFORMANCE

Keep a file for each of your employees and continually enter notes describing specific instances of accomplishments and behaviours. Include dates and details. When the time comes for you to conduct formal employee appraisals, you'll have a comprehensive history of each employee's performance record during the appraisal period. This will minimize the recency error, increase the accuracy of your ratings, and provide you with specific documentation to support your assessments.

USE BEHAVIOURALLY BASED MEASURES

As we've noted previously, behaviourally based measures are superior to those developed around traits. Many traits often considered to be related to good performance may, in fact, have little or no performance relationship.

Traits such as loyalty, initiative, courage, and reliability are intuitively appealing as desirable characteristics in employees. But the relevant question is: Are employees who are evaluated as high on these traits higher performers than those who rate low? We can't answer that question. We know that there are employees who rate high on these characteristics and are poor performers. And we can find others who are excellent performers but don't score well on traits such as these. Our conclusion is that traits like loyalty and initiative may be prized by organizations, but there is no evidence to support the view that certain traits will be adequate substitutes for performance in a large cross-section of jobs. Additionally, as we noted previously, traits suffer from weak agreement among multiple raters. What you consider "loyalty," I may not.

Behaviourally based measures can deal with both of these objections. Because they deal with specific examples of performance—both good and bad—you avoid the problem of using inappropriate substitutes. Moreover, because you're evaluating specific behaviours, you increase the likelihood that two or more evaluators will see the same thing. You might consider a given employee as "friendly" while I rate her "standoffish." But when asked to rate her in terms of specific behaviours, we might both agree that she "frequently says 'good morning' to customers," "rarely gives advice or assistance to coworkers," and "almost always avoids idle chatter with coworkers."

COMBINE ABSOLUTE AND RELATIVE STANDARDS

A major drawback to absolute standards is that they tend to be biased by inflationary pressures—evaluators lean toward packing their subjects into the high part of the rankings. On the other hand, relative standards suffer when there is little actual variability among the subjects.

The obvious solution is to consider using appraisal methods that combine absolute and relative standards. For example, you might want to use the graphic rating scale and the individual ranking method. It's much more meaningful to compare two employees' performance records when you know that Supervisor A gave Bob Carter an overall rating of 86, which ranked fourth in a department of 17; while Supervisor B gave Tina Blackstone the same overall rating—an 86—but ranked her twelfth in a department of 14. It's possible that Supervisor B has higher-performing employees than Supervisor A. But Supervisor B's ratings may also suffer from inflationary pressures. By providing both absolute and relative assessments, it is easier to more accurately compare employees across departments.

USE MULTIPLE RATERS

As the number of evaluators increases, the probability of attaining more accurate information increases. If rater error tends to follow a normal curve, an increase in the number of appraisers will tend to find the majority congregating about the middle. You see this approach being used in athletic competitions in such sports as diving, gymnastics, and figure skating. A set of evaluators judges a performance, the highest and lowest scores are dropped, and the final performance appraisal is made up from the cumulative scores of those remaining. The logic of multiple raters applies to organizations as well (hence the increasing popularity of an approach known as 360-degree feedback).

FIGURE 7-11

Figure skating performances are judged by multiple raters in order to increase accuracy.

If an employee has had ten supervisors, nine having rated her excellent and one poor, the one poor appraisal takes on less importance. Multiple raters, therefore, increase the reliability of results by tending to lessen the importance of rater biases—leniency, similarity, and central tendency errors.

RATE SELECTIVELY

As an employee's direct supervisor, you are not always in a position to comprehensively appraise all the key aspects of that employee's job. You should only rate in those areas where you have significant job knowledge and have been able to observe, first-hand, the employee's job performance. If you appraise only those dimensions which you are in a good position to rate, you make the performance appraisal a more valid process.

Multisource performance appraisal, 360-degree feedback
http://www.cudenver.edu/~ldeleon/pad5220/resources/papers/msa.html

If there are important parts of an employee's job in which you aren't able to make accurate judgments, you should supplement your appraisal with self-appraisals, peer evaluations, or even customer appraisals, if that's more appropriate. For instance, a number of sales supervisors use customer input as part of their evaluation of sales representatives. And where supervisors have to be away from their work areas frequently, thus limiting their opportunities to observe their employees' job behaviour, the use of peer reviews can improve the validity of the appraisal process.

PARTICIPATE IN APPRAISAL TRAINING

Good appraisers aren't necessarily born. If your appraisal skills are deficient, you should participate in performance-appraisal training because there is evidence that training can make you a more accurate rater.

Common problems such as leniency and halo errors have been minimized or eliminated in workshops where supervisors practise observing and rating behaviours. These workshops typically run from one to three days, but allocating many hours to training may not always be necessary. For instance, one case has been cited where both halo and leniency errors were decreased immediately after exposing evaluators to explanatory training sessions lasting only five minutes.[5] But the effects of training appear to diminish over time, which suggests the need for regular refresher sessions.

WHAT ABOUT TEAM PERFORMANCE APPRAISALS?

Performance appraisal concepts have been almost exclusively developed with the individual employee as the focus point. This reflects the historic belief that individuals are the core building block around which organizations are built. But as we've noted a number of times in this book, more and more organizations are restructuring themselves around teams: self-managed teams, cross-functional teams, task forces, and the like (see Supervision in Action)

In team-based departments, job performance is a function of each individual's contribution to the team, and of his or her ability to be a good team player. Both these performance dimensions are often better assessed by the team's members than by the team's supervisor. We suggest, therefore, that supervisors include peer evaluations from team members in the performance appraisals of those whose jobs are inherently designed around team work. This enhances the autonomy of the team, reinforces the importance of cooperation, and increases the validity of the appraisal process. Additionally, supervisors should consider the benefits of downplaying individual contributions by substituting group performance measures. Where teams have clear responsibilities for achieving specific objectives, it makes more sense to appraise the team's overall performance than to focus on its individual members.

NOW WHAT? RESPONDING TO PERFORMANCE PROBLEMS

The Employee Assistance Program Resource Site
http://www.intr.net/masi/eap/

Employee counselling
An emphasis on encouraging training and development efforts in a situation where an employee is unwilling or unable to perform his or her job satisfactorily

You've completed your employees' performance appraisals. What if you've identified a significant performance deficiency? What are your options? You can provide personal coaching, attempt to increase employee motivation, provide skill training, reassess the employees, or try to eliminate external performance barriers. Which option you select depends on the reason why performance is lacking.[7]

If you realize the performance problem is ability-related, your emphasis becomes one of encouraging training and development efforts. However, when the performance problem is desire-related, whether the unwillingness to correct the problem is voluntary or involuntary, **employee counseling** is the next logical approach.[8]

WHAT DO YOU NEED TO KNOW ABOUT COUNSELLING EMPLOYEES?

Although employee counselling processes differ, some fundamental steps should be followed when couselling an employee (see Figure 7-12).

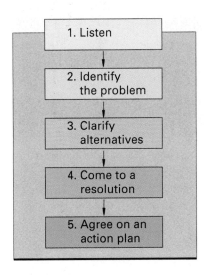

FIGURE 7-12

The counselling process

1. Listen
2. Identify the problem
3. Clarify alternatives
4. Come to a resolution
5. Agree on an action plan

LISTEN TO WHAT THE EMPLOYEE HAS TO SAY

You can't effectively counsel others unless you listen to what they have to say.[9] Your actions should be tailored to the needs, demands, and personality of your employee. These factors can't be accurately assessed without active listening.

When you sit down with your employee, demonstrate your willingness and desire to be helpful. Then, listen to what he or she has to say. Also, listen to what is not being said. How is the employee framing the problem? Who does the employee think is to blame? Are his or her emotions driving out rational thinking? Don't make judgments too quickly. Try to grasp the employee's perception of the situation without agreeing or disagreeing with that perception. At this point, it's not so important to determine whether the employee is right or wrong as it is to try to fully understand the problem from his or her point of view.

IDENTIFY THE PROBLEM

After you've listened to your employee's initial assessment of the situation, begin the search to identify the problem and its causes. What does the employee think is the problem? Who or what is the cause? How is this problem affecting the employee? What, if any, responsibility is your employee taking for the problem? You must remember, though, you're attacking some behaviour, not the employee!

CLARIFY ALTERNATIVES

Problems come with options. In most cases there are a number of alternative actions that can correct the problem. These need to be explored and clarified. At this step, a participative approach can be particularly valuable because you may see and know things that escape the employee. As a result, the merging of both your insights and those of the employee can result in a larger number of quality options.

Performance Appraisals in Contemporary Organizations

The foundation of the performance appraisal process is the concept that performance standards are clearly identified.[6] This fundamental fact implies that for workers to perform effectively, they must know and understand what is expected of them. This concept, however, applies only where clear job descriptions and specifications exist, and where variations to the job are minimal. In other words, conventional performance appraisals were designed to fit the needs of the traditional organization. But what happens when the organization is far from traditional? Let's look at some possibilities.

First, setting goals for an employee could become a thing of the past. Your workers may go from project to project, with the demands and requirements of their work rapidly changing. No formalized performance appraisal system may be able to capture the complexities of the jobs being done. Second, employees will likely have several bosses, not just you. Who, then, will have the responsibility for the performance appraisal? It is more likely to be the team members themselves—setting their own goals and evaluating each other's performance. One can even speculate that this will take the format of an ongoing informal process, rather than some formal "ritual" held every twelve months. All in all, while we surmise a drastic change in the performance appraisal process, it should not be interpreted that you will become less concerned with evaluating employee performance. On the contrary, individual performance will still matter most. The major difference is that employee performance information is likely to be collected from a number of sources—from anyone who's familiar with the employee's work.

Once alternatives are identified, they need to be evaluated. What are the strengths and weaknesses of each? Again, two heads are better than one. Your goal should be to have the employee weigh the pluses and minuses of each course of action.

COME TO A RESOLUTION

What's the best option for the employee? Remember, the best option for one employee is not necessarily the best option for another. The solution should reflect the unique characteristics of the employee. And ideally, both you and the employee will agree on the solution. You want to be sure the employee buys into the final choice, whether that final choice was made by you, the employee, or jointly. A terrific solution that's not accepted by the employee is unlikely to result in any meaningful change in the problem.

AGREE ON AN ACTION PLAN

Finally, the employee needs to develop a concrete plan of action for implementing the solution. What, specifically, is the employee going to do? When will he or she do it? What resources, if any, will be needed?

It's usually a good idea to end a couselling session with the employee summarizing what has taken place and the specific actions he or she plans on taking. You should establish a follow-up point at some specific date in the future for reassessing the employee's progress. If a formal meeting isn't needed, request a short memo from the employee updating you on his or her progress. This can be effective as a reminder to the employee that progress is expected, and as a control device for you to assess the employee's progress.

IS YOUR ACTION ETHICAL?

What business do you have delving into an employee's personal life? That's a valid question, and it requires us to look at the ethics of couselling.

Employees bring a multitude of problems and frustrations from their personal lives to their jobs. They have difficulty finding quality day care for infants. A teenage child is expelled from high school. They have fights with their spouses. A family member suffers a nervous breakdown. They get behind in their bills and they're harassed by creditors. A close friend is seriously hurt in an automobile accident. A parent is diagnosed with Alzheimer's disease.

It may seem wise to keep your nose out of your employees' personal lives, but that is often unreasonable. Why? Because there is no clear demarcation that separates personal and work lives. Consider the following scenario involving one of your employees, Denise. Denise's son was arrested last night for possession of drugs. She spent most of the night with police and lawyers. Today, at work, she is tired and psychologically distant. She has trouble concentrating. Her mind is not on her job. It's naive to believe that employees can somehow leave their personal baggage at the door when they come to work each morning.

5. As a supervisor, you evaluated two of your employees. Employee A received an evaluation of 90; employee B, an evaluation of 92. Which of the following statements is the best interpretation of these results?
   a. Employee B is superior to Employee A.
   b. You give inflated performance evaluations.
   c. There is probably no significant difference between the two employees.
   d. Both employees are ready for promotion.
6. Identify six means by which you can help reduce the barriers to effective performance appraisals.
7. Evaluating employee performance in terms of traits is often a weak predictor of performance. True or false?
8. The process designed to help employees overcome performance-related problems when the problem is related to unwillingness to do the job is called:
   a. performance appraisal
   b. employee counselling
   c. employee assistance
   d. team appraisals

Employees have a right to privacy. However, when personal problems interfere with work performance, you should not consider it beyond your jurisdiction to inquire about the problem, offer yourself as an open ear, and genuinely seek to help with the problem. If your offer is rejected, don't push. If the employee understands how his or her personal problem is affecting work performance, and you make clear what the consequences will be if the work performance doesn't improve, you've reached the ethical limit of your involvement. If the employee is protective of his or her personal life, your rights as a supervisor don't extend to helping solve his or her personal problems. However, you do have the right and the obligation to make sure employees understand that if personal problems interfere with their work, they need to solve those personal problems—and you're there to help, if asked.

CONDUCTING THE APPRAISAL
REVIEW INTERVIEW

ASSESSING YOURSELF: CONDUCTING
THE APPRAISAL INTERVIEW

For each of the following questions, check the answer that best describes your relationship with subordinates. Remember to respond as you have behaved or would behave, not as you think you should behave. If you have no supervisory experience, answer the questions assuming you are a supervisor.

WHEN CONDUCTING AN EMPLOYEE'S PERFORMANCE APPRAISAL REVIEW, I:

	Usually	Sometimes	Seldom
1. Try to put the employee at ease.	❏	❏	❏
2. Make sure I fully understand the employee's job duties and responsibilities.	❏	❏	❏
3. Encourage the employee to engage in self-evaluation.	❏	❏	❏
4. Do most of the talking.	❏	❏	❏
5. Avoid criticism.	❏	❏	❏
6. Focus discussion on the employee's behaviour rather than on his or her personal characteristics.	❏	❏	❏
7. Use specific examples to support my judgments.	❏	❏	❏
8. Try to get the appraisal over with as quickly as possible.	❏	❏	❏

For questions 1, 2, 3, 6, and 7, give yourself 3 points for "Usually," 2 points for "Sometimes," and 1 point for "Seldom." For questions 4, 5, and 8, give yourself 3 points for "Seldom," 2 points for "Sometimes," and 1 point for "Usually."

Add up your points. A score of 21 or higher indicates excellent performance appraisal skills. Scores in the 16–20 range imply some deficiencies in this skill. Scores below 16 denote that you have considerable room for improvement.

Skill Basics

There are three basic approaches to conducting the performance review: 1. tell and sell, 2. tell and listen, and 3. problem solve.[10] With *tell and sell*, the supervisor acts as a judge. That is, the supervisor tells the employee how well he or she is doing and then persuades the employee to change in the way the supervisor desires. The *tell and listen* approach is similar, except that the supervisor conveys assessments of the strengths and weaknesses in the employee's performance and then lets the employee respond to these statements. The supervisor tries to understand the employee's feelings by being a good listener and by displaying empathy. The *problem-solving* approach takes a very different tack. In this approach, the supervisor acts as a partner and works jointly with the subordinate to develop the employee's performance. It requires the supervisor to practise both joint goal setting and effective listening.

Most contemporary discussions of the performance review advocate the problem-solving approach. We acknowledge our debt to this approach in developing many of the following guidelines.

1. **Schedule the formal appraisal review in advance and be prepared.** Many supervisors treat the entire performance appraisal as a lark. They put neither time nor thought into it.

   If a performance review is to be effective, planning must precede it. Review the employee's job description. Go over your rating sheet. Have you carefully considered the employee's strengths as well as weaknesses? Can you substantiate, with specific examples, all points of praise and criticism? Given your past experiences with the employee, what problems, if any, do you anticipate cropping up in the review? How do you plan to react to these problems?

   Once you have worked out these kinds of issues, you should schedule a specific time and place for the review and give the employee ample advance notice. You should also do whatever is necessary—close your office door, have your phone calls held, and the like—to ensure there are no outside interruptions once the review begins.

2. **Put the employee at ease.** Regardless of your personal feelings about performance reviews—and many supervisors feel uncomfortable judging others, or fear that being honest will create resentment among their employees—you are responsible for creating a supportive climate for the employee. The performance review can

be a traumatic experience for the best of employees. People don't like to hear their work criticized. On the other hand, many employees have little confidence that the organization's performance-appraisal system will accurately assess their contribution. Add the fact that people tend to overrate themselves (approximately 60 per cent place their own performance in the top 10 per cent[11]) and you have the ingredients for tension and confrontation. Recognize that the employee is probably uptight, so be supportive and understanding.

3. **Be sure that the employee understands the purpose of the appraisal review.** What's the purpose of the review? Is it to be used for personnel decisions or to promote the employee's growth and development? The former purpose warrants focusing on the past, while the latter points to the future. In the problem-solving approach, the review is seen as an opportunity to provide recognition for those things the employee is doing well and to discuss any job-related problems that the employee may be experiencing. Regardless of the purpose, however, you should clarify at the start any uncertainty the employee may have about what will transpire during the review and the resulting consequences.

4. **Minimize threats.** You will want to create a helpful and constructive climate. The review should not be an inquisition. Try to maximize encouragement and support, while minimizing threats.

5. **Obtain employee participation.** Effective performance reviews are characterized by high employee participation. Let the employee do the majority of the talking. The evidence indicates the more the employee talks, the more satisfied he or she will be with the appraisal.[12]

6. **Have the employee engage in self-evaluation.** Consistent with high participation, encourage the employee to evaluate his or her own performance. If the climate is supportive, the employee may well openly acknowledge performance problems you've identified, thus eliminating your need to raise them. Further, the employee may offer viable solutions to these problems. By encouraging self-evaluation and being a good listener, you become a partner who is helping the employee perform better, rather than a "boss" who is looking for negatives to criticize. The employee might be the best person to identify a training plan or program that will improve his or her own performance.

FIGURE 7-13

"Providing negative feedback is difficult for me to do," comments Hal Espo of Dialog. "It's never fun telling someone they're not doing well."

Dialog
http://www.dialog.com/

7. **Criticize performance but not the person.** If you need to criticize, direct the criticism at specific job-related behaviours that negatively affect the employee's performance. Never criticize the employee. It's the person's performance that is unsatisfactory, not the person.

8. **Soften the tone when criticizing, but not the message.** Many of us find it difficult to criticize others. If you believe criticism is necessary, don't water down the message, don't dance around the issue, and certainly don't avoid discussing a problem in the hope that it'll just go away. State your criticism thoughtfully and show concern for the employee's feelings, but don't soften the message. Criticism is criticism, even if it's constructive. When you try to sell it as something else, you're liable to create ambiguity and misunderstanding.

9. **Don't exaggerate**. Many of us have a tendency to make extreme statements in order to make our point. Don't stretch the facts. If an employee has been late for four out of five recent meetings, don't say, "You're always late for meetings." Whenever possible, avoid absolutes like "always" or "never." Such terms encourage defensiveness and undermine your credibility. An employee only has to introduce one exception to your "always" or "never" statement to destroy the entire statement's validity. Instead, list the four occasions on which the employee was late for the meeting.

10. **Use specific examples to support your ratings.** Document your employee's performance ratings with specific examples. This adds credibility to your ratings and helps employees to better understand what you mean by "good" and "bad" performance. If you use critical instances to record specific actions in each employee's file, it will be easier to support your rating.

11. **Give positive as well as negative feedback.** No matter how poorly an employee is performing, he or she will have exhibited some strengths worthy of recognition. State what was done well and why it deserves recognition. What you want to avoid is turning the performance review into a totally negative feedback session. Interestingly, research indicates that those areas of job performance that are most criticized are least likely to show an improvement.[13] Of course, you want to avoid the other extreme, too, of unjustified blanket praise. If blanket praise is given, the employee is reinforced for mediocre as well as excellent behaviour.

12. **Have the employee sum up the appraisal review.** As the review nears its conclusion, encourage the employee to summarize the discussion that has taken place. This gives your subordinate an opportunity to put the entire review into perspective. It will also tell you whether you have succeeded in clearly communicating your evaluation.

13. **Detail a future plan of action.** Where there are serious performance deficiencies, the final part of the review should be devoted to helping the employee draft a detailed, step-by-step plan to correct the situation. Your role should be supportive: "What can I do to provide assistance?" Do you need to make yourself more available to answer questions? Do you need to give the employee more freedom or responsibility? Would securing funds to send the employee to professional meetings, workshops, or training programs help? The object is to demonstrate your support for the employee by asking him or her where you can provide assistance and then committing to provide that assistance. In effect, you fulfill your partnership role by helping employees clear the obstacles on the road toward their goals. Remember, outstanding employees also need to know future plans for their own advancement.

APPLYING YOUR SKILLS

Break the class into groups of three. One student will play the role of DANA (Employee Relations Supervisor); the other student will be CHRIS (Junior Research Analyst). Students are to read *only* their own character's role. They then have up to 15 minutes to conduct the role play.[14] A member using the Observer's sheet will record Dana's skill.

The person playing the role of Dana should consciously attempt to practise the appraisal review skills described on the Observer's Sheet.

> **DANA'S role:** You are the Employee Relations Supervisor for a manufacturing firm. You are well thought of in the firm and have an excellent rapport with your boss, the Vice President for Human Resources. Chris is a junior research analyst in your department. You know that Chris is reasonably good at his/her job. But you also know that Chris believes his/her job performance to be "outstanding," which isn't true. Chris is scheduled to have a performance review session with you in five minutes,

and you would like to establish clearer communication, as well as to convince Chris to adopt a less grandiose self-image.

You believe that Chris is on the right track, but it will take him/her about two years to reach the stage at which he/she can be promoted to senior analyst. As to Chris's performance, you have received some good reports, as well as three letters of complaint. Chris prepared four research reports that you considered above average, but to keep him/her motivated and happy, you exaggerated and said they were "excellent." Maybe that was a mistake.

You are worried about the impact on other employees, whose performance is nearly as good as Chris's, if Chris is promoted. So you plan to set meaningful targets for Chris this year, evaluate his/her performance one or two years from now, and then recommend the promotion if it's deserved.

As you look up, Chris is entering your office.

CHRIS'S role: You are a junior research analyst in the Employee Relations Department of a manufacturing firm. Dana is your supervisor and head of the department. You know that you are one of the best performers in your department, and may even be the best. However, you were not promoted to senior analyst last year, even though you expected to be. So you would like to be promoted this year.

You expect your supervisor to raise some obstacles to your promotion. Dana is bound to mention three letters of complaint against you, for instance. Dana seems to point out only your errors. Up front, you plan to remind Dana that you wrote four research reports that Dana said were "excellent." If Dana tries to delay your promotion unnecessarily, you plan to confront him/her and, if necessary, take the issue to Dana's boss, the Vice President for Human Resources. You think there have been many instances in which you were rated better on performance than your colleagues in the department. You have decided you will press your point of view firmly, but also rationally, in a professional manner.

Dana has called you to his/her office. The subject: your performance review. This role play begins as you enter Dana's office.

OBSERVER'S SHEET

As the role play proceeds, record Dana's skill in applying the actions to make performance appraisals more effective.

	1 not used	2	3	4 used very well
1. Put employee at ease	❏	❏	❏	❏
2. Clearly set out the purpose of the interview	❏	❏	❏	❏
3. Obtain employee participation	❏	❏	❏	❏
4. Ask for self-evaluation	❏	❏	❏	❏
5. Criticize performance, not the person	❏	❏	❏	❏
6. Soften the tone, not the message, when criticizing	❏	❏	❏	❏
7. Don't exaggerate	❏	❏	❏	❏
8. Use specific examples	❏	❏	❏	❏
9. Give positive feedback	❏	❏	❏	❏
10. Detail a future plan	❏	❏	❏	❏

Notes:

SUMMARY

This summary is organized by the Learning Objectives.

1. Performance appraisal is both an evaluation/development tool and a legal document. It reviews past performance to identify accomplishments and deficiencies; it offers a detailed plan to improve future performance through training and development. It also becomes a legal document that can be used to justify or support personnel actions.

2. Formal performance appraisals are regular, planned meetings where the supervisor and employee discuss and review the latter's work performance. Informal performance appraisal is the day-to-day assessment a supervisor makes of an employee's performance and the ongoing feedback the supervisor gives to the employee about that performance.

3. To minimize legal problems, supervisors should make sure that they carefully follow all performance appraisal policies and procedures set forth in the organization's handbooks (if any), and make every effort to avoid prejudice and discrimination.

4. The three most popular sets of criteria used by supervisors in appraisals are individual task outcomes, behaviours, and traits. The first two are almost always preferable to the third.

5. Absolute standards compare the employee's performance against specific traits or behaviours rather than against other people. In contrast, relative standards compare employees against other employees.

6. The graphic rating scale lists a set of factors—traits or behaviours—that are related to job performance. The rater then uses a 5-to-10-point scale to rate the employee on each of these factors.

7. Behaviourally anchored rating scales have received increased interest because they focus on job-related behaviours specific to a given job. This tends to reduce rating error and increase the validity of findings.

8. Common human errors that can distort appraisals include leniency, halo, similarity, recency, central tendency, and inflationary pressures.

9. The three variables that most often result in employee performance deficiencies are inadequate skills, low levels of effort, and unfavourable external conditions.

KEY TERMS AND CONCEPTS

Behaviourally anchored
rating scales·(BARS)
Central tendency error
Checklist
Critical incidents
Employee counselling
Extrinsic feedback
Graphic rating scale
Group order ranking

Halo error
Individual ranking
Intrinsic feedback
Leniency error
Performance appraisal
Recency error
Similarity error
Written essay

REVIEWING YOUR KNOWLEDGE

1. Why do many supervisors dislike and even avoid giving employees performance feedback?
2. Contrast the advantages of supervisor-conducted appraisals, self-evaluations, and peer appraisals.
3. What is the relationship between goal setting and performance appraisal?
4. Contrast intrinsic and extrinsic feedback.
5. If appraising behaviours is superior to appraising traits, why do you think so many organizations evaluate their employees on criteria such as effort, loyalty, and dependability?
6. Do formal performance appraisals replace informal ones? Discuss.
7. Compare written essay appraisals with BARS.
8. Would human errors in the appraisal process be eliminated in small organizations where one person does all the appraisals?
9. What can a supervisor do to minimize distortions in the appraisal process?

ANSWERS TO THE POP QUIZZES

1. **b. to determine if employees are in need of training.** One dimension of performance appraisals is to recognize weaknesses and use that information for employee training and development.

2. Intrinsic feedback involves getting information on performance on a daily basis simply by doing the job. It is built into the job in terms of numbers produced, daily goals, and the like. Extrinsic feedback is provided to an employee by an outside source—such a supervisor, a quality inspector, or a customer.

3. **True.** This is one of the guiding principles of performance evaluations. It involves you and the employee establishing standards that, when accomplished, will lead to successful performance and departmental goal attainment.

4. **d. All of the above.** Each response deals with a particular documentation concern. Having performance appraisal policies that are consistent and able to withstand review by external agencies; having bias-free processes; and demonstrating that what is appraised and evaluated is job-related.

5. **c. There is probably no significant difference between the two employees.** Although a 92 is higher than a 90, the difference is relatively small. Accordingly, there is probably no significant difference between the two employees.

6. The six ways to reduce the barriers to effective performance appraisals are: 1. continually documenting employee performance; 2. using behaviourally-based measures; 3. combining absolute and relative standards; 4. using multiple raters; 5. rating selectively; and 6. participating in appraisal training.

7. **True.** This is one of the difficulties with using only traits. The reason is that traits refer to potential predictors of performance, not performance itself. Additionally, traits typically have a strong subjective component. They may mean different things to different people.

8. **b. employee couselling.** This question and response reflects the definition of employee counselling.

CASE 7.A

Operating from Home Base

Scott Burton is the District Sales Manager, Toronto West, for Carlton Cards of Canada. Scott's job is unusual in that he manages his staff of eleven account managers, six merchandisers, and forty-five part-time merchandisers from an office in his own home. Citing satisfaction with the basic function of servicing retail outlets with Carlton Cards products, Scott says the excitement and challenge of his job is never knowing what's coming in a competitive and changing industry.

Given the sales orientation of his department, Scott uses monthly and quarterly sales reports to track the performance of each account manager, with quarterly bonuses to reward achievement. The need to provide security to staff in challenging economic times has tipped the balance of pay back to base salary, though bonuses of up to 20 per cent of pay are still available.

Scott has set up a structured weekly reporting process, assigning designated times to each account manager for "call in" telephone meetings. Even better, Scott has made every manager aware of all the time slots, encouraging them to call ahead of scheduled appointments so he can assist them in passing on information to other account managers. His meetings are scheduled in advance of corporate mailing schedules and reporting deadlines, giving Scott the time to react quickly from an informed and updated position on each manager's performance.

Backed with corporate training in performance appraisals, and supported by monthly and quarterly sales reports, Scott feels confident in the appraisal system at Carlton Cards. As territory-by-territory targets are set during planning sessions, Scott feels that the system might be strengthened by more input from the account-manager level. Like most industries that are service-oriented, some of the best planning input resides with those frontline representatives who deliver the product.

RESPONDING TO THIS CASE

1. Prepare a list of the advantages and disadvantages of a performance appraisal system based on sales quotas.
2. What advice would you give to Scott Burton in preparing a recommendation to increase the account managers' input in planning the quotas? What resistance might he face from top management?

CASE 7.B

Cutting Costs at Great Western

Dave Petrosky and his coworkers are experiencing a lot of stress from the knowledge that their supervisor, Loretta Reynolds, is planning to implement an employee evaluation system. They have had several discussions about the process. They are concerned about whether a formal evaluation system will be a fair assessment of their work performance. They have fears that it will be more quantity-driven than based on the quality of their work. They are concerned about when it will be conducted. However, probably their greatest question is why a performance appraisal system is needed at all. They have never had any problems in the past, even though there has been no formal process. They wonder what the real reason is behind management wanting to implement an employee evaluation system.

Dave's coworkers, Denise Lorenz and Rodney Sabrsula, are even more concerned about employee evaluations because they have been with Great

Western Pipe and Steel Inc. less than a year, giving them the shortest tenure. They know that many businesses have been downsizing, but Great Western has not laid anyone off in over ten years. In recent months, however, there has been a lot of discussion about tight budgets and ways to cut costs of production.

RESPONDING TO THIS CASE

1. Why are Great Western employees so concerned about the implementation of a performance appraisal system?

2. What suggestions would you give Loretta Reynolds to lessen the fears her employees have about employee evaluation?

3. Identify the appraisal criteria that should be considered in designing an employee evaluation system. Why are some of the criteria more difficult to identify than others?

4. In groups of four or five, design an appraisal "instrument" you think would be good for Loretta Reynolds' employees as well as for the management of Great Western. Would you like to be evaluated with this instrument? Why or why not?

8

DEVELOPING YOUR EMPLOYEES

LEARNING OBJECTIVES

After reading this chapter, you should be able to:

1. Define *training*.
2. Identify signs that suggest employee training may be necessary.
3. Describe the role of reinforcement in learning.
4. Explain the learning curve.
5. Describe four on-the-job training methods.
6. Describe four off-the-job training methods.
7. List three skill deficiency categories.
8. Explain the importance of evaluating training effectiveness.
9. Identify two popular types of diversity training.
10. List five positive outcomes of ethics training.

CHAPTER OUTLINE

As Human Resources and Training Manager for Motorola's Wireless Data Division, Betti Clipsham's role has changed dramatically over the past eight years. Betti spent six years in the Richmond, B.C. facility, where her primary role was to bring Motorola's training initiatives into an organization that had been acquired by the Motorola Corporation. The HR department distributed Motorola University course catalogues, brought in programs, and assisted managers and employees (now called "associates") to complete the required forty hours of relevant training in three key skill areas: technical, interpersonal and business. The Richmond site also offers training to develop "core competencies" for each of the job groups.

Betti has spent the last two years of her role in Seattle, Washington. She's had to immerse herself in a new culture and learn a whole new set of HR laws and procedures. For the twenty-first century, Betti predicts increasing use of alternative learning methods (e.g., intranet, internet, CD-ROM). The required training hours for associates will likely rise. Betti predicts increasing focus on globalization, cultural diversity, and managing change. She's looking forward to more exciting, challenging times ahead for "learning organizations" and the people who work for them.

EMPLOYEE TRAINING: WHAT IS IT AND WHY IS IT IMPORTANT?

Chrysler Canada
http://www.
chryslercanada.ca/

Training
Learning experience that results in a relatively permanent change in an individual that improves his or her ability to perform on the job

As we'll show in this chapter, employee training and development is more important today than ever. It's relevant to big companies and small ones, and for businesses and nonprofit organizations alike. Additionally, organizations are increasingly looking to supervisors to identify employee training needs, recommend programs, and even conduct training sessions.

Employee **training** refers to a learning experience that results in a relatively permanent change in an individual that improves his or her ability to perform on the job. It can involve changing skills, knowledge, attitudes, or behaviour. It includes obvious development of technical skills such as operating sophisticated equipment or using new software programs. But it also includes learning other, more subtle, behaviours. For instance, Chrysler Corporation has essentially redesigned its organization around teams. This has required extensive training so employees and supervisors can learn how to work effectively as part of a team.

To maintain friendly customer service, the Tattered Cover Book Store gives two weeks of training to new employees. This photo pictures Ann Marie Martin (centre) instructing new hires.

In today's fast-changing world, victory increasingly goes to the company whose entire workforce can solve problems and make good decisions. That means investing in training. As companies seek continuous process improvements, employees must be trained to use control charts and other statistical tools. And as technology rapidly transforms the workplace, employees must upgrade or alter their skills to allow new technologies to realize their full potential in increasing productivity.

At the dawn of the new century, training is becoming an integral part of most jobs. The goals of high productivity and avoidance of obsolescence require that employees be in a constant state of learning and adapting. In this chapter, we want to present the fundamental aspects of training and the supervisor's role in these efforts.

NEEDS ASSESSMENT

As a supervisor, how do you tell whether an employee could benefit from training? Begin by assuming that *every* new employee needs orientation training. Joining a new organization and settling into a new job is typically an uncomfortable experience. There are new people to meet and new policies to learn—the "right way" to do a job in one company is not necessarily the "right way" in another company or even in a different department at the same company. Provide initial orientation training to new members in order to reduce their anxiety and to allow them to become comfortable in their new surroundings.

Beyond orientation training, look for signals that suggest employee training may be necessary. What are some of these signals?

1. The introduction of new equipment or processes that may affect an employee's job
2. An increase in the number of errors
3. An increase in the number of questions that employees ask you or their colleagues
4. An increase in complaints by customers or coworkers.
5. A rise in the number of accidents.
6. A drop in individual or group productivity.

If you see any of these signs, should you automatically assume the solution is increased training? Not necessarily! As we noted in the previous chapter, training is not the only response to performance problems. If the problem is lack of motivation, a poorly designed job, or external conditions, training is not likely to offer much help. For example, training is not likely to be the answer if a performance deficiency is caused by low salaries, inadequate benefits, a poorly designed work layout, or the trauma of layoffs associated with corporate downsizing.

When you have determined that training is necessary, specify training goals. What explicit changes or results do you expect the training to achieve? These goals should be clear to both you and the employee. For example, the new service assistant at a Kinko's Copy Center is expected to be able to 1. use all photocopying equipment, 2. enlarge and shrink copies, 3. send and receive domestic and international faxes, 4. operate the passport photo machine, 5. operate and answer technical questions about the Macintosh computer rentals, 6. answer all technical questions regarding photo processing and differences in paper quality, and 7. operate the cash register and make change. These goals then guide the design of the training program and can be used after the program is complete to assess its effectiveness.

Kinko's
http://www.kinkos.com/

ALLOCATING TRAINING RESPONSIBILITIES

You are primarily responsible for training the employees who report to you. Since you'll eventually be judged on the performance of the people who work for you, it is your responsibility to ensure that they are properly trained.

This doesn't mean, however, that you must necessarily conduct all the training yourself. Exactly what role you play in training your employees will generally depend on the size of your organization, your training budget, and your own training skills. The larger your organization, the more likely it is that there will be a separate training department or training specialists in the human resources group. As you'll see, they can provide valuable support resources and may perform some centralized training functions. Additionally, the size of your departmental training budget will have a large bearing on your role. The more generous the budget, the more you can look to specialists outside your department for assistance. Finally, supervisors vary in their abilities to conduct effective training sessions. The higher your skills, the more of the actual training you can do yourself.

In addition to yourself, there are three other training resources you should consider. As previously noted, where available, you should consult with your firm's *in-house training specialists*. They can help you identify training needs, design specific programs for your employees, provide

- *You* can provide training for people in your department
- *In-house training specialists* are often available in large organizations
- *Outside trainers* can be hired to provide specialized expertise
- *Your employees* often are capable of training their peers

FIGURE 8-2

Where to look for training resources

advice on teaching methods, and assist you in assessing the effectiveness of your training efforts. In most large organizations, these in-house specialists will also conduct centralized training on general issues affecting all employees. For instance, specialists at Walt Disney, Motorola and AT&T Canada provide organization-wide training on issues such as company history and policies, employee benefits, basic business economics, math and literacy skills, and interpersonal skills. Job-specific training is then typically left to the responsibility of departmental supervisors.

In small organizations or in cases where very specialized expertise is required, supervisors will rely on *outside trainers*. Outsiders, for instance, may be the best source for teaching your people about the implications of new legislation or for improving their communication skills.

Last, but not least, don't forget the potential of *your employees* to train their peers. You may want to delegate some training activities to skilled and experienced employees. If you do so, remember that just because employees can do their own job well, it is no assurance that they can teach others. Just as the best athletes don't always make the best coaches, the best workers don't always make the best trainers. The experienced employee must not only know the job, but also know how to train others. So if you use employees as trainers, make sure that they have been properly prepared for these added responsibilities.

DESIGNING THE PROPER TRAINING PROGRAM: UNDERSTANDING HOW PEOPLE LEARN

You're developing a training program for your department. You want the program to be effective. That is, you want to create a learning experience that results in changing employees so it improves their ability to perform their jobs. Toward this end, you should understand how people learn. An understanding of learning principles can help you to structure effective training experiences.

The following suggestions highlight what we know about how people learn.[1]

LEARNING IS ENHANCED WHEN THE LEARNER IS MOTIVATED

You can lead a horse to water but you can't make it drink! Merely exposing an employee to a learning experience is no guarantee that learning will take place. The employee must be motivated to learn! This is best achieved by linking the learning experience to one or more employee goals. Show the employee, for example, how completion of the course will lead to higher pay, promotion opportunities, heightened departmental status, increased protection against layoffs, or other benefits.

LEARNING REQUIRES FEEDBACK

Feedback on results is necessary so learners can correct mistakes. Only by getting information about how they're doing can they compare results against goals and correct any deviations. Feedback is best when it is immediate rather than delayed: the sooner a learner has some knowledge of how well he or she is performing, the easier it is to correct deficiencies.

REINFORCEMENT INCREASES THE LIKELIHOOD THAT A LEARNED BEHAVIOUR WILL BE REPEATED

Behaviours that are rewarded tend to be repeated and sustained. For instance, if employees are verbally praised when they have properly performed a task, they are likely to continue doing the task this way and be motivated to strive toward performing better work. On the other hand, punishment tends to only temporarily suppress a behaviour. Moreover, punishment merely tells someone what they're doing wrong; it doesn't convey the right way to do something.

PRACTICE INCREASES A LEARNER'S PERFORMANCE

When learners actually practise what they have read or seen, they gain confidence and are less likely to make errors or forget what they have learned. Active involvement through practice should therefore be made part of any learning experience.

There are basically two ways an employee can practise a job. One is to practise the whole job at once. The other is to break the job into parts and practise each part independently. Which way is best? It depends on the type of job being done. It appears that if the job is narrowly defined and relatively simple—for example, stocking shelves in a grocery store—practice should cover the whole job. If the job is complicated—for example, tracking space satellites—it is better to practise the parts of the job independently.

LEARNING BEGINS RAPIDLY, THEN LEVELS OFF

Learning rates can be expressed as a curve that usually begins gradually and is followed by a steep rise, then increases at a decreasing rate until a plateau is reached. Learning is very fast near the beginning, but then levels off as opportunities for improvement are reduced.

The **learning curve** concept can be illustrated by observing individuals in training to run the mile. At first, their time improves rapidly as they get into shape. Then, as their conditioning develops, their improvement reaches a plateau. Obviously, knocking one minute off a ten-minute mile is a lot easier than knocking one minute off a five-minute mile. If you have ever learned to type, you may have had an experience that somewhat follows the pattern shown in Figure 8-3.

Notice the shape of the curve in Figure 8-3. During the first three months, the rate of increase is slow as the subject learns the technique and becomes familiar with the keyboard. During the next three months, learning accelerates as the subject works on developing speed. After six months, learning slows as progress evolves into refinement of technique.

Learning curve
Learning begins gradually, followed by a steep rise, then increases at a decreasing rate until a plateau is reached.

LEARNING MUST BE TRANSFERABLE TO THE JOB

It doesn't make much sense to perfect a skill in the classroom and then find that you can't successfully transfer it to the job. Therefore training should be designed for transferability.

This means that the learning environment should simulate the work situation as closely as possible. In cases where learning is done on the job—such as when a senior employee spends a week with a new worker, showing the new employee specifically what to do and watching as he or she perfects the skill—the transferability requirement is not a relevant issue. Neither is it much of a problem where the off-site simulation is

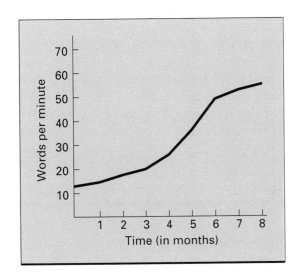

FIGURE 8-3

Learning curve for keyboarding

FIGURE 8-4

Pilot flight-training simulators improve the transferability of training from the classroom to the job.

incredibly realistic—as is the case with today's sophisticated flight simulators used to train pilots. Transferability becomes a problem when the learning environment is considerably unlike that of the actual work situation. If a medical surgeon's training was made up completely of reading books and attending lectures on anatomy and physiology, you'd rightly question whether the surgeon could transfer that knowledge to actually operating on a real patient. This explains why surgical training includes a large segment of actual practice and several years of internship—it ensures transferability of surgical skills.

DESIGNING TRAINING PROGRAMS

The previous section provides insights into how to structure training experiences for your employees. It tells us that you should provide motivation by tying the learning experience into the employee's goals. Employees should have the opportunity to perfect their skills. They should receive feedback on how well the training is progressing, as well as praise and other rewards for each step of progress. And if the training takes place off the job, the employees should have some opportunity to transfer to the job what has been learned, either through actual on-the-job practice or through practice in a highly realistic, simulated job environment.

TRAINING METHODS

Training employees in an economy of constant change has challenged supervisors to react faster and more creatively in preparing employees to perform other jobs. Supervisors are looking for newer, faster, and more effective ways to keep their staff trained to meet the challenges of an increasingly customer-driven market. In this section we'll briefly review various on-the-job and off-the-job training methods and then show that the choice of training methods should reflect the type of problem that needs fixing.

On-the-Job Training

Most training takes place on the job. This is because it's easy to do and gives the impression of being low in cost. **On-the-job training** places employees in actual work situations and makes them appear to be immediately productive. It is learning by doing. For jobs that either are difficult to simulate or can be learned quickly by watching and doing, on-the-job training makes sense.

On-the-job training
Training that places employees in actual work situations

One of the drawbacks of on-the-job training can be low productivity while employees develop their skills. Another drawback can be the errors made by the trainees while they learn. However, when the damage the trainees can do is minimal, where training facilities and personnel are limited or costly, and where it is desirable for the employees to learn the job under normal working conditions, the benefits of on-the-job training frequently offset its drawbacks.

SIMULATION TRAINING

CAE Inc. Home Page
http://www.cae.ca/

C.A.E. Electronics of Montreal designed a $15 million computer simulator of a "virtual flying experience" to train Boeing 777 pilots. The simulator gives its novice pilots a wild run—mimicking 35 airports, complete with the roar of engines, bumps from turbulent air, snow, birds hitting the windshield, heavy traffic and warning lights. While the simulator's price tag might seem steep, it costs only $500 per hour to run, a fraction of the $14 000 an hour it costs to fly the real thing.[2]

APPRENTICESHIPS

People seeking to enter skilled trades—to become, for example, plumbers, electricians, or ironworkers—are often required to undergo **apprenticeships** before they are accepted to expert status. Typically, this apprenticeship period lasts from one to five years. For instance, a cosmetician's apprenticeship is two years, a bricklayer's is three years, machinists and printers spend four years, and a patternmaker's apprenticeship requires five years.

Apprenticeship
A program covering a period of time—typically one to five years—when an individual is considered to be training to learn a skill

Apprenticeship programs put the trainee under the guidance of a master worker. The argument for apprenticeships is that the required job knowledge and skills are so complex as to rule out anything less than a period of time where the trainee understudies a skilled master.

FIGURE 8-5

At Corning, apprentices learn on the job but also in the classroom. Most training is done by ordinary employees. This is consistent with the company's goal of preparing workers in their new roles as teachers, coaches, and leaders.

One disadvantage of apprenticeships is that they are designed solely around the skills of a specific trade; they are not tailored to the needs of a specific organization. So when hired, apprentices typically have to be retrained to an organization's specific job requirements. The other disadvantage is that apprenticeships are at odds with the current trend toward cross-training and teamwork. Today's employees need versatility. They need to be able to move quickly between a number of jobs as situations change. Apprenticeships grew out of a time when one learned a specific skilled trade and then practised it for a lifetime. Today's jobs require a broader range of skills that must be continually updated.

COACHING

Coaching
Day-to-day, hands-on process of helping employees recognize opportunities to improve their work performance

One of the most significant changes in the supervisor's job over the past few years has been the increased importance placed on coaching employees. **Coaching** is a day-to-day, hands-on process of helping employees recognize opportunities to improve their work performance. A coach analyzes the employee's performance; provides insight as to how that performance can be improved; and offers the leadership, motivation, and supportive climate to help the employee achieve that improvement. In From Concepts to Skills, at the end of this chapter, we'll carefully describe the specifics involved in developing effective coaching skills.

Eric White, a sales trainer for Appletree Wholesale Decorating is enthusiastic about the one-on-one coaching provided by his company. Upon joining Appletree (which has offices in Vancouver, Calgary, Ottawa, and Toronto), Eric was coached on the job by his branch manager through a program designed to partner new employees with experienced sales reps. Employees are also encouraged to request single day "retrain" sessions, with bonuses for training days.

MENTORING

Most work groups foster a buddy system where more experienced employees informally show recent hires new skills and help them out when they have problems. **Mentoring** formalizes the buddy system. In formal mentoring programs, senior employees are assigned junior protégés to whom they lend the benefit of their experience. Mentors are tutors, coaches, counsellors, and guides to less experienced associates.

Mentoring
Senior employees tutor, coach, counsel, and guide less experienced associates

Not every experienced or high-performing employee makes an effective mentor. Successful mentors are good teachers. They can present ideas clearly, listen well, and empathize with the problems of their protégés. In some cases, supervisors will become formal mentors to one or more of the people who work for them. However, this is not typically a good idea. It can create morale problems among other employees who perceive that protégés are getting favoured treatment. The best mentors for operative employees are other operative employees in their department or work group.

JOB ROTATION

Job rotation is an excellent way to broaden employees' perspectives and turn specialists into generalists. It allows employees to increase their experience and absorb new skills.

Job rotation
Moving employees horizontally to broaden their skills, knowledge, or abilities; turning specialists into generalists

Job rotation can take one of two forms: planned or situational. *Planned rotation* describes a formal program of sequential moves. For instance, an accountant at Xerox may spend six months working in the tax area, then six months in cost analysis, then six months on auditing activities, and so forth. Japanese companies have relied extensively on job rotation to build a labour force of generalists who can perform a wide range of company functions on a variety of teams. *Situational rotation* is more informal—employees are moved to different jobs when their current one is no longer challenging, or in order to meet the needs of work scheduling. Many supervisors use the summer months, when employees typically take vacations, as an opportunity to broaden their staff's skills by situationally rotating people into and out of different jobs to cover for those on vacation.

While job rotation fits well with today's increased need for employee flexibility and cross-training, it comes with some serious drawbacks. Initial productivity often suffers when an employee moves into a new job.

POP QUIZ

Are You Comprehending What You're Reading?

1. Supervisors should train their own employees. True or False?
2. Which of the following is true of learning?
   a. Learning requires feedback.
   b. Learning begins slowly, then speeds up and continues to accelerate.
   c. Learning is enhanced by the use of punishment.
   d. All of the above.
3. List advantages and disadvantages of training on the job.
4. "Moving employees horizontally to broaden their skills, knowledge or abilities" describes:
   a. mentoring
   b. job rotation
   c. apprenticeship
   d. simulation training

And an extensive job-rotation program can result in a vast number of employees situated in positions where their job knowledge is very limited. The organization must therefore be equipped to deal with the day-to-day problems that result when inexperienced personnel perform new tasks. That usually means supervisors must be readily available to help with problems.

OFF-THE-JOB TRAINING

Off-the-job training
Training that takes place outside the direct work area

Chrysler contracted training for 3000 employees in communications, group motivation and stress management through Sheridan College, a community college in southwestern Ontario. Training sessions were held outside of scheduled production shifts, beginning at 6:00 in the morning or 7:00 in the evening. This training partnership allowed Chrysler to use the expertise of college professors who designed and tailored the **off-the-job training** program directly to the company's needs.

VESTIBULE TRAINING

In **vestibule training**, employees learn their jobs on the equipment they will be using, but the training is conducted away from the actual work floor. Many large retail chains train cashiers on their new computer cash registers—which are much more complex because they control inventory and perform other functions in addition to ringing up orders—in specially created vestibule labs that simulate the actual checkout-counter environment. While expensive, vestibule training allows employees to get a feel for doing tasks without real-world interferences such as noise, distractions, and time pressures. Additionally, it minimizes the problem of transferring learning to the job, because vestibule training uses the same equipment the trainee will use on the job.

Vestibule training Employees learn their jobs on the equipment they will be using, but away from the actual work floor

SEMINARS AND CONFERENCES

Giving employees the opportunity to participate in seminars and conferences is an effective way of conveying specific information such as corporate policies, job procedures, business economic data, and industry trends. The presentations tend to rely on a mixed bag of techniques, for example, lectures, videos, demonstrations, case studies, role plays, and group exercises. They are widely used when orienting large groups of new employees. Organizations also rely on seminars and conferences as ways of keeping professional employees up to date in their fields.

Paul Hickey, Human Resources Supervisor for Island Tel in Charlottetown, P.E.I., uses the new technology of Picture Tel for conferences with other maritime telecommunications companies. Conference members are linked with interactive visual and audio capability so they can share information from their independent locations.

PROGRAMMED INSTRUCTION

A popular self-paced instructional method is called **programmed instruction**. Trainees are exposed to a small block of information and then tested immediately to see if the material has been understood. When trainees answer correctly, they move on to another block of information. Incorrect answers require repeating the cycle.

Programmed instruction Individuals learn a small block of information and are then tested immediately to see if the material has been understood.

Programmed instruction can be in the form of manuals, teaching machines, or video displays. But they all have a common characteristic: they condense material to be learned into highly organized, logical sequences, which require the trainee to respond.

A good illustration of programmed learning is the tutorial programs that often accompany the purchase of computer software. The tutorial walks the user through the software application, giving the individual opportunities to experiment with the various functions the program can perform.

OUTSIDE READING

It's so basic that it's often overlooked: providing reading material for employees to review in their nonworking hours. Supervisors, for example, can request and purchase subscriptions to job-relevant periodicals and have them mailed to employees' homes. Or, more typically, books, journals, and magazines are provided in rest areas, lunch rooms, and other places where employees may informally gather.

INDUSTRIAL SECTOR TRAINING

Canadian Automotive Parts Manufacturers' Association
http://www.capma.com/

Canadian Auto Workers Union
http://www.caw.ca/

In a unique partnership between management and union, a certificate program was developed to cooperatively address training needs within the independent automotive parts manufacturing industry in Canada. The partners, Automotive Parts Manufacturers' Association (management) and the Canadian Auto Workers Union, must both approve the content and instruction methods. The ultimate aim is to deliver effective long-term training in an integrated curriculum that focuses on communication, industry and technology. The program relies heavily on the use of peer trainers—production workers recruited from industry. The trainers work at gaining mutual respect for the agendas of management, labour, employers and workers with an orientation towards the auto parts manufacturing sector. The certificate informational brochure states:

> Management representatives see the value of this process in increased willingness and ability of their employees to participate in changes occurring at their workplace. Labor representatives see its value in increased empowerment of their members to play a leading role in making and implementing decisions about workplace change. Both agree, however, that the title of the program— "Opening Doors"—expresses its essential purpose.[3]

MATCHING TRAINING PROGRAMS TO OBJECTIVES

Supervisors shouldn't select training methods arbitrarily. Each method has certain strengths and weaknesses. A good deal of the success of any training or development program can be attributed to properly selecting a method that fits your objective.

Most skill deficiencies fall into one of three categories: technical, decision-making, or interpersonal. *Technical deficiencies* address the ability to use the tools, equipment, processes, and techniques needed to perform a job. *Decision-making deficiencies* encompass the abilities to identify problems, develop alternatives, analyze and evaluate alternatives, and arrive at effective solutions. *Interpersonal deficiencies* are concerned with abilities to work and communicate with others. In addition,

FIGURE 8-6

- *Technical.* Encompasses the ability to use tools, equipment, processes, and techniques.

- *Decision making.* Encompasses the ability to identify problems, develop alternatives, analyze and evaluate alternatives, and arrive at effective solutions.

- *Interpersonal.* Encompasses the ability to work and communicate with others.

FIGURE 8-6

Categories of skill deficiencies

learning in each of these categories may be from a cognitive or experiential perspective. **Cognitive learning** relies on mental processes. When you learn by reading, watching, or thinking, you're engaged in cognitive learning. When training focuses on actually practising, experiencing, or doing something, then you're engaged in **experiential learning**. As we noted earlier in the chapter, surgical training relies both on cognitive concepts and experiential practice.

On-the-job training methods are either experiential or a combination of cognitive and experiential learning. These are the preferred methods for learning technical skills and for practising interpersonal skills. Vestibule training, while off-the-job, requires learning by doing. It is an excellent means of dealing with technical deficiencies. Programmed learning can be either cognitive or experiential. For example, when you read about computers, it's cognitive. When you practise what you've learned, it's experiential. Seminars and conferences can likewise be designed along either perspective. Lecturing, for instance, relies on cognitive processes for learning. Role plays, on the other hand, incorporate learning by doing. Outside reading is an example of a purely cognitive learning activity.

When you want to merely know about something, cognitive learning methods are most effective. If you want to understand what a business plan is, or the pros and cons of putting your department on flexible work hours, or the proper steps to take in disciplining an employee, cognitive learning methods work well. However, if you want to actually write a business plan, or learn to implement flexible work hours, or practise disciplining, you should focus on experiential techniques.

Before you choose a training method, ask yourself what it is you want your trainee to learn. What specifically is the skill deficiency? Then design a training program that will most effectively facilitate the learning of that skill.

Returning to Island Tel, Paul Hickey reports that the current training challenge is to build "business savvy" in the increasingly competitive environment of the telecommunications industry. Island Tel holds a one-day

Cognitive learning
Learning that occurs via mental processes such as reading, watching, and thinking

Experiential learning
Learning that relies on practising, experiencing, or doing something

conference that encourages employees to look at new ways of dealing with competition, change and challenges. The conference focuses on face-to-face engagement with Island Tel customers who are major business leaders in the province. "Simply Better," another training program, coaches employees to promote Island Tel services to its customers. These two programs assist the company and its employees to achieve its objectives in a competitive business environment.

EVALUATING TRAINING EFFECTIVENESS

It's relatively easy to offer a new training program. But training must be cost-effective. You won't know if it's cost-effective unless you evaluate the training that's taking place. You must be able to show that the benefits gained from the training outweigh the costs of providing the learning experience. The only way to do this is to analyze the outcomes training may have generated.

Is there a way in which training programs are typically evaluated? Frequently, the following scenario takes place. Several individuals—usually representatives from the training department and a group of workers—are asked to critique a recently completed training program. If the comments are generally positive, the program gets a favourable evaluation. Based on that evaluation, the program continues, until something occurs that causes it to be changed or eliminated.

The accuracy of these reactions, however, is questionable. The participants' opinions are often heavily influenced by factors that have little to do with actual training effectiveness—factors like difficulty, entertainment value, or the personality of the instructor. Obviously, that's not the type of evaluation we're talking about. Rather, you must be certain that employee performance improves. Accordingly, training programs must be evaluated on some performance-based measures. This can be achieved by evaluating how well employees perform their jobs after they have received training, or the differences found between pre- and post-training performance.

HOW IS EMPLOYEE DEVELOPMENT DIFFERENT FROM EMPLOYEE TRAINING?

Employee development Preparation of employees for future positions that require hgiher-level skills, knowledge, or abilities

In many organizations, the terms *training* and *development* are often used synonymously. In many respects, that may be correct. But employee development is different. Whereas employee training focuses its attention on the skills needed to do one's current job, **employee development** is more future-oriented. That is, it deals with preparing employees for future positions that require higher level skills, knowledge, or abilities—like the analytical, human, conceptual, political, and specialized skills needed by all supervisors, which we introduced in Chapter 1. Although the methods of delivering employee development programs are similar to training methods, they focus more heavily on employees' personal growth.

It is important to consider one critical component of employee development in today's organizations. All employees, no matter what their level, can be developed. Historically, development was reserved for supervisory personnel, and those aspiring to be such. Although there's no question that development still must include preparing these individuals, the processes of downsizing, reengineering, and empowering have shown us that nonsupervisory personnel need such skills as planning, organizing, leading, and controlling, too. For instance, the use of work teams, workers' greater opportunity to participate in decision making, and the greater emphasis on customer service and quality have all led to development being "pushed" down in the organization. Like training, development efforts must also be evaluated to ensure that the organization is getting its money's worth.

CURRENT ISSUES IN TRAINING AND DEVELOPMENT

Informal discussions with practising supervisors reveal that, in addition to basic job skills, two other issues are high on their list of training needs. One is *diversity training*. Work groups are increasingly made up of individuals of mixed gender and diverse ethnic backgrounds. Employees need training to help them learn to accept people who are different from themselves and to become aware of the advantages diversity can bring to a work group. The other issue is *ethics training*. Many employees are no longer sure that "doing the right thing" at work is in their best interest. They get mixed signals from management, coworkers, friends, elected officials, and the media. As a result, supervisors are increasingly seeing the need to provide ethical training.

DIVERSITY TRAINING

While some organizations rely on outside consultants to provide diversity training, others are doing it in-house with their own employees. Take Pacific Gas & Electric, for example. It has trained 110 of its employees—including supervisors—as diversity-awareness trainers.[4] They understand what is meant by "valuing differences" and take on the task of showing employees the economic, competitive, and business reasons for managing diversity.

FIGURE 8-7

This informal, small group training session focuses on increasing diversity awareness among participants.

The two most popular types of diversity training focus on increasing awareness and building skills. Awareness training tries to create an understanding of the need for, and meaning of, managing and valuing diversity. Skill-building training educates employees about specific cultural differences in the workplace.[5]

ETHICS TRAINING

Ethics training is currently "in" in large companies.[6] You don't have to look far to understand why. We find reports of ethical transgressions almost daily in our newspapers. Employees are caught lying on their job résumés or fudging expense reports. Members of Parliament are found to be taking under-the-table financial kickbacks to vote a certain way. Stockbrokers profit from insider information. College students buy prewritten term papers or cheat on exams. As a result, organizations are offering ethics workshops in which employees review company codes of ethics, share common ethical dilemmas, and participate in games and exercises that allow them to address their ethical standards and practise their understanding of the organization's ethical code. Most of these ethical training programs are directed by middle-level and upper-level managers; however, supervisors often lead ethics workshops with members of their department.

What do proponents of ethics training expect to achieve with these programs? It's a noble goal to want to stimulate moral thought, identify ethical dilemmas, create a sense of moral obligation, develop problem-solving skills, and teach workers to tolerate or reduce ambiguity. But can you *teach* ethics? Critics argue that ethics is based on values, and value systems are fixed at an early age. The critics also claim that ethics cannot be formally taught, but must be learned by example. Leaders set ethical examples by what they say and do. If this is true, then ethics training is relevant only as part of leadership training.

But an increasing amount of evidence suggests that we can teach ethics. Values *can* be learned and changed after early childhood. Moreover, ethics training gets employees to think about ethical dilemmas and become more aware of the ethical issues underlying their actions. Finally, comprehensive studies made on the effectiveness of ethics training programs have found that they do improve ethical awareness and reasoning skills.

The Shift to Customer Orientation

As the Canadian economic base becomes more focused on sales and service, supervisors will be challenged to instill a different orientation to customer satisfaction in employees who are accustomed to process-driven jobs. As we look at recent advertising themes in our market, companies are pushing the truth of "the customer is always right!" And companies such as Wal-Mart and Nissan, with proven records of price and quality satisfaction for their clients, have been making their mark on the Canadian market.

Scotiabank
http://www.scotiabank.ca/

The Bank of Nova Scotia tackled the issue of promoting this new orientation among its employees, changing from an audit-driven focus to an emphasis on sales and service. The bank developed in-branch training for mass delivery across its distribution system, including prepackaged training units and accompanying videos. Account manager Leigh Enlund says, "In reality, the focus needs to be on motivating employees to accept the switch to a sales and service orientation." She estimated that it would take two to three years before the real commitment to a sales orientation is achieved.

5. Trainees who pace their own instruction, learning a small block of information (usually from a computer or manual), getting tested immediately, and then moving on to the next block of information, are learning by which technique?
   a. vestibule training
   a. sector training
   c. programmed instruction
   d. simulation training

6. Getting several participants to critique a recently completed training program is an effective way to evaluate the training. True or False?

7. Which one of the following statements best reflects the difference between employee training and employee development?
   a. Employee training primarily involves off-the-job training methods whereas employee development tends to use on-the-job methods.
   b. Training focuses on potential employees whereas employee development focuses on current employees.
   c. Employee training focuses on the skills needed for current jobs whereas employee development focuses on the skills needed for future postions.
   d. Employee training and development mean the same thing.

8. Explain why diversity training is offered.

COACHING

ASSESSING YOURSELF: WHAT IS EFFECTIVE COACHING?

For each of the following statements, answer either True (T) or False (F).

AN EFFECTIVE COACH SHOULD:

1.	Tell employees the right way to do a job.	T	F
2.	Suspend judgment and evaluation.	T	T
3.	Be a role model.	T	F
4.	Provide long-term career planning.	T	F
5.	Use a collaborative style.	T	F
6.	Never use threats.	T	F
7.	Respect an employee's individuality.	T	F
8.	Focus on getting each employee's performance up to a minimum standard.	T	F
9.	Dismiss mistakes.	T	F
10.	Delegate responsibility for coaching outcomes to the employee.	T	F

SCORING KEY

Give yourself one point for each correct answer: 1. F; 2. T; 3. T; 4. F; 5. T; 6. T; 7. T; 8. F; 9. F; and 10. F. Scores of eight or above indicate you have quite a bit of valid knowledge about coaching.

SKILL BASICS

Effective supervisors have learned how to coach their employees. That is, through coaching you help your employees to improve their performance.

Is *coaching* synonymous with *counselling*? Both deal with day-to-day issues rather than the long term. But they're different. Coaching deals with ability issues. As a coach, you provide instruction, guidance, advice, and encouragement to help employees improve their job performance. Counselling by contrast deals with personal problems. When employee attitudes or personality are the problem, you need to provide counselling.

Another important dimension of coaching is that it requires you to suspend judgment and evaluation. Supervisors, in the normal routine of carrying out their jobs, regularly express judgments about performance in relation to previously established goals. As a coach, you focus on accepting employees the way they are and helping them to make continual improvement toward the goal of developing to their full potential.

There are three general skills that supervisors should exhibit if they are to help their employees generate breakthroughs in performance.[7] The following reviews these general skills and the specific behaviours associated with each.

1. **Ability to analyze ways of improving an employee's performance and capabilities.**

   a. Observe your employee's behaviour on a day-to-day basis.

   b. Ask questions of the employee: Why do you do a task this way? Can it be improved? What other approaches might be used?

   c. Show genuine interest in the person as an individual, not merely as an employee. Respect his or her individuality. The insight you have into the employee's uniqueness is more important than any technical expertise you can provide about improving job performance.

   d. Listen to the employee. You can't understand the world from an employee's perspective unless you listen.

2. **Ability to create a supportive climate.** It's the coach's responsibility to reduce barriers to development and facilitate a climate that encourages performance improvement.

   a. Create a climate that contributes to a free and open exchange of ideas.

   b. Offer help and assistance. Give guidance and advice when asked.

   c. Encourage your employees. Be positive and upbeat. Don't use threats.

   d. Focus on mistakes as learning opportunities. Change implies risk and employees must not feel that mistakes will be punished. When failure occurs, ask: "What did we learn that can help us in the future?"

   e. Reduce obstacles. What factors do you control that, if changed, would help the employee to improve his or her job performance?

f. Express to the employee the value of his or her contribution to the department's goals.

g. Take personal responsibility for the outcome, but don't rob employees of their full responsibility. Validate the employees' efforts when they succeed, and point to what was missing when they fail. Never blame the employees for poor results.

3. **Ability to influence employees to change their behaviour.** The ultimate test of coaching effectiveness is whether an employee's performance improves. But this is not a static concept. We are concerned with ongoing growth and development.

a. Encourage continual improvement. Recognize and reward small improvements and, consistent with TQM, treat coaching as helping employees to continually work toward improvement. There are no absolute upper limits to an employee's job performance.

b. Use a collaborative style. Employees will be more responsive to accepting change if they participate in identifying and choosing among improvement ideas.

c. Break difficult tasks down into simpler ones. By breaking down more complex jobs into a series of tasks of increasing difficulty, discouraged employees are more likely to experience success. Achieving success on simpler tasks encourages them to take on more difficult ones.

d. Model the qualities you expect from your employees. If you want openness, dedication, commitment, and responsibility from your employees, you must demonstrate these qualities yourself. Your employees will look to you as a role model, so make sure your deeds match your words.

APPLYING YOUR SKILLS

Read the following scenario. Depending on the instructions given, be prepared to either write a three- or four-page report or discuss in class how you would handle Todd Corsetti based on the coaching skills in this chapter.

SITUATION

You work for a large mortgage brokering company. They have thirty offices in western Canada. You're supervisor of the Edmonton office and have seven mortgage brokers, an assistant, and a secretary reporting to you. Your business entails helping home buyers find mortgages and acting as a link between lenders and borrowers in getting loans approved and processed.

Todd Corsetti is one of your brokers. He has been in the office for two-and-a half years. Before that, he sold commercial real estate. You've been in your Edmonton job for fourteen months, prior to which you supervised a smaller office for the same company.

You have not been pleased with Todd's job performance, so you decided to review his personnel file. His first six-month review stated: "Todd is enthusiastic. He is a bit disorganized but willing to learn. Seems to have good potential." After a year, his previous supervisor had written, "Todd seems to be losing interest. Seems frequently disorganized. Often rude to clients. Did not mention these problems to him. Hope he'll improve. His long-term potential now much more in question."

You have not spent much time with Todd. Your offices are far apart. But probably the real reason is that he's not a person who's easy to talk to and you have little in common. When you took this job, you decided that you'd wait some time before tackling any problems to make sure you had a good grasp of the people and the situation.

But Todd's problems have gotten too visible to ignore. He is consistently missing his quarterly sales projections. Based on mortgages processed, he is your lowest performer. In addition, his reports are constantly late. After reviewing last month's performance reports, you made an appointment yesterday to meet him today at 9:00 a.m. But he wasn't in his office when you arrived for that appointment. You waited fifteen minutes and gave up. Your secretary tells you that Todd regularly comes in late for work in the morning and takes extra long coffee breaks. Last week, Valerie Oletta, who has the office next to Todd's, complained to you that Todd's behaviour was demoralizing her and some of the other brokers.

You don't want to fire Todd. It wouldn't be easy to find a replacement. Moreover, he has a lot of contacts with new-home builders, which brings in a number of borrowers to your office. In fact, maybe 60 per cent of the business generated by your entire office comes from builders who have personal ties to Todd. If Todd were to leave your company and go to a competitor, he'd probably be able to convince the builders to take their business somewhere else.

DISCUSSION

Using the three general skills in coaching employees, detail a plan of action that you, as Todd's supervisor, might follow in a coaching seminar.

SUMMARY

This summary is organized by the Learning Objectives.

1. *Training* is defined as a learning experience that results in a relatively permanent change in an individual that improves his or her ability to perform on the job.

2. Signs that suggest employee training may be necessary include the entry of a new employee, the introduction of new equipment or processes, an increase in the number of employee errors, an increase in the number of questions employees ask, an increase in complaints by customers or coworkers, a rise in the number of accidents, or a drop in individual or group productivity.

3. The use of reinforcement encourages the repetition of a behaviour. When a new behaviour is exhibited, it can be sustained by use of reinforcement.

4. The learning curve describes the speed with which learning occurs over time. Learning is very fast near the beginning, which means the curve is steep. Then learning levels off as opportunities for improvement lessen.

5. Four on-the-job training methods are apprenticeship, coaching, mentoring, and job rotation.

6. Four off-the-job training methods are vestibule training, seminars and conferences, programmed instruction, and outside reading.

7. Three skill deficiency categories are technical, decision-making, and interpersonal.

8. Evaluating training effectiveness is an important tool to ensure that training dollars are spent on programs that positively influence employee job performance. Rigorous evaluation can help determine if training makes any difference and whether the improvement justifies the cost.

9. Two popular types of diversity training are awareness training and skill-building training.

10. Five positive outcomes of ethics training are stimulating moral thought, recognizing ethical dilemmas, creating a sense of moral obligation, developing problem-solving skills, and tolerating or reducing ambiguity.

KEY TERMS AND CONCEPTS

Apprenticeship
Coaching
Cognitive learning
Experiential learning
Job rotation
Learning curve

Mentoring
Off-the-job training
On-the-job training
Programmed instruction
Vestibule training

REVIEWING YOUR KNOWLEDGE

1. Why is training important?
2. When might training not be the solution to ineffective job performance?
3. What is the supervisor's responsibility regarding training?
4. How can you use learning principles to make training more effective?
5. Discuss this statement in terms of designing a training program:
   "I hear and I forget. I see and I remember. I do and I understand."
6. What are the advantages of on-the-job training? Off-the-job training?
7. What's the best approach for evaluating training? Why?
8. Is it possible to teach ethics? Explain.

ANSWERS TO THE POP QUIZZES

1. **False.** Whether the supervisor is involved in training depends on training budget, time, the supervisor's training skills, the size of the organization and the availability of other training resources.

2. **a. Learning requires feedback.** Learners must be aware of how effective their performance is in order to correct mistakes and focus on improving.

3. Advantages of training on the job include ease, transferability to job and apparent low cost. Disadvantages include low productivity during training and the costs incurred by errors.

4. **b. job rotation**

5. **c. programmed instruction**

6. **False.** Their critiques are subjective and may be unrelated to actual changes in performance, which must be the focus in evaluating the training.

7. **c. Employee training focuses on the skills needed for current jobs whereas employee development focuses on the skills needed for future positions.**

8. Diversity training is aimed at creating a more tolerant and productive workforce. The workforce is increasingly diverse and it is felt that training can help people better accept and appreciate this diversity.

CASE 8.A

Ahmad's Oriental Carpet Bazaar

Ahmad's Oriental Carpet Bazaar is a direct importer of oriental and antique rugs, and is owned and operated by Syed Ahmad. The company does appraisals and exchanges on oriental rugs and has an expert cleaning and repair service. Ahmad's Bazaar prides itself on its interior design services and its elegant showroom displaying a wide range of Persian antique rugs, tapestries, kilims, needlepoint, and chain-stitch rugs.

Recently Mr. Ahmad has been reading a lot about the value of training for employees and has come to the conclusion that a training program is needed for his company. Obviously, there are quite a few questions that need to be answered before a training program can be implemented for Mr. Ahmad's twenty-eight employees.

Mr. Ahmad feels that Laura Disrude and Sedric Abraham are the logical employees to develop and conduct the training program. Laura and Sedric are extremely competent, supervise several people, work well with customers, and are admired and respected by company employees. Laura, a very creative and outgoing person, has been an interior designer with the company for twelve years. Sedric, a very laid-back individual with a quiet and warm personality, has been an appraiser and buyer/salesperson with Ahmad's Bazaar for nine years. Both Laura and Sedric are highly valued employees.

RESPONDING TO THIS CASE

1. What factors might have led Mr. Ahmad to the decision that a training program is needed for his employees?
2. Are Laura and Sedric the best people to develop and implement a training program? Why or why not?
3. What factors are important for Laura and Sedric to consider as they begin this new project?
4. How would a needs assessment help Laura and Sedric in designing a training program?
5. Divide into small groups to discuss the elements that will help assure success for Laura and Sedric in designing and implementing a training program. Identify the questions Mr. Ahmad needs to have answered about the direction (development, design, implementation, facilitation, evaluation, etc.) of the proposed program. Share and compare the results of group discussions.

CASE 7.B

Tenneco, Inc.

Darla Malone is a graphics communication technologist who works for Tenneco, Inc. Last month she was promoted to a supervisory position in her unit.

As long as Darla can remember, training has been an important aspect of developing employees at Tenneco. Darla recalls that her first "training" experience at Tenneco was her participation in the excellent new employee orientation four years ago when she joined the large company.

Since then Darla has had several other training opportunities and experiences, which have expanded her skills and knowledge. For example, she has had training sessions—on issues from safety to quality—conducted by company trainers and her manager. Her employer has encouraged and supported her participation in out-of-company graphics communication seminars and conferences as well as her enrollment in the management program at a local community college. Darla has also become active in a local printing industries association where she has made a couple of presentations on colour press techniques and desktop publishing.

Darla is an expert in the intricacies of colour press operations and is extremely good at solving problems that arise in producing quality print media for Tenneco. Darla has always worked well with other employees in her unit and is enthusiastic and optimistic about the increased responsibility in her new supervisory position. The first "formal" training she will provide to her employees will centre on the new Heidelberg press that will be installed in her unit.

RESPONDING TO THIS CASE

1. Discuss the factors that point to Darla's likely success in training her employees.

2. What are some of the learning guidelines of which Darla should be aware as she takes on new training endeavours? What words of caution can you give to Darla in her new position?

3. What steps should Darla follow in training her employees?

4. Identify the various training methods Darla could use in training her employees. Discuss the pros and cons of each method.

5. Form groups, then assign to each group one or more of the training methods discussed in this chapter. Each group should make a list of the strengths and weaknesses of the training method(s) assigned. Then determine why the method(s) would or would not be recommended for Darla to use. Discuss findings and conclusions with the class.

6. How should Darla evaluate her training effectiveness?

Part III: Organizing, Staffing and Employee Development

Mary Jo Romportl
Teller Supervisor, Western Bank

Mary Jo was a teller at Western before being promoted to teller supervisor. There was dissension within the department. The former supervisor had personal problems and she seemed to bring many of those problems to work. She was cold and critical toward employees, and teamwork suffered. Most of the tellers felt they could not talk to their supervisor.

One of Mary Jo's first tasks is to build up the morale and teamwork in her department. There are serious problems with teamwork and absenteeism, and none of the tellers want to work overtime. Customer service is very poor because the tellers suffer from negative attitudes.

1. What are the main goals Mary Jo has set for her department?

2. Do you think Mary Jo has set realistic goals? Why or why not?

3. Why is it important to conduct an assessment of a team's effectiveness? What can be learned from it? Which role should a supervisor play in such an assessment?

4. Discuss the elements that need to be considered in developing an employee performance appraisal system.

5. Discuss some of the most effective ways to improve morale, to build trust and teamwork, and to motivate employees to contribute to the organization's goal.

PART FOUR

STIMULATING INDIVIDUAL AND GROUP PERFORMANCE

9

MOTIVATING YOUR EMPLOYEES

LEARNING OBJECTIVES

After reading this chapter, you should be able to:

1. Define *motivation*.
2. Identify and define five personality characteristics relevant to understanding the behaviour of employees at work.
3. Explain the elements and the focus of the three early theories of motivation.
4. Identify the characteristics that stimulate the achievement drive in high achievers.
5. Explain how reinforcement is related to motivation.
6. Describe the role that equity can play in motivation.
7. Identify the three relationships in expectancy theory that determine an individual's level of effort.
8. List those actions a supervisor can take to maximize employee motivation.
9. Contrast the challenges in motivating low-pay service workers versus professional employees.

CHAPTER OUTLINE

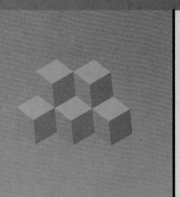

Sean Hartman is a hard-driving, competitive person. He gives a maximum effort on everything he does—at his job, his summer softball team, in cleaning and waxing his classic 1963 Porsche. In contrast, his good friend Don Avery seems to have no discipline in his life. People who know him think he's lazy. While Don is smart and highly capable, he has trouble holding a job because of his inability to put forth much sustained effort. Sean summed up his appraisal of Don: "He can't stay with anything for more than a half-hour or so. He gets bored and distracted easily."

Supervisors like having Sean Hartman types working for them. Such people are essentially self-motivated. You don't have to do much to get them to produce a full day's effort. The Don Averys of the world are another story. They're a supervisor's nightmare. It's a challenge to develop creative ways to motivate them.

Most employees aren't like either Sean or Don. They're more like Molly Hubert. On some activities, Molly is incredibly motivated. For example, she reads two or three novels a week and she gets up at 5:30 every morning and religiously runs three or four miles before showering and going to work. But at her sales job at the local Footlocker shoe store, she seems bored and unmotivated. Most people are like Molly in that their levels of motivation vary across activities.

What can supervisors do to increase the motivation of people like Don Avery and Molly Hubert? In this chapter, we'll provide you with some insights and tools that can help answer this question.

WHAT IS MOTIVATION?

Motivation
The willingness to do some action. It is conditioned by this action's ability to satisfy some need for the individual.

Need
A physiological or psychological deficiency that makes certain outcomes seem attractive

First, what do we mean by the term *motivation*? **Motivation** is the willingness to do something and is conditioned by this action's ability to satisfy some need for the individual. A **need**, in our terminology, means a physiological or psychological deficiency that makes certain outcomes seem attractive.

An unsatisfied need creates tension, which sets off a drive to satisfy that need. The greater the tension, the greater the drive or effort that will be required to reduce that tension. So when we see employees working hard at some activity, we can conclude that they're driven by a desire to satisfy one or more needs that they value.

UNDERSTANDING INDIVIDUAL DIFFERENCES

An error that new supervisors commonly make is to assume that other people are like them. If they're ambitious, they think others are also ambitious. If they place a high value on spending evenings and weekends with their family, they assume that others feel the same way. Big mistake! People are different. What's important to me is not necessarily important to you. Not everybody, for instance, is driven by the desire for money. Yet a lot of supervisors believe a bonus or the opportunity for a pay increase should make every employee want to work harder. If you're going to be successful in motivating people, you have to begin by accepting and trying to understand individual differences. And you have to be willing to treat different people differently.

To make our point, let's look at personality. Most of us know people who are loud and aggressive. We know others who are quiet and passive. A number of personality characteristics have been singled out as having relevance to understanding the behaviour and motivation of employees at work. These include locus of control, Machiavellianism, self-esteem, self-monitoring, and risk propensity.

Some people believe that they are masters of their own fate. Other people see themselves as pawns of fate, believing that what happens to them in their lives is due to luck or chance. **Locus of control** in the first case is internal; these people believe they control their destiny. Those who see their life controlled by outsiders have an external locus of control. Studies tell us that employees who rate high in externality are less satisfied with their jobs, more alienated from the work setting, and less involved in their jobs than are internals. For instance, employees with an external locus of control may be less enthusiastic about their jobs because they believe that they have little personal influence on the outcome of their performance appraisals. If they get a poor appraisal, they're apt to blame it on their supervisor's prejudice, their coworkers, or other events outside their control.

The characteristic of **Machiavellianism** (Mach) is named after Niccolo Machiavelli, who wrote in the sixteenth century on how to gain and manipulate power. An individual exhibiting strong Machiavellian tendencies is manipulative and believes ends can justify means. Some might even see these people as ruthless. High Machs tend to be motivated on jobs that require bargaining (such as labour negotiator) or where there are substantial rewards for winning (as in commissioned sales). But they can get frustrated in jobs where there are specific rules that must be followed or where rewards are based more on using the proper means rather than on the achievement of outcomes.

People differ in the degree to which they like or dislike themselves. This trait is called **self-esteem**. Studies confirm that people high in self-esteem (SE) believe that they possess more of the ability they need in order to succeed at work. But the most significant finding on self-esteem is that low-SEs

FIGURE 9-1

"Management is people," says Michelle Chung, a Calgary store manager. "One plus one equals two? No, it doesn't work that way when you're dealing with people's emotions, their ups and downs. You have to be really good with people."

Locus of control
The degree to which people believe they are masters of their own fate

Machiavellianism
The degree to which an individual is manipulative and believes ends can justify means

Self-esteem
The degree to which individuals like or dislike themselves

are more susceptible to external influence than are high-SEs. Low-SEs are dependent on receiving positive evaluations from others. As a result, they are more likely to seek approval from others and more prone to conform to the beliefs and behaviours of those they respect than are high-SEs.

Some individuals are very adaptable and can easily adjust their behaviour to changing situations. Others are rigid and inflexible. The personality trait that captures this difference is called **self-monitoring**. Individuals high in self-monitoring show considerable adaptability in adjusting their behaviour to external situational factors. They are highly sensitive to external cues and can behave differently in different situations. High self-monitors are capable of presenting striking contradictions between their public personas and their private selves. Low self-monitors can't disguise themselves this way. They tend to display their true feelings and beliefs in every situation. The evidence tells us that high self-monitors tend to pay closer attention to the behaviour of others and are more capable of conforming than are low self-monitors. Additionally, because high self-monitors are flexible, they adjust better than low self-monitors to job situations that require individuals to play multiple roles in their work groups.

People differ in their willingness to take chances. Individuals with a high **risk propensity** make more rapid decisions and use less information in making their choices than low risk-propensity individuals. Not surprisingly, high-risk seekers tend to prefer, and are more satisfied in, jobs such as stockbroker or firefighter on an oil platform.

Self-monitoring
A personality trait that measures an individual's ability to adjust his or her behaviour to external, situational factors

Risk propensity
The degree to which people are willing to take chances

HOW CAN AN UNDERSTANDING OF PERSONALITY HELP YOU BE A MORE EFFECTIVE SUPERVISOR?

The major value of understanding personality differences probably lies in selection. You are likely to have higher performing and more satisfied employees if consideration is given to matching personality types with compatible jobs. In addition, there may be other benefits. By recognizing that people approach problem solving, decision making, and job interactions differently, you can better understand why, for instance, an employee is uncomfortable making quick decisions or insists on gathering as much information as possible before addressing a problem. You can also anticipate that individuals with an external locus of control may be less satisfied with their jobs than "internals," and also that they may be less willing to accept responsibility for their actions.

EARLY APPROACHES TO MOTIVATION

Once we accept individual differences, we begin to understand why there is no single motivator that applies to all employees. Because people are complex, any attempt to explain their motivations will also tend to be complex. We see this in the number of approaches that have been taken in developing theories of employee motivation. In the following pages, we'll review the most popular of these approaches.

FOCUS ON NEEDS

The most elementary approach to motivation was developed by Abraham Maslow.[1] He identified a set of basic needs which, he argued, were common to all individuals; and he said individuals should be evaluated in terms of the degree to which these needs are fulfilled. According to Maslow's **hierarchy of needs theory**, a satisfied need no longer creates tension and therefore doesn't motivate. The key to motivation then, according to Maslow, is to determine where an individual is located on the needs hierarchy and focus motivation efforts at the point where needs become essentially unfulfilled.

Hierarchy of needs theory
There is a hierarchy of five needs—physiological, safety, social, esteem, and self-actualization. As each need is sequentially satisfied, the next need becomes dominant.

Maslow proposed that within every human being there exists a hierarchy of five needs. These needs are:

1. **Physiological**—includes hunger, thirst, shelter, sex, and other bodily needs.
2. **Safety**—includes security and protection from physical and emotional harm.
3. **Social**—includes affection, a sense of belonging, acceptance, and friendship.
4. **Esteem**—includes internal factors such as self-respect, autonomy, and achievement; and external factors such as status, recognition, and attention.
5. **Self-actualization**—the drive to become what one is capable of becoming; includes growth, achieving one's potential, and self-fulfillment.

As each of these needs becomes substantially satisfied, the next need becomes dominant. In terms of Figure 9-3, the individual moves up the hierarchy. From the standpoint of motivation, the theory would say that although no need is ever fully gratified, a substantially satisfied need no longer motivates.

A number of studies to test the validity of Maslow's theory have been made over the years. Generally, these studies have not been able to support the theory. We can't say, for example, that everyone's need structure is organized along the dimensions Maslow proposed. So, while this theory has been around for a long time and is certainly well known, it is probably not a very good guide for helping you motivate your employees.

FOCUS ON THE NATURE OF PEOPLE

Some supervisors believe their employees are hard working, committed, and responsible. Other supervisors view their employees as essentially lazy,

FIGURE 9-2

Today, almost all permanently employed workers have their lower-order needs met.

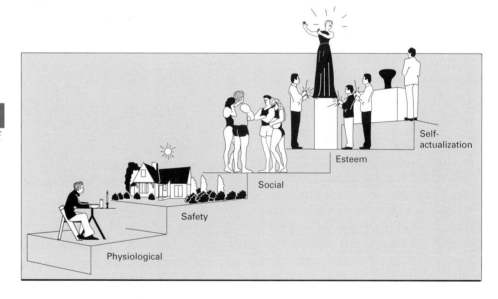

FIGURE 9-3

Maslow's Hierarchy of Needs. (*Source:* By permission of the Modular Project of Organizational Behavior and Instructional Communications Centre. McGill University, Montreal, Canada.)

Self-actualization

Esteem

Social

Safety

Physiological

Theory X-Theory Y
Two diametrically opposed views of human nature. Theory X assumes people are essentially lazy, irresponsible, and lacking ambition; Theory Y assumes people are hard working, committed, and responsible.

irresponsible, and lacking ambition. This observation led Douglas McGregor to propose his **Theory X-Theory Y** view of human nature and motivation.[2]

McGregor argued that a supervisor's view of the nature of human beings is based on a certain grouping of assumptions, and that supervisors tend to mold their behaviour toward subordinates according to these assumptions.

Under Theory X, the four assumptions held by supervisors are:

1. Employees inherently dislike work and, whenever possible, will attempt to avoid it.

2. Since employees dislike work, they must be coerced, controlled, or threatened with punishment to achieve desired goals.
3. Employees will shirk responsibility and seek formal direction whenever possible.
4. Most workers place security above all other factors associated with work, and will display little ambition.

In contrast to these negative views toward the nature of human beings, McGregor listed four other assumptions that he called Theory Y:

1. Employees can view work as being as natural as rest or play.
2. Employees will exercise self-direction and self-control if they are committed to the objectives.
3. The average person can learn to accept, even seek, responsibility.
4. The ability to make good decisions is widely dispersed throughout the population, and not necessarily the sole province of those in management.

What are the motivational implications of Theory X-Theory Y? McGregor argued that Theory Y assumptions were more valid than those of Theory X. As a result, he proposed ideas such as participation in decision making, responsible and challenging jobs, and good group relations as approaches that would maximize an employee's job motivation.

Unfortunately, there is no evidence to confirm that either set of assumptions is valid, or that acceptance of Theory Y assumptions and altering one's actions accordingly will lead to more motivated workers. As will become evident later in this chapter, either Theory X or Theory Y assumptions may be appropriate in a particular situation.

Focus on Satisfaction and Dissatisfaction

"First, describe situations in which you felt exceptionally good about your job. Second, describe situations in which you felt exceptionally bad about your job." Beginning in the late 1950s, Frederick Herzberg asked these two questions of a number of workers. He then tabulated and categorized their responses. What he found was that the replies people gave when they felt good about their jobs were significantly different from the replies given when they felt bad. As shown in Figure 9-4, certain characteristics tend to be consistently related to job satisfaction (when they felt "good"), and others to job dissatisfaction (when they felt "bad"). Intrinsic factors such as achievement, recognition, the work itself, responsibility, and advancement seemed to be related to job satisfaction. When those questioned felt good about their work, they tended to attribute these characteristics to themselves. On the other hand, when they were dissatisfied, they tended to cite external factors, such as company policy and administration, supervision, interpersonal relations, and working conditions.

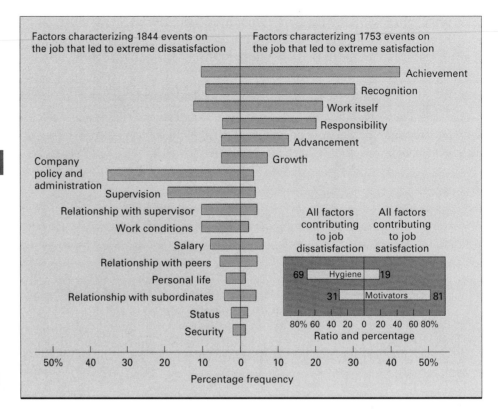

Motivation-hygiene theory
Intrinsic factors are related to job satisfaction, while extrinsic factors are associated with dissatisfaction.

Herzberg took these results and formulated what he called **motivation-hygiene theory**.[3] He said the responses suggest that the opposite of satisfaction is not dissatisfaction, as was traditionally believed. Removing dissatisfying characteristics from a job does not necessarily make the job satisfying. Herzberg proposed that his findings indicate the existence of a dual continuum: the opposite of "Satisfaction" is "No Satisfaction," and the opposite of "Dissatisfaction" is "No Dissatisfaction" (see Figure 9-5).

According to Herzberg, the factors leading to job satisfaction are separate and distinct from those that lead to job dissatisfaction. Therefore, supervisors who seek to eliminate factors that can create job dissatisfaction may bring about peace, but not necessarily motivation. They will be placating their employees rather than motivating them. As a result, such characteristics as company policy and administration, supervision, interpersonal relations, working conditions, and salary have been characterized by Herzberg as *hygiene factors*. When they're adequate, people will not be dissatisfied; however, neither will they be satisfied. If we want to motivate people on their jobs, Herzberg suggests emphasizing achievement, recognition, the work itself, responsibility, and growth. These *motivating factors* are the characteristics that people find intrinsically rewarding.

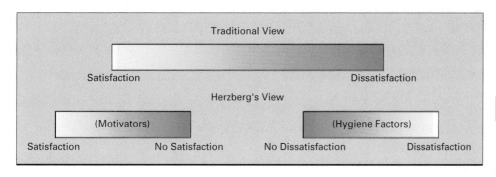

FIGURE 9-5

Contrasting views
of satisfaction–
dissatisfaction

The motivation-hygiene theory is important because it was the primary initiating force encouraging managers, beginning in the 1960s, to redesign jobs in order to make them more intrinsically interesting and challenging for employees. However, we should point out that the theory is concerned with job satisfaction rather than directly with motivation. That is, it seeks to predict what factors contribute to job satisfaction and dissatisfaction. A large body of research allows us to say, rather definitively, that satisfied workers are not necessarily motivated or productive workers.[4] For example, high job satisfaction tends to result in reduced absenteeism and turnover, but the effect of satisfaction on productivity is minimal. So motivation-hygiene theory should be considered a more valuable guide to an employee's level of job satisfaction than to his or her level of motivation.

CONTEMPORARY THEORIES OF MOTIVATION

While the previous theories are well known, they unfortunately have not held up well under close examination. However, all is not lost. Some contemporary theories have one thing in common: each has a reasonable degree of valid supporting documentation. The following theories represent the current "state-of-the-art" explanations of employee motivation.

FOCUS ON ACHIEVEMENT

Some people have a compelling drive to succeed, but are striving for personal achievement rather than the rewards of success. They have a desire to do something better or more efficiently than it has been done before. This drive is the **need for achievement**. Those people with a high need for achievement (*nAch*) are intrinsically motivated.[5] As you'll see, when high achievers are placed into jobs that stimulate their achievement drive, they are self-motivated and require little of a supervisor's time or energy.

Need for achievement
The need to do things
better or more effi-
ciently than they have
been done before

1. The motto "Let each become all he/she is capable of being" best illustrates:
   a. the expectancy theory of motivation
   b. the relationship between needs and tension
   c. self-actualization needs
   d. Theory Y
2. Describe how needs affect the motivation process.
3. Theory X is basically a positive view of employees, assuming that they are creative, while Theory Y is a negative view of human nature, assuming that employees dislike work. True or False?
4. Motivation-hygiene theory factors that eliminate dissatisfaction are called:
   a. motivators
   b. social needs
   c. eliminators
   d. none of the above

High achievers differentiate themselves from others by their desire to do things better. They seek situations where they can attain personal responsibility for finding solutions to problems, where they can receive rapid and unambiguous feedback on their performance so they can tell easily whether they are improving or not, and where they can set moderately challenging goals. High achievers are not gamblers; they dislike succeeding by chance. They prefer the challenge of working at a problem and accepting the personal responsibility for success or failure, rather than leaving the outcome to chance or the actions of others. They avoid what they perceive to be very easy or very difficult tasks.

High achievers perform best when they perceive their probability of success as being 0.5; that is, when they estimate that they have a 50–50 chance of success. They dislike gambling with high odds because they get no achievement satisfaction from accidental success. Similarly, they dislike low odds (high probability of success) because then there is no challenge to their skills. They like to set goals that require them to stretch themselves a little. When there is an approximately equal chance of success or failure, there is the optimum opportunity to experience feelings of accomplishment and satisfaction from their efforts.

What proportion of the workforce is made up of high achievers? In developed countries, the answer appears to be between 10 and 20 per cent. The percentage is considerably lower though in third-world countries. The reason is that the cultures of developed countries tend to socialize more people toward striving for personal achievement.

Based on an extensive amount of achievement research, we can draw three reasonably well-supported conclusions. First, individuals with a high *nAch* prefer job situations with personal responsibility, feedback, and an intermediate degree of risk. When these characteristics are prevalent, high achievers will be strongly motivated. The evidence consistently demonstrates, for instance, that high achievers are successful in entrepreneurial activities such as running their own businesses as well as in many sales positions.

Second, a high need to achieve does not necessarily lead to being a good supervisor or manager, especially in large organizations. High *nAch* salespeople do not necessarily make good sales supervisors, and the good manager in a large organization does not typically have a high need to achieve. The reason seems to be that high achievers want to do things themselves rather than lead others toward accomplishments.

Lastly, employees have been successfully trained to stimulate their achievement need. If a job calls for a high achiever, you can select a person with a high *nAch* or develop your own candidate through achievement training. Achievement training focuses on teaching people to act, talk, and think like high achievers by having them write stories emphasizing achievement, play simulation games that stimulate feelings of achievement, meet with successful entrepreneurs, and learn how to develop specific and challenging goals.

FOCUS ON REINFORCEMENT

In Chapter 8, in our discussion of learning principles, we said that reinforcement increases the likelihood that a learned behaviour will be repeated. The concept of reinforcement also has application as an approach to motivation.

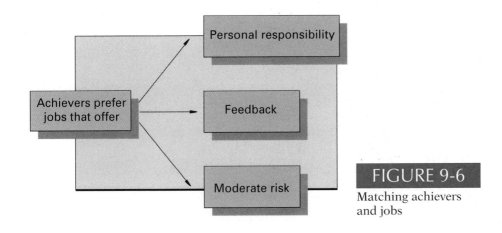

FIGURE 9-6

Matching achievers and jobs

Reinforcement theory
People will exert higher levels of effort in tasks that are reinforced.

Reinforcement theory states that people will exert higher levels of effort in tasks that are reinforced. A reinforcer is any consequence that, when immediately following a response, increases the probability that the behaviour will be repeated. This would include piece-rate pay plans where workers are paid a fixed sum for each unit of production completed, prizes given to employees for achieving perfect attendance, and compliments to employees when they do something nice for a customer.

The current popularity of pay-for-performance programs in organizations is clearly a direct response to the logic of reinforcement theory. Instead of compensating people on the basis of, for example, seniority, paying workers for performance outcomes increases their effort because the higher their performance, the larger their compensation. But in its pure form, reinforcement theory totally ignores the inner state of an individual and concentrates solely on what happens to a person when he or she takes some action. It's hard to believe that feelings, attitudes, expectations, and similar cognitive variables have no impact on behaviour, but that's what reinforcement theory proposes. Our conclusion is that you should recognize that reinforcement undoubtedly has an important influence on motivation but it is not the only influence.

FOCUS ON EQUITY

Your company just hired someone new to work in your department, doing the same job as you are doing. That person is about the same age as you, with almost identical educational qualifications and experience. The company is paying you $3500 a month (which you consider very competitive). How would you feel if you found out that the company is paying the new person—whose credentials are not one bit better than yours—$4000 a month? You'd probably be upset and angry. You'd probably think it wasn't fair. You're now likely to think you're underpaid. And you might direct your anger into actions such as reducing your work effort, taking longer coffee breaks, or taking extra days off by calling in "sick."

Your reactions illustrate the role that equity plays in motivation. People make comparisons of their job inputs and outcomes relative to others, and inequities have a strong bearing on the degree of effort that employees exert.[6]

Equity theory
Employees perceive what they get from a job situation (outcomes) in relation to what they put into it (inputs), then compare their input-outcome ratio with the input-outcome ratio of others; and then respond so as to eliminate any inequities.

Equity theory states that employees perceive what they can get from a job situation (outcomes) in relation to what they put into it (inputs), and then compare their input–outcome ratio with the input–outcome ratio of others. If they perceive their ratio to be equal to the relevant others with whom they compare themselves, a state of equity is said to exist. They feel their situation is fair, and that justice prevails. If the ratios are unequal, inequity exists; that is, the employees tend to view themselves as underrewarded or overrewarded. When inequities occur, employees will attempt to correct them.

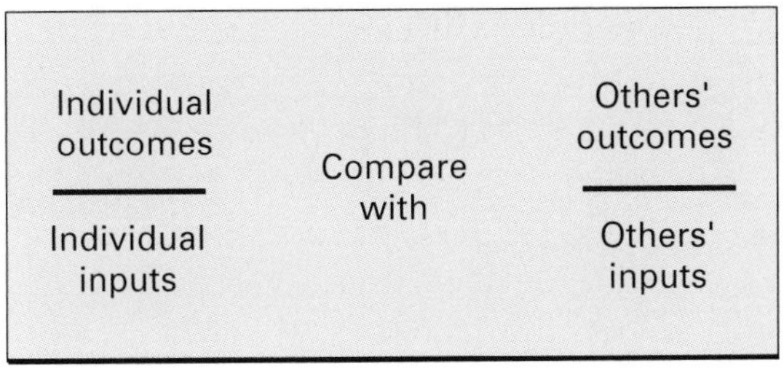

Individual
outcomes
———————
Individual
inputs

Compare
with

Others'
outcomes
———————
Others'
inputs

FIGURE 9-7

Equity theory

Equity theory recognizes that individuals are concerned not only with the absolute amount of rewards they receive for their efforts, but also with the relationship of this amount to what others receive. They make judgments based on the relationship between their inputs and outcomes and the inputs and outcomes of others. Inputs such as effort, experience, education, and competence can be compared to outcomes such as salary levels, raises, recognition, and other factors. When people perceive an imbalance in their input–outcome ratio relative to others, tension is created. This tension provides the basis for motivation, as people strive for what they perceive as equity and fairness.

There is substantial evidence to confirm the equity thesis: Employee motivation is influenced significantly by relative rewards as well as by absolute rewards. It helps to explain why, particularly when employees perceive themselves as underrewarded (we all seem to be pretty good at rationalizing being *over*rewarded), they may reduce their work effort, produce lower quality work, sabotage the system, skip work days, or even resign.

FOCUS ON EXPECTANCIES

The final perspective we'll present is an integrative approach to motivation. It focuses on expectations. Specifically, **expectancy theory** argues that individuals analyze three relationships: effort–performance, performance–rewards, and rewards–personal goals. Their level of effort depends on the strengths of their expectations that these relationships can be achieved.[7] According to expectancy theory, an employee will be motivated to exert a high level of effort when he or she believes that effort will lead to a good performance appraisal; that a good appraisal will lead to organizational rewards like a bonus, a salary increase, or a promotion; and that the rewards will satisfy the employee's personal goals. The theory is illustrated in Figure 9-8.

Expectancy theory has proven to provide a powerful explanation of employee motivation. It helps explain why a lot of workers aren't motivated on their jobs and merely do the minimum necessary to get by. This can be made clearer if we look at the theory's three relationships in

Expectancy theory
The strength of a tendency to act depends on the strength of an expectation that the act will be followed by a given outcome and on the attractiveness of that outcome to the individual.

FIGURE 9-8

Expectancy theory

a little more detail. We'll present them as questions which, if supervisors want to maximize employee motivation, need to be answered affirmatively by those employees.

1. **If I give maximum effort, will it be recognized in my performance evaluation?** For a lot of employees, the answer is no. Why? Their skill level may be deficient, which means that no matter how hard they try, they're not likely to be a high performer. Or the company's performance appraisal system may be poorly designed—assessing traits, for example, rather than behaviours—making it difficult or impossible for the employee to achieve a strong evaluation. Still another possibility is that the employee, rightly or wrongly, perceives that her supervisor doesn't like her. As a result, she expects to get a poor appraisal regardless of her level of performance. These examples suggest that one possible source of low employee motivation is the belief, by the employee, that no matter how hard she works, the likelihood of getting a good performance appraisal is low.

2. **If I get a good performance appraisal, will it lead to organizational rewards?** Many employees see the performance–reward relationship in their job as weak. The reason is that organizations reward a lot of things besides just performance. For example, when pay is allocated to employees based on factors such as seniority, being cooperative, or "kissing up" to the boss, employees are likely to see the performance–reward relationship as being weak and demotivating.

3. **If I'm rewarded, is the reward one that I find personally attractive?** The employee works hard in hope of getting a promotion, but gets a pay raise instead. Or the employee wants a more interesting and challenging job, but receives only a few words of praise. Unfortunately, many supervisors are limited in the rewards they can distribute. This makes it difficult to tailor rewards to individual employees. Still other supervisors incorrectly assume that all employees want the same thing, thus overlooking the motivational effects of differentiating rewards. In either case, employee motivation is submaximized.

APPLYING MOTIVATION CONCEPTS

We've presented a number of approaches to motivation in this chapter. If you're a supervisor, concerned with motivating your employees, how do you apply the various concepts introduced? While there is no simple, all-encompassing set of guidelines, the following suggestions provide valuable insight.

RECOGNIZE INDIVIDUAL DIFFERENCES

If there is one thing we've learned over the years, it's that employees are not homogeneous. People have different needs. While you may be driven by the need for recognition, I may be far more concerned with satisfying my desire for security. And we identified earlier in the chapter that a minority of employees have a high need for achievement. But if one or more of the people working for you are high achievers, make sure you design their jobs so as to provide them with the personal responsibility, feedback, and intermediate degree of risk that is most likely to provide them with motivation. Your job as a supervisor includes learning to recognize the dominant needs of each of your employees. "You have to listen to them and find out what they're looking for. Some are there for life, some a short time. Figure out how the company can meet their needs and, when you have the opportunity, offer them something that will suit them," says Carolyn Hendricks, a supervisor at The Gap's Canadian distribution centre in Brampton, Ontario.

MATCH PEOPLE TO JOBS

There is abundant evidence to support the idea that motivational benefits accrue from carefully matching people to jobs. Some people prefer routine work with repetitive tasks, while others need constant new challenges to keep them interested. Many people enjoy being part of a team, while others do their best work when they're isolated from other people and able to do their jobs independently. Since jobs differ in terms of autonomy, the variety of tasks to be done, the range of skills they demand, and the like, you should try to match employees to jobs that best fit with their capabilities and personal preferences.

SET CHALLENGING GOALS

We talked in Chapter 2 about the importance of goals. In that discussion, we showed how challenging goals can be a source of motivation. When people accept and are committed to a set of specific and difficult goals, they

FIGURE 9-9

Stephen Fraser, a manager with a packaged goods manufacturer, says "There's a real learning curve in adapting to different personalities, strengths and weaknesses. There are many different types of good salespeople."

The Gap
http://www.gap.com/

FIGURE 9-10

W. L. Gore & Associates, the maker of Gore-Tex fabrics, is a strong proponent of participation. All employees are encouraged to participate actively in all key decisions that affect them. Here you're watching a production meeting in progress.

Gore-Tex: Outerwear & Gore Fabrics Home Page
http://www.gorefabrics.com/

will work hard to achieve them. While we haven't directly addressed goals as motivators in this chapter, our earlier review of the evidence clearly indicates the power of goals in influencing employee behaviour. Based on that earlier evidence, we suggest that you sit down with each of your employees and jointly set tangible, verifiable, and measurable goals for a specific time period; and then create a mechanism by which these employees will receive ongoing feedback on their progress toward achieving these goals. If done properly, this goal-setting process should act to motivate employees.

ENCOURAGE PARTICIPATION

"I motivate my staff by making sure they're an integral part of decisions that affect them," says Joanne Hawrylyshyn, manager of records and freedom of information at the Regional Municipality of Hamilton-Wentworth. Participation is empowering. It allows people to take ownership of decisions. Examples of decisions in which employees might participate include setting work goals, choosing their own benefit packages, and selecting preferred work schedules and assignments. Participation, of course, should be the option of the employee. No one should feel compelled to participate in decision making. While participation is associated with increasing employee commitment and motivation, consistent with our earlier discussion of individual differences, some people may prefer to waive their rights to participate in decisions that affect them. Those preferences should be heeded. If you ask for participation, make sure the involvement is real and not just a token request. Otherwise you may create cynicism and a resistance to getting involved in the future.

INDIVIDUALIZE REWARDS

Since employees have differing needs, what acts as a reinforcer for one may not work for another. You should use your knowledge of individual differences to customize the rewards over which you have control. Some of the

FIGURE 9-11

A Canadian senior sales director with Mary Kay Cosmetics Inc., Denise Baynton (seen here, left, with Mary Kay) knows that setting frequent, challenging goals and linking rewards to goal achievement is a big part of the organization's success.

Dealing with a Difficult Issue

REWARDING APPROPRIATE BEHAVIOUR

You have just been hired as a supervisor at Quality Travel Agency. When customers call to arrange travel plans, your employees look up airline flights, times, and fares on their computers. They help customers make travel reservations that work best for them. Customers also often want assistance in reserving rental cars or finding suitable hotel accommodations.

The car rental agencies and hotels frequently run contests for the sales representative who reserves the most cars for a particular firm or books the most clients for a specific hotel chain. The rewards for doing so are very attractive, too. One car rental firm offers to place employees' names in a monthly draw to win $2500 if they book just twenty reservations. If they book a hundred in the same amount of time, they're eligible for a draw with a $10 000 prize. If they book two hundred clients, they receive an all-expenses-paid, four-day Caribbean vacation for two. These incentives are attractive enough for your employees to "steer" customers toward those companies, even though they might not be the best or the cheapest for them. Yet, as the supervisor, you don't discourage participation in these programs. In fact, you view it as a bonus for your agency's hard work.

Do you believe there is anything wrong with your firm doing business with these car rental and hotel firms that offer "kickbacks" to employees? What ethical issues do you see in this case for a) you and b) your customers? How could you design a performance reward system that would encourage employees to attain high levels of bookings without compromising good ethical practices?

more obvious rewards that supervisors allocate include pay, job assignments, work hours, and the opportunity to participate in goal setting and decision making (see Dealing with a Difficult Issue). The difficulty here may be in ensuring that rewards that are different are still perceived to be equal.

GIVE RECOGNITION

In many jobs, it is difficult to measure degrees of success or failure because there's no bottom line figure or hard data directly related to performance. People working in such jobs may have difficulty feeling a sense of achievement or progress, so the supervisor, who is one of the few people aware of their efforts, is an important source of recognition. Bruce Condie, a manager in the Toronto Board of Education's Adult Basic Education Unit, says, "I can't offer money as a reward. But I can give recognition. I've always found personally that the supervisor can give a powerful reward in simply acknowledging where you've been successful and discussing what you'll work on next."

LINK REWARDS TO PERFORMANCE

In both reinforcement theory and expectancy theory, motivation is maximized when supervisors make rewards contingent on performance. To reward factors other than performance will only act to reinforce and encourage those other factors. Key rewards such as pay increases and promotions should be allocated for the attainment of the employee's specific goals. To maximize the impact of the reward contingencies, supervisors should look for ways to increase the visibility of rewards. Publicizing performance bonuses and allocating annual salary increases in a lump sum (rather than spreading them out over the entire year) are examples of actions that will make rewards more visible and potentially more motivating.

CHECK FOR EQUITY

Rewards or outcomes should be perceived by employees as equalling the inputs they give. At a simplistic level, this should mean that experience, abilities, effort, and other obvious inputs should explain differences in pay, responsibility, and other obvious outcomes. The problem, however, is complicated by the fact that there are dozens of inputs and outcomes, and that employee groups place different degrees of importance on them. This suggests that one person's equity is another's inequity, so an ideal reward system should probably weight inputs differently in order to arrive at the proper rewards for each job. In many cases, communication of rewards can reduce perceived inequities in employees' minds. As a supervisor, it can help to announce who is being rewarded and why.

DON'T IGNORE MONEY!

Our last suggestion may seem incredibly obvious. But it's easy to get so caught up in setting goals or providing opportunities for participation that you can forget that money is a major reason why most people work. So the allocation of performance-based wage increases, piece-work bonuses, and other pay incentives are important in determining employee motivation. Maybe the best case for not overlooking money as a motivator is a review of eighty studies evaluating motivational methods and their impacts on employee productivity.[8] Goal setting alone produced, on average, a 16 per cent increase in productivity; efforts to redesign jobs in order to make them more interesting and challenging yielded 8 to 16 per cent increases; employee participation in decision making produced a median increase of less than 1 per cent; while monetary incentives led to an average increase of 30 per cent.

CHALLENGES FOR MOTIVATING TODAY'S EMPLOYEES

Today's supervisors have challenges in motivating their employees that their counterparts of thirty or forty years ago didn't have. This is most evident when we look at some of the fastest growing employee subgroups.

MOTIVATING A DIVERSIFIED WORKFORCE

Don Connelly (not his real name) supervises four workers in a government office located in Toronto that deals with the public all the time. One employee is Colombian, another Chinese, one is African-Canadian and the fourth is Jamaican. Two are male and two are female. Their skills in written and spoken English vary widely as does their motivation to improve these skills. They have different ideas about punctuality and what constitutes a full day's work. Don feels vulnerable as a white male in this supervisory situation. To him, it seems he is constantly being monitored for any inkling of racism or sexism in his actions or words. The supervisory job alone is tough enough to handle without this extra complication. Like many managers, he says it's impossible to please everyone no matter how hard he tries.

Diversity has become the norm in organizations. You are likely to supervise departments that include women and men, ethnic minorities, immigrants, people who are physically disabled, senior citizens, and others from diverse groups. This diversity presents a number of motivation challenges. For instance, diverse group members often have different needs and expectations. If you're going to maximize motivation, you've got to understand and respond to this diversity (see Supervision in Action).

The key word to guide you should be *flexibility*. Be ready to design work schedules, benefits, physical work settings, and the like to reflect your employees' varied needs. This might include offering child care, flexible work hours, and job sharing for employees with family responsibilities. You might offer flexible leave policies for immigrants who want to return occasionally to their homelands. Or consider allowing employees who are going to school to be able to vary their work schedules from semester to semester.

Supervision in Action

Motivating a Diverse Workforce

The flexibility required to motivate a diverse workforce includes being aware of *cultural* differences. The theories of motivation we have identified were developed largely by North American psychologists and validated by studying North American workers. Therefore, these theories need to be modified for different cultures.[9]

For instance, the self-interest concept is consistent with capitalism and the extremely high value placed on oneself in countries like Canada and the United States. Because almost all the motivation theories presented in this chapter are based on the self-interest motive, they should also be applicable to employees in such countries as Great Britain and Australia, where capitalism and self-interest are highly valued. In more collective-oriented nations, such as Venezuela, Singapore, Japan, and Mexico, the individual's loyalty to the organization or society takes precedence over his or her self-interest. Employees in collective-oriented cultures are likely therefore to be more receptive to team-based job design, group goals, and group-performance evaluations. Reliance on the fear of being fired in such cultures is likely to be less effective, even if the laws in these countries allow managers to fire employees.

The need-for-achievement concept provides another example of a motivation theory with a North American bias. The view that a high need for achievement acts as an internal motivator presupposes the existence of two cultural characteristics: a willingness to accept a moderate degree of risk and a concern with performance. However, results of several recent studies among employees in countries outside North America indicate that some aspects of motivation theory are transferable.[10] For instance, motivational techniques presented earlier in this chapter were shown to be effective in changing performance-related behaviours of Russian textile mill workers. However, we shouldn't assume that motivation concepts are universally applicable. The technique of recognizing and embarrassing the worst sales clerks by giving them awards—used by a large department store in Xian, China—may be effective in China.[11] But an action that humiliates employees isn't likely to work in North America or Western Europe.

MOTIVATING LOW-PAY SERVICE WORKERS

You're supervising counter workers at McDonalds, clerks at Blockbuster Video, orderlies in a hospital, or a building maintenance crew. These examples represent some of the fastest growing job categories. Such jobs represent a challenge: how do you motivate people in low-paying jobs that offer limited opportunities for advancement? In contrast to low-skill, blue-collar manufacturing jobs that paid $10 to $15 an hour in the 1960s, today's low-skill service jobs are paying $7 or $8 an hour—barely enough to satisfy basic needs and far from allowing the worker to move into the middle class.

So what can you do? Pay might be increased a bit, but significantly higher basic wages can't be passed on to consumers. The public isn't ready yet for the $10 Big Mac. So what you're left with are options such as offering job flexibility and variety, providing recognition, and capitalizing on the role of social support. Give employees flexibility in choosing their work hours. Increase variety by allowing them to change tasks and rotate among jobs. And build group cohesiveness, support, and commitment by encouraging employees to be part of a winning team.

FIGURE 9-12

Colin Kirby spent the summer supervising fifteen students painting campus buildings. What motivated them? Colin made their duties clear, pitched in and helped, used humour and challenges; plus they got a bonus for finishing the job.

MOTIVATING PROFESSIONALS

How do you motivate the professional librarian, civil engineer, registered nurse, or lawyer? How do you get the most effort from the C.A. at Price Waterhouse, the software programmer at Corel, or the Calgary Flames hockey player making $1 million a year?

Professional employees provide a unique challenge in terms of motivation. Money, in an absolute sense, does not tend to be high on their needs list. They tend to be sensitive to the design of their jobs. And they're more likely to attach their identity to their profession than to the organization that employs them.

Since professionals tend to be relatively well paid, money is more likely to be an issue of equity than of absolute amount. Many professionals are equity sensitive; they are likely to compare their salary, job assignments, benefit packages, office furnishings, and the like with those of their colleagues and associates. A $5000 bonus tends to carry significantly more weight to a $25 000-a-year blue-collar worker than to a $75 000-a-year professional.

Professionals tend to place a high value on job factors such as autonomy, personal growth, recognition, and challenging work. Their motivation is closely tied to the degree to which their job satisfies these needs. Much of the discussion that follows on designing motivating jobs is particularly relevant to professionals.

Finally, one characteristic that typically differentiates professional employees from others is that professionals put their allegiance to their

FIGURE 9-13

When asked about motivation issues, Heather Cook (manager of Halton Region Children's Assessment and Treatment Centres) said of the psychologists and social workers, "We deal more with the other end of the continuum. People tend to take on too much; they push themselves because it's hard to say no to urgent, difficult cases."

field of expertise ahead of their allegiance to the organization. A corporate attorney who works for MacMillan Bloedel will tend to see his or her identity as being more closely tied to the legal profession than to MacMillan Bloedel. This presents a challenge to supervisors, because the rewards offered outside the organization often take precedence over those from within. For example, recognition by professional peers through articles in newsletters, awards, appointment to important committees, or election to a high-ranking office within the professional organization can be powerful motivators to the professional employee. Unfortunately, the typical supervisor has little influence over these outside sources of rewards.

SHOULD EMPLOYEES BE PAID FOR PERFORMANCE OR FOR TIME ON THE JOB?

What's in it for me? That's a question every person consciously or unconsciously asks before engaging in any form of behaviour. Our knowledge of motivation tells us that people do what they do to satisfy some need. Before they do anything, therefore, they look for a payoff or reward. Although there may be many different rewards offered by organizations, most of us are concerned with earning an amount of money that allows us to satisfy our needs and wants. Because pay, as one type of reward, is an important variable in motivation, we need to look at how we can use pay to motivate high levels of employee performance. This principle explains the intent and logic behind pay-for-performance programs.

Pay-for-performance programs are compensation plans that pay employees on the basis of some performance measure.[12] Piece-rate plans, gainsharing, wage incentive plans, profit sharing, and lump sum bonuses are examples of pay-for-performance programs.[13] What differentiates these forms of pay from more traditional compensation plans is that instead of paying an employee for *time* on the job, pay is adjusted to reflect some measures of *performance*. These performance measures might include such things as individual productivity, team or work group productivity, departmental productivity, or the overall organization's profits for a given period.

Performance-based compensation is probably most compatible with expectancy theory. That is, employees should perceive a strong relationship between their performance and the rewards they receive if motivation is to be maximized. If rewards are allocated solely on nonperformance factors—such as seniority, job title, or across-the-board cost-of-living raises—then employees are likely to reduce their efforts.[14]

Pay-for-performance programs are gaining in popularity in organizations. Their growing popularity can be explained in terms of both

Pay-for-performance programs
Compensation plans that pay employees on the basis of some performance measure

motivation and cost control. From a motivation perspective, making some or all of a worker's pay conditional on performance measures focuses his or her attention and effort on that measure, then reinforces the continuation of that effort with rewards. However, if the employee, team, or organization's performance declines, so too does the reward.[15] Thus, there's an incentive to keep efforts and motivation strong. For instance, employees at Hallmark Cards, Inc. have up to 10 per cent of their pay at risk. Depending on their productivity on such performance measures as customer satisfaction, retail sales, and profits, employees turn that 10 per cent into rewards as high as 25 per cent.[16] However, failure to reach the performance measures can result in the forfeiture of the 10 per cent of salary placed at risk. Companies like Saturn, Hewlett-Packard, and duPont use similar formulas in which employee compensation is comprised of base and reward pay.[17] On the cost-savings side, performance-based bonuses and other incentive rewards avoid the fixed expense of permanent—and often annual—salary increases. The bonuses do not accrue to base salary, which means that the amount is not compounded in future years. As a result, they save the company money!

Hallmark
http://www.hallmark.com/

Hewlett-Packard (Canada) Ltd.
http://hpclweb.external.hp.com/

HOW CAN EMPLOYEE STOCK OWNERSHIP PLANS AFFECT MOTIVATION?

Many companies are using employee stock ownership plans for improving and motivating employee performance. An **employee stock ownership plan** (ESOP) is a compensation program in which employees become part owners of the organization by receiving stock as a performance incentive. Millions of employees in such companies as British Petroleum, Avis, and Starbucks participate in ESOPs.[18] Also, many ESOPs allow employees to purchase additional stocks at attractive, below-market prices. Under an ESOP, employees are often motivated to give more effort because they are owners who will share in any gains and losses. The fruits of their labours are no longer just going into the pockets of some unknown owners—the employees *are* the owners!

Do ESOPs positively affect productivity and employee satisfaction? The answer appears to be yes. The research on ESOPs indicates that they increase employee satisfaction and frequently result in higher performance.[19] However, other studies showed that productivity in organizations with ESOPs does increase, but the impact is greater the longer the ESOP has been in existence.[20] You shouldn't expect immediate increases in employee motivation and productivity if an ESOP is implemented. But over time, employee productivity and satisfaction should go up.

Employee stock ownership plan (ESOP) A compensation program that allows employees to become part owners of an organization by receiving stock as a performance incentive

5. The degree to which an individual believes that working at a particular level will generate a desired outcome is defined by the expectancy theory as:
   a. attractiveness
   b. performance–reward linkage
   c. effort–performance linkage
   d. value
6. Describe the motivational implications of equity theory.
7. The primary motivational effect of ESOPs comes from the fact that employees become part owners of the organization by receiving stock as a performance incentive. True or False?
8. The key to motivating today's diversified work force lies in
   a. creativity
   b. goal-setting
   c. support
   d. flexibility

DESIGNING MOTIVATING JOBS

ASSESSING YOURSELF: IS ENRICHMENT FOR YOU?

People differ in what they like and dislike in their jobs. Following are twelve pairs of jobs. For each pair, indicate which job you would prefer. Assume that everything else about the jobs is the same—pay attention only to the characteristics actually listed for each pair of jobs. If you would prefer the job in the left-hand column (Column A), indicate how much you prefer it by putting a check mark in a blank to the left of the Neutral point. If you prefer the job in the right-hand column (Column B), check one of the blanks to the right of Neutral. Check the Neutral blank only if you find the two jobs equally attractive or unattractive. Try to use the Neutral blank rarely.

COLUMN A		COLUMN B
1. A job that offers little or no challenge	Strongly Prefer A — Neutral — Strongly Prefer B	A job that requires you to be completely isolated from coworkers
2. A job that pays very well	Strongly Prefer A — Neutral — Strongly Prefer B	A job that allows considerable opportunity to be creative and innovative
3. A job that often requires you to make important decisions	Strongly Prefer A — Neutral — Strongly Prefer B	A job in which there are many pleasant people to work with
4. A job with little security in a somewhat unstable organization	Strongly Prefer A — Neutral — Strongly Prefer B	A job in which you have little or no opportunity to participate in decisions that affect your work
5. A job in which greater responsibility is given to those who do the best work	Strongly Prefer A — Neutral — Strongly Prefer B	A job in which greater responsibility is given to loyal employees who have the most seniority
6. A job with a supervisor who sometimes is highly critical	Strongly Prefer A — Neutral — Strongly Prefer B	A job that does not require you to use much of your talent
7. A very routine job	Strongly Prefer A — Neutral — Strongly Prefer B	A job in which your coworkers are not very friendly
8. A job with a supervisor who respects you and treats you fairly	Strongly Prefer A — Neutral — Strongly Prefer B	A job that provides constant opportunities for you to learn new and interesting things
9. A job that gives you a real chance to develop yourself personally	Strongly Prefer A — Neutral — Strongly Prefer B	A job with excellent vacations and fringe benefits
10. A job in which there is a real chance you could be laid off	Strongly Prefer A — Neutral — Strongly Prefer B	A job with very little chance to do challenging work
11. A job with little freedom and independence to do your work in the way you think best	Strongly Prefer A — Neutral — Strongly Prefer B	A job with poor working conditions
12. A job with very satisfying teamwork	Strongly Prefer A — Neutral — Strongly Prefer B	A job that allows you to use your skills and abilities to the fullest extent

Table source: J. R. Hackman and G. R. Oldham (1974), *The Job Diagnostic Survey: The Instrument for the Diagnosis of Jobs and the Evaluation of Job Redesign Projects.* Technical Report No. 4. New Haven, Conn.: Yale University, Department of Administrative Sciences. With permission.

SCORING DIRECTIONS

This twelve-item questionnaire taps into the degree to which you have a strong versus weak desire to obtain growth satisfaction from your work.

Each item on the questionnaire yields a score from 1 to 7 (that is, "Strongly prefer A" scores 1; "Neutral" scores 4; and "Strongly prefer B" scores 7). To obtain the score for your individual growth-need, average the twelve items as follows:

> #1, #2, #7, #8, #11, #12 (direct scoring)
> #3, #4, #5, #6, #9, #10 (reverse scoring)

Average scores for typical respondents are close to the midpoint of 4.0. High scores suggest that you will respond to an enriched job because you have a high growth need. Low scores suggest that you wouldn't find enriched jobs satisfying or motivating.

SKILL BASICS

One of the more important factors that influence an employee's motivational level is the structure of his or her work. Is there a lot of variety or is the job repetitive? Is the work closely supervised? Does the job allow the employee discretion? The answers to questions like these will have a major impact on the motivational potential of the job and hence the level of productivity an employee can expect to achieve.

Job design
The way that tasks are combined to form complete jobs

We use the term **job design** to refer to the way that tasks are combined to form complete jobs. Some jobs are routine because the tasks are standardized and repetitive; others are nonroutine. Some require a large number of varied and diverse skills; others are narrow in scope. Some jobs constrain the employee by requiring him or her to follow very precise procedures; others allow employees substantial freedom in how they do their work. The point is that jobs differ in the way tasks are combined, and these different combinations create a variety of job designs.

What are the key characteristics that define a job? There are five, and together they comprise the core dimensions of any job:[21]

1. **Skill variety:** The degree to which the job requires a variety of different activities, enabling the worker to use a number of different skills and talents.

2. **Task identity:** The degree to which the job requires completion of a whole and identifiable piece of work.

3. **Task significance:** The degree to which the job has a substantial impact on the lives or work of other people.

4. **Autonomy:** The degree to which the job provides substantial freedom, independence, and discretion to the individual in scheduling the work and in determining the procedures to be used in carrying it out.

5. **Feedback:** The degree to which carrying out the work activities required by the job results in the individual obtaining direct and clear information about the effectiveness of his or her performance.

Figure 9-14 offers examples of job activities that rate high and low for each characteristic.

When these five characteristics are all present in a job, the job becomes enriched and potentially motivating. Notice that we said *potentially* motivating. Whether that potential is actualized is largely dependent on the employee's growth-need strength (refer back to Assessing Yourself exercise at the beginning of this section). Individuals with a high growth need are more likely to be motivated in enriched jobs than their counterparts with a low growth need.

Job enrichment increases the degree to which a worker controls the planning, execution, and evaluation of his or her work. An enriched job organizes tasks so as to allow the worker to perform a complete activity, increases the employee's freedom and independence, increases responsibility, and provides feedback, so an individual will be able to assess and correct his or her own performance.

PRACTISING THE SKILL

So what can you do, as a supervisor, to enrich your employees' jobs and increase their motivation? We can suggest five specific actions (see Figure 9-15):

1. **Combine tasks.** Supervisors should seek to take existing and fractionalized tasks and put them back together to form a new and larger module of work. This increases skill variety and task identity.

Skill variety
The degree to which the job requires a variety of different activities so the worker can use a number of different skills and talents

Task identity
The degree to which the job requires completion of a whole and identifiable piece of work

Task significance
The degree to which the job has a substantial impact on the lives or work of other people

Autonomy
The degree to which the job provides substantial freedom, independence, and discretion to the individual in scheduling the work and in determining the procedures to be used in carrying it out

Feedback
The degree to which carrying out the work activities required by the job results in the individual obtaining direct and clear information about the effectiveness of his or her performance

Job enrichment
Increasing the degree to which a worker controls the planning, execution, and evaluation of his or her work

FIGURE 9-14

Examples of high and
low job characteristics
Source: G. Johns,
*Organizational
Behavior:
Understanding Life
at Work*, 3rd ed.
(New York: Harper
Collins, 1992), p. 216.
With permission.

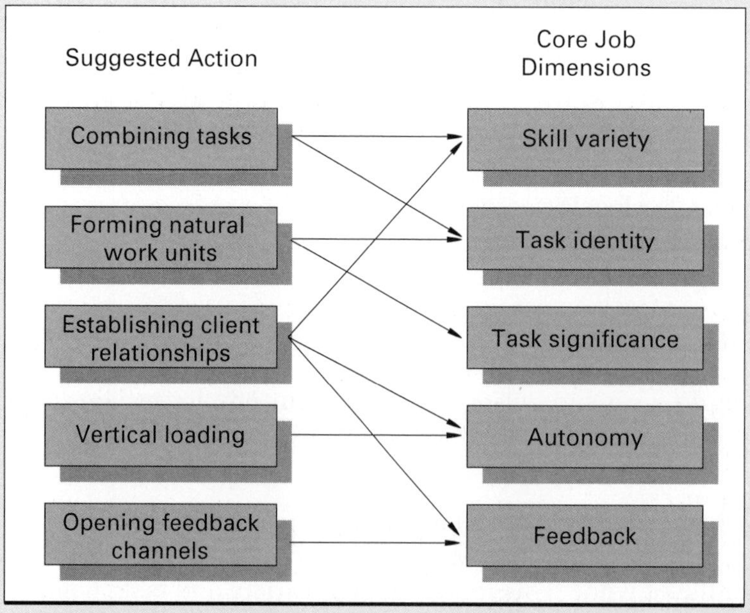

Skill Variety

High variety	An owner-operator of a garage who does electrical repair, rebuilds engines, does body work, and interacts with customers
Low variety	A body shop worker who sprays paint eight hours a day

Task Identity

High identity	A cabinet maker who designs a piece of furniture, selects the wood, builds the object, and finishes it to perfection
Low identity	A worker in a furniture factory who operates a lathe solely to make table legs

Task Significance

High significance	Nursing the sick in a hospital intensive care unit
Low significance	Sweeping hospital floors

Autonomy

High autonomy	A telephone installer who schedules his or her own work for the day, makes visits without supervision, and decides on the most effective techniques for a particular installation
Low autonomy	A telephone operator who must handle calls as they come according to a routine, highly specified procedure

Feedback

High feedback	An electronics factory worker who assembles a radio and then tests it to determine if it operates properly
Low feedback	An electronics factory worker who assembles a radio and then routes it to a quality control inspector who tests its proper operation and makes needed adjustments

FIGURE 9-15

Guidelines for enrich-
ing a job. (Source:
Improving Life at Work
by J. R. Hackman and
J. L. Suttle. Copy-
right ©1977 by Scott,
Foresman and
Company. Reprinted
by permission.)

Suggested Action	Core Job Dimensions
Combining tasks	Skill variety
Forming natural work units	Task identity
Establishing client relationships	Task significance
Vertical loading	Autonomy
Opening feedback channels	Feedback

2. **Create natural work units.** The creation of natural work units means that the tasks an employee does form an identifiable and meaningful whole. This increases employee ownership of the work and improves the likelihood that employees will view their work as meaningful and important rather than as irrelevant and boring.

3. **Establish client relationships.** The client is the user of the product or service that the employee works on. Wherever possible, supervisors should try to establish direct relationships between workers and their clients. This increases skill variety, autonomy, and feedback for the employee.

4. **Expand jobs vertically.** Vertical expansion refers to giving employees responsibilities and control that were formerly reserved for supervisors and other managers. For example, let employees set work schedules, have a hand in budgeting, select work methods, check quality, and decide how to solve problems.

5. **Open feedback channels.** By increasing feedback, employees not only learn how well they are performing their jobs, but also whether their performance is improving, deteriorating, or remaining at a constant level. Ideally, this feedback about performance should be received directly as the employee does the job, rather than from the supervisor on an occasional basis.

The suggestions we've offered in this section refer to the design of individual jobs. But don't forget that we can also design jobs around work teams: in Chapter 5, we discussed how teams can enrich jobs at the group level, and how they can increase motivation and productivity.

Applying Your Skills

Break into groups of four or five. You are a consulting team that has been hired by Citibank to help them solve a motivation/performance problem.

Citibank employs several hundred people in its back office to process all the company's financial transactions. These jobs have been split up so each person performs a single, routine task over and over again. These include:

- opening courier bags
- sorting transactions into business, consumer, foreign and internal Citibank piles
- delivering transactions to processing areas

- sorting transactions into numerical order
- verifying dates and signatures
- reconciling transactions to computer journals (daily reports)
- investigating discrepancies
- filing transactions in appropriate accounts
- submitting correction reports

Employees have become dissatisfied with these mundane jobs, and this dissatisfaction shows in their work. Severe backlogs have developed, and error rates are unacceptably high. Your team's task is to:

1. Redesign these jobs in order to resolve these problems, and

2. Identify how these changes are likely to affect the jobs of supervisors in this department.

Your team has thirty minutes to complete this task.

SUMMARY

This summary is organized by the Learning Objectives.

1. Motivation is the willingness to do something and is conditioned by this action's ability to satisfy some need for the individual.
2. Five personality characteristics relevant to understanding the behaviour and motivation of employees are: 1. locus of control—the degree to which people believe they are masters of their own fate; 2. Machiavellianism—the degree to which an individual is manipulative and believes ends can justify means; 3. self-esteem—an individual's degree of liking or disliking for himself or herself; 4. self-monitoring—an individual's ability to adjust his or her behaviour to external, situational factors; and 5. risk propensity—the degree of an individual's willingness to take chances.
3. Maslow focused on the self. His hierarchy of needs proposes that there are five needs (physiological, safety, social, esteem and self-actualization) and as each is sequentially satisfied, the next need becomes dominant.

    Theory X-Theory Y proposes two views of human nature, then argues that employees are essentially hard working, committed, and responsible. Therefore, to maximize motivation, employees should be allowed to participate in decision making and be given responsible and challenging jobs; and supervisors should strive to achieve good group relations among employees.

    According to the motivation-hygiene theory, if you want to motivate employees, you have to emphasize achievement, recognition, the work itself, responsibility, and growth, These are the characteristics people find intrisically rewarding.
4. High achievers prefer jobs that give them personal responsibility for finding solutions to problems, where they can receive rapid and unambiguous feedback on their performance, and where they can set moderately challenging goals.
5. Reinforcement theory proposes that people will exert high levels of effort in tasks that are reinforced.
6. People don't only look at absolute rewards they receive from their job. They also look at relative rewards. A focus on equity deals with this fact.
7. The three relationships in expectancy theory that determine an individual's level of effort are effort–performance, performance–rewards, and rewards–personal goals.
8. To maximize employee motivation, supervisors should recognize individual differences, match people to jobs, set challenging goals,

encourage participation, individualize rewards, give recognition, link rewards to performance, check for equity, and not ignore money.

9. Low-pay service workers suffer both from essentially permanent low pay and limited promotional opportunities. They are most likely to respond to job flexibility and variety, recognition, and social support. In contrast, money is relevant to professionals mostly from an equity perspective. Professionals prefer enriched jobs. Additionally, their loyalty to their profession typically overrides their loyalty to their employer.

KEY TERMS AND CONCEPTS

Autonomy	Need
Equity theory	Need for achievement
Expectancy theory	Reinforcement theory
Feedback	Risk propensity
Hierarchy of needs theory	Self-esteem
Job design	Self-monitoring
Job enrichment	Skill variety
Locus of control	Task identity
Machiavellianism	Task significance
Motivation	Theory X-Theory Y
Motivation–hygiene theory	

REVIEWING YOUR KNOWLEDGE

1. How does an unsatisfied need create motivation?
2. Contrast behavioural predictions between people with an internal versus an external locus of control.
3. Contrast behavioural predictions between high and low self-monitors.
4. Compare the assumptions of Theory X with Theory Y.
5. What is the importance of the dual-continuum in the motivation–hygiene theory?
6. What does a supervisor need to do to motivate a high achiever?
7. Describe expectancy theory.
8. What motivational challenges does a diversified work force create for supervisors?
9. What are the five core dimensions in a job?
10. What is job enrichment?

ANSWERS TO THE POP QUIZZES

1. **c. self-actualization needs.** Self-actualization in Maslow's theory means reaching one's full potential. "Being all you can be" reflects this attainment, and thus, the self-actualization needs.

2. Motivation is the willingness to exert high levels of effort in order to satisfy some individual need. The motivation process begins with an unsatisfied need, which creates tension and drives an individual to search for goals that, if attained, will satisfy the need and reduce the tension.

3. **False.** It's just the reverse. Theory X reflects the negative view of human nature, assuming that they dislike work. Theory Y, on the other hand, is basically a positive view of employees, assuming that they are creative.

4. **d. none of the above.** Motivation-hygiene theory factors that eliminate dissatisfaction are called **hygiene factors**.

5. **c. effort-performance linkage.** The degree to which an individual believes that working at a particular level will generate a desired outcome reflects the effort that individual must expend in order to perform successfully.

6. In equity theory, individuals compare their job's inputs-outcomes ratio to those of colleagues and other relevant individuals. If they perceive that they are underrewarded, their work motivation declines. When individuals perceive that they are overrewarded, they may be motivated to work harder in order to justify their pay.

7. **True.** ESOPs enable employees to receive incentives that are directly tied to their performance. Because they are "part owners," this incentive creates a motivational effect.

8. **d. flexibility.** Employees from diverse cultures have differing needs. To be able to motivate them, and meet their needs, supervisors must be flexible in their dealings with their workers.

CASE 9.A

Motivating Molly Hubert

Molly Hubert really likes novels. In fact you may recall from the opening of this chapter that Molly reads two or three novels every week. She frequently stops by the bookstore during her lunch break or after work to browse and buy the books she reads in the evening.

You may also recall that Molly gets up early at 5:30 every morning so she can have a three- to four-mile run before showering and going to work. Molly has a high energy level, part of which can be attributed to her daily exercise routine.

Molly's motivation and drive for reading and exercise is truly commendable. Her motivation, however, seems to stop there and doesn't carry over to her sales position at Footlocker shoe store. In fact, if her supervisor, Ken Luong, could see Molly's determination away from the store, he would be amazed.

As a salesperson, Molly does an average job—no more, no less than necessary. She is friendly and helpful with customers, but doesn't go out of her way to help them. Molly gets along quite well with her coworkers and usually does her share of work around the store. It is rather obvious that there are several tasks, such as replacing inventory, that she doesn't like, and she puts off these tasks as long as possible. Her coworkers will usually help her with some of the tasks she doesn't like, but they know that she probably will not volunteer to "pay back" her coworkers unless it is work she really likes.

All in all, her work habits can be characterized as very neutral—with very few highs and lows. Her attitude at work seems to be "what happens, happens; there isn't a real reason to try to influence an outcome; and anyway, a paycheque is a paycheque."

RESPONDING TO THIS CASE

1. Describe Molly's characteristics in relation to the following terms: locus of control, self-esteem, and self-monitoring. Why is it important for Mr. Luong to understand these and other factors in relation to Molly and his other employees?
2. Which motivation theory/approach in the text do you think provides the best insights into Molly's behaviour? Defend your choice.
3. If Molly is essentially doing her job, why should Mr. Luong look for ways to motivate Molly?
4. What suggestions do you have for Mr. Luong to motivate Molly in her job? How will this affect Molly's coworkers?

CASE 9.B

Job Completion at Centennial Mutual

Most of the employees at the home office of Centennial Mutual Insurance, Inc. know that there are many opportunities for job advancement at CMI. Presently there is a supervisory position open in the commercial division, which will go either to Jill Mata or Leon Pollard.

In the past four months, Jill Mata has applied for two supervisory positions. She is anxious to move into a supervisory job for two reasons: to get a salary increase and to get the opportunity to supervise other people. Jill has not been with the company long, but she has worked hard to learn about the insurance business. She is a competent, thorough worker and has done well as a personal liability claims agent for the past year. She has accomplished her personal goal of learning about several types of insurance coverage, including general liability, workers' compensation, and life and health insurance, even though she does not process claims in these areas.

Leon Pollard is a personal property claims agent. He, too, is competent and precise in his work. He, too, has learned a lot about the insurance business, but has slightly different goals in applying for the supervisory position. He wants to make some changes around the office. He thinks there is too much duplication and that there should be more interaction among agents and departments. He thinks he can facilitate the change that other supervisors have not considered important enough to tackle.

RESPONDING TO THIS CASE

1. Describe the motivators that are driving Jill and Leon to apply for the supervisory position.

2. What are the job characteristics that appear to be stimulating the achievement drive for Jill? For Leon?

3. Assuming that Jill was given the job, describe how you believe she will motivate her employees. What if Leon were given the job?

4. What suggestions would you give to Jill (Leon) as she (he) assumes the new responsibilities of the supervisory position?

5. If there are factors that would appear to indicate one individual would be a better supervisor than the other, what are they? Which person do you think would do the best job in the position? Why?

6. For which person would you like to work? Why? Is gender an issue for you? Why or why not?

10 PROVIDING LEADERSHIP

LEARNING OBJECTIVES

After reading this chapter, you should be able to:

1. Define *leadership*.
2. Describe traits generally associated with leadership.
3. Identify traits associated with charismatic leadership.
4. Contrast task-centred and people-centred styles of leadership.
5. Identify and describe three types of participative leadership styles.
6. Explain situational leadership.
7. Explain the differences in how men and women lead.

CHAPTER OUTLINE

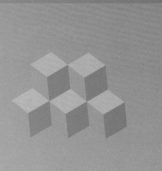

**Halton Regional
Police Service**
http://www.worldchat.
com/hrp/

The concept of leadership has changed over the past thirty years. In the 1960s, when the majority of jobs were still in the manufacturing sector and less than 20 per cent of the labour force had attended college, leaders were described in terms such as *strong, forceful, tough,* and *in charge.* Jobs and workers are different at the dawn of the new century, and so are leaders. The majority of today's workers are employed in the service sector. They're more likely to be working in an office than in a steel mill. And an increasing proportion of workers have been to college. They have ideas and opinions, and expect to be able to express them. They have little tolerance for authoritarian leaders. Today, you're much more likely to hear leaders described in terms such as *visionary, enthusiastic, knowledgeable, coach,* or *empowering.*

The shift we're describing has been widespread. For instance, Staff Sergeant Jackie Gordon of the Halton Regional Police Service describes how leadership has changed in police work—a field where you might expect authoritarian leadership to still be pervasive:

> During the last ten years we've shifted from a paramilitary organization to one with a more participative style. Not everything is communicated "top down." Issues are discussed in management teams. Items that affect constables are now being discussed by platoons and their ideas are forwarded to the administration and then incorporated into the final decision. For example, traditionally police officers have been issued military-style boots. Little consideration was given to the practical use or the warmth of this footwear in winter. As a result of input by uniform management teams, other footwear such as running shoes and thermal boots are now being tested to ensure that this equipment can meet the demands placed upon a uniformed patrol officer.

In this chapter, we'll look at whether leaders have common traits and which, if any, leadership styles are most effective. We'll also review the topic of charismatic leadership and show you what you can do to be perceived as charismatic by others.

Leadership
The ability to influence others to act in a particular way through direction, encouragement, sensitivity, consideration, and support

WHAT IS LEADERSHIP?

Leadership is the ability you demonstrate when you encourage others to act in a particular way. Through direction, encouragement, sensitivity, consideration, and support, you inspire your followers to accept challenges and achieve goals that may be viewed as difficult to achieve. As a leader, you're also someone who sees and can get the best out of others—helping them develop a sense of persona and professional accomplishment. Being a leader means building commitment to goal attainment among those being led, as well as a strong desitre for them to continue to follow your leadership.

When you think of leaders, you may often view them as those individuals who are in charge of others. These people would include yourself, as an authority over your employees, your boss, and anyone else who holds a position of power over you—like your professor in this class. Obviously, through a variety of actions, you and the other leaders have the ability to influence. Yet, leadership frequently goes beyond formal positions. In fact, sometimes this person of power is not around, yet leadership may still exist (see Dealing with a Difficult Issue). Let's look at this pair of issues.

LEADERS AND SUPERVISORS

Let's begin by clarifying the distinction between those who supervise others and those we call leaders. The two are frequently used as if they mean the same thing, but they do not.

Those who supervise others are appointed by the organization. They have legitimate power that allows them to reward and punish their employees. Their ability to influence employees is based on the formal authority inherent in their positions. In contrast, leaders may either be appointed or emerge from within a group. Leaders can influence others to perform beyond the actions dictated by formal authority.

Should all those who supervise others be leaders? Conversely, should all leaders be individuals who formally direct the activities of others? Because no one yet has been able to demonstrate through research or logical argument that leadership ability is a hindrance to those who supervise, we can state that anyone who supervises employees should ideally be a leader. However, not all leaders necessarily have capabilities in other supervisory functions, and thus not all should have formal authority. Therefore when we refer to a leader in this chapter, we will be talking about anyone who is able to influence others.

SOMETIMES "NO" LEADER IS OKAY

Given that as a supervisor you should ideally be a leader, we might expect you to exhibit leadership ability. But that may not be the case. Although you have the formal authority to oversee employee activities, your leadership skills may be lacking. While that may not be the best of situations, can your employees survive if you provide little or no leadership? The answer is *yes*. In fact, leadership may not always be important. Many research studies have concluded that, in many situations, a leader's

INFLUENCING WITHOUT POWER

Leadership is about your influence over others—especially in those instances where you don't have formal authority over them—and the "power" you wield. The use or misuse of power can generate ethical questions about right and wrong. For instance, consider the following scenario.

Your boss has been dissatisfied with the way one of your fellow supervisors is handling a project. She has reassigned the project to you, but your colleague hasn't been told of this action. You've been told to work with this colleague to find out what he's already done, discuss any other necessary information that he might have, and to prepare a project report by the end of next month.

Your colleague is not giving you the information you need to even start, much less complete, the project. He finds your questions unusual. After all, it's his project, and he doesn't have time to stop and talk to you. That would delay him more—and jeopardize the success of his department. However, without this information, you won't be able to meet your deadline either. If that happens, you both may lose.

Do you see any problem in talking to your colleague and telling him the reason you're getting involved? How can you influence him in gaining his cooperation? What would you do in this situation?

behaviour may be irrelevant to goal attainment. That is, certain individual, job, and organizational factors can act as "substitutes for leadership." As a result, the "person in charge" has little influence on others.[1]

Employee characteristics such as experience, skill levels and training, "professional" orientation, or the need for autonomy, can neutralize the effect of leadership. These characteristics can replace the need for a leader's support. The drive to succeed in these cases comes from within, so no external stimulus is needed. Similarly, jobs that are well defined and routine require less leadership influence. In this case, employees know exactly what is expected and how it is to be done. In such cases, it generally doesn't take an inspirational leader to enforce compliance. Also, in jobs that are intrinsically satisfying, employees may have less need to be influenced, because the job itself provides the influence to excel. Finally, organizational characteristics such as explicit and formalized goals, rigid rules and procedures, or cohesive work groups can act in the place of formal leadership.

"Henry! Our party's total chaos! No one knows
when to eat, where to stand, what to....
Oh, thank God! Here comes a border collie!"

FIGURE 10-1

(*Source:* Gary Larson,
Weiner Dog Art.
Kansas City: Andrews
& McMeel, 1990, p. 11.)

Although the previous paragraph cites instances where leadership may be irrelevant, don't take this to mean that your leadership is not important in today's world of work. Rather, recognize that these "substitutions" for leadership are the exceptions. In most organizations, leadership is critical for organizational survival. That's why we will spend the rest of this chapter looking at what makes a good leader, and at the kinds of things a good leader does.

ARE YOU BORN TO LEAD?

Ask the average person what comes to mind when he or she thinks of leadership. You're likely to get a list of qualities such as intelligence, charm, decisiveness, enthusiasm, strength, bravery, integrity, and self-confidence. In fact, these are probably some of the same characteristics you may have listed yourself. The responses that we get, in essence, represent **leadership traits**. The search for traits or characteristics that separate leaders from nonleaders dominated the early research efforts in the study of leadership.

Leadership traits
Qualities such as intelligence, charm, decisiveness, enthusiasm, strength, bravery, integrity, and self-confidence.

Is it possible to isolate one or more traits in individuals who are generally acknowledged to be able to influence others—people like Jean Chrétien, Nelson Mandela, or Mother Theresa—that nonleaders do not possess? You may agree that these individuals meet the fundamental definition of a leader, but they represent individuals with widely varying characteristics. If the concept of leadership traits was to prove valid, there would have to be identifiable characteristics that all leaders are born with.

TRAITS OF SUCCESSFUL LEADERS

Hospital for Sick Children, Toronto
http://www.sickkids.
on.ca/

Research efforts at isolating specific traits resulted in a number of dead ends. Attempts failed to identify a set of traits that would always differentiate leaders from followers and effective leaders from ineffective leaders. Perhaps it was a bit optimistic to believe that a set of consistent and unique personality traits could apply across the board to all effective leaders—in such widely diverse organizations as Grant MacEwan Community College, The Hospital for Sick Children, Schneider National Carriers Ltd., and Toyota.

Attempts to identify traits consistently associated with those who are successful in influencing others has been more promising. For example, six traits on which leaders are seen to differ from nonleaders include: drive, the desire to influence others, honesty and moral character, self-confidence, intelligence, and relevant knowledge (see Figure 10-2).[2]

A person's *drive* reflects his or her desire to exert a high level of effort to complete a task. This type of individual often has a strong need to achieve and excel in what they do. Ambitious, this leader demonstrates high energy levels in his or her endless persistence in all activities. Furthermore, a person with drive frequently shows a willingness to take

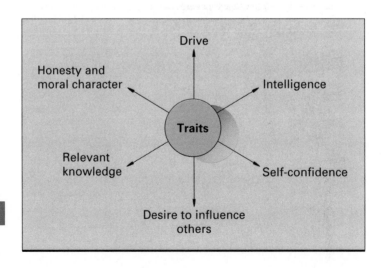

FIGURE 10-2

Six traits of effective leaders

FIGURE 10-3

What traits characterize supervisory leaders? Research has identified six: drive, the desire to lead, honesty and integrity, self-confidence, intelligence, and job-related knowledge.

initiative. Leaders have a clear *desire to influence others*. Often, this desire to lead is viewed as a willingness to accept responsibility for a variety of tasks. A leader is also someone who builds trusting relationships with those he or she influences. This is done by being truthful and by showing a high consistency between spoken words and actions. In other words, people are more apt to be influenced by someone whom they view as *honest and having high moral character*.

A person who leads is also someone who shows *self-confidence*, and thus is able to convince others of the correctness of goals and decisions. It has been shown that employees prefer to be influenced by individuals who are free of self-doubt. In other words, they are influenced more by a supervisor who has a strong belief as opposed to one who frequently wavers on decisions. Influencing others requires a level of *intelligence*, too. To successfully influence others, one needs to be able to gather, synthesize, and interpret a lot of information. The leader must also be able to create a vision (a plan), communicate it in such a way that others understand it, solve problems, and make good decisions. Many of these "intelligence" requirements derive from education and experience. Finally, an effective leader is someone who has a high degree of *relevant knowledge* about the department and the unit's employees. This in-depth knowledge assists the supervisor in making well-informed decisions, as well as understanding the implications those decisions have on others in the department.

FIGURE 10-4

"Whether it's a house or a satellite you're constructing, you have to be able to visualize what it is you want at the end and how you're going to get there," says Joe Sferrazza, a man who has built both. "As a manager, you have to know your stuff, have an eye out for costs all the time, be confident, optimistic, and have a good relationship with your subordinates."

What Is This Thing Called Charisma?

What do people as diverse as former Prime Minister Pierre Trudeau, dancer Karen Kain and TV personality Don Cherry have in common? They all have something in their personality construct called *charisma*. Charisma is a magnetism that, among other things, inspires followers to go the "extra mile" to reach goals that are perceived as difficult or unpopular. Being charismatic, however, is not attributed to a single factor. It too evolves from one's possession of several characteristics.[3]

Over the past two decades, several authors have attempted to identify the personal characteristics associated with the **charismatic leader**. Some of the earlier writings focused on such attributes as confidence level, dominance, and strong convictions in one's beliefs.[4] More charismatic dimensions were added when Warren Bennis, after studying ninety highly effective and successful leaders, found they had four common competencies. These were the individual's compelling vision or sense of purpose; an ability to communicate that vision in clear terms that their followers could readily understand; a demonstrated consistency and focus in the pursuit of their vision; and an understanding of their own strengths.[5]

The most recent and comprehensive analysis has been completed by two researchers from McGill University.[6] Among their conclusions (see Figure 10-5), they propose that charismatic leaders have an idealized goal that they want to achieve, and are able to communicate it to others in a way that they can understand. That goal, however, is something quite different from the "status quo." It's a better "state" for the future, something that will significantly improve the present situation. Of course, the charismatic leader has a strong personal commitment to achieving that goal. This leadership trait also includes behaving in a way that is viewed as unconventional, or at best, out of the ordinary. A charismatic leader often does things that come as a surprise to the followers.

A charismatic leader is also assertive and self-confident. As previously noted, it is not surprising that a charismatic leader would have these traits. The individual's personal conviction and ability to convince others that he or she is leading them in the right direction provide followers with a sense that the leader knows best.

In Chapter 9, we introduced the personality dimension called self-monitoring. As you'll recall, we described high self-monitors as individuals who can easily adjust their behaviour to different situations. They can read verbal and nonverbal social cues and alter their behaviour accordingly. This ability to be a "good actor" has been found to be associated with charismatic leadership (see From Concepts to Skills, at the end of the chapter). Because high self-monitors can accurately read a situation, understand the feelings of employees, and then exhibit behaviours that match employees' expectations, they tend to emerge as effective and charismatic supervisors.[7]

Charismatic leader An individual with a compelling vision or sense of purpose, an ability to communicate that vision in clear terms that followers can understand, a demonstrated consistency and focus in pursuit of his or her vision, and an understanding of his or her own strengths

1. **Idealized goal.** Charismatic leaders have vision that proposes a future better than the status quo. The greater the disparity between this idealized goal and the status quo, the more likely that followers will attribute extraordinary vision to the leader.

2. **Ability to help others understand the goal.** They are able to clarify and state the vision in terms that are understandable to others. This explanation demonstrates an understanding of the followers' needs, and acts as a motivating force.

3. **Strong convictions about their goal.** Charismatic leaders are perceived as being strongly committed, and willing to take on high personal risk, incur high costs, and engage in self-sacrifice to achieve their vision.

4. **Behaviour that is unconventional.** They engage in behaviour that is perceived as being novel, out of the ordinary, and counter to norms. When successful, these behaviours evoke surprise and admiration in followers.

5. **Assertive and self-confident.** Charismatic leaders have complete confidence in their judgment and ability.

6. **High self-monitoring.** They can easily adjust their behaviour to different situations.

7. **Appearance as a change agent.** They are perceived as agents of radical change rather than as caretakers of the status quo.

FIGURE 10-5

Key characteristics of charismatic leaders (*Source:* Conger, Jay A. and Kanungo, Rabindra N., "Behavioral Dimensions of Charasmatic Leadership," adaptation as submitted of Table 1, p. 91. In J. A. Conger, R. N. Kanungo, and Associates, *Charasmatic Leadership: The Elusive Factor in Organizational Effectiveness.* Copyright 1988 Jossey-Bass Inc., Publishers.)

Finally, a charismatic leader is often perceived as an agent of radical change. His or her refusal to be satisfied with the status quo means that everything is open to change. In the end, his or her vision, conviction, and unconventional nature of doing things leads to an admiration by the followers—and success for the charismatic leader.

What can be said about the charismatic leader's effect on his or her followers? There is increasing belief that there is a strong link between charismatic leadership and high performance and satisfaction among followers.[8] That is, people working for charismatic leaders are motivated to exert extra work effort and, because they like their leader, express greater satisfaction.

HOW DO YOU BECOME A LEADER?

Although traits of successful leaders have been identified over the years, these traits alone do not adequately explain leadership effectiveness. If they were an adequate explanation, then leaders could be identified right from birth. But while you may have been the natural line leader in kindergarten—exhibiting your influencing abilities at an early age—true leadership requires more than such traits. The problem with focusing solely on traits is that it ignores the skills leaders must have, as well as the behaviours they must demonstrate in a vareity of situations. Fortunately, skills and behaviours are both learned! Therefore, it is more correct to say that leaders are made than born.

Whether or not you currently hold a formal position of authority over others, you can be in a position where you are able to influence others. Becoming a leader, however, requires certain skills (as well as possessing many of the traits described above). These are technical, conceptual, networking, and human relations skills. You're probably thinking you've heard these before. If you are, congratulations. You're paying close attention. Some of these are the competencies that effective supervisors need—as we discussed in Chapter 1. Because of their importance to leadership, let's look at them again—this time with an eye on leadership!

TECHNICAL SKILLS

It's a rare occurrence when you can influence others even though you have absolutely no idea of what they are doing. Although people may respect you as a person, when it comes to influencing them, they would like to believe you have the experience to make recommendations. This experience generally comes from your technical skills.

Technical skills are those tools, procedures, and techniques that are unique to your specialized situation. You need to "master" your job in your attempt to be viewed as a source of help—the "expert." Others generally won't come to you unless they need assistance. It's often the exceptions that they can't—or are ill-equipped to—handle. That's when they'll look to you for guidance. By having the technical skills, you're able to assist. But imagine if you didn't. You'd constantly have to ask someone else for the information. When you got it, you might be unable to adequately explain it to your employee who has requested it. At some point, employees may simply go around you, and talk directly to the "source" of the technical information. When that happens, you've lost some of your influence!

You can't overemphasize the importance of the technical skills related to your job. Those seen as being "in the know" do influence others, so if you want "followers" to have confidence in your advice and the direction you give, they've got to perceive you as a technically competent supervisor.

CONCEPTUAL SKILLS

Conceptual skills are your mental ability to coordinate a variety of interests and activities. Having conceptual skills means having the ability to think in the abstract, analyze lots of information, and make connections

FIGURE 10-6

Pat Lancaster, second from left, demonstrates his leadership skills when he works with his employeees to find better ways to improve their department's production. As a result, their unit—which manufactures machines that wrap large items in plastic—has witnessed better production numbers and higher-quality units produced.

between the data. Earlier, we described an effective leader as someone who could create a vision. In order to do this, you must be able to think critically and conceptualize how a situation *could be*, as well as understanding how it presently *is*.

Thinking conceptually is not as easy as you may believe. For some, it may be impossible! That's because to think conceptually, you must look at the "big picture." Too many times, we get caught up in the daily grind, focusing our attention on the minute details. Not that focusing on the details isn't important—without it, little may be accomplished. But setting long-term directions requires you to think about the future. It requires you to deal with uncertainty and the risk of the unknown. To be a good leader, then, you must be able to make some sense out of this chaos and envision what could be.

NETWORKING SKILLS

Networking skills are your ability to socialize and interact with outsiders—those not associated with your unit. It's understood that as a leader, you cannot do everything by yourself. Therefore, you need to know where to go to get the things your followers need. This may mean "fighting" for more resources or establishing relationships outside your area that will provide some benefit to your followers. Networking, if you're making the connection, means having good political skills. That's a point that shouldn't be overlooked.

Your employees will often look to you to provide them what they need to do an excellent job. If they can depend on you for giving them the tools (or "running the interference" they need), then you'll once again inspire a level of confidence in them. They are also likely to respond better if they know you're willing to fight for them.

HUMAN RELATIONS SKILLS

Human relations skills focus on your ability to work with, understand, and motivate those around you. As you've been reading this book, you'll notice that these skills have been highlighted. Good human relations skills require you to be able to effectively communicate—and especially to communicate your vision—with your employees and those outside your unit. They also involve listening to what others have to say. A good leader is not a "know it all," but rather someone who freely accepts and encourages involvement from his or her followers.

Human relations skills are those "people skills" that are frequently mentioned in today's discussion of effective supervision. They lie in the coaching, the facilitating, and supporting of others around you;[9] in understanding yourself, and being confident in your abilities; in your honesty in dealing with others and the values you live by; in your confidence in knowing that by helping others succeed—and letting them get the credit—you're doing the right thing for them, the organization, and yourself.

If you fail as a leader, it most likely won't be because you lack technical skills. Rather, it's more likely that your followers, as well as others, have lost respect for you because of your lack of human relations skills. If that ever happens, your ability to influence others will be seriously impaired.

LEADERSHIP BEHAVIOURS AND STYLES

One of the interesting aspects of leadership is that its defining traits and skills are difficult for followers to detect. As a result, they define your leadership by the *behaviours* they see in you. As the adage goes, "actions speak louder than words." It's what you do that matters. Therefore, you need to understand leadership behaviours.

The inability to explain leadership solely in terms of traits and skills has led researchers to look at the behaviours and styles that specific leaders exhibit. Researchers wondered whether there was something unique in the behaviour of effective leaders, and the style in which they practised their "craft." For example, do leaders tend to be more participative than autocratic?

A number of studies looked at behavioural styles. The most comprehensive of the behavioural theories resulted from research that began at Ohio State University in the late 1940s.[10] This study (as well as others) sought to identify independent dimensions of leader behaviour. Beginning with more than a thousand dimensions, they eventually narrowed the list down to two categories that accounted for most of the leadership behaviour described by employees. These are best identified as task-centred and employee-centred behaviours.[11]

TASK-CENTRED BEHAVIOURS

A **task-centred leader** is an individual who has a strong tendency to emphasize the technical or task aspects of the job. This individual's major concern is ensuring that employees know precisely what is expected of them and providing any guidance necessary for goals to be met. Employees, as viewed by this leader, are a means to an end. That is, in order to achieve goals, employees have to do their jobs. As long as they do what is expected, this leader is happy.

> **Task-centred leader** An individual with a strong tendency to emphasize the technical or task aspects of a job

Calling such a production-oriented person a leader may be something of a misnomer. This individual may not lead in the classic sense, but simply ensures compliance with stated rules, regulations, and production goals. In motivational terms, a production-oriented leader is someone who frequently exhibits a Theory X orientation (see Chapter 9) or an autocratic/authoritarian leadership style.

An **autocratic leader** is someone who can best be described as a task master. This individual leaves no doubt as to who's in charge and who has the authority and power in the group. He or she makes all the decisions affecting the group and tells others what to do. This telling frequently happens in the form of orders—mandates that are expected to be followed. Failure to obey these orders usually results in some negative reinforcement at the hands of the authoritarian leader.

> **Autocratic leader** A task master who leaves no doubt as to who is in charge and has authority and power in the group

Autocratic leadership is clearly inappropriate in today's organizations—right? Well, maybe not. There are leaders in all types of organizations—including business, government, and the military—who have found the autocratic style to work best.

PEOPLE-CENTRED BEHAVIOURS

A **people-centred leader** is a person who emphasizes interpersonal relations with those he or she leads. This leader takes a personal interest in the needs of employees, and is concerned for employees' welfare. Interactions between this leader and his or her employees are characterized as trusting, friendly, and supportive. Furthermore, this leader is very sensitive to the concerns and feelings of employees. From a motivational

> **People-centred leader** An individual who emphasizes interpersonal relations with those he or she leads

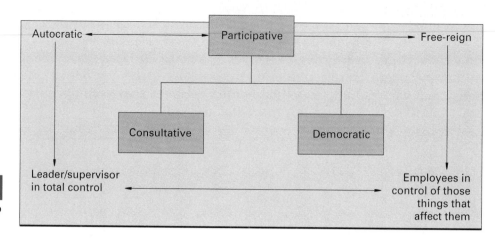

FIGURE 10-7

Supervisory leadership behaviours

point of view, a people-centred leader is one who exhibits more Theory Y orientations. As a result, this individual often exhibits a participative (or democratic) leadership style.

A **participative leadership** style is one where input from followers is actively sought for many of the activities in the organization. This means that establishing plans, solving problems, and making decisions is not done solely by the supervisor. Instead, the entire work group participates. The only question that really remains is who has the final say. That is, participative leadership can be viewed from two perspectives. First is one where the leader seeks input, hears the concerns and issues of the followers, but makes the final decision himself or herself. In this capacity, the leader is using the input as an information-seeking exercise. We call this **consultative-participative leadership**. On the other hand, a participative leader may allow the followers to have a say in what's decided. Here, decisions are made truly by the group. This is referred to as **democratic-participative leadership**.

There is one other behavioural leadership style beyond participative leadership. This is often referred to as free-reigning leadership. A **free-reign** (or laissez-faire) **leader** is someone who gives employees total autonomy to make the decisions that will affect them. After overall objectives and general guidelines have been established, the employees are free to establish their own plans for achieving their goals. This is not meant to imply that there's a lack of leadership. Rather, it implies that the leader is removed from the day-to-day activities of the employees—but is always available to deal with the exceptions.

WHAT BEHAVIOUR SHOULD YOU EXHIBIT?

In today's organizations, many employees appear to prefer to work for a supervisor with a people-centred leadership style. However, just because this style appears "friendlier" to employees, we cannot make a sweeping

Participative leadership
The leadership style of an individual who actively seeks input from followers for many of the activities in the organization

Consultative-participative leadership
The leadership style of an individual who seeks input, hears the concerns and issues of the followers, but makes the final decision himself or herself, using input as an information-seeking exercise

Democratic-participative leadership
A leadership style that allows followers to have a say in what is decided

Free-reign leader
An individual who gives employees total autonomy to make decisions that will affect them

FIGURE 10-8

Would this basketball coach's leadership style be effective in all situations? Although he's found success in using his task-centred style for winning basketball games, that doesn't mean it would work elsewhere.

generalization that a people-centred leadership style will make you a more effective supervisor. There has actually been very little success in identifying consistent relationships between patterns of leadership behaviour and successful organizational performance. In some cases, people-centred styles generate both high productivity and high follower satisfaction. However, in others, followers are happy, but productivity suffers. What is sometimes overlooked in trying to determine the superiority of one style over the other is the plethora of the situational factors that influence effective leadership.

EFFECTIVE LEADERSHIP

It became increasingly clear to those studying leadership that predicting leadership success involves something more complex than isolating a few traits or preferable behaviours. The failure to find answers led to a new focus on situational influences. The relationship between leadership style and effectiveness suggested that under condition a, style X would be appropriate, whereas style Y would be more suitable for condition b, and style Z for condition c. But what were the conditions a, b, c, and so forth? It was one thing to say that leadership effectiveness depends on the situation and another to be able to isolate those situational conditions. The key to many of these situational theories was their inclusion of followers in the leadership equation.

KEY SITUATIONAL MODELS OF LEADERSHIP

Some approaches to isolating key situational variables have proven more successful than others and, as a result, have gained wider recognition.[12] The first comprehensive model, developed by University of Washington professor Fred Fiedler, proposed that effective leadership is a function of a proper match between the leader's style of interaction with followers and the degree to which the situation gives control and influence to the leader.[13] According to Fiedler, a leader's style can be identified based on how the leader describes an individual he or she least enjoys working with. When a leader describes this person in favourable terms, it indicates that the leader is interested in good relationships. Accordingly, that leader's style would tend to be more people-centred. On the other hand, describing this least-preferred individual in unfavourable terms indicates more of a task-centred style. Fiedler believed that an individual's style is fixed. Using three situational factors (degree of respect for employees, structured jobs, and influence over the employment process) he identified eight situations where either the task- or people-centered styles would work best. That is, these situational factors would dictate which leadership style would be more effective (see Figure 10-9).

One of the more respected approaches to situational leadership was developed by Robert House. It is called the **path-goal theory** of leadership.[14] The basis of this model is that it's the leader's job to assist his or her followers in attaining their goals. This is done by providing the necessary direction and/or support to ensure that their goals are compatible with the overall objectives of the group or organization. The leader clarifies the path by which employees may get from where they are to a point where they will have achieved their goals—assisting them also by reducing potential roadblocks and pitfalls.

A few examples will illustrate how you can use the path-goal approach. If your employees have considerable experience and perceive themselves to have the ability to do their jobs, they don't need task-centred leadership. They know how to do their work, so people-centred leadership is appropriate. In contrast, new employees, those lacking confidence in their abilities, or those who are insecure will appreciate the help provided through task-centred leadership. Similarly, when an employee's job is unstructured and ambiguous, a task approach to leadership is appreciated. But if the employee has clear job goals, structured tasks, and a supportive work group that provides assistance, task-centred leadership will be seen at best as redundant and maybe even as overbearing and controlling.

In summary, path-goal theory demonstrates that employees are likely to be most productive and satisfied when their supervisor compensates for things lacking in either the employee or the work setting. However, the supervisor who spends time explaining tasks when those tasks are already clear or when the employee has the ability and experience to handle them without interference is likely to be ineffective. The employee will see this behaviour as redundant or even insulting. The fundamental issue, then, is to adjust your style to the needs of your employees.

Path-goal theory
The leader's job is to assist followers in overcoming obstacles in the way of attaining the goals by promoting the proper leadership style.

Situational Factors	I	II	III	IV	V	VI	VII	VIII
Respect for Followers	Good	Good	Good	Good	Poor	Poor	Poor	Poor
Structured Jobs	High	High	Low	Low	High	High	Low	Low
Influence Over Employment Process	Strong	Weak	Strong	Weak	Strong	Weak	Strong	Weak
Preferred Leader Behaviour	Task Centred	Task Centred	Task Centred	People Centred	People Centred	People Centred	Task Centred	Task Centred

FIGURE 10-9

Fiedler's leadership findings

One situational model of leadership that has been getting much attention lately was proposed by Paul Hersey and Kenneth Blanchard. Called simply **situational leadership**, its emphasis is on adjusting leadership style to specific situations.[15] Specifically, given that without employees there is no leader, situational leadership shows how you should adjust your leadership style to reflect employees' needs.

Although similar in nature to Fiedler's theory, there are a couple of differences worth noting. First, situational leadership places much attention on what is called the **readiness** of employees. Readiness in this context reflects how able and willing an employee is to do a job. Hersey and Blanchard have identified four stages of follower readiness. These are:

R1: An employee is both unable and unwilling to do a job.

R2: An employee is unable to do the job, but willing to perform the necessary tasks.

R3: An employee is able to do the job, but unwilling to be told by a leader what to do.

R4: An employee is both able and willing to do the job.

A point should be made here concerning willingness and unwillingness. Unwillingness, as defined for example in R1, is not the same unwillingness that you would associate with an employee being insubordinate. Rather, it's an unwillingness that stems from the individual's lack of confident and competence enough to do a job. You'll see how this works in a moment.

A second component of the model focuses on what you do as a leader. Depending on the readiness level of an employee, you as a leader will exhibit a certain behaviour. Behaviour in this model is best described as the type of communication taking place. Task behaviour can be seen as one-way communication—*from* you *to* the employee. Relationship behaviour, on the other hand, reflects two-way communication—*between* you and the employee. Given that high and low degrees of each of these two behaviours can exist, Hersey and Blanchard identified four specific leadership styles based on the maturity of the follower. Let's see how this model works by going through an example of a new employee in your department, and her first day on the job (see Figure 10-10).

When this employee first arrives at work, she is anxious. She's uncertain about what she is getting into and how to handle the job responsibilities. You feel that the employment process worked well in properly matching her to the job and orienting her to the organization. Now it's time for her to start the job she was hired to do. Imagine if at this point you just assigned a list of tasks for her to complete and walked away! She would probably have some difficulty. Why? Because at this time, she's not ready (R1). It's doubtful she even knows the right questions to ask. Communications between you and the employee, at this point, need to be

Situational leadership
A leadership model that emphasizes adjusting leadership style to specific situations

Readiness
How willing and able an employee is to do a job

College of Business Ohio University Alumni Newsletter interview with Paul Hersey: "Situational Leadership 'Guru' Returns To Campus" http://sirius.cba.ohiou. edu/www/news/ spring97/indextext. htm#anchor494445

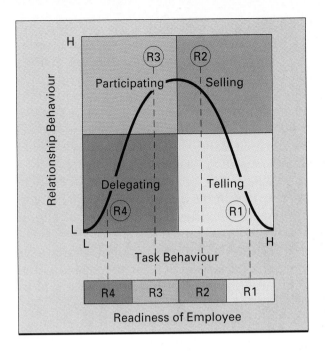

FIGURE 10-10

Situational leadership

one-way: you need to tell her what to do and give her specific directions on how to do it. According to situational leadership, at this stage you are using a *telling* style of leadership.

But this new employee won't stay at R1 forever. After having been provided with ample directions and becoming more familiar with the job, she's moving to stage **R2**. At the R2 stage of work development, the employee is becoming more involved in her job, but she still lacks some ability. She's not yet fully trained. She's asking questions about things she may not fully understand. She may question why certain things have to be done as you have asked. Accordingly, you may need to *sell* this employee on some of your ideas to get her to accept them. At this point, high degrees of both one-way and two-way communication are happening simultaneously.

At some later point (R3), this employee has become the expert on her job. She knows her duties better than anyone else, and she's beginning to put her special mark on things. You no longer need to tell her what to do, but the reality is, you still need to be involved in what she's doing. She has not quite reached the point where you can feel comfortable leaving her totally alone. That's not an insult—it's just that you recognize that this employee still has some developing to do. Accordingly, you will best deal with this situation by being supportive of her and not being overly task-centred. Hersey and Blanchard refer to this as a *participating* style of leadership.

Finally, this employee has fully developed. She has your trust and can carry out her duties with little, if any, direction (R4). In this situation, she basically needs to be left alone. At this *delegating* stage of leadership, you simply assign the tasks and let her do her job. You now know—based on your appraisal of her performance—that she can and will get the job done. If she needs help, you're always available to deal with the exceptions.

An important aspect of situational leadership is that an employee can be in all four quadrants at the same time. To lead properly, you must be able to exhibit the correct leadership style given what each employee needs. If a seasoned employee generally at stage R4 gets a new assignment, you cannot assume that he or she will necessarily be at R4 for the new tasks. In fact, the employee may need to be clearly directed in these new taks—and that implies a telling style of leadership. If that doesn't occur, problems may arise. On the other hand, if an employee who has been at R4 for some time gets additional assignments that require a telling style, problems will arise if that individual is treated like an R1 employee on *all* aspects of his or her job. If all of a sudden, the employee is being told how to do what he or she has been doing for many months or years, it can have the effect of implying that you perceive the employee as not doing the job properly—which isn't true! The point is, you need to demonstrate a leadership style that's consistent at all times with your employees' abilities (see Supervision in Action).

CONTEMPORARY LEADERSHIP ROLES

Let's turn our attention to some important issues that every effective supervisor today is, and will continue to be, concerned about. Specifically, how do you build credibility and trust with your employees and how can you become a more empowering supervisor?

CREDIBILITY AND TRUST

Credibility
Supervisory qualities of honesty, competence, and the ability to inspire

Trust
The belief in the integrity, character, and ability of a leader

Followers want leaders who are credible and whom they can trust. But what do these terms—*credibility* and *trust*—really mean?

The most dominant component of **credibility** is honesty. In addition, credible supervisors have been found to be competent and inspiring. By inspiring, we mean that they are able to effectively communicate their confidence and enthusiasm to their employees. So employees judge their supervisors' credibility in terms of their honesty, competence, and ability to inspire.

Trust is so closely linked with the concept of credibility that the two terms are frequently used interchangeably. We define trust as belief in the integrity, character, and ability of a leader. When employees trust their

National Culture Could Affect Your Leadership Style

One general conclusion that surfaces from learning about leadership is that you shouldn't use any single leadership style in every case. Instead, you should adjust your style to the situation. Although not mentioned specifically in any of the theories we've presented, national culture is clearly an important situational variable in determining which leadership style will be most effective for you.

National culture affects leadership by way of your employees. You cannot choose your leadership styles at will. Rather, you are constrained by the cultural conditions your employees come to expect.[16] For example, an autocratic leadership style is more compatible with cultures where power is unequal, such as those found in Arabic, Far Eastern, and Latin countries. This cultural "power" ranking should be a good indicator of employees' willingness to accept participative leadership. Participation is likely to be most effective in cultures where power is more equally distributed—such as those in Norway, Finland, Denmark, and Sweden.

It's important to remember that most leadership theories were developed by North American researchers using North American subjects. Canada, the United States, and the Scandinavian countries all rate below average on the "power" criterion. This fact may help explain why our theories tend to favour more participative and empowering styles of leadership. Accordingly, you need to consider national culture as yet another contingency variable in determining your most effective leadership style.

supervisor, they're willing to be vulnerable to their supervisor's actions because they're confident that their rights and interests won't be abused.[17] Recent evidence has identified five dimensions that underlie the concept of trust.[18] These are *integrity, competence, consistency, loyalty,* and *openness* (see Figure 10-11).

FIGURE 10-11

Five dimensions of trust.
Source: Modified and reproduced with permission of authors and publishers from Schindler, P. L., & Thomas, C. C., "The Structure of Interpersonal Trust in the Workplace," *Psychological Reports*, 1993, 73, pp. 563–73. © Psychological Reports 1993

- Integrity: Honesty and truthfulness
- Competence: Technical and interpersonal knowledge and skills
- Consistency: Reliability, predictability, and good judgment in handling situations
- Loyalty: Willingness to protect and save face for a person
- Openness: Willingness to share ideas and information freely

WHY ARE CREDIBILITY AND TRUST IMPORTANT?

The top rating of honesty as an identifying characteristic of admired supervisors indicates the importance of credibility and trust to leadership effectiveness.[19] This has probably always been true. However, recent changes in the workplace have reignited interest and concern with supervisors building trust.

The trend toward empowering employees and creating work teams has reduced or removed many of the traditional control mechanisms used to monitor employees.[20] For instance, employees are increasingly free to schedule their own work, evaluate their own performance, and in some cases even make their own team hiring decisions. Therefore, trust becomes critical. Employees have to trust supervisors to treat them fairly and supervisors have to trust employees to conscientiously fulfill their responsibilities.

Supervisors are increasingly having to lead others who are not in their direct line of authority—members of project teams, individuals who work for suppliers, customers, and people who represent other organizations through such arrangements as corporate partnerships. These situations don't allow supervisors to fall back on their formal positions to enact compliance. Many of the relationships, in fact, are dynamic. The ability to quickly develop trust may be crucial to the success of such relationships.

How can you build trust? We've listed several suggestions in Building a Supervisory Skill.

PLAYING FAVOURITES

You might think that a sure way to undermine employees' trust in you would be to be seen as someone who plays favourites. In many cases you'd be right. But many supervisors, it appears, do in a sense play favourites, in that they don't treat all their employees in the same manner.[21]

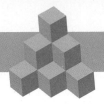

BUILDING TRUST

ABOUT THE SKILL

Given the importance trust plays in the leadership role today, supervisors should actively seek to build trust among their employees. Here are some suggestions for achieving that goal.[22]

PRACTISING THE SKILL

1. **Practise openness.** Mistrust comes as much from what people don't know as from what they do know. Openness leads to confidence and trust. Keep people informed, make the criteria on how decisions are made overt and clear, explain the rationale for your decisions, be candid about problems, and fully disclose relevant information.
2. **Be fair.** Before making decisions or taking actions, consider how others will perceive them in terms of objectivity and fairness. Give credit where it's due, be objective and impartial in performance appraisals, and pay attention to equity perceptions when you distribute rewards.
3. **Speak your feelings.** Supervisors who convey only hard facts come across as cold and distant. If you share your feelings, others will see you as real and human. They'll know who you are and their respect for you will increase.
4. **Tell the truth.** Because honesty is critical to credibility, you must be perceived as someone who tells the truth. Employees are more tolerant of learning something they "don't want to hear" than of finding of out that their leader lied to them.
5. **Show consistency.** Employees want predictability. Mistrust comes from not knowing what to expect. Take the time to think about your values and beliefs. Then let them consistently guide your decisions. When you know your central purpose, your actions will follow accordingly, and you'll project a consistency that earns trust.
6. **Fulfill your promises.** Trust requires that employees believe you're dependable. So you need to ensure that you keep your word. Promises made must be promises kept.
7. **Maintain confidences.** You trust those whom you believe to be discreet and whom you can rely on. Employees feel the same way. If they make themselves vulnerable by telling you something in confidence, they need to feel assured that you won't discuss it with others or betray that confidence. If employees perceive you as someone who leaks personal confidences or someone who can't be depended on, you won't be perceived as trustworthy.
8. **Demonstrate confidence.** Develop the admiration and respect of others by demonstrating technical and professional ability. Pay particular attention to developing and displaying your communication, negotiation, and other interpersonal skills.

You're likely to have favourite employees who make up your "in" group. You'll have a special relationship with this small group. You'll trust them, give them a lot of your attention, and often give them special privileges. Not surprisingly, they'll perceive themselves as having preferred status. Be aware that this creation of a favoured in-group can undermine your credibility, especially among those employees outside this group.

Be cautious of this tendency to create favourites in your department. You're human, so you'll naturally find some employees you feel closer to and with whom you want to be more open. What you need to think through is whether you want this favouritism to show. When this favoured-employee status is granted to someone based on nonperformance criteria—for example, you share similar interests or common personality traits—it is likely to lessen your leadership effectiveness. However, favouritism may have a place when it falls on those employees who are high performers. In such cases, you are rewarding a behaviour you want to reinforce. But always be careful when you follow this practice. Unless performance measures are objective and widely visible, you may be seen as arbitrary and unfair.

LEADING THROUGH EMPOWERMENT

Several times in different sections of this book, we've stated that supervisors are increasingly leading by empowering their employees. Millions of individual employees and teams of employees are making key operating decisions that directly affect their work. They are developing budgets, scheduling workloads, controlling inventories, solving quality problems, evaluating their own performance, and so on—activities that until very recently were viewed exclusively as part of the supervisor's job.

The increased use of empowerment is being driven by two forces. The first is the need for quick decisions by those people who are most knowledgeable about the issues. If organizations are to successfully compete in a dynamic global village, they have to be able to make decisions and implement changes quickly. That requires, at times, moving decision making to the employee level. The second force is the reality that the downsizing and restructuring of organizations through the mid-1990s left many supervisors with considerably larger spans of control than they had before. In order to cope with the demands of an increased workload, supervisors have to empower their people. As a result, they are sharing power and responsibility with their employees.[23] This means their role is to show trust, provide vision, remove performance-blocking barriers, offer encouragement, and motivate and coach employees.[24]

Does this wholesale support of shared leadership appear strange given the attention paid earlier to contingency theories of leadership? If it doesn't, it should. Why? Because empowerment proponents are essentially advocating a noncontingent approach to leadership. That means they claim that empowerment will work anywhere. Such being the case, directive, task-oriented, autocratic leadership is out.

The problem with this kind of thinking is that the current empower-ment movement ignores the conditions that facilitate successful shared leadership and the extent to which leadership can be shared. Because of factors such as downsizing, which results in the need for higher-level employee skills, commitment of organizations to continuous training, implementation of continuous improvement programs, and introduction of self-managed teams, the need for shared leadership is certainly increasing. But that is not true in all situations, and blanket acceptance of empowerment or any universal approach to leadership is inconsistent with the best and most current evidence we have on the subject.

LEADERSHIP ISSUES TODAY

We'll finish this chapter by looking at two current debates about leader-ship. These are 1. the issue of differing leadership styles between men and women, and 2. the movement from transactional to transformation-al leadership.

DO MEN AND WOMEN LEAD DIFFERENTLY?

Are there differences in leadership styles based on gender? Are men more effective leaders or does that honour belong to women? Just asking these questions is certain to evoke emotions on both sides of the debate. Before we attempt to respond to them, let's set down one important fact: the bot-tom line is that the two sexes are more alike than different in terms of the way they lead.[25] Much of this similarity is based on the fact that leaders, irrespective of gender, perform similar activities in influencing others. That's their job, and both sexes do it equally well. This is similar to what can be said of nurses. Although the stereotypical nurse is a woman, men are equally effective—and successful—in this career choice.

However, there are notable differences between men and women as leaders. The most common difference lies in leadership style. Women have a tendency to lead more with a democratic style. This implies that they encourage participation of their followers and are willing to share their positional power with others. In addition, women tend to influence others best through their "charisma, expertise, contacts, and their inter-personal skills."[26] Men, on the other hand, tend to use a task-centred leadership style. Their directing of activities and reliance on their posi-tional power to control the organization's activities tend to dominate the way they influence others. And yet even this difference is blurred, because other things being equal, when a woman leads in a traditionally male-dominated job (like that of a police officer), she too tends to lead in a manner that is more task-centred.[27]

FIGURE 10-12

Are Army leadership styles changing with the times? Previously, drill instructors—primarily men—were typically autocratic leaders. They gave orders and structured recruits' activities from sunrise to bedtime. They emphasized task accomplishment, accepting authority and obeying orders. The "new" Army still focuses on these values, but is also taking into consideration factors like sensitivity training, which are more frequently associated with women's leadership characteristics.

Further compounding this issue is the changing role of supervisors in today's organizations. With more emphasis on teams, employee involvement, and interpersonal skills, democratic leadership styles are more in demand. Supervisors need to be more sensitive to their employees' needs, be more open in their communication, and build more trusting relationships. Ironically, many of these are behaviours that women have typically grown up developing.

Women are still not accepted as leaders as readily as men and must be prepared to deal with this, preferably with a sense of humour. Della Tardif, as the corporate credit manager at IPSCO in Regina, found that being a woman in management is a challenge. For example, she got a call from a customer who wanted to "talk with the f---ing credit manager, not his secretary." She replied calmly, "I am the f---ing credit manager. If you'd like to speak with my assistant who is male, that's fine. But I do have to approve his decisions." He apologized and dealt cooperatively with her.

TRANSACTIONAL AND TRANSFORMATIONAL LEADERS

The second issue is the interest in differentiating transformational leaders from transactional leaders.[28] As you'll see, because transformational leaders are also charismatic, there is some overlap between this topic and the preceding discussion on charismatic traits.

Transactional leaders Leaders who guide or motivate their employees in the direction of established goals by clarifying role and task requirements

Most of the leadership models address **transactional leaders**. These leaders guide or motivate their employees in the direction of established goals by clarifying role and task requirements. There is another type of leader who inspires followers to transcend their own self-interest for the good of the organization. This type of leader is capable of having a

Go to the library and find two or three recent articles that discuss the issue of gender differences in leadership. Summarize these articles. Then, respond to the following: Do you believe that in today's organizations, both "masculine" and "feminine" approaches to leadership are equally important? Discuss. Also, explain how the specific situation one faces may affect one's leadership style.

profound and extraordinary effect on his or her followers. They are called **transformational leaders**. They pay attention to the concerns and developmental needs of employees; they change employees' awareness of issues by helping them to look at old problems in new ways; and they are able to excite, arouse, and inspire followers to put out extra effort to achieve group goals.

Transactional and transformational supervision should not be viewed as opposing approaches to getting things done.[29] Rather, transformational supervision is built on top of transactional supervision. Transformational supervision produces levels of employee effort and performance that go beyond what would occur with a transactional approach alone. Moreover, transformational supervision is more than charisma. "The purely charismatic [leader] may want employees to adopt the charismatic's world view and go no further. The transformational supervisor will attempt to instill in employees the ability to question not only established views but eventually those established by the leader."[30]

The evidence supporting the superiority of transformational supervision over the transactional variety is overwhelmingly impressive. In summary, it indicates that transformational supervision leads to lower turnover rates, higher productivity, and higher employee satisfaction.[31]

Transformational leaders
Leaders who inspire followers to transcend self-interest for the good of the organization and who are capable of having a profound and extraordinary effect on their followers

5. According to the theory of situational leadership, when an employee is both unable and unwilling to perform the duties of his or her job, which supervisory leadership style would work best?
   a. delegating
   b. telling
   c. selling
   d. participating
6. Describe how credibility and trust affect leadership.
7. Empowering supervisors share power and responsibility with their employees. True or False?
8. Which one of the following statements about gender differences in leadership is correct?
   a. There are no differences in leadership based on gender.
   b. Women leaders have a tendency to lead using a directive leadership style.
   c. Men have a tendency to use a leadership style that encourages participation of their followers.
   d. None of the above statements about gender differences is correct.

PROJECTING CHARISMA

ASSESSING YOURSELF: DO YOU SELF-MONITOR?

Indicate the degree to which you think the following statements are true or false by circling the appropriate number; for example, if a statement is always true, you would circle the 5 next to that statement.

5 = Always true
4 = Generally true
3 = Somewhat true, but with exceptions
2 = Somewhat false, but with exceptions
1 = Generally false
0 = Always false

1. In social situations, I have the ability to alter my behaviour if I feel that something else is called for.	5	4	3	2	1	0
2. I am often able to read people's true emotions correctly through their eyes.	5	4	3	2	1	0
3. I have the ability to control the way I come across to people, depending on the impression I wish to give them.	5	4	3	2	1	0
4. In conversations, I am sensitive to even the slightest change in the facial expression of the person I'm conversing with.	5	4	3	2	1	0
5. My powers of intuition are quite good when it comes to understanding others' emotions and motives.	5	4	3	2	1	0
6. I can usually tell when others consider a joke in bad taste, even though they may laugh convincingly.	5	4	3	2	1	0
7. When I feel that the image I am portraying isn't working, I can readily change it to something that does.	5	4	3	2	1	0
8. I can usually tell when I've said something inappropriate by reading the listener's eyes.	5	4	3	2	1	0
9. I have trouble changing my behaviour to suit different people and different situations.	5	4	3	2	1	0

10.	I have found that I can adjust my behaviour to meet the requirements of any situation I find myself in.	5	4	3	2	1	0
11.	If someone is lying to me, I usually know it at once from that person's manner of expression.	5	4	3	2	1	0
12.	Even when it might be to my advantage, I have difficulty putting up a good front.	5	4	3	2	1	0
13.	Once I know what the situation calls for, it's easy for me to regulate my actions accordingly.	5	4	3	2	1	0

SCORING DIRECTIONS

This questionnaire measures your self-monitoring score.[32] To obtain your total score, add up the numbers circled, except reverse scores for questions 9 and 12. On those, a circled 5 becomes a 0, 4 becomes 1, and so forth.

Scores of approximately 53 or higher indicate a high self-monitor. The lower your score, the greater your rigidity. This questionnaire can provide you insights into your ability to project charisma. That's because the skill may require you to engage in behaviours that are not natural to you. The higher your score, the easier it should be for you to comfortably and effectively project behaviours associated with charismatic leadership.

SKILL BASICS

There's good news! People have been successfully trained to exhibit charismatic behaviour.[33] In this section, we'll review the basic behaviours that you need to project in order to be perceived as a charismatic leader.

PROJECT A POWERFUL, CONFIDENT, AND DYNAMIC PRESENCE

This has both verbal and nonverbal components. You'll want to use a captivating and engaging voice tone. It should convey confidence. You'll also want to talk directly to people, maintaining direct eye contact, and holding your body posture in a way that says you're sure of yourself. When you speak, act as if you're in control. Speak clearly, don't stammer, and avoid sprinkling your sentences with noncontent phrases such as "ahhh" and "you know."

ARTICULATE AN OVERARCHING GOAL

You need a vision for the future, unconventional ways of achieving the vision, and the ability to communicate the vision to others.

Your vision should be a clear statement of where you want your department to go and how you're going to get there. Of course, this vision must be relevant to your people. They must see it as important. So part of your job is to persuade them how the achievement of this vision will benefit them and your department.

The means for accomplishing the vision can't be a rehash of what has been done in the past. Look for fresh and radically different approaches to problems. The road to achieving your vision should be novel but appropriate to the context.

It's not enough to have a vision. You must be able to get others to buy into it. The real power of Martin Luther King, Jr. was not that he had a dream, but that he could articulate it in terms that made it accessible to millions.

COMMUNICATE HIGH PERFORMANCE EXPECTATIONS AND CONFIDENCE IN FOLLOWERS

You help demonstrate your confidence in people by stating ambitious goals for them individually and as a group. Make sure you convey your absolute belief that they will achieve your expectations. For instance, this statement reflects such confidence: "I'm sure you've established a well-thought-out plan for the project and that you'll do a great job."

BE SENSITIVE TO THE NEEDS OF FOLLOWERS

A charismatic leader gets to know each of his or her followers individually. This allows the leader to understand their individual needs and to be able to develop an intensely personal relationship with each one. By being sensitive to the needs of his or her followers, the charismatic leader builds a unique bond—where followers give unquestioned obedience, loyalty, commitment, and devotion to the leader.

How do you become sensitive? By encouraging followers to express their points of view, by being approachable, by genuinely listening to and caring about your followers' concerns, and by asking questions so you can learn what is really important to them.

APPLYING YOUR SKILLS

The class is to break into pairs. Each member of the pair will practise exhibiting behaviours associated with charismatic leadership.

EXERCISE 1

Student A's task is to "lead" Student B through a new-student orientation to your college. The orientation should last about ten to fifteen minutes. Assume Student B is a brand-new student and is unfamiliar with the campus. Remember, Student A should attempt to project himself or herself as charismatic.

EXERCISE 2

Student B's task is to "lead" Student A in a ten-to-fifteen-minute program on how to study more effectively for college exams. Take a few minutes to think about what has worked well for you and assume that Student A is a new student and interested in improving his or her study habits. As with the first exercise, Student B should attempt to project himself or herself as charismatic.

When both exercises are complete, each pair should assess how well they did in projecting charisma and how they might improve.

SUMMARY

This summary is organized by the Learning Objectives.

1. Leadership is the ability to influence others. The main difference between a leader and a supervisor is that a supervisor is appointed. A supervisor has legitimate power that allows him or her to reward and punish. A supervisor's ability to influence is founded upon the formal authority inherent in his or her position. In contrast, a leader may either be appointed or emerge from within a group. A leader can influence others to perform beyond the actions dictated by formal authority.

2. Six traits have been found that distinguish leaders differ from nonleaders: drive, the desire to influence others, honesty and moral character, self-confidence, intelligence, and relevant knowledge. Yet possession of these traits is no guarantee of leadership because situational factors are also important.

3. Charisma is a magnetism that inspires employees to reach goals that are perceived as difficult or unpopular. Charismatic leaders are self-confident, possess a vision of a better future, have a strong belief in that vision, engage in unconventional behaviours, have a high degree of self-monitoring, and are perceived as agents of radical change.

4. Task-centred leadership behaviours focus on the technical or task aspects of a job. People-centred leadership behaviours focus on interpersonal relations among the employees.

5. The three types of participative leadership styles are consultative (seeking input from employees); democratic (giving employees a role in making decisions); and free-reign (giving employees total autonomy to make the decisions that affect them).

6. Situational leadership involves adjusting one's leadership style to the readiness level of the employee for a given set of tasks. Given an employee's ability and willingness to do a specific job, a situational leader will use one of four leadership styles—telling, selling, participating, or delegating.

7. While there are some differences, men and women are more alike than different in how they lead. The differences that do exist lie in leadership styles. Women tend to rely on charisma, expertise, and interpersonal skills to influence others. Men, on the other hand, tend to use positional power to direct and control organizational activities.

KEY TERMS AND CONCEPTS

Autocratic leader

Charismatic leader

Consultative-participative
leadership

Democratic participative
leadership

Free-reign leader

Leadership

Leadership traits

Participative leadership

Path-goal theory

People-centred leader

Readiness

Situational leadership

Task-centred leader

REVIEWING YOUR KNOWLEDGE

1. "All supervisors should be leaders but not all leaders should be supervisors." Do you agree or disagree? Support your position.

2. How is intelligence related to leadership?

3. What is charismatic leadership? Why might high self-monitors be more effective leaders? Discuss.

4. What is the difference between a task-centred and a people-centred supervisor? Which one do you believe employees would rather work for? Why? Which one would you prefer to work for? Explain.

5. Compare and contrast consultative, democratic, and free-reign styles of participative leadership.

6. How can supervisors be both flexible and consistent in their leadership styles? Aren't these contradictory? Explain.

7. How could a professor apply situational leadership with students in a classroom setting?

8. If leaders play favourites, is it good or bad for their department's performance? Discuss.

9. "Given the emphasis on caring for employees, women may be more effective supervisors." Do you agree or disagree? Support your position.

ANSWERS TO THE POP QUIZZES

1. **d. All leaders should be supervisors.** Leaders do not have to be supervisors, nor serve in any supervisory capacity whatsoever.

2. Six traits have been found on which leaders differ from nonleaders—drive, the desire to lead, honesty and integrity, self-confidence, intelligence, and job-relevant knowledge. Yet possession of these traits is no guarantee of leadership because situational factors must also be considered.

3. **False.** A supervisor who gets input from his or her staff but makes the decision himself or herself would be classified as a consultative-participative leader.

4. **c. A strong commitment to the status quo.** A charismatic supervisor does what is necessary to make changes to move his or her department/organization forward. In doing so, this individual looks beyond the current state of events—the status quo.

5. **b. telling.** The unwillingness and inability to do the job reflects an employee in the R1 stage of readiness. Therefore the telling style of supervisory leadership would be best used.

6. Credibility and trust do influence leadership effectiveness. If employees do not view their supervisor as being honest, competent, consistent, loyal, open, and having the ability to inspire them, they may not have a strong sense of unity—nor a commitment to their jobs or the organization.

7. **True.** Empowering supervisors share power and responsibility with their employees. That's one of the basic concepts of empowering supervisors.

8. **d. None of the above statements about gender differences is correct.** Although men and women do, in some cases, demonstrate similar leadership styles, they are different in their style orientation. Women tend to use a leadership style that encourages participation of their followers. Men, on the other hand, have a tendency to lead using a directive leadership style.

CASE 10.A

From Boot Camp to a Shoe Company?

Where do the graduates of Canada's military colleges go?[34] Into the Canadian Forces as officers, yes. But many ex-cadets (who may leave the forces after five years service) have found their way into influential positions in business. They're good at much more than commanding military units, and those leadership skills are recognized widely.

The quality of military college graduates has much to do with the rigorous selection procedures which ensure that only able and motivated individuals enter Royal Military College in Kingston, or Collège militaire royal de St-Jean in St-Jean-sur-Richelieu. But the training itself is also highly demanding. Before entering college, recruits must endure the gruelling seven weeks of Basic Officers Training at Chilliwack, B.C. About twenty per cent of the candidates don't make it to the next step, which is a six-week indoctrination course at the college. Here every moment from 6:30 a.m. to 11 p.m. is scheduled, and intense physical and mental challenges push the recruits and force them to work as a team. Upon completion of the course (marked by an obstacle race), the fully fledged cadets have four years of college ahead of them which is not only rigorous academically, but also features compulsory athletics and a rigid dress code. Additionally, off-campus visits are restricted for the first two years, and cadets' performance in all aspects is continually appraised. They virtually govern themselves through a system by which senior cadets train, monitor, and sometimes discipline more junior cadets. And they are thrust into leadership positions early on and frequently.

Graduates now in business form a powerful network whose strength is due not only to their shared experiences but also to their unwritten code of honour, which says that they are expected to help each other and be honest in those dealings.

RESPONDING TO THIS CASE

1. Why do you think military college graduates are considered highly desirable employees and potential leaders by many businesses?
2. What leadership style is likely to be more typical of military college graduates: task- or people-centred? Why?
3. Explain why that style is suitable in the military. Refer to theory to support your explanation. Speculate what businesses or circumstances in business would also benefit from this style.
4. Discuss how students who are interested in management but are not in military college could attempt to duplicate some of the experiences and learning of the military college graduates.

CASE 10.B

Steelworkers Team Up

With the construction of their new pipefinishing mill in the spring of 1994, a western Canadian steel company and the United Steelworkers took the opportunity to begin a process called worker empowerment. In this mill there are crews of twelve to thriteen members, each with their own elected leader. Unlike the traditional setup with a centralized maintenance department, all crew members have been trained to do basic maintenance and repair on their own equipment. And on each shift there are a millwright and an electrician, who are also operators but can assist where needed when breakdowns occur. Jim Clarke is the 24″ finishing line foreman. He does no direct supervising but coordinates the crews through their leaders:

> My role is more of a coach. The most important thing I can do is to share as much information with the crews as possible: what expectations are regarding quality and performance, and how well we're actually performing. Because it's a new facility, we're still making lots of changes. We couldn't see exactly where bottlenecks would occur until we were operational. Each crew has its own ideas but we have to establish a routine, a method of operation, so I have to get the crew leaders to come to a consensus. But they work on different shifts (we operate twenty-four hours a day, seven days a week) so I act as mediator.

> We want our crew leaders to exercise direction on the floor, coordinating the flow of pipes through the building. For example, this means asking the leaders to stagger the lunches of guys in different areas according to the flow. For some leaders, this is still tough to do, asking a fellow worker to work another half hour rather than go for lunch at the same time he's used to.

> I'm optimistic it's going to work over time but right now we're feeling our way. I'd say about two-thirds of my staff are excited about being in a new mill and about achieving their own objectives. The other one-third are more accustomed to working in an environment with a direct supervisor in a white hard hat who tells them what to do; these people aren't as focused or as willing to take initiative on their own.

> What skills do I need? Strong analytical skills. We've eliminated all the paper on the floor and have become totally computerized. I have to be able to sit down at the computer and figure out what has happened overnight; use the tools provided by the computer to figure out where we are and what the problems are; and follow up. For example, if a pipe was rejected, I need to know why. What caused it? I have to follow up fast.

> In terms of the staff themselves, it's important to be fair and consistent. There was one leader elected that I wouldn't have chosen but I went and had a good chat with him. A week later, I was hearing good feedback about him. So I can't let my personal preferences enter into decision making.

> As a manager you have to use your skills and know when to call on help from others. You can come from almost any background. For example, my background is more Human Resources and Collective Bargaining whereas another foreman is from Maintenance and a third is from Metallurgy. Don't be afraid to seek help, even from the workers on the floor.

> You may have to overcome the desire to handle things in a punitive way. Some people are cooperative on the floor and then when they're promoted, they wield their authority too much.

RESPONDING TO THIS CASE

1. Describe how Jim's positon as foreman requires him to show technical, conceptual, networking and human relations skills.
2. Apply the path-goal theory of leadership to Jim's positon.
3. Discuss why it would be difficult for some leaders to simply ask workers to eat lunch at a different time.
4. What characteristics are apparent in Jim Clarke which indicate his suitability for supervising in a *team* environment?
5. What challenges does this worker empowerment pose for a leader like Jim?

11

COMMUNICATING EFFECTIVELY

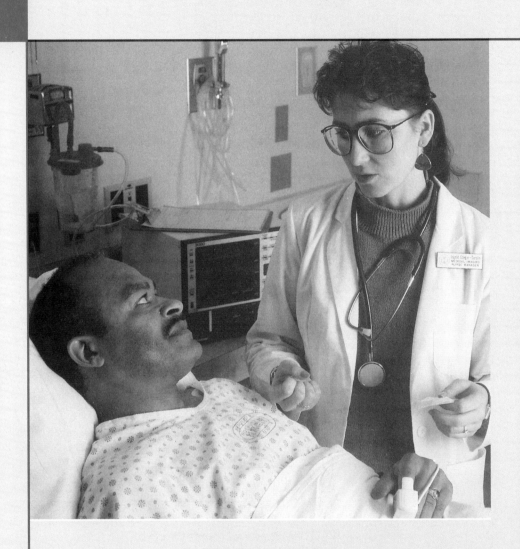

LEARNING OBJECTIVES

After reading this chapter, you should be able to:

1. Define *communication*.
2. Contrast formal and informal communication.
3. Explain how electronic communications affect the supervisor's job.
4. Identify four grapevine patterns.
5. List barriers to effective communication.
6. Describe techniques for overcoming communication barriers.
7. List the essential requirements for active listening.
8. Explain what behaviours are necessary for providing effective feedback.

CHAPTER OUTLINE

PERFORMING EFFECTIVELY

WHAT IS COMMUNICATION?

METHODS OF COMMUNICATION
Oral Communication
Written Communication
Something to Think About
Electronic Communication
Nonverbal Communication
The Grapevine

THE SUPERVISOR'S DAY-TO-DAY COMMUNICATION

BARRIERS TO EFFECTIVE COMMUNICATION
Language
Poor Listening Habits
Lack of Feedback
Differences in Perception
Role Requirements
Choice of Information Medium
Lack of Honesty
Dealing with a Difficult Issue: Should You Tell the Whole Truth?
Emotions

IMPROVING YOUR COMMUNICATION EFFECTIVENESS
Think First!
Constrain Emotions
Learn to Listen
Tailor Language to the Receiver
Match Words and Actions
Supervision in Action: Communication Differences in a Global Village
Utilize Feedback
Participate in Assertiveness Training
Pop Quiz

THE IMPORTANCE OF FEEDBACK SKILLS
What's the Difference Between Positive and Negative Feedback?
How Do You Give Effective Feedback?

FROM CONCEPTS TO SKILLS: ACTIVE LISTENING
Assessing Yourself: Do You Listen Actively?
Skill Basics
Applying Your Skills
Pop Quiz

UNDERSTANDING THE BASICS
Summary
Key Terms and Concepts
Reviewing Your Knowledge
Answers to the Pop Quizzes

PERFORMING YOUR JOB
Case 11.A: Fact, Fiction, or Interpretation at IBM
Case 11.B: Cynthia Raises Expectations

BUILDING A PORTFOLIO
Al Bunge, Production QA Manager and Doris Dresson, Controller, Josten's (Manufacturing)

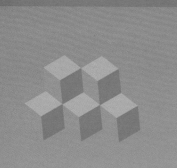

Kerrie Preete is a service team leader for Schneider National Carriers Inc. at their Canadian base in Guelph, Ontario. At only 23, her job is to ensure things go smoothly for the forty truck drivers that are her responsibility, that loads arrive on time and that the drivers' needs are met. Kerrie rarely sees the long-distance drivers in person. Most of her ten-hour day is spent on the phone and computer, so communication skills are critical to her effectiveness.

"It was a challenge getting to know my drivers and learning how to interact with each one. Their English skills vary. So do their personalities. Some want you to spell everything out. Others are insulted by that. Some I can joke with, others I can't."

The interactions with drivers vary from resolving problems at customs to giving directions, from ensuring they get their scheduled time at home to dealing with performance issues.

"I've had to learn how to give critical feedback—for example, get the driver to explain what happened and why he did it. Ask if he thought it was appropriate and then explain how the situation needs to be handled in future and why. Then get a commitment from him and follow up later. But I can't come across as angry. I have to reinforce what he's doing well and be straight with him regarding problems."

Kerrie's employer knows how important communication skills are to anyone in her position. That's why the selection process she went through involved interviews with a number of people and role plays to see how she would handle situations. This emphasis on communications has continued in her early on-the-job training, in the regular feedback she gets from her manager, and in the ten-day formal training she recently received.

All supervisors need strong communication skills. They may not spend most of their day on the phone like Kerrie, but they are involved in frequent communication with employees, peers, their immediate manager, customers, people in other departments and others in order to get their department's objectives accomplished. The communication can be face-to-face, by e-mail, phone, memo, or formal report. Regardless of the form, the wrong words, the wrong tone, or an insensitivity to the audience can have dire consequences. Communication skills alone don't make an effective manager but ineffective communication skills can lead to a continuous stream of problems for the supervisor.

WHAT IS COMMUNICATION?

Communication involves the transfer of meaning. If no information or ideas have been conveyed, communication has not taken place. The speaker who is not heard or the writer who is not read does not communicate.

However, for communication to be successful, the meaning must not only be imparted, but must also be understood. A memo addressed to me in German (a language of which I am totally ignorant), cannot be considered a communication until I have it translated. Therefore, **communication** is the *transference* and *understanding* of meaning. Perfect communication, if such a thing were possible, would exist when a transmitted thought or idea was perceived by the receiver *exactly* as it was envisioned by the sender (see Figure 11-1).

A final point before we move on: *Good communication* is often erroneously defined by the communicator as "agreement" instead of "clarity of understanding." If someone disagrees with us, many of us assume the person just didn't fully understand our position. In other words, many of us define good communication as having someone accept our views. But I can understand very clearly what you mean and *not* agree with what you say. In fact, when a supervisor concludes that a lack of communication must exist because a conflict between two of her employees has continued for a prolonged time, a closer examination often reveals that there is plenty of effective communication going on. Each fully understands the other's position. The problem is one of erroneously equating effective communication with agreement.

Communication
The transference and understanding of meaning

FIGURE 11-1

What is communication?

METHODS OF COMMUNICATION

Formal communication
Addresses task-related issues and tends to follow the organization's authority chain

Informal communication
Moves in any direction and is as likely to satisfy social needs as to facilitate task accomplishments

Grapevine
The means by which informal communication takes place

Supervisors participate in two types of communication. One is **formal communication**. It addresses task-related issues and tends to follow the organization's authority chain. When supervisors give orders to an employee, provide advice to a team in their department, are offered suggestions by employees, interact with other supervisors on a project, or respond to a request made by their boss, they are engaged in formal communication. The other type is **informal communication**. This type of communication moves in any direction, skips authority levels, and is as likely to satisfy social needs as it is to facilitate task accomplishments.

Supervisors engage in formal communication through speech, written documents, electronic media, and nonverbal behavior. Informal communication takes place on the **grapevine**.

ORAL COMMUNICATION

Supervisors rely heavily on oral communication. They meet one-on-one with an employee, they give a speech to their department, they engage in a problem-solving session with a group of employees, or they talk on the phone to a disgruntled customer.

What are the advantages of oral communication? You can transmit information quickly through the spoken word, and oral communications include a nonverbal component that can enhance the message. A phone call, for instance, conveys not only words but also tone and mood. A one-on-one meeting further includes gestures and facial expressions. Additionally, today's supervisors are becoming increasingly aware that not only are oral communications an effective means for quickly conveying information, but they also have positive symbolic value. In contrast to a memo or e-mail message, the spoken word is more personal. It conveys more intimacy and caring. As a result, some of the best supervisors rely extensively on oral communication even when the use of written or electronic channels would seem to be as effective. They have found, through experience, that reliance on oral communication tends to build trust with employees and creates a climate of openness and support (see Something to Think About).

WRITTEN COMMUNICATION

When your message is intended to be official, when it has long-term implications, and when it is highly complex, you'll want to convey it in written form. Introducing a new departmental procedure, for instance, should be conveyed in writing so there will be a permanent record to

Do men and women communicate in the same way? The answer is no! The differences in communication styles between men and women may lead to some interesting insights. When men talk, they tend to do so to emphasize status and independence; whereas women tend to use communications to create connections and intimacy. For instance, men frequently complain that women talk too much about their problems. Women, however, criticize men for not listening. What's happening is that when a man hears a woman talking about a problem, he frequently asserts his desire for independence and control by providing solutions. Many women, in contrast, view conversing about a problem as a means to promote closeness. The woman presents the problem to gain support and connection—not to get the male's advice.

Because effective communication between the sexes is important to all supervisors for meeting departmental goals, how can you manage the differences in communication style? Preventing gender differences from becoming persistent barriers to effective communication requires acceptance, understanding, and a commitment to adaptive communication across gender lines. Both men and women need to acknowledge that there are differences in communication styles, that one style isn't better than the other, and that it takes real effort to "talk" with each other successfully.

What do you think? Do men and women really communicate differently?

which all employees can refer. Providing a written summary to employees following performance reviews is a good idea because it helps reduce misunderstandings and creates a formal record of what was discussed. Departmental reports that contain lots of detailed numbers and facts are best conveyed in writing because of their complexity.

The fact that written communications provide better documentation than the spoken word is both a plus and a minus. On the plus side, written documents provide a reliable "paper trail" for decisions or actions that are later called into question. They also reduce ambiguity for recipients. But on the negative side, obsessive concern with documenting everything in writing leads to risk avoidance, decision paralysis, and creation of a highly politicized work environment. At the extreme, task accomplishment becomes subordinated to "covering your rear" and making sure that no one person is held responsible for any questionable decision.

ELECTRONIC COMMUNICATION

Computers and digitalization are dramatically increasing a supervisor's communication options. Today, you can rely on a number of sophisticated electronic media to carry your communications. These include electronic mail (e-mail), intranets, electronic paging, cellular telephones, video conferencing, modem-based transmissions, and other forms of network-related communications.

Supervisors are increasingly using many of these technological advances. E-mail and voice mail allow people to transmit messages twenty-four hours a day. Even though you're away from your office, others can still leave messages for you to review on your return. And for important and complex communiqués, a permanent record of e-mail messages can be obtained by printing out a hard copy. Cellular phones are dramatically changing the role of the telephone as a communication device. In the past, telephone numbers were attached to physical locations. Now, with cellular technology, the phone number attaches to the individual. As such, supervisors can be in constant contact with department members, other supervisors, and key members of the management team, regardless of where they are physically located. Network-related communications allow supervisors to monitor the work of employees whose jobs are done on computers, to participate in electronic meetings, and to communicate with suppliers and customers on interorganizational networks.

NONVERBAL COMMUNICATION

Some of the most meaningful communications aren't spoken, written, or transmitted on a computer. These are **nonverbal communications**. A loud siren or a red light at an intersection tells you something without words. When a supervisor is conducting a training session, he doesn't need words to tell him that people are bored when eyes get glassy. Similarly, he can tell in an instant by his boss's body language and verbal intonations whether she's angry, upbeat, anxious, or distracted.

Body language refers to gestures, facial configurations, and other movements of the body. A snarled face, for example, says something different from a smile. Hand motions, facial expressions, and other gestures can communicate emotions or temperaments such as aggression, fear, shyness, arrogance, joy, and anger.

Verbal intonation refers to the emphasis someone gives to words or phrases. To illustrate how intonations can change the meaning of a message, consider the employee who asks a colleague a question. The colleague replies, "What do you mean by that?" The employee's reaction will vary, depending on the tone of the colleague's response. A soft, smooth tone creates a different meaning from one that is abrasive and puts a

FIGURE 11-2

Mary Jean Giroux, a supervisor for London Life Insurance, uses electronic mail as a response to the grapevine. "If I hear a rumour that I know isn't true, I will do an electronic piece of mail to the whole department to try to set their minds at ease."

Nonverbal communications
Communication that sends messages without words

Body language
Gestures, facial configurations, and other movements of the body

Verbal intonations
The emphasis someone gives to words or phrases

FIGURE 11-3

Words, either written or spoken, don't have to exist for meaning to be transferred. This sign tells you plenty.

strong emphasis on the last word. Most of us would view the first intonation as coming from someone who sincerely sought clarification, whereas the second suggests that the person is being aggressive or defensive.

The fact that every oral communication also has a nonverbal message cannot be overemphasized. Why? Because the nonverbal component is likely to carry the greatest impact. One study found that 55 per cent of an oral message is derived from facial expression and physical posture, 38 per cent from verbal intonations, and only 7 per cent from the actual words used.[1] Most of us know that animals respond to the way we say something rather than the content of what we say. Apparently, people aren't much different.

THE GRAPEVINE

The grapevine is active in almost all organizations. In fact, studies typically find that the grapevine is the means of communication by which most operative employees first hear about important changes introduced by management. It rates ahead of supervisors, official memoranda, and other formal sources.

Is the information that flows along the grapevine accurate? The evidence indicates that about 75 per cent of what is carried is accurate.[2] But what conditions foster an active grapevine? What gets the rumour mill rolling?

It is frequently assumed that rumours start because they make titillating gossip. Such is rarely the case. Rumours have at least four purposes:

- to structure and reduce anxiety;
- to make sense of limited or fragmented information;
- to serve as a vehicle to organize group members, and possibly outsiders, into coalitions; and
- to signal a sender's status (I'm an insider and you're not) or power (I have the power to make you into an insider).

Studies have found that rumours emerge as a response to situations that are *important* to us, where there is *ambiguity*, and under conditions that arouse *anxiety*. Work situations frequently contain these three elements, which explains why rumours flourish in organizations. The secrecy and competition that typically prevail in large organizations—around such issues as the appointment of new bosses, the relocation of offices, the realignment of work assignments, and layoffs—create conditions that encourage and sustain rumours on the grapevine. A rumour will persist either until the wants and expectations creating the uncertainty underlying the rumour are fulfilled or the anxiety is reduced.

What can we conclude from this discussion? Certainly that the grapevine is an important part of any group or organization's communication system and is well worth understanding. Moreover, it's never going to be eliminated, so supervisors should use it in beneficial ways.

Given that only a small set of employees typically passes information to more than one other person, supervisors can analyze grapevine information and predict its flow. Certain messages are likely to follow predictable patterns (see Figure 11-4). Supervisors might even consider using the grapevine informally to transmit information to specific individuals by planting messages with key people who are active on the grapevine and are likely to find a given message worthy of passing on.

Supervisors should not lose sight of the grapevine's value for identifying issues that employees consider important and that create anxiety among them. It acts as both a filter and a feedback mechanism, picking up issues that employees consider relevant, and planting messages that employees want passed on to upper management. For instance, the grapevine can tap employee concerns. If the grapevine is abuzz with a rumour of a mass layoff, and if you know the rumour is totally false, the message still has meaning. It reflects the fears and concerns of employees, and hence should not be ignored.

THE SUPERVISOR'S DAY-TO-DAY COMMUNICATION

Chapter 2, Supervisory Planning and Time Management, described the value of planning. It was suggested that supervisors schedule their time in order to minimize interruptions and block out segments of time to focus

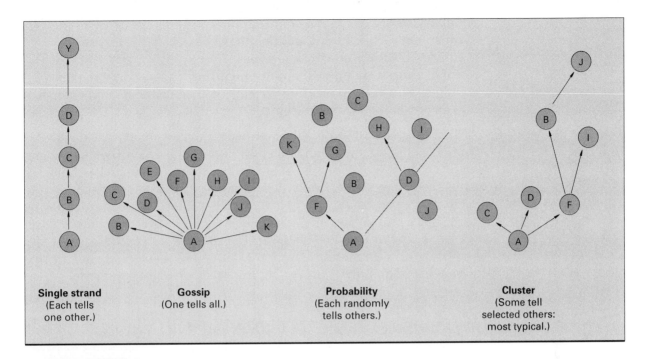

Single strand
(Each tells
one other.)

Gossip
(One tells all.)

Probability
(Each randomly
tells others.)

Cluster
(Some tell
selected others:
most typical.)

FIGURE 11-4

Grapevine patterns. (*Source:* John W. Newstrom and Keith Davis, *Organizational Behavior: Human Behavior at Work*, 9th ed., New York: McGraw Hill, 1993, p. 445. Reproduced with permission.)

FIGURE 11-5

Informal discussions "around the water cooler" are part of the grapevine.

on high-priority activities. In practice, this is very hard to do. Diaries and observations of supervisory activities reveal three interesting findings that relate to communication.[3]

1. **Supervisors are busy.** The typical supervisor's day is made up of hundreds of separate incidents. Instead of planning their days in great detail, supervisors are often forced to react to events and people on the spur of the moment.

2. **Supervisory work is fragmented.** Interruptions are frequent in supervisory work, allowing little time to be devoted to any single activity. Tasks are completed quickly.
3. **Supervisors rely on oral communication.** Supervisors spend most of their time communicating verbally on the telephone, in meetings, or in one-on-one personal contacts.

Taken together, these findings remind us that a supervisor's day-to-day communications are made up of literally dozens of brief encounters punctuated by constant interruptions. At any given moment, a supervisor might be reading correspondence, involved in a phone conversation, responding to an e-mail message, participating in a formal or informal meeting, taking an observational tour, or cornered in a hallway by his or her immediate manager or by an employee with a question. The effective supervisor learns to differentiate important messages from the unimportant ones and not to let the constant disruptions deter him or her from the pursuit of paramount goals.

BARRIERS TO EFFECTIVE COMMUNICATION

As noted earlier, the goal of perfect communication is to transmit a thought or idea from a sender to a receiver so that it is perceived by the receiver exactly as it was envisioned by the sender. That goal is almost never achieved because of distortions and other barriers. In this section, we will describe some of the more serious barriers that hinder effective communication. In the following section, we'll offer some suggestions for how to overcome these barriers.

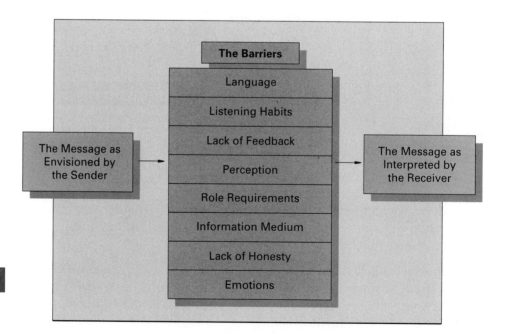

FIGURE 11-6

Barriers to effective communication

LANGUAGE

Words means different things to different people. Age, education, and cultural background are three of the more obvious variables that influence the language people use and the definitions they give to words. In an organization, employees usually come from diverse backgrounds. Furthermore, horizontal differentiation creates specialists who develop their own jargon or technical language. In large organizations, members are often widely dispersed geographically, and those in each locale will use terms and phrases that are unique to their area. Vertical differentiation can also cause language problems. For instance, differences in the meaning of words such as *incentives* and *quotas* occur at different levels of management. Top managers often speak about the need for incentives and quotas, yet these terms have been found to imply manipulation and create resentment among supervisors.

The point is that while you and I may both speak the same language (English), our use of that language is far from uniform. A knowledge of how each of us modifies the language would minimize communication difficulties. The problem is that you don't know how your various employees, peers, superiors, customers, and others with whom you interact have modified the language. Senders tend to assume that the words and terms they use mean the same to the receiver as they to do them. This, of course, is often incorrect, and thus creates communication difficulties.

POOR LISTENING HABITS

Most of us hear but we always don't listen! Hearing is merely picking up sound vibrations. Listening is making sense out of what we hear. That is, listening requires that you pay attention, interpret, and remember what is being said.

Most of us are pretty poor listeners. As a result, we've included a skill module on listening at the end of this chapter (see From Concepts to Skills). At this point, it suffices to say that if you don't have good listening skills, you're not going to get the full message as the sender meant to convey it. For example, there are common flaws that many of us share regarding listening. We get distracted and end up hearing only parts of a message. Instead of listening for meaning, we listen to determine whether we agree or disagree with what's being said. We begin thinking about our response to what's being said rather than listening for the complete message. Each of these flaws in our listening habits contributes to messages being received differently from the way the sender intended.

LACK OF FEEDBACK

Effective communication means the transference and *understanding* of meaning. But how do you know if someone has received your message and comprehended it in the way that you meant? The answer is: Use feedback. When a supervisor requests that each member of her staff submit a specific report, receipt of the report is feedback. When your instructor tests you on the material in this book, he gets feedback on your understanding of the text material and his lectures.

When a sender fails to use feedback, he or she never knows if the message has been received as intended. So lack of feedback creates the potential for inaccuracies and distortions.

Differences in Perception

Our attitudes, interests, past experiences, and expectations determine how we organize and interpret our surroundings. This explains how we can look at the same things and perceive them differently (see Figure 11-7). In the communication process, the receiver selectively sees and hears messages based on his or her background and personal characteristics. The receiver also projects his or her interests and expectations into communications when interpreting them. Since senders and receivers of communications each bring their own set of perceptual biases, the messages they seek to transfer are often subject to distortions.

Role Requirements

Roles
Behaviour patterns that go with the position one occupies in the organization

People in organizations play **roles**. They engage in behaviour patterns that go with the position they occupy in the organization. Managerial jobs, for instance, come with role identities. Managers know they are

FIGURE 11-7

What do you see— an old woman or a young girl?

supposed to be loyal to, and defend, their boss and the organization. Union leaders' roles typically require loyalty to union goals such as improving employee security. Marketing roles demand efforts to increase sales, while the roles of people working in the credit department emphasize minimizing losses from bad debts.

With the differening role requirements of different members come communication barriers. Each role comes with its own jargon that sets the role apart from others. Additionally, fulfilling role requirements often requires individuals to *selectively* interpret events. They hear and see the world in a way that is consistent with their role requirements. The result is that people in different roles often have difficulty communicating with each other. Marketing people say they want to "increase sales." So, too, do the people in credit. The difference is that the marketing people want to sell everything to anybody, while credit only wants to sell to those who are creditworthy. Labour and management representatives have difficulty negotiating because their roles encompass very different language and interests. A lot of internal communication breakdowns in organizations are merely individuals enacting behaviours consistent with the roles they are playing.

CHOICE OF INFORMATION MEDIUM

The amount of information transmitted in a face-to-face conversation is considerably greater than that received from a flyer posted on a bulletin board. The former offers multiple information cues (words, posture, facial expressions, gestures, intonation), immediate feedback, and the personal touch of "being there," all of which the flyer lacks. This reminds us that media differ in the **richness of information** they transmit. Figure 11-9 illustrates the hierarchy of information richness. The higher a medium rates in richness, the more information it is capable of transmitting.

Richness of information The amount of information a medium is capable of transmitting.

FIGURE 11-8

Union-management negotiations, such as those between Ford and the Canadian Auto Workers, require the parties to play roles.

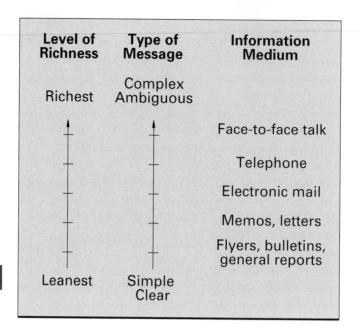

FIGURE 11-9

Hierarchy of
information richness

Level of Richness	Type of Message	Information Medium
Richest	Complex Ambiguous	Face-to-face talk
		Telephone
		Electronic mail
		Memos, letters
Leanest	Simple Clear	Flyers, bulletins, general reports

Generally speaking, the more ambiguous and complicated the message, the more the sender should rely on a rich communication medium. For example, as a supervisor, if you want to share with your employees a major new product line that your company will be introducing—and which will affect everyone in your department—your communication is more likely to be effective in a face-to-face departmental meeting than through use of a memo. Why? Because this message is likely to initiate apprehension among employees and require clarification. In contrast, a modest change in tomorrow's departmental production schedule can be effectively communicated in a memo. Unfortunately, people in organizations don't always match the medium to the message, and thereby create communication problems.

LACK OF HONESTY

A colleague asks you what you think of the ideas he suggested in the recent team meeting in which you both participated. You personally think his suggestions were weak. But you don't tell him that. Rather, you compliment his ideas and said how much they contributed to the final results.

A good deal of what passes as "poor communication" is nothing other than individuals purposely avoiding honesty and openness (see Dealing with a Difficult Issue). To avoid confrontations and hurting others' feelings, some organizational members engage in practices such as conveying ambiguous messages, saying what they think others want to hear, or cutting off communication altogether.

Dealing with a Difficult Issue

SHOULD YOU TELL THE WHOLE TRUTH?

Effective communications in both your personal life and work life is built on the expectation that appropriate and accurate information is being given. In any communications encounter, people should be afforded the respect and dignity of being given complete and factual information. Under what circumstances, then, is it appropriate to withhold information from someone?

One instance that calls for discretion in conveying information is when the issue of confidentially is involved. The decision to withhold confidential information is sometimes a must—especially at work. Take a situation where one of your employees has just been diagnosed with a treatable form of cancer. He's confided in you about the status of his health. He's also asked you not to say a word to anyone because he considers his health to be a personal matter.

Over the next few months, your employee is absent frequently, especially during his radiation treatments. Because of the circumstances surrounding his illness, you do not feel his absences are a major problem. In part, that's because some of his duties involve direct computer work, which he can do while at home and forward electronically to the appropriate people. You've also discreetly divided the rest of his work among other employees in your work unit. Your employees, though, are wondering what is wrong. Many have come to you to you to find out. You simply, and politely, decline to discuss the issue about this employee with his coworkers. However, a number of them think that you're giving him preferential treatment, and they are ready to go to your boss to complain. You know that if they only knew what was going on, they'd understand, but you can't reveal the reason for his absence. On the other hand, if some individuals begin to make trouble for you or for this employee, it could create more problems for him. That's something he doesn't need right now in his life.

Is it ever appropriate to withhold or filter information in an organization? Should you tell your other employees the whole story? What do you think? Would your views change if this employee had a contagious disease and was working in close contact with his coworkers?

Some people run from confrontation. They want everyone to like them. As such, they avoid communicating any messages they think might be displeasing to the receiver. What they end up doing is increasing tension and further hindering effective communication.

EMOTIONS

How the receiver feels at the time of receipt of a message will influence how he or she interprets it. A message received negatively when you're angry or distraught is likely to be interpreted differently when you're in a neutral disposition. Extreme emotions such as jubilation or depression are most likely to hinder effective communication. In such instances, we are most prone to disregard our rational and objective thinking processes and to substitute emotional judgments. These are also the times we're most likely to use inflammatory language that we later regret.

IMPROVING YOUR COMMUNICATION EFFECTIVENESS

A few of the barriers we've described are part of organizational life and will never be fully eliminated. Perceptual and role differences, for example, should be recognized as barriers but should not be considered easy to correct. However, most barriers to effective communication can be overcome. The following suggestions provides you with some guidance.

THINK FIRST!

"Think before you speak!" That cliché can be expanded to include all forms of communication. Before you speak or write, ask yourself: What message am I trying to convey? Then ask: How can I organize and present my message so that it will achieve the desired outcome?

Most of us follow the "think first" rule when writing a message. The formal and deliberate process of writing encourages thinking through what we want to say and how best to say it. The concept of "working on a draft" implies that the written document will be edited and revised. But few of us give anywhere near the same attention to our verbal communications. That's a mistake. Before you speak, make sure you know what you want to say. Then present your message in a logical and organized fashion so it will be clear and understood by your receiver.

CONSTRAIN EMOTIONS

It would be naive to assume that supervisors always communicate in a fully rational manner. Yet we know that emotions can severely cloud and distort the transference of meaning. If you as a supervisor are emotionally upset over an issue, you are more likely to misconstrue incoming messages and fail to clearly and accurately express outgoing messages. What can you do? The simplest answer is to desist from further communication until you have regained composure.

LEARN TO LISTEN

"It's more important that a manager be a good listener than a good talker," says Rundell Seaman of Seaman's Beverages in Charlottetown, P.E.I.

We stated earlier that most of us are poor listeners. But that doesn't mean we can't improve our listening skills. There are specific behaviours that have been found to be related to effective listening. We present those skills in the From Concepts to Skills section at the end of this chapter.

TAILOR LANGUAGE TO THE RECEIVER

Since language can be a barrier, supervisors should choose words and structure their messages in ways that will make them clear and understandable to the receiver. The supervisor needs to simplify his or her language and consider the audience to whom the message is directed, so the language will be tailored to the receivers (see Figure 11-10). Remember that effective communication is achieved when a message is both received and *understood* (see Supervision in Action). Understanding is improved in many cases by simplifying the language used. This means, for example, that a nursing supervisor should always try to communicate in clear and easily understood terms, and that the language used in messages to a patient should be purposely different from that used with the medical staff. Jargon can facilitate understanding when used with those who know what it means, but it can cause innumerable problems when used outside that group.

MATCH WORDS AND ACTIONS

If actions speak louder than words, then it's important to watch your actions to make sure they align with and reinforce the words that go along with them. We noted that nonverbal messages carry a great deal of weight. Given this fact, the effective supervisor watches his or her nonverbal cues to ensure that they too convey the message desired.

FIGURE 11-10

Supervising a group of animators at Nelvana, Brian Lemay sometimes used cartoon memos to get his message across—a vivid example of tailoring the message to the audience.

Remember, also, that as a supervisor, your employees will look at your behaviour as a model. If your verbal comments are backed up by your actions, you will gain credibility and build trust. If, on the other hand, you say one thing and do another, your employees will ignore what you say and model themselves on what you do. At the extreme, people stop listening because they no longer believe your words have credibility. Incidentally, this is a problem that often plagues politicians.

Communication Differences in a Global Village

It's important to recognize that communication isn't conducted in the same way around the world.[3] For example, contrast countries that place a high value on individualism (such as Canada) with countries where the emphasis is on collectivism (such as Japan).[5]

Owing to the emphasis on the individual in countries such as the Canada, communication patterns are individual-oriented and rather clearly spelled out. For instance, North American supervisors rely heavily on memoranda, announcements, position papers, and other formal types of communication to stake out their positions in the organization. They also often hoard secret information in an attempt to promote their own advancement and as a way of inducing their employees to accept decisions and plans. For their own protection, lower-level employees also engage in this practice.

In collectivist countries such as Japan, there is more interaction for its own sake and a more informal manner of interpersonal contact. The Japanese manager, in contrast to Canadian managers, will engage in extensive verbal consultation over an issue first and will draw up a formal document later, only to outline the agreement that was made. Face-to-face communication is encouraged. Additionally, open communication is an inherent part of the Japanese work setting. Work spaces are open and crowded with individuals at different levels in the work hierarchy. In contrast, Canadian organizations emphasize authority, hierarchy, and formal lines of communication.

Utilize Feedback

Many communication problems can be directly attributed to misunderstandings and inaccuracies. These problems are less likely to occur if the supervisor uses feedback. This feedback can be verbal or nonverbal.

If a supervisor asks a receiver, "Did you understand what I said?" the response represents feedback. But feedback should include more than yes

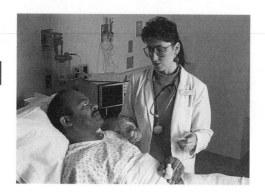

FIGURE 11-11

A nursing supervisor needs to adjust his or her language used when talking with a patient from that used when talking to her medical staff.

and no answers. The supervisor can ask a set of questions about a message in order to determine whether the message was received as intended. Better yet, the supervisor can ask the receiver to restate the message in his or her own words. If the supervisor then hears what was intended, understanding and accuracy should be enhanced. Feedback includes subtler things than the direct asking of questions or summarizing of messages. General comments can give a supervisor a sense of the receiver's reaction to a message. Of course, performance appraisals, salary reviews, and promotions also represent forms of feedback.

Feedback does not have to be conveyed in words. The sales supervisor who sends his staff a directive, in which he describes a new monthly sales report that all sales personnel will need to complete, receives feedback if some of the salespeople fail to turn in the new report. This feedback suggests that he needs to clarify further the initial directive. Similarly, when you give a speech to a group of people, you watch their eyes and look for other nonverbal clues to tell you whether they are getting your message or not. This may explain why television performers on comedy shows prefer to tape their programs in front of a live audience. Immediate laughter and applause, or their absence, convey to the performer whether the message is getting across as intended.

PARTICIPATE IN ASSERTIVENESS TRAINING

Many people have no trouble asserting themselves. Being open and honest comes naturally to them. Some, in fact, are too assertive. They cross over the line to become aggressive and abrasive. Other individuals suffer from a constant fear of upsetting others and fall back on avoidance or ambiguous communication, when what they need is to be open and assertive. Such people would benefit from participation in assertiveness training. An effective supervisor needn't always be assertive, but should be capable of being so when it's needed.

Assertiveness training Training designed to make people more open and self-expressive

Assertiveness training is designed to make people more open and self-expressive. Assertive people confront issues in a straightforward manner. They say what they mean, but without being rude or thoughtless.

1. Good communication does not require:
   a. transference
   b. agreement
   c. understanding
   d. meaning
2. What value can a grapevine offer to a supervisor?
3. The advantage of oral communication is that it creates an accurate and permanent record of the communication that took place. True or False?
4. Communication is distorted when:
   a. body language and verbal intonation are used
   b. e-mail, which lacks feedback opportunities, is used
   c. body language and intonation are not aligned
   d. the information is complex

Individuals who take assertiveness training learn verbal and nonverbal behaviours that enhance their ability to communicate openly and unambiguously. These behaviours include direct and unambiguous language; the use of "I" statements and cooperative "we" statements; a strong, steady, audible voice; good eye contact; facial expressions matched to the message; an appropriately serious tone; and a comfortable but firm posture.

THE IMPORTANCE OF FEEDBACK SKILLS

Ask a supervisor about the feedback he or she gives to employees, and you're likely to get a qualified answer. If the feedback is positive, it's likely to be given promptly and enthusiastically. Negative feedback is often treated very differently. Like most of us, supervisors don't particularly enjoy communicating bad news. They fear offending or having to deal with the receiver's defensiveness. The result is that negative feedback is often avoided, delayed, or substantially distorted.[6] The purposes of this section are to show you the importance of providing both positive and negative feedback and to identify specific techniques to help make your feedback more effective.

WHAT'S THE DIFFERENCE BETWEEN POSITIVE AND NEGATIVE FEEDBACK?

We stated that supervisors treat positive and negative feedback differently. So too do receivers. You need to understand this fact and adjust your feedback style accordingly.

Positive feedback is more readily and accurately perceived than negative feedback. Furthermore, while positive feedback is almost always accepted, you can expect negative feedback to meet resistance. Why? The logical answer appears to be that people want to hear good news and block out the rest. Positive feedback fits what most people wish to hear and already believe about themselves.

Does this mean, then, that you should avoid giving negative feedback? No! What it means is that you need to be aware of potential resistance and learn to use negative feedback in situations in which it's most likely to be accepted.[7] That is, negative feedback should be used when it's supported by hard data—numbers, specific examples, and the like.

HOW DO YOU GIVE EFFECTIVE FEEDBACK?

There are six specific suggestions that we can make to help you become more effective in providing feedback, which we will discuss below.

FOCUS ON SPECIFIC BEHAVIOURS

Feedback should be specific rather than general. Avoid such statements as "You have a bad attitude" or "I'm really impressed with the good job you did." They're vague and, while they provide information, they don't tell the receiver enough to correct the "bad attitude" or on what basis you concluded that a "good job" has been done so the person knows what behaviours to repeat.

KEEP FEEDBACK IMPERSONAL

Feedback, particularly the negative kind, should be descriptive rather than judgmental or evaluative. No matter how upset you are, keep the feedback focused on job-related behaviours and never criticize someone personally because of an inappropriate action. Telling people they're incompetent, lazy, or the like is almost always counterproductive. It provokes such an emotional reaction that the performance deviation itself is apt to be overlooked. When you're criticizing, remember that you're censuring job-related behaviour, not the person. You might be tempted to tell someone he or she is rude and insensitive (which might just be true); however, that's hardly impersonal. It's better to say something more specific like, "You've interrupted me three times with questions that weren't urgent when you knew I was talking long distance to a customer in Brazil."

KEEP FEEDBACK GOAL-ORIENTED

Feedback should not be given primarily to "unload" on another person. If you have to say something negative, make sure it's directed toward the receiver's goals. Ask yourself whom the feedback is supposed to help. If the answer is essentially you—"I've got something I just want to get off my chest"—bite your tongue and hold the comment. Such feedback undermines your credibility and lessens the meaning and influence of future feedback sessions.

MAKE FEEDBACK WELL TIMED

Feedback is most meaningful to a receiver when there is a very short interval between his or her behaviour and the receipt of feedback about that behaviour. For example, a new employee who makes a mistake is more likely to respond to suggestions for improving right after the mistake or at the end of the work day—rather than during a performance review session six months later. If you have to spend time recreating a situation and refreshing someone's memory of it, the feedback you're providing is likely to be ineffective.[8] Moreover, if you're particularly concerned with changing behaviour, delays in providing timely feedback on the undesirable actions lessens the likelihood that the feedback will be effective in bringing about the desired change. Of course, making feedback prompt merely for promptness's sake can backfire if you have insufficient information or if you're emotionally upset. In such instances, "well timed" might be better defined as "somewhat delayed."

ENSURE UNDERSTANDING

Is your feedback concise and complete enough that the receiver clearly and fully understands your communication? Remember, every successful communication requires both transference and understanding of meaning. If feedback is to be effective, you need to ensure that the receiver understands it. Consistent with our discussion of listening techniques, you should have the receiver rephrase the content of your feedback to find out whether it fully captured the meaning you intended.

DIRECT NEGATIVE FEEDBACK

Negative feedback should be directed toward behaviour the receiver can do something about. There's little value in reminding a person of some shortcoming over which he or she has no control. For instance, to criticize an employee who's late for work because she forgot to set her alarm clock would be valid. To take her to task for being late for work when the subway she takes to work every day had a power failure, stranding her for ninety minutes, would be pointless. There's nothing she could have done to correct what happened—short of finding a different means of travel, which may be unrealistic.

In addition, when negative feedback is given concerning something that the receiver can control, it might be a good idea to indicate specifically what can be done to improve the situation. This takes some of the sting out of the criticism and offers guidance to employees who understand the problem, but don't know how to resolve it.

FROM CONCEPTS TO SKILLS

ACTIVE LISTENING

This chapter has repeatedly noted that most of us suffer from poor listening skills. Listening is difficult and often more tiring than talking. It demands intellectual effort and concentration. The average person speaks at a rate of about 150 words per minute, whereas we have the capacity to listen at the rate of over 1000 words per minute. The difference leaves idle time for the brain and opportunities for the mind to wander.

This section is designed to help you correct and improve your listening habits.

ASSESSING YOURSELF: DO YOU LISTEN ACTIVELY?

For each of the following questions, select the answer that best describes your listening habits.

	Usually	Sometimes	Seldom
1. I maintain eye contact with the speaker.	❑	❑	❑
2. I determine whether a speaker's ideas are worthwhile solely by his or her appearance and delivery.	❑	❑	❑
3. I try to align my thoughts and feelings with those of the speaker.	❑	❑	❑
4. I listen for specific facts rather than for "the big picture."	❑	❑	❑
5. I listen for both factual content and the underlying emotion.	❑	❑	❑
6. I ask questions for clarification and understanding.	❑	❑	❑
7. I withhold judgment of what the speaker is saying until he or she is finished.	❑	❑	❑
8. I make a conscious effort to evaluate the logic and consistency of what is being said.	❑	❑	❑
9. While listening, I think about what I'm going to say as soon as I have my chance.	❑	❑	❑
10. I try to have the last word.	❑	❑	❑

SCORING KEY AND INTERPRETATION

For questions 1, 3, 5, 6, 7, and 8, give yourself three points for Usually, two points for Sometimes, and one point for Seldom. For questions 2, 4, 9, and 10, give yourself three points for Seldom, two points for Sometimes, and one point for Usually.

Total up your points. A score of 27 or higher means that you're a good listener. A score of 22 to 26 suggests you have some listening deficiencies. A score below 22 indicates that you have developed a number of bad listening habits.

SKILL BASICS

Passive listening
Absorbing information as it is literally transmitted

Active listening
Listening with intensity, empathy, acceptance, and a willingness to take responsibility for completeness

Effective listening is active rather than passive. In **passive listening**, you are much like a tape recorder. You absorb the information given. If the speaker provides you with a clear message and makes his or her delivery interesting enough to keep your attention, you'll probably get most of what the speaker is trying to communicate. But **active listening** requires you to understand the communication from the speaker's point of view.

There are four essential requirements for active listening. You need to listen with

1. intensity,
2. empathy,
3. acceptance, and
4. a willingness to take responsibility for completeness.

Because listening presents the opportunity for the mind to wander, the active listener concentrates intensely on what the speaker is saying and tunes out thousands of miscellaneous thoughts (work deadlines, money, personal problems) that create distractions. What do active listeners do with their idle brain time? Summarize and integrate what has been said! They put each new bit of information into the context of what has preceded it.

Empathy requires you to put yourself in the speaker's shoes. Try to understand what the speaker wants to communicate rather than what you want to understand. Notice that empathy demands from you both knowledge of the speaker and flexibility. Suspend your own thoughts and feelings and adjust what you see and feel to your speaker's world. In that way, you increase the likelihood that you will interpret the message being spoken in the way the speaker intended.

An active listener demonstrates acceptance. He or she listens objectively without judging content. This is no easy task. It is natural to be distracted by the content of what a speaker says, especially when we disagree with it. When we hear something we disagree with, we begin formulating mental arguments to counter what is being said. Of course, in doing so, we miss the rest of the message. The challenge for the active listener is to absorb what is being said and to withhold judgment on content until the speaker is finished.

The final ingredient of active listening is taking responsibility for completeness. That is, the listener does whatever is necessary to get the full intended meaning from the speaker's communication.

The following guide summarizes fourteen specific techniques to use for effective listening.

1. **Be motivated.** If a listener is unwilling to exert the effort to hear and understand, no amount of additional advice is likely to improve listening effectiveness. As we previously noted, active listening is hard work. So your first step toward becoming an effective listener is a willingness to make the effort.

2. **Make eye contact.** How do you feel when somebody doesn't look at you when you're speaking? If you're like most people, you're likely to interpret this as aloofness or lack of interest. It's ironic that while "you listen with your ears, people judge whether you are listening by looking at your eyes."[9] Making eye contact with the speaker focuses your attention, reduces the likelihood that you will become distracted, and encourages the speaker.

3. **Show interest.** The effective listener shows interest in what is being said. How? Through nonverbal signals. Affirmative head nods and appropriate facial expressions, when added to good eye contact, convey to the speaker that you're listening. Verbal signals —comments such as "I see," "Yes," and "I know what you mean"— offer even more direct evidence that you are listening.

4. **Avoid distracting actions.** The other side of showing interest is avoiding actions that suggest your mind is somewhere else. When listening, *don't* look at your watch, shuffle papers, play with your pencil, or engage in similar distractions. They make the speaker feel you're bored or uninterested. Maybe more importantly, they indicate that you aren't fully attentive and may be missing part of the message that they want to convey.

5. **Empathize.** We said the active listener tries to understand what the speaker sees and feels by putting herself in his shoes. Don't project your own needs and intentions onto the speaker. When you do so, you're likely to hear what you want to hear. So ask yourself: Who is this speaker and where is he coming from? What are his attitudes, interests, experiences, needs, and expectations?

6. **Take in the whole picture.** The effective listener interprets feelings and emotions as well as factual content. If you listen to words alone and ignore other vocal cues and nonverbal signals, you will miss a wealth of subtle messages. To test this point, read the script of a play. Then go and see that play live in a theatre. The characters and the message take on a much richer meaning when you see the play acted on stage.

7. **Ask questions.** The critical listener analyzes what he or she hears and asks questions. This behaviour provides clarification, ensures understanding, and assures the speaker that you're listening.

8. **Paraphrase.** Paraphrasing means restating what the speaker has said *in your own words*. The effective listener uses phrases like: "What I hear you saying is …" or "Do you mean …?" Why rephrase what's already been said? Two reasons! First, it's an excellent control device with which to check whether you're listening carefully. You can't paraphrase accurately if your mind is wandering or if you're thinking about what you're going to say next. Second, it's a control for accuracy. By rephrasing what the speaker has said in your own words and feeding it back to the speaker, you verify the accuracy of your understanding.

9. **Don't interrupt.** Let the speaker complete his or her thought before you try to respond. Don't try to second-guess where the speaker's thoughts are going. When the speaker is finished, you'll know it!

10. **Integrate what's being said.** Use your spare time while listening to better understand the speaker's ideas. Instead of treating each new piece of information as an independent entity, put the pieces together. Treat each part of the message as if it were an additional piece of a puzzle. By the time the speaker is done, instead of having ten unrelated bits of information, you'll have ten integrated pieces of information that form a comprehensive message. If you don't, you should ask the questions that will fill in the blanks.

11. **Don't overtalk.** Most of us would rather speak our own ideas than listen to what someone else says. Too many of us listen only because it's the price we have to pay to get people to let us talk. While talking may be more fun and silence may be uncomfortable, you can't talk and listen at the same time. The good listener recognizes this fact and doesn't overtalk.

12. **Confront your biases.** Evaluate the source of the message. Notice such things as the speaker's credibility, appearance, vocabulary, and speech mannerisms. But don't let them distract you. For instance, all of us have "red flag" words that prick our attention or cause us to draw premature conclusions. Examples might include terms such as *racist, gay, chauvinist, conservative, liberal, feminist,* or *Moral Majority.* Use information about the speaker to improve your understanding of what he or she has to say, but don't let your biases distort the message.

13. **Make smooth transitions between speaker and listener roles.** In most work situations, you're continually shifting back and forth between the roles of speaker and listener. The effective listener makes transitions smoothly from speaker to listener and back to speaker. From a listening perspective, this means concentrating on what a speaker has to say and practising not thinking about what you're going to say as soon as you get your chance.

14. **Be natural.** An effective listener develops a style that is natural and authentic. Don't try to become a compulsive listener. If you exaggerate eye contact, facial expressions, the asking of questions, showing of interest, and the like, you'll lose credibility. A good listener is not a manipulator. Use moderation and develop listening techniques that are effective and fit well with your interpersonal style.

APPLYING YOUR SKILLS

This is a role play to practise listening skills. Break into groups of three. One person will be the observer. He or she will evaluate the two other role players and provide feedback on their listening skills using the fourteen points listed. The second person will take the role of Lee Wilson. Lee is a regional sales supervisor with the Campbell Soup Company, who is spending the month recruiting on campuses. Lee joined Campbell Soup three

Campbell's Community
http://www.
campbellsoup.com/

Abbreviated Job Description

Title: Marketing Management Trainee—Biscuit and Bakery Division

Reports to: Regional Sales Supervisor

Duties and Responsibilities: Completes formal training program, and thereupon:

- calls on retail stores
- introduces new products to store personnel
- distributes sales promotion materials
- stocks and arranges shelves in stores
- takes sales orders
- follows up on complaints or problems
- completes all necessary sales reports

Abbreviated Résumé

Name: Chris Bates

Age: 23

Education: B.Comm. in Business

Major: Marketing. Minor: Economics

Work Experience: Worked 15 hours a week during school and summer vacations at The Gap and at B. Dalton Bookseller

Honours: Dean's Honour Roll (ranked in top 5 per cent of business class)

Extracurricular activities: Intercollegiate tennis team; Vice President, University Marketing Club

---

years ago, directly out of college, and went through the company's marketing-management training program. The third person in the group is Chris Bates. Chris is graduating at the end of this semester from university.

The observer should read both Lee's and Chris's roles. The people playing Lee and Chris, however, should read *only* their own roles. After all have read their appropriate roles, begin the exercise. You have up to fifteen minutes. When completed, the observer should provide feedback to both of the role players.

Note to the role players: The role descriptions in this exercise establish each character. Follow the guidelines. Don't lie about or change the facts you're given. But within the guidelines, try to involve yourself in the character.

SITUATION

Preliminary interview (in a college placement centre) for a marketing management-trainee position with Campbell Soup. A brief job description and Chris's résumé follow.

LEE WILSON'S ROLE. You will be interviewing approximately 150 students over the next six weeks to fill four trainee positions. You're looking for candidates who are bright, articulate, ambitious, and have management potential. The Campbell training program is eighteen months in length. Trainees will be sales representatives calling on retail stores, and will spend the first six weeks taking formal Campbell classes at the head office. The compensation to start is $33 000 a year plus a car. You are to improvise other information as needed.

Examples of questions you might ask include: Where do you expect to be in five years? What's important to you in a job? What courses did you like best in university? Like least? What makes you think you would do well in this job?

CHRIS BATES'S ROLE. Review your résumé. You are a very good student whose previous work experience has been limited to selling in retail stores part time while going to school and full time during the summers. This is your first interview with Campbell's, but you're very interested in their training program. Fill in any gaps in the information as you see fit.

5. What should active listeners do with idle brain time?
   a. summarize and integrate what has been said
   b. organize their schedules for the next few hours
   c. plan how to ask questions of the speaker
   d. rest and prepare to receive future communication
6. Identify the six elements of giving feedback.
7. Empathy in communications means you listen objectively without judging content. True or False?
8. The greatest value of feedback is that it:
   a. forces the sender to think twice about what is communicated
   b. allows for further discussions between the sender and receiver
   c. is not necessary in written communication because the message is tangible and verifiable
   d. improves communication by reducing the chance of misunderstandings

SUMMARY

This summary is organized by the Learning Objectives.

1. Communication is the transference and understanding of meaning.

2. Formal communication addresses task-related issues and tends to follow the organization's authority chain. Informal communication moves in any direction, skips authority levels, and is as likely to satisfy social needs as it is to facilitate task accomplishments.

3. Electronic communications allow supervisors to transmit messages twenty-four hours a day and stay in constant contact with department members, other supervisors, and key members of the management team regardless of where they are physically located. Networks also allow supervisors to participate in electronic meetings and interact with key people outside the organization.

4. The four grapevine patterns are the single strand, gossip, probability, and cluster. The cluster—some people pass a message to a selected group of other people—is most typical.

5. Barriers to effective communication include language differences, poor listening habits, lack of feedback, differences in perception, role requirements, poor choice of information medium, lack of honesty, and emotion.

6. Techniques for overcoming communication barriers include thinking through what you want to say before communicating, constraining emotions, learning to listen, tailoring language to the receiver, matching words and actions, utilizing feedback, and participating in assertiveness training.

7. The essential requirements for active listening are: 1. intensity, 2. empathy, 3. acceptance, and 4. a willingness to take responsibility for completeness.

8. Behaviours that are necessary for providing effective feedback include focusing on specific behaviours; keeping feedback impersonal, goal-oriented, and well-timed; ensuring understanding; and directing negative feedback toward behaviour that the recipient can control.

KEY TERMS AND CONCEPTS

Active listening	Informal communication
Assertiveness training	Nonverbal communication
Body language	Passive listening
Communication	Richness of information
Formal communication	Roles
Grapevine	Verbal intonation

REVIEWING YOUR KNOWLEDGE

1. "Everything a supervisor does involves communicating." Build an argument to support this statement.
2. Why isn't agreement necessarily a part of good communication?
3. When is a written communication superior to an oral one?
4. "Do what I say, not what I do." Analyze this phrase in terms of supervisors being effective communicators.
5. How can nonverbal messages be powerful communicators?
6. What are the purposes of rumours?
7. Can supervisors control the grapevine? Discuss.
8. Given all the barriers to communication, how is it possible for any two people in an organization to accurately transfer information?
9. "A supervisor should always select the information medium that rates highest in information richness." Do you agree or disagree? Discuss.
10. Contrast passive and active listening.

ANSWERS TO THE POP QUIZZES

1. **b. agreement.** Good communication involves transference of meaning—which enables understanding between the parties. It does not require agreement. In fact, two individuals can be in complete agreement, yet still not be communicating.

2. The grapevine can indicate to a supervisor that employees perceive certain problems in the organization. Although the grapevine may not be totally accurate, information flowing through the grapevine can be valuable to a supervisor.

3. **False.** The advantage of oral communication is that it creates a chance for timely feedback. An advantage of written communications is that it creates an accurate and permanent record of the communication that took place.

4. **c. body language and intonation are not aligned.** Effective communications requires that body language and intonation be aligned. Otherwise, they send mixed signals and create a barrier to effective communications.

5. **a. summarize and integrate what has been said.** This response is one of the basic elements of active listening.

6. The six elements of giving feedback are: 1. focus on specific behaviours; 2. keep feedback impersonal; 3. keep feedback goal-oriented; 4. make feedback well timed; 5. ensure understanding; and 6. direct negative feedback toward behaviour that the receiver can control.

7. **False.** Empathy in the communications process means trying to understand what the speaker wants to communicate rather than what you want to understand.

8. **d. improves communication by reducing the chance of misunderstandings.** Reducing the chance of misunderstandings—thus helping the transference of meaning—is the foundation of effective feedback.

CASE 12.A

Fact, Fiction, or Interpretation at IBM

When Nancy Mullins arrived at her IBM office job one Wednesday morning, Kevin O'Connor, a coworker, told her he had heard that their unit was going to be eliminated. Nancy was devastated. Kevin assured Nancy he couldn't believe it either, but that's what he had heard from Iris Gomez and Iris usually knew about most of the "realities" at IBM. In fact, Iris had keen interest in most industry changes. Iris always seemed to know about mergers and downsizing of all types of organizations—from airlines to oil companies. Iris knew a lot about business and the national economy, mainly from being an avid reader of the business section of the newspaper. She kept up with the status of which companies were facing bankruptcy, what takeovers were emerging, which industries were anticipating significant layoffs, and similar news.

Nancy and Kevin continued their discussion at lunch with another coworker, Trish Powell. Trish had not heard anything about the IBM downsizing and wondered if it would affect her department too. As they talked, Nancy and Kevin came to the conclusion that they understood now what their supervisor, Opal Reed, had meant in a memo a few days ago. Ms. Reed had told them their unit needed to have "more interaction with other units to ensure that they were all working toward the same goal."

Trish was bothered by the discussion, especially the "working together" element that Nancy and Kevin had mentioned. She kept thinking about that element all afternoon and

nearly came unglued when her supervisor, Huong Pham, asked her if the inventory report was ready. Mr. Pham had a very worried look on his face when he said he needed the report for a meeting with other departments the next morning. Trish responded that she would have the report ready by the end of the day, but thought to herself, "Why would the inventory report be needed for a meeting with other departments?"

On her way home from work, Trish realized that what Nancy and Kevin were saying was about to happen immediately! A decision had already been made. She was angry that Mr. Pham had said nothing to her. Apparently the supervisor/employee relationship she had with Mr. Pham was not as good as she thought it was. No doubt she would have to be much more cautious with Mr. Pham. She decided that she should be rather coy with him and try to be alert in "picking up" little bits and pieces she needed about the upcoming layoff and reorganization so she could complete the puzzle.

RESPONDING TO THIS CASE

1. In small groups, discuss the facts of this situation. What do you know for sure about this situation? Share your group's thoughts with the class. Did all groups come to the same conclusion about the situation? Why or why not?

2. Describe the method(s) of communication that have been used to "send messages" in this situation. In relation to the communication methods you identified, discuss the different ways the employees could interpret the elements of each of the "messages" they received.

3. Why is it easy to come to a conclusion about a situation without having all the facts? Why is it dangerous to do so?

4. Based on Trish's reaction, how might Mr. Pham have been a better communicating supervisor?

IBM information in Canada
http://www.can.ibm.com/

CASE 12.B

Cynthia Raises Expectations

Doris Patterson was excited about the salary increase she was going to receive. In a department meeting, Doris and her fellow workers had just been informed by their supervisor, Cynthia Lamberti, that salary increases would be based on the third- and fourth-quarter profits for their company, Comfort Mobile Home Factory. Ms. Lamberti's meeting had been upbeat; and it was, of course, good news to her employees that probable salary increases would be known before the end of the year. The third-quarter report would be released next week.

Doris and her fellow workers talked about what they were going to do with their increases. They talked about how high the percentage increases might be. They talked about how soon they would get their increases. And they talked about what additional increases they might expect. It had been a long time since Doris and her friends had had significant salary raises. They had always had cost-of-living increases, but additional raises were never very great. It was time! Now, she thought, her company's pay would be comparable with other employees in the Calgary region.

When Ms. Lamberti had not received the third-quarter report by the end of the following week, she talked to each of her employees individually and assured them the report would be forthcoming. When the report was still not ready by the end of the second week, Ms. Lamberti's response to each of her employees was not to worry because the report was certain to be ready in a few days. Ms. Lamberti was beginning to wish she had waited with the good news until the report was actually in her hands. In fact, she remembers from the supervisors' meeting with her vice president that the supervisors were cautioned against sharing the news of the salary increase with employees.

RESPONDING TO THIS CASE

1. What methods of communications were used in this case? Describe the effectiveness of each. What other methods could have been used?
2. What led you to believe that Ms. Lamberti has good rapport with her employees? Has Ms. Lamberti lost any of her effectiveness as a supervisor as a result of this situation? Explain.
3. What barriers to communication may have played a significant role in this case? Why?
4. What action should Ms. Lamberti take now?

Al Bunge, Production QA Manager
and Doris Dresson, Controller
Josten's (Manufacturing)

The Josten's plant makes the molds (called tools) for rings the company produces. The plant switched to a work team approach a few years ago, and has had great success with it. The plant employs a hundred people, divided into five self-managed teams. The plant runs twenty-four hours a day, six days a week. Teams can include members from two or even three different shifts. They receive and process orders directly from customers. Each self-managed team has a designated leader.

Al and Doris supervise these teams together. Al is responsible for day-to-day production. Doris is responsible for budgeting, orders, and other tasks. They each attend team meetings and teams can address both of them with problems. Doris has more experience with products; Al has more experience with work teams.

In a team environment, cross-training is necessary. Vacations and absenteeism are managed by moving team members from one position to another. Cross-training helps when there is extra work or there are rush jobs. It helps team members understand different positions on the team, what functions the team can perform, and how a team can be reorganzied or streamlined.

In a traditional factory, the supervisor would simply assign someone to be involved in cross-training. In a team environment, Al and Doris need to let the teams work out problems on their own.

Al and Doris had trouble convincing the teams to cross-train. Everyone was willing to train to a higher skill level, but employees with higher skill levels were unwilling to share their knowledge. Nobody wanted to learn a lower-level job. When the workload is heavy, there is little time to take trained team members off regulars tasks to teach them a new skill.

1. Describe the pros and cons of a) self-managed teams; b) cross-training.

2. What factors do you believe contribute to Al's and Doris's success as they manage their teams?

3. Which leadership traits are needed to lead a team? Which of these traits can you see in the story of Al and Doris?

4. Explain why the supervisory approach used by Al and Doris does not violate the rule: Employees should report to only one supervisor.

5. Contrast communications in the self-managed approach with a more traditional supervisory approach.

12

MANAGING CONFLICT AND POLITICS

LEARNING OBJECTIVES

After reading this chapter, you should be able to:

1. Define *conflict*.
2. Identify the three general sources of conflict.
3. List the five basic techniques for resolving conflict.
4. Describe how a supervisor could stimulate conflict.
5. Define *politicking*.
6. Explain the existence of politics in organizations.
7. Describe the situational factors that determine political options.
8. List specific guidelines for developing and improving political skills.
9. Contrast distributive and integrative bargaining.

CHAPTER OUTLINE

"I want him out of here," Todd Escobar, a production supervisor in the animation group at Northern Studios, was yelling into the phone. "I've tried my best to work with him for two years. It's not working. You've got my recommendation and the paperwork. Transfer him, fire him, I don't care. We just can't get along!"

"Calm down, Todd," came the voice from the other end. The voice belonged to Tina Wells in the Human Resources division. "I know you want Sirota out of your department. I'm doing my best. But it's not easy. He's been with the company for four years. His performance reviews haven't been bad. It's just personality differences between you two."

"You're darn right it's personality differences. He whines and complains all the time. He argues with every decision I make. He disrupts the department. I want him out of here! I don't care what you do with him, just get him out of my hair!"

"Todd, listen to me," Tina pleaded. "I'm doing my best. But don't expect miracles. You may have to learn to live with Mike Sirota, at least for another four or five months."

"Over my dead body!" Todd screamed into the phone, and then slammed down the receiver.

Dealing with conflict is a part of every supervisor's job. Those who learn how to manage conflict properly are likely to reap significant benefits. For instance, one study of a group of managers looked at twenty-five skill and personality factors to determine which, if any, were related to managerial success (defined in terms of ratings by one's boss, salary increases, and promotions).[1] Of the twenty-five measures, only one—the ability to handle conflict—was positively related to managerial success.

In this chapter, we'll define conflict, explore what brings it about, and examine the various ways supervisors can handle it. Then we'll discuss organizational politics—why understanding politics is important for all supervisors and how you can make politics work for you.

WHAT IS CONFLICT?

Conflict
A process in which one party consciously interferes in the goal-achievement efforts of another party

Conflict is a process in which one party consciously interferes in the goal-achievement of another party. This interference can be between a supervisor and a member of his or her department. It might alternatively be between two employees within a department. Conflicts can exist between a supervisor and his or her boss, or involve interdepartmental parties, such as two supervisors in separate departments. In our opening dialogue, you saw evidence of two conflicts: one between Todd Escobar and Mike Sirota, and the other between Todd and Tina Wells. The first is an *intra*departmental conflict; the second is an *inter*departmental conflict.

ARE ALL CONFLICTS BAD?

Most of us have grown up with the idea that all conflicts are bad. We were told not to argue with our parents or teachers, to get along with our brothers and sisters, and that countries spent billions of dollars on military outlays to preserve peace. But conflicts aren't *all* bad, especially in organizations.[2]

Conflict is a natural phenomenon of organizational life. It can't be completely eliminated. Why? For the following reasons:

1. Organizational members have different goals.
2. There are scarce resources, such as budget allocations, which various people want and are willing to fight over.
3. People in organizations don't all see things alike, as a result of their diverse backgrounds, education, experiences, and interests.

However, the existence of conflict in organizations has a positive side. It stimulates creativity, innovation, and change. And only through change can an organization adapt and survive (see Figure 12-1). For instance, a positive level of conflict in an organization supports disagreements, the open questioning of others, and challenging the status quo. If organizations were completely devoid of conflict, they would become apathetic, stagnant, and unresponsive to change.

Supervisors should consider conflict as having an upside as well as a downside. They should encourage enough conflict to keep their departments viable, self-critical, and creative. Of course, too much conflict *is* bad and should be reduced. The supervisor's goal should be to have enough conflict in the department to keep the unit responsive and innovative, but not so much as to hinder departmental performance (see Figure 12-2).

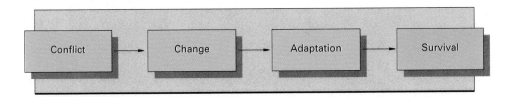

FIGURE 12-1
The positive role of conflict

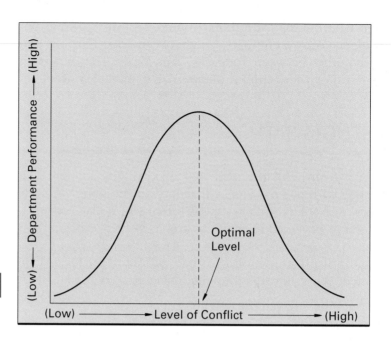

FIGURE 12-2

Conflict and department performance

SOURCES OF CONFLICT

Conflicts don't pop out of thin air. They have causes. These causes can be separated into three general categories: communication differences, structural differences, and personal differences.

COMMUNICATION DIFFERENCES

Communication differences encompass those conflicts arising from misunderstandings and different meanings attached to words.

One of the major myths that most of us carry around with us is that poor communication is the main reason for conflicts—"If we could just communicate with each other, we could eliminate our differences." Such a conclusion is not unreasonable, given the amount of time each of us spends communicating. Poor communication is certainly not the source of all conflicts, though there is considerable evidence to suggest that problems in the communication process act to hinder collaboration and stimulate misunderstanding.

STRUCTURAL DIFFERENTIATION

As explained earlier in this book, organizations are horizontally and vertically differentiated. Management divides up tasks, groups common tasks into departments, and establishes rules and regulations to facilitate standardized practices between departments.

FIGURE 12-3

Workforce diversity is likely to increase conflicts based on communication and personal differences. But that conflict can be beneficial when it stimulates change and attacks apathy.

This structural differentiation often causes conflicts. Individuals disagree over goals, decision alternatives, performance criteria, and resource allocations. These conflicts, however, are not due to poor communication or personal animosities. Rather, they are rooted in the structure of the organization itself. The "goodies" that people want—budgets, promotions, pay increases, additional staff, office space, influence over decision—are scarce resources that must be divided up. The creation of horizontal units (departments) and vertical levels (the management hierarchy) brings about efficiencies through specialization and coordination, but at the same time produces the potential for structural conflicts.

PERSONAL DIFFERENCES

The third source of conflict is personal differences. These include value systems and personality characteristics that account for individual idiosyncrasies and differences.

For example: Your values emphasize acquiring material possessions, while mine focus on developing close family ties. An employee in your department thinks salary increases should be based on seniority. You think the criterion should be job performance. These value differences stimulate conflicts. Similarly, the chemistry between some people makes it hard for them to work together. Factors such as background, education, experience, and training mold each individual into a unique personality. Some personality types are attracted to each other, while some types are like oil and water—they just don't mix. The result is that some people may be perceived by others as abrasive, hard to work with, untrustworthy, or strange. This creates interpersonal conflicts.

TECHNIQUES FOR MANAGING CONFLICT

As a supervisor, you want to have the optimum level of conflict in your department. That means you need to manage it. You'll want to *resolve*

Institute for Conflict Analysis and Resolution
http://www.gmu.edu/departments/ICAR/

Mediation Training Institute International
http://mediationworks.com/mti/

Program on Negotiation
http://www.law.harvard.edu/Programs/PON/

Conflict management
The application of resolution and stimulation techniques to achieve the optimum level of departmental conflict

conflict when it is too high and disrupts your department's performance. You'll want to *stimulate* conflict when it's too low. So **conflict management** is defined as the application of resolution and stimulation techniques to achieve the optimum level of departmental conflict.

RESOLUTION TECHNIQUES

What options are available to eliminate or reduce conflicts? You have five basic approaches or techniques to resolving conflict: avoidance, accommodation, force, compromise, and collaboration. As shown in Figure 12-4, they differ in terms of the emphasis they place on concern for others versus concern for oneself. Each technique has particular strengths and weaknesses, and no single technique is ideal for every situation. You should consider each technique as a tool in your conflict management tool chest. While you may be better at using some tools than others, the skilled supervisor knows what each tool can do and when it is likely to be most effective.

AVOIDANCE

Avoidance
The desire to withdraw from or suppress a conflict

Sometimes **avoidance** is the best solution—just withdrawing from the conflict or ignoring its existence. When would that be? When the conflict is trivial, when emotions are running high and time can help cool things down, or when the potential disruption from a more assertive action outweighs the benefits of resolution. The thing to be concerned about with this approach is that some supervisors believe that they can run away

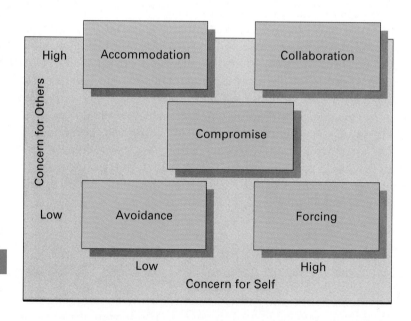

FIGURE 12-4

Basic techniques for resolving conflicts

from *all* conflicts. These conflict avoiders are often very poor supervisors. They frustrate their employees and usually lose their respect. There *are* times when the best action is no action, but that shouldn't be the way you respond to every conflict.

ACCOMMODATION

The goal of **accommodation** is to maintain harmonious relationships by placing another's needs and concerns above your own. You might, for example, yield to another person's position on an issue or try to defuse a conflict by focusing on points of agreement. This approach is most viable when the issue under dispute isn't too important to you or when you want to build up "credits" for possible later issues.

Accommodation
The willingness of one party in a conflict to place the opponent's interests above his or her own

FORCING

With **forcing**, you attempt to satisfy your own needs at the expense of the other party. In organizations, this is most often illustrated by supervisors and managers using their formal authority to resolve a dispute. The use of physical threats, intimidation, majority-rule voting, or stubborn refusal to give in on your position are other examples of force. Force works well 1. when you need a quick resolution, 2. on important issues where unpopular actions must be taken, and 3. where commitment by others to your solution is not critical.

Forcing
The desire to satisfy your own needs at the expense of the other party

COMPROMISE

A **compromise** approach requires each party to give up something of value. This is typically the approach taken by management and unions in negotiating a new labour contract. Supervisors often use compromise to deal with interpersonal conflicts. For instance, a supervisor in a small printing company wanted one of his employees to come in over a weekend to finish an important project. The employee didn't want to spend his whole weekend at work. After considerable discussion, they arrived at a compromise solution: the employee would come in on Saturday only, the supervisor would also come in and help out, and the employee would get eight hours of overtime pay plus the following Friday off.

When should a supervisor look to compromise as an option? When conflicting parties are about equal in power, when it is desirable to achieve a temporary solution to a complex issue, or when time pressures demand an expedient solution.

Compromise
A situation in which each party to a conflict is willing to give up something of value

COLLABORATION

The ultimate win-win solution is **collaboration**. All parties to the conflict seek to satisfy their interests. This technique is typically characterized by open and honest discussion among the parties, intensive listening in order

Collaboration
A situation where the parties to a conflict each desire to satisfy fully the concerns of all parties

to understand differences and identify areas of mutual agreement, and careful deliberation over a full range of alternatives in order to find a solution that is advantageous to all. When is collaboration the best conflict approach? When time pressures are minimal, when all parties seriously want a solution, and when the issue is too important to be compromised.

At P.E.I.'s Island Telephone, management and union representatives use collaboration in resolving many conflicts that arise from the daily operations of the business. A number of joint committees have been established, cochaired by union and management people on a rotating basis. These committees include the Health and Safety Committee, the E.A.P. (Employee Assistance Program) Advisory Committee, and the Pay Equity Committee. Paul Hickey, the Human Resources Manager, indicates that the competitive pressure of the telecommunications industry has played a role in motivating the successful partnership of management and union groups in solving conflicts.

WHICH CONFLICTS SHOULD YOU TACKLE?

Not every conflict justifies your attention. Some might not be worth the effort; others might be unmanageable. While avoidance might appear to be a "cop-out," it can sometimes be the most appropriate response. You can improve your overall management effectiveness, and your conflict management skills in particular, by avoiding trivial conflicts. Choose your battles judiciously, saving your efforts for the ones that count.

Regardless of our desires, reality tells us that some conflicts are unmanageable.[3] When antagonisms are deeply rooted, when one or both parties wish to prolong a conflict, or when emotions run so high that constructive interaction is impossible, your efforts to manage the conflict are unlikely to meet with much success. Don't be lured into the naive belief that a good supervisor can resolve every conflict effectively. Some aren't worth the effort. Some are outside your realm of influence. Still others may be functional and, as such, are best left alone. Those you choose to handle, you need to know how to handle in the best way possible.

CHOOSING THE APPROPRIATE RESOLUTION TECHNIQUE

Now that you're familiar with your options, how should you proceed if you find you have a conflict that needs resolving?

Start by considering your *preferred conflict-handling style* (see Assessing Yourself, page 453). Each of us has a basic approach to handling conflict with which we feel most comfortable. Do you try to postpone dealing with conflicts, hoping they'll go away (avoidance)? Do you prefer soothing the other party's feelings so the disagreement doesn't damage your relationship (accommodation)? Are you stubborn and determined to get your way (forcing)? Do you look for middle-ground solutions (compromise)? Or do you prefer to sit down and discuss differences in order to find a solution that will make everybody happy (collaboration)?

Everyone has a basic resolution approach that reflects his or her personality. You should understand what yours is. But most people aren't held prisoner by that approach. They're flexible and can use different approaches if they need to. Unfortunately, some people are extremely rigid and incapable of adjusting their styles. These people are at a severe disadvantage because they can't use all the resolution options. You should know your basic resolution style and try to show flexibility in using others. However, keep in mind that when push comes to shove, most of us fall back on our basic approach because it's the one we know best and feel most comfortable with.

The next thing you should look at are your *goals*. The best solution is closely intertwined with your definition of *best*. Three goals dominate the preceding discussion of resolution approaches: the *importance* of the conflict, concern over maintaining long-term *interpersonal relations*, and the *speed* with which you need to resolve the conflict. All other things held constant, if the issue is critical to your unit's success, collaboration is preferred. If sustaining supportive relationships is important, the best approaches, in order of preference, are accommodation, collaboration, compromise, and avoidance. If it's crucial to resolve the conflict as quickly as possible, then force, accommodation, and compromise—in that order—are preferred.

Lastly, you need to consider the *source of the conflict*. The resolution technique that works best depends, to a large degree, on the cause of the conflict. Communication-based conflicts revolve around misinformation and misunderstandings. Such conflicts lend themselves to collaboration. In contrast, conflicts based on personal differences arise out of disparities between the parties' values and personalities. Such conflicts are most susceptible to avoidance because these differences are often deeply entrenched. When supervisors have to resolve conflicts rooted in personal differences, they frequently rely on force—not so much because it placates the parties, but because it works! The third category, structural conflicts, offers opportunities to use most of the conflict approaches.

This process of blending your personal style, your goals, and the source of the conflict should result in identifying the approach or set of approaches most likely to be effective for you in any specific conflict.

Scott Burton, Toronto West District Manager for Carlton Cards, prefers to accommodate the needs of others in resolving conflict. However, when the store manager of a retail outlet wanted to reduce the card counter by 5 metres (Scott calculates that each meter generates $3000 in sales), Scott was faced with an immovable opponent. Try as he might to educate the rookie store manager, Scott's message of current trends and profit margins fell on deaf ears. Although the problem was resolved in Scott's favour at the corporate level, he regretted that he had not been able to reach a satisfactory resolution on his own.

Carlton Cards OnLine
http://www.
carltoncards.com/

FIGURE 12-5

In resolving conflict, Scott Burton of Carlton Cards prefers to accommodate the needs of others.

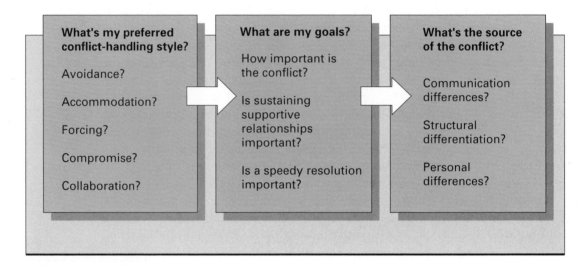

What's my preferred conflict-handling style?	What are my goals?	What's the source of the conflict?
Avoidance?	How important is the conflict?	Communication differences?
Accommodation?	Is sustaining supportive relationships important?	Structural differentiation?
Forcing?		
Compromise?	Is a speedy resolution important?	Personal differences?
Collaboration?		

FIGURE 12-6

Choosing the appropriate resolution technique

STIMULATION TECHNIQUES

What about the other side of conflict management—situations that require supervisors to *stimulate* conflict? The notion of stimulating conflict is often difficult to accept. For almost all of us, the term *conflict* has a negative connotation, and the idea of purposely creating conflict seems to be counter to good supervisory practices. Few of us personally enjoy being in conflictual situations. Yet there are situations where an increase in conflict is constructive. Figure 12-7 provides a set of questions that can help you to determine whether a situation might justify conflict stimulation. An affirmative answer to one or more of the questions suggests that an increase in conflict might help your unit's performance.

YOUR PREFERRED CONFLICT-HANDLING STYLE

Instructions: Indicate how often you do the following—by checking *seldom, sometimes,* or *usually*—when you differ with someone.

	Seldom	Sometimes	Usually
1. I explore our differences, not backing down, but not imposing my view either.	❑	❑	❑
2. I disagree openly, then invite more discussion about our differences.	❑	❑	❑
3. I look for a mutually satisfactory solution.	❑	❑	❑
4. Rather than let the other person make a decision without my input, I make sure I am heard and also that I hear out the other person.	❑	❑	❑
5. I agree to a middle ground rather than look for a completely satisfying solution.	❑	❑	❑
6. I admit I am half wrong rather than explore our differences.	❑	❑	❑
7. I have a reputation for meeting a person halfway.	❑	❑	❑
8. I expect to get out about half of what I really want to say.	❑	❑	❑
9. I give in totally rather than try to change another's opinion.	❑	❑	❑
10. I put aside any controversial aspects of an issue.	❑	❑	❑
11. I agree early on, rather than argue about a point.	❑	❑	❑
12. I give in as soon as the other party gets emotional about an issue.	❑	❑	❑

	Seldom	Sometimes	Usually
13. I try to win the other person over.	❏	❏	❏
14. I work to come out victorious, no matter what.	❏	❏	❏
15. I never back away from a good argument.	❏	❏	❏
16. I would rather win than end up compromising.	❏	❏	❏

SCORING

Total your choices as follows: give yourself five points for "Usually," three points for "sometimes," and one point for "seldom." Then total them for each set of statements grouped as follows:

Set A:	Items 13–16	Set B:	Items 9–12
Set C:	Items 5–8	Set D:	Items 1–4.

WHAT THE ASSESSMENT MEANS

Treat each set separately. A score of 17 or above on any set is considered high; scores of 12–16 are moderately high; scores of 8–11 are moderately low; and scores of 7 or less are considered low. Sets A, B, C, and D represent different conflict-resolution strategies.

A = Forcing: I win, you lose
B = Accommodation: I lose, you win
C = Compromise: Both you and I win some and lose some
D = Collaboration: Both you and I win

Everyone has a basic underlying conflict-handling style. Your highest scoring set(s) in this exercise indicates the strategy or strategies you rely on most.

1. Are you surrounded by "yes people"?

2. Are subordinates afraid to admit ignorance and uncertainties to you?

3. Do you and department members concentrate so hard on reaching a compromise that you lose sight of key values, long-term objectives, or the organization's welfare?

4. Do you believe that it is in your best interest to maintain the impression of peace and cooperation in your unit, regardless of the price?

5. Is there an excessive concern in your department not to hurt the feelings of others?

6. Do people in your department believe that popularity is more important for obtaining rewards than competence and high performance?

7. Is your department unduly enamoured of obtaining consensus for all decisions?

8. Do employees show unusually high resistance to change?

9. Is there a lack of new ideas?

10. Is there an unusually low level of employee turnover?

FIGURE 12-7

Is conflict stimulation needed? An affirmative answer to any or all of these questions suggests that it may be. (*Source:* Adapted from Stephen P. Robbins, "'Conflict Management' and 'Conflict Resolution' Are Not Synonymous Terms," *California Management Review*, Winter 1978, p. 71.)

We know a lot more about resolving conflict than about stimulating it. However, the following are some suggestions you might want to consider if you find your department is in need of an increased level of conflict.

USE COMMUNICATION

Politicians are well known for using communication to stimulate conflict. Senior officials float trial balloons by "planting" possible decisions with the media through the infamous "reliable source" route. For example, a policy draft is "leaked" to determine public support. However, if the media or the public do not support the intent of the policy, some high-level official will invariably come forward and make a formal statement such as, "At no time was this policy under consideration."

You can use rumours and ambiguous messages to stimulate conflict in your department. Information that some employees might be transferred, that serious budget cuts are coming, or that a layoff is possible can reduce apathy, stimulate new ideas, and force reevaluation—all positive outcomes as a result of increased conflict.

BRING IN OUTSIDERS

A widely used method for shaking up a stagnant department is to bring in—either by hiring from outside or by internal transfer—individuals whose backgrounds, values, attitudes, or personalities differ from those of present members. One of the major benefits of the diversity movement (encouraging the hiring and promotion of people who are different) is that it can stimulate conflict and improve an organization's performance.

RESTRUCTURE THE DEPARTMENT

We know that structural variables are a source of conflict. It is therefore only logical that supervisors look to structure as a conflict stimulation device. Centralizing decisions, realigning work groups, and increasing formalization are examples of structural devices that disrupt the status quo and act to increase conflict levels.

APPOINT A DEVIL'S ADVOCATE

Devil's advocate
A person who purposely presents arguments that run counter to those proposed by the majority or against current practices

A **devil's advocate** is a person who intentionally presents arguments that run counter to those proposed by the majority or against current practices. He or she plays the role of the critic, even to the point of arguing against positions with which he or she actually agrees.

A devil's advocate acts as a check against groupthink and practices that have no better justification than "that's the way we've always done it around here." When thoughtfully listened to, the advocate can improve the quality of group decision making. On the other hand, others in the group often view advocates as time-wasters; appointment of an advocate is almost certain to delay any decision process.

A WORD OF CAUTION

Even though there are situations in which departmental performance can be enhanced through conflict stimulation, it may not be in your best career interests to use stimulation techniques.

If your organizational culture or your immediate superior view *any* kind of conflict in your department as a negative reflection on your supervisory performance, think twice before stimulating conflict or even allowing low levels of conflict to exist. Where upper management believes that all conflicts are bad, it's not uncommon for lower-level managers and supervisors to be evaluated on how peaceful and harmonious conditions are in their department. While a conflict-free climate tends to create stagnant and apathetic organizations, and eventually lower performance, it is important for your survival to adopt a conflict-management style that's compatible with your organization. In some cases, that might mean using only resolution techniques.

Are You Comprehending
What You're Reading?

1. Which one of the following situations best suggests the need for a manager to stimulate conflict?
   a. when a supervisor is surrounded by "yes people"
   b. when employees in a department lack specific expertise
   c. when the work unit is peaceful and cooperative
   d. when creativity and innovation are present
2. Describe why all conflict cannot be completely eliminated in organizations.
3. The ultimate win-win conflict resolution technique is accommodation, which seeks to satisfy each party's interests. True or False?
4. A person who purposely presents arguments that run counter to those proposed by the majority or against current practices is called a(n) ——————————.
   a. conflict stimulator
   b. devil's advocate
   c. external consultant
   d. all of the above

UNDERSTANDING ORGANIZATIONAL POLITICS

"If your organization's senior management views all conflicts as bad, don't use conflict stimulation techniques, even if they improve your department's performance." This summary of the previous paragraph acknowledges the political nature of organizations. You're not always rewarded for doing the right things. In the real world of organizations, the good guys don't always win. Demonstrating openness, trust, objectivity, support, and similar humane qualities in relationships with others doesn't always lead to improved supervisory performance. There will be times when, to get things done or to protect your interests against the maneuvering of others, you'll have to engage in politicking. Effective supervisors understand the political nature of organizations and adjust their actions accordingly.

Politicking
The actions you can take to influence, or attempt to influence, the distribution of advantages and disadvantages within your organization

Politics relates to who gets what, when, and how. **Politicking** is the actions you can take to influence, or attempt to influence, the distribution of advantages and disadvantages within your organization. Some examples of political behaviour include withholding key information from decision makers, whistle-blowing, spreading rumours, leaking confidential information about organizational activities to the media, exchanging favours with others in the organization for mutual benefit, and lobbying on behalf of or against a particular individual or decision alternative.

One of the most interesting insights about politics is that what constitutes a political action is almost entirely a judgment call. Like beauty, politics is in the eye of the beholder. A behaviour that one person labels "organizational politics" is very likely to be characterized as an instance of "effective management" by another. This doesn't mean that effective management is necessarily political, though in some cases it might be. Rather, a person's reference point determines what he or she classifies as organizational politics. Take a look at the contrasting labels in Figure 12-8 that are used to describe the same activities.

POLITICAL LABEL		EFFECTIVE MANAGEMENT LABEL
1. Blaming others	or	Fixing responsibility
2. Kissing up	or	Developing working relationships
3. Apple-polishing	or	Demonstrating loyalty
4. Passing the buck	or	Delegating authority
5. Covering your rear	or	Documenting decisions
6. Creating conflict	or	Encouraging change and innovation
7. Forming coalitions	or	Facilitating teamwork
8. Whistleblowing	or	Improving efficiency
9. Nitpicking	or	Meticulous attention to detail
10. Scheming	or	Planning ahead

FIGURE 12-8

Is it politics or effective management? You make the call!

WHY IS THERE POLITICS IN ORGANIZATIONS?

Can you conceive of an organization that is free of politics? It's possible but most unlikely.

Organizations are made up of individuals and groups with different values, goals, and interests. This sets up the potential for conflict over resources. Departmental budgets, space allocations, project responsibilities, and salary adjustments are just a few examples of the resources about whose allocation organizational members will disagree.

Resources in organizations are limited, which often turns potential conflict into real conflict. If resources were abundant, then all the various interests within the organization could satisfy their goals. But because they're limited, not everyone's interests can be provided for. Further, gains by one individual or group are often perceived, accurately or not, as being at the expense of others within the organization. These forces create competition among members for the organization's limited resources.

Maybe the most important factor leading to politics within organizations is the realization that most of the "facts" that are used to allocate the limited resources are open to interpretation. What, for instance, is "good" performance? What's a "good" job? What's an "adequate" improvement? The manager of any major league baseball team knows a .400 hitter is a high performer and a .125 hitter a poor performer. You don't need to be a baseball genius to know you should pay your .400 hitter and send the .125 hitter back to the minors. But what if you have to choose between players who hit .280 and .295? Then other factors—less objective ones—come into play: fielding, attitude, potential, ability to perform in the clutch, and so on. Most managerial decisions in organizations more closely resemble choosing between a .280 and a .295 hitter than deciding between a .125 and a .400 hitter. It is in this large and ambiguous middle ground of organizational life—where the facts *don't* speak for themselves—that politics takes place.

Finally, because most decisions have to be made in a climate of ambiguity (where facts are rarely fully objective, and thus are open to interpretation), people within the organization will use whatever influence they can to taint the facts to support their goals and interests. That, of course, creates motivation for the activities we call politicking.

THE ETHICS OF "PLAYING POLITICS"

Not all political actions are necessarily unethical. To help guide you in differentiating ethical from unethical politicking, there are some questions you should consider (see Figure 12-9, which illustrates a decision tree to guide ethical actions). The three questions are illustrated by the following examples.

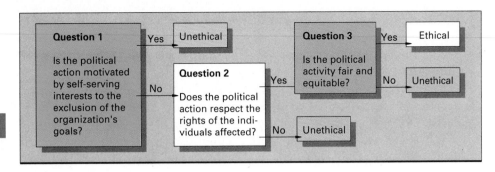

FIGURE 12-9

Is a political action
ethical?

The first question you need to answer addresses self-interest versus
organizational goals. Ethical actions are consistent with the organization's goals. Spreading untrue rumours about the safety of a new product
introduced by your company, in order to make that product's design
group look bad, is unethical. However, there may be nothing unethical if
you, as a department head, exchange favours with your division's purchasing manager, in order to get a critical contract processed quickly.

The second question is concerned with the rights of other parties. If
you went down to the mail room during your lunch hour and read through
the mail directed to the purchasing manager with the intent of "getting
something on him" so he'd expedite your contract, you'd be acting unethi-
cally. You would have violated the purchasing manager's right to privacy.

The final question you need to address relates to whether the political activity conforms to standards of equity and justice. If you inflate the
performance evaluation of a favoured employee and deflate the evaluation of a disfavoured employee, and then use these evaluations to justify
giving the former a big raise and nothing to the latter, you have treated
the disfavoured employee unfairly.

ASSESSING THE POLITICAL LANDSCAPE

Before you consider your political options in any situation, you need to
evaluate that situation. The key situational factors are your organization's
culture, the power of others, and your own power.

YOUR ORGANIZATION'S CULTURE

The place to begin is an assessment of your organization's culture, to
determine which behaviours are desirable and which aren't.

Culture
A system of shared
meaning

Every organization has a system of shared meaning called its **culture**.
This culture is a set of unwritten norms that members of the organization
accept and understand, and that guide their actions. For example, some

organizations' cultures encourage risk taking, accept conflicts and disagreements, allow employees a great deal of autonomy, and reward members according to performance criteria. But there are cultures that differ by 180 degrees: they punish risk taking, seek harmony and cooperation at any price, minimize opportunities for employees to show initiative, and allocate rewards to people according to such criteria as seniority, effort, or loyalty. The point is that every organization's culture is somewhat different, and if a political strategy is to succeed, it must be compatible with the culture.

Working with his brother as a partner in S.C.I.L., a family-owned construction and renovation company, Don Bray has learned to handle the politics of working with a more experienced, older sibling. At S.C.I.L, everyone accepts the "culture" that gives the older sibling more authority. When his brother insists on his way, Don falls back on individual specialty skills to clear the right path. In a recent conflict, Don asked their contracted plumber to explain why Don couldn't seal a floor as his brother was insisting. By soliciting an expert opinion, Don was able to show that his brother's request was not reasonable.

THE POWER OF OTHERS

People are either powerful or they're not, right? Wrong! On some issues, a person may be very powerful. Yet that same person may be relatively powerless on other issues. What you need to do, therefore, is determine which individuals or groups will be powerful in a given situation.

Some people will have influence as a result of their formal position in the organization. So that is probably the best place to begin your power assessment. What decision or issue do you want to influence? Who has formal authority to affect that issue? The answer to that question is only the beginning. After determining who has formal authority, consider others—individuals, coalitions, or departments—who may have a vested interest in the decision's outcome. Who might gain or lose as a result of one choice being selected over another? This helps to identify the power players—those motivated to engage in politicking. It also pinpoints your likely adversaries.

Now you need to specifically assess the power of each player or group of players. In addition to each one's formal authority, evaluate the resources each controls and his or her location in the organization. The control of scarce and important resources is a source of power in organizations. Control and access to key information, expert knowledge, and possession of special skills are examples of resources that may be scarce and important to the organization; hence, they become potential means of influencing organizational decisions. In addition, being in the right place in the organization can be a source of power. This explains, for example, the frequent power of secretaries. They are often in the direct flow of key information and control the access of others to their bosses.

Ingrid Hann, V. P. Human Resources, Spar Aviation, · describes herself as a "hands on" manager.

Assess your boss's influence in any power analysis. What is his or her position on the issue under concern? For, against, or neutral? If it's for or against, how intense is your boss's stand? What is your boss's power status in the organization—strong or weak? Answers to these questions can help you assess whether the support or opposition of your boss will be relevant.

Ingrid Hann, V. P. Human Resources, Spar Aviation, describes a political situation at her former employer. The customer relations department was assigned to Ingrid, while the former director went on to other responsibilities within the company. The former director, however, continued to exercise power over Ingrid's newly reassigned staff. Ingrid's style is best described as "hands on." She proceeded to implement new business practices with the fifty-six employees in the customer relations area, with a focus on working smarter.

Ingrid understood the feelings of "ownership" of the former director toward the customer service department. The employees, too, were more comfortable with the previous director, because he and his style were very familiar to them. With the former director still part of the company, Ingrid decided to patiently ride out the storm, confident that her new employees would eventually see the gains from her approach to workplace excellence.

YOUR POWER

After looking at others' power, assess your own power base. What is your personal power? What power does your supervisory position in the organization provide? Where do you stand relative to others who hold power?

Your power can come from several sources. If you've got a charismatic personality, for instance, you can exert power because others will want to know your position on issues, your arguments will often be persuasive, and your position is likely to carry considerable weight in others' decisions. Another frequent source of power for supervisors is access to important information that others in the organization need.

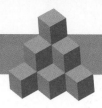

BECOMING POLITICALLY SMART

ABOUT THE SKILL

Although there are few clear-cut ways to avoid getting involved in office politics, here are some suggestions that we offer to help you become more politically smart. These recommendations, however, are not designed to teach you how to take advantage of someone else or of a given situation. Rather, they are intended to help you develop a personal profile, which can assist you if you find yourself in a political situation.

1. **Frame arguments in terms of organizational goals.** Effective politicking requires covering up self-interest. No matter that your objective is self-serving; all the arguments you marshal in support of it must be framed in terms of the benefits that will accrue to the organization. People whose actions appear to blatantly further their own interests at the expense of the organization's are almost universally denounced, are likely to lose influence, and often suffer the ultimate penalty of being expelled from the organization.

2. **Portray the proper image.** What others think about you is important to your political success. You need to understand the organization's culture and act accordingly. Accept and demonstrate the values, norms, and behaviours that the organization wants. Doing so shows that you know what is important for organizational survival. Portraying the proper image also increases the likelihood that when you do raise an issue, others may give it more legitimacy. An "outcast" who's always complaining rarely gets an audience—even if he or she is right.

3. **Gain control of organizational resources.** The control of organizational resources that are scarce and important is a source of power. Knowledge and expertise are particularly effective resources to control. They make you more valuable to the organization, and therefore more likely to gain security, advancement, and a receptive audience for your ideas.

4. **Make yourself appear indispensable.** Since we're dealing with appearances rather than objective facts, you can enhance your power by appearing to be indispensable. That is, you don't have to *really* be indispensable, so long as key people in the organization believe that you are. If the prime decision makers believe there is no ready substitute

for what you are giving the organization, they are likely to go to great lengths to ensure that your desires are satisfied. How do you make yourself appear indispensable? The most effective means is to develop expertise (through experience, contacts, secret techniques, and natural talents) that is perceived as critical to the organization's operations and that key decision makers believe no one else possesses to the extent that you do.

5. **Be visible.** Because the evaluation of supervisory effectiveness has a substantial subjective component, it is important that your boss and those in power in the organization be made aware of your contribution. If you are fortunate enough to have responsibilities that bring your accomplishments to the attention of others, it may not be necessary to take direct measures to increase your visibility. But your department may handle activities that are low in visibility, or your specific contribution may be indistinguishable because you're part of a team endeavour. In such cases—without creating the image of a braggart—you'll want to call attention to yourself by giving progress reports to your boss and others, being seen at social functions, being active in your professional associations, developing powerful allies who speak positively about your accomplishments, and similar tactics. Of course, the skilled politician actively and successfully lobbies to get those projects that will increase his or her visibility.

6. **Find a mentor.** Nothing helps you avoid land mines better than someone who knows where the land mines are. Getting them to navigate your path makes things so much safer. In organizations, this navigator is called a *mentor*. A mentor is someone who is usually a more experienced and more senior member of the organization. The mentor is usually already part of the "power" group, and his or her role is to be your support system. Mentors are also people who can vouch for you in the organization. They often are able to get you exposure to the power-brokers in the organization, and provide you advice on how to effectively manoeuvre through the system. From a political point of view, a mentor can act as a sounding-board for you, providing vital suggestions and feedback on how to survive and succeed.

7. **Develop powerful allies.** It helps to have powerful people in your camp. In addition to a mentor, you can cultivate contacts with potentially influential people above you and among other supervisors. They can provide you with important information that may not be available through normal channels. Additionally, there will be times

when decisions will be made by those with the greatest support. Sometimes—though not always—there is strength in numbers. Having powerful allies can provide you with a coalition of support if and when you need it.

8. **Avoid tarnished individuals.** In almost every organization, there are fringe members whose status is questionable. Their performance and/or loyalty is under close scrutiny. Such individuals, while they are under the microscope, are "tainted." Carefully keep your distance from them. We all tend to judge others by the company they keep. Given the reality that effectiveness has a large subjective component, your own effectiveness might be called into question if you are perceived as being too closely associated with tainted people.

9. **Support your boss.** Your immediate future is in the hands of your current boss. Since he or she evaluates your performance, you will typically want to do whatever is necessary to have your boss on your side. You should make every effort to help your boss succeed and look good. Provide support if he or she is under siege and spend the time to find out what criteria will be used to assess your effectiveness. Don't undermine your boss. Don't speak negatively of him or her to others. If the individual is competent, visible, and in possession of a power base, she or he is likely to be on the way up in the organization. By being perceived as supportive, you increase the likelihood that you will be pulled along.

Gaining political power and building a power base in an organization is often fostered with the help of a mentor. In the past, however, most of those who were "supported" by an experienced, senior member of the organization often shared something in common. That is, they were usually male and white. But what about women and people of colour? What opportunities lie ahead for them to find and gain this support?

Finding or getting a mentor is rarely easy. In fact, more often than not, you are approached by the other person. What can serve as the "attraction" to bring the two of you together? In the past, it was something a potential mentor saw in you—which was often something they saw in themselves years ago. But how can a male properly relate to a female or vice versa? How can individuals from different races or national origins identify with each other when there's no foundation of commonality between them? Unquestionably, these can be major issues—many of which we've highlighted in previous chapters. Organizations are attempting to bridge this gap. Many recognize that leaving it up to nature just won't work. There needs to be some system in place such as a program that encourages senior members to take junior members under their wing. Even when such programs exist, other problems still may arise. For example, is the male supervisor mentoring a younger female employee exhibiting appropriate mentoring behaviour, or is she getting special treatment because she's a woman? If the two of them develop a close, personal work relationship is there a risk of them crossing the line into sexual harassment?

Despite the potential difficulties diversity offers for mentoring, the fact remains that each of us needs this support. Therefore, if someone doesn't approach you, you must make every effort to find a mentor yourself. In either case, being mentored requires work on your part. That effort will only be magnified when your mentor is someone who has personal attributes different from yours.

What do you think about this diversity issue?

NEGOTIATION

As a supervisor, your success in resolving conflict and playing politics will be influenced by your negotiating skills. We know that lawyers and car salesmen spend a lot of time negotiating, but so do supervisors. They have to negotiate salaries for incoming employees, bargain over budgets, work out differences with associates, and resolve conflicts with subordinates. This section will help you to improve your negotiating skills.

ASSESSING YOURSELF: DO YOU UNDERSTAND WHAT IT TAKES TO BE AN EFFECTIVE NEGOTIATOR?

For each of the following statements, indicate your degree of agreement or disagreement by circling one of the five responses.

SA = Strongly agree
A = Agree
U = Undecided
D = Disagree
SD = Strongly disagree

1. I believe everything is negotiable.	SA	A	U	D	SD
2. In every negotiation, someone wins and someone loses.	SA	A	U	D	SD
3. I try to get as much information as possible about the other party prior to negotiation.	SA	A	U	D	SD
4. The other party's initial offer shapes my negotiating strategy.	SA	A	U	D	SD
5. I try to open negotiations with a positive action such as offering a small concession.	SA	A	U	D	SD
6. I build an image of success by focusing on winning as much as possible in every bargaining situation.	SA	A	U	D	SD

SCORING DIRECTIONS AND KEY

For questions 1, 3, and 5, give yourself five points for SA, four points for A, three points for U, two points for D, and one point for SD. For questions 2, 4, and 5, reverse the scoring; that is, give yourself one point for SA, two points for A, and so forth.

A score of 25 or above suggests you have a basic understanding of how to be an effective negotiator. Scores of 19 to 24 indicate you have room for improvement. Those who scored 18 or less should find the following discussion and exercise very valuable in improving their overall supervisory effectiveness.

SKILL BASICS

Negotiation
A process in which two or more parties exchange goods or services and attempt to agree upon the exchange rate for them

What is **negotiation**? It's a process in which two or more parties exchange goods or services and attempt to agree upon the exchange rate for them. For our purposes, we'll also use the term interchangeably with *bargaining*.

BARGAINING STRATEGIES

There are two general approaches to negotiation: *distributive bargaining* and *integrative bargaining*.

Distributive bargaining
Zero-sum negotiations where any gain by one is at the expense of the other

You see a used car advertised for sale in the newspaper. It appears to be just what you're looking for. You go out to see the car. It's great and you want it. The owner tells you the asking price. You don't want to pay that much. The two of you then negotiate over the price. The negotiating process you are engaging in is called **distributive bargaining**. Its most distinctive feature is that it operates under zero-sum conditions. That is, any gain I make is at your expense, and vice versa. Every dollar you can get the seller to cut from the car's price is a dollar you save. Conversely, every dollar more he or she can get from you comes at your expense. Thus the essence of distributive bargaining is negotiating over who gets what share of a fixed pie.

Probably the most widely cited example of distributive bargaining is in labour-management negotiations over wages and benefits (see Chapter 15). Typically, labour's representatives come to the bargaining table determined to get as much as they can from management. Because every cent more that labour negotiates increases management's costs, each party bargains aggressively and often treats the other as an opponent who must be defeated.

Figure 12-11 depicts the distributive bargaining strategy. Parties A and B represent the two negotiators. Each has a *target point* that defines what he or she would like to achieve. Each also has a *resistance point*, which marks the lowest outcome that is acceptable—the point below which he or she would break off negotiations rather than accept a less favourable settlement. The area between their resistance points is the settlement range. As long as there is some overlap in their aspiration ranges, there exists a settlement area where each one's aspirations can be met.

When engaged in distributive bargaining, your tactics should focus on trying to get your opponent to agree to your specific target point or to get as close to it as possible. Examples of such tactics are persuading your opponent of the impossibility of getting to his or her target point and the advisability of accepting a settlement near yours; arguing that your target is fair, while your opponent's isn't; and attempting to get your opponent to feel emotionally generous toward you and thus to accept an outcome close to your target point.

Now let's look at **integrative bargaining**. Assume a sales representative for a women's sportswear manufacturer has just closed a $15 000 order from a small clothing retailer. The sales rep calls in the order to her firm's credit department. She is told that the firm can't approve credit to this customer because of a past slow-pay record. The next day, the sales rep and the firm's credit supervisor meet to discuss the problem. The sales rep doesn't want to lose the business. Neither does the credit

Integrative bargaining Bargaining under the assumption that there is at least one settlement option that can create a win-win solution.

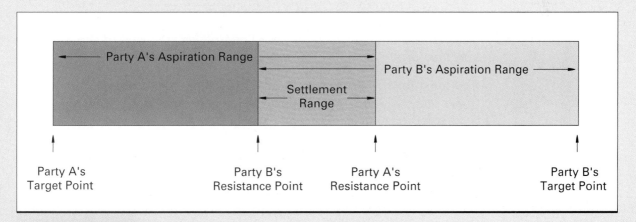

FIGURE 12-11

Staking out the bargaining zone

supervisor, but he also doesn't want to get stuck with an uncollectable debt. The two openly review their options. After considerable discussion, they agree on a solution that meets both their needs: The credit supervisor will approve the sale, but the clothing store's owner will provide a bank guarantee that will assure payment if the bill isn't paid within sixty days.

The sales-credit negotiation is an example of integrative bargaining. In contrast to distributive bargaining, integrative problem solving operates under the assumption that there is at least one settlement that can create a win-win solution.

In general, integrative bargaining is preferable to distributive bargaining. Why? Because the former builds long-term relationships and facilitates working together in the future. It bonds negotiators and allows each to leave the bargaining table feeling that he or she has achieved a victory. Distributive bargaining, on the other hand, leaves one party a loser. It tends to build animosities and deepen divisions between people who have to work together on an ongoing basis.

Why, then, don't we see more integrative bargaining in organizations? The answer lies in the conditions necessary for this type of negotiation to succeed. These conditions include openness with information and frankness between parties; sensitivity on the part of each party to the other's needs; the ability to trust one another; and a willingness by both parties to maintain flexibility. Because many organizational cultures and interpersonal relationships are not characterized by openness, trust, and flexibility, it isn't surprising that negotiations often take on a win-at-any-cost dynamic.

BECOMING AN EFFECTIVE NEGOTIATOR

The essence of effective negotiation can be summarized in the following six guidelines.

1. **Consider the other party's situation.** Acquire as much information as you can about your opponent's interests and goals. What is his or her strategy? This information will help you understand your opponent's behaviour, predict his or her responses to your offers, and frame solutions in terms of his or her interests. Additionally, when you can anticipate your opponent's position, you are better equipped to counter his or her arguments with the facts and figures that support your position.

2. **Have a concrete strategy.** Treat negotiation like a chess match. Expert chess players have a strategy. They know ahead of time how they will respond to any given situation. How strong is your situation

and how important is the issue? Are you willing to split differences to achieve an early solution? If the issue is very important to you, is your position strong enough to let you play hardball and show little or no willingness to compromise? These are questions you should address before you begin bargaining.

3. **Begin with a positive overture.** Studies on negotiation show that concessions tend to be reciprocated and lead to agreements. As a result, begin bargaining with a positive overture—perhaps a small concession—and then reciprocate your opponent's concessions.

4. **Address problems, not personalities.** Concentrate on the negotiation issues, not on the personal characteristics of your opponent. When negotiations get tough, avoid the tendency to attack your opponent. It's your opponent's ideas or position that you disagree with, not him or her personally. Separate the people from the problem, and don't personalize differences.

5. **Pay little attention to initial offers.** Treat an initial offer as merely a point of departure. Everyone has to have an initial position. These initial offers tend to be extreme and idealistic. Treat them as such.

6. **Emphasize win-win solutions.** Bargainers often assume that their gain must come at the expense of the other party. As noted with integrative bargaining, that needn't be the case. There are often win-win solutions. But assuming a zero-sum game means missed opportunities for trade-offs that could benefit both sides. So if conditions are supportive, look for an integrative solution. Frame options in terms of your opponent's interests and look for solutions that can allow your opponent, as well as yourself, to declare a victory.

APPLYING YOUR SKILLS

Break into pairs. This is a role-play exercise. One person will play the role of TERRY, the department supervisor. The other person will play DALE, Terry's boss.

THE SITUATION

Nike
http://www.nike.com/

Terry and Dale work for Nike. Terry supervises a research laboratory. Dale is the manager of research and development. Terry and Dale are former college runners who have worked for Nike for more than six years. Dale has been Terry's boss for two years.

One of Terry's employees has greatly impressed Terry. This employee is Lisa Roland. Lisa was hired eleven months ago. She is twenty-four years old and holds a master's degree in mechanical engineering. Her entry-level salary was $32 500 a year. She was told by Terry that, in accordance with corporate policy, she would receive an initial performance evaluation at six months and a comprehensive review after one year. Based on her performance record, Lisa was told she could expect a salary adjustment at the time of the one-year evaluation.

Terry's evaluation of Lisa after six months was very positive. Terry commented on the long hours Lisa was putting in, her cooperative spirit, the fact that others in the lab enjoyed working with her, and that she was making an immediate positive impact on the project she had been assigned. Now that Lisa's first anniversary is coming up, Terry has again reviewed Lisa's performance. Terry thinks Lisa may be the best new person the R&D group has ever hired. After only a year, Terry has rated Lisa as the number three ranked performer in a department of eleven.

Salaries in the department vary greatly. Terry, for instance, has a basic salary of $57 000, plus eligibility for a bonus that might add another $5000 to $8000 a year. The salary range of the eleven department members is $26 400 to $51 350. The lowest salary is a recent hire with a bachelor's degree in physics. The two people that Terry has rated above Lisa earn base salaries of $47 700 and $51 350. They're both twenty-seven years old and have been at Nike for three and four years, respectively. The median salary in Terry's department is $42 660.

TERRY'S ROLE. You want to give Lisa a big raise. Though she's young, she has proven to be an excellent addition to the department. You don't want to lose her. More importantly, she knows in general what other people in the department are earning and she thinks she's underpaid. The company typically gives one-year raises of three per cent, although five per cent is not unusual and eight to ten per cent increases have been approved on occasion. You'd like to get Terry as large an increase as Dale will approve.

DALE'S ROLE. All your supervisors typically try to squeeze you for as much money as they can for their people. You understand this because you did the same thing when you were a supervisor. But your boss wants to keep a lid on costs. He wants you to keep raises for recent hires generally in the two to four per cent range. In fact, he's sent a memo to all managers and supervisors saying this. However, your boss is also very concerned with equity and paying people what they're worth. You feel assured that he will support any salary recommendation you make, as long as it can be justified. Your goal, consistent with cost reduction, is to keep salary increases as low as possible.

Terry has a meeting scheduled with Dale to discuss Lisa's performance review and salary adjustment. Take ten minutes to set your negotiation strategies, referring to the six points of effective negotiation. Also consider the points on ethical politicking as part of your strategy. Then take up to fifteen minutes to conduct your negotiation. When your negotiation is complete, the class will compare the various negotiation strategies used and pair outcomes.

5. Which one of the following is not an example of political behaviour that exists in an organization?
   a. leaking confidential information about organizational activities to the media
   b. using informal communications channels to expedite important messages
   c. whistleblowing
   d. withholding key information from decision makers
6. What situational factors lead to office politics?
7. The most distinctive feature of distributive bargaining is that it operates under zero-sum conditions. True or False?
8. The process in which two or more parties who have different preferences must make a joint decision to come to an agreement is called —————————.
   a. delegation
   b. empowerment
   c. conflict-handling
   d. none of the above

SUMMARY

This summary is organized by the Learning Objectives.

1. Conflict is a process in which one party consciously interferes in the goal-achievement efforts of another party.
2. Conflicts generally come from one of three sources: communication differences, structural differences, or personal differences.
3. The five basic techniques for resolving conflict are avoidance, accommodation, force, compromise, and collaboration.
4. A supervisor could stimulate conflict by communicating ambiguous messages, bringing in outsiders with different backgrounds or personalities, restructuring the department, or appointing a devil's advocate.
5. Politicking is the actions you can take to influence, or attempt to influence, the distribution of advantages and disadvantages within your department.
6. Politics exist in organizations because individuals have different values, goals, and interests; because organizational resources are limited; because the criteria for allocating the limited resources are ambiguous; and because individuals seek influence so they can shape the criteria to support their goals and interests.
7. The situational factors that determine political options are 1. your organization's culture, 2. the power of others, and 3. your own power.
8. To develop and improve your political skills, you should frame arguments in terms of organizational goals; develop the right image; gain control of organizational resources; make yourself appear indispensable; be visible; get a mentor; develop powerful allies; avoid "tainted" members; and support your boss.
9. Distributive bargaining creates a win-lose situation because the object of negotiation is treated as fixed in amount. Integrative bargaining treats available resources as variable, and hence creates the potential for win-win solutions.

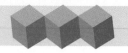
KEY TERMS AND CONCEPTS

Accommodation

Avoidance

Collaboration

Compromise

Conflict

Conflict management

Culture

Devil's advocate

Distributive bargaining

Forcing

Integrative bargaining

Negotiation

Politicking

REVIEWING YOUR KNOWLEDGE

1. How can conflict benefit an organization?
2. How can an organization's structure create conflict?
3. What is conflict management?
4. When should you avoid conflict? When should you seek compromise?
5. What is a devil's advocate? How does an advocate affect conflict in a department?
6. Can an organization be free of politics? Explain.
7. Is it unethical to "play politics"?
8. How do you assess another person's power in an organization?
9. Why does effective politicking require covering up self-interest?
10. How can increased visibility enhance a person's power?

ANSWERS TO THE POP QUIZZES

1. **a. when a supervisor is surrounded by "yes people."** This is one of the situations listed in Exhibit 12-7, indicating a need to stimulate conflict. Response b) indicates a need for training. Responses c) and d) are preferred unit characteristics.

2. All conflict cannot be completely eliminated in organizations because it is a natural phenomenon of organizational life. That's because 1. organizational members have different goals; 2. there are scarce resources, like budget allocations, which various people want and are willing to fight over; and 3. people in organizations don't all see things alike as a result of their diverse backgrounds, education, experiences, and interests.

3. **False.** The ultimate win-win conflict resolution technique, which seeks to satisfy each party's interests, is **collaboration**.

4. **b. devil's advocate.** This is the definition of the actions of a devil's advocate.

5. **b. using informal communications channels to expedite important messages.** This choice was not identified as an example of political behaviour. The other responses were examples.

6. Situational factors leading to office politics include individuals with different backgrounds and values, conflict over limited resources, and the realization that most of the "facts" that are used to allocate the limited resources are open to interpretation.

7. **True.** The most distinctive feature of distributive bargaining is that it operates under zero-sum conditions. That is, any gain one makes is at the expense of the other person, and vice versa.

8. **d. none of the above.** The process in which two or more parties who have different preferences must make a joint decision to come to an agreement is called **negotiation**.

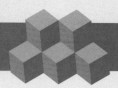

CASE 14.A

Change—A Shift in Political Power

At the Honeywell plant in Scarborough, Ontario, the recent introduction of self-directed work teams led to many other unexpected changes.

The plant was previously run in a "traditional" assembly line mode. Then, the introduction of work teams changed every aspect of production, creating new positions that involved each employee in all the aspects of production, not just one small piece of assembly in a long process. These self-directed teams not only assemble products, they also test, package, and control whole assembly lines. Teams also take responsibility for daily routines including work assignments, ordering materials, maintaining equipment and training.

As expected, this significant change resulted in chaos and conflict as the plant adjusted to its new format. Managers were threatened with a reduction in their power (and indeed one-third of the salaried positions have now disappeared); workers were challenged to take on managerial functions; and the communication and authority lines within the company were scrambled as the old hierarchy was broken down. The empowerment of line workers also meant the right to question higher management, and the entrenchment of face-to-face discussion and justification of decisions. At these discussions, employees from diverse areas (engineering, assembly, sales) now need the negotiation and communication skills to deal with a much wider audience. Indeed, these groups might never have talked to each other under the old hierarchical structure, but rather would have used their respective managers to convey their messages. Now, work groups can put the brakes on the assembly line at any time for a consultation to fix a problem. One recent half-hour shutdown saved the company thousands of dollars in reworking.

According to Honeywell employees, the trick is to teach team members how to handle conflict in dealing with a new set of problems and circumstances which were never part of their jobs in the past.

RESPONDING TO THIS CASE

1. a) Describe the specific causes of conflict (using terms from the chapter) that arose with the introduction of work teams.
   b) Consider those same issues now that work teams are operational.
2. Now that work teams are used at the Honeywell plant, which style of conflict resolution is likely to be adopted by the company. Why?
3. How will the political game change at Honeywell? Consider the impact of work teams on the organization's culture, the power of others, and the individual power of each employee.

CASE 14.B

Eduardo Ortega's Promotion

Eduardo Ortega was flattered to be asked to become supervisor of the office staff at VideoCom Home Entertainment, Inc. Most of Eduardo's coworkers agreed that he was the ideal person to get the promotion. Eduardo got along with everyone. He was the "informal leader" among his six coworkers.

Honeywell Limited
http://www.
honeywell.ca/

For example, when Carlos and Victoria argued over how a customer's order should have been processed, it was Eduardo who would get "both sides of the story"—usually first from Carlos and then from Victoria. When Imtez was unhappy about something or someone around the office—which was most of the time—Imtez would turn to Eduardo for a sounding board.

And when Rosalie wanted some information about the "facts" of a rumour, she would go to Eduardo. Rosalie found Eduardo very level-headed about most situations. Eduardo and Rosalie had some good discussions, and she would frequently ask his opinion about a lot of things—from changes occurring in management and the organization to conflicts within the office staff and among other employees in the store. Yes, Eduardo was the person for the job—even Mary and Liesl spoke up to say that Eduardo would be able to represent their interests to management better than any other person in the office. In her heart, however, Liesl had really wanted the job for herself.

RESPONDING TO THIS CASE

1. Identify some of Eduardo's potential conflict problems in this case and discuss ways to resolve them.

2. Apply the five basic conflict-resolution techniques to the conflicts you identified.

3. Do you think Eduardo will need to stimulate conflict in his department? Why or why not?

4. What are some of the ethical ways Eduardo can use politicking to his advantage? What pitfalls should he avoid that may have undertones of unethical politicking?

5. How do you think Eduardo's relationships will change with his coworkers when he becomes their supervisor? How should he prepare for this change?

6. What advice would you give Eduardo about politics and conflict to assure his department runs smoothly and he is successful as a supervisor?

13

MANAGING CHANGE AND STRESS

LEARNING OBJECTIVES

After reading this chapter, you should be able to:

1. Contrast the old and contemporary views of change.
2. Explain why people resist change.
3. Identify ways supervisors can reduce resistance to change.
4. List the steps in changing negative employee attitudes.
5. Define *stress*.
6. Explain what brings about employee stress.
7. Contrast Type A and Type B behaviour.

CHAPTER OUTLINE

PERFORMING EFFECTIVELY

FORCES FOR CHANGE
New Technologies
Environmental Dynamics
Internal Forces
Assessing Yourself: How Ready Are You for Coping with Work-Related Change?
Can You Serve as a Change Agent?

CHANGING PERSPECTIVES ON CHANGE
The Old View of Change
The Contemporary View of Change
Will You Face a World of Constant and Chaotic Change?

RESISTANCE TO CHANGE
Habit
Threat to Job or Income
Fear of the Unknown
Selective Perception
Threat to Expertise
Threat to Established Power Relationships
Threat to Interpersonal Relationships

REDUCING RESISTANCE TO CHANGE
Build Trust
Pop Quiz
Open Channels of Communication
Involve Employees
Provide Incentives

WORK STRESS
Building a Supervisory Skill: Changing Employee Attitudes
What Is Stress?

Sources of Work Stress
The Symptoms of Stress
Companies Take Action on Stress
Something to Think About

FROM CONCEPTS TO SKILLS: STRESS REDUCTION
Assessing Yourself: How Well Can You Identify Stressful Events?
Skill Basics
Applying Your Skills
Pop Quiz

UNDERSTANDING THE BASICS
Summary
Key Terms and Concepts
Reviewing Your Knowledge
Answers to the Pop Quizzes

PERFORMING YOUR JOB
Case 13.A: AutoZone
Case 13.B: Tax Time at Arthur Andersen

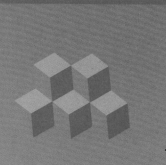

Nick Thomas was a bit tired. He'd spent the previous night partying into the wee hours with a group of close friends from work. They were celebrating Nick's thirtieth anniversary at the Alcoa plant. He said, "I came to work here right out of college, as a production scheduler. The supervisor at the time was seriously injured in a car accident that November and had to take early retirement. I was promoted to supervisor. I've been in the job ever since."

When asked to recall how his job had changed over thirty years, he smiled. "Boy, other than my title, I don't think anything is the same. In those early days, I had a secretary. She typed all my correspondence and made up the schedules and reports. Had to make three copies of everything—and she did that with carbon paper. Do you remember carbon paper? If I wanted to know the status of an order or whether a certain product was in inventory, I'd have to make a few calls.

"Like now, I spent a lot of time in meetings. But the meetings are different nowadays. And, of course, the people in my department are very different now. When I started, I had six people reporting to me. All were high school graduates, but I was the only one who had any college or university. They were all hourly people. They had to punch in and out on a time clock. They looked to me for answers all the time. They expected me to tell them what to do.

"Oh yeah, I almost forgot. We used to get this quarterly newsletter from the head honcho. He'd describe all the things the company was planning to do. Now we have a closed-circuit television system throughout the company and the top brass put on question-and-answer sessions every Friday afternoon.

"It's a different world here today. I have no secretary. I do all my own correspondence and reports on my computer. The photocopier replaced carbon paper; then a few years back, e-mail replaced making paper copies. It used to take four days to get a physical order form from a sales office. We relied on the mail back then. Now we receive orders by fax—we have them minutes after the salesperson closes a deal. Thirty years ago, it would take a couple of phone calls and a half-hour or more to check on the status of an order. It takes me about twenty seconds to do it now. Our information system tracks every order and I can access that data from the computer here on my desk. While I still spend an hour or more every day in meetings, for most of them I never leave my office. Our computers are all networked, so we just do electronic meetings.

Alcoa Home
http://www.alcoa.com/

"But maybe the biggest change has to do with the people I work with. My boss and his boss all have graduate degrees. Everyone in my department is a college or university graduate. They're a lot smarter than the schedulers we had thirty years ago. And they want to be challenged more. I let them organize and monitor their own work. They're all paid on a monthly basis rather than hourly. They come and go as they wish. They're very responsible. If they need to work an hour or two extra or come in on Saturdays to get a project complete, they do it. Instead of telling them what to do, I'm basically here to coordinate production jobs, provide direction for the department, communicate with upper management, and help solve problems that my people need help with. I'm sort of a resource person."

FIGURE 13-1

Production scheduling at this Alcoa plant has changed dramatically over the last thirty years.

If it weren't for *change*, the supervisor's job would be relatively easy. Planning would be without problems because tomorrow would be no different from today. Given that the environment would be free from uncertainty, there would be no need to adapt. Decision making would be dramatically simplified because the outcome of each alternative could be predicted with almost certain accuracy. It would, indeed, simplify the supervisor's job if, for example, no new products were introduced, government regulations were never modified, technology remained the same, or employees' needs didn't change.

However, change is an organizational reality. Handling change is an integral part of every supervisor's job. The forces that are "out there" simply demand it!

FORCES FOR CHANGE

FIGURE 13-2

To cope with the stress of a pharmaceutical business growing at 30 per cent per month, Neil Skelding, former President of Pharmex, moved the company to premises that will accommodate five-year growth expectations.

NEW TECHNOLOGIES

Fax machines, e-mail, and computers are technological changes that have affected Nick Thomas's job. If you talk to supervisors at Canada Post, they'll tell you how automated readers and sorters have changed the jobs of those responsible for sorting the mail. Take a look at today's automobile assembly lines. Thousands of jobs on these assembly lines have been replaced with automated robots. Few jobs today have not been directly affected by technological change.

The introduction of new equipment, tools, methods, automated machinery, and computerization allows employees and supervisors to do their jobs better and faster. We can expect that technological changes will continue to modify the way work is done. Most importantly, because these technological changes tend to be focused at the operating level, supervisors will have the primary responsibility for introducing and managing these change efforts.

ENVIRONMENTAL DYNAMICS

Changes going on outside the organization can affect supervisors. These changes include new government regulations, changing social and political trends, new tax laws, changes in labour market conditions, and new strategies taken by competitors. For example, when human rights legislation was passed, many supervisors had to fill out additional reports, modify historical hiring criteria, and participate in the redesign of physical facilities to reduce barriers for the disabled. Similarly, the trend toward supervisors having wider spans of control has been largely driven by global competition and the need for organizations to cut costs.

Don Bray, partner in S.C.I.L., a construction and renovation company serving the Greater Toronto area, says high unemployment impacted their business in two ways. First, the recession dried up the bigger construction projects. Second, many unemployed professionals turned "handyman," undercutting the bidding process. Add in the underground economy that developed in reaction to the G.S.T., and business became a challenge.

INTERNAL FORCES

In addition to technological and environmental factors, internal forces can stimulate the need for change. These internal forces include changes in the organization's overall strategy, reorganizations, changes in the composition of the workforce, introduction of new equipment, and the need to modify employee attitudes.

When top management redefines or modifies its strategy, it often introduces a host of changes. As an example, Hughes Aircraft Co. has recently converted its strategy from focusing almost exclusively on defence contracts, to applying its military expertise in satellites and electronics to commercial products. In so doing, Hughes management has had to restructure its research and development, production, and marketing units. An organization's workforce is rarely static. Its composition changes in terms of age, education, gender, and ethnicity. The increasing number of women and minorities in the workforce has required many supervisors to become more sensitive to diversity and to change some of their previous practices. The introduction of new equipment represents another internal force for change. Employees may have their jobs redesigned, need to undergo training to operate the new equipment, or be required to establish new interaction patterns within their formal work group. Employee attitudes, such as increased job dissatisfaction, may lead to increased absenteeism, more voluntary resignations, and even strikes. Such events will, in turn, often lead to changes in supervisory practices.

Assessing Yourself

HOW READY ARE YOU FOR COPING WITH WORK-RELATED CHANGE?

Instructions: Listed below are some statements a supervisor made about working in a large, successful corporation. If your job had these characteristics, how would you react to them? After each statement are five letters, A to E. Circle the letter that best describes how you think you would react according to the following scale:

A I would enjoy this very much; it's completely acceptable.
B This would be enjoyable and acceptable most of the time.
C I'd have no reaction to this feature one way or another,
   or it would be about equal parts enjoyable and unpleasant.
D This feature would be somewhat unpleasant for me.
E This feature would be very unpleasant for me.

1. I regularly spend 30 to 40 per cent
    of my time in meetings.   A   B   C   D   E

2. A year and a half ago, my job did not exist,
    and I have been essentially inventing it as
    I go along.   A   B   C   D   E

3. The responsibilities I either assume or am assigned consistently exceed the authority I have for discharging them.

A B C D E

4. At any given moment in my job, I have on the average about a dozen phone calls to be returned.

A B C D E

5. There seems to be very little relationship in my job between the quality of my performance and my actual pay and benefits.

A B C D E

6. About two weeks a year of formal supervisory training is needed in my job just to stay current.

A B C D E

7. Because we have very effective equal employment opportunity (EEO) in my company and because it is thoroughly multinational, my job consistently brings me into close working contact at a professional level with people of many races, ethnic groups, and nationalities and of both sexes.

A B C D E

8. There is no objective way to measure my effectiveness.

A B C D E

9. I report to three different bosses for different aspects of my job, and each has an equal say in my performance appraisal.

A B C D E

10. On average, about a third of my time is spent dealing with unexpected emergencies that force all scheduled work to be postponed.

A B C D E

11. When I have to have a meeting of the people who report to me, it takes my secretary most of a day to find a time when we are all available, and even then, I have yet to have a meeting where everyone is present for the entire meeting.

A B C D E

12. The college degree I earned in preparation for this type of work is now obsolete, and I probably should go back for another degree.

    A   B   C   D   E

13. My job requires that I absorb 100–200 pages per week of technical materials.

    A   B   C   D   E

14. I am out of town overnight at least one night per week.

    A   B   C   D   E

15. My department is so interdependent with several other departments in the company that all distinctions about which departments are responsible for which tasks are quite arbitrary.

    A   B   C   D   E

16. I will probably get a promotion in about a year to a job in another department that has most of these same characteristics.

    A   B   C   D   E

17. During the period of my employment here, either the entire company or the department I worked in has been reorganized every year or so.

    A   B   C   D   E

18. While there are several possible promotions I can see ahead of me, I have no real career path in an objective sense.

    A   B   C   D   E

19. While there are several possible promotions I can see ahead of me, I think I have no realistic chance of getting to the top levels of the company.

    A   B   C   D   E

20. While I have many ideas about how to make things work better, I have no direct influence on either the business policies or the personnel policies that govern my department.

    A   B   C   D   E

21. My company has recently put in an "assessment centre" where I and all other supervisors will be required to go through an extensive battery of psychological tests to assess our potential.

    A   B   C   D   E

22. My company is a defendant in an antitrust suit, and if the case comes to trial, I will probably have to testify about some decisions that were made a few years ago.   A   B   C   D   E

23. Advanced computer and other electronic office technology is continually being introduced into my division, necessitating constant learning on my part.   A   B   C   D   E

24. The computer terminal and screen I have in my office can be monitored in my bosses' offices without my knowledge.   A   B   C   D   E

SCORING

Give yourself four points for each A, three points for each B, two points for each C, one point for each D, and no points for each E. Compute your total, and divide that score by 24. Round your answer to one decimal place.

WHAT THE ASSESSMENT MEANS

While the results of this assessment are not intended to be more than suggestive, the higher your score, the more comfortable you appear to be with change. The test's author suggests analyzing scores as if they were grade point averages. In this way, a 4.0 average is an "A," a 2.0 is a "C," and scores below 1.0 "flunk." Using replies from nearly 500 students and individuals new to supervisory positions, the range of scores was found to be relatively narrow: between 1.0 and 2.2. The average score was between 1.5 and 1.6—a D+/C− sort of grade!

Source: Peter B. Vail, *Managing as a Performing Art: New Ideas for a World of Chaotic Change,* Exhibit 1, pp. 8–9. © 1989 Jossey-Bass, Inc., Publishers.

CAN YOU SERVE AS A CHANGE AGENT?

Changes within an organization need a catalyst. People who act as catalysts and assume the responsibility for overseeing the change process are called **change agents**.

Any supervisor can be a change agent. The change agent can also be a nonmanager—for example, an internal staff specialist or outside consultant whose expertise is in change implementation. For major systemwide changes, company officials will often hire outside consultants to provide advice and assistance. Because they are from the outside, they often can offer an objective perspective usually lacking in insiders. However, outside consultants may be at a disadvantage because they have an inadequate understanding of the organization's history, culture, operating procedures, and personnel. Outside consultants are also prone to initiate more drastic changes than insiders—which can be either a benefit or a disadvantage— because they do not have to live with the repercussions of the change after it is implemented. In contrast, supervisors who act as change agents may be more thoughtful (and possibly more cautious) because they must live with the consequences of their actions.

Change agents
People who act as catalysts and assume the responsibility for overseeing the change process

CHANGING PERSPECTIVES ON CHANGE

Supervisors historically treated the management of change as a periodic activity with a distinct beginning and end. A problem surfaced that required a change. That change would then be introduced, and the situation would return to a state of equilibrium. This perspective on change is no longer very accurate. Today's supervisor is increasingly finding that change is a constant. It has no distinct beginning or end. Supervisors are having to learn to manage in a world of continuous change.

THE OLD VIEW OF CHANGE

The old view of change is best illustrated in the classic three-step model of the **change process**[1] (See Figure 13-3).

Change process
Unfreezing the status quo, changing to a new state, and refreezing the new change to make it permanent

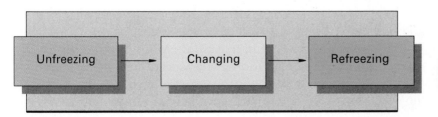

Unfreezing → Changing → Refreezing

FIGURE 13-3
The three step change process

According to this model, successful change requires unfreezing the status quo, changing to a new state, and refreezing the new change to make it permanent. The status quo can be considered an equilibrium state. To move from this equilibrium, unfreezing is necessary. It can be achieved in one of three ways:

1. The driving forces that direct behaviour away from the status quo can be increased.
2. The restraining forces that hinder movement from the existing equilibrium can be decreased.
3. The two approaches can be combined.

Once unfreezing has been accomplished, the change itself can be implemented. However, the mere introduction of change does not ensure that it will take hold. The new situation therefore needs to be *refrozen* so that it can be sustained over time. Unless this last step is attended to, there is a very strong chance that the change will be short-lived and that employees will revert to the previous equilibrium state. The objective of refreezing, then, is to stabilize the new situation by balancing the driving and restraining forces.

Note how this three-step process treats change as a break in the organization's equilibrium state. The status quo has been disturbed and change is necessary to establish a new equilibrium state. This view might have been appropriate to the relatively calm environment that most organizations faced in the 1950s, 1960s, and early 1970s. But this model does not describe the world in which current supervisors must manage.

THE CONTEMPORARY VIEW OF CHANGE

The contemporary view of change takes into consideration that environments are both uncertain and dynamic. To get a feeling for what directing change might be like when you have to continually manoeuvre in uninterrupted rapids, consider going on a ski trip and facing the following scenario: The ski slopes that are open vary in length and difficulty. Unfortunately, when you start a "run," you don't know what the ski course will be. It might be a simple course, or one that is very challenging. Furthermore, you've planned your ski vacation assuming that the slopes will be open. After all, it's January—and that is prime ski time at the resort. But the course does not always open. As if that were not bad enough, on some days the slopes are closed for no apparent reason at all. Oh yes, and one more thing—lift ticket prices can change dramatically on the hour. And there is no apparent pattern to the price fluctuations.

To succeed under these conditions, you would have to be incredibly flexible and be able to respond quickly to every changing condition. Those who were too slow or too structured would have difficulty—and clearly no fun!

A growing number of supervisors are coming to accept that their job is much like what one might face on such a ski vacation. The stability and predictability of the traditional view of change may not exist. Disruptions in the status quo are not occasional and temporary, and followed by a return to "calm waters." Many of today's supervisors never get out of the rapids. They face constant change, bordering on chaos. These supervisors are being forced to play a game they've never played before, which is governed by rules that are created as the game progresses.[2]

WILL YOU FACE A WORLD OF CONSTANT AND CHAOTIC CHANGE?

Not every supervisor faces a world of constant and chaotic change. However, the set of supervisors who don't is dwindling rapidly. Few supervisors today can treat change as the occasional disturbance in an otherwise peaceful world. Doing so can put you at great risk: too much is changing too fast for anyone to be complacent. As business writer Tom Peters has aptly noted, the old saying "If it ain't broke, don't fix it" no longer applies. In its place, he suggests "If it ain't broke, you just haven't looked hard enough. Fix it anyway."[3]

RESISTANCE TO CHANGE

One of the most well-documented findings in the study of people at work is that individuals resist change. As one person once put it, "most people hate any change that doesn't jingle in their pockets."

Resistance to change surfaces in many forms. It can be overt, implicit, immediate, or deferred. It is easiest for supervisors to deal with resistance when it is overt and immediate. For instance, a change is proposed and employees quickly respond by voicing complaints, engaging in a work slowdown, threatening to go on strike, or the like. The greater challenge is managing resistance that is implicit or deferred. Implicit resistance efforts are more subtle (loss of loyalty to the organization, loss of motivation to work, increased errors or mistakes, increased absenteeism due to "sickness"), and hence more difficult to recognize. Similarly, deferred actions cloud the link between the source of the resistance and the reaction to it. A change may produce what appears to be only a minimal reaction at the time it is initiated, but then resistance surfaces weeks, months, or even years later. A single change that in and of itself might have little impact can become the straw that breaks the camel's back. Reactions to change can build up and then explode in some response that seems totally out of proportion to the particular change action it follows. The resistance, of course, has merely been deferred and stockpiled. What surfaces is a response to an accumulation of previous changes.

So why do people resist change? There are a number of reasons (see Figure 13-4).

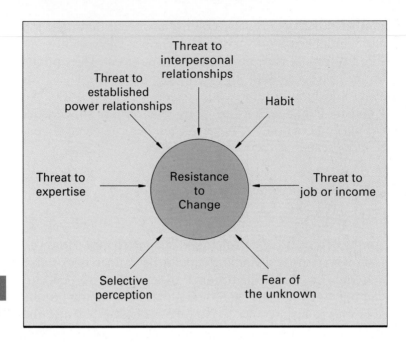

FIGURE 13-4

Why employees resist change

HABIT

As human beings, we're creatures of habit. Life is complex enough; we don't need to consider the full range of options for the hundreds of decisions we have to make every day. To cope with this complexity, we all rely on habits or programmed responses. But when confronted with change, our programmed responses are no longer appropriate. So when your department is moved to a new office building across town, it means your employees are likely to have to change many habits: waking up ten minutes earlier, taking a new set of streets to work, finding a new parking place, adjusting to the new office layout, developing a new lunch-time routine, and so on.

THREAT TO JOB OR INCOME

Employees fear any change they think may reduce their job security or income. New labour-saving equipment, for instance, may be interpreted as the forerunner of layoffs. People are also often threatened by changes in job tasks or established work routines if they are fearful that they won't be able to perform them successfully. This is particularly threatening where pay is closely tied to productivity.

FEAR OF THE UNKNOWN

Human beings don't like ambiguity. But changes substitute ambiguity and uncertainty for the known. If the introduction of a desktop publishing

FIGURE 13-5

Labour-saving equipment, like assembly-line robots, have replaced thousands of workers in automobile plants. Many auto workers fear changes because they're afraid their jobs might be eliminated.

system by a small book publisher means that editorial staff will have to learn to do their entire jobs on computers, some of these people may fear that they will be unable to learn the intricacies of the system. They may, therefore, develop a negative attitude toward working with desktop publishing or behave dysfunctionally—complaining, purposely working slowly, undermining department morale—if required to use the system.

SELECTIVE PERCEPTION

Individuals shape the world through their perceptions. Once they have created this world, it resists change. So individuals are guilty of selectively processing what they see and hear in order to keep their perceptions intact. They often hear what they want to hear. They ignore information that challenges the world they've created. For example, the book editors faced with the introduction of desktop publishing may ignore the arguments their supervisors make in explaining why the new equipment has been purchased or what potential benefits the change will provide them.

THREAT TO EXPERTISE

Changes in organizational policies and practices may threaten the expertise of specialized groups and departments. The introduction of decentralized personal computers, which allow supervisors and managers access to information directly from a company's mainframe, is an example of a change that was strongly resisted by many information systems departments in the early 1980s. Why? Because decentralized end-user computing was a threat to the specialized skills held by those in the centralized information systems departments.

THREAT TO ESTABLISHED POWER RELATIONSHIPS

Any redistribution of decision-making authority can threaten existing power relationships within an organization. Efforts by top management to empower operating employees or introduce self-managed work teams have frequently been met by resistance from supervisors who are threatened by a loss of power.

THREAT TO INTERPERSONAL RELATIONSHIPS

Work is more than a means to earn a living. The interpersonal relationships that are part of a person's job often play an important role in satisfying the individual's social needs. We look forward to going to work to interact with coworkers and make friends. Change can be a threat to those relationships. Reorganizations, transfers, and restructuring of work layouts change the people that employees work with, report to, and regularly interact with. Since such changes are often seen as threats, they tend to be resisted.

REDUCING RESISTANCE TO CHANGE

The resistance we've described to change can be overcome. We offer four specific techniques:

1. Build trust.
2. Open channels of communication.
3. Involve employees.
4. Provide incentives.

Resistance is most likely to be eliminated when supervisors implement all four of the techniques. The techniques are discussed below.

BUILD TRUST

If employees trust and have confidence in you, they're less likely to be threatened by changes you propose.

The implementation of self-directed work teams at a beverage processing plant initially met with considerable resistance because employees didn't trust management. For years, supervisors hadn't trusted their employees to make decisions; then, all of a sudden, these same supervisors were telling workers to make their own decisions. It took more than a year for employees to accept responsibility for solving their own problems.

Trust takes a long time to develop. It's also very fragile; it can be destroyed easily. What can you do to build trust? Be fair and impartial. Be consistent and predictable in your decisions and in the way you treat your employees. Develop a reputation for making good on your promises, both explicit and implied. Be supportive. Employees trust supervisors who offer praise, are good listeners, exhibit confidence in their people, and protect their interests. Finally, be candid and honest. Your people should believe that you'll tell them the truth.

OPEN CHANNELS OF COMMUNICATION

Resistance can be reduced by communicating with employees to help them see the logic of a change.

When employees receive the full facts and get misunderstandings cleared up, resistance often fades. This explains why, for example, management at Apex Environmental allows any of its 100 employees to review the company's profit and loss statements and get questions answered about the firm's financial performance. Opening communication channels,

Apex Environmental
http://www.apexenv.com/

however, will only be effective when there is a climate of trust and where the organization is truly concerned with the welfare of its employees. Improved communication is particularly effective in reducing threats created by ambiguity. For instance, when the grapevine is active with rumours of cutbacks and layoffs, honest and open communication of the true facts can be a calming force. Even if the news is bad, a clear message often wins points and opens people to accepting change. When communication is ambiguous and people are threatened, they often contrive scenarios that are considerably worse than the actual "bad news."

INVOLVE EMPLOYEES

Many organizations are asking employees to participate in planning major change programs. Why? It's difficult for individuals to resist a change decision in which they have participated. So solicit employee inputs early in the change process. When employees have been involved in a change from its beginning, they will usually actively support the change. No one wants to oppose something that he or she helped develop.

PROVIDE INCENTIVES

Our last suggestion is to make sure that people see how supporting a change is in their best interests. What's the source of their resistance? What do you control that might overcome that resistance? Are they afraid they won't be able to do a new task? Provide them with new-skills training. Or maybe provide a short paid leave of absence so they'll have time to rethink their fears, calm down, and come to the realization that their concerns are unfounded. Similarly, layoffs can become opportunities for those who remain. Jobs can be redesigned to provide new challenges and responsibilities. A pay increase, a new title, flexible work hours, or increased job autonomy are additional examples of incentives that can help reduce resistance. Polaroid Corp., for instance, wants employees to broaden their skills and become more flexible. To encourage this, it offers pay premiums of up to 10 per cent to employees who develop new skill competencies.

Polaroid
http://www.polaroid.com/

WORK STRESS

There are few places as stressful as the control tower at a major international airport where traffic controllers handle thousands of flights a day. The typical controller at Toronto's Pearson airport lands a plane every two minutes while simultaneously monitoring a half-dozen more. The pressure to keep traffic moving while, at the same time, maintaining proper

Lester B. Pearson International Airport
http://www.lbpia.toronto.on.ca/

Canadian Air Traffic Control Association
http://www.catca.ca/

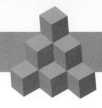

CHANGING EMPLOYEE ATTITUDES

ABOUT THE SKILL

Every employee has hundreds of attitudes on dozens of subjects. These attitudes affect department morale. Furthermore, employees tend to seek consistency between attitudes and behaviour.

STEPS IN PRACTISING THE SKILL

1. **Identify the attitude you want to change.** The place to begin is to clearly identify the dysfunctional attitude. What specifically is it that you want to change?
2. **Determine what sustains the attitude.** Once a negative attitude is identified, you will want to find out where it comes from. If you're going to change it, you need to know its source and what sustains it. Typically, attitudes grow out of 1. beliefs held by parents, teachers, and friends, which were communicated to us early in our lives; 2. previous experiences; 3. group pressures; or 4. incorrect information.
3. **Unfreeze the attitude.** Once the roots of an undesirable attitude are clear, you can begin to weaken the assumptions that underlie it. You can, for instance, provide new information, clarify incorrect assumptions, provide opportunities for the employee to gain new experiences that will counter his or her prevailing attitude, or reorganize the formal work group if it's the source of the problem.
4. **Offer an alternative attitude.** It's not enough to unfreeze a current attitude. It must then be replaced with a new, more appropriate, one.
5. **Refreeze the new attitude.** Unless the new attitude is reinforced and supported, it's likely to fade over time.

spacing and avoiding any mistakes takes a heavy toll on these controllers. Most exhibit signs of chronic stress: ulcers, high blood pressure, headaches, and upset stomachs. Others have more severe stress-related symptoms such as alcoholism, drug abuse, depression, persistent nightmares, and acute anxiety. Many controllers quit within five years on the job and few ever reach ten years.

Transport Canada conducted an investigation into sick days taken by air traffic controllers. Because of understaffing, sick days at the major Canadian airports ranged from a high of eighteen per year (Edmonton) to a low of twelve per year (Toronto). Other figures were seventeen per year (Vancouver), sixteen per year (Winnipeg) and fourteen per year (Montreal). These absences are high given a Canadian workforce average of 6.7 sick days per year.

How would you like to be an air traffic control supervisor? If you were, is there anything you could do to lessen the stress your employees experience? There *are* some things you could do, and we'll discuss them at the end of this chapter.

Work stress seems to be a growing problem. A recent survey of North American workers found that 46 per cent felt their jobs were highly stressful and 34 per cent reported that the stress was so bad they were thinking of quitting. High-stress jobs include air traffic controllers, police officers, fire fighters, emergency-room physicians, and assembly-line workers. But employees in all types of jobs are reporting increased stress levels. And change seems to be a major contributor to this increase in stress levels. In addition, the uncertain environment characterized by takeovers, mergers, restructurings, forced retirements, and mass layoffs has created a large number of employees who are overworked and stressed out. Therefore, stress is an issue that all supervisors need to pay attention to.

QUALITY TIME By Gail Machlis

FIGURE 13-6

(Drawing by Machlis. © 1993 Chronicle Features.)

WHAT IS STRESS?

The formal definition of **stress** is complex: an adaptive response resulting from any environmental action, situation, or event that places excessive psychological and/or physical demands on a person.[2] Essentially, the adaptive response we typically associate with stress includes things such as tension, anxiety, or a rush of adrenaline. The demands refer to the potential loss of something that a person desires; for instance, respect, his or her job, or a promotion.

Two conditions are necessary for a potentially stressful situation to create actual stress for a person. There must be uncertainty over the outcome and the outcome must be important. Stress is highest for those who don't know whether they will win or lose and lowest for those who think that winning or losing is a certainty. But importance is also critical. If winning or losing is an unimportant outcome, there is no stress. If keeping your job doesn't hold any importance to you, you have no reason to feel stress over having to undergo a performance review. Athletes typically experience greater stress during championship competition because there is increased importance placed on the outcome.

Keep in mind that stress, like conflict, isn't all bad. While it's typically discussed in a negative context, stress has positive value. Consider, for example, the superior performance that an athlete or stage performer gives in clutch situations. Such individuals often use stress positively to rise to the occasion and perform at or near their maximum. For many employees, the high demands associated with stress create the adrenaline kick they depend on to accomplish high quantities of work and to meet ambitious deadlines.

Neil Skelding, former president of Pharmex—a mail order drug delivery company—says resourcefulness and teamwork are keys to handling stressful situations. When a supplier cancelled a shipment without warning, Neil's staff phoned hundreds of clients, informed them of an out-of-stock situation and offering to transfer their prescriptions to another pharmacy. Neil reports, "The key was good phone communication and immediate response." From hundreds of clients, only two orders switched to another pharmacy.

SOURCES OF WORK STRESS

Work-related stress is brought about by both organizational and individual factors. As shown in Figure 13-7, these in turn are influenced by individual differences. That is, not all people in similar situations experience similar levels of stress.

If we return to S.C.I.L., Don Bray's construction company, Don points out his remedy to reduce employee stress. He feels that "employees need to know what they are expected to do in specific terms, and why."

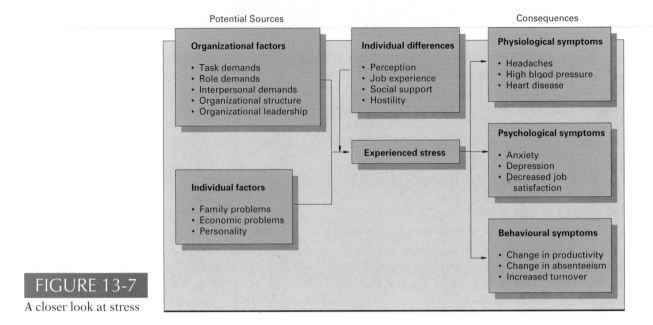

FIGURE 13-7

A closer look at stress

Don recommends that supervisors need to remove the guesswork—either let employees know that the supervisor has made the decision (no guesswork), or let them know the parameters that you, as a supervisor, have set for them to make the decision on their own. Above all, don't leave employees to guess at things that have already been decided!

ORGANIZATIONAL FACTORS

There is no shortage of factors within the organization that can cause stress. Pressures to avoid errors or complete tasks in a limited time period, a demanding supervisor, and unpleasant coworkers are a few examples (see Figure 13-8). The discussion that follows organizes stress factors into five categories: task, role, and interpersonal demands; organizational structure; and organizational leadership.

Task demands are factors related to an employee's job. They include the design of the job (autonomy, task variety, degree of automation), working conditions, and the physical work layout. Assembly lines can put pressure on people when the line's speed is perceived as excessive. The more interdependence between a person's tasks and the tasks of others, the more potential stress there is. Autonomy, on the other hand, tends to lessen stress. Jobs where temperatures, noise, or other working conditions are dangerous or undesirable can increase anxiety. So, too, can working in an overcrowded room or in a location where interruptions are constant.

Role demands relate to pressures placed on an employee as a function of the particular role he or she plays in the organization. **Role conflicts** create expectations that may be hard to reconcile or satisfy. **Role overload**

Role conflicts
Situations in which individuals are confronted by divergent role expectations

Role overload
Situations where an employee is expected to do more than time permits

What factors cause the most stress on the job? A *Wall Street Journal* survey reported:	
Factor	**Percentage Response***
Not doing the kind of work I want to	34
Coping with current job	30
Working too hard	28
Colleagues at work	21
A difficult boss	18

* Percentages exceed 100 as a result of some multiple responses.

FIGURE 13-8

Primary causes of stress at work. (*Source:* "Worries at Work," *Wall Street Journal*, April 7, 1988, p. 27. Reprinted by permission of Wall Street Journal, ©1988 Dow Jones & Company, Inc. All rights reserved worldwide.)

is experienced when the employee is expected to do more than time permits. **Role ambiguity** is created when role expectations are not clearly understood and the employee is not sure what he or she is to do.

Interpersonal demands are pressures created by other employees. Lack of social support from colleagues and poor interpersonal relationships can cause considerable stress, especially among employees with a high social need.

Organizational structure can increase stress. Excessive rules and an employee's lack of opportunity to participate in decisions that affect him or her are examples of structural variables that might be potential sources of stress.

Organizational leadership represents the managerial style of the organization's senior executives. Some chief executive officers create a culture characterized by tension, fear, and anxiety. They establish unrealistic pressures to perform in the short run, impose excessively tight controls, and routinely fire employees who don't measure up. This style of leadership flows down through the organization to affect all employees.

Role ambiguity
A situation where role expectations are not clearly understood and the employee is not sure what he or she is to do

INDIVIDUAL FACTORS

The typical employee works about forty hours a week. The experiences and problems that people encounter in the remaining nonwork hours each week can spill over to the job. Our other category, then, encompasses factors in the employee's personal life. Primarily, these factors are *family issues, personal economic problems*, and *inherent personality characteristics*.

Surveys consistently show that people hold family and personal relationships dear. Marital difficulties, the breaking off of a relationship, discipline troubles with children, and relatives with serious illnesses are examples of relationship problems that create stress for employees and that aren't left at the front door when they leave for work.

Economic problems created by individuals overextending their financial resources are another set of personal troubles that can create stress for employees and distract their attention from their work. Regardless of income level (people who make $80 000 a year seem to have as much trouble handling their finances as those who earn $18 000), some people are poor money managers or have material desires that always seem to exceed their earning capacity.

Recent studies have found that stress symptoms reported prior to beginning a job don't change much from those reported nine months later. This has led to the conclusion that some people may have an inherent tendency to accentuate negative aspects of the world in general. If true, then a significant individual factor influencing stress is a person's basic disposition. That is, stress symptoms expressed on the job may actually originate in the person's personality (see Something to Think About, page 505).

Stress factors are additive. A fact that tends to be overlooked when stress factors are reviewed individually is that stress is an additive phenomenon. Stress builds up. Each new and persistent stressor adds to an individual's stress level. A single stressor may seem relatively unimportant in and of itself, but if it is added to an already high level of stress, it can be "the straw that breaks the camel's back."

INDIVIDUAL DIFFERENCES

Some people thrive on stressful situations, while others are overwhelmed by them. What is it that differentiates people in terms of their ability to handle stress? Four individual difference factors have been found to be important: perception, experience, social support, and hostility.

One person's fear that he'll lose his job because his company is laying off personnel may be perceived by another as an opportunity to get a large severance allowance and start his own business. Similarly, what one employee perceives as an efficient and challenging work environment may be viewed as threatening and demanding by others. So stress potential doesn't lie in objective conditions. Rather, it lies in an employee's *perception* and interpretation of those conditions.

Experience is said to be a great teacher. It can also be a great stress-reducer. Think back to your first date or your first few days in college. For most of us, the uncertainty and newness of these situations created stress. But as we gained experience, that stress disappeared or at least significantly decreased. The same phenomenon seems to apply to work situations. Why? One explanation is the process of selective withdrawal. Voluntary turnover is more likely among people who experience more stress. Therefore, people who remain with the organization longer are those with more stress-resistant traits, or those who are more resistant to the stress characteristics of their organization. A second explanation is that people eventually develop coping mechanisms to deal with stress. Because this takes time, senior members of the organization are more likely to be fully adapted and experience less stress.

FIGURE 13-9

The social support that these workers at a Goodyear plant give each other buffers the impact of stress.

There is increasing evidence that *social support*—collegial relationships with coworkers and supervisors—can buffer the impact of stress. The logic underlying this conclusion is that social support acts as a palliative, lessening the negative effects of even high-stress jobs.

For much of the 1970s and 1980s, a great deal of attention was directed at what became known as **Type A behaviour**. It was frequently seen as the primary individual difference factor in explaining who would be affected by stress. Type A behaviour is characterized by feelings of a chronic sense of time urgency and by an excessive competitive drive. Type As try to do more and more in less and less time. The opposite of Type A is **Type B behaviour**. Type Bs never suffer from time urgency or impatience. Until quite recently, it was believed that Type As were more likely to experience stress on and off the job. A closer analysis of the evidence, however, has produced new conclusions. It has been found that only the *hostility* and anger associated with Type A behaviour is actually associated with the negative effects of stress. The chronically angry, suspicious, and distrustful person is the one at risk of stressing out.

Type A behaviour
Aggressive involvement in a chronic, incessant struggle to achieve more and more in less and less time

Type B behaviour
The behaviour of a person who is rarely harried by the desire to obtain a wildly increasing number of things or participate in an endlessly growing series of events in an ever-decreasing amount of time

THE SYMPTOMS OF STRESS

What signs indicate that an employee's stress level might be too high? There are three general ways that stress reveals itself. These include physiological, psychological, and behavioural symptoms.

Most of the early interest over stress focused heavily on health-related or *physiological* concerns. This was attributed to the realization that high stress levels result in changes in metabolism, increased heart and breathing rates, increased blood pressure, headaches, and increased risk of heart attacks. Because detecting many of these symptoms requires the skills of trained medical personnel, their immediate and direct relevance to supervisors is negligible.

Of greater importance to supervisors are psychological and behavioural symptoms of stress. These are things that can be witnessed in the person. The *psychological symptoms* can be seen as increased tension and anxiety, boredom, or procrastination—which can all lead to productivity decreases. So too, can the *behaviourally-related symptoms*—changes in eating habits, increased smoking or substance consumption, rapid speech, or sleep disorders. The astute supervisor, upon witnessing such symptoms, does what he or she can to assist the employee in reducing stress levels.

COMPANIES TAKE ACTION ON STRESS

With the annual cost of stress in Canadian companies exceeding $12 billion, Canadian companies are implementing a variety of stress-reducing options including flextime (49 per cent of employers), job sharing (19 per cent), and part-time pro-rated benefits (30 per cent). These companies are responding to the needs of a very different workforce in which:

- 62 per cent of all husband-and-wife families have both spouses working
- 66 per cent of all women with children under 16 work outside the home
- 16 per cent of workers report that they care for elderly members of their family

Much of the stress in the Canadian workforce seems to be centred on the new generation of working moms and dads. This group is vulnerable to work/family stress caused by raising their own families as well as caring for elder family members. Companies are beginning to look at options to give greater flexibility in handling both work and personal responsibilities.

Bank of Montreal
http://www.bmo.com/

For example, the Bank of Montreal has implemented a number of policies to help its employees deal with stress. Policies include family emergency days; unpaid leaves of up to two years for personal reasons; flexible work options; telecommuting; condensed work weeks; and child care and elder-care referral services.

In a similar way, Island Telephone in Charlottetown, P.E.I. has a number of supportive programs to help its employees deal with stress. The company offers stress management seminars targeting both front line and management employees. In addition, the company subsidizes fitness memberships, and funds a complete E.A.P. (Employee Assistance Program) with a variety of counselling services.

Work/Family Directions, Inc.
http://www.wfd.com/

Although many firms have recognized the need to address work/family stress, Hal Morgan of Work/Family Directions says that widespread support for work/family programs is a gradual process. Ambitious programs remain few and far between. In many cases, employers have adopted some benefits, but have resisted the global rethink of their employee policies that's necessary for real change to occur.

Below are twenty statements. Use the following scale in responding to each statement:

4 = all the time
3 = often
2 = sometimes
1 = never

1. I'm exhausted by daily demands at work, college, and home. 4 3 2 1

2. My stress is caused by outside forces beyond my control. 4 3 2 1

3. I'm trapped by circumstances that I just have to live with. 4 3 2 1

4. No matter how hard I work to stay on top of my schedule, I can't get caught up. 4 3 2 1

5. I have financial obligations that I can't seem to meet. 4 3 2 1

6. I dislike my work, but I can't take the risk of making a career change (or if not working: I dislike college, but can't take the risk of dropping out). 4 3 2 1

7. I'm dissatisfied with my personal relationships. 4 3 2 1

8. I feel responsible for the happiness of people around me. 4 3 2 1

9. I'm embarrassed to ask for help. 4 3 2 1

10. I don't know what I want out of life. 4 3 2 1

11. I'm disappointed that I have not achieved what I had hoped for. 4 3 2 1

12. No matter how much success I have, I feel empty. 4 3 2 1

13. If the people around me were more competent, I would feel happier. 4 3 2 1

14. People let me down. 4 3 2 1

15. I stew in my anger rather than express it.	4	3	2	1
16. I become enraged and resentful when I am hurt.	4	3	2	1
17. I can't take criticism.	4	3	2	1
18. I'm afraid I'll lose my job (or fail school).	4	3	2	1
19. I don't see the value of expressing sadness or grief.	4	3	2	1
20. I don't trust that things will work out.	4	3	2	1

After rating each statement, total your score for the twenty items. Scores of 20–29 indicate a high degree of control, self-esteem, and low stress levels. Scores of 30–49 suggest that your occasional negative self-talk causes you to feel anxious in stressful situations, thus causing moderate levels of stress. Scores of 50–69 indicate a relatively high level of stress. This might indicate you feel trapped. Scores of 70 or more indicate very high stress levels—indicating life has become one crisis and struggle after another for you.

Using this questionnaire as a guide, describe the kinds of things that are causing stress in your life. How are you handling this stress? Do you feel successful? Why or why not? For those who have low stress, what tips could you offer to others for coping with the stress?

Source: From *Stress to Strength,* by R. S. Eliot, M.D. © 1994 by Robert S. Eliot, M.D. Used by permission of Bantam Books, a division of Bantam Doubleday Dell Publishing Group, Inc.

STRESS REDUCTION

If employee stress levels are too high in your department, is there anything you can do? The answer is a resounding yes. In this section, we'll review some of your options.

ASSESSING YOURSELF: HOW WELL CAN YOU IDENTIFY STRESSFUL EVENTS?

Which life events typically create the greatest stress? To test your knowledge, rank-order the following twelve events from the most stressful (rank number 1) to least stressful (number 12). Note that positive events can cause stress as well as negative ones.

		Rank
1.	Divorce	_____
2.	Being fired at work	_____
3.	Minor violation of the law such as receiving a traffic ticket	_____
4.	Changing to a different line of work	_____
5.	Death of a spouse	_____
6.	Outstanding personal achievement	_____
7.	Major changes in working hours or conditions	_____
8.	Foreclosure on a mortgage or loan	_____
9.	Gaining a new family member through birth, adoption, or a relative moving in	_____
10.	Major personal injury or illness	_____
11.	Major change in responsibilities at work such as a promotion, demotion, or lateral transfer	_____
12.	Marriage	_____

Source: Based on T.H. Holmes and R.H. Rahe, "The Social Readjustment Scale," *Journal of Psychosomatic Research,* 11 (1967), p. 216.

SCORING DIRECTIONS AND KEY

To find out how you did, transpose your ranking numbers to Column A below. The numbers in Column B represent the correct ranking (from most to least stressful). Now subtract Column B from Column A for each event and put that number in Column C. In Column D, calculate the square of the difference you calculated in Column C e.g., $3^2=9$).

Event	Column A	Column B	Column C	Column D
1	___	5	___	___
2	___	1	___	___
3	___	10	___	___
4	___	12	___	___
5	___	2	___	___
6	___	9	___	___
7	___	4	___	___
8	___	8	___	___
9	___	11	___	___
10	___	6	___	___
11	___	7	___	___
12	___	3	___	___

Total ___ ÷ 12 = _____

Sum up the total of Column D and divide by 12. The result is a measure of variation. The lower the number, the better you are at identifying the stressfulness of various events. An excellent variation score would be 10 or less.

SKILL BASICS

Low-to-moderate levels of employee stress may not require your attention. The reason, as we noted earlier in the chapter, is that such levels of stress can be functional and can lead to higher employee performance. But high levels of stress, or even low levels sustained over long periods of time, can lead to reduced employee performance and thus require supervisory action.

While a limited amount of stress may benefit an employee's performance, don't expect employees to see it that way. From the individual's standpoint, even low levels of stress are likely to be perceived as undesirable. It's not unlikely, therefore, that you and your employees will differ on what constitutes an acceptable level of stress on the job. What you may consider a positive stimulus that keeps the adrenaline running may be seen as excessive pressure by your employees. Keep this in mind as we discuss techniques for reducing stress.

SELECT EMPLOYEES WITH THE SPECIFIC JOB IN MIND

While certain jobs are more stressful than others, we know that individuals differ in their response to stress situations. Selection and placement decisions should take these facts into consideration. Match personalities to the demands of the job. And remember that, especially in stressful jobs, experienced individuals are likely to adapt better and perform their jobs more effectively.

USE GOALS

In Chapter 2, you learned that individuals perform better when they have specific and challenging goals, and receive feedback on how well they are progressing toward these goals. The use of goals can also reduce stress. Specific goals that employees believe are attainable reduce the stress caused by unrealistic expectations. Additionally, goal feedback reduces uncertainties as to actual job performance. The result is less employee frustration, role ambiguity, and stress.

ENCOURAGE TIME MANAGEMENT

As discussed in Chapter 2, many people manage their time poorly. However, the well-organized employee can often accomplish twice as much as the person who is poorly organized. The understanding and use of basic time-management principles can help individuals better cope with job demands.

REDESIGN JOBS TO ALIGN WITH INDIVIDUAL PREFERENCES

Redesigning jobs to give employees more responsibility, meaningful work, autonomy, and increased feedback can reduce stress because these factors give the employee greater control over work activities and lessen dependence on others. Of course, not all employees want enriched jobs. The right job redesign for some employees might then be *less* responsibility and *increased* division of labour. If individuals prefer structure and routine, standardizing the job should also reduce uncertainties and stress levels.

LET EMPLOYEES PARTICIPATE IN DECISION MAKING

Role stress is detrimental to a large extent because employees feel uncertain about goals, expectations, how they'll be evaluated, and the like. By giving employees a voice in those decisions that directly affect their job performance, you can increase employee control and reduce this role stress.

PROVIDE SOCIAL SUPPORT

Having friends, family, or colleagues to talk to provides an outlet when stress levels become excessive. Helping employees expand their social support networks can be a means to reduce tension. Having someone else to hear a problem can provide a more objective perspective on a given situation. Interestingly, the value of social support in lessening stress may be an important, but rarely mentioned, advantage provided by work teams.

INCREASE FORMAL COMMUNICATION

Increasing formal communication with employees reduces uncertainty by lessening role ambiguity and role conflict. When employees think they're being kept "in the dark,'" stress levels rise. When you provide "the light," stress should decline.

ENCOURAGE EMPLOYEES TO EXERCISE AND RELAX

Noncompetitive physical exercise such as aerobics, race walking, jogging, swimming, and riding a bicycle have long been recommended by physicians as a way to deal with excessive stress levels. These forms of exercise increase heart capacity, lower at-rest heart rate, provide a mental diversion from work pressures, and offer a means to "let off steam."

Employees can also be encouraged to practice relaxation techniques such as meditation, hypnosis, and biofeedback. Fifteen or twenty minutes a day of deep relaxation releases tension and provides a person with a pronounced sense of peacefulness.

Some organizations offer wellness programs that focus on the employees' total physical and mental condition. For example, they typically provide workshops to help people quit smoking, control alcohol use, lose weight, and eat better. If your organization offers such programs, encourage your employees to participate.

APPLYING YOUR SKILLS

Complete the following questionnaire by circling one number in each line across. To what extent does each of the following sentences fit as a description of you?

	Very true	Quite true	Some-what true	Not very true	Not at all true
1. I "roll with the punches" when problems come up.	1	2	3	4	5
2. I spend almost all of my time thinking about my work.	5	4	3	2	1
3. I treat other people as individuals and care about their feelings and opinions.	1	2	3	4	5
4. I recognize and accept my own limitations and assets.	1	2	3	4	5
5. There are quite a few people I could describe as "good friends."	1	2	3	4	5
6. I enjoy using my skills and abilities both on and off the job.	1	2	3	4	5
7. I get bored easily.	5	4	3	2	1
8. I enjoy meeting and talking with people who have different ways of thinking about the world.	1	2	3	4	5
9. Often in my job I "bite off more than I can chew."	5	4	3	2	1
10. I'm usually very active on weekends with projects or recreation.	1	2	3	4	5
11. I prefer working with people who are very much like myself.	5	4	3	2	1
12. I work primarily because I have to survive, not necessarily because I enjoy what I do.	5	4	3	2	1
13. I believe I have a realistic picture of my personal strengths and weakness.	1	2	3	4	5
14. Often I get into arguments with people who don't think my way.	5	4	3	2	1
15. Often I have trouble getting much done on my job.	5	4	3	2	1
16. I'm interested in a lot of different topics.	1	2	3	4	5

	Very true	Quite true	Some-what true	Not very true	Not at all true
17. I get upset when things don't go my way.	5	4	3	2	1
18. Often I'm not sure how I stand on a controversial topic.	5	4	3	2	1
19. I'm usually able to find a way around anything that blocks me from an important goal.	1	2	3	4	5
20. I often disagree with my boss or others at work.	5	4	3	2	1

SCORING AND INTERPRETATION

The author of this questionnaire believes that people who cope with stress effectively have five characteristics.

1. They know themselves well and accept their own strengths and weaknesses.
2. They have a variety of interests off the job, and they are not total "workaholics."
3. They exhibit a variety of reactions to stress, rather than always getting a headache or always becoming depressed.
4. They are accepting of others who have values or styles different from their own.
5. They are active and productive both on and off the job.

Add together the numbers you circled for the four questions contained in each of the five coping scales.

Coping scale	Add together your responses to these questions	Your score (write in)
Knows self	4, 9, 13, 18	_____
Many interests	2, 5, 7, 16	_____
Variety of reactions	1, 11, 17, 19	_____
Accepts other's values	3, 8, 14, 20	_____
Active and productive	6, 10, 12, 15	_____

Then, add the five scores together for your overall total score: _____

Scores on each of the five areas can vary between 5 and 20. Scores of 12 or above suggest that it might perhaps be useful to direct more attention to the area.

The overall total score can range between 20 and 100. Scores of 60 or more may suggest some general difficulty in coping on the dimensions covered.

Source: McLean, A. A. *Work Stress* (Reading, MA: Addison-Wesley, 1979), pp. 126–27. Copyright © 1976 by Management Decision Systems, Inc. Reprinted by permission.

GROUP INTERACTION

Break into groups of three or four. Compare your scale and total scores. Discuss what you might be able to do if your score is high.

Have the two people in each group with the highest score and lowest score enact a role play. The person with the lowest score is the supervisor; the person with the highest is the employee. Assume that the supervisor has concluded that the employee seems to be acting strangely recently on his or her job. You think high stress may be part of the problem. Conduct a counselling session with the employee to discuss what you (the supervisor) might do to help the employee reduce his or her stress level.

5. For potential stress to become actual stress, which two conditions must exist?
   a. uncertainty and importance
   b. people and organizations
   c. certainty and importance
   d. uncertainty and risk
6. What are the three symptoms of stress? Which one is least important to detect in those one supervises?
7. Role conflict refers to a situation where jobs are ill-defined. True or False?
8. Indicate which of the following statements is true:
   a. The use of goals can reduce stress.
   b. Enriched jobs will always reduce stress.
   c. Letting employees participate in decisions that affect their performance will give them more control and, therefore, more stress.
   d. Increasing formal communication will create more stress through overwhelming people with information.

SUMMARY

This summary is organized by the Learning Objectives.

1. The old view of change treats change as a break in the organization's equilibrium state. Change is initiated and then stabilized at a new equilibrium. The contemporary view of change is that it is constant. Disequilibrium is the natural state.

2. People resist change out of habit, fear of the unknown, selective perception, or if they perceive the change as a threat to their job, income, expertise, established power relationships, or interpersonal relationships.

3. Supervisors can reduce resistance by building trust, opening channels of communication, involving employees in the change decisions, and by providing incentives to employees for accepting change.

4. The five steps in changing attitudes are:
   1. Identify the attitude you want to change.
   2. Determine what sustains the attitude.
   3. Unfreeze the attitude.
   4. Offer an alternative attitude.
   5. Refreeze the new attitude.

5. Stress is an adaptive response resulting from any environmental action, situation, or event that places excessive psychological and/or physical demands on a person.

6. Stress comes from organizational factors such as task and role demands, interpersonal demands, and structural variables; it can also be caused by individual factors such as family problems, economic problems, and personality variables.

7. Type A behaviour is characterized by a chronic sense of time urgency and an excessive competitive drive. Type B behaviour is the opposite—characterized by an absence of time urgency or impatience.

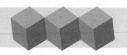
KEY TERMS AND CONCEPTS

Attitudes
Change agents
Change process
Role ambiguity
Role conflict

Role overload
Stress
Type A behaviour
Type B behaviour

REVIEWING YOUR KNOWLEDGE

1. Give several examples of environmental forces that might affect supervisors and require changes in a department.
2. Describe the three-step model of the change process.
3. What signals or cues might tell you that an employee is resistant to a change you're planning to implement?
4. What is selective perception and how is it related to change resistance?
5. How does building trust lessen change resistance?
6. Why should supervisors be concerned with an employee's work-related attitudes?
7. What happens if an attitude change is not refrozen?
8. Is all stress bad? Discuss.
9. How can supervisors reduce employee stress?
10. Do supervisors have the right to inquire about, or try to help employees deal with, stresses that result from factors outside the job? Discuss.

ANSWERS TO THE POP QUIZZES

1. **a. a change agent.**
2. According to Tom Peters, supervisors must recognize that the work world is rapidly changing. Fighting to maintain the status quo may prove harmful to a department. Consequently, supervisors must continually look for ways to do things better and more effectively—even those things that appear to work well now. The issue is: will it work well tomorrow given the "chaos" surrounding the department? Peters's quote implies that a supervisor must always be preparing for "tomorrow."
3. **False.** The correct order of the traditional view of change is unfreezing—changing—refreezing.
4. **b. is consistent with dynamic environmental forces.** The rapidly changing environmental forces often create a chaotic work environment, one similar to "shooting the rapids."
5. **a. uncertainty and importance.** These two elements are critical in creating stressful situations.
6. There are three general ways that stress reveals itself. These include physiological, psychological, and behavioural symptoms. Because detecting such things as changes in metabolism, increased heart and breathing rates, increased blood pressure, headaches, and increased risk of heart attacks requires the skills of trained medical personnel, the immediate and direct relevance of physiological stress symptoms to supervisors is negligible.
7. **False.** Role conflict refers to a situation where role expectations are hard to reconcile or satisfy.
8. **a. The use of goals can reduce stress.** Through the process of setting goals, the employee better understands expectations, reducing ambiguity and frustration.

CASE 13.A

AutoZone

Ramesh Patel really enjoys his supervisory job at AutoZone because he enjoys helping people. Ramesh is what AutoZone calls an "extra miler"—he does what is necessary to get the job done. Ramesh and his coworkers like sharing success stories and "cheering" their company. Ramesh also enjoys change—for example, learning to use the electronic training manuals that can be updated easily and are accessible at point-of-sale terminals.

Ramesh likes to tell people about AutoZone, a major provider of auto parts for vehicle maintenance and services such as free testing of starters, alternators, and batteries. Ramesh is proud of the work he does and wears the AutoZone uniform proudly.

However, Ramesh is concerned about one of his employees, Manuel Fuentes. Ramesh believes Manuel has a lot of potential, but he seems preoccupied most of the time. Manuel is reluctant to troubleshoot problems for customers and is having more and more difficulty organizing his work. He almost had to be forced to use the point-of-sale terminals when they were installed. And there is other electronic equipment at Manuel's disposal, but he avoids anything that is new or requires change in his work. In fact, Manuel will not try any of the ideas that so many of the company employees share with each other, and, of course, Manuel never shares any of his ideas.

Ramesh has tried to get Manuel to become friends with some of the other workers, but the more Ramesh tries, the farther Manuel seems to retreat into his shell. Ramesh is worried about Manuel's success at AutoZone, or anywhere for that matter, if he continues to insulate himself from his coworkers and the technological changes that are occurring so rapidly around him.

RESPONDING TO THIS CASE

1. What are some of the resistors to change that Manuel seems to be facing?
2. What does Ramesh need to learn about Manuel to understand why he is so resistant to change? Why should Ramesh be concerned?
3. How can Ramesh help Manuel reduce his resistance to change?
4. Outline the sources of stress that may be affecting Manuel's behaviour. What can Ramesh do to help Manual deal with his stress?

CASE 13.B

Tax Time at Arthur Andersen

Tax time is always the busiest time of the year for the accountants and most other employees at Arthur Andersen & Co., one of the "Big Six" chartered accounting firms. Harold Rabalais, one of the supervisors of an information processing centre at Arthur Andersen & Co., knows that the hassles of tax time will be rolling around soon. It is his job to ensure the centre's electronic equipment is serviced prior to their busy season. He must be certain he has the necessary materials and supplies that will be so crucial at this time. He also must hire part-time employees and schedule regular employees for longer hours.

Harold sees to it that work is scheduled, processed, and disseminated accurately and efficiently. Timing is vital because so many people depend on his department for production of the completed documents. And the tax deadline means there is no room for delays. Harold really likes his job, but it seems that tax time is becoming more and more stressful for him and his employees. It seems that during the tax period, absenteeism increases significantly among his employees—a problem that complicates departmental scheduling. He also thinks the annual tax time is becoming longer each year—at least the employees talk about it more. Most of the employees feel that the extra pay they can get with overtime doesn't reduce the pressures and stress that tax time brings with it.

Arthur Andersen
http://www.
arthurandersen.com/

RESPONDING TO THIS CASE

1. Describe why stress may be costly to Arthur Andersen & Co. Support your answer.
2. Discuss the factors that are contributing to the building of stress among information processing centre workers.
3. How does change enter into the situation described here?
4. How can Harold help to reduce the resistance to change?
5. How can Harold help to reduce stress for himself and his employees?

14

DISCIPLINING EMPLOYEES

LEARNING OBJECTIVES

After reading this chapter, you should be able to:

1. Define *discipline*.
2. Identify the four most common types of discipline problems.
3. List the typical steps in progressive discipline.
4. Explain the "hot stove" rule.
5. Describe the role of extenuating circumstances in applying discipline.
6. Explain the three legal dismissal situations.
7. Describe how a collective bargaining agreement affects the disciplining of unionized employees.

CHAPTER OUTLINE

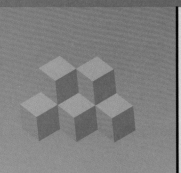

Regardless of how good a supervisor you are or how able and motivated the group of people in your department are, here is the hard truth: at some time or another, you will have to discipline a problem employee. How effective you are in performing your disciplining skills can literally have life or death consequences.

Patrick Dombroskie worked at Ontario Glove Manufacturing Company for eight years, keeping to himself as he conscientiously performed his duties. Having made his work his life, he was seething with anger when his plant supervisor "dressed him down for failing to be a team player." Known as a loner who never made waves, no one could have predicted that Dombroskie would kill the three people who played a part in his suspension. On Monday, February 3, Patrick Dombroskie casually strolled into the vice president's office and shot him in the chest. He then searched out and shot a woman who had complained about him to the plant supervisor. The third victim was that supervisor, Dombroskie's own distant cousin.

Any form of discipline can create fear or anger in employees. But the supervisor who can make the discipline process less painful for the employee, who behaves with compassion and treats the employee with dignity, is likely to find that more severe forms of disciplinary action become unnecessary. And in those cases where termination does occur, the employee is better able to handle it.

WHAT IS DISCIPLINE?

What specifically do we mean when we use the term **discipline** in the workplace? It refers to actions taken by a supervisor to enforce the organization's standards and regulations. It generally follows a typical sequence of four steps: verbal warning, written warning, suspension, and dismissal (see Figure 14-1).

The mildest form of discipline is the **verbal warning**. A verbal warning is a temporary record of a reprimand, which is placed in the supervisor's file. This verbal warning typically states the purpose, date, and outcome of the feedback session with you. If the verbal warning is effective, no further disciplinary action is needed. However, if an employee fails to improve their performance, they'll encounter more severe action—the written warning. The **written warning** is the first formal stage of the disciplinary procedure. This is because the written

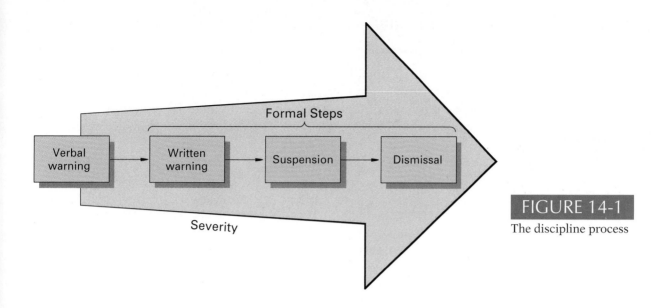

Formal Steps

Verbal warning → Written warning → Suspension → Dismissal

Severity

FIGURE 14-1
The discipline process

warning becomes part of an employee's official personnel file. In all other ways, however, the written warning is similar to the verbal warning. That is, the employee is advised in private of the violation, its effects, and potential consequences of future violations. Also, after a period of time if no further disciplinary problems arise, the warning is removed from the file.

A **suspension** or time off without pay may be the next disciplinary step, usually taken only if the prior two steps have not achieved the desired results—although exceptions do exist where suspension may be given without any prior verbal or written warning if the infraction is of a serious nature. Why would you suspend an employee? One reason is that a short lay-off, without pay, is potentially a rude awakening. It may convince the employee that you are serious, and may help him or her to fully understand and accept responsibility for following the organization's rules.

Suspension
Time off without pay; this step is usually taken only if neither verbal nor written warnings have achieved desired results.

Your ultimate disciplinary punishment is terminating employment. While **dismissal** is often used for the most serious offences, it may be the only feasible alternative if your employee's behaviour seriously interferes with a department or the organization's operation.

Dismissal
Termination of employment

While many organizations may follow the process described above, recognize that it may be bypassed if an employee's behaviour is extreme. For example, stealing, or attacking another employee with intent to inflict serious harm, may result in immediate suspension or dismissal. Regardless of any action taken, however, discipline should be fair and consistent. That is, the punishment an employee receives should be appropriate to what he or she did, and others doing the same thing should be disciplined in a like manner.

TYPES OF DISCIPLINE PROBLEMS

Employee Discipline in Small Firms
http://cber.nlu.edu/DBR/
GULBRO.htm

With very little difficulty, we could list several dozen or more infractions that supervisors might believe require disciplinary action. For simplicity's sake, we have classified the more frequent violations into four categories: attendance, on-the-job behaviours, dishonesty, and outside activities.

ATTENDANCE

The most common disciplinary problems facing supervisors undoubtedly involve attendance. For instance, in a study of 200 organizations, 60 per cent of which employed over 1000 workers, absenteeism, tardiness, abuse of sick leave, and other aspects of attendance were rated as the foremost problems by 79 per cent of the respondents.[1] Importantly, attendance problems appear to be even more widespread than those related to productivity (carelessness in doing work, neglect of duty, and not following established procedures).

ON-THE-JOB BEHAVIOURS

This blanket label includes insubordination, horseplay, fighting, gambling, failure to use safety devices, carelessness, and two of the most widely discussed problems in organizations today—alcohol and drug abuse.

DISHONESTY

Although it is not one of the more widespread employee problems confronting a supervisor, dishonesty has traditionally resulted in the most severe disciplinary actions. One study found that 90 per cent of surveyed organizations would discharge an employee for theft, even if it was only a first offence. Similarly, 88 per cent would discharge employees who were found to have falsified information on their employment applications.[2] These findings reflect the strong cultural norm against dishonesty in North America.

OUTSIDE ACTIVITIES

Our final problem category covers activities that employees engage in outside of work, but which either affect their on-the-job performance or generally reflect negatively on the organization's image. Included here are unauthorized strike activity, outside criminal activities, and working for a competing organization.

DISCIPLINE ISN'T ALWAYS THE SOLUTION

Just because you have a problem with an employee, don't assume that discipline is the automatic answer. Before you consider disciplining an employee, be sure that the employee has both the ability and the influence to correct his or her behaviour.

If an employee doesn't have the ability—that is, he or she *can't* perform—disciplinary action is not the answer. Similarly, if there are external factors beyond the employee's control that block goal attainment—for example, inadequate equipment, disruptive colleagues, or excessive noise—discipline doesn't make much sense. If an employee *can* perform but won't, then disciplinary action is called for. However, ability problems should be responded to with solutions such as skill training, on-the-job coaching, job redesign, or a job transfer. Serious personal problems that interfere with work performance are typically best met with professional counselling or a medical referral. And, of course, if there are external obstacles in the employee's way, you should act to remove them. The point is that if the cause of an employee's problem is outside his or her control, then discipline is not the answer.

BASIC TENETS OF DISCIPLINE

Based on decades of experience, supervisors have learned what works best when administering discipline. In this section, we'll review some of the lessons learned. We'll present the basic groundwork that needs to be laid prior to any punitive action, the importance of making discipline progressive, and how the "hot stove" rule can guide your actions.

Lay the Groundwork

Any disciplinary action you take should be perceived as fair and reasonable. This increases the likelihood that the employee will change his or her behaviour to align with the organization's standards, and also prevents unnecessary legal entanglements. The foundation of a fair and reasonable disciplinary climate is created by ensuring that employees are given adequate advance notice of disciplining rules and that a proper investigation precedes any action.

ADVANCE NOTICE
"The best surprise is no surprise." This phrase, used a number of years ago by a national hotel chain to describe their rooms and service, is a valid guide for supervisors. Employees have a right to know what is

expected of them and the probable consequences should they fail to meet those expectations. They should also understand just how serious different types of offences are. This information can be communicated in employee handbooks, company newsletters, posted rules, or labour contracts. It is always preferable to have these expectations in writing. This provides protection for you, the organization, and your employees.

PROPER INVESTIGATION

Fair treatment of employees demands that a proper investigation precede any decision. Employees should be treated as innocent until proven guilty. And importantly, no judgment should occur before all the relevant facts have been gathered.

As the employee's supervisor, you will typically be responsible for conducting the investigation. However, if the problem includes an interpersonal conflict between you and the employee, a neutral third party should be chosen to conduct the investigation.

The investigation should focus not only on the event that might lead to discipline but also on any related matters. This is important because these related concerns may reveal mitigating factors that will need to be considered. And, of course, the employee must be notified of the offence with which he or she is being charged so that a defence can be prepared. Remember, you have an obligation to listen objectively to the employee's interpretation and explanation of the offence. A fair and objective investigation will include identification and interviewing of any witnesses and documentation of all evidence that is uncovered.

Failure to conduct a full and impartial investigation can carry high costs. A good employee may be unjustly punished, the trust of other employees may be severely jeopardized, and you may place your organization under possible risk for financial damages should the employee file a suit.

MAKE DISCIPLINE PROGRESSIVE

The SOHO Guidebook I: Progressive Discipline
http://www.toolkit.cch. com/text/P05_7250.stm

Progressive discipline Penalties are made progressively stronger if, or when, an offence is repeated.

Punishment should be applied in steps. That is, penalties should get progressively stronger if or when an offence is repeated. As outlined at the start of this chapter, progressive disciplinary action typically begins with a verbal warning, and then proceeds through written reprimands, suspension, and finally, in the most serious cases, dismissal (see Figure 14-1). At London Life Insurance, for example, employees are given three written warnings, followed by suspension or dismissal.

The logic underlying **progressive discipline** is twofold. First, stronger penalties for repeated offences discourage repetition. Second, progressive discipline is consistent with court and arbitration rulings that mitigating factors (such as length of service, past performance record, or ambiguous organizational policies) be considered when taking disciplinary action.

FIGURE 14-2

At London Life Insurance, employees are given three written warnings. This procedure is dictated by the procedures issued by the company's Human Resources department.

FOLLOW THE "HOT STOVE" RULE

The **"hot stove" rule** is a frequently cited set of principles that can guide you in effectively disciplining an employee.[3] The name comes from the similarities between touching a hot stove and administering discipline.

Both are painful, but the analogy goes further. When you touch a hot stove, you get an *immediate* response: the burn you receive is instantaneous, leaving no doubt in your mind about the cause and the effect. You have ample *warning*: you know in advance what happens if you touch a red-hot stove. Further, the result is *consistent*: every time you touch a hot stove, you get the same response—you get burned. Finally, the result is *impartial*. Regardless of who you are, if you touch a hot stove, you will be burned. The analogy with discipline should be apparent, but let's briefly expand on each of these four points because they are central tenets in developing your disciplining skills.

"Hot stove" rule Principles that can guide disciplining; the action should be immediate, offer advance warning, be consistent, and impartial.

IMMEDIACY

The impact of a disciplinary action will be reduced as the time between the infraction and the penalty's implementation lengthens. The more quickly the discipline follows the offence, the more likely it is that the employee will associate the discipline with the offence rather than with you as the imposer of the discipline. Therefore, it is best to begin the disciplinary process as soon as possible after you notice a violation. Of course, the immediacy requirement should not result in undue haste. Fair and objective treatment should not be compromised for expediency.

ADVANCE WARNING

As we noted earlier, you have an obligation to give advance warning before initiating formal disciplinary action. This means the employee must be aware of the organization's rules and accept its standards of

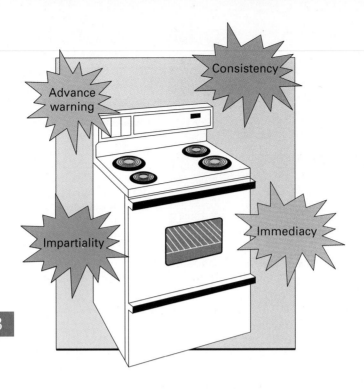

FIGURE 14-3

The "hot stove" rule

behaviour. Disciplinary action is more likely to be interpreted as fair by employees when they have received clear warning that a given violation will lead to discipline and when they know what that discipline will be.

CONSISTENCY

Fair treatment of employees demands that disciplinary action be consistent. If you enforce rule violations in an inconsistent manner, the rules will lose their impact. Morale will decline and employees will question your competence. Productivity will suffer as a result of employee insecurity and anxiety. Your employees will want to know the limits of permissible behaviour and they will look to your actions for guidance. If John is reprimanded today for an action he took last week, at which time nothing was said, these limits become blurry. Similarly, if Tina and Jennifer are both goofing around at their desks and only Tina is reprimanded, Tina is likely to question the fairness of the action. The point, then, is that discipline should be consistent. This need not result in treating everyone exactly alike, because that would mean ignoring mitigating circumstances. But it does put the responsibility on you to clearly justify disciplinary actions that may appear inconsistent to employees.

IMPARTIALITY

The last guideline that flows from the "hot stove" rule is to keep the discipline impartial. Penalties should be connected with a given violation, not with the personality of the violator. That is, discipline should be directed

1. The first formal step in the discipline process is _____ .
   a. verbal warning
   b. written warning
   c. suspension
   d. dismissal
2. What is the purpose of suspension in the disciplinary process?
3. There are circumstances in which an employee's behaviour justifies immediate suspension or dismissal, bypassing the normal sequence of discipline. True or False?
4. Which one of the following statements would not indicate a need for discipline?
   a. attendance problems
   b. insubordination
   c. inability to do the job
   d. illegal strike activity

at what the employee has done, not at the employee. As a supervisor, you should make it clear that you are avoiding personal judgments about the employee's character. You are penalizing the rule violation, not the individual. And all employees commiting the violation can be expected to be penalized. Further, once the penalty has been imposed, you must make every effort to forget the incident. You should attempt to treat the employee in the same manner you did prior to the infraction.

FACTORS TO CONSIDER IN DISCIPLINING

Defining what is "reasonable in relation to the offence" is one of the most challenging aspects of the discipline process. Why? Because infractions vary greatly in terms of severity. Suspending an employee is considerably more stringent than issuing a verbal warning. Similarly, the decision to fire someone—the organizational equivalent of the death penalty—is dramatically more punitive than a two-week suspension without pay. If you fail to recognize relevant extenuating factors and

FIGURE 14-4

Relevant factors
determining the
severity of penalties

- Seriousness of the problem

- Duration of the problem

- Frequency and nature of the problem

- Employee's work history

- Extenuating circumstances

- Degree of warning

- History of the organization's discipline practices

- Implications for other employees

- Upper-management support

make the proper adjustments in the severity of penalties, you risk having your action perceived as being unfair. The following factors (summarized in Figure 14-4) should be taken into consideration when applying discipline:

1. **Seriousness of the problem.** How severe is the problem? Dishonesty, for example, is usually considered a more serious infraction than reporting to work twenty minutes late.
2. **Duration of the problem.** Have there been other discipline problems with this employee, and if so, over how long a time span? A first occurrence is usually viewed differently from a third or fourth offence.
3. **Frequency and nature of the problem.** Is the current problem part of an emerging or continuing pattern of discipline infractions? Continual infractions may require a different type of discipline from that applied to isolated instances of misconduct.
4. **Employee's work history.** How long has the employee worked for the organization, and what has been the quality of his or her performance? For many violations, the punishment will be less severe for those who have developed a strong track record.
5. **Extenuating circumstances.** Are there extenuating factors, such as influences outside the employee's control, that lessen the severity of the infraction? The employee who missed the plane for an important meeting because his wife went into labour with their first child is likely to have his violation assessed more leniently than would his peer who missed the same plane because he overslept.
6. **Degree of warning.** To what extent has the employee been previously warned about the offence? Did he or she know and understand the rule that was broken? As we have noted several times previously,

discipline severity should reflect the degree of knowledge the violator holds of the organization's standards of acceptable behaviour. In addition, an organization that has formalized written rules governing employee conduct is more justified in aggressively enforcing violations than is an organization whose rules are informal or vague.

7. **History of the organization's discipline practices.** How have similar infractions been dealt with in the past within your department? Within the entire organization? Equitable treatment of employees must take into consideration precedents within the unit where the infraction occurs, as well as previous disciplinary actions taken in other units within the organization.

8. **Implications for other employees.** What impact will the discipline selected have on other workers in the unit? There is little point in taking a certain action against an employee if it will have a major dysfunctional effect on others within the unit. The result may be to convert a narrow and single disciplinary problem into a severe supervisory headache. Conversely, failure to impose discipline where it's justified can reduce departmental morale, undermine your credibility, and lessen employee concern for obeying the rules. For instance, more than 40 per cent of respondents to a survey felt their managers were too lenient with poor performers, which generated resentment among hard-working employees.[4]

9. **Upper-management support.** If a disciplined employee decides to appeal the case to a higher level of management, will you have reasonable evidence to justify your decision? If you have the data to support your action, can you count on your superiors backing you up? Your disciplinary actions aren't likely to carry much weight if violators believe that they can get your decision overridden.

DISCIPLINE AND THE LAW

Making a mistake when disciplining an employee can have very serious repercussions for an organization. As a result, most large organizations have specific procedures that supervisors are required to follow. Supervisors typically are provided training in how to handle the discipline process. Moreover, they are encouraged to work closely with staff specialists in the human resources department.

Most large corporations have specific rules to follow, including documentation and progressive steps, in cases that might lead to eventual dismissal. As a supervisor, it is your responsibility to defend your disciplinary actions. Proper documentation is the best protection against employees who claim, "I never knew there was any problem," or, "I was treated unfairly." In addition, you will want to obey **due process** when taking any disciplinary action. This includes:

Due process
Assuming an employee is innocent until proved otherwise; giving the employee the right to be heard; and invoking disciplinary action that is reasonable in relation to the offence involved.

1. a presumption of innocence until reasonable proof of an employee's role in an offence is substantiated;
2. the right of the employee to be heard, and in some cases to be represented by another person; and
3. discipline that is reasonable in relation to the offence involved.

Does the threat of legal action then prevent companies from letting employees go? Certainly not. In Canada, there are three basic ways to dismiss employees.

DISMISSAL WITH JUST CAUSE

These cases involve employees with documented offences such as disobedience of a lawful and reasonable order, gross negligence, or criminal activities. The supervisor must have documented proof of such offences.

DISMISSAL WITH REASONABLE NOTICE

An employee can be discharged, even if performance is entirely satisfactory, as long as reasonable notice is given. Provincial Employment Standards Acts and the federal Labour Code define the minimum notice periods. Since these regulations change frequently, supervisors need to take care to keep abreast of the legislative updates.

DISMISSAL WITH REASONABLE COMPENSATION

Again, a satisfactory employee might be let go immediately, with reasonable compensation in lieu of notice. Provincial and federal acts again outline the conditions of minimum compensation.

UNIONIZATION

Collective Bargaining Review
http://labour.hrdc-drhc.
gc.ca/bli/eng/cbr.html-ssi

What if your employees are unionized and are protected by a collective bargaining agreement? How does this affect the disciplinary process?

Where employees belong to a union, there will be a *collective bargaining agreement*. This agreement, among other things, will outline rules governing the behaviour of union members. It will also identify disciplinary procedures and clarify the steps members are to follow if they believe that they are receiving arbitrary or unfair treatment.

The collective bargaining agreement will typically define what represents a rule violation and what penalties are applicable. Keep in mind that the more serious actions—suspension or dismissal of an employee—usually can be expected to be vigorously opposed by both the employee and the union.

Most collective-bargaining agreements

1. stipulate that employees can only be disciplined for "just cause";
2. provide a grievance procedure; and
3. afford opportunities for third-party review if employees believe they have been wronged.

Disciplining unionized employees, therefore, tends to be a more quasi-legal undertaking than disciplining nonunion employees. The bargaining contract, the existence of a grievance procedure, the right to have differences evaluated and resolved by a third party, and the whole quasi-legal labour-management relationship all act to reduce your authority as a supervisor in taking disciplinary action.

Union leaders tend to argue in favour of resolution of problems rather than discipline, except in the case of criminal actions by employees. Depending on the maturity of the workplace relationship, the union can play a role in helping to solve the problem. Many unions view discipline as a draconian system that represses the workers, and if coupled with a lean operating philosophy, discipline measures often come down hard on absenteeism. A real problem can develop if legitimate time off is challenged. Increased pressure is felt by all workers because those at work are expected to produce despite a workforce depleted by absent employees. Union members would prefer to look at resolving the bigger issue of what causes absenteeism than face discipline for days away from work.

POP QUIZ

Are You Comprehending What You're Reading?

5. Which one of the following is not a recommended guideline in administering discipline?
   a. Make it immediate.
   b. Make it progressive.
   c. Make it corrective.
   d. Make it visible.
6. What are the two keys to the groundwork of the discipline process?
7. It is sometimes necessary to discipline an employee in public—especially when that employee's inappropriate actions were witnessed by other employees in the department. True or False?
8. In Canada, the following are all bases for dismissal, except:
   a. dismissal with reasonable compensation
   b. dismissal with reasonable notice
   c. dismissal with just cause
   d. dismissal with guaranteed rights

DISCIPLINING

Let's translate what you've learned about disciplining into specific skills you can apply on the job. As we've done throughout this book, we'll begin by testing your current basic skill level.

ASSESSING YOURSELF: ARE YOU EFFECTIVE AT DISCIPLINING?

For each of the following statements, select the answer that best describes you. Remember to respond as you have behaved or would behave, not as you think you *should* behave. If you have no supervisory experience, answer the statements assuming you were a supervisor.

WHEN DISCIPLINING AN EMPLOYEE:	Usually	Sometimes	Seldom
1. I provide ample warning before taking formal action.	❏	❏	❏
2. I wait for a pattern of infractions before calling it to the employee's attention.	❏	❏	❏
3. Even after repeated offences, I prefer informal discussion about correcting the problem rather than formal disciplinary action.	❏	❏	❏
4. I delay confronting the employee about an infraction until his or her next performance-appraisal review.	❏	❏	❏
5. In discussing an infraction with the employee, my style and tone are serious.	❏	❏	❏
6. I explicitly seek to allow the employee to explain his or her position.	❏	❏	❏
7. I remain impartial in allocating punishment.	❏	❏	❏
8. I allocate stronger penalties for repeated offences.	❏	❏	❏

SCORING KEY AND INTERPRETATION

For questions 1, 5, 6, 7, and 8, give yourself three points for Usually, two points for Sometimes, and one point for Seldom.

For questions 2, 3, and 4, give yourself three points for Seldom, two points for Sometimes, and one point for Usually.

Total up your points. A score of twenty-two points or higher indicates excellent skills at disciplining. Scores in the nineteen–to–twenty-one range suggest some deficiencies. Scores below nineteen indicate considerable room for improvement.

SKILL BASICS

The following dozen principles should guide you when you have to discipline an employee.

1. **Before you accuse anyone, do your homework.** What happened? If you didn't personally see the infraction, investigate and verify any accusations made by others. Was it completely the employee's fault? If not, who or what else was involved? Did the employee know and understand the rule or regulation that was broken? Document the facts: date, time, place, individuals involved, mitigating circumstances, and the like.

2. **Provide ample warning.** Before you take formal action, be sure you've provided the employee with reasonable previous warnings and that those warnings have been documented. Ask yourself: if challenged, will my action be defensible? Did I provide ample warning to the employee before taking formal action? It's very likely that applying stiffer punitive actions later on will be judged as unjust by the employee, an arbitrator, and the courts if it is determined that these punitive actions could not be readily anticipated by the employee. New supervisors, whose predecessors were lax on discipline, often move quickly to tighten discipline practices. Their frequent mistake is failing to provide adequate notice to employees of this change. In these cases, employees have a good basis for claiming arbitrary and discriminatory practices.

    The preliminary warning should typically be informal and of the verbal variety. That is, you point out the rule violation, the problem that this infraction has caused, what the correct behaviour should be, and the specific consequences if the infraction is repeated.

It's a good idea to make a temporary record of this oral reprimand and place it in the employee's file. Once the employee has corrected the problem, the record of the reprimand can be removed. Of course, if this warning is ineffective, you have documentation of your warning.

3. **Act in a timely fashion.** When you become aware of an infraction and it has been supported by your investigation, do something and do it quickly. Delay weakens the link between actions and consequences, sends the wrong message to others, undermines your credibility with your subordinates, creates doubt that any action will be taken, and invites repetition of the problem.

4. **Conduct the discipline session in private.** Praise employees in public but keep punishment private. Your objective is not to humiliate the violator. Public reprimands embarrass an employee and are unlikely to produce the change in behaviour you desire.

5. **Adopt a calm and serious tone.** Many interpersonal situations are facilitated by a loose, informal, and relaxed manner on the part of a supervisor. The idea in such situations is to put the employee at ease. Administering discipline is not one of those situations. Avoid anger or other emotional responses, and convey your comments in a calm and serious tone. But do not try to lessen the tension by cracking jokes or making small talk. Such actions are only likely to confuse the employee because they send out conflicting signals.

6. **Be specific about the problem.** When you sit down with the employee, indicate that you have documentation and be specific about the problem. Define the violation in exact terms instead of just citing company regulations or the union contract. Explain why the behaviour can't be continued by showing how it specifically affects the employee's job performance, the unit's effectiveness, and the employee's coworkers.

7. **Keep it impersonal.** Criticism should be focused on the employee's behaviour rather than on the individual personally. For instance, if an employee has been late for work several times, point out how this behaviour has increased the workload of others or has lowered departmental morale. Don't criticize the person for being thoughtless or irresponsible.

8. **Get the employee's side of the story.** Regardless of what your investigation has revealed, due process demands that you give the employee the opportunity to explain his or her position. From the employee's perspective, what happened? Why did it happen? What was his or her perception of the rules, regulations, and circumstances? If there are significant discrepancies between your version of the violation and the employee's, you may need to do more investigating. Of course, you'll want to document your employee's response for the record.

   Keep an open mind and use your active listening skills. It is possible that your initial information on the violation was biased or in error. Additionally, there might be extenuating circumstances of which you were unaware. The point is that you should not merely go through the motions to meet "due process" requirements; rather, you should solicit the employee's explanation to ensure that you have all the relevant facts.

9. **Keep control of the discussion.** In most interpersonal exchanges with employees, you want to encourage open dialogue. You want to give up control and create a climate of communication between equals. This won't work in administering discipline. Why? Violators are prone to use any leverage to put you on the defensive. In other words, if you don't take control, they will. Disciplining, by definition, is an authority-based act. You are enforcing the organization's standards and regulations. So take control. Ask the employee for his or her side of the story. Get the facts. But don't let the employee interrupt you or divert you from your objective.

10. **Agree on how mistakes can be prevented next time.**
    Disciplining should include guidance and direction for correcting the problem. Let the employee state what he or she plans to do in the future to ensure that the violation isn't repeated. For serious violations, have the employee draft a step-by-step plan to change the problem behaviour. Then set a timetable, with follow-up meetings in which progress can be evaluated. If the employee is genuinely unable to develop a satisfactory solution to the problem, you may be called upon to become a counsellor. You might need to help the employee understand the problem, identify courses of corrective action, assess the advantages and disadvantages of each, and plan a specific strategy for improving the situation. When the root of the problem is personal (relationships, children, financial, or the like) or has considerable emotional content, you may need to direct the employee to a professional counsellor.

11. **Select progressive disciplinary action and consider mitigating circumstances.** Choose a punishment that is appropriate to the crime. For the typical minor infraction, begin with a verbal warning, and then progress up the disciplinary chain. For more serious violations (for example, stealing, falsification of records, sabotage, gross insubordination, selling drugs at the work site, or attacking another employee with the intent to do serious harm) stronger punishments are justified from the outset. The punishment you select should be viewed as fair and consistent. But once you've arrived at your decision, tell the employee what the action will be, your reasons for taking it, and when it will be carried out.

12. **Fully document the disciplinary session.** To complete your disciplinary action, make sure that your ongoing documentation (what occurred, the results of your investigation, your initial warnings, the employee's explanation and responses, the discipline decision, and the consequences of further misconduct) is complete and accurate. This full documentation should be made part of the employee's permanent file. In addition, it's a good idea to give the employee a formal letter that highlights what was resolved during your discussion, specifics about the punishment, future expectations, and what actions you are prepared to take if the behaviour isn't corrected or the violation is repeated.

APPLYING YOUR SKILLS

The class should break into pairs. The following role play takes place between Chris Thomas (the supervisor) and Pat Nystrom (the employee). One member of the pair will play the role of Chris; the other will play Pat. Each role player should read the following background material and then *only* his or her role. Do *not* read the other person's role. When you've both read your respective roles, begin the role play. This should take approximately ten minutes to complete. Incorporate as many of the twelve points above as possible in your role play.

BACKGROUND

Pat Nystrom works on the quality inspection line at a toy manufacturing firm and has held the same job for two years. Pat's job is to inspect finished stuffed animals for defects as they go down the conveyor belt toward the boxing and shipping department. Pat's supervisor, Chris Thomas, is new on the job. Chris was hired from another company and has been with the toy firm for only two weeks. Upon being hired, Chris called the entire quality inspection staff together and talked about his/her management philosophy. One point Chris emphasized was the need for people to explicitly follow the company rules. Chris then proceeded to give a copy of the rules and procedures manual to everyone.

Pat's performance evaluations have been consistently good and Pat has no prior history of problems. Today Pat walked away from the conveyor belt for a few minutes. Pat left without asking permission. Company rules state that assembly-line employees are not to leave their work stations unless they ask for and get permission from their supervisor. Pat has now returned to the conveyor belt.

PAT NYSTROM'S ROLE: You left the conveyor belt—for what you thought was about five minutes—to check with your daughter's nursery school. You are a single parent and your daughter has been sick for the past few days. Although you left your work station without asking permission, you didn't consider it a problem because everyone leaves their jobs on the line for a few minutes without getting permission. You like your job and, as a single parent, depend on your weekly pay cheque to pay the bills. You're an emotional person. If challenged or reprimanded, you are prone to get very upset and become argumentative.

CHRIS THOMAS' ROLE: As a new supervisor, you are determined to do a good job. One problem that concerns you is that employees leave their workstations without asking permission. The previous supervisor apparently looked the other way and let employees break the rules. Well, no more! You're going to shape up the quality inspection department. You glanced at your watch when Pat left the conveyor belt—it was 10:20. Pat returned at 10:40.

To you, leaving a workstation without permission is serious for three reasons:

1. It increases the workload for others;
2. It means defective items have a lower probability of being caught; and
3. The company rule is well known and flaunting it creates a breakdown in authority. You want to make the right decision. It is now 10:45— five minutes after Pat has returned to the line. Your office, which is only thirty feet from the conveyor line, provides privacy should you think this is necessary.

SUMMARY

This summary is organized by the chapter Learning Objectives.

1. *Discipline* refers to actions taken to enforce the organization's rules and standards.
2. The most common disciplinary problems facing supervisors relate to attendance issues such as absenteeism, tardiness, and abuse of sick leaves. The other major types of discipline problems are on-the-job behaviours (including insubordination and substance abuse), dishonesty, and outside activities that affect on-the-job performance or reflect poorly on the organization.
3. The typical steps in progressive discipline are: 1. a verbal warning, 2. written reprimands, 3. suspension, 4. demotion or a pay cut, and 5. dismissal.
4. The "hot stove" rule states that discipline should be administered in the same way that people are burned by a hot stove. The response should be immediate; there should be a warning; the result should be consistent; and the result should be impartial.
5. Fairness demands that extenuating circumstances be considered before applying negative discipline. Factors such as the duration of the problem, the employee's work history, and past discipline practices in the organization are all legitimate factors that can influence the degree of disciplinary action.
6. The three methods of dismissal permitted by law are dismissal with just cause, dismissal with reasonable notice, and dismissal with reasonable compensation.
7. In disciplining unionized employees, the bargaining contract, the existence of a grievance procedure, the right to have differences evaluated and resolved by a third party, and the entire quasi-legal labour-management relationship all act to reduce a supervisor's range of discretion.

KEY TERMS AND CONCEPTS

Discipline
Dismissal with just cause
Dismissal with reasonable
  compensation
Dismissal with reasonable
  notice

Due process
"Hot stove" rule
Progressive discipline
Suspension
Verbal warning
Written warning

REVIEWING YOUR KNOWLEDGE

1. "A good supervisor will never have to use discipline." Do you agree or disagree with this statement? Discuss.
2. Is punishment consistent with 1. having confidence in employees, 2. team work, and 3. empowerment? Discuss.
3. Why is it common for an organization to immediately dismiss a high-performing employee who lied about his educational qualifications on his application but take less harsh action against an average employee who misses a day of work to go fishing? Is this fair?
4. Why isn't discipline always the solution?
5. If you see a violation of an organizational rule by one of your employees with your own eyes, do you still need to investigate? Discuss.
6. Why is it so important to document, in writing, any disciplinary action you take against an employee?
7. What authority, if any, do you think human resource departments should have over a supervisor's disciplinary practices?
8. What should you do to follow due process when taking disciplinary action?

ANSWERS TO THE POP QUIZZES

1. **b. written warning.** This is the first formal step of the discipline process because it is the first step in which a record of the discipline is placed in the employee's personnel file. The first step of the discipline process, the verbal warning, results in documentation that is informally kept in the supervisor's file on the employee.

2. The purpose of a suspension—a short lay-off, typically without pay—is to create a rude awakening for the employee. It is designed to convince the employee that the supervisor is serious about the action being taken. Furthermore, it is designed to help the employee fully understand and accept responsibility for following the organization's rules.

3. **True.** Examples are stealing and attack with intent to seriously harm another employee.

4. **c. inability to do the job.** Lack of ability to do the job is not the same thing as a lack of desire to do it. Inability to do a job is best dealt with through training—not discipline.

5. **d. make it visible.** All discipline should be handled privately. It's a matter of respecting the individual, even though disciplinary action is taking place.

6. The keys to the discipline process are that the process be perceived as being both fair and reasonable.

7. **False.** All discipline should be conducted in private. The fact that the inappropriate behaviours were witnessed by other employees does not give the supervisor the freedom to discipline in public.

8. **d. dismissal with guaranteed rights.** The three acceptable approaches to dismissing employees are dismissal with just cause, dismissal with reasonable notice and dismissal with reasonable compensation.

CASE 14.A

Patsy Hartley at Coastal Savings and Loan

Patsy Hartley was an excellent receptionist at the Coastal Savings and Loan Corporation. She greeted each person who walked through the front door as if that person were the only one who mattered to the company. Her friendly voice reflected exactly the same enthusiasm and sincerity when she answered the phone. Patsy gave personal attention to every single visitor and caller—she was a valued, conscientious ambassador for Coastal.

As a matter of fact, Patsy was the best salesperson that Coastal had—frequently she was the first contact a potential client would have with the company, and it seemed that Patsy was fielding more and more calls with each passing day. Patsy's supervisor, Bill Westermeier, was pleased that Patsy seemed so happy in her job. He would have to be sure to put a special notation on her performance review.

About three months later, when Bill was having a conversation with two other supervisors, they asked Bill if Patsy was okay. Patsy seemed to be absent a lot and, when she was at work, her performance seemed to have fallen off. They complained of messages being taken incorrectly. They were having more and more clients telling them how difficult it was to reach the company, let alone reaching a specific Coastal employee or agent. Also, Patsy really looked tired and worn out.

Bill couldn't believe his ears. Patsy was busier than ever. She never had time to help with any of the overflow typing that she had done from time to time in past months. Yes, she did seem a bit pale and had taken off a few days from work, but the work load was always heavy this time of year. She seemed cheerful enough— how could anyone think something might be wrong? However, he had better talk with Patsy if others seemed to perceive there was a problem.

(Patsy's problem is identified in question 3 below; however, it is recommended that questions 1 and 2 be answered first before referring to question 3.)

RESPONDING TO THIS CASE

1. What explanation might be offered as to why Bill was not seeing Patsy's work deteriorating as others did?

2. How can Bill find out if Patsy has a problem? If Bill considers the four types of discipline problems with which most supervisors are confronted, which ones might apply to Patsy?

3. Problem: Patsy was an excellent receptionist, but was not challenged in her job. Because she didn't feel she had job security at Coastal and her job didn't pay enough to support her, she responded to a newspaper ad seeking at-home direct mail representatives. As a direct mail representative she made follow-up phone calls for the direct mail company. At first she made only a few of the calls at work. But when she found it easier to contact people during the day, she made more and more of her calls from the office. After all, she rationalized, she wasn't that busy at her job, everyone liked her work, and her supervisor wanted her to keep busy. One thing led to another and before she realized it, she was on the phone more for her direct mail business than she was for Coastal. And this gave her more time to be with her friends during weekday evenings. Given these facts, what are some of the factors Bill should consider in disciplining Patsy? Discuss how the steps in progressive discipline are complicated by Bill not being "on top" of the situation earlier?

4. Are there any extenuating circumstances or other factors that would influence the type of action Bill should take in Patsy's case? If so, what are they? Why?

5. In groups of two or three, discuss the action Bill should take in this case. As each group shares its action plan with the class, each group should explain its reasons for recommending its plan of action.

CASE 14.B

Hydro Mississauga Deals with Discipline

Hydro Mississauga, located in the Greater Toronto Area, has a corporate aim to be "the best utility in Ontario." The company backs up this objective with a focus on cost-effectiveness, lowest rates in Greater Toronto, reliability, and a commitment to safety and training. Indeed, the company's literature carries the slogan, "Our Safety—We Care."

Over several years, Ingrid Hann, then the Director Employee and Customer Relations, dealt with disciplinary situations within a unionized workplace. She believes that the basis for fair discipline is consistency. If employees are aware of procedures, and those procedures are not followed, then a consistent disciplinary action must follow.

In one case, through the use of an elevated hydraulic boom, a hydro worker was working on a high hydro line. One of the tools used by the crew is a hilti gun, which uses an explosive shell to drive rivets. Due to horseplay that ignored all company safety procedures, one worker dropped a shell forty feet to the concrete below. The crew member on the ground suffered a permanent 20 per cent hearing loss due to the sound of the exploding cap. Although Ingrid negotiated for a two-day suspension (she preferred a week), the union successfully grieved to have the suspension reduced to one day. However, from Ingrid's perspective, this does establish documentation that sets up more severe discipline on any further safety infraction.

RESPONDING TO THIS CASE

1. Do you feel that the one-day suspension was sufficient penalty for the safety infraction?
2. Discuss the basic tenets of discipline that apply to an organization in a union environment.
3. Interview four local managers to discuss their company's discipline policy. Make sure you interview two from a non-union workplace and two from a union workplace. Compare and contrast the discipline policies.

15 THE SUPERVISOR'S ROLE IN EMPLOYEE RELATIONS

LEARNING OBJECTIVES

After reading this chapter, you should be able to:

1. Describe the current status of labour unions in Canada.
2. Explain the appeal of unions to employees.
3. Describe the importance of labour legislation.
4. Identify the primary purpose of collective bargaining.
5. Describe the supervisor's role in labour legislation.
6. Discuss the C.A.W.'s perspective on labour issues.
7. Describe the steps for handling a grievance.

CHAPTER OUTLINE

Nick Tomaski has been a maintenance supervisor at a major airline for nearly eleven years. Nick's job is to make sure his work crews keep the planes operating safely and efficiently. In a recent interview, Nick talked about his job and contrasted it to that of his brother, Dom, who works for a tree-cutting service. Dom is also a supervisor, but unlike Nick, Dom's employees don't belong to a union.

"Last Sunday, Dom and his family were down visiting. We were sitting in the living room and got around to comparing our jobs. Dom supervises a small group of tree trimmers. They meet at a central location every morning. Then Dom drives them to their various work locations. Dom's boss imposes very few rules on him or the work group. Dom has the major say-so in who he hires, how much they get paid, what tasks people should do, when they take breaks, and the like. If an employee gives him any trouble, he gives a warning. If they don't shape up, he fires them. When they're working on a job, Dom runs the show. There is no question about who's the boss.

"The maintenance people I oversee are all members of the machinists' union. They have a contract with the airline that covers just about anything that could come up. For instance, I have no influence on pay or in reassigning people to different tasks. That's negotiated at the time of the contract by union and company representatives. If I need some people to work overtime so we can get a plane repaired and turned around, the contract specifies that I have to offer the overtime to employees based on their seniority, I have to give them twenty-four hours' notice, and they have the right to refuse if they've worked at least eighty hours in the past fourteen days. I have to fill out dozens of forms and the employees have all kinds of appeal procedures. Dom told me that he fired one of his people because he caught him drinking hard liquor during his afternoon break. The guy had been warned once about the company's rule about no drinking on the job. If one of my people were caught drinking, I'd be required to issue three written warnings, then if the employee still didn't shape up, he'd be sent for counselling. Even if the employee continued with his drinking problem, it would take six or nine months to go through all the appeals that the union contract provides before the person would actually be terminated."

As Nick Tomaski vividly describes, supervising unionized workers is different from supervising nonunionized employees. In this chapter, we'll discuss why employees join unions, review the key labour laws you need to know about, and then consider the role that supervisors play in labour matters.

WHAT IS EMPLOYEE RELATIONS?

Employee relations includes all the activities within a company that involve dealing with a union and its members. But what's a **union**? It's an organization that represents workers and seeks to protect their interests through collective bargaining.

In Canada, union membership has increased from 30 per cent of the workforce in the 1960s to 37 per cent in the 1990s. The pattern of current membership varies widely as we look across Canada:

Newfoundland	53%
Quebec	41%
British Columbia	38%
Ontario	33%
Alberta	24%

Union membership in the major industrialized countries, led primarily by the U.S., as a percentage of the civilian workforce, has been declining for more than thirty-five years. A number of factors have contributed to this decline. The economic sectors where union strength has traditionally been greatest—particularly blue-collar manufacturing jobs in the automobile, steel, rubber, and chemical industries—have significantly cut their North American workforces. Many of these jobs have been eliminated through automation or exported to countries with lower labour costs. The growth in the labour force since the late 1960s has been among women, professionals, government employees, and service workers—groups that have been more resistant to labour's effort to organize them. And, of course, unions have suffered directly as a result of their own success. Labour union growth in the 1930s and 1940s was largely a result of responding to the depressed status of the working class. But as unions succeeded in raising wages and improving working conditions, the reasons for their very existence became less obvious.

However, in many key industries (for instance, mining, construction, railroads, and trucking) the majority of workers are unionized. Most importantly, we can't overlook the **spillover effect**. Successes made by unions at the negotiating table spill over to influence the wages, working conditions, and terms of employment for workers who are not unionized (particularly in the same industry).

A BASIC QUESTION: WHY WOULD EMPLOYEES JOIN A UNION?

What do employees seek to gain when they join a union? The answer to this question varies with the individual and the union context, but the following captures the most common reasons.

Employee relations
All activities within a company that involve dealing with a union and its members

Union
An organization that represents workers and seeks to protect their interests through collective bargaining

Spillover effect
Successes made by unions at the negotiating table influence the wages, working conditions, and terms of employment for workers who are not unionized.

Canadian Labour Congress
http://www.clc-ctc.ca/

Ontario Federation of Labour
http://www.ofl-fto.on.ca/

HIGHER WAGES AND BENEFITS

There's power in numbers. As a result, unions are often able to obtain higher wages and benefit packages for their members than these employees would be able to negotiate individually. One or two employees walking off the job over a wage dispute is unlikely to significantly affect most businesses, but hundreds of workers going out on strike can temporarily disrupt or even close down a company. Additionally, professional bargainers employed by the union may be able to negotiate more skillfully than any individual could do on his or her own behalf.

GREATER JOB SECURITY

Unions provide members with a sense of independence from management's power to arbitrarily hire, promote, or fire. The collective bargaining contract will stipulate rules that apply to all members, thus providing fairer and more uniform treatment.

INCREASED OPPORTUNITIES TO INFLUENCE WORK RULES

Where a union exists, workers are provided with an opportunity to participate in determining the conditions under which they work, and an effective channel through which they can protest conditions they believe are unfair. Therefore, a union not only represents the worker but also provides rules that define channels through which complaints and concerns of workers can be registered. Grievance procedures and rights to third-party arbitration of disputes are examples of practices that are frequently defined and regulated as a result of union efforts.

COMPULSORY MEMBERSHIP

Union shop
A workplace where employees must join the union

Agency shop
A workplace where employees do not have to join the union but must pay union dues if they want to keep their jobs

Many labour agreements require that individuals must join the union (such a workplace is referred to as a **union shop**) or at least pay dues (an **agency shop**) if they want to keep their jobs. These requirements are typically imposed by the unions themselves on free riders (employees who gain the benefits of union membership without paying fees and dues).

UNHAPPINESS WITH A SUPERVISOR

Setting aside the other reasons why employees join a union, there appears to be one common factor—you, the supervisor. If employees are upset with the way you handle problems or the way you disciplined one of their co-workers, they are likely to seek help from a union. In fact, research has shown that when employees vote to unionize, it's often a vote against their immediate supervisor rather than a vote in support of a particular union.

LABOUR LEGISLATION YOU NEED TO KNOW ABOUT

Supervisors don't need to be labour lawyers to deal with legal issues surrounding union-management relations. But there are some basic laws with which you need to be familiar.

In Canada, there are three legislative areas that deal with the relationships among employees, unions and employers: the federal Labour Relations Act, provincial Labour Relations Acts and the federal Charter of Rights and Freedoms. Again, as with other legislation, the jurisdiction will be largely determined by the nature of the company.

FEDERAL AND PROVINCIAL LABOUR RELATIONS ACTS

The labour relations acts set out the responsibilities and rights of employees and their unions, generally outlining the following issues:

- rules for starting a union
- rules for joining a union
- supporting or not supporting a union
- collective bargaining procedures
- administration of collective agreements
- unfair labour practices

These acts specifically prohibit employers from:

1. interfering with, restraining, or coercing employees in the exercise of the rights to join unions and bargain collectively
2. dominating or interfering with the formation or administration of any labour organization
3. discriminating against anyone because of union activity
4. discharging or otherwise discriminating against any employee because he filed charges or gave testimony under the act
5. refusing to bargain collectively with the representatives chosen by the employees

These acts also prohibit union actions that may not be in the best interests of the employees. Specifically, a union may not:

1. force an employee to bargain through it if the union is not the bargaining agent
2. participate or interfere with the administration of the company
3. attempt, at the workplace or during working hours, to persuade an employee to become a union member, except with the employer's consent

4. expel or suspend an employee from the union by applying union membership rules in a discriminatory manner
5. penalize a member for filing a complaint or testifying pursuant to the code

Each jurisdiction has a labour relations board that regulates the actions of both unions and companies, playing a role in settling disputes in contract administration and collective bargaining.

THE CHARTER OF RIGHTS AND FREEDOMS

The Charter of Rights and Freedoms, passed by the federal government in 1982, also influences the relationship between employees and their union representative. Any action that contravenes an individual's fundamental freedom can be challenged. For example, fundamental freedoms include freedom of religion; freedom of expression; freedom of association; freedom of peaceful assembly; and freedom of thought, belief and opinion. By joining a union, an employee does not surrender these fundamental freedoms guaranteed by the charter.

THE 1990s: FROM CONFLICT TO COOPERATION

Historically, the relationship between labour and management was built on conflict. The interests of management and labour were seen as basically at odds; each treated the other as the enemy.

But times have changed. Management has become increasingly aware that successful efforts to increase productivity, improve quality, and lower costs require employee involvement and commitment. And labour unions have come to recognize that they can help their members more by cooperating with management than by fighting them.

According to Ingrid Hann, formerly Director Employee and Customer Relations at Hydro Mississauga, Ontario, the union has become more collaborative because partnership is necessary to solve situations in a unionized environment. The union is motivated to build more cooperative relationships with management because its members expect results based on mutual respect, not confrontation. The management at Hydro Mississauga also invites the union to join in problem solving, implanting more operational initiatives and evaluating results and progress.

Ironically, current labour laws, passed in an era of mistrust and antagonism between management and labour, have become barriers to these parties putting their differences aside and becoming cooperative partners.

Are You Comprehending
What You're Reading?

1. Which one of the following is not a reason for an individual to join a union?
   a. better wages and benefits
   b. good supervision
   c. compulsory union membership
   d. ability to influence work rules
2. Explain the spillover effect.
3. A union organizer's best weapon for convincing workers to join a union is poor supervision. True or False?
4. Rules for starting a union and for joining a union, collective bargaining procedures and unfair labour practices are set out in:
   a. the federal and provincial labour relations acts
   b. the Charter of Rights and Freedoms
   c. municipal bylaws
   d. all of the above

AN OVERVIEW OF THE COLLECTIVE BARGAINING PROCESS

As a supervisor, you won't typically be directly involved in the collective bargaining process. You will, however, be affected by the process and outcome. The next section will describe things you can and cannot legally do during the period when a union is attempting to organize employees in your company; it will also show how you play a major part in the administration of the final union contract. So you need a basic understanding of collective bargaining.

Collective bargaining is a process for negotiating a union contract and for administrating the contract after it has been negotiated (see Figure 15-1). The following discussion briefly summarizes how the process typically flows in the private sector.

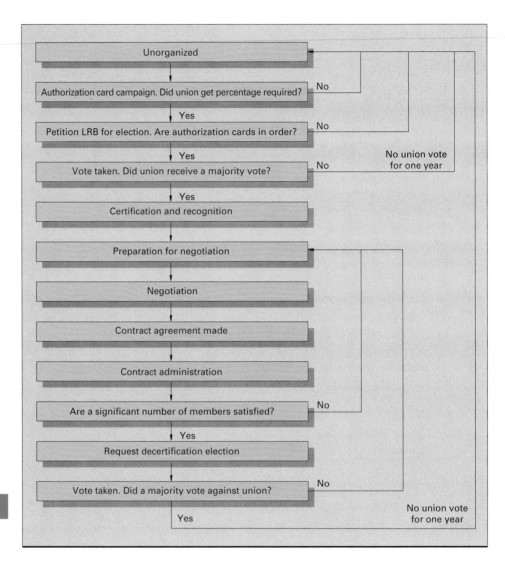

FIGURE 15-1

The collective
bargaining process

ORGANIZATION AND CERTIFICATION

Efforts to organize a group of employees may begin when employee
representatives ask union officials to visit the employees' organization
and solicit members or when the union itself initiates a membership
drive. Either way, the law requires that a union must secure signed
authorization cards from a specified percentage of the employees it
desires to represent. If the percentage goal is achieved, either the union
or management will file a petition with the Labour Relations Board
(LRB), requesting a representation election. The percentage of employees needed to hold an election varies from a low of 35 per cent in
Quebec to a high of 40 per cent in Ontario.

When the LRB receives the required number of authorization cards, it evaluates them, verifies that legal requirements have been satisfied, and then clarifies the appropriate **bargaining unit**; that is, it identifies which employees the union will represent if it wins the election.

A secret-ballot election is usually called within twenty-five days after the LRB receives the authorization cards. If the union gets a majority in this election, the LRB certifies the union and recognizes it as the exclusive bargaining representative for all employees within the specified bargaining unit. Should the union fail to get a majority, another election cannot be held for one year.

Occasionally, employees become dissatisfied with a certified union. In such instances, employees may request a decertification election by the LRB. If a majority of the members vote for decertification, the union is out. However, recognize two things about decertification. First, most contracts forbid it during the contract's term. Second, union members cannot decertify today and bring in another union tomorrow. In most cases, at least one year must transpire between votes.

> **Bargaining unit**
> Identifies which employees the union will represent if it wins an election

OK, THE UNION WON—WHAT NOW?

After a union has been certified—meaning it won the election and was successful in organizing a group of workers—the collective bargaining process commences. **Collective bargaining** is a process for negotiating a union contract and for administering the contract after it has been negotiated. It includes preparing to negotiate, the actual contract negotiations, and administering the contract after it has been ratified.[1]

The people who do the negotiating for both the union and the company are referred to as the negotiations teams. The company's representatives will often depend on the size of the organization. In a small firm, for instance, bargaining is probably done by the president—and probably some other staff the president feels are necessary participants. In larger organizations, there is usually an industrial relations expert. In such cases, you can expect the company to be represented by the senior official for industrial relations, other company executives, and company lawyers—with support provided by legal and economic specialists in wage and salary administration, labour law, benefits, and so forth.

On the union side, you typically can expect to see a bargaining team made up of an officer of the local union, local shop stewards, and some representation from the union. Again, as with the company, representation is modified to reflect the size of the bargaining unit. If negotiations involve a contract that will cover many employees at company locations throughout Canada, the team will be dominated by several union officers, with a strong supporting cast of economic and legal experts employed by the union. In a small firm or for local negotiations covering special issues at the plant level for a nationwide organization, bargaining representatives for the union might be the local officers and a few specially elected committee members.

> **Collective bargaining**
> A process for negotiating a union contract and for administrating the contract after it has been negotiated. It includes preparing to negotiate, the actual contract negotiations, and administering the contract after it has been ratified.

Preparation for Negotiation

Once a union has been certified, management will begin preparing for negotiations. It will gather information on the economy, copies of recently negotiated contracts between other unions and employers, cost-of-living data, labour market statistics, and similar external factors. It will also gather internal information on complaints and accident records, employee performance reports, and overtime figures.

This information will tell management their organization's current labour-performance status, what similar organizations are doing, and what it can anticipate from the economy in the near term. Management then uses these data to determine what it can expect to achieve in the negotiation. What can it expect the union to ask for? What is management prepared to give?

Negotiation

Negotiation customarily begins when the union delivers a list of demands to management. These are typically ambitious in order to create room for trading in the later stages of negotiation. Not surprisingly, management's initial response may be to counter by offering little more than the terms of the previous contract or, in an increasing number of cases, to even propose reductions in current wages, benefits, and previously agreed-to conditions.

These introductory proposals usually initiate a period of long and intense bargaining. Compromises are made, and after an oral agreement is achieved, it is converted into a written contract. Finally, negotiation concludes with the union's representatives submitting the contract to its members for ratification.

Contract Administration

Once a contract is agreed upon and ratified, it must be administered. The way in which it will be administered is specified in the contract itself.

Probably the most important element of contract administration—particularly in terms of the supervisor's job—has to do with the spelling out of a procedure for handling contractual disputes. Almost all collective bargaining agreements contain formal procedures for resolving grievances over the interpretation and application of the contract.

THE SUPERVISOR'S ROLE IN LABOUR MATTERS

Now let's turn our attention to the various demands placed on supervisors as a result of labour-management relations.

ORGANIZING DRIVES

If your employees aren't currently unionized, you may experience a union organizing drive. If that happens, be very careful about what you say and do. For example, the law is clear in stating that you can't threaten or intimidate employees in order to get them to vote against the union.

Because supervisors are the closest level of management to the workers, you represent the best source of information about intentions and actions. So pay attention. If you see that union-organizing activities are taking place among employees, report your observations to your boss or to the human resources department. Early detection can allow your company to plan a proper response.

Figure 15-2 provides a list of guidelines to lessen the likelihood that you'll break the law or hinder your company's response to the union's

- If your employees ask for your opinion on unionization, respond in a neutral manner. For example, "I really have no position on the issue. Do what you think is best."

- You can prohibit union organizing activities in your workplace during work hours only if they interfere with work operations.

- You can prohibit outside union organizers from distributing union information in the workplace.

- Employees have the right to distribute union information to other employees during break and lunch periods.

- Don't question employees publicly or privately about union-organizing activities. For example, "Are you planning to go to that union rally this weekend?" But if an employee freely tells you about the activities, you may listen.

- Don't spy on employees' union activities, for example, by standing in the lunchroom to see who is distributing pro-union literature.

- Don't make any threats or promises that are related to the possibility of unionization. For example, "If this union effort succeeds, upper management is seriously thinking about closing down this plant. But if it's defeated, they plan to push through an immediate wage increase."

- Don't discriminate against any employee who is involved in the unionization effort.

- Be on the lookout for efforts by the union to coerce employees to join its ranks. This is illegal. If you see this occurring, report it to your boss or the human resources department. Your company may want to file a complaint against the union with the LRB.

FIGURE 15-2

Supervisory guidelines during a union organizing drive

organizing effort. You are free to express your views and opinions about unions to your employees. But the law forbids you from interfering in your employee's right to choose a union to represent them. And because the line is often vague about where your free speech becomes interference, you've got to be cautious.

NEGOTIATION

Supervisors typically play a minor part in the actual negotiation of the contract. Basic responsibility for this activity lies with specialists in the human resource department and top management.

The supervisor's role during the negotiation period tends to be limited to that of a resource person. You may be called upon to provide your organization's negotiators with departmental information on past problems with work-shift schedules, seniority rights, transfers, discipline, or ambiguous terminology in the current contract. This suggests that it's important for you to keep careful records of labour problems you experience during the current contract period so that these problems can be addressed during the next contract negotiation.

CONTRACT ADMINISTRATION

Once a formal agreement is in place, you must manage your department within the framework established by that contract. This means that you must fully understand all the "fine print" in the contract—and you need to make sure departmental members have the contract information, too.

Large and small organizations alike will hold supervisory training sessions and meetings to help you understand the contract and to clarify new provisions. You'll be given a copy of the agreement to study, an opportunity to get questions answered, and procedures to follow when problems arise.

Why do organizations place so much emphasis on ensuring that supervisors know and understand the contract? Because supervisors are the primary link between management and the employees. For the typical unionized employee, the supervisor is his or her sole contact with management. What supervisors say and do, then, largely determines the labour-management climate in the organization. If you misinterpret a contract provision, treat an employee unfairly, or engage in a similar contract violation, the consequences for you and the company might be immediate, or they might be postponed until the next negotiation. The union's representatives will be keeping track of these incidents and they'll use them to help win concessions in the next contract.

Keep in mind that working under a labour contract and supervising unionized employees does not take away your rights to make decisions or manage your people. What it does is spell out limitations to your authority and establish procedures for employees to challenge any action you take that they see as a violation of the labour agreement. So, for instance, you can still assign work schedules, make job transfers, and discipline problem employees—but you must do so within the framework defined in the labour contract.

Remember, too, that the labour contract is a bilateral agreement. It also specifies responsibilities for employees, and procedures you can take when employees fail to comply with provisions in the contract. So the labour agreement constrains employees as well as management.

Depending on the relationship that has been built between the supervisor and workers, a looser interpretation of the contract can lead to agreement in solving day-to-day problems. HR specialist Ingrid Hann advises front-line supervisors to focus on understanding their employees. If a supervisor can perceive the wants and needs of each individual worker, and try to fulfill those needs, the contract can become secondary as employees develop job ownership and empowerment in solving problems.

RELATIONS WITH THE UNION STEWARD

The **union steward** in your department is essentially to the union what you are to the company. Just as you're there to protect the rights of management, he or she is an employee who is the elected representative of the employees in your work unit, and is there to protect the rights of the union members.

Union steward
An employee who is the elected representative of the employees in a work unit, and is there to protect the rights of the union members

What authority does a union steward have in running your department? Very little to none! The steward cannot tell you or any employee what to do. The only authority stewards have is to give advice. They can offer advice to you and employees as to their understanding of how the contract limits your actions.

Just because union stewards have limited formal authority doesn't mean they can't be troublesome. Poor relations with your steward are likely to result in increased challenges to your actions and increased grievance filings. So getting along with your union steward tends to make your life at work a lot more pleasant.

The role of steward comes with certain expectations from employees. The steward is *their* representative. He or she is elected to protect *their* rights. You have to expect the steward's loyalties to lie with the union members. That doesn't mean, however, that you can't attempt to minimize hostilities with your steward. The best means for developing a cooperative relationship is to show respect for the steward and to keep him or her informed of problems you're having and of any changes that will affect the people in your department. A good supervisor-steward relationship can allow problems to be resolved quickly in the department and avoid the stress and cost associated with a lengthy dispute.

Strike
A situation in which employees leave their jobs and refuse to come to work until a contract has been signed

Lockout
A company action equivalent to a strike; occurs when management denies unionized employees access to their jobs.

Conciliation
An impasse-resolution technique in which a third party acts as a go-between with the aim of keeping negotiations ongoing

Mediation
An impasse-resolution technique in which a mediator attempts to pull together the common ground that exists and make settlement recommendations for overcoming the barriers that exist between the two sides in a conflict

Sometimes representatives of management and labour cannot reach an agreement on a new contract. When this happens, the union may choose to call a strike. In a **strike**, employees leave their jobs and refuse to come to work until a contract has been signed. Realize, too, that there's a company equivalent to a strike. It's called a **lockout**. That is when management denies unionized employees access to their jobs.

Historically, the strike was a potent weapon. By withholding labour, the union could impose financial hardships on an employer. However, beginning in the early 1980s, strikes began to lose much of their potency. For one thing, public sentiment supporting their use by unions has declined. But more importantly, management in recent years has become much more aggressive in replacing striking workers. A strike by flight attendants at American Airlines in November 1993 didn't completely stop American from flying. Although many flights had to be cancelled, supervisors and other employees with flight-attendant training temporarily took some of their places. A few years earlier, when TWA flight attendants participated in a lengthy strike against their employer, TWA's management went out and recruited replacements. The present law in some Canadian jurisdictions allows managers to replace striking workers, but replacement workers are currently banned in Quebec, British Columbia and Ontario.

When labour and management cannot reach a satisfactory agreement themselves, they may need the assistance of an objective third-party individual. This assistance comes in the form of conciliation and mediation, fact-finding, or interest arbitration.

Conciliation and **mediation** are two very closely related impasse resolution techniques. Both are techniques whereby a neutral third party attempts to get labour and management to resolve their differences. Under conciliation, the role of the third party is to keep the negotiations ongoing. In other words, this individual is a go-between—advocating a

American Airlines flight attendants walk the picket line while on strike.

voluntary means through which both sides can continue negotiating. Mediation goes one step further. The mediator attempts to pull together the common ground that exists and make settlement recommendations for overcoming the barriers that exist between the two sides. A mediator's suggestions, however, are only advisory. That means that the suggestions are not binding on either party.

Fact-finding is a technique whereby a neutral third-party individual conducts a hearing to gather evidence from both labour and management. The fact-finder then renders a decision as to how he or she views an appropriate settlement. Similar to mediation, the fact-finder's recommendations are only suggestions—they, too, are not binding on either party.

The final impasse resolution technique is called **interest arbitration**. Under interest arbitration, generally a panel of three individuals—one neutral and one each from the union and management—hears testimony from both sides. After the hearing, the panel renders a decision on how to settle the current contract negotiation dispute. If all three members of the panel are unanimous in their decision, that decision may be binding on both parties. Interest arbitration is found more frequently in public-sector collective bargaining; its use in private-sector labour disputes is rare.

There is little you can do to directly resolve a strike. However, if your employees go out on strike, you may be called upon to assume an increased number of nonsupervisory tasks in order to keep the business going. Or if management decides to replace striking workers, you will have to train and orient the new employees.

A more troublesome situation for supervisors is the **wildcat strike**. This is an illegal strike where employees refuse to work during the term of a binding contract. Such strikes can be brought about by a number of factors, but they usually involve ambiguities in the current contract. For instance, employee concerns over management's right to contract out some assembly work has resulted in wildcat strikes at several electronic-component manufacturers. The key point to remember is that wildcat strikes are illegal. Grievance procedures exist precisely to settle such differences. Should you find yourself in the middle of a wildcat strike, Figure 15-4 provides you with some guidelines to follow.

When the Canada Labour Relations Board ruled that Royal Oak Mines in Yellowknife had acted in bad faith, the final chapter in one of Canada's most bitter labour disputes was written.

The management of Royal Oak Mines was ruled to have encouraged a union raid, with the apparent aim of getting a rival union to take over. This would have eliminated the need to negotiate with the original union, which had been a tough adversary. The Board ruled that negotiations were to resume with the original union. In this famous case, the relationship between Royal Oak and the union deteriorated to the point that nine men (strikebreakers) were killed while working the mine. A union member who was out on strike was charged in their deaths.

Fact-finding
A technique whereby a neutral third-party individual conducts a hearing to gather evidence from both labour and management

Interest arbitration
Arbitration in which a panel of three individuals hears testimony from both sides and renders a decision on how to settle the current contract negotiation dispute

Wildcat strike
An illegal strike where employees refuse to work during the term of a binding contract, often due to ambiguities in the current contract

Royal Oak Mines Inc. – Giant Mine
http://www.
royal-oak-mines.
com/giant.html

Dying For Gold: The True Story Of The Giant Mine Murders
http://www.
harpercollins.com/
canada/0002557541.htm

FIGURE 15-4

Supervisory guidelines for handling wildcat strikes. (*Source:* L. W. Rue and L. L. Byars, *Supervision: Key Link to Productivity,* 4th ed., Homewood, IL: Richard D. Irwin, 1993, p. 325. With permission.)

- Stay on the job.
- Notify higher management by telephone or messenger.
- Carefully record the events as they happen.
- Pay strict attention to who the leaders are and record their behaviour.
- Record any lack of action by union officials.
- Report all information as fully and as soon as possible to higher management.
- Encourage employees to go back to work.
- Ask union officials to instruct employees to go back to work.
- Don't discuss the cause of the strike.
- Don't make any agreements or say anything that might imply permission to leave work.
- Make it clear that management will discuss the issue when all of the employees are back at work.

THE OTHER SIDE: CAW PERSPECTIVE ON LABOUR MATTERS

Herman Rosenfeld, the National Representative, Education Department for the Canadian Auto Workers union, outlines the labour perspective of a union representing 214 000 members. Herman has been a national representative since January 1994. Before that, he worked on the CAW technology project. He also has experience in a GM van assembly plant, working on the line and acting as a committee person and member of the bargaining committee for ten years.

HOW HAS NAFTA AFFECTED UNION MEMBERSHIP?

In general, the North American Free Trade Agreement (NAFTA) hasn't yet led to large number of plant closings, at least in industries where we are organized. We know, however, that many of our employers have begun to make long-term investment decisions based upon their expectations of the effects of North American free trade. One aspect of this is the increasing concerns with relative costs by our employers.

On the other hand, it has certainly affected the way our members perceive their futures. Workers know that a free trade environment will make it easier for many employers to move to lower cost manufacturing areas, or at least to use the threat of competition from lower-cost manufacturers to drive down wage and benefit levels.

We see NAFTA and the FTA as a threat to workers for a number of reasons. They are part of a whole series of policies which have increased capital mobility and decreased the ability of democratic institutions to intervene in the operation of the economy. Both FTA and NAFTA have helped to carry this agenda forward and institutionalize these policies.

It is not as if we are opposed to increasing levels of trade. Our union argued for a managed trade environment, modeled on the US-Canada Auto Pact, where workers in the U.S., Canada, and Mexico would have basic job level guarantees. We feel that NAFTA and FTA aren't principally concerned with trade, but are more concerned with capital mobility and further deregulating the economic system.

The movement of a number of manufacturers to low-wage areas, increased investment in financial and other low-wage service sectors, and the privatization of public services have cost jobs in Canada. They also constitute a threat to overall unionization levels. Certainly, unionization levels have decreased throughout much of the industrialized world.

FIGURE 15-5

Herman Rosenfeld, National Representative, Education Department, CAW, has many years experience in union matters, at the manufacturing level and as part of the union/management team.

Notes on NAFTA: The Masters of Mankind
http://daisy.uwaterloo. ca/~alopez-o/politics/ chomnafta.html

North American Free Trade Agreement
http://www.accent.net/ advocate/nafta.htm

On the other hand, unionization levels haven't dropped in Canada. Certainly in the industries that we organize we haven't seen this in quite the same way that some others have, especially in auto parts and auto assembly, where we have, more or less, held our own. This is true for a number of reasons, not the least of which has been the lowering of the value of the Canadian dollar, the resurgence of U.S. auto markets and the fundamental soundness and strategic location of our auto industry.

HOW DOES THE UNION VIEW TQM AND REENGINEERING PROGRAMS?

In our view, total quality management programs, reengineering projects and the like are part of a wave of workplace change that has more to do with cost reduction and attempts to shed labour than with any desire to provide better quality goods and services to consumers.

Based upon the principles originally developed in Japan, at Toyota, they attempt to analyze production processes in order to squeeze labour out of production and time out of labour. The result has been twofold: we have seen an increasing number of layoffs in our workplaces, related not to declines in market shares or in the number of users of products or through new technology, but through reorganizing the production unit to run with fewer workers; second, those that remain in the workplace suffer from increasing levels of work and stress.

I think it is important to emphasize that we as a union and most unionized workers in Canada care deeply about the quality of the products we produce and the services we provide to the public. Our objections to efforts to "lean out" the workplace are based upon our view that this has little to do with quality and "empowerment" of workers.

WHAT WOULD BE YOUR ADVICE TO SUPERVISORS IN A UNIONIZED WORKPLACE?

First, respect the collective agreement. It was negotiated to make sure that production could be carried out without sacrificing the rights of workers. Collectively bargained work rules do work.

Second, remember that, as the first-line supervisor, you are close to the workers. An important aspect of your working conditions is how they treat you. And how they treat you will be determined in part by how you treat them.

Third, there are tremendous pressures these days from upper management to look for ways to reduce the number of workers, increase workloads, and try to get the workers to "buy in" to some form of "continuous improvement" activities. We realize the pressures that you are under from your bosses, but don't work to undermine our working conditions or change our way of thinking.

Fourth, respect our legitimate needs for washroom relief, time to socialize with each other, time off the job, and desire to choose our overtime hours. Make every effort to accommodate our needs in this area.

Fifth, don't play favourites and don't try to develop straw bosses.

Sixth, try to resolve our grievances and complaints on the shop floor before they get out of hand.

Finally, respect the union. If you have a problem with the way things are going, talk to the union rep. Keep in mind the fact that we probably look at the company, its role, and a whole series of things differently than you do. Respect these differences and live with them.

OVER HISTORY, UNIONS HAVE FOUGHT DIFFERENT BATTLES. WHAT DO YOU FORESEE AS THE BATTLES OR CAUSES OF THE FUTURE?

First, unions must become leaders in the struggle for policies to reassert the right to secure full-time, socially useful jobs. Full employment is the fundamental basis of a sound and just economy. To attain this, unions must also fight for the development of new democratic institutions to limit corporate power and intervene in the overall investment process that allows capital to leave Canada.

Second, unions will lead the battle for shorter work time. We see this as an alternative to the present reality where individual businesses increase productivity through shedding the labour of some and intensifying the labour of others, reaping the windfall in the form of profits and highly-paid top executives.

Third, unions will have to find ways to organize the unorganized, both in manufacturing and service sectors.

Fourth, in this period of increasing social insecurity and social stress, unions are becoming a critical force in the struggle for social justice, equality, tolerance and human rights.

Fifth, unions will have to become leaders in the struggle to protect the environment, through that elusive thing called "sustainable growth."

Finally, unions will be at the forefront of the struggle for deepening access to quality, universal, and life-long education.

WHAT IS THE MOST IMPORTANT ISSUE FOR CANADIAN STUDENTS TO APPRECIATE ABOUT UNIONS?

Unions have played a critical role in changing the face of both the workplace and society as a whole. They are the single most responsible force for safe, secure, well-paid and humane workplaces. As well, they are the basic social force that brought us most of the things that have made Canada a good place to live: medicare, a relatively open and democratic political system, decent jobs, the social safety net. To the extent that unions are weakened, these things will be watered down or lost.

HANDLING GRIEVANCES

We've used the term *grievance* at several points in this chapter. But how does a supervisor go about handling a grievance? Of all the activities that supervisors of unionized employees get involved in, none are more important than the handling of grievances. In this section, we'll help you develop your grievance-handling skills.

ASSESSING YOURSELF: ARE YOU AN EFFECTIVE GRIEVANCE-HANDLER?

Answer each of the following questions as you have or would behave, not as you think you *should* behave.

	Strongly Agree	Agree	Undecided	Disagree	Strongly Disagree
1. If an employee has a grievance, the first thing I do is review the relevant clause in the union contract.	❏	❏	❏	❏	❏
2. As soon as an employee informs me of a grievance, to avoid escalation I specifically provide him or her with management's side of the story.	❏	❏	❏	❏	❏
3. If I'm unsure about wording or an interpretation in the contract, I contact a labour specialist in the organization for counsel.	❏	❏	❏	❏	❏
4. I make sure I get all the facts pertinent to the dispute, regardless of how much time it may take.	❏	❏	❏	❏	❏
5. I avoid letting personalities or personal preferences influence my decision on a grievance.	❏	❏	❏	❏	❏
6. If a grievance has merit, I assume I have the authority to take immediate corrective action.	❏	❏	❏	❏	❏
7. I keep comprehensive records on every grievance in expectation that my decision will be appealed.	❏	❏	❏	❏	❏

SCORING DIRECTIONS AND KEY

For questions 3, 5, and 7, give yourself five points for Strongly Agree, four points for Agree, three points for Undecided, two points for Disagree, and one point for Strongly Disagree. For questions 1, 2, 4, and 6, reverse the scoring (for example, one point for Strongly Agree). Add up your total score. The range will be between 7 and 35. Scores of 30 and above indicate good grievance-handling skills. Scores of 25 to 29 indicate room for improvement. Scores of less than 25 suggest a strong need to work on these skills.

SKILL BASICS

Almost all collective bargaining agreements contain formal procedures to be used in resolving disputes surrounding the interpretation and application of the contract. These procedures are typically designed to resolve disputes as quickly as possible and at the lowest level in the organization. Whenever possible, then, the supervisor is encouraged to resolve employee grievances without involving upper levels of management and senior union officials.

Consistent with this belief that grievances should be handled at the lowest level possible in the organization, the typical grievance procedure looks like Figure 15-6. An employee's first efforts should be directed at attempting to resolve the complaint with his or her immediate supervisor.

If dissatisfied with the supervisor's response, the grievance typically escalates through the following stages: the supervisor and union steward discuss the complaint; the supervisor and a labour specialist from the human resources department discuss the complaint with the chief union steward or union grievance committee; the facilities manager and the labour specialist meet with the union grievance committee; the organization's top management meet with the union grievance committee and a representative of the national union to try to work out a solution. If the grievance still cannot be resolved, the dispute will be referred to an impartial third-party **arbitrator** who will hear the case and make a ruling. In practice, 98 per cent of all collective-bargaining agreements provide for arbitration as the final step in an impasse. Grievance arbitration usually focuses on one of two issues—contract interpretation and discipline and discharge. The party claiming that the contract language has been improperly interpreted has the burden of going forward in presenting its case. In discipline and discharge cases, because the action was initiated by the company, the company officials have the burden of showing that they had just cause. As for who pays the arbitrator, it's often dependent

Arbitrator
An impartial third party who hears grievances and makes rulings on them

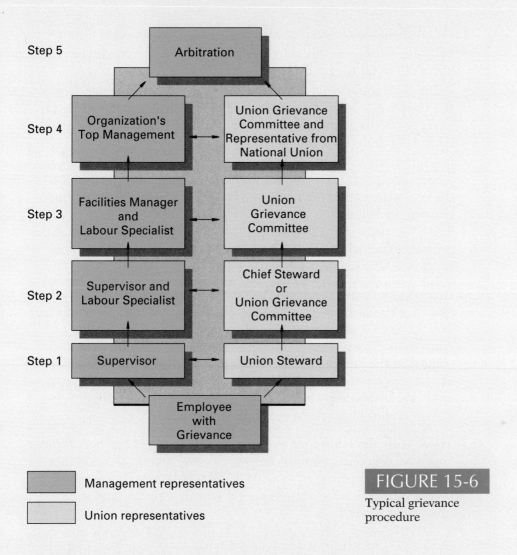

Step 5

Step 4

Step 3

Step 2

Step 1

Arbitration

Organization's Top Management

Union Grievance Committee and Representative from National Union

Facilities Manager and Labour Specialist

Union Grievance Committee

Supervisor and Labour Specialist

Chief Steward or Union Grievance Committee

Supervisor

Union Steward

Employee with Grievance

Management representatives

Union representatives

FIGURE 15-6

Typical grievance procedure

on who's raising the issue. More often, though, the labour agreement will stipulate who pays, or how the costs of arbitration will be divided.

The previous steps describe the overall grievance procedure. But our concern is in building supervisory skills. So we need to address a more specific question: how should you, as a supervisor, respond if an employee or union steward presents a formal grievance? We suggest you do the following:

1. **Listen to the employee's complaint.** Don't be defensive and don't take the complaint personally. Employees regularly have grievances and you're the first contact point in the process that represents the organization.

- Calmly listen to the employee's complaint. Keep an open mind.
- Very importantly at this stage, don't argue with the employee. What you want to do is gain understanding.
- Using your active listening skills will help you better understand the employee's complaint. Additionally, hostilities and tensions are likely to become subdued as you honestly demonstrate your willingness to understand the grievance.
- Ask questions to make sure you get to the real problem. Is the employee complaining about unfair allocation of overtime when the real issue is that the employee is having serious personal financial problems and was counting on lots of overtime to help pay bills? You want to make sure you fully understand the details of the grievance and what specific provision of the labour contract the employee believes is involved.

2. **Investigate to get the facts.** You want to separate facts from opinions. Are the facts, as presented by the employee, complete and factual? Interview any key people who may be able to verify the employee's claims. Review all pertinent documents. Go over the clauses in the labour contract that apply to the employee's complaint. If you're unsure about the contract's language or how a relevant clause should be interpreted, get counsel from a labour specialist in your human resources department.

3. **Make your decision and explain it clearly.** You need to complete your investigation promptly so you can reach your decision in a relatively short period of time. Why? Because most labour agreements specify a definite time period within which a grievance must be answered.

- If you determine that the grievance is unfounded, verbally give the employee and union steward your interpretation. Be sure to back up your decision with specific reasons for denying the grievance, citing evidence from your investigation and/or language from the contract. You should then follow up the verbal answer with a written response.
- If the grievance has merit, provide a written response to the employee and union steward stating this fact. Additionally, you should describe the corrective action you plan to take. But before you write this response, be sure that your remedy is consistent with established practices, doesn't set any new precedents, and is within your authority. When in doubt, get approval from your boss or a

manager in human resources. You should be very careful about making individual exceptions to past practices. This might seem like an easy way to make the grievance disappear, but you could end up setting a precedent that might seriously hurt the organization in future contract negotiations or in future arbitration decisions.

4. **Keep records and documents.** It's important to document everything you do relating to a grievance. Remember that the labour agreement is a binding, legal contract. As such, formality is important. You have to follow the language of the contract. To protect yourself and the organization against charges that you have not followed the contract as intended, you must keep all the records that you've accumulated on every grievance.

5. **Be prepared for appeals.** If you rule against the employee, you should expect the employee or the union steward to appeal your decision to a higher level. Be prepared to be questioned by union officials and various labour specialists from your organization's human resource group. Don't let this shake you. And don't let an employee or union representative's threat of appeal influence your decision.

The grievance procedure is essentially a formal appeals system. It is designed to protect an employee's rights. Your judgment may be overruled at a higher level. But that's OK. If you've followed the contract's procedures, made your decision in good faith, and carefully documented your actions, you've correctly fulfilled your obligations in the grievance procedure.

APPLYING YOUR SKILLS

Break the class into groups of three. This role play requires one person to play the role of the supervisor (Alex), another the role of the employee (Pat), and the third will play the union steward (C.J.).

All players should read the following scenario and the excerpt from the union's contract. Then you are to role-play a meeting in Alex's office. This role play should take no more than fifteen minutes.

SCENARIO

The head of security guards has recently been focusing attention on the possession of drugs at the company's workplace. One morning last week, the guard suspected the possession of a controlled substance by an employee, Pat Davis. The guard, noticing Pat placing a bag in his/her personal locker, searched the locker for drugs. The guard found a variety of pills, some of which he thought were non-prescription amphetamines.

As Pat was leaving work for the day, the security guard stopped him/her and requested Pat to empty the contents of the bag. Pat was not told why the request was being made. Pat refused to honour the request, stormed out the door, and left the company premises. Pat was informed the next morning that he/she was being terminated for refusing to obey the legitimate order of a plant security guard.

Alex has just gone into a meeting with Pat and C.J. Alex wishes to enforce management's decision to terminate Pat, and justify the reason for it. C.J. and Pat, on the other hand, claim this action is a violation of the contract.

RELEVANT CONTRACT LANGUAGE

The following is extracted from the union-management contract.

> An employee who fails to maintain proper standards of conduct at all times, or who violates any of the following rules, shall subject him- or herself to disciplinary action:

> *Rule 4.* Bringing illegal substances or intoxicating liquors onto company premises, using or possessing these on company property, or reporting to work under the influence is strictly prohibited.

> *Rule 11.* Refusal to follow supervisory orders, or in any way act insubordinate to any management agent, is strictly prohibited.

5. Which one of the following is not part of the collective bargaining process?
   a. interpretation of a written agreement
   b. negotiations of a written agreement
   c. approval of a written agreement by the LRB
   d. administration of a written agreement

6. Bargaining in good faith means that the company and labour union must negotiate until they've reached an agreement acceptable to both parties. True or False?

7. Explain what is meant by the terms *conciliation, mediation,* and *fact-finding.* When are any of the three used?

8. The procedure used in resolving disputes surrounding the interpretation and application of the contract is called _____.
   a. the grievance procedure
   b. interest arbitration
   c. a strike or a lockout
   d. none of the above

SUMMARY

This summary is organized by the Learning Objectives.

1. The overall percentage of the labour force that belongs to a union has been declining since the mid-1950s. But this decline should not be interpreted as implying that labour union influence has declined similarly. Labour unions still represent the majority of workers in many key industries. Additionally, wages and benefits won by labour unions typically spill over to influence the wages and benefits of nonunionized employees.

2. Unions are appealing to employees because their power offers the promise of higher wages and benefits, greater job security, and increased opportunities to influence work rules.

3. The federal and provincial labour relations acts provide guidelines for both companies and unions. The Charter of Rights and Freedoms further protects all individual rights of every Canadian.

4. The primary purpose of collective bargaining is to negotiate a union contract and spell out the terms for administering that contract.

5. The supervisor plays a very important role in contract administration. He or she needs to know the details of the contract in order to interpret it and carry out its procedures. What supervisors say and do largely determines the labour-management climate in the organization.

6. Herman Rosenfeld explained the C.A.W. opinion that:
   a) Although NAFTA has not affected Canadian unionization levels yet, it is a threat to the security of workers' futures.
   b) TQM, reengineering, etc. are based more on concern for cost reduction than improving quality and are linked with heavy downsizing.
   c) Supervisors should respect the union and the collective agreement, treat workers well, accommodate to their legitimate needs, not play favourites, try to resolve problems on the shop floor, and be wary of pressures to cut costs and undermine workers.
   d) In future, unions will focus on protecting jobs, working shorter hours, organizing more workers, and fighting for better access to education, environmental protection and protection of human rights.
   e) Students need to appreciate the critical and constructive role unions have played in our society.

7. The steps involved in handling a grievance are: 1. listen to the employee's complaint; 2. investigate to get the facts; 3. make your decision and explain it clearly; 4. keep records and documents; and 5. be prepared for appeals.

UNDERSTANDING THE BASICS

KEY TERMS AND CONCEPTS

Agency shop
Arbitration
Arbitrator
Bargaining unit
Collective bargaining
Conciliation
Employee relations
Fact-finding
Interest arbitration

Lockout
Mediation
Spillover effect
Strike
Union
Union shop
Union steward
Wildcat strike

REVIEWING YOUR KNOWLEDGE

1. What might explain the decline in union membership over the past thirty-five years?
2. Contrast agency and union shops.
3. How are labour issues impacted by legislation?
4. Describe the supervisor's role in the collective bargaining process.
5. "An employer might not want to stifle a union organizing effort. In fact, an employer might want to encourage his employees to join a union." Do you agree or disagree with this statement? Discuss.
6. What is collective bargaining?
7. What is the purpose of a grievance procedure? Describe the typical steps in the grievance process.
8. "You can predict strikes. Union administrators have to call a strike every now and then just to demonstrate to their membership that they're fighting hard for them." Do you agree or disagree with this statement? Explain.
9. How would the existence of a union and a collective-bargaining contract affect a) employee recruitment and selection, b) compensation, and c) discipline?

ANSWERS TO THE POP QUIZZES

1. **b. good supervision.** Where supervision and supervisory practices are "good," there's less likely a chance for a successful union organizing campaign.

2. The conditions negotiated by unionized workers influence the wages and terms of employment of nonunionized workers.

3. **True.** As in question 1, where supervision is good, the likelihood of having a union is low; where supervisory practices are poor, a union is likely to be encouraged to represent the workers.

4. **a. the federal and provincial labour relations acts.**

5. **c. approval of a written agreement by the LRB.** The LRB does not approve labour-management agreements. Final approval of a contract is the province of the rank-and-file members who are to ratify a contract before it is binding.

6. **False.** Bargaining in good faith means the company and labour union must negotiate in an attempt to reach an agreement acceptable to both parties. Reaching an agreement is not guaranteed, however.

7. Conciliation, mediation, and fact-finding are three impasse-resolution techniques. Conciliation and mediation involve a neutral third party who attempts to get labour and management to resolve their differences. Fact-finding is a technique whereby a neutral third-party individual conducts a hearing to gather evidence from both labour and management. The fact-finder then renders a decision as to how he or she views an appropriate settlement. Suggestions from all three techniques, however, are not binding on either party.

8. **a. the grievance procedure.** This is the definition of the process used in labour-management relationships to resolve disputes surrounding the interpretation and application of the contract.

CASE 15.A

Up Against the Golden Arches

When Sarah Inglis took on McDonald's in an attempt to establish the first unionized franchise in North America, she learned about the power of big organizations and the politics of union drives. The initial success of the membership card drive (a majority of 67 of 102 workers) should have lead to immediate certification. But the ensuing battle ended with McDonald's the victor.

Her drive to unionize the Orangeville McDonald's failed in a private vote, agreed to after lengthy arguments at the Ontario Labour Board. McDonald's anti-union machine was effective. It ran the gamut from "warm fuzzies" of praise for previously mistreated employees, to free Big Macs, promotional Olympic hats for each employee, hassle-free changes to work schedules, staff parties, and a miraculous transformation in the work relationship between management and the predominantly teenaged workers. With a pricey Toronto lawyer working on the campaign, McDonald's dragged out proceedings at the Ontario Labour Board. The company used the extra time to persuade the young workers that it was in their best interest to vote "No." On the night before the vote, the store manager hosted a rally. Its aim was to build morale and pep for a store that really cared about its staff, and to apologize for any perception of ill will.

McDonald's
http://www.
mcdonalds.com/

McSpotlight
www.mcspotlight.
org/media/press/
toronto_13feb98.html

The *Labour Times* reported that Sarah Inglis was let down by the labour movement. The Canadian Auto Workers' union wouldn't take her side. According to Gary Fane, director of organizing, "We are not in the fast-food industry in Ontario." When the Service Employees International Union (SEIU) did join her, it was reported that Sarah did not get adequate support against the strength of McDonald's. To unionize a major international corporation, it takes alliances of unions to pool their resources to develop grassroots, broad-based organizing drives. This practice is extremely uncommon in Canadian labour movements. It is suggested, however, that as the traditional union membership continues to shrink, the very livelihood of unions in Canada rests with Sarah's generation working in the fast food service sector.

In retrospect, Sarah Inglis says, "Either way it went, we won. We changed the working conditions 100 per cent," gaining respect, dignity, and job security for the McDonalds' crew.

RESPONDING TO THIS CASE

1. Review the certification process to determine why the Labour Board would have allowed a private vote in this case. In groups, discuss whether it was fair, or not, to decide the fate of the union drive by a private vote versus the membership card drive.

2. Review the actions of McDonald's. Did they abide by the rules governing a company's actions when faced with certification?

3. In teams, research this case more fully. Acting as consultants, develop a strategy that you would propose if the situation arose to unionize another McDonalds' franchise. You may want to interview union representatives in local companies to identify successful union drive actions.

CASE 15.B

Applying Union Rules at GM

Lindsey Stevenson works for General Motors as a production line supervisor. She likes her job because she has excellent rapport with the workers she supervises. Probably one of her greatest assets is keeping lines of communication open with her employees. She attributes to her own manager her success in knowing what her employees think. That is, she has learned from him that being a strong manager is built on employee trust and a positive attitude. He willingly shares information with supervisors and is a good listener.

Lindsey has particularly good rapport with one of her assembly-line employees, Tyson Miller. Tyson has become a good informal leader and helps Lindsey ward off potential problems. He isn't afraid of suggesting things that may be of concern to other employees and Lindsey listens. Tyson is quite attuned to the "big picture" too, partially because of his friendship with Kareem Rifaat, a manager at a local bank.

Due to the popularity of a GM truck model that was introduced recently, GM has increased its production to meet customer demands. Lindsey and her employees know it is important to respond to the increased productivity emphasis of top management, but the union contract also must be considered. She has had many conversations with her manager, peers, and employees about this important balance.

GM Canada
http://www.gmcanada.
com/

In fact, only this morning Tyson told her that he heard GM was going to initiate a large recruitment effort to expand the number of production line assemblers. He wanted to know what that meant to him and his coworkers. Lindsey felt he was hinting that maybe the lines of communication may not be as open as she thought they were.

RESPONDING TO THIS CASE

1. How should Lindsey respond to the information Tyson just gave her?

2. How might GM employees, especially Lindsey's employees, benefit from an increase in production? What might be some of the drawbacks or negative implications of such action?

3. Looking at some of the items you identified in question 2, what implications or concerns are there for the GM management and employees that hinge on labour management issues? Why?

4. What outcomes could result from the issues and actions you identified in questions 2 and 3? In view of the direction this scenario seems to be going, what advice would you give to Lindsey about her role in labour matters and the collective bargaining process?

5. Form groups of four to six students. Assume that GM (or any company) may be entering into the collective bargaining process.
   a) What should Lindsey (or any supervisor) know about contract negotiations?
   b) Identify the information a supervisor (especially Lindsey) needs to gather in preparing for negotiation.
   c) Identify some of the challenges a supervisor faces in gathering information for negotiations, as well as in supervising union employees.

Part V: Coping with Workplace Dynamics

Jan Holman, Maintenance Manager
Metropolitan Transit Commission

Jan supervises two kinds of workers—mechanics and cleaners.

According to the union, a supervisor can ask an employee to perform tasks at or below his or her level.

Because the Metropolitan Transit Commission (MTC) sometimes has a shortage of cleaners, Jan will ask the mechanics to clean the buses. One morning Jan called in mechanics on overtime to do repairs. At the same time, some buses needed to be cleaned. Because all cleaners were busy, Jan asked a mechanic on overtime to clean the buses. A cleaner filed a grievance with the union. He claimed it was unfair to call in mechanics to do a cleaner's job.

Jan and the MTC maintained that they had the right to ask the mechanic to clean the bus. It had been an emergency situation. The bus needed to go out and there were no cleaners available. The problem was taken to the third level of grievance in front of the MTC's Chief Administrator.

1. What is Jan Holman's main source of conflict? Why?

2. What are some of the problems and challenges Jan Holman faces as he considers implementing change at the MTC? What do you consider his biggest challenge and why?

3. When are problems and conflicts within a unionized organization sometimes handled differently than in a nonunionized business? In such cases, are supervisors expected to solve all problems that arise? Why or why not?

4. What course of action may be necessary when a formal grievance is filed within a unionized organization? What role, if any, does the supervisor assume in such action? How does this apply to Jan Holman's situation?

5. What can a supervisor do to help employees reduce conflict and stress, cope with change, and improve their working environment? Which of these "solutions" would be helpful to Jan Holman and his employees?

PART SIX

PERSONAL DEVELOPMENT

16. MANAGING YOUR CAREER

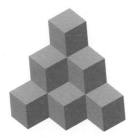

16 MANAGING YOUR CAREER

LEARNING OBJECTIVES

After reading this chapter, you should be able to:

1. Define *career*.
2. Describe the traditional career path.
3. Explain why traditional career paths are disappearing.
4. Identify your basic talents and strengths.
5. Describe your interests.
6. Indicate the size of organization you prefer.
7. Match your individual personality to an organizational culture.
8. Define your career goals.
9. Identify the path from where you are now to your career goals.

CHAPTER OUTLINE

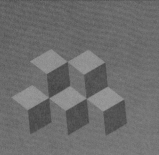

Reckitt and Colman Canada, Ltd.
http://www. foodserviceworld. com/reckitt/

Com-Dev Inc.
http://www. com-dev.com/

Pat McCallum, 40, has spent her entire working career at Air Canada. After receiving her B.B.A. from St. Francis Xavier University, she began as a passenger agent at Halifax airport and ten months later became a field auditor. Pat progressed through three levels of responsibility there, ending up in charge of field auditing. In 1986, Pat became the supervisor of commercial receivables, in 1988 she moved to Winnipeg as Manager of Refund Services, and in 1997 she became Manager of Sales Accounting, responsible for the processing of all Air Canada ticket transactions. Pat also sits on various industry committees (e.g., IATA) representing Air Canada.

Stephen Fraser, 35, has had several employers. After getting a college diploma in business followed by a B.A. from Wilfrid Laurier, Stephen went to Reckitt and Colman. In his three years there he went from sales representative to key account manager. Then he moved to J.B. Foods as a key account manager. After two years there Stephen became a district sales manager for a packaged goods manufacturer. His success there led to his becoming first their private label sales manager, and then national sales manager.

Joe Sferrazza, 40, has had not only several employers but several different professions. After earning his B.Eng. and M.Eng. at McMaster, he spent two years on a federal strategical grant implementing new technologies in various companies. Then he went to Com-Dev as a research engineer designing products for satellites, later becoming a production engineer supervising sixteen technicians. During these years, Joe also had a sideline buying and renovating homes for resale. From Com-Dev he went to A.I.C. Investment Company for whom he ran a small company. When it went into receivership, Joe was hired by Northern Telecom as a group leader. He had another stint running a company for A.I.C. followed by yet another stretch with Northern Telecom (now as a manager) after which he moved to De Santis Developments to be a project coordinator for residential construction. This required him to go back to school part-time for a year and a half to learn civil engineering skills. After five years with De Santis, the death of his wife led to Joe's quitting so he could spend more time with his children. He has now taken the entrepreneurial plunge, heading up his own property development company.

Pat's, Stephen's, and Joe's careers vary widely. Pat has followed a steady progression up the organization with one employer. Stephen has moved from sales into sales management but did so through changing employers and the products he sells. Joe has had several management positions but is now on his own and he has used his varying skills in two totally different industries. Your career is likely to look a lot more like that of Stephen or Joe than that of Pat. You can expect to change employers, move laterally as well as upward, and not to restrict yourself to a single "profession." You're also likely to need some retraining along the way.

WHAT IS A CAREER?

The term *career* has a number of meanings. In popular usage, it can mean advancement ("his career is progressing nicely"), a profession ("she has chosen a career in medicine"), or a lifelong sequence of jobs ("his career has included fifteen jobs in six different organizations"). For our purposes, we define a **career** as the sequence of positions occupied by a person during his or her lifetime. By this definition, it is apparent that we all have, or will have, careers. Moreover, the concept is as relevant to transient unskilled labourers as to engineers or physicians.

Many of you are currently pursuing, or plan to pursue, a career in management. That typically begins with a supervisory job. So success as a supervisor is almost always a prerequisite to assuming higher-level management positions.

Are you well suited to a career in management? What type of organization is best matched to your particular management style and most likely to lead to your being successful? What can you do to better prepare yourself for an increasingly changing and uncertain world? We'll try to answer these questions in the remainder of this chapter.

Career
The sequence of positions occupied by a person during his or her lifetime

THE TRADITIONAL CAREER PATH

Pat McCallum pursued a **traditional career path** at Air Canada. She started in a nonmanagerial job and then progressed through a sequence of management positions with increasing responsibilities. The traditional career path is characterized by relative predictability, upward movement, and the organization taking responsibility for your career development.

Figure 16-1 illustrates a traditional career path that a college or university graduate of the early 1960s might have experienced. Graduating at age 21 or 22, with a degree in business and little or no work experience, this graduate went to work for a large corporation such as Canadian Pacific, Bell Canada, Ford, Stelco or, Imperial Oil. Along with fifty or more other young graduates, the new employee was put into the company's management training program. Trainees would begin in one department—for example, production control—and proceed in lockstep fashion from department to department for two or three years. Never staying in any department for more than four to six months, the trainee got to see many different facets of the company and was able to find the area where he and the company believed he could make the largest contribution. Companies treated their trainees as soft clay, to be shaped into the type of person whose skills and management style fit their corporate mold. General Motors, for instance, sought conservative people who could sublimate their individuality to the larger corporate team. Committees made the key decisions at GM; individual stars were discouraged.

Traditional career path
A sequence of management positions with increasing responsibilities; characterized by relative predictability, upward vertical movement, and the organization taking responsibility for employee career development.

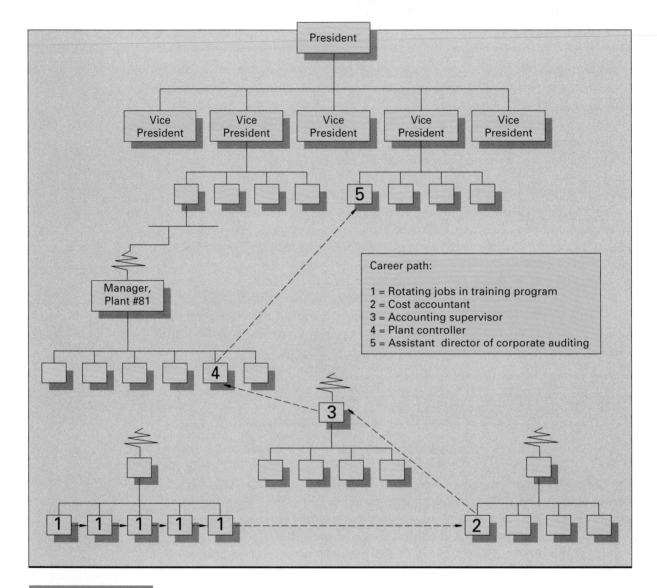

FIGURE 16-1

An example of the traditional career path

CIBC Home Page
http://www.cibc.
com/index.html

For someone accepted to be an officer-in-training at the CIBC, a six-month training program would lead to a posting in a bank branch with low-level supervisory responsibilities (typically accounting). After being rotated through the various supervisory positions (at the same or different branches) in order to get supervisory experience in all areas, the trainee would become a branch manager of a small branch. His or her career would then consist of managing progressively larger branches. Some people, of course, reached plateaus along the way. They were rarely fired; instead, further promotion opportunities simply disappeared.

FIGURE 16-2

The traditional career path historically began for college graduates with a visit to their career placement centre.

The tall pyramid shape of these large corporations meant there were lots of promotion opportunities for good workers. Additionally, rapid growth and expansion further opened the doors to continuous promotions. The traditional career path allowed people to spend their work lives in only one or two organizations and eliminated the need for them to worry about their future. The company's human resources group (then called the personnel department) developed replacement charts, succession tracking systems, and individual career progression plans. Responsibility for career development essentially fell on the company rather than on the individual employee.

THE NEW CAREER PATH

Some large corporations still have formal management training programs for new college graduates. And there are some current employees who will experience a relatively uninterrupted ascent up a single organization's managerial hierarchy. But such corporations and employees are increasingly rare. What we're seeing is corporations that have cut costs by reducing layers of management; widening spans of control; and significantly shrinking, and in some cases eliminating, entry-level management training programs. As a result, you should not expect to follow the traditional career path we've described. More likely, you'll pursue a different path, one which will be characterized by unpredictability, lateral and interorganizational moves, occasional bouts of stagnation, and the continual need for educational updating and retraining. Finally, you must be prepared to do what's necessary on your own to advance your career. We'll offer some guidelines later in this chapter.

UNPREDICTABILITY

The traditional career path offered predictability. This was possible because companies faced relatively stable environments. In the 1960s, for instance, General Motors' competition essentially came from only

Ford and Chrysler. Established brand names such as Chevrolet, Buick, and Cadillac, plus strong customer loyalty, assured GM of high sales year after year. With nearly a 50 per cent share of the North American automobile market, GM could offer its managers a stable, predictable, and upward career path.

Today, GM faces aggressive competition from dozens of automakers. Consumers demand high quality, innovative features, and maximum value for the dollar. In this competitive world, GM is no longer able to pass along its inefficiencies or higher development and production costs to consumers. So GM has had to restructure its organization. It has cut tens of thousands of jobs and reorganized the work of those whose jobs remain.

What has taken place at GM has gone on at almost every major corporation in the world. Continual efforts at cost cutting and reorganization have eliminated the traditional management career path. In fact, career paths in large corporations are increasingly looking like those in small business, where rapid change and uncertainty create a wide range of diverse career paths.

LATERAL AND INTERORGANIZATIONAL MOVES

In the traditional career path, individuals expected a sequence of steady promotions. In companies such as GM or IBM, it was not unusual for managers to get promoted every two to three years. Success, in fact, was defined more by the speed of one's promotions than by the promotions themselves. Except during early training, lateral transfers were perceived as nearly equivalent to a demotion.

Your career is very likely to include a number of lateral moves. New challenges will come from taking on different rather than greater responsibilities.

In addition, the restructuring and downsizing that corporations have undergone during the past decade have reduced the loyalty bonds that previously held employees to organizations. As corporations have shown less commitment to employees, employees have shown less commitment to them. So while your father or grandfather may have spent his entire working career with one employer, you're likely to change employers as conditions change and new opportunities arise.

PLATEAUING

Plateauing
A lack of further upward movement in one's career with their current employer

Reduced promotion opportunities translate into increased career **plateauing**. After only one or two promotions, employees are increasingly finding that there is not likely to be any further upward movement in their career with their current employer.

Plateauing is increasingly becoming a way of life for many managers. In the traditional career path, plateauing occurred, but it usually didn't hit until the manager reached his or her late 40s or early 50s. Nowadays, many managers are plateauing as early as their mid-20s. Downsizing, fewer management levels in the organization, less turnover in the upper-management ranks, and fewer job opportunities elsewhere have made plateauing a fact of life for millions of supervisors and middle-level managers.

Ambitious employees will be finding new paths to job satisfaction and personal growth. Success is less likely to be defined solely in terms of promotions. Jobs will be redesigned to increase diversity and challenge. Regular lateral moves will become commonplace. Compensation plans will be reworked to pay people more for their contribution than for their title. And we can expect to see many employees turning more attention toward their families or hobbies as a means of finding life gratification.

SKILL UPDATING

The usable life span of your skills is rapidly shrinking. The computer skills you learned five years ago have become obsolete. Recently enacted laws affecting civil rights and employees with disabilities require supervisors to change some of their practices. Corporate efforts at empowering employees mean supervisors need to learn empowerment skills. The changing workforce demands that supervisors learn how to manage diversity. Organizations implementing TQM expect their supervisors to understand its techniques and methods.

ZIGGY By Tom Wilson

© 1993, Ziggy and Friends, Inc./Distributed by Universal Press Syndicate

FIGURE 16-3

(*Source: Los Angeles Times*, January 19, 1993. Universal Press Syndicate.)

Lifelong learning
The need to
continually upgrade
skills through reading,
seminars, and formal
education

Future success in supervisory and managerial positions will require individuals to pursue **lifelong learning**. You'll be expected to read extensively and keep current on new management concepts, business practices, and changes in your industry. You'll regularly attend company seminars, industry workshops, and evening college classes to upgrade your skills. You may even need to take occasional sabbaticals from work in order to go back to school for advanced certificates and degrees.

TAKING CONTROL OF YOUR CAREER

While career development has been an important topic in business-related courses for the past three decades, we have witnessed some drastic changes over the years. Years ago, career development programs were designed to assist you in advancing your work life. The focus was to provide the information and assessment you needed to realize your career goals. Career development was also a way for the organization to attract and retain highly talented personnel. But those programs are all but disappearing in today's contemporary organizations—for many of the reasons we mentioned previously—downsizing, restructuring, and reengineering. As a result, one significant conclusion can be drawn about career development: you—and not the organization—are responsible for your career! Many employees have learned that the hard way over the past few years. As one supervisor aptly put it, "I've got to look out for Number One. No one else is going to."

How do you take control of your own career? The next section provides a detailed guide for helping you do personal career development.

PERSONAL CAREER DEVELOPMENT

Personal career planning doesn't provide any guarantees that you'll optimize your career potential. However, many years ago, a wise friend suggested that "opportunity knocks two or three times in every person's life. The difference between those who are able to take advantage of these opportunities and those who aren't is preparation." Further, the friend said, "the person we typically call 'lucky' is usually just someone who was ready when the right situation came around." **Personal career planning** can prepare you to be ready when opportunity does knock.

Personal career
planning
Preparing oneself to
take advantage of
career opportunities
through assessing
talents, strengths,
needs, and interests;
identifying the best
organizational fit;
identifying career
goals and developing a
strategy for achieving
these goals

WHAT ARE MY TALENTS AND STRENGTHS?

The place to begin is by assessing your basic strengths. What is it that you do best? What skill or skills do you excel at? Writing, speaking, concentrating, interacting with people, organizing things, and logical reasoning

Are You Comprehending What You're Reading?

1. Which one of the following is not considered part of the definition of a career?
   a. advancement
   b. profession
   c. position
   d. lifelong sequence of jobs
2. The traditional career path often resulted in individuals progressing through a sequence of positions with increasing responsibilities in the same organization. True or False?
3. Describe what types of careers are increasingly replacing the tradtional career path.
4. All of the following were identified as a cause hindering the traditional career path except:
   a. company responsibility for development employees' careers
   b. unpredictability
   c. more emphasis on lateral moves
   d. continual need for educational updating and retraining

are just a few skills to consider. Figure 16-4 provides a list that might help you. You might also reflect on classes in school where you did particularly well and comments from friends or relatives as to where they thought your talents lay.

Everyone has certain things that he or she does better than other things. What are yours? The idea here is to play off your strengths.

WHAT ARE MY NEEDS AND INTERESTS?

Next, determine what it is you *like* to do. Forget, for a moment, what you're good at and think about what "turns you on." Do you like to talk to people? Be left alone? Participate in sports? Read? Explain things to others? Research subjects? Do something risky?

If nothing comes immediately to mind, think back over previous courses you've taken in school or past work experiences that you found particularly interesting. You might also find Figure 16-5 helpful. It identifies six personality types and the characteristics associated with each. Which one of these best describes you?

Analytical skills: Comparing, evaluating, and understanding complex problems or situations

Interpersonal communication skills: Speaking with clarity, clarifying misunderstandings, and listening effectively

Making presentations: Presenting ideas to groups of people with a clear and logical presentation

Writing skills: Writing with clarity and conciseness

Manipulating data and numbers: Processing information and numbers skillfully; handling budgets and statistical reports

Entrepreneurial skills and innovation: Recognizing and seizing opportunities for new ideas or products, creating new services or processes or products

Leading and managing others: Inspiring others, assessing others' abilities, delegating effectively, motivating others to achieve a set of goals

Learning skills: Grasping new information quickly, using common sense to deal with new situations, using feedback effectively

Team membership skills: Working well on teams and committees, incorporating a variety of perspectives toward a common goal

Conflict resolution skills: Dealing with differences, confronting others effectively

Human development skills: Encouraging, guiding, and evaluating others; explaining and/or demonstrating new ideas or skills, creating an environment for learning and growth

FIGURE 16-4

Where does your strength lie? (*Source:* Adapted from Dorothy Marcic, *Organizational Behavior: Experiences and Cases*, 3rd ed. St. Paul, MN: West Publishing, 1992, pp. 315–16.)

MERGING STRENGTHS AND INTERESTS

Now, try to merge what you do *best* with what you *like* to do (see Figure 16-6).

If you're a good writer but like to be left alone, maybe your life's work should be as a novelist or researcher. If your strength is writing but you like to interact with people, maybe you should consider journalism. Think about linking jobs with your strengths and preferences. For example, supervisors and managers need analytical, interpersonal, leading, and team skills. Conventional and social personalities are probably better matched to a management career than are artistic types. If you're good at organizing things, management or a career as a library cataloguer may be

TYPE	PERSONALITY CHARACTERISTICS
Realistic: Prefers physical activities that require skills, strength, and coordination	Shy, genuine, persistent, stable, conforming, practical
Investigative: Prefers activities that involve thinking, organizing, and understanding	Analytical, original, curious, independent
Social: Prefers activities that involve helping and developing others	Sociable, friendly, cooperative, understanding
Conventional: Prefers rule-regulated, orderly, and unambiguous activities	Conforming, efficient, practical unimaginative, inflexible
Enterprising: Prefers verbal activities where there are opportunities to influence others and attain power	Self-confident, ambitious, energetic, domineering
Artistic: Prefers ambiguous and unsystematic activities that allow creative expression	Imaginitive, disorderly, idealistic, emotional, impractical

FIGURE 16-5

Personality types. (*Source:* Based on John L. Holland, *Making Vocational Choices*, 2nd ed. Englewood Cliffs, NJ: Prentice Hall, 1985)

FIGURE 16-6

Merging strengths and interests

right for you. If you like sports, coaching is a possibility. If you like to explain things, you'd probably find a great deal of satisfaction in teaching; or you might combine this with an interest in management by pursuing a career in educational administration. These examples only break the surface of potential job opportunities. Keep in mind that the *National Occupational Classification*, published by the federal government, lists over 25 000 job titles!

Once you've got a set of jobs that you think you'd like and would also do well at, ask yourself: Where do I want to work? There is a popular myth that a good employee or manager will succeed anywhere. In truth, you can do a job in one organization and be considered a superstar and do the same job in another organization and be rated a poor performer. Why? Because organizations value different types of attitudes and behaviours. You increase the chances of your contribution being positively valued by an organization if you properly match your talents and personality to that organization. So choose organizations whose size and culture fits your style.

SIZE

Working in a large organization, with thousands of employees, is different from working in a small one. Large organizations tend to have more job specialization, more rules and regulations, more fixed duties, and more formal communication channels. Additionally, large organizations generally provide fewer opportunities for supervisors and operative employees to participate in decision making, less proximity and identification with the organization's goals, and less ability to see the link between individual effort and the final goods or services the organization produces.

Noting these differences is not meant to imply that small organizations are better places to work or have happier employees. In reality, some people find themselves more comfortable working in large bureaucracies, while others prefer smaller, less formal organizations.

Figure 16-7 is a twenty-item, bureaucratic-orientation questionnaire that measures whether your personal preferences better match a large or small organization. Individuals with a high degree of bureaucratic orientation tend to place a heavy reliance on higher authority, prefer formalized and specific rules, and prefer formal relationships with others on the job. Those individuals with a low degree of bureaucratic orientation are better suited to small organizations with adaptable duties, informal communication, and minimal rules and regulations. How did *you* score on Figure 16-7? What size of organization is best for *you*?

ORGANIZATIONAL CULTURE

The better the match between your personal style and the culture of your employing organization, the more likely you are to receive favourable performance reviews and rewards such as pay raises and promotions. Given this reality, a critical decision in your career plans is choosing employers where there is a good individual-organization fit.

What is organizational culture? As briefly described in Chapter 4, it's the organization's personality. It's a set of characteristics that distinguishes one organization from another. The Canadian steel industry offers two

Instructions: For each statement, check the response (either Mostly Agree or Mostly Disagree) that best represents your feelings.

	Mostly Agree	Mostly Disagree
1. I value stability in my job.	____	____
2. I like a predictable organization.	____	____
3. The best job for me would be one in which the future is uncertain.	____	____
4. Revenue Canada would be a nice place to work.	____	____
5. Rules, policies, and procedures tend to frustrate me.	____	____
6. I would enjoy working for a company that employed 85 000 people worldwide.	____	____
7. Being self-employed would involve more risk than I'm willing to take.	____	____
8. Before accepting a job, I would like to see an exact job description.	____	____
9. I would prefer a job as a freelance house painter to one as a clerk for the Department of Motor Vehicles.	____	____
10. Seniority should be as important as performance in determining pay increases and promotion.	____	____
11. It would give me a feeling of pride to work for the largest and most sucessful company in its field.	____	____
12. Given a choice, I would prefer to make $50 000 per year as a vice president in a small company to $55 000 as a staff specialist in a large company.	____	____
13. I would regard wearing an employee badge with a number on it as a degrading experience.	____	____
14. Parking spaces in a company lot should be assigned on the basis of job level.	____	____
15. An accountant who works for a large organization cannot be a true professional.	____	____
16. Before accepting a job (given a choice), I would want to make sure that the company had a very fine program of employee benefits.	____	____
17. A company will probably not be successful unless it establishes a clear set of rules and procedures.	____	____
18. Regular working hours and vacations are more important to me than finding thrills on the job.	____	____
19. You should respect people according to their rank.	____	____
20. Rules are meant to be broken.	____	____

SCORING

Compute your bureaucratic-orientation score by giving yourself one point for each statement which you responded to in the bureaucratic direction:

1. Mostly agree	8. Mostly agree	15. Mostly disagree
2. Mostly agree	9. Mostly disagree	16. Mostly agree
3. Mostly disagree	10. Mostly agree	17. Mostly disagree
4. Mostly agree	11. Mostly agree	18. Mostly agree
5. Mostly disagree	12. Mostly disagree	19. Mostly agree
6. Mostly disagree	13. Mostly disagree	20. Mostly disagree
7. Mostly agree	14. Mostly agree	

What does your score mean? A very high score (fifteen and over) suggests that you would enjoy working in a bureaucracy. A very low score (five or lower) indicates that you would be frustrated by working in a bureaucracy and might be better off in business for yourself or working in a small organization.

FIGURE 16-7

Bureaucratic orientation test. (*Source:* Adapted from Andrew J. DuBrin, *Human Relations: A Job-Oriented Approach*. Reston, VA: Reston Publishing Co., 1978, pp. 687–88. Reprinted with permission.)

contrasting cultures. Both Dofasco and Stelco are large, long-established steel manufacturers based in Hamilton, Ontario, and both have undergone radical downsizing and reorganizing recently. Yet their cultures differ markedly, much of it related to the fact that Stelco is unionized and Dofasco is not. Dofasco has the world's largest employee Christmas party, has an extensive recreational centre for employee use and is strongly involved in the community through sponsorship of cultural events. Its successful experimentation with the team approach is now being extended further in the organization. There's a feeling of esprit de corps. By contrast, the management and union at Stelco have a fairly adversarial relationship and much time has been lost in strikes over the years. It's more difficult for management at Stelco to initiate change because of the constraints of the union contract and the political aspects of working with a union.

Figure 16-8 presents a labelling typology for classifying organizational cultures.[1] An *academy* is the place for steady climbers who want to thoroughly master each new job they hold. These companies like to recruit young college graduates, provide them with much special training, and then carefully steer them through a myriad of specialized jobs within a particular function. These cultures, incidentally, were the primary populizers of the traditional career path. Companies that typify the academy culture include Canadian Pacific, Seagram's, IBM, General Motors, and Procter & Gamble.

A *club* places high value on fitting in, loyalty, and commitment. Seniority is the key at clubs. Age and experience count. In contrast to an academy, the club grooms managers as generalists. Examples of clubs are United Parcel Service, the Bell operating companies, government agencies, and the military.

Type	Description
Academy	Employees stay within a narrow functional specialty and are promoted after they thoroughly master a new job.
Club	Employees are trained as generalists and are promoted on the basis of seniority.
Baseball team	Employees are rewarded for what they produce; risk-taking and innovation is highly valued.
Fortress	These cultures are preoccupied with survival, offer little job security, and reward employees who can reverse the organization's sagging fortunes.

FIGURE 16-8

Four types of cultures

FIGURE 16-9

Brokerage firms are an example of a "baseball team."

FIGURE 16-10

The strong team culture at Seaman's Beverages in P.E.I. is part of the company's success. At Seaman's there's a sense of mutual respect for each player on the team and a work ethic to do whatever needs to be done but still have fun. "We're hard on people who don't enjoy themselves."

Baseball teams are entrepreneurially oriented havens for risk takers and innovators. They seek out talented people of all ages and experiences, then reward them for what they produce. Because they offer huge financial incentives and great freedom to their star performers, job-hopping among these organizations is commonplace. Organizations that fit the baseball team description are common in accounting, law, investment banking, consulting, advertising, software development, and bioresearch.

While baseball teams prize inventiveness, *fortresses* are preoccupied with survival (see Dealing with a Difficult Issue). Many were once academies, clubs, or baseball teams, but fell on hard times and are now seeking to reverse their sagging fortunes. Fortresses offer little job security, yet they can be exciting places to work for those who like the challenge of a turnaround. Fortress organizations include large retailers, hotels, and oil and natural gas exploration firms.

Research has shown that each of these four cultural types tends to attract certain personalities and that the personality-organizational culture match affects how far and how easily a person will move up the management ranks. For instance, a risk-taker will thrive at a baseball team, but fall flat on his or her face at an academy. Job offers, performance appraisals, and promotions are strongly influenced by the individual-organization fit, that is, whether the attitudes and behaviour of the applicant or employee are compatible with the culture of the organization. Additionally, employee satisfaction will be significantly higher when there is a good match between individual needs and the culture.

WHAT ARE MY CAREER GOALS?

Once you understand your strengths and interests, and the type of organization that fits you best, you need to address your career goals. Where do you want to be in five years? Ten years? Twenty years?

WILL ONLY THE STRONG SURVIVE?

In the animal kingdom, there's a saying that only the strong survive. In the wild, the animal that is the quickest, or the strongest, has the advantage of being toward the top of the "food chain." Being more powerful or the swiftest, then, is handsomely rewarded. But what about humans? Is survival in our world based on being the strongest?

Many cases can be built to support this premise. Military strength has been shown to help a nation defend itself or avert invasions by an opposing country. Professional sports, as well as the entertainment industry, reinforce that being very competitive has its advantages. Those who want success more—who have the strongest desire to climb to the top—frequently succeed. And this success is often achieved at the expense of someone else's mistakes. Take a football running back who fumbles deep in his own end of the field. As a result of his misfortune, the opponent has now received great field position. This is not a result of their great ability to move the ball down field. Rather, it's because they capitalized on an opponent's mistake.

Obviously in professional sports, or even military matters, there's a good reason for this behaviour. It's how the "game" is played. Can this be applied to organizations where there is competition for positions of responsibility or for generating a good bottom line? Does one have to be *over*-competitive? Can you achieve your career goals by working with others as opposed to being out for yourself? If you help others succeed, do you believe you'll be overrun by those who are willing to take advantage of your kindness? Does acting in an ethical manner have a justifiable place when your career is at stake? Or does ethics begin to matter only when everything else is in place—like the bottom line being met. What do you think?

In today's rapidly changing workplace, very specific goals are likely to be limiting, as well as widely off-target. Things are changing too fast to make detailed goals very meaningful. What you need are goals that can give your career direction. Identify the general type of job you want, the size of the organization, the appropriate culture, approximate responsibilities, preferred geographic location, and the like. So, for instance, you might set a ten-year goal to hold a management position in a small but fast-growing biotechnology firm, where performance rather than seniority is valued, located in Western Canada. Notice how these goals contrast with the comparable ten-year goals your counterpart might have set back in the early 1970s—for example, to be a branch manager or higher at a CIBC office within a thirty-mile radius of Vancouver.

WHERE AM I NOW?

Before you can define the path that will get you to your goals, you need to take stock of where you are now. What's your level of education? Work experience? What are your skill strengths and weaknesses? As part of this assessment, if you're preparing for a career in supervision and management, take a moment to complete the supervisory inventory in Figure 16-11. This provides a summary of the skills you've been introduced to in this book and a checklist of your competency level for each.

Skill	LEVEL OF COMPETENCE		
	Weak	Needs Improvement	Strong
Goal setting	☐	☐	☐
Budgeting	☐	☐	☐
Creative problem solving	☐	☐	☐
Developing control charts	☐	☐	☐
Empowering others through delegation	☐	☐	☐
Employment interviewing	☐	☐	☐
Conducting the performance appraisal interview	☐	☐	☐
Coaching	☐	☐	☐
Designing motivating jobs	☐	☐	☐
Projecting charisma	☐	☐	☐
Active listening	☐	☐	☐
Conducting a group meeting	☐	☐	☐
Negotiating	☐	☐	☐
Stress reduction	☐	☐	☐
Counselling	☐	☐	☐
Disciplining	☐	☐	☐
Handling grievances	☐	☐	☐

FIGURE 16-11

Supervisory skills inventory

The final issue you need to address in personal career development is laying out a plan that will help you achieve your goals. The journey of a thousand miles begins with the first step. Once you know where you want to go, you have to take the initiative to begin that journey. Remember, don't count on your boss or organization to take responsibility for your career. If they offer assistance, then great. But you're far less likely to be disappointed and far more likely to achieve your goals if you treat career planning as a self-development project.

SELECT YOUR FIRST JOB JUDICIOUSLY

Not all first jobs are alike. Where you begin in the organization has an important effect on your subsequent career progress. Specifically, evidence suggests that if you have a choice and you are ambitious, you should select a powerful department as the place to start your supervisory career.[2] A power department is one where crucial and important organizational decisions are made. If you start out in departments that are high in power within the organizations, you're more likely to advance rapidly throughout your career.

DO GOOD WORK

Good work performance is a necessary (but not sufficient) condition for career success. The marginal performer may be rewarded in the short term, but his or her weaknesses are bound to surface eventually and cut off career advancement. Your good work performance is no guarantee of success, but without it, the probability of a successful career is low.

PRESENT THE RIGHT IMAGE

Assuming that your work performance is in line with that of other successful supervisors, the ability to align your image with that sought by the organization is certain to be interpreted positively. You should assess the organization's culture so you can determine what the organization wants and values. Then you need to project that image in terms of style of dress; organizational relationships that you should and should not cultivate; whether you should project a risk-taking or risk-averse stance; the leadership style you should use; whether you should avoid, tolerate, or encourage conflict; the importance of getting along well with others; and so forth.

LEARN THE POWER STRUCTURE

The authority relationships defined by the organization's formal structure, as shown by an organizational chart, explain only part of the influence patterns within an organization. It is of equal or greater importance to know and understand the organization's power structure. You need to learn "who's really in charge, who has the goods on whom, what are the major debts and dependencies"—all things that won't be reflected in neat boxes on the organization chart. Once you have this knowledge, you can work within the power structure with more skill and ease.[3]

GAIN CONTROL OF ORGANIZATIONAL RESOURCES

The control of scarce and important organizational resources is a source of power. Knowledge and expertise are particularly effective resources to control. They make you more valuable to the organization and therefore more likely to gain job security and advancement.

STAY VISIBLE

Because the evaluation of supervisory effectiveness can be very subjective, it is important that your boss and those in power in the organization be made aware of your contributions. If you're fortunate enough to have a job that brings your accomplishments to the attention of others, taking direct measures to increase your visibility might not be needed. However, your job may require you to handle activities that are low in visibility, or your specific contribution may be indistinguishable because you're part of a group endeavour. In such cases, without creating the image of a braggart, you'll want to call attention to yourself by giving progress reports to your boss and others. Other tactics include being seen at social functions, being active in professional associations, and developing powerful allies who speak positively of you.

DON'T STAY TOO LONG IN YOUR FIRST JOB

The evidence indicates that, given a choice between staying in your first supervisory job until you've "really made a difference" or accepting an early transfer to a new job assignment, you should go for the early transfer. By moving quickly through different jobs, you signal to others that you're on the fast track. This, then, often becomes a self-fulling prophecy. The message for you is to start fast by seeking early transfers or promotions from your first supervisory job.

FIND A MENTOR

A *mentor* is someone from whom you can learn and who can encourage and help you. The evidence indicates that finding a sponsor who is part of the organization's power core is essential for you to make it to top levels of management.[4]

SUPPORT YOUR BOSS

Your immediate future is in the hands of your current boss. He or she evaluates your performance, and you're unlikely to have enough power to successfully challenge this manager. Therefore, you should make the effort to help your boss succeed, be supportive if your boss is under siege from other organizational members, and find out how he or she will be assessing your work effectiveness. Don't undermine your boss. Don't speak negatively of your boss to others. If your boss is competent, visible, and in possession of a power base, he or she is likely to be on the way up in the organization. Being perceived as supportive, you might find yourself pulled along too. If your boss's performance is poor and his or her power is low, you need to transfer to another unit. A mentor may be able to help you arrange this. It's hard to have your competence recognized or your positive performance evaluation taken seriously if your boss is perceived as incompetent.

STAY MOBILE

You're likely to move up more rapidly if you indicate your willingness to move to different geographical locations and across functional lines within the organization. Career advancement may also be facilitated by your willingness to change organizations. Working in a slow-growth, stagnant, or declining organization makes mobility even more important to you.

THINK LATERALLY

The suggestion to think laterally acknowledges the changing world of business. Because of organizational restructurings and downsizings, there are fewer rungs on the promotion ladder in many large organizations. To survive in this environment, it's a good idea to think in terms of lateral career moves.[5] It's important to recognize a point previously mentioned—that lateral movers in the 1960s and 1970s were presumed to be mediocre performers. That presumption doesn't hold today. Lateral shifts are now a viable career consideration. They give you a wider range of experiences which enhance your long-term mobility. In addition, these moves can help energize you by making your work more interesting and satisfying. So if you're not moving ahead in your organization, consider a lateral move internally or a lateral shift to another organization.

FIGURE 16-12

You're never too old to go back to school and enhance your educational credentials.

FOCUS ON ACQUIRING AND UPGRADING SKILLS

Organizations need employees who can readily adapt to the demands of the rapidly changing marketplace. By focusing on skills that you currently have and continuing to learn new skills, you can establish your value to the organization. It is employees who don't add value to an organization whose jobs (and career advancement) are in jeopardy.

WORK HARD AT DEVELOPING A NETWORK

Our final suggestion is based on the recognition that having a network of friends, colleagues, neighbours, customers, suppliers, etc., can be a useful tool for career development. If you spend some time cultivating relationships and contacts throughout your industry and community, you'll be prepared if worst comes to worst and your current job is eliminated. Even if your job is in no danger of being cut, having a network can prove beneficial in getting things done.

POP QUIZ

Are You Comprehending What You're Reading?

5. Which of the following are characteristic of a "club" organizational culture?
   a. loyalty and commitment
   b. entrepreneurial spirit
   c. specialized jobs
   d. survival
6. Why is career planning important?
7. Starting out in a department that is high in power within the organization often hinders your career growth. True or False?
8. Which of the following advice is offered regarding personal career development?
   a. Rely on your boss to ensure your career progresses.
   b. Stay away from powerful departments early in your career.
   c. Stay in your first job until you've made a major impact, rather than accepting an early transfer to a new job assignment.
   d. Spend time cultivating relationships in your company, industry and community.

SUMMARY

This summary is organized by the chapter Learning Objectives.

1. A career is a sequence of positions occupied by a person during his or her lifetime.
2. The traditional career path is characterized by relative predictability, upward movement, and the organization taking responsibility for employee career development.
3. The traditional career path is disappearing because organizations have cut costs by reducing layers of management, widening spans of control and cutting back on entry-level management programs. The new career path is characterized by unpredictability, lateral and interorganizational moves, occasional bouts of plateauing, the continual need for educational updating and retraining, and personal assumption of responsibility for career planning.
4. Everyone has specific talents and strengths. Examples include writing, speaking, concentrating, interacting with people, organizing things, and reasoning.
5. You can identify your interests by looking at courses you've taken in school or past work experiences that you found particularly interesting.
6. Some people prefer to work in large organizations, while others prefer small ones. Size creates very different work climates and it's important for individuals to understand where they best fit.
7. Make sure the culture of any organization you choose to work for fits well with your style and personality. The better the match, the more likely you are to receive favourable performance reviews and rewards such as pay raises and promotions.
8. You should define career goals for five, ten, and twenty years into the future. These goals should be more directional than specific.
9. The final step in personal career development is laying out a plan that will take you from where you are to where you want to be. This might include finding a mentor, acquiring and upgrading skills, developing a network, and exploring possible moves (lateral or upward).

KEY TERMS AND CONCEPTS

Career
Lifelong learning
Personal career planning
Plateauing
Traditional career path

REVIEWING YOUR KNOWLEDGE

1. Can you plan a career? Discuss.
2. Can a small company—with 50 or 100 employees—provide traditional career paths? Discuss.
3. Do you think the decline of the traditional career path increases or decreases organizational politics? Explain.
4. What can an employee do if he or she faces a mid-career plateau?
5. Why must employees assume personal responsibility for their career planning?
6. List six personality types and describe each. Which fits you best?
7. For each of the six personality types, identify a job that you think would be a good match.
8. "Most people would prefer to work in a small organization." Build an argument to support this statement, then negate that argument.
9. Contrast the four types of organizational cultures.
10. What is the relationship between organizational culture and successful careers?

ANSWERS TO THE POP QUIZZES

1. **c. position.** The specific job one holds is not necessarily a component of one's career. The other three are dimensions identified as part of the definition of a career.

2. **True.** This statement reflects the predictability that was associated with traditional career pathing.

3. More workers today are plateauing, rather than advancing in job level, and making lateral moves to different kinds of jobs or to different organizations.

4. **a. company responsibility for developing employees' careers.** On the contrary, it is the employee, not the company, that is responsible for ensuring career goals are met.

5. **a. loyalty and commitment.** Entrepreneurial spirit is more associated with a "baseball" culture; specialized jobs with an academy culture; and survival with a fortress culture.

6. Career planning is important because it can prepare you to be ready when career opportunities present themselves.

7. **False.** Starting out in a department that is high in power has the opposite effect. That is, you're more likely to advance rapidly throughout your career.

8. **d. spend time cultivating relationships in your company, industry and community.** This network can help you get things done and learn of career opportunities.

CASE 16.A

Going for It

Nathalie Brunet was excited at the prospect of finally becoming financially secure. Someone told her that in her first year as an account manager for Kodak Canada, she might be able to make $35 000. Right out of university! In fact, by the end of that first year Nathalie had made much more than that, as well as earning a ring for reaching 100 per cent of her sales target and a watch for surpassing the 150 per cent mark.

Nathalie's success in getting hired by Kodak was just as spectacular. A rookie out of university with no industry experience, she was hired despite extremely stiff competition for one of the few openings that year.

It was at Lakehead University that she first thought of working for Kodak. She was spending a year there to earn her B.A., after completing a three-year marketing diploma at Sheridan College. A Lakehead alumnus came to Nathalie's sales class to make a presentation on Kodak's training program, which is highly regarded in the industry. The more Nathalie heard, the more she liked: sales reps got an excellent training program (during which they were paid), a company car, a laptop computer, a good benefits package plus the opportunity to make a lot of money. So Nathalie approached Brian, the speaker, to ask him for a contact at Kodak.

Kodak Canada home page
http://www.kodak.com/
aboutKodak/regions/kci/
kciHomePage.shtml

When she followed up his lead, she found herself simply confused by the woman's description of the company's restructuring. So Nathalie again contacted Brian and asked him to go for coffee and explain the restructuring. In fact, he met with her several more times and offered help, including passing on to her a Kodak newsletter which included all the information about the restructuring. He also suggested who to contact. Nathalie sent her résumé to many Kodak managers and persistently phoned the H.R. manager, leaving her messages. Finally she was granted an "information exchange" with that H.R. manager. During this meeting she discovered two things; first, the manager had a whole file of Nathalie's résumés passed on to her by other managers with notes attached, and second, a possible job opening was coming up. Then came an interview with a second H.R. person (who also tested Nathalie's fluency in French) and a series of five interviews in one afternoon with various managers. During that afternoon she was also put into a room with a competing candidate with much more experience than she had. They were given five minutes to come up with individual presentations on a given topic. Nathalie got the job.

RESPONDING TO THIS CASE

1. What conclusions can you draw from reading about Nathalie that would be good advice in planning your own career?
2. Discuss how there seems to be a good match between Nathalie's interests, skills and personality and the culture of a sales department.
3. During one of her interviews Nathalie was asked if she had any questions. Her response was "Many. First, what criteria are you using to assess the candidates for this job?" What do you think of her asking this question, and why?

A Tough Decision for Lydia Marrder

When Lydia Marrder registered with her school's career planning and placement office, she was advised to develop a personal career development plan. She was also encouraged to participate in their résumé-writing and interviewing workshops, attend job fairs, and register for campus recruitment interviews. The campus recruitment interviews were conducted by representatives of large and small companies—many from her community, such as Klineman Industries, but others, including Sears and Shell Oil, that had opportunities all over the country and maybe even the world.

Lydia had always dreamed of travelling to far-away places. She even fantasized about being a business tycoon who could influence the world with her innovative ideas and timely, informed decisions. She had lots of talents and strengths—she was an ideal, all-round student. She liked debate and was good at it—a talent that she dreamed could expand her part-time job at a local radio station into a job as a T.V. talk show host or a sportscaster. She liked all types of sports, especially their competitive aspect. She was an extremely good soccer player and competed in tennis tournaments at a community tennis club. Lydia also liked the visual arts and had creative ability. Probably Lydia's biggest dilemma was not being able to decide on what she really wanted to do in life.

1. Why it is of value to Lydia (and to you) to develop a personal career plan? What elements should be included in such a plan?

2. If Lydia were to decide she wanted to work for Sears, Shell Oil, or Klineman Industries (a fabric design firm of 70 employees), what advice would you give her?

3. For a person such as Lydia who appears to have many talents, how can she possibly define a career path? How can focus help or hinder her in her defining her career goals? Why?

4. Identify your strengths and talents. Then in groups of four or five, have your classmates identify what they see your strengths and talents to be. Do the two lists agree with each other? Why or why not?

5. Starting from where you are right now and using the information from question 4, develop a career plan that you think is realistic for you.

6. Research and write a report about a career of your choice. Include why the career appeals to you and what career mobility skills you probably will need.

**Shell Canada
Home Page**
http://www.shell.ca/

Part VI: Managing Your Career

Andrea Gurley
Associate Director, Skills Survival Institute

Andrea is the supervisor at a non-profit day care centre for at-risk children. She was lead teacher in the preschool program. When Andrea was promoted to supervisor, another lead teacher, who had many years of experience, resented it. The teacher did not want to take orders from Andrea and she criticized Andrea to other staff members.

When the lead teacher was asked to reorganize her program in order for the centre to renew its licence, additional resentment was evident. Andrea knew the new licensing rules required a dynamic play area set in the teacher's classroom, but the teacher did not want this.

Andrea called team meetings to present these proposals to the staff. She wanted the staff to support the changes. The lead teacher made sarcastic comments during the meeting, undermining Andrea's authority. Andrea knew that the lead teacher was wonderful with the children. Because she was afraid the teacher would quit, Andrea did not confront the woman directly. Instead, Andrea called in an outside consultant to analyze the centre's physical setup. The outside consultant made the same recommendations that Andrea had made about the play area. The lead teacher still refused to make the changes.

1. When an employee is promoted to a leadership position, what are some of the problems that face the new supervisor?

2. How can the supervisor overcome some of these problems?

3. What can new supervisors do to prepare themselves for their new careers?

4. What are some of the ways a new supervisor can gain the trust, respect, and confidence of other employees? Why is this necessary for a new supervisor who has newly-gained authority?

Chapter 1

[1] L. Smith, "Rubbermaid Goes Thump," *Fortune*, October 2, 1995, p. 91.

[2] Allen I. Kraut and others. "The Role of the Manager: What's Really Important in Different Management Jobs," *Academy of Management Executive* (November 1989), pp. 286–93.

[3] This section is based on Linda A. Hill, *Becoming a Manager: Mastery of a New Identity* (Boston: Harvard Business School Press, 1992).

[4] Robert L. Katz, "Skills of an Effective Administrator," *Harvard Business Review* (September–October 1974), pp. 90–102.

[5] D. Farrell and J. C. Petersen, "Patterns of Political Behavior in Organizations," *Academy of Management Review* (July 1982), p. 405.

[6] R. E. Boyatzis, *The Competent Manager: A Model for Effective Performance* (New York, NY: John Wiley & Sons, 1982), p. 33.

[7] Based on John W. Newstrom and Keith Davis, *Organizational Behavior: Human Behavior at Work*, 9th ed. (New York: McGraw-Hill, 1993), p. 239.

[8] See Richard E. Crandall, "First-Line Supervisors: Tomorrow's Professionals," *Personnel* (November 1988), pp. 24–31.

[9] M. Saskin and K. J. Kiser, *Total Quality Management* (Seabrook, MD: Ducochon Press, 1991).

[10] Geert Hofstede, Culture's Consequences: International Differences in Workplace Values (Gage Publications, 1997).

[11] Hofstede called this last dimension masculinity–femininity. We've changed it because of the sexist connotation of the choice of terms.

[12] M. Hammer and J. Champy, *Reengineering the Corporation* (New York, NY: HarperCollins, 1993).

[13] T. A. Stewart, "Reengineering: The Hot New Managing Tool," *Fortune* (August 23, 1993), pp. 41–43.

[14] Ibid, p. 42.

[15] S. E. O'Connell, "The Virtual Workplace Moves at Warp Speed," *HRMagazine*, (March 1996), pp. 51–53; and "Managing the Reinvented Work Place Becomes a Hot Topic," *The Wall Street Journal* (March 20, 1996), p. A-1.

[16] T. Roberts, "Who are the High-Tech Home Workers?" *Inc. Technology*, 1994, p. 31.

[17] Adapted from C. M. Solomon, "Managing the Baby Busters," *Personnel Journal* (March 1992), p. 56.

[18] See, for example, S. Ratan, "Why Busters Hate Boomers," *Fortune* (October 4, 1993), pp. 56–70.

[19] L. Thornburg, "The Age Wave Hits: What Older Workers Want and Need," *HRMagazine* (February 1995), pp. 43–4.

[20] "Office Hours," *Fortune* (November 5, 1990), p. 184.

[21] T. Peters, *Thriving on Chaos: Handbook for a Management Revolution* (New York, NY: Knopf, 1987).

Chapter 2

[1] A. Tanzer, Studying at the Feet of the Masters," *Forbes*, May 10, 1993, p. 43.

[2] H. Mintzberg, *The Rise and Fall of Strategic Planning* (New York, NY: Free Press, 1994).

[3] Ibid.

[4] K. Rebello and P. Burrows, "The Fall of an American Icon," *Business Week*, Februrary 5, 1996, pp. 34–42.

[5] D. Miller, "The Architecture of Simplicity," *Academy of Management Review*, January 1993, pp. 116–138.

[6] See, for example, H. G. DeYoung, "Thieves Among Us," *Industry Week* (June 17, 1996), pp. 12–16.

[7] Cited in Harold E. Fearon and others, *Fundamentals of Production/Operations Management*, 3rd ed. (St. Paul, Minn.: West Publishing, 1986), p. 97.

[8] Cited in Ross A. Webber, *To Be a Manager* (Homewood, Ill.: Richard D. Irwin, 1981), p. 373.

Chapter 3

[1] Based on "Harley Hogs the Spotlight," *Small Business Reports*, November 1994, p. 58; B. S. Moskal, "Born to Be Real," *Industry Week*, August 2, 1993, p. 58; "On the Road Again," ABC News 20/20, January 25, 1991; and "How Harley Beat Back the Japanese," *Fortune*, September 25, 189, pp. 155–164.

[2] This list is based on James J. Semrodek, Jr., "Nine Steps to Cost Control," *Supervisory Management*, April 1976, pp. 29–32.

[3] Cited in G. Bylinsky, "How Companies Spy on Employees," *Fortune*, November 4, 1991, pp. 131–40.

[4] Cited in Archie B. Carroll, "In Search of the Moral Manager," *Business Horizons*, March–April 1987, p. 7.

Chapter 4

[1] A. Williams, "Career Planning: Building on Strengths, Strengthening Weaknesses," *Black Collegian*, September–October 1993, pp. 82–3.

[2] Alan J. Rowe, James D. Boulgarides, and Michael R. McGrath, *Managerial Decision Making*, Modules in Management Series (Chicago: SRA, 1984), pp. 18–22.

[3] Saul W. Gellerman, "Why 'Good' Managers Make Bad Ethical Choices," *Harvard Business Review*, July–August 1986, p. 89.

[4] Adapted from Laura L. Nash, "Ethics Without the Sermon," *Harvard Business Review*, November–December 1981, p. 81.

[5] See William M. Bulkeley, "'Computizing' Dull Meetings Is Touted As an Antidote to the Mouth that Bored," *The Wall Street Journal*, January 28, 1992, p. B1.

[6] R. Richards and others, "Assessing Everyday Creativity: Characteristics of the Lifetime Creativity Scales and Validation with Three Large Samples," *Journal of Personality and Social Psychology*, March 1988, pp. 476–85.

[7] Adapted from J. Calano and J Salzman, "Ten Ways to Fire up Your Creativity," *Working Woman* (July 1989), pp. 94–5.

Chapter 5

[1] R. Henkoff, "Getting Beyond Downsizing," *Fortune* (January 10, 1994), pp. 58–62.

[2] Henry Mintzberg, *Structure in Fives: Designing Effective Organizations* (Englewood Cliffs, NJ: Prentice-Hall, Inc., 1983), p. 157.

[3]J. A. Byrne, "The Horizontal Corporation," *Business Week*, December 20, 1993, pp. 76–81.

[4]"A Master Class of Radical Change," *Fortune* (December 13, 1993), p. 83.

[5]Ibid, p. 88.

[6]Ibid.

[7]Jon R. Katzenbach and Douglas K. Smith, *The Wisdom of Teams* (Boston: Harvard Business School Press, 1993), pp. 43–64.

[8]See James A. Shepperd, "Productivity Loss in Performance Groups: A Motivation Analysis," *Psychological Bulletin*, January 1993, pp. 67–81.

[9]Fernando Bartolomé, "Nobody Trusts the Boss Completely—Now What?" *Harvard Business Review*, March–April 1989, pp. 135–42.

[10]This questionnaire is adapted from L. Steinmetz and R. Todd, *First Line Management*, 4th ed. (Homewood, IL: Irwin, 1986), pp. 64–67. With permission.

Chapter 6

[1]This case is based on Michael P. Cronin and Stephanie Gruner, "Hiring: The Devil You Know?", *Inc.*, April 1994, p. 109.

[2]Allan Halcrow, "Employees Are Your Best Recruiters," *Personnel Journal*, November 1988, pp. 42–49.

[3]Wayne F. Cascio, *Applied Psychology in Personnel Management*, 4th ed. (Englewood Cliffs, N.J.: Prentice Hall, 1991), p. 265.

[4]John B. Miner, *Industrial and Organizational Psychology* (New York: McGraw-Hill, 1991), pp. 504–11.

[5]Walter C. Borman and Glenn L. Hallman, "Observation Accuracy for Assessors of Work Sample Performance: Consistency Across Task and Individual Differences Correlates," *Journal of Applied Psychology*, February 1991, pp. 11–18.

[6]See Robert L. Dipboye, *Selection Interviews: Process Perspectives* (Cincinnati: South-Western, 1992), Chapter 2.

[7]Irwin L. Goldstein, "The Application Blank: How Honest Are the Responses?" *Journal of Applied Psychology*, October 1971, pp. 491–92.

[8]Cited in "If You Can't Say Something Nice…," *Wall Street Journal*, March 4, 1988, p. 25.

[9]See, for example, S. L. Premack and J. P. Wanous, "A Meta-Analysis of Realistic Job Preview Experiments," *Journal of Applied Psychology*, November 1985, pp. 706–20.

Chapter 7

[1]Gary P. Latham and Kenneth N. Wexley, *Increasing Productivity Through Performance Appraisal* (Reading, MA: Addison-Wesley, 1981), p. 80.

[2]Peter M. Blau, *The Dynamics of Bureaucracy*, rev. ed. (Chicago: University of Chicago Press, 1963).

[3]See, for example, Michael J. Kavanagh, "Evaluating Performance," in K. M. Rowland and G. R. Ferris, eds., *Personnel Management* (Boston: Allyn & Bacon, 1982), pp. 187–226.

[4]K. R. Murphy and V. A Pardaffy, "Bias in Behaviorally Anchored Rating Scales: Global or Scale Specific," *Journal of Applied Psychology*, April 1989, pp. 343–46; and M. J. Piotrowski, J. L. Barnes-Farrell, and F. H. Esris, "Behaviorally Anchored Bias: A Replication and Extension of Murphy and Constans," *Journal of Applied Psychology*, October 1988, pp. 827–28.

[5]H. John Bernardin, "The Effects of Rater Training on Leniency and Halo Errors in Student Rating of Instructors," *Journal of Applied Psychology*, October 1975, pp. 550–55.

[6]W. Bridges, "The End of the Job," *Fortune*, September 19, 1984, p. 64.

[7]This discussion is based on Scott A. Snell and Kenneth N. Wexley, "How to Make Your Performance Appraisals More Effective, *Personnel Administrator*, April 1985, pp. 117–28.

[8]J. Wisinski, "A Logical Approach to a Difficult Employee," *HR Focus*, January 1992, p. 9.

[9]G. D. Cook, "Employee Counseling Session," *Supervision*, Agust 1989, p. 3.

[10]Norman R. F. Maier, *The Appraisal Interview: Three Basic Approaches* (La Jolla, CA: University Associates, 1976).

[11]"How Do I Love Me? Let Me Count the Ways," *Psychology Today*, May 1980, p. 16.

[12]Ronald J. Burke, R. J. Weitzel, and T. Weir, "Characteristics of Effective Employee Performance Review and Development Interviews: Replication and Extension," *Personnel Psychology*, Winter 1978, pp. 903–19.

[13]Latham and Wexley, *Increasing Productivity*, p. 151.

[14]Based on Srinivasan Umapathy, "Teaching Behavioural Aspects of Performance Evaluation: An Experiential Approach," *The Accounting Review*, January 1985, pp. 107–08.

Chapter 8

[1]This is based on Albert Bandura, *Social Learning Theory* (Englewood Cliffs, N.J.: Prentice Hall, Inc., 1977).

[2]*Toronto Star*, June 2, 1994

[3]Auto Parts Certificate, Automotive Parts Sectoral Training Council, Jeffry Piker, Educational Consultant

[4]Ronita B. Johnson and Julie O'Mara, "Shedding New Light on Diversity Training," *Training and Development Journal*, May 1992, pp. 45–52.

[5]J. E. Ellis, "Monsanto's New Challenge: Keeping Minority Workers," *Business Week*, July 8, 1991, p. 61.

[6]P. F. Miller and W. T. Coady, "Teaching Work Ethics," *Education Digest*, February 1990, pp. 54–55.

[7]Charles D. Orth, Harry E. Wilkinson, and Robert C. Benfari, "The Manager's Role as Coach and Mentor," *Organizational Dynamics*, Spring 1987, p. 67.

Chapter 9

[1]Abraham Maslow, *Motivation and Personality* (New York: Harper and Row, 1954).

[2]Douglas McGregor, *The Human Side of Enterprise* (New York: McGraw-Hill, 1960).

[3]Frederick Herzberg, B. Mausner, and B. Snyderman, *The Motivation to Work* (New York: John Wiley and Sons, 1959).

[4]See Raymond A. Katzell, Donna E. Thompson, and Richard A. Guzzo, "How Job Satisfaction and Job Performance Are and Are Not Linked," in C. J. Cranny, Patricia Cain Smith, and Eugene F. Stone, *Job Satisfaction* (New York: Lexington Books, 1992), pp. 195–217.

[5]David C. McClelland, *The Achieving Society* (New York: Van Nostrand Reinhold, 1961).

[6]J. Stacey Adams, "Inequity in Social Exchanges," in L. Berkowitz (ed.), *Advances in Experimental Social Psychology*, Vol. 2 (New York: Academic Press, 1965), pp. 267–300.

[7]Victor H. Vroom, *Work and Motivation* (New York: John Wiley, 1964).

[8]Edwin A. Locke and others, "The Relative Effectiveness of Four Methods of Motivating Employee Performance," in K. D. Duncan, M. M. Gruneberg, and D. Wallis, eds., *Changes in Working Life* (London: John Wiley, Ltd., 1980), pp. 363–83.

[9]G. Hofstede, "Motivation, Leadership, and Organizations: Do American Theories Apply Abroad?" *Organizational Dynamics*, Summer 1980, p. 55.

[10]D. H. B. Walsh, F. Luthens, and S. M. Sommer, "Organizational Behavior Modification Goes to Russia: Replicating an Experimental Analysis Across Cultures and Tasks," *Journal of Organizational Behavior Management*, Fall 1993, pp. 15–35; and J. R. Baum, et al., "Nationality and Work Role Interactions: A Cultural Contrast of Israel and U.S. Entrepreneurs' Versus Managers' Needs," *Journal of Business Venturing*, November 1993, pp. 499–512.

[11]A. Ignatius, "Now if Ms. Wong Insults a Customer, She Gets an Award," *Wall Street Journal*, January 24, 1989, p. A-1.

[12]A. M. Dickinson and K. L. Gillette, "A Comparison of the Effects on Productivity: Piece-Rate Pay Versus Base Pay Plus Incentives," *Journal of Organizational Behavior Management*, Spring 1994, pp. 3–82.

[13]See, for example, D. Fenn, "Compensation: Bonuses That Make Sense," *Inc.*, March 1996, p. 95.

[14]G. Grib and S. O'Donnell, "Pay Plans that Reward Employee Achievement," *HRMagazine*, July 1995, pp. 49–50.

[15]"Compensation: Sales Managers as Team Players," *Inc.*, August 1994, p. 102.

[16]D. Fenn, "Compensation: Goal-Driven Incentives," *Inc.*, August 1996, p. 91; M. A. Verespej, "More Value for Compensation," *Industry Week*, June 17, 1996, p. 20.

[17]S. Overman, "Saturn Teams Working and Profiting," *HRMagazine*, March 1995, p. 72.

[18]K. Capell, "Options for Everyone," *Business Week*, July 22, 1996, pp. 80–88.

[19]See, for example, T. R. Stenhouse, "The Long and the Short of Gainsharing," *Academy of Management Executive*, Vol. 9, No. 1 (1995), pp. 77–78.

[20]S. A. Lee, "ESOP is a Powerful Tool to Align Employees with Corporate Goals," *Pension World*, April 1994, pp. 40–42.

[21]J. Richard Hackman and Greg R. Oldham, "Motivation Through the Design of Work: Test of a Theory," *Organizational Behavior and Human Performance*, August 1976, pp. 250–79.

Chapter 10

[1]For example, see J. P. Howell, D. E. Bowen, P. W. Dorfman, S. Kerr, and P. M. Podsakoff, "Substitutes for Leadership: Effective Alternatives to Ineffective Leadership," *Organizational Dynamics*, Summer 1990, pp. 21–38.

[2]S. A. Kirkpatrick and E. A. Locke, "Leadership: Do Traits Matter?" *Academy of Management Executive*, May 1991, pp. 48–60.

[3]See, for example, Patricia Sellers, "What Exactly is Charisma?" *Fortune*, January 15, 1996, pp. 68–75.

[4]R. J. House, "A 1976 Theory of Charismatic Leadership," in J. G. Hunt and L. L. Larson, eds., *Leadership: The Cutting Edge* (Carbondale, IL: Southern Illinois University Press, 1977), pp. 189–207.

[5]W. Bennis, "The 4 Competencies of Leadership," *Training and Development Journal*, August 1984, pp. 15–19; see also Marshall Loeb, "Where Leaders Come From," *Fortune*, September 19, 1994, p. 241.

[6]J. C. Conger and R. N. Kanungo, "Behavioural Dimensions of Charismatic Leadership," in J. A. Conger, R. N. Kanungo and Associates, *Charismatic Leadership* (San Francisco, CA: Jossey-Bass, 1988), p. 79.

[7]G. H. Dobbins aet al, "The Role of Self-Monitoring and Gender on Leader Emergence: A Laboratory and Field Study," *Journal of Management*, September 1990, pp. 609–18.

[8]R. J. House, J. Woycke, and E. M. Fodor, "Charismatic and Noncharismatic Leaders: Differences in Behavior and Effectiveness," in Conger and Kanungo, *Charismatic Leadership*, pp. 103–104.

[9]See, for example, S. Camminiti, "What Team Leaders Need To Know," *Fortune*, February 20, 1995, pp. 93–100.

[10]R. M. Stogdill and A. E. Coons, eds., *Leader Behavior: Its Description and Measurement*, Research Monograph No. 88 (Columbus, OH: Ohio State University, Bureau of Business Research, 1951).

[11]Ibid; and R. Kahn and D. Katz, "Leadership Practices in Relation to Productivity and Morale," in D. Cartwright and A. Zander, eds., *Group Dynamics: Research and Theory*, 2nd ed. (Elmsford, NY: Row, Paterson, 1960).

[12]For a good review of the Fielder Contingency Model, Path-Goal Theory, and Leader-Participation Model, see S. P. Robbins and D. A. De Cenzo, *Fundamentals of Management* (Englewood Cliffs, NJ: Prentice-Hall, Inc., 1995), pp. 300–306.

[13]F. E. Fiedler, *A Theory of Leadership Effectiveness* (New York, NY: McGraw-Hill, 1967).

[14]R. J. House and T. R. Mitchell, "Path-Goal Theory of Leadership," *Journal of Contemporary Business*, Autumn 1974, pp. 81–97.

[15]P. Hersey and K. H. Blanchard, *Management of Organizational Behavior: Utilizing Human Resources*, 5th ed. (Englewood Cliffs, NJ: Prentice-Hall, Inc., 1988). For those who wish to look at both sides of the debate on the validity of situational leadership, you are encouraged to read W. R. Norris and R. P Vecchio, "Situational Leadership Theory: A Replication," in *Group and Organization Management*, September 1992, pp. 331–42; and W. Blank, J. R. Weitzel, and S. G. Green, "A Test of the Situational Leadership Theory," *Personnel Psychology*, Autumn 1990, pp. 579–97.

[16]G. Hofstede, "Motivation, Leadership, and Organization: Do American Theories Apply Abroad?" *Organizational Dynamics* (Summer 1980), p. 57; and A. Ede, "Leadership and Decision Making: Management Styles and Culture," *Journal of Managerial Psychology* (July 1992), pp. 28–31.

[17]Based on L. T. Hosmer, "Trust: The Connecting Link Between Organizational Theory and Philosophical Ethics," *Academy of Management Review*, April 1995, p. 393; and R. C. Mayer, J. H. Davis, and F. D. Shoorman, "An Integrative Model of Organizational Trust," *Academy of Management Review*, July 1995, p. 712.

[18]P. L. Schindler and C. C. Thomas, "The Structure of Interpersonal Trust in the Workplace," *Psychological Reports*, October 1993, pp. 563–73.

[19]T. A. Stewart, "The Nine Dilemmas Leaders Face," *Fortune*, March 18, 1996, p. 113.

[20]See, for example, W. H. Miller, "Leadership at a Crossroads," *Industry Week*, August 19, 1996, pp. 43–44.

[21]D. Duchon, S. G. Green, and T. D. Taylor, "Vertical Dyad Linkage: A Longitudinal Assessment of Antecedents, Measures, and Consequences," *Journal of Applied Psychology*, February 1986, pp. 56–60.

[22]This skills box is based on F. Bartolome, "Nobody Trusts the Boss Completely—Now What?" *Harvard Business Review*, March–April 1989, pp. 35–142; and J. K. Butler, Jr., "Toward Understanding and Measuring Conditions of Trust: Evolution of a Condition of Trust Inventory," *Journal of Management*, September 1991, pp. 643–63.

[23]L. Holpp, "Applied Empowerment," *Training*, February 1994, pp. 39–44.

[24]See, for example, R. Wellins and J. Worklan, "The Philadelphia Story," *Training,* March 1994, pp. 93–100.

[25]G. N. Powell, *Women and Men in Management,* 2nd ed. (Thousand Oaks, CA: Sage, 1993).

[26]S. P. Robbins. *Organizational Behavior: Concepts, Controversies, and Applications,* 7th ed. (Englewood Cliffs, NJ: Prentice-Hall, Inc., 1996), p. 441.

[27]Ibid.

[28]B. M. Bass, "From Transactional to Transformational Leadership: Learning to Share the Vision," *Organizational Dynamics,* Winter 1990, pp. 19–31.

[29]See, for example, J. Seitzer and B. M. Bass, "Transformational Leadership: Beyond Initiation and Consideration," *Journal of Management,* December 1990, pp. 693–703

[30]B. J. Avolio and B. M. Bass, "Transformational Leadership: Charisma and Beyond," working paper, School of Management, State University of New York, Binghamton (1995), p. 14.

[31]Ibid.

[32]Source: R. D. Lennox and R. N. Wolfe, "Revision of the Self-Monitoring Scale," *Journal of Personality and Social Psychology,* June 1984, p. 1361. with permission.

[33]Jane M. Howell and Peter J. Frost, "A Laboratory Study of Charismatic Leadership," *Organizational Behavior and Human Decision Processes,* April 1989, pp. 243–69.

[34]Source: Adapted from Alexander Ross, "Where Industry Gets Captains", *Canadian Business,* January 1993.

Chapter 11

[1]Albert Mehrabian, "Communication Without Words," *Psychology Today,* September 1968, pp. 53–55.

[2]Keith Davis, cited in R. Rowan, "Where Did That Rumor Come From?," *Fortune,* August 13, 1979, p. 134.

[3]See, for example, Morgan W. McCall, Jr., Ann M. Morrison, and Robert L. Hannan, *Studies of Managerial Work: Results and Methods,* Technical Report No. 9 (Greensboro, NC: Center for Creative Leadership, 1978), pp. 7–9; and Fred Luthans and Janet K. Larsen,

"How Managers Really Communicate," *Human Relations,* February 1986, pp. 161–78.

[4]See, for example, L. K. Larkey, "Toward a Theory of Communicative Interactions in Culturally Diverse Workgroups," *Academy of Management Review,* June 1996, pp. 463–91; R. V. Lindahl, "Automation Breaks the Language Barrier," *HRMagazine,* March 1996, pp. 79–82; D. Lindorff, "In Beijing the Long March Is Just Starting," *Business Week,* February 12, 1996, p. 68; and L. Miller, "Two Aspects of Japanese and American Coworker Interaction: Giving Instructions and Creating Rapport," *Journal of Applied Behavioral Science,* June 1995, pp. 141–61.

[5]Based on S. D. Saleh, "Relational Orientation and Organizational Functioning: A Cross-Cultural Perspective," *Canadian Journal of Administrative Sciences,* September 1987, pp. 276–93.

[6]C. Fisher, "Transmission of Positive and Negative Feedback to Subordinates," *Journal of Applied Psychology,* October 1979, pp. 433–540.

[7]F. Bartolome, "Teaching About Whether to Give Negative Feedback," *The Organizational Behavior Teaching Review,* vol. 9, no. 2, 1986–1987, pp. 95–104.

[8]K. S. Verderber and R. F. Verderber, *Inter-Act: Using Interpersonal Communication Skills,* 4th ed. (Belmont, CA: Wadsworth, 1986).

Chapter 12

[1]J. Graves, "Successful Management and Organizational Muggings," in J. Papp, ed., *New Directions in Human Resource Management* (Englewood Cliffs, N.J.: Prentice-Hall Inc., 1978).

[2]See Stephen P. Robbins, *Managing Organizational Conflict: A Nontraditional Approach* (Englewood Cliffs, N.J.: Prentice-Hall Inc., 1974).

[3]L. Greenhalgh, "Managing Conflict," *Sloan Management Review,* Summer 1986, pp. 45–51.

Chapter 13

[1]Kurt Lewin, *Field Theory in Social Science* (New York: Harper & Row, 1951).

[2]See, for instance, T. Peters, *Thriving on Chaos* (New York, NY: Alfred A. Knopf, 1987).

[3]Ibid., p. 3.

[4]Kurt Lewin, *op. cit.*

Chapter 14

[1]*Employee Conduct and Discipline,* Personnel Policies Forum, Survey No. 102 (Washington, D.C.: Bureau of National Affairs, August 1973).

[2]*Employee Conduct and Discipline,* Personnel Policies Forum, Survey No. 102 (Washington, D.C.: Bureau of National Affairs, August 1973).

[3]Douglas McGregor, "Hot Stove Rules of Discipline," in George Strauss and Leonard Sayles, eds., *Personnel: The Human Problems of Management* (Englewood Cliffs, N.J.: Prentice-Hall Inc., 1967).

[4]A study by the Wyatt Company cited in *Boardroom Reports,* April 1, 1989, p. 2.

Chapter 15

[1]This section is based on D. A. De Cenzo and S. P. Robbins, *Human Resource Management,* 5th ed. (New York, NY: John Wiley & Sons, Inc., 1996), pp. 494–97.

Chapter 16

[1]Described in C. Hymowitz, "Which Culture Fits You?" *Wall Street Journal,* July 17, 1989, p. B1.

[2]J. E. Sheridan, J. W. Slocum, Jr., R. Buda, and R. C. Thompson, "Effects of Corporate Sponsorship and Departmental Power on Career Tournaments," *Academy of Management Journal* (September 1990), pp. 578–602.

[3]C. Perrow, *Complex Organizations: A Critical Essay* (Glenwood, IL: Scott, Foresman, 1972), p. 43.

[4]G. F. Dreher and R. A. Ash, "A Comparative Study of Mentoring Among Men and Women in Managerial, Professional, and Technical Positions," *Journal of Applied Psychology* (October 1990), pp. 539–46.

[5]D. T. Hall and Associates, *The Career is Dead—Long Live the Career: A Relational Approach to Careers* (San Francisco, CA: Jossey-Bass, 1996).

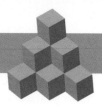

GLOSSARY

Absenteeism Failure to report to work.

Accept errors Accepting those candidates who subsequently perform poorly on the job.

Accommodation The willingness of one party in a conflict to place the opponent's interests above his or her own.

Accountability Holding a person to performing an assignment in a satisfactory manner.

Active listening Listening with intensity, empathy, acceptance, and a willingness to take responsibility for completeness.

Activities Time or resources required to progress from one event to another on a PERT chart.

Agency shop Work setting in which employees do not have to join the union but they must pay union dues if they want to keep their jobs.

Agenda A written statement of a meeting's purpose, who will be in attendance, and the issues that will be discussed.

Apprenticeships A program covering a period of time—typically from one to five years—when an individual is considered to be training to learn a skill.

Arbitrator An impartial third party who hears grievances and makes rulings on them.

Assertiveness training Training designed to make people more open and self-expressive.

Assignable causes Nonchance variations.

Attitudes Evaluative statements or judgments concerning objects, people, or events.

Attribute charts Charts that measure a product characteristic in terms of whether it is good or bad.

Authority The managerial right to give orders and expect the orders to be obeyed.

Authority after discussion Decision making by a group leader after weighing group members' decisions.

Autocratic leader A task master who leaves no doubt as to who's in charge, and who has the authority and power in the group.

Autonomy The degree to which the job provides substantial freedom, independence, and discretion to the individual in scheduling the work and in determining the procedures to be used in carrying it out.

Avoidance The desire to withdraw from or suppress a conflict.

Baby-boomers The largest group in the workforce; they are regarded as the career climbers—at the right place at the right time. Mature workers view them as unrealistic in their views and workaholics.

Baby-busters A group of workers less committed, less rule-bound, and more into self-gratification, with an intolerance of baby-boomers and their attitudes. They are viewed as selfish and not willing to play by the rules.

Bargaining unit Identifies which employees the union will represent if it wins an election.

Behaviorally anchored rating scales (BARS) A performance appraisal technique in which an evaluator rates employees on specific job behaviours derived from performance dimensions.

Benchmarking The continuous process of measuring products and practices against the toughest competition and those companies recognized as world class leaders.

Body language Gestures, facial configurations, and other movements of the body.

Bottom-up budgeting Budgeting in which budget requests are prepared by those who implement them and are then sent to higher levels of management for approval.

Brainstorming An idea-generation process that specifically encourages any and all alternatives while withholding any criticism of those alternatives.

Budgets Numerical plans.

Career The sequence of positions occupied by a person during his or her lifetime.

Career counselling Guiding an individual's future within the organization and general career path.

Cause-effect diagrams Diagrams that depict the causes of a certain problem and group them according to common categories.

Central limit theorem A sampling distribution approaches normality as the size of the sample increases.

Central tendency error A reluctance by an evaluator to use the extremes of the appraising scale.

Chance causes Variations caused by randomness in the process.

Change agents People who act as catalysts and assume the responsibility for overseeing the change process.

Change process Unfreezing the status quo, changing to a new state, and refreezing the new change to make it permanent.

Charismatic leadership An attribution made of individuals with self-confidence, vision, the ability to articulate the vision, strong convictions in the vision, novel or unconventional behaviour, and the perception that they are agents of radical change.

Checklist A performance appraisal technique where an evaluator uses a list of behavioural descriptions and checks off those behaviours that apply to the employee.

Coaching Day-to-day, hands-on process of helping employees recognize opportunities to improve their work performance.

Code of ethics A formal document that states an organization's primary values and the ethical rules it expects employees to follow.

Cognitive learning Occurs via mental processes such as reading, watching, and thinking.

Cohesiveness The degree to which members are attracted to each other and are motivated to stay in the group.

Collaboration A situation where the parties to a conflict each desire to satisfy fully the concerns of all parties.

Collective bargaining A process for negotiating a union contract and for administrating the contract after it has been negotiated.

Communication The transference and understanding of meaning.

Compromise A situation in which each party to a conflict is willing to give up something of value.

Conceptual competence The mental ability to analyze and diagnose complex situations.

Conciliation An impasse-resolution technique that states that the role of the third party is to keep the negotiations ongoing and to act as a go-between.

Concurrent controls Controls that are enacted while an activity is in progress.

Conflict A process in which one party consciously interferes in the goal-achievement efforts of another party.

Conflict management The application of resolution and stimulation techniques to achieve the optimum level of departmental conflict.

Consensus Agreement to support a decision by all members of a group.

Consultative participative leadership The leadership style of an individual who seeks input, hears the concerns and issues of the followers, but makes the final decision him- or herself, using input as an information-seeking exercise.

Control by exception Strategic control devices should call attention only to exceptions from standard.

Control charts Charts that show plotting of results over a period of time, with statistically determined upper and lower limits.

Control process Measuring actual performance, comparing results with standards, and taking corrective action.

Controlling Monitoring activities to ensure that objectives are being met as planned and correcting any significant deviations.

Corrective control Provides feedback, after an activity is finished, to prevent any future deviations.

Counselling Discussion of a problem (usually one with emotional content) with an employee in order to resolve the problem or, at a minimum, help the employee to cope with it better.

Counselling process The five steps that describe how a counselling session should be conducted.

Credibility Supervisor qualities of honesty, competence, and the ability to inspire.

Critical incidents A performance appraisal technique in which an evaluator lists key behaviours that separate effective from ineffective job performance.

Critical path The longest sequence of events and activities in a PERT chart.

Cross-functional teams Managers and employees from different levels and different parts of the organization form teams to solve problems.

Culture A system of shared meaning.

Customer Everyone internally or externally who interacts with the organization's product or service.

Customer departmentalization Grouping activities on the basis of common customers.

Data Raw, unanalyzed facts.

Decision trees A diagrammatic technique for analyzing decisions by assigning probabilities to various outcomes and calculating payoffs for each.

Decision-making process The seven steps to making rational decisions.

Delegation A four-step process of allocating duties, delegating authority, assigning responsibility, and creating accountability.

Delphi technique A group decision technique where members act independently but need not be physically present for discussion.

Democratic participative leadership A leadership style that allows followers to have a say in what's decided.

Departmentalization Grouping departments based on work functions, product or service, target customer or client, geographic territory, or the process used to turn inputs into outputs.

Devil's advocate A person who purposely presents arguments that run counter to those proposed by the majority or against current practices.

Discipline Actions taken by a supervisor to enforce the organization's rules and standards.

Discretionary time The portion of a supervisor's time that is under his or her control.

Dismissal Termination of one's employment.

Distributive bargaining Zero-sum negotiations, where any gain by one is at the expense of the other.

Division of labour The breakdown of jobs into narrow, repetitive tasks.

Downsizing A reduction in the workforce and reshaping of operations to create "lean and mean" organizations. The goals of organizational downsizing are greater efficiency and reduced costs.

Due process Assuming an employee is innocent until proved otherwise; giving the employee the right to be heard; and invoking disciplinary action that is reasonable in relation to the offence involved.

85-15 rule Eighty-five per cent of what goes wrong is due to the system, while fifteen per cent is attributed to the employees who operate the system.

Effectiveness Doing a task right; goal attainment.

Efficiency Doing a task right; also refers to the relationship between inputs and outputs.

Electronic meeting A group of individuals make decisions by communicating anonymously on computer terminals.

Emergent leaders Leaders who arise out of a group but who have no formal authority in the organization.

Employee Assistance Programs (EAPs) Programs designed to act as a first stop for individuals seeking psychiatric or substance-abuse help, with the goal of getting productive employees back on the job as swiftly as possible.

Employee counselling An emphasis on encouraging training and development efforts in a situation in which employee unwillingness or inability to perform his or her job satisfactorily is either voluntary or involuntary.

Employee development Preparation of employees for future positions that require higher level skills, knowledge, or abilities.

Employee stock ownership plan (ESOP) A compensation program that allows employees to become part owners of an organization by receiving stock as a performance incentive.

Employee training Changing skills, knowledge, attitudes, or behavior of employees. Determination of training needs is made by supervisors.

Empowered work teams The primary working units in a TQM program who have hands-on involvement in process improvement.

Empowerment Increasing an employee's involvement in making decisions and taking responsibility for work outcomes.

End-users Individuals who take responsibility for accessing and analyzing information they need on their personal computers.

Equity theory Employees perceive what they get from a job situation (outcomes) in relation to what they put into it (inputs), and then compare their input-outcome ratio with the input-outcome ratio of others; then respond so as to eliminate any inequities.

Employee relations All activities within a company that involve dealing with a union and its members.

Ethical dilemmas Situations requiring one to define right and wrong conduct.

Ethics Rules or principles that define right and wrong conduct.

Events End points on a PERT chart that represent the completion of major activities.

Expectancy theory The strength of a tendency to act depends on the strength of an expectation that the act will be followed by a given outcome and on the attractiveness of that outcome to the individual.

Expected value analysis Calculating the expected value of a particular alternative by weighting its possible outcomes by the probability of

achieving the alternative, then summing up the totals derived from the weighting process.

Experiential learning Relies on practising, experiencing, or doing something.

Expert A person with special skill or knowledge in a particular field.

Extrinsic feedback Performance feedback provided by an outside source.

Fact-finding A technique whereby a neutral third-party individual conducts a hearing to gather evidence from both labour and management.

Feedback The degree to which carrying out the work activities required by the job results in the individual obtaining direct and clear information about the effectiveness of his or her performance.

Fiedler's contingency theory A leadership theory; proposes that effectiveness depends upon a proper match between a leader's style of interacting with subordinates and the degree to which the situation gives control and influence to the leader.

First-level managers Supervisors.

Flow charts Visual representations of the sequence of events for a particular process.

Forcing The desire to satisfy your own needs at the expense of the other party.

Formal communication Addresses task-related issues and tends to follow the organization's authority chain.

Formal group A work group where objectives and work assignments are defined by management.

Free-reign leader An individual who gives employees total autonomy to make decisions that will affect them.

Functional authority Rights over individuals outside one's own direct areas of responsibility.

Functional departmentalization Grouping activities by functions performed.

Gantt chart A bar graph, with time on the horizontal axis and activities to be scheduled on the vertical axis, that shows planned and actual activities.

Geographic departmentalization Grouping activities on the basis of territory.

Grapevine The means by which informal communication takes place; rumour mill.

Graphic rating scale A performance-appraisal technique in which an evaluator rates a set of performance factors on an incremental scale.

Grievance procedures Procedures designed to resolve disputes as quickly as possible and at the lowest level in the organization.

Group Two or more people who come together to achieve a particular objective.

Group order ranking A performance appraisal approach that groups employees into ordered classifications.

Groupthink Group members withhold different views in order to appear to be in agreement.

Halo error A tendency to rate an individual high or low on all factors due to the impression of a high or low rating on some specific factor.

Hierarchy of needs theory Theory that thre is a hierarchy of five needs—physiological, safety, social, esteem, and self-actualization. As each need
is sequentially satisfied, the next need becomes dominant.

Histograms Bar charts used to show the frequency with which something occurs.

Horizontal structures Very flat structures used in small businesses as well as giant companies in which job-related activities cut across all parts of the organization.

"Hot stove" rule Principles that can guide disciplining; the action should be immediate, offer advance warning, and be consistent and impartial.

Human resource planning Ensuring that a department has the right personnel, who are capable of completing those tasks that help the department reach its objectives.

Immediate corrective action Action that adjusts something right now and gets things back on track.

Incident rate A measure of the number of injuries, illnesses, or lost workdays as it relates to a common base rate of 100 full-time employees.

Incremental budget A budget that develops out of the previous budget.

Individual ranking A performance appraisal approach that ranks employees in order from highest to lowest.

Informal communication Moves in any direction and is as likely to satisfy social needs as to facilitate task accomplishments.

Informal group Natural formations in the work place that are neither formally structured nor defined by management.

Information Analyzed and processed data.

Integrative bargaining Assumes there is at least one settlement option that can create a win-win solution.

Interest arbitration Arbitration in which a panel of three individuals hears testimony from both sides and renders a decision on how to settle the current contract negotiation dispute.

Intermediate-term plans Plans that cover from one to five years.

Interpersonal competence The ability to work with, understand, and motivate other people, both individually and in groups.

Intrinsic feedback Self-generated feedback on performance provided by the work itself.

Job description A written statement of what a jobholder does, how the job is done, and why it is done.

Job design The way tasks are combined to form complete jobs.

Job enrichment Increasing the degree to which a worker controls the planning, execution, and evaluation of his or her work.

Job rotation Moving employees horizontally to broaden their skills, knowledge, or abilities; turning specialists into generalists.

Job specification The minimum acceptable qualifications an applicant must possess to perform a given job successfully.

Justice view of ethics Decisions that seek fair and impartial distribution of benefits and costs.

Just-in-time (JIT) inventory system A system in which inventory items arrive when they are needed in the production process instead of being stored in stock. See also Kanban.

Kanban In Japanese, a "card" or "sign." Shipped in a container, a kanban is returned to the supplier when the container is opened, initiating the shipment of a second container that arrives just as the first container is emptied.

Lateral thinking A creativity-stimulation technique; using zig-zag thinking instead of rational or vertical reasoning.

Leader-member relations The degree of confidence, trust, and respect subordinates have in their leader.

Leadership The ability to influence a group toward the achievement of goals.

Leading Directing and coordinating people.

Learning curve Learning begins with a steep rise, then increases at a decreasing rate until a plateau is reached.

Leniency error The tendency to appraise a set of employees too high (positive) or too low (negative).

Lifelong learning The need to continually upgrade skills through reading, seminars, and formal education.

Line authority The authority that entitles a supervisor to direct the work of his or her direct reports and to make certain decisions without consulting others.

Lockout A company action equivalent to a strike; when management denies unionized employees access to their jobs.

Locus of control The degree to which people believe they are masters of their own fate.

Long-term plans Plans covering more than five years.

Machiavellianism Degree to which an individual is manipulative and believes ends can justify means.

Majority vote Agreement to a decision by at least 51 per cent of a group's members.

Management The process of getting things done, effectively and efficiently, through and with others.

Management by objectives (MBO) A system in which subordinates jointly determine specific performance objectives with their superiors, progress toward objectives is periodically reviewed, and on the basis of which rewards are allocated.

Management competencies General categories of skills necessary to successfully perform a managerial job.

Management functions Planning, organizing, leading, and controlling.

Management information system (MIS) A mechanism to provide managers with needed and accurate information on a regular and timely basis.

Management process The four managerial functions of planning, organizing, leading, and controlling.

Marginal analysis Analyzing decisions in terms of their incremental costs.

Matrix A structural design that assigns specialists from functional departments to work on one or more projects that are led by a project manager.

Mature workers A group of workers born prior to 1946 who are security-oriented and have a committed work ethic.

Mediation An impasse-resolution technique where a mediator attempts to pull together the common ground that exists, and makes settlement recommendations for overcoming the barriers that exist between two sides in a conflict.

Mentors Senior employees who tutor, coach, counsel, and guide less experienced associates.

Middle managers All employees below the top-management level who manage other managers.

Minority vote Decision-making power held by a sub-group of a larger group.

Motivation The willingness to do something; is conditioned by this action's ability to satisfy some need for the individual.

Motivation–hygiene theory Intrinsic factors are related to job satisfaction, while extrinsic factors are associated with dissatisfaction.

Need A physiological or psychological deficiency that makes certain outcomes seem attractive.

Need for achievement The need to do things better or more efficiently than they have been done before.

Negative discipline The supervisor identifies employee performance problems and initiates sanctions to correct them.

Negotiation A process in which two or more parties exchange goods or services and attempt to agree upon the exchange rate for them.

Networking Developing contacts (could be in organization, industry, community) for potential use in future.

Nominal group technique A group decision technique in which all members are present but operate independently.

Nonverbal communications Communication that sends messages without words.

Normal distribution Variations are assumed to follow a bell-shaped distribution curve.

Norms Acceptable standards of behaviour within a group that are shared by the group's members.

Off-the-job training Training that takes place outside the direct work area.

On-the-job training Training that places employees in actual work situations.

Operative employees Rank-and-file workers who physically produce an organization's goods and services.

Organization A systematic grouping of people brought together to accomplish some specific purpose.

Organizational culture A shared perception of the organization's values.

Organizing Arranging and grouping jobs, allocating resources, and assigning work in a department so that activities can be accomplished as planned.

Orientation An expansion on information a new employee obtained during the recruitment and selection stages; an attempt to familiarize new employees with the job, the work unit, and the organization as a whole.

Pareto charts Simple bar charts that rank causes of a problem by their quantity over a certain time.

Participative leadership The leadership style of an individual who actively seeks input from followers for many of the activities in the organization.

Passive listening Absorbing information as it is literally transmitted.

Path-goal theory The leader's job is to assist followers in overcoming obstacles in the way of attaining their goals by providing the proper leadership style.

Pay-for-performance programs Compensation plans that pay employees on the basis of some performance measure.

People-centred leaders Emphasize good interpersonal relations.

Performance appraisal An evaluation and development tool. Involves reviewing past performance to identify accomplishments and deficiencies, and creating detailed plans to improve future performance.

Personal career planning Preparing oneself to take advantage of career opportunities through assessing talents, strengths, needs, and interests; identifying the best organizational fit; identifying career goals and developing a strategy for achieving these goals.

PERT chart A technique for scheduling complex projects.

Planning Defining objectives and the means for attaining them.

Plateauing A lack of further upward movement in one's career with the current employer.

Policies Broad guidelines for managerial action.

Political competence A supervisor's ability to enhance his or her power, build a power base, and establish the "right" connections in the organization.

Politicking The actions you can take to influence, or attempt to influence, the distribution of advantages and disadvantages within your organization.

Polychronicity The degree to which a person prefers doing two or more things simultaneously.

Position power The degree of influence a leader has over factors such as hiring, firing, discipline, promotions, and salary increases.

Positive discipline A technique that attempts to reinforce the good work behaviours of an employee, while simultaneously emphasizing to the employee the problems created by undesirable performance.

Preventive control Controls that anticipate and prevent undesirable outcomes.

Problem A discrepancy between an existing and a desired state of affairs.

Procedure A series of steps for responding to a recurring problem.

Process departmentalization Grouping activities on the basis of product or customer flow.

Product departmentalization Grouping activities by product line.

Program A single-use set of plans for a specific major undertaking.

Programmed instruction Individuals learn a small block of information and are then tested immediately to see if the material has been understood.

Progressive discipline Action that begins with a verbal warning, and then proceeds through written reprimands, suspension, and finally, in the most serious cases, dismissal.

Quality Defined as what the customer says the term means.

Quality control Identification of mistakes that may have occurred; monitoring quality to ensure that it meets some preestablished standard.

Range of variation The degree of acceptable variation between actual performance and the standard.

Readiness The ability and willingness of an employee to complete a task.

Realistic Job Preview Information given to job applicant during hiring process which includes both positive and negative information about the job and company; it creates realistic expectations.

Recency error The tendency for evaluators to recall and give greater importance to employee job behaviours that have occurred near the end of the performance-measuring period.

Reengineering Radical or quantum change that occurs when most of the work being done in an organization is evaluated, and then altered. Reengineering requires organizational members to rethink what work should be done, how it is to be done, and how to best implement these decisions.

Reinforcement theory People will exert higher levels of effort in tasks that are reinforced.

Reject errors Rejecting candidates who would later perform successfully on the job.

Reliability The ability of a selection device to measure the same thing consistently.

Response time Responding to requests, demands, and problems initiated by others.

Responsibility An obligation to perform assigned activities.

Richness of information A measure of the amount of information that is transmitted based on multiple information cues (words, posture, facial expressions, gestures, intonations), immediate feedback, and the personal touch.

Rights view of ethics Decisions emphasize respecting and protecting the basic rights of individuals.

Risk propensity The degree to which people are willing to take chances.

Role ambiguity A situation where role expectations are not clearly understood and the employee is not sure what he or she is to do.

Role conflicts Situations in which individuals are confronted by divergent role expectations.

Role overload Situations where an employee is expected to do more than time permits.

Roles Behaviour patterns that go with the position one occupies in the organization.

Rule An explicit statement that tells a manager what he or she ought or ought not to do.

Run charts The results of a process plotted over a period of time.

Scatter diagrams Illustrate the relationship between two variables.

Scheduling Determining what activities have to be done, the order they are to be done in, who is to do each, and when they are to be completed.

Self-esteem The degree to which individuals like or dislike themselves.

Self-monitoring A personality trait that measures an individual's ability to adjust his or her behavior to external, situational factors. High self-monitors are adaptable in adjusting their behaviour to external situational factors, and are capable of presenting striking contradictions between public personas and private selves. Low self-monitors tend to display their true feelings and beliefs in every situation.

Sexual harassment Sexually suggestive remarks, unwanted touching and sexual advances, requests for sexual favours, and other verbal and physical conduct of a sexual nature.

Short-term plans Plans that are less than one year in length.

Similarity error Giving special consideration when rating others to those qualities that the evaluator perceives in himself or herself.

Simple structure A non-elaborate structure low in complexity, with little formalization, and with authority centralized in a single person; a "flat" organization with only two or three levels.

Single-use plans Detailed courses of action used once or only occasionally.

Skill The ability to demonstrate a system and sequence of behavior that is functionally related to attainment of a performance goal.

Skill variety The degree to which the job requires a variety of different activities so the worker can use a number of different skills and talents.

Social loafing The tendency of group members to do less than they are capable of individually when their individual contribution is not measured.

Social network analysis A process of graphically mapping social interactions to identify meaningful patterns.

Span of control The number of subordinates a supervisor can direct efficiently and effectively.

Spillover effect Successes made by unions at the negotiating table influence the wages, working conditions, and terms of employment for workers who are not unionized.

Staff authority A limited authority that supports line authority by advising, servicing, and assisting.

Standard deviation A measure of variability in a group of numerical values.

Standing plans Plans used over and over again for recurring activities.

Status A social rank or the importance one has in a group.

Strategic planning Covering the entire organization, it establishes overall goals and positions the organization's products or services against the competition.

Stress An adaptive response resulting from any environmental action, situation, or event that places excessive psychological and/or physical demands on a person.

Strike Employees leave their jobs and refuse to come to work until a contract has been signed.

Supervisors First-level managers who oversee the work of operatives or nonmanagement employees.

Supervisory competencies Conceptual, interpersonal, technical, and political capabilities.

Suspension Time off without pay; this disciplinary step is usually taken only if neither verbal nor written warnings have achieved desired results.

Tactical planning Specific plans on how overall goals are to be achieved.

Task identity The degree to which the job requires completion of a whole and identifiable piece of work.

Task significance The degree to which the job has a substantial impact on the lives or work of other people.

Task structure The degree to which job assignments are structured and procedurized.

Task-centred leaders Leaders who emphasize the technical or task aspects of the employee's job.

Team A workgroup whose members are committed to a common purpose, have a set of specific performance goals, and hold themselves mutually accountable for the team's results.

Team discipline Discipline is imposed by group control rather than supervisory control.

Technical competence The ability to apply specialized knowledge or expertise.

Telecommuting The linking by computer and modem of workers at home with coworkers and management at an office.

Test-retest method Evaluating training effectiveness by giving participants a test before training begins, a test after training is complete, and assessing the difference in test scores.

Theory X-Theory Y Two diametrically-opposed views on human nature. Theory X assumes people are essentially lazy, irresponsible, and lacking ambition; Theory Y assumes people are hard-working, committed, and responsible.

Time management A personal form of scheduling; maximizing the allocation of the use of time.

Top management The highest level of management. Those people responsible for establishing the organization's overall objectives and developing the policies to achieve those objectives.

Top-down budgeting Budgets that are initiated, controlled, and directed by top management.

Total quality management (TQM) A philosophy of management that is driven by the constant attainment of customer satisfaction through the continuous improvement of all organizational processes.

Traditional career path A sequence of management positions with increasing responsibilities; characterized by relative predictability, upward vertical movement, and the organization taking responsibility for employee career development.

Traditional objective setting Objectives are set at the top and then broken down into subgoals for each level in the organization.

Training Learning experience that results in a relatively permanent change in an individual that improves his or her ability to perform on the job.

Traits Specific characteristics held by individuals that allow them to effectively lead others.

Transactional leaders Leaders who guide or motivate their employees in the direction of established goals by clarifying role and task requirements.

Transformational leaders Leaders who inspire followers to transcend self-interests for the good of the organization and who are capable of having a profound and extraordinary effect on their followers.

Trust Team members believe in the integrity, character, and ability of each other.

Type A behaviour Aggressive involvement in a chronic, incessant struggle to achieve more and more in less and less time.

Type B behaviour Rarely harried by the desire to obtain a wildly increasing number of things or participate in an endlessly growing series of events in an ever-decreasing amount of time.

Union An organization that represents workers and seeks to protect their interests through collective bargaining.

Union shop Requires that employees must join the union.

Union steward An employee who is the elected representative of the employees in a work unit, and is there to protect the rights of the union members.

Unity of command The principle that a subordinate should have one and only one superior to whom he or she is directly responsible.

Utilitarian view of ethics Decisions are based solely on the basis of their outcomes; the goal is to provide the greatest good for the greatest number.

Validity The proven relationship that exists between a selection device and some relevant criterion.

Variable charts Measure a characteristic on a continuous scale.

Verbal intonation The emphasis someone gives to words or phrases.

Vestibule training Employees learn their jobs on the equipment they will be using, but away from the actual work floor.

Wellness programs Any type of program that is designed to keep employees healthy, focusing on such things as smoking cessation, weight control, stress management, physical fitness, nutrition education, high blood-pressure control, and so on.

Wildcat strike An illegal strike where employees refuse to work during the term of a binding contract.

Work sampling A selection device in which job applicants are presented with a miniature replica of a job and are asked to perform tasks central to that job.

Workforce diversity The increasing heterogeneity of organizations with the inclusion of different groups.

Work specialization Also known as division of labour. The process of breaking down a job into a number of steps, with each step being completed by a separate individual.

Written essay A performance appraisal technique in which an evaluator writes out a description of an employee's strengths, weaknesses, past performance, and potential and then makes suggestions for improvement.

Written warning The first formal stage of the disciplinary procedure; the warning becomes part of an employee's official personnel file.

Wrongful discharge Improper or unjust termination of an employee.

Zero-base budget A budget that makes no reference to previous appropriations; all items must be justified.

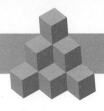

P

Parkinson's Law, 70
participation:
  as motivator, 344
  by employee in performance
    reviews, 285
  in appraisal training, 277
  in change programs to reduce
    resistance, 496
  in MBO goal setting, 67
participative leader, 378
path-goal theory of leadership, 381
pay-for performance programs,
  350-351
people-centred leader, 377-378
performance appraisal, 253-294
  absolute standards measurements,
    266-269
    behaviourally-anchored rating
      scales, 269
    checklists, 267
    critical incidents, 267
    graphic rating scales, 268
    written essay, 267
  and counselling, 278-281
  and goal setting, 271
  criteria, 263-265
    behaviours, 265
    individual task outcomes, 265
    traits, 265
  conducting, 284-287
  documentation, 258-259
  ethics in, 281-282
  formal reviews, 257
  forms for, 258-259
  frequency of, 257
  informal appraisals, 257
  legal issues in, 262-263
  methods of, 266-272
  multiple raters in 276-277
  overcoming hurdles, 275-277
  performance data, gathering,
    265-266
  performance expectations, setting,
    259
  performance feedback, 259, 262
  potential problems in, 272-275
    central tendency errors, 274
    halo errors, 272-273
    inflationary pressures, 274-275
    leniency errors, 272
    recency errors, 274
    similarity errors,
  purpose of, 256-257
  relative standards measurements,
    269-271
    group order ranking, 269-271
    individual ranking, 271

self-evaluations, 258
  supervisor's role in, 258-262
  team appraisals, 278
performance-based compensation,
  350-351
performance measurement, 88-90
  acceptable ranges, 90
  cause and effect diagrams, 92, 93
  control charts, 94-95
  flow charts, 92, 93
  scatter diagrams, 92, 94
  sources of information, 88
    oral reports, 88
    personal observation, 88
    statistical reports, 88
    written reports, 88
  what is measured, 89-90
performance feedback, 259, 262
  in MBO, 67
performance problems, 278-282
  counselling employees, 278-282
performance simulation tests, 240
personal career planning, 590
personal differences, as a source of
  conflict, 447
personality characteristics, and
  stress, 501-502
PERT chart, 60, 62-64
  activities, 62
  critical path, 62
  events, 62
  history of, 62
physical examinations, and employee
  selection, 241-242
physiological symptoms of stress,
  500, 503
planning, 7, 50-67
  breadth, 53, 56
  formal, 54
  key guides, 56-63
  linkages in organizational levels, 56
  single-use plans, 59-64
    budgets, 59-60
    programs, 59
    schedules, 60-64
  standing plans, 57-58
    policies, 57-58
    procedures, 58
    rules, 58
  time frame, 56
plateauing, 588-589
playing favourites, 386, 388
policies, 56, 57-58
political competence, 16, 17
politics, organizational, 457-466
  and organizational culture,
    460-461
  becoming politically smart,
    463-465

  ethics of, 459-460
  why inevitable, 459
polychronicity, 70
potential team, 200
power distance, 27
preventive control, 95-96
problem-solving and decision-
  making, 126-169
procedures, 58
process departmentalization, 189
product departmentalization, 186
productivity cycle, 70
professionals, motivating, 349
programmed instruction, 309
programs, 59
pseudoteam, 200
psychological symptoms of stress,
  500, 504
pyramid, 5

Q

quality control, 100-101
quality of life, 28
quantity of life, 28

R

range of variation, 90
readiness, employee, 382
realistic job preview, 244
realistic type, 593
recency error, 274
recruiting, 230-235
  advertisements, 231
  casual or unsolicited applicants,
    235
  employee referrals, 232
  employment agencies, 233
  internal search, 231
  professional organizations,
    234-235
  schools, colleges, universities, 234
  unemployment centres and
    agencies, 235
reengineering, 30-32
  and supervisors, 33-34
  compared to TQM, 31
referrals, employee, 232
reinforcement theory, 340
reject errors, 236
relative standards performance
  measurements, 269-271
  group order ranking, 269271
  individual ranking, 271